D1130985

A
CHECKLIST OF
AMERICAN IMPRINTS
1820-1829

TITLE INDEX

compiled by

M. Frances Cooper

The Scarecrow Press, Inc.
Metuchen, N.J.   1972

ISBN 0-8108-0513-8

RICHARD HESTON SHOEMAKER, 1907-1970*

Some men have monuments erected to them after their death;
the monuments stand, but the men they memorialized have been for-
gotten. Other men build their own monuments during their lifetime;
they last and their creators are not iorgotten. Richard Heston Shoemaker will be remembered as long as anyone buys, sells, catalogues
or studies any American imprint between 1801 and 1830. That, I
can predict, will be a long, long time.

Dick Shoemaker would have been the first to have chuckled at
the idea of a larger than life-size statue of himself outside the
School of Library Service. He could only have been portrayed
against a cluttered background of reference works, stooping a bit
from a lifetime of catalogue searching, but firmly clutching in his
hand a box of imprint slips. Bronze would have been a difficult
medium in which to express Dick's gentleness and kindness to bibliographical peers and beginning students alike. How could one re-
produce the twinkle in his eye which seemed to say: "I may look
like a fuddy-duddy compiler of fuddy-duddy lists, but, you know,
it's really an exciting thing to do." His only frustration was not in
his work, but in the failure of some to understand how important it
was. The product of enthusiastic patience is his monument.

Born in a suburb of Philadelphia in 1907, Dick Shoemaker
graduated from the University of Pennsylvania and began his library
career in 1938 at Temple University. He received the stamp of
professional approval in the form of a degree in Library Science
from Columbia that same year. When the WPA undertook to catalogue a number of the old, neglected libraries in Philadelphia, Dick
was put in charge of the project at the Mercantile Library. The
appearance of the sigil PPM in the National Union Catalogue in con-
nection with a surprising number of rare and unusual works is due
to his early diligence.

Then he moved South. After eight years as head cataloguer and assistant librarian at Washington and Lee University, where he earned a master's degree in English Literature, in 1947 Dick Shoemaker came to Rutgers. For almost a quarter of a century until his death last year, first at Newark where he was librarian and then here at New Brunswick where he was professor in the Graduate School of Library Service, Rutgers was his well-loved professional and academic home. Nothing pleased him more than the growth of the Rutgers Library and the Library School. He saw the infants of the post-war period grow to positions of national importance as the library and the school expanded rapidly in quantity and quality. He was proud of Rutgers and Rutgers had every reason to be proud of him.

It was as a bibliographer, however, that Dick Shoemaker made his international reputation. When Clifford K. Shipton in 1959 completed the last volume of the American Bibliography begun by Charles Evans in 1903, the chronologically arranged catalogue of books printed in the United States through the year 1800 was finished. But Evans had projected his work through 1820 and the constellations had moved inexorably on their courses. Whereas once upon a time, with the exception of a few high spots, only 17th and 18th-century American-printed books had been considered worth collecting, listing and studying, the mid-20th century expanded its interests temporally. There was a vacuum in American bibliography for twenty years until Roorbach's woefully incomplete list picked up in 1820.

With the kind of intestinal fortitude long associated with battles rather than books, Ralph R. Shaw and Richard H. Shoemaker, working out of Rutgers, determined to continue Evans to 1820. The concept was so vast that the undertaking seemed almost foolhardy. Yet, working with slips compiled all over the country by the WPA, supplemented by the locations in the National Union Catalogue and shelf-lists of a few libraries, notably the American Antiquarian Society, Shaw and Shoemaker began. The volume for 1801 appeared over the imprint of The Scarecrow Press in 1958, and by 1963 1819 was issued; supplementary volumes of indices and additions and corrections subsequently appeared. The work was modestly called "A Preliminary Checklist." No one, and foremost among the critics, Dick Shoemaker, saw this as more than a pioneer compilation, subject to refinement and expansion, of the astonishing number of 50,192 entries. That nineteen volumes could have been produced in so short a time was a bibliographical miracle. We may not have all the tiny atolls pinpointed on Shaw and Shoemaker's map; a few creeks and headlands may have been misplaced; yet a whole terra incognita in all its main and most of its minor elements has been charted. Librarians, collectors and booksellers can now find their way.

When Ralph Shaw decided that other and eventually more distant pastures were greener, Dick Shoemaker decided to carry on the project himself through 1830. My friendship with Dick began when he came to the Library Company to check a few problem slips. Consequently I was privy to his criticism of the earlier volumes and his determination in the continuation selectively to check as many of the actual titles as he could in the handful of libraries from Worcester to Washington where the great majority of them was found. For years thereafter, Dick Shoemaker would make his appearance, brandishing his boxes of slips in a welcoming wave, with a cheery: "Well, here I am again." We shelve our Americana chronologically and alphabetically by author within each year, so that our shelves are in "Shoemaker" order. I can assure you that there are few librarians, bibliographers or scholars whom I would permit to work in our rare-book stacks. Dick was one of the few. His project was so important and so in line with our own interests. Moreover, how could anyone not want to help so pleasant, industrious and lovable a man? As he went along he pointed out an anonymous work for which he had found an author, but we had not; or he helped us put a date on an undated imprint. We enjoyed his visits; we enjoyed him; we were always delighted to hear that "Well, here I am again."

The first volume of Shoemaker, covering the year 1820, came out in 1964. Persistently ploughing through thousands of catalogue slips, he continued on and on. By the time one volume was in print another had been edited and a third was in the process of being gathered. Dick's life was not one of bibliographical frenzy; he was careful, calm and methodical, as every good bibliographer should be. In 1969 he acquired from the Library Company an assistant in the person of Gayle Cooper, who helped Dick in his last year and finished off the volumes for 1828 and 1829 which he had almost readied. The 41,633 entries of Shoemaker's Checklist of American Imprints, 1820-1829, are in print. His preliminary slips for 1830 await editing and publication.

How important was Dick Shoemaker's end result? (For of the making of bibliographies, as of books, there is no end.) The best answer to my question is Socratically to ask another: how important is the history of the United States for the first three decades of the 19th century? Shaw and Shoemaker, and Shoemaker attempted to list every book, pamphlet and broadside printed in the country during that period. Nothing printed was alien to them. As a result, the full range of political life is covered, from Jefferson to John Quincy Adams, the War of 1812, the pioneer American expeditions across the continent, the rise of a significant native American literature, the beginnings of the American industrial system, piety and crime, medicine and internal improvements, the whole mixture of the important and the trivial which made life during the period and is history today. A key has been given to the American historian which he at his scholarly peril will neglect.

On thousands of catalogue cards all over the country Shoemaker numbers have begun to appear. The greatest accolade dealers give a book is to boast, "Not in Shoemaker," or to state, "Only two copies located by Shoemaker." In days to come there will not be those who can associate the bibliography with the kindly bibliographer, but in times to come there will be many who will bless his name.

---

*From the First Annual Richard H. Shoemaker Memorial Lecture on Bibliography, delivered November 3, 1971 at Rutgers University by Edwin Wolf 2nd, Librarian, The Library Company of Philadelphia.

Title Index

A

grammar developing the principles of the English language
... 4847

An abridgment of the American system of English grammar...
12002; 23942

An abridgment of the Catholic
doctrine... 29177

An abridgment of the Christian
doctrine... 16486

An abridgement of the General
history of the Baptist denomination in America... 384

An abridgment of the History of
England.   8844; 8845; 8846;
8847; 16310; 16311; 20688;
20689; 38766

An abridgement of the law of nisi
prius... 14080

An abridgment of the laws of
Pennsylvania... 13696

An abridgment of The new Robinson Crusoe... 15633

An abridgment of the writings of
Lewis Cornaro... 15874

Abrogation of the Jewish Sabbath.
28560

Absence.   [Song.] 3067

Absence.   Air Rosseau's dream.
2213

Absence.   The words adapted to
the favorite air of Rousseau's
dream.   10147; 17861; 17862;
17863; 22140; 22141; 22142

Absent friends.   A canzonet.
3190; 14098

Absent friends.   Duetto. 12170

Abstract from the ninth annual
report of the Boston Society
for the Religious and Moral Instruction of the Poor... 19825

Abstract from the proceedings of
the board of visitors of the
Maryland Hospital. 39440

Abstract from the returns of
banks in Massachusetts...
39487

Abstract of a correspondence with
the executive, relative to the
rank or command of Major-
Generals Scott and Macomb.
31876

Abstract of a journal kept by E.

Bacon... 15148

Abstract of a journal of E. Bacon... 4517; 7859

An abstract of a new theory of
the formation of the earth.
12827

Abstract of American seamen...
30870; 35586

Abstract of an essay "On the
economy of farm yard ma-
nure." 503

Abstract of returns from the
school committees... 25251

Abstract of sacred history...
7732; 11520; 15011; 20647;
33337

Abstract of the annual return of
the Militia of the State of
Ohio... 2580; 6330

An abstract of the Bible history.
35571

Abstract of the bill of mortality,
of the town of Boston. 8125

An abstract of the census of Alabama, taken in 1827. 27765

An abstract of the condition of
granting of lands in Maryland.
15582; 19886

An abstract of the eighth annual
report of the Society of the
Protestant Episcopal Church
for the advancement of Christianity in Pennsylvania. 3264

Abstract of the fifth annual report of the Tract Association
of Friends.   6988

Abstract of the laws for the regulation of licensed houses...
5266

An abstract of the laws, relative
to the duty of assessors, in
the city of New York. 17355

An abstract of the ninth annual
report of the trustees of the
Society of the Protestant Episcopal Church for the Advancement of Christianity in Pennsylvania. 6558

Abstract of the number of Convicts in the Massachusetts
State Prison... 2143; 9432

Abstract of the proceedings of
ancient Free-Masons of South

Carolina... 24625

An abstract of the proceedings of the annual meetings of the Corporation for the Relief of the Widows and Children of Clergymen of the Protestant Episcopal Church in the State of New Jersey... 12263

An abstract of the proceedings of the board of trustees of the General Theological Seminary in the United States... 17410; 21685

Abstract of the proceedings of the Grand lodge of Ancient free Masons of South-Carolina... 5398; 8766; 12613; 16225; 20594; 28952; 33274; 38672

Abstract of the proceedings of the Grand Lodge of Georgia, Ancient York Masons... 1289

An abstract of the proceedings of the Grand Lodge of the most ancient and honorable fraternity of free and accepted Masons of the state of New York... 28945; 38658

An abstract of the proceedings of the R.W. Grand Lodge of the state of New York... 38659

Abstract of the proceedings of the right worshipful G. Lodge of Maryland... 12592

Abstract of the report of the joint committee of the Legislature, appointed to examine into the state of the Bank of Pennsylvania. 39990

Abstract of the returns of the school districts of Maine... 39388

Abstract of the returns of the selectmen of the several towns, and assessors of plantations in the state. [Me.] 39389

Abstract of the returns of the selectmen of towns and assessors of plantations of the number of school districts. [Me.] 39390

Abstract of third and fourth annual reports. [Tract Association, Philadelphia] 3467

Abstracts of the proceedings of the Grand Lodge of Maryland ... 1301

The absurdities of Methodism. 9835

The acacia bower. 4507

Academician and professor of dancing, respectfully informs the citizens of Williamsburg... 8578

Academies of arts. 29816

The acceptable sacrifice. 4758

The accomplishment of the Saviour's precious promise... 4392

An account of a boy who died at the age of 12 years... 15012

Account of a collection of plants from the Rocky Mountains and adjacent countries. 30818

An account of a new method of making dried anatomical preparations. 3370

An account of a revival of religion in Jerusalem... 14265

Account of Abigail Hutchinson... 1081; 1082

Account of an expedition from Pittsburgh to the Rocky Mts. 9135; 12942

Account of Charles Dunsdon. 22494

An account of Elizabeth Radden. 5

An account of four species of stormy petrels. 15492

Account of John Boltwood... 7733

Account of John Schureman Sutphen. 15013

An account of memorials presented to Congress... 6; 37354; 37355

Account of Mrs. Emerson. 8618

Account of premium awarded in 1825... 24443

An account of some eudiometers ... 1513; 20810

An account of some further experiments to determine the absorbing power of the veins and lymphatics. 13073; 13074

An account of some of the steamboats navigating the Hudson River... 34996

An account of sundry missions performed among the Senecas and Munsees... 27801

An account of surveys and examinations... relative to the projected Chesapeake and Ohio, and Ohio and Lake Erie canals. 17981

An account of the alarming & destructive fire in Yorkminster ... 37356

An account of the apprehension, trial, conviction, and condemnation of Manuel Philip Garcia ... 5870

An account of the asylum for the insane. 21872; 23197

An account of the attempt made by Jesse A. Bynum, attended by several armed associates, to murder Robert Potter... 21955

An account of the Boston Asylum for Indigent Boys...11932

Account of the ceremony and dedication of Washington Hall... 7734

An account of the ceremony of laying the corner stone of St. Thomas' Church... 15014

An account of the Christian denominations in the United States. 28523

An account of the controversy in the First Parish in Cambridge. 38030

An account of the destruction of the city of Jerusalem... 15015

Account of the dinner given to Professor List... 27767

An account of the dreadful fire, which occurred at the orphan asylum... 7735

An Account of the execution of Samuel Green... 7736

An account of the expenses that have accrued in the House of Correction in the county of Worcester... 27709

An account of the formation and proceedings of the Auxiliary Foreign Mission Society of Worcester... 19480

Account of the great fire in Broad Street... 6231

Account of the great Jackson meeting in Baltimore. 39374

An account of the High School for Girls, Boston... 23887

An account of the illegal seizure on the high seas, of the American brig Phoenix... 37357

Account of the jeffersonite... 9181

An account of the last hours of the lives of the three Thayers ... 19360

An account of the last sickness and death of Mr. George W. Thompson... 10136

An account of the late intended insurrection among a portion of the blacks of this city. 8315; 8316; 8317.

An account of the loss of the Essex... 20029

An account of the loss of the Wesleyan Missionaries... 29375

Account of the Maine Charity School... 2083

An account of the manuscript papers of George Washington... 30679

An account of the meetings of Friends in the Yearly meeting of New-England... 20610

An account of the natives of the Tonga Islands... 2107

An account of the New-York hospital. 3262

An account of the origin and progress of the Pennsylvania Institution for the Deaf and Dumb... 6431

Account of the overseers of the poor. 19797

Account of the Penitentiary and Penal Code of Pennsylvania... 11522

An account of the plan and regulation of the Newburyport Female Charitable Society. 9769

An account of the prediction of the dreadful disaster which is to take place in the City of New York. 27656

An act additional to the several acts now in force, to organize, govern and discipline the militia. 25188

Act and by-laws and rules of the Parker River Bridge Corporation... 30152

An act authorising the construction of a rail road from the State prison at Auburn to the Erie canal. 34468

An act authorizing the sale within this State of a limited number of tickets in the lottery... 2472

An act concerning parishes. 5906

An act concerning religious and other corporations. 31858

An act concerning the Erie and Champlain canals. 21647

An act concerning the revised statutes... 34469

An act concerning the students of Yale College... 8424

An act establishing a fire dept. in the city of Boston... 19798

An act, establishing a free bridge in the city of Boston. 25252

An act establishing an equitable mode of levying the taxes of this state... 21721

An act establishing the law of the road. 16986

An act for assessing and collecting the revenue. 16656

An act for disciplining the militia of the state of Ohio... 9755

An act for erecting the lower part of the county of Sussex in New Jersey, into a separate county... 13516

An act for establishing a health office... 30168

An act for facilitating the communication from Elizabeth-Town... 17340

An act for incorporating the Bank of Virginia... 32099

Act for incorporating the Society formed for the relief of poor aged & infirm masters of

ships... 30657

An act for regulating elections ... 9664

An act for regulating marriage ... 5907

An act for the better employment, relief, and support of the poor... 17357; 17358

An act for the better regulation of the militia... 39441

An act for the better regulation of the militia of the city of Baltimore... 17033

An act for the consolidation & amendment of the laws, as far as they respect the poor of the city of Philadelphia... 13742

An act for the entire abolition of slavery in Pennsylvania. 25683

An act for the establishment and support of public schools in the city of Baltimore. 21338; 21339

An act for the establishment of a College at Uniontown... 29587

An act for the establishment of free schools in the state of Delaware... 38359

An act for the further organization of the Supreme Court... 13191

An act for the further relief and support, employment and removal of the poor. 2074

An act for the instruction and education of youth. 5911

An act for the maintenance and protection of the Erie and Champlain Canals ... 2473

Act for the regulation of the militia of the commonwealth of Pennsylvania... 6406; 9837; 34672

An act for the relief and employment of the poor of the city of Philadelphia... 34740

An act for the relief of certain persons whose lands, bank

stock, &c., have been sold for taxes... 5680

An act for the relief of poor debtors arrested on execution. 5908; 9330

The act for the support of common schools... 9665

An act, further regulating the storage, safe keeping, and transportation of gunpowder, in the town of Boston... 5965

An act further to amend the character of the town of Alexandria. 23450

An act imposing a duty on sales at auction. 25189

An act, in addition to an act, entitled, "An Act, ascertaining what shall constitute the legal settlement, and for providing for the relief and support, employment and removal of the poor." 9331

An act in addition to an act entitled "An Act establishing a Supreme Judicial Court within this state"... 13192

An act in addition to an act entitled "An act establishing the city of Boston." 15497

An act in addition to the several acts now in force for the regulation of innholders, retailers and common victuallers. 25190

An act in addition to the several acts now in force, to organize, govern and discipline the militia of this state... 21298; 21299

Act incorporating the city of Cincinnati... 32711

The act incorporating the Dover Bank... 16000

An act... incorporating the Exeter Manufacturing Company... 33109

The act incorporating the House of Refuge... 40048

An act making further provisions for the survey of routes for canals between the Delaware and Ohio. 21804

An act of assembly, incorporating the Mutual Assurance Company of the City of Norwich... 29876

Act of incorporation... [Roxbury Charitable Soc.] 3071

Act of incorporation and by-laws [Academy of Natural Sciences] 31878

Act of incorporation and by-laws. [Merrimack Co. Bank] 21427

Act of incorporation and by-laws adopted by the Grand Royal Arch Chapter of Maine... 16197

Act of incorporation, and by-laws adopted for the government of the officers and members of the Grand Royal Arch Chapter of Maine... 38646

The act of incorporation, and by-laws, for the government and management of the master, wardens and members of the Grand Lodge of Maine... 5382

Act of incorporation and by-laws of the Central Universalist Society in Boston. 11936

Act of incorporation and by-laws of the First Church, Boston. 37906

An act of incorporation and by-laws of the First Universalist Society, in Boston. 33177

Act of incorporation and by-laws of the Gloucester Canal Corporation... 8840

Act of incorporation and by-laws of the Mine Hill and Schuylkill Haven Rail Road Company. 39601

Act of incorporation, and by-laws of the New England Society for the Promotion of Manufactures and Mechanic Arts. 25504

The act of incorporation, and by-laws of the Tremont Theatre... 28255

Act of incorporation, and by-laws, of the West-Newbury Mutual Fire Insurance Company. 41476

The act of incorporation and bye-laws. [Cumberland Co. Society for the Promotion of Agriculture and Domestic Manufactures] 5116

Act of incorporation and bye-laws [Ministers' Annuity Society] 21471

Act of incorporation and bye-laws of the Salem Laboratory Company. 6703

Act of incorporation and list of subscribers [Society for the Relief of the Insane] 14158

Act of incorporation and minutes of the Baptist Convention of the State of Rhode-Island... 37669

Act of incorporation and scale of valuation of pews... [Roxbury, Mass. First Religious Society] 22151

Act of incorporation and stated rules of the Society of the Brethren for Propagating the Gospel among the Heathen. 21518

The act of incorporation and supplementary acts, with the by-laws of the Medical and Chirurgical Faculty of Maryland. 9447

The act of incorporation & the constitution of the Connecticut Historical Society... 20173

Act of incorporation, by-laws and orchestral regulations [Musical Fund Society of Philadelphia] 25473

The act of incorporation, by-laws, rules and regulations, for the government and management of the master, wardens and members, of the Grand Lodge of Massachusetts. 24603

The act of incorporation, constitution, and by-laws, of the New Hampshire Historical Society. 13510

The act of incorporation, constitution and by-laws, of the Salem Society for the Moral and Religious Instruction of the Poor. 26010

An act of incorporation for that part of the Northern Liberties lying between the middle of 6th St. and the river Delaware... 17602

Act of incorporation for the Kensington district of the Northern Liberties... 6407; 11523; 34741

Act of incorporation, New England Yearly Meeting. 12624

Act of incorporation of the Bank of North America. 27961

The act of incorporation of the Cincinnati Academy of Fine Arts. 32712

Act of incorporation of the city of Cincinnati. 4991

Act of incorporation of the Farmington Canal Company... 8425; 8680; 20165

The act of incorporation, of the Twelfth Congregational Society. 23898

An act of incorporation of the village of Rochester... 25961

The act of incorporation, regulations, and members... [Mass. Congregational Charitable Society] 21368

The act of incorporation rules and by-laws... [R. I. Medical Society] 6638

The act of incorporation, the deed of settlement, and articles of association of the Cincinnati Equitable Insurance Company. 28496

The act of incorporations [sic] with the supplement thereto, and the constitution and by-laws of the Medical Society of Delaware... 17086

An act of the commonwealth of Massachusetts... 34050

An act passed by the Legislature of Pennsylvania... 34673

An act, providing for the collection of taxes. 17319

An act providing for the government of the state prison. 16987

An act, recommending a convention of the people of this state ... 6238

An act regulating the militia, of

the state of Indiana... 16657

Act regulating the storage of gunpowder [Boston] 4769

An act, relating to the calling of
a convention of delegates.
2144

An act relating to the punishment
of convicts. 16988

An act relating to the purchase of
lands... 39783

An act relative to the Delaware
and Raritan canal... 21805

An act suspending executions...
5681

An act to abolish the Circuit
Courts of Common Pleas.
[Maine] 5910; 5912

An act, to alter the organization
of the Common Council...
13535

An act to amend an act, entitled,
"An act concerning distresses
..." 2474

Act to amend an act, entitled "An
act to incorporate and vest
certain powers in the freeholders and inhabitants of the
village of Brooklyn, in the
County of Kings..." 17359

An act to amend the Act for disciplining the militia of the state
of Ohio... 6331

The act to amend the act for the
support of common schools...
9666

An act to amend the charter of
Alexandria... 4445

An act... to authorize the Baltimore and Ohio Railroad Company to construct a railroad
through Pennsylvania... 32087

An act to authorize the Hampshire
and Hampden Canal Company to
construct a canal... 33467

An act, to authorize the proprietors of Union wharf to extend
the same. 39488

An act, to confirm an act of the
General Assembly of the state
of Vermont [Mass.] 25253;
29659

Act to confirm an act of the General Assembly of the state of

Vermont [N.H.] 25505

An act, to confirm "An act to
provide for improving the navigation in the valley of Connecticut River. 25254

An act to continue in force "An
act to protect the commerce of
the United States, and punish
the crime of piracy..." 3519

An act to empower the inhabitants
of Salem to choose Board of
Health and for removing and
preventing nuisances. 14033

An act to enable the Hebrew Congregation... to lease on ground
rent a lot of ground, in the
city of Philadelphia... 34136

An act to establish a company under the names of "The Philadelphia, Dover and Norfolk
Steam-Boat & Transportation
Company..." 20284

An act to establish a Court of
Common Pleas for the state
[Maine] 9332

An act to establish a permanent
fund for the support of public
schools [Mass.] 2145

An act to establish the Boston
and Roxbury Mill Corporation.
2146

An act to establish the city of
Boston. 9400

An act to establish the Kennebec
and Androscoggin Canal Association. 25191

An act to establish the Massachusetts Rail Road Corporations.
39489

An act to establish the Warren
Bridge Corporation. 29660

An act to extend the Charter of
the Philadelphia Bank. 13746

An act to facilitate the construction of a rail-road from the
city of Boston to the Hudson
River. 34470

An act to give effect to the provisions of the Constitution of
the United States... 25684

An act to improve the navigation
of the River Lehigh... 9250

An act to incorporate a company

An act to incorporate the St. Andrew's Society. 22176

An act to incorporate the Salem Lead Manufacturing Company. 17044

An act to incorporate the Salem Mill-Dam Corporation. 26008

An act to incorporate the stockholders of the Mechanics' Bank of Baltimore. 6005

An act to incorporate the stockholders of the New-York Insurance Company. 2475

An act to incorporate the stockholders of the Philadelphia Arcade. 40043

An act to incorporate the subscribers to the Consolidated Association of the Planters of Louisiana. 28583; 38261

An act to incorporate the Traders' Insurance Company. 21648

An act to incorporate the Union Bank. 21302

An act to incorporate the United States Fire Insurance Company. 17363

An act to incorporate the Watervliet Turnpike Company. 34474

An act to lay out and improve a road through the Buffalo Indian reservation. 39785

An act to organize, govern, and discipline the militia of the State of Maine. 5913; 16989;

An act to organize, govern, and discipline the militia of this state. 5909

An act to organize the militia. [Mich.] 21443; 21444

An act to organize the militia [N. Y.] 6239; 13543

An act to prevent kidnapping. 2682

An act to prevent resistance to legal process. 25192

An act to prevent the creation of unnecessary costs in criminal prosecutions. 13193

An act to prevent the introduction of paupers from foreign ports or places. 2147

An act to promote the sale and settlement of the public land. 16991

An act to provide against infectious and pestilential diseases. [N. Y.] 2476; 13544

An act to provide for taking future enumerations of the inhabitants of this state. [N. Y.] 21649

An act to provide for taking the fourth census. 3521

An act to provide for the distribution and safe keeping of the public arms. [Ohio] 17471

An act to provide for the instruction of youth. 29661

An act to provide for the public instruction of youth. [Md.] 13225

An act to provide for the support and better regulation of common schools. [Ohio] 39897

An act to provide for the support of common schools. [Vt.] 31596

An act to re-charter certain banks. [Pa.] 17550; 17551; 17552; 22207; 23600

An act to redeem the paper currency. 34567; 35388

An act to reduce the law incorporating the village of Brooklyn. 28287

An act to regulate banks and banking. 39490

An act to regulate sales by public auction. 17364

An act to regulate the administration of justice within the county of Suffolk. 9401

An act to regulate the exportation of flour. 15059

An act to remove the unconstitutional obstructions which have been thrown in the way of the Court of Appeals. 29412

An act to submit to the people of this state certain amendments proposed to the constitution. [N. Y.] 25541

Acte d'incorporation de l'association Consolidée des Cultiva-

teurs de la Louisiane. 28584;
38262

Acte pour amender l'acte intitule,
"Acte pour incorporer l'Association Consolidée des Cultiva-
teurs de la Louisiane. 32817

Actes, relatifs aux townships, aux
grands chemins, aux elections,
&c. 29744

Acting American theatre. 25139;
25140

Active benevolence. 31972

The actor of all work. 8393

The actor, or Guide to the stage.
11524

Acts amendatory of the Militia
Law of the State of Tennessee.
3413

Acts and ordinances relating to
the fire department in the town
of Providence. 40191

The acts and proceedings of the
classis and general synod of
the True Reformed Dutch
Church. 18246

The acts and proceedings of the
extra and stated sessions of
the general synod of the Reformed Dutch Church. 34972

The acts and proceedings of the
general synod of the Reformed
Dutch Church in North America. 2955; 2956; 6601; 10073;
13912; 17772; 22044; 22045;
22046; 25908; 30413; 40227

Acts and proceedings of the general synod of the True Reformed Dutch Church, in the
United States. 22524; 26249;
30843; 35562; 40687

Acts and proceedings of the government of the state of Ohio.
34597

The acts and proceedings of the
Synod of the German Reformed
Church of the United States.
34975

Acts and Resolutions of the General Assembly of the State of
South Carolina. 3276; 6826;
10310; 14166; 18052; 22328;
26105; 30663; 35357; 40486

Acts and resolves passed by the

General Court of Massachusetts. 29662

Acts and resolves, passed by the
Legislature of Massachusetts.
39491

Acts for the relief of the poor
within the County of Baltimore.
205; 5951

Acts incorporating the town of
Wheeling. 41489

Acts of a general nature [Ohio]
2581; 2582; 9756; 13618;
17472; 21722; 39898

Acts of a local nature [Ohio]
2583; 9757; 13619; 17473;
21723; 39899

Acts of a local or private nature
[Tenn.] 3414; 30777

Acts of a public or general nature [Tenn.] 3415

Acts of Alabama. 15047

Acts of assembly and ordinances
relating to the water works.
9839

Acts of Assembly, concerning the
Lancaster, Elizabethtown and
Middletown Turnpike road.
9838

The acts of assembly, incorporating the city of St. Louis.
35091a

Acts of assembly relative to the
board of wardens, of the port
of Philadelphia. 39991

Acts of General Assembly, May
1827. 30440

Acts of incorporation and acts
regulating the practice of
physick and surgery, with the
by-laws and orders of the
Massachusetts Medical Society.
9426; 25276

The acts of incorporation, and
by-laws of the Cocheco Manufacturing Company. 28529

The acts of incorporation, and
by-laws of the Nashua Manufacturing Company. 29883

Acts of incorporation and ordinances of the village of Buffalo. 23961

Acts of incorporation, bye-laws
and ordinances of the borough

of Kentucky. 1844; 5754; 21105; 25027; 29413; 33766; 39187

Acts passed at the... General Assembly of the state of Ohio. 6332; 9758

Acts passed at the... General Assembly of the State of Tennessee. 6945; 10425; 14266; 18165; 26186; 30778; 30779

Acts passed at... the General Assembly of the State of Alabama. 52; 4431; 7762; 11557; 15048; 19383; 23438; 27794; 31912; 37393

Acts passed at the... legislative council of the territory of Michigan. 17141; 34126; 39580;

Acts passed at the... Legislature of the State of Louisiana. 2012; 5859; 9295; 13142; 16938; 21249; 25144; 29537; 33906; 39326

Acts passed at the... session of the ... Congress of the United States. 3522; 7041; 10514

Acts passed by the General Assembly of the state of North Carolina. 17437; 21700; 25600; 30070; 34568; 39854

Acts passed by the General Assembly of the territory of Arkansas. 7831; 15120

Acts, passed by the legislative council of the territory of Michigan. 21446; 25333

Acts passed by the Legislature of the State of Vermont. 4087; 7506; 11291; 14775; 19129; 23151; 27501; 31597; 37003; 41369

Acts passed... by the Legislature ... respecting the Canals from Lake Erie to the Hudson River. 2477

Acts, relating to circuit courts in Pennsylvania. 25687

Acts relative to Bowdoin College. 23910

Acts, relative to townships, highways, & elections. 29745

Acts, resolves and reports passed at the General Assem-

bly...[R.I.] 22073

Ad favetium nobilissimum ac illustrissimum, galliae decus, nec non humani generis... 18026

Adam und Eva im Paradies. 13

Adam's Latin grammar. 15020; 19363; 19364; 27771; 27772; 27773; 31881; 37358

Adam's new arithmetic. 27775; 27776; 31882; 31883; 37360

Addenda, No. III, to the catalogue of books of James Eastburn & Co. 1068

Addition to the article "Russia." 39539

Addition to the Fourth memorial of Joseph W. Brackett and Samuel Leggett... 15538

An additional act for the relief of poor debtors. 16990

Additional documents, in relation to the differences between the late Commodore O.H. Perry, and Captain J.D. Elliott... 4405

Additional executive department. 26332; 26333

Additional facts, remarks, and arguments, illustrative of the advantage to the people of the United States, of a national circulating medium. 7741

Additional ground for Fort Washington. 40777

Additional hymns, intended as an appendix to Watts and Rippon. 28269

Additional inquiries respecting the Indian languages. 696

Additional naval force. 26334

Additional report of spoliations on the commerce of the United States. 40778

Additional report of the Committee on the Public Buildings. 3523

Additional reports of the committee of ways and means. 13226

An additional supplement to the Catalogue of the Library of Congress. 35637

Additions and amendments to the Civil code of the state of

Louisiana. 13143

Additions et amendemens au code civil de l'état de la Louisiane. 13144

Additions to the general anatomy of Xavier Bichart. 11772

Additions to the ornithology of the United States. 19786

Address... [New Haven, Conn.] 717

Address. [Maryland State Colonization Society.] 2132

An address adopted at a meeting of citizens of Philadelphia. 37368

Address and invitation to ministers. 25390

An address and prayer, on laying the corner stone of the intended wing to the Orphan House. 14188

Address and resolutions of the American Institute. 31961

Address and rules of the South-Carolina Society, for Promoting and Improving Agriculture. 6831

An address, at Northampton, October 11, 1826. 24359

Address at the dedication of the building in Chalmers Street. 38846

An address at the dedication of the Second Church in Waltham. 5621

An address, at the first stated meeting of the Indiana Colonization Society. 37856

Address, at the interment of R. W. James Davenport. 16448

An address at the laying of the corner stone of the First Universalist Church. 23962

Address before Mount Carmel Lodge. 5322

Address before the Agricultural Society of Bucks County. 4341

Address before the American Home Missionary Society. 41362

An address before the Attleborough Agricultural Society. 23333

An address before the Kennebunk

Temperance Society. 40443

Address before the Meridian Sun Lodge. 14999

Address before the Middlesex Association for the Promotion of Temperance. 40382

Address before the Ontario Agricultural Society. 5522

An address by Daniel Burnham. 8219

Address by David Trimble. 14318

An address, by Thomas B. Reed. 30409

Address, commencement of Hamilton College. ... 32903

An address delivered and published at the request of the Young Men's Auxiliary Education Society of Newburyport. 11435

An address, delivered at a meeting of the citizens of Cincinnati. 38296

An address delivered at a meeting of the citizens of Trenton. 18109

An address, delivered at a meeting of the Republican electors of the ninth ward. 33353

An address, delivered at a public installation of the officers of Menominie Lodge. 27928

Address delivered at a public meeting... Franklin Institute, Phila. 30139

Address delivered at Amesbury. 38325

An address, delivered at Bath. 23356

An address delivered at Bennington. 39175

An address delivered at Bloomington. 41602

An address, delivered at Bowdoin College. 8363

An address delivered at Brunswick [Bartlett] 28065

An address delivered at Brunswick [Mann] 13209

An address delivered at Cambridge [Spooner] 10323

An address delivered at Charlestown [Everett] 24454

An address, delivered at commencement, August 27, 1828.
[Davis] 38346

An address, delivered at Concord
[Hill] 33543

An address, delivered at Cummington [Robinson] 10127

An address, delivered at Faneuil
Hall, Boston, January 8, 1828
[Greene] 33417

An address delivered at Fanueil
Hall, July 4, 1828 [Prince]
34885

An address, delivered at Hadlyme [Griswold] 33444

An address delivered at Hanover
[Lord] 33903

An address delivered at Hanson,
Mass. [Hitchcock] 38993

An address delivered at Hopkinton [Moore] 9531

Address delivered at Jefferson
Hall [Greenleaf] 33419

An address delivered at Kennebunk [Ware] 37080

An address, delivered at Limington [Greene] 8886

An address delivered at Lynn
[Cushing] 24267

An address delivered at Lyons
[Holley] 39015

An address delivered at Minot
[Hill] 20886

An address delivered at New
Castle, Del. [Read] 22038

An address delivered at Newbury,
Vt. [Wallace] 14815

An address, delivered at Newburyport [Cleaveland] 15782

An address delivered at Northampton [Truair] 30841

An address delivered at Pembroke [Allen] 27807

An address delivered at Plymouth [Carter] 24030

An address, delivered at Portland, February 6, 1824 [Ladd]
16837a

An address, delivered at Portland, on the decease of John
Adams, and Thomas Jefferson
[Daveis] 24300

An address, delivered at Port-

land, on the 27th December,
A. L. 5819 [Sias] 3222

An address, delivered at Portsmouth, N. H. 34823

Address, delivered at Roxbury
[Harrington] 1523

An address delivered at Roxbury
[Warren] 7585

An address delivered at St.
Paul's Church, Buffalo.
[Moulton] 6128

An address delivered at Somersworth, Great Falls [Holmes]
39019

An address, delivered at Springfield, before the Hampden
colonization socıety [Peabody]
34661

An address, delivered at Springfield, N. J. on the fiftieth anniversary of American independence [Cooke] 24214

Address delivered at Taunton
[Hamilton] 24784

Address delivered at the anniversary celebration of the Franklin Typographical Society.
24118

An address, delivered at the anniversary of the issue of the
first number of "The mechanic's free press." 37369

An address delivered at the annual commencement of the
Berkshire Medical Institution.
19492

An address, delivered at the annual meetıng of the Hartford
Benevolent Society. 1825

Address delivered at the annual
visitation of Amicable Lodge.
38982

An address delivered at the annual visitation of Union Lodge.
16600

An address delivered at the celebration of American independence at West Point. 18006

An address delivered at the celebration of the festival of St.
John the Evangelist. 11659

An address delivered at the celebration of the fiftieth anniversary of the independence of the United States. 26181

An address delivered at the close of the private school in Dixfield Village. 32403

An address, delivered at the close of the Sabbath School on Norwich Plain. 183

An address, delivered at the closing of a Sunday School in Maine. 15029

An address, delivered at the Collegiate Institution in Amherst. 12890

An address, delivered at the Columbian College, in the District of Columbia. 24971

An address delivered at the commencement of the General Theological Seminary [Croes] 24242

An address delivered at the commencement of the General Theological Seminary [Kemp] 21102

An address delivered at the commencement of the General Theological Seminary [White] 31733; 37164; 41502

An address, delivered at the consecration and installation of Mount Zion Royal Arch Chapter. 6640

An address delivered at the consecration of Golden Rule Lodge. 39315

An address, delivered at the consecration of Olive Branch Lodge. 11768

An address delivered at the dedication of the Town Hall in Worcester. 20269

Address, delivered at the eighth anniversary of the Massachusetts Peace Society. 15402

Address delivered at the eleventh anniversary of the Massachusetts Peace Society. 28982

An address, delivered at the erection of a monument to John Harvard. 33100

Address, delivered at the fifth anniversary of the Massachusetts Peace Society. 2927; 6579; 6580

Address delivered at the fifth anniversary of the Peace Society of Minot. 33729

An address, delivered at the first anniversary meeting of the Elizabeth-Town Apprentices' Library Association. 12986

An address delivered at the first anniversary meeting of the United Agricultural Society of South Carolina. 35135

An address delivered at the first anniversary of the Library Society of Edisto Island. 17496

An address delivered at the first anniversary of the Porter Rhetorical Society. 20377

Address, delivered at the formation of the Lycurgan Association. 2303

Address, delivered at the fourth anniversary of the Massachusetts Peace Society. 1350

An address delivered at the funeral of John Gorham, M.D. 39108

Address delivered at the funeral of the Hon. George Partridge. 33764

Address delivered at the Ichthyon Feast at Greenwich-Village. 24560

An address, delivered at the installation of officers, in Massachusetts Lodge. 8289

An address, delivered at the installation of Social Harmony Lodge. 13306

An address delivered at the installation of the officers of Belfast Lodge. 23446

Address, delivered at the installation of the officers of La Fayette Encampment. 16598

An address delivered at the installation of the officers of Mount Zion Royal Arch Chapter, Stoughton. 39054

An address, delivered at the installation of the officers of St. Paul's Royal Arch Chapter. 5645

An address delivered at the installation of the Worcester County Encampment. 23363

An address delivered at the interment of the Rev. Philander Chase. 17874

An address delivered at the laying of the cap-stone, of the ten combined locks at Lockport. 20221

An address delivered at the laying of the corner stone of the Bunker Hill monument. 23265; 23266; 23267; 23268; 23269

Address delivered at the laying of the corner stone of the Second Congregational Unitarian Church. 23217

An address delivered at the laying of the corner stone of the West Meetinghouse in Andover. 24406

An address delivered at the Meeting House in Bennington. 13307

Address, delivered at the Methodist Chapel in Norwich. 33552

Address delivered at the opening of Boston Mechanics' Institution. 28784

An address; delivered at the opening of Campbell Academy. 33600

An address delivered at the opening of Chauncy-Hall. 35486

Address, delivered at the opening of late convention of the Protestant Episcopal Church in Maryland. 12993

Address delivered at the opening of the Columbian College. 10336

An address, delivered at the opening of the 11th exhibition of the American Academy of Fine Arts. 21176; 25070

An address delivered at the opening of the late convention of the Protestant Episcopal Church in Maryland. 12994

An address delivered at the opening of the Medical College, in Charleston, S. C. 24415

An address delivered at the opening of the tenth exhibition of the American Academy of the Fine Arts. 23158

An address, delivered at the opening of the town-hall in Springfield, March 24, 1828. 32400

An address delivered at the opening of the twelfth exhibition of the American Academy of the Fine Arts. 25674

An address delivered at the ordination of the Reverend John Bell. 37095

Address delivered at the organization of Dickinson College. 9396

Address, delivered at the organization of the faculty of Dickinson College. 9395

Address delivered at the republican dinner at Lamprey River. 39983

An address delivered at the request of a committee of the citizens of Washington. 4400

An address, delivered at the request of Lodge no. 5, Middletown. 17760

Address delivered at the request of the Board of Directors of the first section of the first school district. 20346

An address, delivered at the request of the board of managers before the Fredericksburg Auxiliary Colonization Society. 32391

An address, delivered at the request of the committee of arrangements for celebrating the anniversary of independence. 4401; 4402

An address, delivered at the request of the Franklin Temperance Society. 40368

An address delivered at the request of the Mount-Moriah Lodge. 9038

An address, delivered at the request of the Republican Committee of arrangements. 9293

Address, delivered at the seventh

anniversary of the Massachusetts Peace Society. 14239

An address, delivered at the South meeting house in Carver. 32234

Address delivered at the tenth anniversary of the Massachusetts Peace Society. 25057

Address delivered at the thirteenth anniversary of the Massachusetts Peace Society. 37868

An address, delivered at the twelfth anniversary of the Massachusetts Peace Society. 37245

An address, delivered at the union celebration of independence, at Sutton, Mass. 16549

An address, delivered at Tinmouth. 33007

An address, delivered at Troy. 39975

An address, delivered at Uxbridge. 4317

An address delivered at Washington, D. C. 24835

Address delivered at Washington Hall. 23437

An address delivered at Watertown. 20043

An address delivered at Windsor, Vt. 24047

An address delivered at Worcester, August 24, 1820. 1415

An address, delivered at Worcester, Sept. 20, A. L. 5825. 25313

Address delivered before a meeting of revolutionary pensioners at Canandaigua. 15454

An address delivered before a number of military companies. 10118

An address delivered before Constellation Lodge. 38047

An address delivered before Lodge no. fifty. 12377

An address delivered before Manchester Lodge. 23704

An address delivered before Montgomery Lodge. 40628

An address delivered before

Mount Carmel Lodge. 8691

An address delivered before Mount Vernon Lodge. 21893

An address delivered before the Academy of Teachers of Philadelphia. 8280

An address delivered before the Adams South Village Temperance Society. 40301

Address delivered before the Adelphic Union Society of Williams College [Everett] 28817

An address, delivered before the Adelphic Union Society, of Williams College [Yale] 31827

An address delivered before the African Grand Lodge. 33549

Address delivered before the Agricultural Society of Bucks County. 13401; 13402

An address, delivered before the Agricultural Society of Susquehanna county. 3054

An address delivered before the Agricultural Society of the County of West Chester. 5530

Address delivered before the alumni of Columbia College [Bard] 23699

Address delivered before the alumni of Columbia College [Milledoler] 34138

Address delivered before the alumni of Columbia College [Moore] 21498

Address delivered before the alumni of Union College. 37275

Address delivered before the American Academy of Fine Arts. [Verplanck] 19139

An address, delivered before the American Academy of the Fine Arts [Ray] 22037

An address delivered before the American Education Society. 20761

Address, delivered before the American Institute of the City of New York [Lockwood] 39312

Address, delivered before the American Institute of the City of New-York [Lynch] 39344

An address delivered before the Anti-masonic Convention of the County of Addison. 37690

An address delivered before the Antiquarian and Historical Society of Illinois. 38889

An address delivered before the associated lodges of free and accepted Masons, meeting at Corinth. 22289

An address delivered before the associated lodges of free and accepted Masons, met at Walpole. 12345

An address, delivered before the Association of the Alumni of Middlebury College. 17012

An address, delivered before the Auxiliary missionary society of Morris. 2266

An address delivered before the Auxiliary New York Bible and Common Prayer Book Society. 16010

Address delivered before the Benevolent Society of Bowdoin College. 25589

An address delivered before the Berkshire Association for the Promotion of Agriculture and Manufactures [Briggs] 37942

An address delivered before the Berkshire Association for the Promotion of Agriculture and Manufactures [M'Kay] 9319

An address delivered before the Berkshire Association for the Promotion of Agriculture and Manufactures [Sedgwick] 14076

An address delivered before the Berkshire Association for the Promotion of Agriculture and Manufactures [Whiting] 31738

Address delivered before the Blockley and Merion Agricultural Society. 32465

An address delivered before the Bridgewater Society for the Promotion of Temperance. 37337

An address, delivered before the

Bristol County Agricultural Society. 10438

An address delivered before the Charleston Protestant Episcopal Sunday School Society [Bowen] 8161

An address delivered before the Charleston Protestant Episcopal Sunday School Society [Mitchell] 21490

An address delivered before the Charleston Protestant Episcopal Sunday School Society [Rutledge] 14026

An address delivered before the Cheraw Literary Society. 24208

An address delivered before the China Rifle Company. 15030

An address, delivered before the Chittenden County Medical Society. 8532

An address, delivered before the citizens of Charleston. 33244

Address, delivered before the citizens of North-Yarmouth. 21405

An address delivered before the citizens of Philadelphia. 35145

Address delivered before the citizens of Providence. 34792

Address delivered before the Columbian Institute. 21173

Address delivered before the Columbian Society. 24248

An address delivered before the convention of the Protestant Episcopal Church. 29233

Address delivered before the Coos Agricultural Society. 4824

An address delivered before the corps of cadets at West-Point. 20857

An address delivered before the corps of cadets of the United States Military Academy. 40288

An address, delivered before the Council of Select Masters. 11353

Address, delivered before the

Danvers Auxiliary Society for the Suppression of Intemperance. 29278

Address delivered before the Delaware Academy of Natural Science. 29017

An address delivered before the Essex Agricultural, at the agricultural exhibition in Topsfield, Oct. 2, 1822. 12425

An address delivered before the Essex Agricultural Society. 7727

Address, delivered before the Essex County Agricultural Society. 22099

An address delivered before the Female Benezet Philanthropic Society. 9259

Address, delivered before the fourth company, eighteenth regiment, Connecticut militia. 34735

An address delivered before the fraternity at Fall River Village. 20276

An address delivered before the fraternity of free and accepted Masons convened at Corinth, Vt. 29171

An address delivered before the General Society of Mechanics and Tradesmen. 9720

An address delivered before the Grafton Agricultural Society. 14886

An address delivered before the Grand lodge of Massachusetts. 23407

An address, delivered before the Hamilton County Agricultural Society. 30609

An address delivered before the Hampshire, Franklin, and Hampden Agricultural Society. 38610

An address delivered before the Hartford County Agricultural Society. 24719

An address delivered before the Hibernian Relief Society. 33969

An address delivered before the Hibernian Society and Association of the Friends of Ireland in Savannah. 38309

An address, delivered before the Hibernian Society of Alexandria, D. C. 20458

An address delivered before the Hibernian Society of the City of Savannah. 20776

An address, delivered before the Hingham Peace Society. 4842

Address delivered before the Hollis branch of Massachusetts Peace Society. 6099

An address, delivered before the inhabitants of Stratford. 30502

An address delivered before the Institutes of medicine and medical jurisprudence. 37755

Address delivered before the Jackson convention of delegates. 15891

An address delivered before the Jefferson County Agricultural Society. 39272

An address delivered before the Kennebec Bible Society. 14286

An address delivered before the Law Academy of Philadelphia. [Hopkinson] 24888

An address delivered before the Law Academy of Philadelphia [Ingraham] 33670

An address delivered before the Leicester Temperance Society. 38599

An address delivered before the Maine Charitable Mechanic Association. 6012

An address delivered before the Marine Bible Society, of New Haven. 30583

An address delivered before the Massachusetts Agricultural Society [Colman] 8396

An address delivered before the Massachusetts Agricultural Society [Quincy] 2928

An address delivered before the Massachusetts Agricultural Society [Pickering] 9934

An address delivered before the Massachusetts Charitable Me-

chanic Association October 4,
1821.   7625

An address delivered before the
Massachusetts Charitable Mechanic Association October 4,
1827.   29217

An address delivered before the
Massachusetts Charitable Mechanic Association October 7,
1823.   15693

An address delivered before the
Massachusetts Horticultural Society.   38354

An address delivered before the
Massachusetts Lodge.   14901

Address delivered before the Massachusetts Peace Society.
23216

An address delivered before the
Massachusetts Society for the
Suppression of Intemperance,
at their annual meeting.   27556

An address delivered before the
Massachusetts Society for the
Suppression of Intemperance.
June, 1826.   23917

An address delivered before the
Massachusetts Society for the
Suppression of Intemperance,
May 31, 1827.   30687; 30688

An address delivered before the
Massachusetts Society for the
Suppression of Intemperance,
May 29, 1828.   33200

Address delivered before the mechanics and working classes
generally of Philadelphia.
29189

An address delivered before the
Medical board of S. Carolina.
5076

An address, delivered before the
Medical Society of the State of
New York, ... Feb. 6, 1821.
6860

An address delivered before the
Medical Society of the state of
New-York... 2d of Feb., 1820.
3312

An address, delivered before the
members of the East-Haddam
branch of the Massachusetts
Peace Society.   510

An address, delivered before the
members of the Franklin Debating Club.   15031

An address, delivered before the
members of the New-Bedford
Lyceum.   38828

Address, delivered before the
members of the New England
Society, in Charleston [Dun-
kin]   1055

Address delivered before the
members of the New-England
Society, in Charleston [Hurl-
but]   9081

An address delivered before the
members of the Suffolk bar.
40552

An address, delivered before the
members of Union Lodge.
10458

An address delivered before the
Middlesex Mechanic Association.   28078

An address delivered before the
most worshipful Grand Lodge
of Massachusetts at the consecration of "Star in the East
Lodge."   15947; 16204

An address, delivered before the
Nantucket Society for the Suppression of Intemperance.
2069

An address, delivered before the
New Bedford Auxiliary Society
for the Suppression of Intemperance.   11442

An address delivered before the
New England Society of Philadelphia [Bond]   15494

An address delivered before the
New England Society of Philadelphia [Nancrede]   2385

Address delivered before the
New-England Society of South-
Carolina.   898

An address, delivered before the
New Hampshire, Franklin and
Hampden Agricultural Society.
2035

An address, delivered before the
Newark   ...   Auxiliary Bible
Society.   9060

An address, delivered before the

Newark Bible Society. 17162

An address, delivered before the Newburgh Lyceum. 14940

An address delivered before the Newton Temperance Society. 33428

An address delivered before the Olive-branch Society of Hampton Academy. 40097

An address, delivered before the Ontario Agricultural Society, at the town house, in Canandaigua. 30723

Address, delivered before the Ontario Agricultural Society... October 3, 1820. 1428

Address, delivered before the Ontario Agricultural Society, at its fifth annual meeting, October 28, 1823. 11534

Address, delivered before the Ontario Agricultural Society, at its fifth [i. e. sixth] annual meeting, October 26, 1824. 15742

Address, delivered before the Ontario Agricultural Society, at its fourth annual meeting. 8221

Address delivered before the Palmetto Society. 20208

Address delivered before the Peace Society of Hartford and vicinity. 33430

Address delivered before the Peace Society of Hartford County. 37922

Address delivered before the Peace Society of Windham County at its annual meeting in Brooklyn. 13730; 34718; 34719

Address delivered before the Peace Society of Windham County, at their semi-annual meeting in Pomfret. 30205

Address delivered before the Pennsylvania Peace Society. 38101

An address, delivered before the Pennsylvania Temperance Society. 33046

An address delivered before the Philadelphia Society for Promoting Agriculture; at its anniversary meeting January 18, 1820. 3441

An address delivered before the Philadelphia Society for Promoting Agriculture: at its anniversary meeting, January 16, 1821. 4844

Address delivered before the Philadelphia Society for Promoting Agriculture, at its annual meeting on the eighteenth of January, 1825. 23147

Address delivered before the Philadelphia Society for Promoting Agriculture, at its annual meeting, on the fifteenth of January, 1822. 8059

Address delivered before the Philadelphia Society for Promoting Agriculture, at its annual meeting, on the twentythird of January, 1823. 13738

Address delivered before the Philadelphia Society for Promoting Agriculture, at its meeting, on the twentieth of July, 1824. 15646; 15647; 15648; 28388

Address, delivered before the Philological Society Middlebury College, on the evening of the 15th August. 26109

Address, delivered before the Philological Society, Middlebury College, on the evening of the 19th August. 13676

An address delivered before the Philomathean Society of the University of Pennsylvania. 27687

An address delivered before the Pittsburgh Philosophical Society. 32501

Address delivered before the Portland Association for the Promotion of Temperance, February 11, 1829. 39705

Address delivered before the Portland Association for the Promotion of Temperance, February 22, 1828. 34557

An address delivered before the

Reading Peace Society. 25724

An address, delivered before the Republicans of Newport. 32227

An address delivered before the Republicans of Portsmouth. 33544

Address delivered before the Rhode Island Society for the Encouragement of Domestic Industry. 30803

An address delivered before the Rockingham Agricultural Society. 6492

Address delivered before the St. John's Lodge. 39954

An address delivered before the Salem Charitable Mechanic Association. 6843

An address, delivered before the school committees. 29180

An address, delivered before the Second Medical Society of the State of Vermont. 593

An address delivered before the social fraternity Phillips Academy. 32737

An address, delivered before the Society for Promoting Temperance, in Haverhill. 34727

An address, delivered before the Society for the Education of Poor & Indigent Children. 40214

An address delivered before the Society of Associated Mechanics and Manufacturers. 24740

An address delivered before the Society of Middlesex Husbandmen and Manufacturers. 11533

An address delivered before the society of the alumni of Williams College. 14966

An address delivered before the Somerset County Bible Society. 1322

An address delivered before the South-Carolina Society. 30406

An address delivered before the Strafford Agricultural Society. [Lyford] 21271

An address delivered before the Strafford Agricultural Society. [Walker] 23196

An address, delivered before the students of the General Theological Seminary. 19266

An address, delivered before the Suffolk Masonic Society. 14139

An address delivered before the teachers of the South Parish Sunday School. 11535; 33504

An address delivered before The Temperance Society of Bath, N. H. 39217; 39218; 39219

An address, delivered before the Temperate Society of Buckfield. 33074

An address, delivered before the trustees and students of the Alma College. 21284

An address, delivered before the trustees, faculty, and students of the General Theological Seminary. 14897

An address, delivered before the trustees, professors, and students of the General Theological Seminary [Onderdonk] 21748

Address delivered before the trustees, professors, and students of the General Theological Seminary [Turner] 14324

Address, delivered before the trustees, professors, and students of the General Theological Seminary [Wilson] 14943

Address delivered before the University in Cambridge at the interment of Professor Frisbie. 9735

An address delivered before the Wareham Lyceum Association. 37725

An address delivered before the Washington Chapter of Royal Arch Masons. 2598

Address delivered before the Windham County Peace Society. 37132

Address delivered before the Worcester Agricultural Society, October 8, 1823. 12554

Address delivered before the Worcester Agricultural Society, October 11, 1826. 31666

Address delivered before the Worcester Agricultural Society, October 13, 1824. 16325

Address, delivered before the
Worcester Agricultural Society,
October 12, 1820. 4707
Address delivered before the
Worcester Agricultural Society,
October 12, 1825. 30850
Address delivered before the
Worcester Agricultural Society,
September 25, 1822. 8538
Address delivered before the
Worcester Agricultural Society,
September 27, 1821. 6685
Address delivered before the
Young Man's Western Auxiliary
Bible Society. 1664
An address delivered before the
Young Men's Missionary So-
ciety of Savannah. 8657
An address delivered before the
Young Men's Missionary So-
ciety of South Carolina. 6649
An address, delivered before
Unity Lodge. 20501
An address, delivered before Ver-
mont Lodge. 24215
An address, delivered by appoint-
ment at Morristown. 32794
An address, delivered by appoint-
ment, in the Episcopal Church,
at the opening of the Appren-
tices' Library, in the city of
Albany. 6833
Address delivered by Gen. Wil-
liam H. Harrison. 16454
An address delivered by His Ex-
cellency Daniel D. Tompkins.
3459
An address delivered by invita-
tion [Union Village] 40497
An address delivered by Isaac
Clinton. 38203
Address delivered by Richard T.
Leech. 33835; 33836
Address delivered by Robert
Owen. 21759
An address delivered by T. J.
O'Malley. 21743
An address delivered in Alexand-
ria. 13080
Address delivered in Bethesda
Lodge. 12880
An address delivered in Brain-
tree. 22386

An address delivered in Burlington. 25228
Address, delivered in Castleton.
15283
An address delivered in Charleston, before the Agricultural
Society of South Carolina, at
its anniversary meeting, on
the 21st of August, 1827.
31668
An address delivered in Charleston before the Agricultural Society of South Carolina, at its
anniversary meeting on Tuesday, the 19th August, 1828.
33593
An address delivered in Chauncey
Place Church. 25037
An address, delivered in Gorham.
13288
An address, delivered in Hallowell. 3291
An address, delivered in Hanover,
N. H. 68
An address, delivered in Haverhill. 40035
An address, delivered in Hing-
ham. 5856
Address, delivered in Leicester.
29909
An address, delivered in Mason-
ick Hall. 24133
An address, delivered in Nash-
ville. 21224
An address delivered in Philadel-
phia. 25818
An address, delivered in Port-
land. 3201
An address, delivered in Ports-
mouth, N. H. 16080
An address delivered in St.
Anne's Church, Annapolis.
33533
An address delivered in St. Mi-
chael's Church. 24278
An address delivered in St.
Paul's Church [Wyatt] 4345
Address delivered in St. Paul's
Church, Radcliffeborough.
35473
An address delivered in St. Phil-
ip's Church. 29132
An address, delivered in St.

Stephen's church.   34611

An address delivered in Springfield.   19926

Address delivered in the Baptist
Meeting-house of Dudley
[Mass.]   33075

An address, delivered in the
Brick meeting house, in Danvers.   2620

An address delivered in the capitol, in Washington City.   37133

An address delivered in the
chapel of Amherst College.
35534

An address delivered in the
chapel of Dartmouth College.
21741

An address delivered in the church
at Princeton; the evening before
the annual commencement of
the College of New-Jersey September 29, 1829.   37771

An address delivered in the
church at Princeton, the evening before the annual commencement of the College of
New-Jersey, September 23,
1828.   33668

An address, delivered in the Congregational meeting-house in
Hansen.   26213

Address delivered in the First
Presbyterian Church, before
the St. Andrew's Society of the
city of Charleston.   39200

An address delivered in the Gaelic
Chapel, Aberdeen.   33405

An address delivered in the Orphan Asylum, New-York.
10331

An address delivered in the
South Dutch Church, Albany.
40508

An address, delivered in Utica.
27792

An address delivered July 4th,
1827.   28061

An address, delivered July 12,
1826.   25971

An address, delivered June 14,
1829.   41520

An address delivered March 8,
1825.   22072

An address, delivered March 2,
1829.   38368

An address delivered May 26,
1829.   38839

An address delivered May 23,
1820.   2649

An address delivered Nov. 12,
1828.   38706; 38707

An address, delivered on Edisto
Island.   35545

An address delivered on the anniversary of St. John the
Baptist.   4311

An address, delivered on the
celebration of the abolition of
slavery, in the state of New-
York.   30154

An address delivered on the commemoration at Fryeburg.
20265

An address, delivered on the 5th
day of July, 1828.   35411

An address delivered on the fifty-
second anniversary of American independence.   35544

An address delivered on the
fourth of July, 1820.   2937

An address delivered on the
Fourth of July, 1828.   33227

An address, delivered on the
opening of the Apprentices' Library of the City of New-York.
2240

Address delivered on the opening
of the New-York High-School
for Females.   24960

An address delivered on the 13th,
May 1824.   16346

Address delivered on the 29th of
September, 1824.   16883

An address delivered on Thursday, the 14th August, 1828.
32241

Address delivered this morning
on the Western Avenue.
12454

An address delivered to the
American Friendly Association.   20976

An address, delivered to the annual convention of the Protestant Episcopal Church in the
state of New-York.   1627; 5598;

12841

An address delivered to the citizens of Bristol, R.I. 5179

An address delivered to the class of graduates of Williams College. 8894

An address, delivered to the Colonization Society of Kentucky. 38195

An address delivered to the graduates of Washington College. 37258

An address delivered to the inhabitants of New Lanark. 21760

An address delivered to the Masonic fraternity of Ark Lodge. 28503

An address delivered to the students of the General Theological Seminary. 33567

Address delivered to the Vergenness Agricultural Society. 4011

An address delivered to the Ware Village Temperance Society. 38269

An address delivered to Warren Lodge. 6000

Address des Missions-Committee. 2963

An address, explanatory and vindicatory, to both parties of the Congregation of St. Mary's. 17490

Address; Feb. 23, 1820. 20

An address, for the benefit of the Greeks. 17161

Address from a meeting of Democratic citizens of Philadelphia. 29903

An address from the administration committee of Hamilton County. 29898

Address from the Choctaw delegation of Indians. 22659

An address from the committee of the New-York Athenaeum. 17401

Address from the Irish Emancipation Society. 40218

An address from the managers of the House of Refuge to their fellow citizens. 25743; 34761

An address from the Monthly Meeting of Friends of Philadelphia. 28966

Address from the standing committee of the Hampshire Sabbath School Union. 29128

An address from the teachers of a Sabbath School. 4406

An address from the Union Society of Queen Ann's County. 30865

An address in behalf of the Juvenile Library Company. 13952

An address in behalf of the temperance cause. 39716

An address, in commemoration of American indendence [sic] Delivered at Sidney. 12376

An address, in commemoration of American independence. Delivered at Palmyra. 14829

An address in commemoration of Lexington battle. 24431

An address in commemoration of the Battle of Bunker Hill. 20411

An address in commemoration of the Boston Massacre. 20412; 20413

An address in commemoration of the independence of the United States. 32212

An address in commemoration of the lives and services of Ledyard. 24760

An address, in commemoration of the sixth of September, 1781. 19850

An address in gospel love. 21

An address in regard to the memorial of the surviving officers of the Revolutionary army. 31889

An address in relation to the subject of Masonry. 37370

An address, intended to promote a geological and mineralogical survey of Pennsylvania. 23951

An address, intended when written, to have been delivered before the district conference of the Baltimore district. 33713

Address introductory to a course of lectures on mechanics. 39150

Address, May 31, 1820. 1707

Address, occasioned by the death of Aaron Bean. 1685

An address occasioned by the death of Nathan Smith. 37423

An address of a bank director to his constituents. 27780

Address of a committee of the board of education. 17685

Address of a convention of delegates of the state of Pennsylvania. 28587

Address of a meeting of citizens of the city and county of Philadelphia. 34752

An address of a minister to the youth of his congregation. 23421

Address of C. A. Wickliffe. 37172

Address of Chief Justice Parker. 34642

The address of David Trimble. 35559

The address of Epaminondas. 1429; 1430; 1431

Address of Erastus Root. 17850

An address of G. Burton Thompson. 40641

The address of Governor Edwards. 24410

The address of Henry Clay to his constituents. 28508

An address of Henry Clay, to the public. 28509; 28510; 32727; 32728; 32729; 32730; 32731; 32732; 32733; 32735

Address of Hon. William Walker. 4152

Address of Hon. William Wallace. 19175

Address of James Barbour. 19605

Address of Jonathan Allen. 4450

Address of Ninian Edwards. 16047; 18374

Address of Republican Members of the Legislature. 1001

Address of Republican members of the Senate and Assembly. 1002

Address of Robert Wickliffe. 31748

Address of students in Union College. 22540

An address of sundry citizens of Colleton district. 35364

Address of the administration convention, held in the capitol at Raleigh. 29896; 34396; 34397

Address of the Administration Convention in Baltimore County. 34375

Address of the Administration standing committee to their fellow-citizens of Indiana. 34369

Address of the Albany Colonization Society. 15052

Address of the Albany Republican corresponding committee. 996

Address of the American Convention for Promoting the Abolition of Slavery. 31955

Address of the American Home Missionary Society. 23483

The address of the board of directors of the Domestic and Foreign Missionary Society. 10026

Address of the board of education to the churches under the care of the synod of Pittsburgh. 34871

Address of the board of education to the Reformed Dutch Churches. 34973

Address of the Board of Health of the city of New-York. 9661; 13536; 25533

Address of the board of managers of the American Bible Society. 37431

Address of the board of managers of the American colonization society. 99

Address of the board of managers of the Brooklyn Temperance Society. 37948

Address of the board of managers of the Infant School Society. 29323

Address of the board of managers

of the Protestant Episcopal
Sunday School Society. 2900

Address of the board of managers
to the emigrants. 16491

Address of the Board of Managers
...to the friends and members
of the church. 14154

Address of the Board of Trustees
of the Protestant Episcopal
Theological Seminary. 10044

Address of the Bunker Hill Monument Association. 15588

Address of the carrier of the African Repository & Colonial
Journal. 31906

Address of the carrier of the
American Mercury. 31963

Address of the carrier of the
Boston Daily Advertiser.
23879; 28240

Address of the carrier of the Boston Patriot and Independent
Chronicle. 11946

Address of the carrier of the Columbian. 32774

Address of the carrier of the Evening Gazette. 23882

Address of the carrier of the Indiana Journal. 33656

Address of the carrier of the Indianapolis Gazette. 39087

Address of the carrier of The
Kentuckian. 39186

Address of the carrier, of the
Kentucky Reporter. 39192

Address of the carrier of the
Long Island Star. 39318

Address of the carrier of the
Nashville Gazette. 21585

Address of the carrier of The
New-York Daily Advertiser.
34535

Address of the carrier of the
Newport Mercury. 9711

Address of the carrier of The
Pennsylvania Intelligencer and
Farmers' and Mechanics' Jour-
nal. 40014

Address of the carrier of the
Pensacola Gazette & West Florida Advertiser. 34717

Address of the carrier of the
Repertory. 34997

Address of the carrier of the
"Republican Advocate." 17791

Address of the carrier, to the
patrons of the Evening Gazette.
38507

Address of the carrier, to the
patrons of The Maysville
Eagle. 13271

Address of the carriers for the
year of our Lord 1826. 23874

The address of the carriers of
Poulson's American Daily Advertiser. 11536; 15032;
21958; 40138

Address of the carriers of the
Albany Gazette. 19371

Address of the carriers of the
Boston Courier. 37903

Address of the carriers of the
Boston Evening Bulletin.
32433

Address of the carriers of the
Christian Mirror. 28484

The address of the carriers of
the Martinsburg Gazette.
29634; 39439

Address of the carriers of the
National Journal. 34367;
39698

Address of the carriers of the
New-Bedford Mercury. 39723

Address of the carriers of the
New-England Galaxy. 2410

Address of the carriers of the
Philadelphia Gazette. 34760

Address of the carriers of the
Savannah Republican. 35103

Address of the carriers of the
United States' Telegraph.
36983; 41345

Address of the carriers of the
Wilmingtonian. 31775

Address of the carriers to the
patrons of the Christian Repository. 15759

Address of the carriers to the
patrons of the New England
Palladium. 29927

Address of the central committee appointed by a convention
of both branches of the legislature. 34376; 34377

Address of the Central Commit-

An address of the Jackson Demo-
cratick committee of correspondence. 32950

Address of the Jackson state convention. 28688

Address of the lay trustees to the
congregation of St. Mary's
Church. 7742

An address of the Lehigh Coal
and Navigation Company. 5811

Address of the male members of
the Methodist Episcopal Church
in Baltimore. 29737

Address of the managers of the
American Sunday School Union.
23494; 23495

Address of the managers of the
Philadelphia Bible Society.
28178

Address of the managers of the
Protestant Episcopal Missionary Society. 2897

Address of the New-Bedford Institute of Instruction. 21601

Address of the New York State
Tract Society. 17423

Address of the pastor of the
Third Church, Newark. 40332

An address of the people of Kentucky. 15957

Address of the people of Louisiana. 32927

Address of the Pennsylvania Society for the Promotion of National Industry. 2714

Address of the President and
Managers of the Schuylkill
Navigation Company. 6731

Address of the president of the
South-Carolina College. 12258

An address of the Republican central committee. 32924

Address of the Republican Committee of Correspondence.
32951

Address of the Republican General Committee of Young Men of
the City and County of New
York. 15962; 32937

Address of the Republican members of the Legislature. 15033

Address of the Republican young
men of the town of Galway.

31890

Address of the Right Rev. Bishop
Hobart. 12842

Address of the Right Rev. Henry
U. Onderdonk. 39927

Address of the Roman Catholics
of New York to John Connolly.
4407

Address of the Society in Hampden county. 1497

Address of the Society of Inquiry
Respecting the Advancement
of Christianity. 18038

Address of the state convention
of delegates from the several
counties of the state of New-
York. 34384

Address of the sufferers of the
Eastern District. 8778

Address of the trustees of St.
Mary's Church. 13751

Address of the Trustees of St.
Peter's School. 10167

Address of the trustees of the
Evangelical Missionary Society. 12477

Address of the trustees of the
Massachusetts General Hospital. 9423

Address of the trustees of the
Missionary Society of Connecticut. 21474

Address of the Trustees of the
Polytechnic and Scientific College. 25796

An address of the trustees of the
Public School Society. 34939

Address of the trustees of the
University of Pennsylvania.
40017

Address of the Wilmington Monthly Meeting of Friends. 28971

Address of the Young Men's Association of Trenton. 34382a

Address of Thomas R. Gold.
1400

An address on ardent spirits.
34359; 39689

Address on church music. 25249;
29657

Address on confirmation. 15909

Address on domestic manufactures. 37141

An address on female education,
delivered in Portsmouth.
28330

An address on female education,
delivered in Zanesville. 20320

An address on female education;
delivered Nov. 21st, 1827.
28992; 33316

Address on infant schools. 40333

Address on intemperance in the
use of ardent spirits. 37383

An address on intemperance.
Pronounced at Nashua Vil-
lage, N. H. 38717

An address on musick. 17650

An address on religion, slavery,
the plantation. 40087

An address on sacred music, as
delivered at the concert of the
Presbyterian Church. 38301

Address on sacred music; delivered at the anniversary of the
Handel and Hastings Society.
29916

An address on the character and
objects of science. 29090

An address on the character and
services of De Witt Clinton.
33618

An address on the death of Alfred Mason. 32656

An address, on the death of the
venerable and illustrious
Adams and Jefferson. 27712

An address on the disorder
which prevailed among the
horned cattle in Orange county. 4496

An address on the emancipation
of slaves. 4904

Address on the expediency and
duty of adopting the Bible as
a class book. 38847

Address on the importance of
charity. 40689

Address on the means of opening
new sources of wealth for the
northern states. 5434

An address on the necessity of
education. 30728

An address on the principles of
Masonry, delivered in the
Church at Frankfort, Ken-

tucky. 5661

An address on the principles of
Masonry, delivered on the 23
of June, 1821. 5369

An address on the progress of
manufactures. 29381

Address on the removal of the
municipal government. 2623

Address on the several subjects
of science. 20644

Address on the state of the public mind. 38332

Address, on the subject of an
"American Academy of Lan-
guages and Belles-Lettres."
672

An address, on the use of ardent spirit. 34552

An address prefatory to the
reading of the Declaration of
Independence. 8539

Address, pronounced at Haddam.
34646

An address, pronounced at Nantucket. 9148

Address pronounced at Natick.
16490

An address, pronounced at the
dedication of the new Masonic
Hall. 387; 1396

An address, pronounced at the
laying of the corner stone of
St. Matthew's Church. 6723

An address, pronounced at the
opening of the New York
Athenaeum. 19256; 23303

An address, pronounced at Wilton. 33884

An address pronounced August 15,
1828. 33160

An address, pronounced before
the Franklin Library Society.
1167

An address pronounced before the
medical graduates of the University of Maryland. 35232;
40456

Address pronounced before the
New-York Horticultural Society. 25404

An address pronounced before the
Union Harmonic Society. 5291

An address, pronounced in Worcester. 19475

An address pronounced on the anniversary of the Concord Lyceum. 38559

Address read before the New-York Horticultural Society. 28415

An address, reported by the Committee appointed at Wilkesboro'. 32947

An address. The following communication from our beloved friend, William Williams. 19296

Address to a child. 15034

An address to all lay exhorters and lay preachers. 6049

An address to back sliders. 23422

An address to children. 22

An address to Christians and ministers. 6025; 17129

An address to earnest seekers of salvation. 5337

An address to Episcopalians. 15139

An address, to every believer in America. 8356

An address to Friends in Great Britain. 14117

An address to friends within the compass of the Yearly Meeting. 28968

Address to his friends and the public in reply to the report of the committee and proceedings of New-Hampshire. 8645

An address to imperfect and perfect believers. 38594

An address to imperfect believers. 5338

An address to masons. 15540

An address to Methodists. 31891

Address to Mothers. 20438

Address to parents and the public. 25492

An address to physicians. 39817

An address to professed Christians. 4835

An address to professed Christians, in two parts. 4905

Address to seamen [Ladd] 29441

An address to seamen [Payson] 6401; 6402; 9829

An address to students of law. 16565

Address to such as inquire; what must we do to be saved? 16157

Address, to the Agricultural Society of Hamilton County. 38491

Address to the Agricultural Society of Maryland. 2190

An address to the Agricultural Society of Portage County. 22497

Address to the Associate Congregations of Ebenezer & Timber Ridge. 20866

An address to the Baptist churches in Maine. 246

An address to the biennial convention of the Eastern Diocess[!]. 1462

An address to the board of aldermen, and members of the common council, of Boston. [Otis] 39943

An address to the board of aldermen and members of the common council, of Boston [Quincy] 17746; 25886; 30395; 32414; 37885; 37886

An address to the brethren of Mount Vernon lodge. 10184

An address to the Brethren of South Elkhorn Church. 4562

An address to the Catholic voters of Baltimore. 33711

Address to the Chester County Cabinet of Natural Science. 27737

Address to the children of Israel in Maryland. 1838

Address to the children of the New York Union Sunday Schools. 2545

An address to the Christian Churches in Kentucky, Tennessee, & Ohio. 6902

An address to the Christian public. 23484

An address to the church and

congregation. 40629

An address to the citizens of
Connecticut. 32920

An address to the citizens of
North Carolina. 12071; 12072

Address to the citizens of Pennsylvania. 21846

An address to the citizens of
Providence, R.I. 20754

Address to the citizens of the
city and county of Philadelphia.
24158

Address to the citizens of the
Commonwealth of Pennsylvania.
21847

An address to the citizens of the
state of Tennessee. 11540

Address to the citizens of the
United States. 8253; 15649

An address to the citizens of the
United States, on the effects
of war and peace. 31737

An address to the citizens of the
United States, on the subject
of ardent spirits. 7743; 19373

Address to the clergy, legislature and wealthy citizens.
16060

Address to the clergy of the
United States. 15035

An address to the Columbian Institute. 33822

Address to the committee appointed by a general meeting
of the citizens of the City of
New York. 37371

An address to the committees on
education of both houses of the
legislature of Kentucky. 645

Address to the community on the
necessity of legalizing the study
of anatomy. 39521

An address to the congregation of
St. Mary's Church. 1639;
5611

Address to the convention of the
Diocese of New-York. 38997

Address to the Danvers Auxiliary
Society, for Suppressing Intemperance and other Vices,
and Promoting Temperance and
General Morality. April 30,
1822. 7731.

Address to the Danvers Auxiliary
Society, for Suppressing Intem-
perance and other Vices, and
Promoting Temperance and
General Morality, April 24,
1821. 10018

Address to the diocesan convention. 33443

Address to the electors of Middlesex County. 34368

Address to the electors of Pennsylvania. 12072a

An address to the electors of the
ninth ward. 31892

Address to the electors of the
senatorial district. 20087

An address to the eleventh convention of the Eastern diocese.
24758

An address, to the Essex Agricultural Society, at their first
cattle show. 6294; 6295

An address to the Essex Agricultural Society, in Massachusetts. 16602

Address to the farmers of Rhode
Island. 31893

Address to the farmers of the
United States. 4913; 4914

An address to the Federalists of
New-Jersey. 33462

An address to the flocks. 23423

An address to the fourteenth convention of the Protestant Episcopal Church. 38864

Address to the free electors of
Pennsylvania. 11541

Address to the free people and
independent citizens of Maryland. 23

An address to the freeman of
Rhode Island. 31894

Address to the freemen of Kentucky. 29890

Address to the freemen of Morgan County. 35495

Address to the freemen of Rhode
Island. 31895

Address to the freemen of the
agricultural and manufacturing
interests of Rhode Island.
40135

Address to the friends of Andrew

Jackson. 32923

Address to the friends of religion. 19407

Address to the friends of sound doctrine. 33816

An address to the graduates in Washington College. 4349

An address to the graduates of Miami University. 37853

An address to the graduates of the Medical College of South Carolina. 40428

Address to the graduates of the South-Carolina College. 5077

An address to the guardians of the Washington Asylum. 27782

Address to the Hampshire, Franklin and Hampden Agricultural Society. 11762

Address to the Hillsborough Agricultural Society. 160

An address, to the honorable the Legislature of the state of New-York. 39265

Address to the humane. 38050

Address to the independent electors of Jefferson County. 19245

Address to the independent Federal electors of New York. 19374

An address to the independent Federal electors of the state of New-York. 24; 25; 26; 27

An address to the inhabitants of Rhode-Island. 19375

An address to the inhabitants of the city of New-York. 39818

Address to the inhabitants of the county of Onondaga. 37482

An address to the KA Society of Hippocrates. 14948

An address to the ladies of St. Mary's Congregation. 4408

Address to the landholders and farmers of Newport County. 37995; 37996

An address to the lay preachers of New Haven. 6050

An address to the legislature of Kentucky. 12287

Address to the liberal and humane. 37372; 37373

Address to the Literary and Philosophical Society of South Carolina. 9156

Address to the members of Solomon's lodge. 11995

An address to the members of the bar of Suffolk, Mass. 22402

An address to the members of the bar of the counties of Hampshire, Franklin and Hampden. 28204

Address to the members of the Episcopal Church. 34077

Address to the members of the first Presbyterian Congregation in Philadelphia. 28

An address to the members of the Methodist Episcopal Church; by a meeting of Methodists. 30278

An address to the members of the Methodist Episcopal Church, on the subject of reform. 27783

Address to the members of the next Legislature of the State of New York. 11542

An address to the members of the Protestant Episcopal Church in Maryland. 37374

An address to the members of the Rochester Athenaeum. 40025

Address to the members of trade societies. 29190

An address to the Middlebury Female Bible Society. 1683

An address to the ministers and members of the Methodist Episcopal Church. 19376

An address to the ministers, of the Unitarian Society. 4409

Address to the officers composing the medical staff. 2304

An address to the parents. 31837

Address to the patrons of the Manufacturer's and Farmer's Journal and Independent Inquirer. 24737

Address to the patrons of the Western Sun. 41485

Address to the people. Anti-

masonic state convention.
40630

An address to the people of
Charles, Calvert and St.
Mary's counties.   32928

Address to the people of Connecticut.   32921

An address to the people of Lincoln County.   11543

An address to the people of
Maine.   29; 30; 2072

An address to the people of
Maryland.   15626

An address to the people of Ohio.
17483

Address to the people of Pennsylvania.   31896

Address to the people of Philadelphia.   38333

An address to the people of Rhode
Island.   36986

Address to the people of the
counties of Columbiana, Stark
and Wayne.   26086

Address...to the people of the
state of New-York.   17425

Address to the people of the
United States [Atlee]   11646

Address to the people of the
United States [Free Trade Con-
vention]   33249

Address to the people of the
United States.   [Mt. Holly]
31897

An address to the people of the
United States, being an examination of a pamphlet, written
by "Aristides."   32502

An address to the people of the
United States, drawn up by order of the National Institution
for the Promotion of Industry.
2391; 6180

An address to the people of the
United States, on the presidential election.   15328

An address, to the people of the
United States, on the subject of
the presidential election.   32784

An address to the people of Winchester.   6907

Address to the people, representatives, and president of the U.S.
23424

An address to the pewholders &
congregation of St. Mary's
Church.   27784

Address to the physicians of
Philadelphia.   4262

The address to the Protestant
Episcopal Sunday School Society.   4957

Address to the public by the
Lackawana Coal Mine and Navigation Co.   15036; 16836

Address to the public by the managers of the Colonization Society of Connecticut.   24162;
32770

An address to the public from the
trustees of the Gardiner Lyceum.   8802

An address to the public of Philadelphia.   16668

Address to the public on the
causes and treatment of disease.   22462

An address to the public on the
subject of establishing a Library and Theological Institution.   31

Address to the public.   Philadelphia, August 20, 1829.   38051

An address to the public, the patrons of literature and religion.
7637

An address to the public, with a
letter to the Rev. Wm. Jackson.   33115

Address to the republican citizens
of the state of New York.
34385

Address to the Republican electors
of the state of New York.
17546

An address to the Republicans and
people of New York, Pennsylvania and Virginia.   15037;
15038; 15039

Address to the Rhode-Island Society for the Encouragement of
Domestic Industry, delivered
at Pawtuxet, October 17, 1821.
8216

Address to the Rhode Island Society for the Encouragement of

Domestic Industry, delivered at Pawtuxet, October 16, 1822. 10117

Address to the Right Rev. the Bishop of Pennsylvania. 677; 678; 8254

An address to the Roman Catholic congregation of New-York. 6943

An address to the Roman Catholics of Philadelphia. 12772

An address to the Roman Catholics of the city of Philadelphia. 13276

An address to the Roman Catholics of the United States. 4410

Address to the Senate and House of Representatives of the United States. 8255

Address to the senior class. 28361

Address to the sinner. 15991

An address to the stockholders of the Bank of Pennsylvania. 37583

Address to the stockholders of the Chesapeake & Delaware Canal. 15650

Address to the Synod of the Reformed Presbyterian Church in America. 29580

Address to the temperate. 38444

An address to the tenth convention of the Eastern diocese. 20766

Address to the trustees of St. Peter's School. 9000

An address to the twelfth convention of the Protestant Episcopal Church. 29092

An address, to the Utica Forum. 16720

An address to the Utica Lyceum. 21061

An address to the Utica Temperance Society. 39143

Address to the Vincennes legislature. 37855

An address to the voters of the electoral district. 31898

An address to the whites. 23906

Address to the young men of the county of Essex. 27785

Address to those on whom heaven has bestowed the goods of fortune. 15651

An address to those who have the care of children. 32

An address to William Tudor. 4915

An address to young people attending Sabbath schools. 27786

An address to young persons after confirmation. 11355

An address to young persons on the great importance of a religious & devotional temper. 14868

An address to youth. 33

Address upon the ceremony of dedicating the new Masonic hall. 28859

An address upon the dominant errors of the agriculture of Maryland. 34354

An address, upon the effects of ardent spirits. 29426; 29427; 33785; 33786; 33787; 33788; 33789; 33790

An address, upon the subject of intemperance. 33791

An address upon the subject of temperance. 33792

Address written at the request of the Association of the Friends of Ireland. 39363

An address, written for the fiftieth anniversary of our independence. 31899

Addresse an das Volk von Dauphin County. 32953

Addresses... [Philadelphia Society for the Promotion of National Industry] 2750

Addresses by Rev. James Appleton. 139

Addresses, delivered at Oxford. 21440

Addresses, delivered at the celebration of the thirteenth anniversary of the victory of New Orleans. 37289

Addresses delivered at the inauguration of the Rev. Robert G. Wilson. 17485

Addresses delivered before the

Association for Religious Improvement. 23551

Addresses, delivered in the Gaelic chapel, Aberdeen. 38806

Addresses delivered on laying the corner stone of the intended penitentiary. 35382

Addresses delivered on various public occasions. 1398; 38763

Addresses; or, The offering of a Sunday school teacher. 31900

Addresses to children. 38035

Addresses to Sabbath-School scholars. 32821

Addresses to the electors of Pennsylvania. 11544

Adelaide, or the rainy evening. 27787.

Adeline; or, The victim of seduction; an affecting tale. 31901

Adeline, the victim of seduction, a melo drama. 9828; 21795

L'adieu. A rondo. 18178

Adieu Auld Robin Gray. 20939

An adjourned meeting of the citizens of Kershaw District. 35365

Adjust claims of South Carolina. 35638

Adjutant general's office, General order. 7044

Adjutant General's office, Orders. 10515

Adlum on making wine. 23425

The administration, and the opposition. 24778

Administration convention. At a convention of members of both branches of the Legislature. 34378

Administration convention of young men. 34386

Administration convention. Proceedings had at a meeting. 29892

Administration meeting in Cooper County. 34379

The administrator's manual and clerk's guide. 38747

Administrator's sale. 11301

Administrators of Andrew Mitchell. 26335

Administrators of John Wilson. 40779

The admired air of Paddy Carey. 1996

Admired cotillions for balls & private parties. 34; 35

The adopted child. 4716

Adopted citizens to your posts! 37375

Adsonville; or, Marrying out. 16614

The advantages and disadvantages of drunkenness. 4412

The advantages of early religion. 29703

The advantages of the proposed canal from Lake Erie, to Hudson's River. 8794

Advantages which man derives from woman. 26137

An adventure in Vermont. 36; 37; 19377

Les adventures de Télemaque. 28865

Adventures, love and constancy of Paul and Virginia. 35092

Adventures of A. Apple Pie. 38

The adventures of a Bible. 11546; 23426

Adventures of a French serjeant. 23689; 28048

The adventures of a king's page. 41494

The adventures of a work-bag. 23427

The adventures of a young rifleman. 23428

The adventures of Boby the Bold. 19781

The adventures of Don Juan. 23429

The adventures of Don Quixote. 4933; 12084; 20015; 32624

The adventures of Gil Blas. 1936; 16884; 29478; 33840; 39273

Adventures of Goody Two Shoes. 39

The adventures of Hajji Baba. 17230; 34199

The adventures of Little Red

dependence of the United States. 23849

Agency of God in the elevation of man.   34924

Agent--lead mines, Missouri and Illinois, &c.   35640

Aggregate amount of each description of persons in the United States 10516

Aggregate amount of persons in the United States.   7046

The agreeable surprise.   17486; 25630

The Agricultural Almanac.   44; 4418; 4419; 4420; 4421; 7726; 7752; 7753; 11548; 11549; 15041; 15042; 15043; 19379; 19380; 23435; 27790; 31908; 31909; 37385; 37386

Agricultural almanac: or the New-York and Upper-Canada Calendar.   4422

An agricultural and economical almanac.   45

The agricultural reader.   15021

The Agricultural Society of Columbia County, offer the following premiums.   4423

Agriculture, commerce and manufactures.   23436

Agriculture of the United States.   30062; 30063

El aguinaldo.   31910; 37388

Ah Country Guy.   20666

Ah did you know enchanting fair. 11483

Ah, se de mali miei.   3058

Ah vous dirai je maman.   15645

Ah! what is the bosom's commotion.   1831

Ah! who sits so sadly.   15311

The Ahiman Rezon, containing a view of the history and polity of Free Masonry.   20590

An ahiman rezon, for the use of the Grand lodge of ancient Free-masons of South-Carolina.   8493

Aids to reflection, in the formation of a manly character. 38222

Ainsi jadis un gran prophète. 13791

Air, avec douze variations pour s'accoutumer à metre les deux mains ensemble.   7759

Air de ballet with variations for the piano forte.   1857; 13007

Air le Joseph.   15482

Air navigation.   29004

The air of the dashing white sergeant.   3019

Air Russe and Cosaque.   14197

Air, with variations for the piano forte [Cathrall] 20007

Air, with variations for the piano forte [Taws] 14258

The airs, songs and chorus's in the popular pantomime of [ ] Brazen mask.   5150

Al Aaraaf, Tamerlane, and minor poems.   40099

The Alabama Almanack.   58; 4436; 7765; 11562

The Alabama justice of the peace.   9018

The Alabama visiter.   38712

Aladdin, a fairy opera.   26095

An alarm to unconverted sinners. 11575; 37416

Alasco: a tragedy, in five acts. 17959; 22260

Albany County agricultural tracts, No. 1.   7767

Albany Daily Advertiser Extra [Circular letter] 15055

The Albany directory.   4442; 4374; 31919; 37404

Albany Grand Canal Ode. 19387

The Albany primer.   11565

Albermarle County Court.   On Tuesday, 7th inst. Messrs. C. Brigham and S. K. Head. 37410

Albertus Magnus, bewährte und approbirte sympatecische und natürliche egyptische Geheimnisse für Menschen und Vieh... 11568

The Albigenses, a romance. 17081

The album.   15057

The album. [Clarke]   768

Album. [Hale] 24774

Aldiborontiphoskyphorniostikos; a round game.   22371

Alejandro, ó la satisfaccion generosa. 31921
Alexander and Rufus. 120
Alexander Claxton. 40780
Alexander Garden. 35641
Alexander Hamilton's report on the subject of manufactures. 30909
Alexander M'Nish. 26338; 26339
Alexander Montgomery. 40781
Alexander Scott. 35642; 40782; 40783
Alexander the Great, a tragedy. 9247
Alexander's feast. 12758
The Alexandria almanac. 70; 7772; 11571
Alfred the Great; an historical tragedy. 9329
Alfred the Great; or, The Patriot king. 39236
Alger's Murray. English grammar. 17263; 25442; 34220;
Alger's Perry. The orthoepical guide to the English tongue. 21864; 34730; 40031
Ali Baba; or, The forty thieves. 31925
Ali Bey. This celebrated horse will stand... 30410
Ali Pacha; or, The signet-ring. 13682
Alice Bradford. 33392
Alice Gray. A ballad. 2261
Alice Gray. With variations. 883
All and sundry. 2945
All for the best. 11573
All hail, Massachusetts! 16125
All hail old hickory!! 35549
All hail to the brave and free! 31926
All hands, unmoor! 34647
All in the dark. 9950
All religions and religious ceremonies. 13959
All that's bright and fair must fade. 14203
All the world's a stage. 9131; 9132
Alleine on the promises. 31928
Allen B. McAlhany. 35643
Allen M'Leod. 30817

Allen's almanac for 1825. 15066
Allen's exposition of the controversy subsisting between Silas Hathaway and himself. 7777
Allen's New England almanack for 1821. 85
Das allgemeine A-B-C-Buchstabir- und Lesebuch. 3118; 17904
Allgemeine Gesetze der Wilhelm Tell's Loge. 30101
Allgemeiner Beweis des polynomischen Lehrsatzes ohne die Voraussetzung bimomischen. 20768
Allgemeines Vieharzneibuch, oder Unterricht, wie der Landmann seine Pferde, sein Rindvieh. 13983
The alliance, Lady Murray's and the pavilion favorite waltzes. 4455; 19398
All's well. A duett. 11976
Allowances to revolutionary officers. 26340
Almack's, a novel. 29268
Almack's revisited. 37163
An almanac. 4456; 4457; 11587; 15068; 19399; 19400; 23462; 23464; 23465; 27812; 27813; 27814; 31940
Almanach de commerce pour la Nouvelle-Orleans. 23463
Almanach de la Louisiane pour 1828. 27811
Almanack, or Christian calendar for 1827. 23466
The almost Christian discovered. 6002; 17083; 29709
Alnwick castle, with other poems. 29117
Alone by the light of the moon. 1653
Alonzo and Melissa. 16692; 34166
Alonzo's dream. 14985
The alphabet, in verse. 11588
The alphabet of Goody Two Shoes. 4458
An alphabet of lessons for children. 86
The alphabet of the primitive language of Spain. 38485
The alphabet of thought. 20820

The alphabet; or, The young
child's first instructor. 23467
Alphabet ou Methode simple &
facile de montrer promptement
a lire aux enfans ainsi qu'aux
etrangers qui veulent appendre
le français. 38121
Alphabetical catalogue of the Li-
brary. 38032
Alphabetical table, of all the
towns and cities in the state of
New-York. 22336
The Alpine maid. 1923; 1924
Alterations and amendments in
the articles and plan of associ-
ation of the proprietors. 6444
Alterations in the Hall. 22660
Always happy: or, Anecdotes of
Felix and his sister Serena.
27817
Ambitious views. 37426
Ambrosio, or the Monk. 9261
Amend the Constitution. 30910
Amend the revenue laws. 26341
Amended charter of incorporation
of St. Johns Methodist Protes-
tant Church. 37578
An amended version of the Book
of Job. 28111
Amendment offered by Mr.
Speaker. 34475
Amendment to chapter I. Of the
third part of the proposed re-
vision, relating to the Court of
Chancery. 34476
Amendments of the constitution of
Massachusetts. 5966
Amendments proposed by the se-
lect committee to Articles two
and three, of Chapter XVI.
31859
Amendments proposed to the fed-
eral constitution. 7526
Amendments to Chapter VI. 31860
Amendments to the Second Chap-
ter of the report of the re-
visers. 31861
America: or, A general survey
of the political situation.
28816
American agricultural almanack.
90
The American almanac and re-

pository of useful knowledge.
37428; 37429
The American almanack. 27818;
27819; 31942; 31943
American and Foreign Agency for
Claims, &c. under the direction
of Aaron H. Palmer. 37430
The American & New Orleans
favorite waltzes. 11651
American anecdotes, characters
and incidents. 11589; 12893
The American annual register.
27820; 31944
The American arithmetic, adapted
to the currency of the United
States. 4239; 7623; 27598;
31702
The American arithmetick; ... al-
so, a short system of book-
keeping. 22114
American atlas. 28873; 31576
American bards. 4153
An American biographical and
historical dictionary.   7785
The American book-keeper.
10269
The American botanist, and fam-
ily physician. 17194
The American builder's compan-
ion.   388; 23743; 28099
The American Caledonian. 19288
The American chancery digest.
32563
The American Chesterfield.
27826; 31953
The American coast pilot. 8115;
23846; 28205
The American common-place book
of prose. 32657; 32658
The American companion. 29175
American Constitutional Law. 101
American cookery.   10279
The American critic.   102
The American definition spelling
book.   1877: 25038
An American dictionary of the
English language.   37115;
41455
The American directory and trav-
eller's companion. 8919
The American dispensatory. 8458;
12280; 20206; 28614
American domestic cookery.

10160; 14014

The American Education Society
is now assisting two hundred
beneficiaries. 4469

American entomology. 17901;
35104

American family physician. 16088

The American farmers' agricultural almanack. 4471

The American Farmers' Almanack.
4472; 7799; 11600; 15084; 19408;
23481; 27834; 31959

The American farrier; or, New-
York horse doctor. 23482

The American first class book.
13776; 17641; 21903; 25775;
34799; 40083

The American gardener;   A
treatise on cultivation of vege-
tables. 12191

The American gardener: containing ample directions for working a kitchen garden. 24659

The American gardener's calendar. 2066; 33959

American goods. 41515

An American grammar. 597;
4848; 32491

The American harmonist. 6692

American hemp, flax, and cotton.
35674

American herpetology. 29137

American ichthyology. 29481

The American instructer [Bent-
ley] 15327; 19664; 23755;
37764

The American instructer [Kelley]
21091; 25017

The American instructer
[Twitchell] 22529

The American Ladies Pocket
Book.   106; 4473; 7800; 15085;
19410; 23486

The American Lady's Preceptor.
107; 4474

American Literary Scientific and
Military Academy, Norwich,
Vermont. 2662

American Lyceum of Science and
the Arts... 23487; 27836

American Lyceum, or Society for
the Improvement of Schools...
39008; 39009

American medical biography.
35480

American medical botany. 460

American military biography.
19411; 23488; 23489; 37866

The American militia officer's
manual. 20357; 20358

American minstrel. 34091

The American missionary register. 18267

American modern practice.
26193

American museum, and repository of arts and sciences, as
connected with domestic manufactures and national industry.
7801; 11601

American natural history. 24696

The American new dispensatory.
6952

American orator. 17995; 32720

The American orchardist. 10430;
22442

American ornithology [Bonaparte]
19787; 19788; 19789

The American ornithology [Hall]
33460

American ornithology [Wilson]
37207

The American penman [Hunting-
ton] 16620; 20979

The American penman [Perkins]
25723; 30204

The American physician, and
family assistant. 26087

The American physician: being
a new system of practice
founded on botany. 17845

American political and military
biography. 19412

American popular lessons...
3029; 11603; 23490; 30465;
37688

The American practical catechism. 4475; 10405

The American practical lunarian.
7840

American precedents of declarations. 4487

The American preceptor improved. 462; 4709; 4710;
11859; 15404; 19732; 23824;
37848

The American primer. 7802
The American pronouncing spelling book. 21130
American psalmody. 39107
The American reader. 1690; 31964; 31965
American school class book. 30261; 34794; 40076
The American school grammar of the English language. 34114
The American school-master's assistant. 12739
American seaman's hymn book. 24307
The American shooter's manual. 27838
American sketches. 7803; 7804
American songster. 37449; 39179
The American speaker. 24563
American speeches. 19654
The American spelling book.
  4221; 4222; 4223; 4224; 4225;
  7612; 7613; 7614; 7615; 11372;
  11373; 11374; 11375; 11376;
  14855; 14856; 14857; 14858;
  19233; 19234; 19235; 19236;
  19237; 23272; 23273; 23274;
  23275; 23276; 23277; 27586;
  27587; 31690; 31691; 31692;
  31693; 31694; 31695; 37116;
  37117; 37118; 37119; 37120;
  37121; 37122; 41456; 41457;
  41458; 41459
American stage. 23493
The American star. 13089
American Statesman and City Register. 19415
The American Sunday School Union. 37450
The American system. 34962
An American system for the protection of American industry. 15091
The American system. Internal improvements and domestic manufactures. 34401
An American system of English grammar. 8186; 19877; 23943; 37957
The American system of practical book-keeping. 390; 15316; 23748; 32267; 37758

The American system, or the effects of high duties on imports. 33454
American taxation. 27843
American taxation. The Primrose Hill. 35091
The American teacher's assistant. 25177
The American teacher's lessons of instruction. 29034
The American telegraph signal book. 11802
The American telescope. 21175
American Theatre, in Mercer-Street. 11606
The American toilet. 21541; 29838
American traveller. New Year's address. 23504
The American traveller; or, National directory. 20872
The American Trenck. 41426
The American tutor's assistant. 109; 5721; 16715; 16716; 21058; 29362; 33715
The American tutor's guide. 6958
The American vine dresser's guide [Loubat] 29533; 39324
The American vine dresser's guide [Dufour] 24373
American water rotted hemp. 30914; 35675
The American's guide. 31988
Americanischer stadt und land calender. 110; 111; 4477; 7808; 11610; 19431; 15095; 15096; 23511; 27854; 31989; 37461
The Americans are robbers. 618
Americans triumphant. 11611
Der Amerikanisch-Teutsch Hausfreund und Baltimore Calender. 4478; 7809; 11612; 15097; 19432; 23512; 27855; 31990
Amherst Academy. Catalogue of the trustees, instructers and students. 27856; 27857; 31991; 31992
Amherst Academy. Exhibition of the Platonic Society. 27860
Amherst Academy. Order of exercises at the exhibition of

the Franklin Society. 27859

Amherst College. 15098

Amherst College. Catalogue of the corporation, faculty and students. 31993

Amherst College. Exhibition of the Alexandrian Society. 27865

Amherst College. Order of exercises at commencement. 31994; 37462

Amherst College. Order of exercises at the exhibition of the Alexandrian Society. 31997; 37465

Amherst College. Order of exercises at the exhibition of the Athenian Society. 31998; 37466

Amherst College. Order of exercises at the Junior exhibition. 31995

Amherst Collegiate Institution. To the public. 15099

Amherst Institution... petition of the founders. 19427

Amir Khan, and other poems. 38341

Amos Binney. 40796

Amos Edwards. 35676

Amos Howe, et al. 40797

Amos Sweet and others. 35677

Amos Wilson, who lived 19 years in a cave secluded from human society. 4301

Amour et toi! or Love and thee! 15313

Amphi-theatre. This evening... (Monday)... December 10, 1821. 4787

Amusements of Western-heath. 15101; 30201

An die Deutchen im Stadt Pennsylvanien. 113

An die freyen Leute von Pennsylvania. 115

An die freyen Leute von Pennsylvanien. 114

ANAAEKTA'EAAHNIKA MEIZONA sive collectanea Graeca majora. 944

Anabaptism disapproved. 4479

The analetic calendar for 1830. 37467

The analogy of religion, natural and revealed. 634; 8227; 28341

Analogy; or, The elements of language. 116

Analyse du jeu des echecs. 6468

Analysis and contents of... the proposed revision of the statute laws of this state. 29965; 29966; 29967; 31862

Analysis of Blackstone's Commentaries on the laws of England. 8701

Analysis of fever. 19922

An analysis of the French alphabet. 21387

Analysis of the game of chess. 25757

An analysis of the memorial of the Delaware and Hudson Canal Company. 38364

An analysis of the mineral waters of Saratoga and Ballston. 22368; 22369; 37339

Analysis of the principles of rhetorical delivery. 30302; 34845

Analysis of the Seneca language. 29296

An analysis of the waters of the Bedford mineral springs. 20075

Analysis of vocal inflections. 17671

Analytic anatomy. 16298

The analytic guide, and authentic key to the art of short hand writing. 12710; 16327; 16328

Analytical arithmetic. 37155

An analytical digest of the reported cases in the courts of equity. 32471

An analytical guide to the art of penmanship. 6317; 25614

Analytical outlines of the English language. 21207

The analytical reader. 30389

Analytical school grammar. 13774; 17637

Analytical spelling-book [Cardell] 12054; 15642

Analytical spelling book [Mulkey] 34214

Analytical system of spelling, reading, and teaching. 39546

The anarchy of the Ranters.
15267
Anastasia o la recompensa de la
hospitalidad.   34017
Anastasia und Theodora. 16432
Anastius; or, Memoirs of a
Greek.   1663
Anatomical investigations, com-
prising descriptions of various
fasciae of the human body.
16299
The anatomist; or, The sham doc-
tor.   10065
The anatomy and physiology of
the human body.   7996; 28098
The anatomy of drunkenness.
33963
Anatomy taught by analysis.
24697
The anatomy of the human ear.
3111; 6719
The anchor's weigh'd.   8171
Ancient and Honourable Fraternity
of Free and Accepted Masons.
Grand Lodge of the State of
Mississippi.   16208
Ancient and Honourable Fraternity
of Free and Accepted Masons.
Grand Lodge of the State of
Tennessee.   5399
An ancient and modern atlas.
118
Ancient atlas adapted to Morse's
New school geography. 9553
The ancient Christians' principle.
119
Ancient documents relative to the
old grist-mill.   38292
Ancient geography.   11425;
31752; 41523
The ancient history of the Egyp-
tians.   3048; 3049; 3050; 3051;
3052; 13984; 17848; 17849;
22120; 22121; 30479; 35066;
40314
The ancient history of the Greeks.
35067
The ancient history of Universal-
ism.   37564
Ancient history, or Annals of
Kentucky.   17751
The ancient order of freemasonry
and liberty of consicence.

35175
Ancient testimony of the people
called Quakers. 5410
Ancient Universalism. 21131
And has she then fail'd in her
truth.   4718
And we're a noddin'.   4074;
4075; 7498; 7499; 14764
And wilt thou weep.   13290
And ye shall walk in silk attire.
19765; 19766; 19767
Andrew Jackson, an interlude in
three acts.   32470
Andrew Jackson's inaugural ad-
dress.   40798
Andrew Turnbull's heirs. 30915
Andrew Westbrook.   30916;
30917
Anecdotes for little boys. 27873
Anecdotes, illustrating the bene-
ficial effects of religious
tracts.   19440
Anecdotes of gamblers. 11385;
19239
Anecdotes of the American Revolution.   33320
Anecdotes of the revolutionary
war in America. 8801
The angel of the world, an Arabian tale.   5110
The angel's salutation to the
shepherds.   9993
Angelia Cutaw and Cecille Boyer.
35678
Animadversions by Dr. Hare on
the review of his theory of
galvanism.   1514
Animadversions on a pamphlet
recently published by... J.
Brooks.   14313
Animadversions on some recent
occurrences in the Presbyteri-
an churches of Cincinnati.
4498
Animadversions on the principles
of the New-Harmony society.
24374
Animadversions upon Mr. Aller-
ton's sermon.   7819
Animal magnetism.   33651
Ann and her little book. 27876
Ann Brashears.   35679
Ann D. Baylor.   26364

Ann of Geierstein. 40369; 40370
Ann of the vale. 16364
Anna Dubord. 35680
Anna Ross; a story for children.
    29400; 29401; 25022; 33753
The annals of America. 39017
Annals of Baltimore. 16349
Annals of liberality, generosity,
    public spirit. 19442; 24000;
    38053
Annals of Nature. 2933
Annals of Portsmouth. 19370
The annals of Salem. 28858
Annals of the American Revolu-
    tion. 17233
Annals of the Lyceum of natural
    history of New York. 17397
Annals of the parish. 1354;
    5420
Annals of the poor. 3010; 35034;
    40277
Annals of the town of Concord.
    17205
Annals of the town of Keene.
    24779
Anniversary address, delivered
    before the Columbian Institute.
    35367
Anniversary address on the prog-
    ress of the natural sciences in
    the United States. 24321
Anniversary celebration of the
    Philermenian Society, Brown
    University. 19885
Anniversary discourse delivered
    before the Columbian Institute.
    27569
An anniversary discourse, deliv-
    ered before the Historical So-
    ciety of New-York. 17891
Anniversary discourse delivered
    before the Historical Society
    of the State of Pennsylvania.
    31589
An anniversary discourse, deliv-
    ered before the Lyceum of
    Natural History of New-York.
    3466
An anniversary discourse deliv-
    ered before the medical and
    chirurgical faculty of Mary-
    land. 16959
An anniversary discourse, deliv-

ered before the New-York His-
    torical Society, December 7,
    1810. (i. e. 1818). 7519
An anniversary discourse, deliv-
    ered before the New-York His-
    torical Society, December 6,
    1826. 39185
An anniversary discourse, deliv-
    ered before the New-York His-
    torical Society, Thursday,
    Dec. 13, 1827. 32404
An anniversary discourse, on the
    state and prospects of the
    Western Museum Society.
    1047
Anniversary discourse pronounced
    before the Philadelphia Forum.
    24853
Anniversary of the Newton Theo-
    logical Institution. 34555
An anniversary oration delivered
    before the Philokrisean So-
    ciety of Baltimore. [Steele]
    6862
An anniversary oration delivered
    before the Philokrisean So-
    ciety of Baltimore [Stewart]
    10350
The anniversary oration of the
    Clariosophic Society. 30257
Anniversary poem delivered in
    New Haven, Conn. 23935
Anniversary poem pronounced be-
    fore the Philermenian Society.
    38824
Anniversary report of the Board
    of Managers, of the Albany
    Bible Society. 59
Anno tertio Georgii IV regis.
    8874
Annot and her pupil. 37985
Annotations on the New Testa-
    ment. 38322
Announcement of an new editio
    of "Appeal to common sense
    and common justice." 8256
Announcement of lectures for the
    winter session. 13563
Announcement of meeting. 19201
Announcement of the fourth im-
    proved edition of "Facts and
    observations..." 8257
Announcement of the Medical Col-

lege of the state of South Carolina.   29715

Announcement of the publication of
the fourth improved edition of
"Prospect before us..." 8258

Annual address delivered before
the Medical Society of the
State of New-York.   32251;
37736

Annual address, delivered before
the Rhode-Island Society for
the Encouragement of Domestic
Industry, October 15, 1823.
24367

Annual address delivered before
the Rhode Island Society for
the Encouragement of Domestic
Industry, October 19, 1825.
25943

Annual address, delivered before
the R.I. Society for the Encouragement of Domestic Industry, Oct. 20, 1824. 24915

Annual address delivered before the
Rhode Island Society for the Encouragement of Domestic Industry, October 24, 1828. 40090

Annual catalogue of fruit and
ornamental trees.   19443;
21462; 40152

Annual catalogue of the officers
and students of Hartwick Theological and Classical Seminary.
29158

The annual catalogue of the officers and students of Westfield
Academy.   41486

Annual catalogue of the officers,
students, and graduates for
the year 1819-1820. [Harvard
University Medical School] 1531

Annual communication, Boston,
Decemer 10, 1828. 38649

Annual communication... Grand
Lodge of Free and Accepted Masons... Massachusetts. 33264

The annual Connecticut register.
23525

The Annual Connecticut Register,
and United States Calendar.
7820; 11625; 15113; 19444

An annual discourse before the
Pennsylvania Academy of the

Fine Arts.   29026

Annual discourse before the Philomathean Society of the University of Pennsylvania. 29327

An annual discourse delivered befor the Historical Society of
Pennsylvania.   34736

Annual discourse delivered before
the Penna. Academy of the
Fine Arts.   1666

Annual Law register of the
United States. 7787; 8896

The annual minutes of the Holland Purchase Baptist Association. 32161; 37649

An annual pocket register, for
the state of Georgia. 19445;
23526

Annual publication Grand Lodge
of the most ancient and honourable fraternity of Free and
Accepted Masons of Pennsylvania.   20591; 24620; 28949;
33272; 38669

The annual register, and military
roster.   6953

The annual report and account
current of the Orphan Asylum
Society in the City of New
York.   6280

Annual report and circular of the
Female Missionary Society of
the Western District, New
York.   38561

Annual report - Commissioner of
Public Buildings.   35681

Annual report for 1829 [Dutchess
County Bible Society] 38432

Annual report, made to the Salem
Society for the Moral and Religious Instruction of the Poor.
6705

Annual report, May 28, 1822
[Massachusetts Missionary So-
ciety] 9429

Annual report of deaths in the
City and County of New York.
2468; 6232; 9662; 13537;
17356; 29962; 34467; 39779

Annual report of the acting superintendent of common schools.
25542; 29968

Annual report of the Apprentices'

Library Company. 25736

Annual report of the Auxiliary Foreign Mission Society. 27908; 27909

The annual report of the Auxiliary Missionary Society, of New-Haven. 27914

Annual report of the Auxiliary Missionary Society of West Association of New Haven County. 32055

The annual report of the Auxiliary Society of Frederick County. 173

Annual report of the Board for Internal Improvements of North-Carolina. 17438; 34569; 39855

Annual report of the Board of Canal Commissioners of Pennsylvania. 17554

The annual report of the board of directors of the Massachusetts Episcopal Missionary Society. 13260

Annual report of the Board of Directors of the Mercantile Library Association of the City of New-York. 2532

Annual report of the board of directors of the Ohio Mechanics' Institute. 39914

Annual report of the board of managers of the Delaware and Hudson Canal Co. 24326

Annual report of the board of managers of the Philadelphia Society for the Establishment and Support of Charity Schools. 30242; 34771; 40476

Annual report of the Board of public improvements of North-Carolina. 2561; 6305

Annual report of the Brattle Street Association for aiding religious charities. 23924

Annual report of the Canal Commissioners [N. Y.] 2480; 6240; 9669; 13545; 17365; 21650; 25543; 29969; 34477; 39786

Annual report of the commissioners of the Canal Fund. 21651

Annual report of the Commission-ers of the Sinking Fund. 3527; 10528; 18381; 22670; 30918

Annual report of the committee of the Foreign Missionary Society of Northampton. 8722; 24558; 33211; 38607

The annual report of the Connecticut Sunday School Union. 20176; 24207; 28580; 32815

Annual report of the convicts in the Massachusetts State Prison. 21358

The annual report of the directors of the Domestic Missionary Society of Connecticut. 5198

Annual report of the directors of the Portsmouth Athenaeum. 30312

Annual report of the executive committee of the Massachusetts Baptist Education Society. 39514

Annual report of the faculty of Brown University. 37967

Annual report of the Female Association in the City of New York. 2528; 6268

The annual report of the finance committee [N. Y.] 6233; 9663

The annual report of the Foreign Missionary Society of Northampton. 1264

Annual report of the inspectors of the Auburn State Prison. 39787

Annual report of the managers of the Union Canal Company. 40707

Annual report of the Mercantile Library Association. 4795

Annual report of the Missionary Society of New Jersey. 25392

The annual report of the Missionary Society of the Reformed Dutch Church. 17773; 22048; 25909

The annual report of the Nassau Hall Bible Society. 21977

Annual report of the New Hampshire branch of the American Education Society. 27831

Annual report of the number of

convicts in the Massachusetts
state prison. 34052

Annual report of the Philadelphia
Society for... Charity Schools.
2749

Annual report of the President and
Directors of the Washington
Canal Company. 22671

Annual report of the president and
managers of the Union Canal
Company. 18262; 22539;
26261; 30863

The annual report of the president
of Harvard University. 29159

Annual report of the Protestant
Episcopal Sunday and Adult
School Society of Philadelphia.
17724; 22002; 30378; 34922

Annual report of the Providence
Young Men's Bible Society.
34935

Annual report of the receipts and
expenditures of the town of
Salem. 26002

Annual report of the regents of
the University, to the legislature of the state of New-York.
30055; 34551; 39788

Annual report of the Superintendent of Common Schools. 17366;
34478

Annual report of the Treasurer of
the University of North Carolina. 39876

Annual report, of the trustees of
the Albany Lancaster School
Society. 37408

Annual report of the trustees of
the Public School Society of
New York. 25876

Annual report of the Unitarian
Book Society of N. Y. 13579

Annual report of the Vermont
Domestic Missionary Society.
31606; 37012; 41373

Annual report of the warden of the
state prison. 25193

Annual report of the Washington
Canal Company. 18382

Annual report on the state of finances. 35682

Annual report... on the subject of
religious services performed

at the new Almshouse and
penitentiary. 6234

Annual report... to the General
Assembly... December 10,
1822. 9726

The annual reports of the Nassau
Hall Bible Tract, & Education
Societies. 17699

The annual reports of the Nassa-
Hall, Tract and Education Societies. 11626

Annual return of the militia.
[U. S.]   26365

Annual return of the militia of
the state of Ohio. 39900

Annual state register, of Connecticut. 32005

Annual statement of the funds of
the University of Pennsylvania.
30199; 34711

The annual visiter and citizen and
farmer's almanac. 127; 7821;
11627

Anonymous sketch of etymology,
syntax. 128

Another candid address to the
Episcopalians of Pennsylvania.
30281

Another card. A card--or rather
a pla-card. 5280

Another humbug! 32006

Another voice from the tomb.
15452

The answer and refutation of S. B.
Griswold to a pamphlet. 16355

Answer of John Eden, an alien,
to the Memorial of sundry persons, opposed to his relief.
5227

The answer of Mr. Sullivan, to
the letter and mis-statements
of the Hon. Cadwallader D.
Colden. 14236; 14237

Answer of the Secretary of the
treasury to the address of
Ninian Edwards. 15892

Answer of the Typographical Society to communications received from Robert Dale Owen.
39839

Answer of William Rector...
17764

Answer to a discourse preached

by Dr. William E. Channing. 29560

An answer to a letter directed to Miles Farmer. 1169

An answer to a pamphlet circulated among members of the Legislature. 129

An answer to a pamphlet entitled "Strictures on Mr. Pattison's reply to certain oral and written criticisms, by W. Gibson." 2666; 2667

An answer, to a paragraph contained in the United States Catholic miscellany. 9027

An answer to "A short reply to 'A defence of the experiments to determine the comparative value of the principal varieties of fuel, &c.' " 32510

An answer, to a work recently published in this country by James Miller. Jun'r. 25104

An answer to all the excuses and pretences which men ordinarily make for their not coming to the Holy Communion. 10393

An answer to an "Address by a Catholic Layman..." 4484

An answer to an essay by W. N. 4485

Answer to Dr. Woods' reply. 11338

Answer to inquiries relative to middle Florida. 29583

An answer to Mr. John L. Sullivan's report. 32763

Answer to Mr. Joseph Moore, the Methodist. 20859

An answer to nine objections made by an anonymous writer against the doctrines of the Catholic Church. 27877

An answer to O'Meara's Napoleon in exile. 12289

An answer to the enquiry, What is Religion? 4486

An answer to the greatest falsehood ever told by a Providence lawyer. 7822

An answer to the letter addressed to the author by the wardens and vestry of Christ Church. 17492

An answer to the highly important question, "What wilt thou have me to do?" 24750

An answer to the question, Why are you a churchman? 40621

An answer to the Rev. G. S. Faber's Difficulties of Romanism. 39271

An answer to the statements contained in Professor Mitchell's printed letter. 22028

An answer to the tract lately published by Professor Cooper of Columbia College. 15860

Answer to the vindicatory address and appeal of Lieutenant Weaver to the public. 18197

Answers of Augustus Storrs, of Missouri, to certain queries. 22672

Answers of the immediate government to questions proposed by a committee of the overseers. 16459

Answers to the articles of impeachment against the judge of probate. 6535

Antediluvian antiquities. 37477

Anthem for Thanksgiving. 27878

Anthony Rollo, the converted Indian. 32007/

Anti-caucus. In consequence of the statements which have gone abroad. 15115

Anti-Christ's kingdom clearly pointed out. 14862

An antidote for the doctrine of universal salvation. 40530

The Antidote; or, Knavery exposed and falsehoods detected. 130

An antidote. Rev. E. Spencer's Defence and testimony. 30683

The Anti-Masonic almanack. 27879; 27880; 32008; 37478; 37479; 37480

Anti-masonic tract, No. 4. 37488

Anti-masonic tract, No. I. 32009; 37486

Anti-Masonic tract, No. 3. 40315

The Antipodean whirligig; or Universal songster. 7824

Antiquarian researches, comprising a history of the Indian wars. 16605

The antiquary. 3134; 6737; 6738; 6739; 17915

Antiquities of the Jews. 12010

Anti-Relief. The following persons voted for Breckinridge. 23527

Antitypical essay, in two parts. 11628

Antoine Prudhomme et al. 40799

Aphorisms concerning the assurance of faith. 12296

Aphorisms of man. 1910

Aphorisms on men, manners, principles and things. 332; 11752

Aphorisms on the application and use of the forceps and vetis. 8535

Apician morsels; or, Tales of the table. 39050

The Apocalypse of St. John. 28622

The apocryphal New Testament. 405; 15339

Apollo Society... concert. 19447; 19449; 19450; 19451; 19452; 19453; 23529; 23530; 23531; 23532; 23533

Apollo thy treasure. Song. 3191

Apologetical discourse on Italy. 5140

An apology for believing in universal reconciliation. 29291

An apology for camp-meetings. 131

Apology for the Baptist sentiments and practice relative to Communion. 132; 13948

An apology for the Bible. 14842; 23228; 37096; 37097; 41445

An apology for the book of Psalms. 5891; 5892

An apology for the Christian divinity. 23698

An apology for the Protestant Methodists. 16973

An apology for the true Christian divinity. 28053

An apology for the United States of America. 37491

An apology for withdrawing from the Methodist Episcopal Church. 33429

The apostate; a tragedy. 30584; 35190

The Apostle Paul a Unitarian. 35401

Apostles' Creed, as contained in (Unitarian) discourses. 133

The apostolic commission. 30697

The apostolic letter of our Holy Father Pope Leo XII. 25088

Apostolic magnanimity. A sermon. 7672

Apostoliches sendschreiben an die Christen Gemeinden in Deutschland. 134

Apostolick origin of episcopacy. 11971

The apparition of a dandy. 12171

An appeal from the denunciations against camp-meetings. 25020

An appeal from the denunciations of the Rev. Dr. Mason. 10230

An appeal from the present popular systems of English philology. 19878; 32492

The appeal for suffering genius. 23954

An appeal in behalf of missions. 40134

An appeal in behalf of religion and learning in Ohio. 24072

An appeal in favor of Sunday schools. 8571; 16005

Appeal, in four articles, with a preamble to the colored citizens of the world. 41409

The Appeal not sustained. 135

Appeal of Joseph Wheaton, late deputy quarter master general and major of cavalry. 4256

The appeal of L. Louaillier, sen., against the charge of high treason. 29534

Appeal of the Cherokees to the people of the United States. 728; 38122

An appeal to common sense and common justice. 8259; 8260; 8261

An appeal to Episcopalians, in behalf of clerical education.

40696

An appeal to his fellow-citizens.
8500

An appeal to liberal Christians
for the cause of Christianity in
India. 23212

An appeal to matter of fact and
common sense. 1254; 24548

An appeal to the American
churches. 31949

Appeal to the bar, and the "freemen of Maryland." 12747

An appeal to the candid of all denominations. 33749

An appeal to the Christian public.
33413

An appeal to the churches containing animadversions on
three ecclesiastical councils.
4425

An appeal to the churches of
Christ. 40685

An appeal to the churches; to defend them against the en-
croachments of associations.
34041

An appeal to the citizens of
Adams County, Ohio. 38667

An appeal to the citizens of Baltimore, containing conclusive
evidence of the base conspiracy
entered into by Moses Swarts.
32004

Appeal. To the citizens of Baltimore in his own vindication.
37338

An appeal to the citizens of Baltimore, recapitulating, generally,
the facts that go to extenuate
the guilt of Morris N. B. Hull.
136

An appeal to the citizens of Caec-
il County. 4488

An appeal to the citizens of
Maryland. 4859

An appeal to the citizens of New
York, in behalf of the Christian Sabbath. 14186

An appeal to the citizens of New
York to show mercy. 37492

Appeal to the citizens of Philadelphia. 19355

An appeal to the citizens of the

United States. 30605

An appeal to the conscience
of Rev. Solomon Aiken.
7709

An appeal to the good sense of
a great people. 19454

An appeal to the good sense of
the legislature. 19455

An appeal, to the inhabitants of
the state of Vermont. 38677;

An appeal to the inhabitants of
Vermont. 38678

Appeal to the justice and human-
ity of the stockholders of the
Chesapeake and Delaware
Canal. 19945; 19946; 19947

An appeal to the lay members of
the Protestant Episcopal
Church in Pennsylvania. 27881

Appeal to the members of the
united churches [of the Protestant Episcopal Church in
Philadelphia] 23534

An appeal to the Methodists.
28217; 28218; 28219

An appeal to the moral & religious of all denominations.
32013

Appeal to the Northern and Eastern churches. 32014

An appeal to the people of Illinois. 11866

Appeal to the people of Maryland. 137; 2118

An appeal to the people of New
York. 4489

An appeal to the people of the
state of Pennsylvania. 32015

An appeal to the people of the
United States. 19456

An appeal to the Presbyterian
Church. 1457

An appeal to the public. [Turn-
bull] 40694

An appeal to the public. At a quarterly conference of the Associate Methodist Church. 41630

An appeal to the public, by William Vans. 31584

An appeal to the public, in consequence of an attack by the
Rev. Nathan H. Hall. 16618

An appeal to the public in general and the people of Virginia in particular, by Matthew H. Rice. 25940

An appeal to the public, in vindication of Universalists. 35233

An appeal to the public, or, An exposition of the conduct of Rev. Isaac Jennison. 33957

Appeal to the Senate of Rhode Island. 37493

An appeal to the temperate. 34589; 34590

An appeal to the unprejudiced judgment of the freemen of Vermont. 32016

An appeal to Universalists. 39224

Appendix, containing an account of the commemoration of the completion of the Erie canal. 25534

Appendix 1818-1828 [to: A manual of the laws of North Carolina] 33511

An appendix, intended to illustrate the merits and objects of A letter of vindication, addressed to the President of the United States. 21089

Appendix, No. IV. Colbert. 28389

An appendix to "An inquiry into the nature and tendency of speculative free-masonry." 35391

Appendix to Musica sacra. 8965

Appendix to the catalogue of the medical library of Bowdoin College. 11964

An appendix to the "Extracts from the journals kept by the Rev. Thomas Smith." 5368

Appendix, to the Journal of the Convention of the Protestant Episcopal Church of Maryland. 13871

Appendix to The outlines of American political economy. 29506

An appendix, to the Rev. Mr. Clowes's pamphlet or Swedenborgianism. 7825

Appendix to the two statements on the part of the United States, respecting the disputed points of boundary between the United States and Great Britain. 40800

Apples of gold for young men and women. 19870

The application of Christianity to education. 33207

The application of Christianity to the commercial and ordinary affairs of life. 4937; 4938; 4939; 8304

Appointment from the members of Congress. 26366

The apprentice. A farce. 17249

The apprentices' dialogues. 37494

Apprentices' library. 17605

Appropriation for the capitol. 30919

Appropriation for the public buildings. 40801

Appropriation-slave trade. 26367

Appropriations and expenditures-- War department 1827. 35685

Appropriations 1st session 19th Congress. 26368

Appropriations - first session, twentieth Congress. 35683

Appropriations for internal improvements. 35686

Appropriations for surveys of roads and canals. 26369

Appropriations for the Navy for 1828. 40803

Appropriations - Naval service. 35684

Appropriations - Second session, Nineteenth Congress. 30920

Appropriations - Second session, twentieth Congress. 40802

Approved Pennsylvania forms. 40328

April election. 17795

The Arabian nights entertainments. 7827; 23535; 27882

Araby's daughter. 25299

Araby's daughter. From "Lalla Rokh." 16796; 16797; 16798; 16799

The arcade. A favorite ballad. 5082

Arcana coelestia or Heavenly mysteries contained in the Sacred Scriptures. 14248

The arcana of arts and sciences. 17520

Archaelogia Americana. 92

Archaeologia graeca. 21953

Archibald W. Hamilton. 30921; 35687

Arden, the unfortunate stranger. 7829; 15119; 27885

Argument addressed to the supreme court of North-Carolina. 25817

Argument against the manufacture of ardent spirits. 1621

Argument and protest against the whole of the proceedings. 30412

Argument before the committee of privileges and elections, in the case of Robert Douthat. 24360

Argument delivered in the Supreme court of errors and appeals, for the state of Tennessee. 37088

Argument for the incorporated company as the best means of developing the Pennsylvania coal fields. 15791

An argument, in a cause depending before the Supreme Court of Louisiana. 29516

Argument in support of the memorial of the Marine Insurance Companies of Baltimore. 26182

Argument in the case of the Brig Sumner. 14954

Argument in the supreme court of the United States, in the case of Ogden versus Saunders. 16373

Argument laid before the Honourable the Board of Commissioners. 15597

The argument of Benj. Faneuil Hunt, in the case of the arrest of the person claiming to be a British seaman. 12892

Argument of counsel in the case of R.W. Meade. 13277

The argument of D. Raymond, Esq. before the Court of appeals of Maryland. 13905

The argument of Domesticus on the question whether a man may marry his deceased wife's sister. 29099

Argument of Mr. Adams, of 5th June, 1822. 26370

Argument of plaintiff's counsel in the case of Willard Peele and others. 25593

Argument on behalf of the president and directors of the Baltimore Insurance Company. 15169

An argument on the cases designated as No. 11. 7685

An argument on the duties of the Vice-President of the U. States, as president of the Senate. 28863

An argument on the powers, duties, and conduct, of the Hon. John C. Calhoun. 28864

Argument on the question of slavery. 3339

Argument on the questions whether the loss, arising from an unlawful seizure preventing the property from reaching its port of destination, ought to be allowed. 15170

Arguments against the justice and policy of taxing the capital stock of banks. 16374

Arguments in the case of Jonathan Hagar vs. E. D. Woodbridge. 15997

Arguments, scriptural and philosophical, proving the divinity of Christ. 24365

Arise each soul! 15774

Aristotle's complete masterpiece. 141

Arithmetic; being a sequel to first lessons in arithmetic. 8378; 12199; 15802; 24149

Arithmetic explained and illustrated. 32253

An arithmetic for beginners. 14136

An arithmetic on the plan of Pestalozzi. 5019

Arithmetic simplified. 11774

Arithmetic, theoretical and practical. 14765

Arithmetic upon the inductive method of instruction. 24150;

28534; 32753; 38211

An arithmetical catechism... 1774;
12938; 16695

The arithmetical expositor. 16898;
39289

Arithmetical foundation. 24966

Arithmetical instructor. 5902

Arithmetical rules and tables, as
used in public schools of the
city of Boston. 11790

Arithmetical rules and tables of
money, weights, measures and
time. 351; 32021; 37730

Arithmetical tables. 142

Arithmetical tables for the use
of schools. 4490; 19458

Arithmetical tables. Most of
which must necessarily be
committed to memory. 23538

Arithmetical tables, rules and
definitions. 27886

The arithmetician's guide. 13168

Arithmetick, theoretically and
practically illustrated. 30855

Arlan, or the force of feeling.
28349

Armories - United States. 40804

Armory on western waters. 22673

Army asylum. 40805

Army list. 7045

Arnold vs. Lea. Contested election. 40806

Arnold's lamentation and St.
Helena. 23546

Arnold's review (of Jackson).
27891

An arrangement of the Psalms,
Hymns and Spiritual Songs, of
the Rev. Isaac Watts. 4189;
4190; 4191; 7599; 7600; 7601;
11357; 14952; 41449

Arrangements for the inauguration
of the Hon. Joseph Story, LL.
D. 38924

Arrangements for the inauguration
of the... President of Harvard
University. 38925

Arsenal at Augusta, Georgia.
26371

Arsenal at Watervliet. 30922

Arsenal - St. Louis. 26372

Arsenal Watervliet. 26373

The art of conjuring made easy.

7841

The art of contentment. 15125

The art of defense on foot.
18159

The art of drawing landscapes.
148

The art of English grammar, in
verse. 2048; 2049; 5880

Art of epistolary composition.
25729

The art of invigorating and prolonging life. 13026; 13027

Art of making fireworks. 5510;
8903

The art of making money plenty.
1273

The art of preserving health.
4492

The art of preserving teeth.
17539; 34660

The art of reading. 27530

The art of short-hand writing.
38802

The art of swimming. 149; 4497

The art of tying the cravat.
33829; 39260

Arthur Monteith: A moral tale.
15457; 35414

Arthur O'Bradley. Giles Scrog-
gin's Ghost. 15126

The article "government," reprinted. 6048

Article second of Title III [N. Y.]
34479

Articles and covenant of the Tabernacle Church in Salem.
6706

Articles and rules of the New
York Association for the Im-
provement of the Breed of
Horses. 13561

Articles containing the rules and
regulations [Worcester Fire
Society] 7712

Articles of amendment to the Constitution of the State of Vermont.
7507

Articles of association of the Bata-
polis Mining Company. 23715

Articles of Association of the
Kennet-Square Library Company. 16779

Articles of association of the

Liverpool Packet Company. 33886

Articles of cession between the United States and Georgia. 40808

Articles of consociation, adopted A.D. 1798. 8421

Articles of faith, adopted by the Congregational Church in Northwood. 39883

Articles of faith adopted by the First Congregational Church in Gilmanton, New-Hampshire. 5460

Articles of faith and a covenant, adopted by the Baptist Church in Bellingham. 7997

Articles of faith and a covenant... adopted by the church in Gorham. 34121

The articles of faith and covenant. [Seekonk] 22234

Articles of faith and covenant [Belchertown] 28097

Articles of faith and covenant, adopted by Danvile Babtist [sic] Association. 19585

Articles of faith and covenant, adopted by the Third Congregational Church of Christ in Portland. 21952

Articles of faith and covenant of the Baptist church. 40308

Articles of faith and covenant of the Baptist Church in Newport and Croydon. 13585

Articles of faith and covenant of the Congregational Church of Christ. 736

The articles of faith and covenant of the Congregational Church, Stoneham, Mass. 40544

The articles of faith and covenant of the Hanover Church, Boston. 23884

The articles of faith and covenant of the Salem Church, Boston. 32444

Articles of faith and covenant of the Second Baptist Church of Christ in Utica. 27491

The articles of faith and covenant of the Trinitarian Congregation-

al Church in Bridgewater, Mass. 23926

The articles of faith and covenant of the Trinitarian Congregational Church in Waltham. 31654

The articles of faith, and covenant, revised, and adopted in its present form by the First Congregational Church in Middleborough, 25358

Articles of faith and form of covenant [Leominster, Mass.] 13088

Articles of faith and form of covenant [Moore] 29794

Articles of faith, and form of covenant, adopted by the Calvinistic Congregational Church in Sandwich. 3105

Articles of faith, and form of covenant adopted by the Congregational Church of Christ, in Townshend, Vt. 35547

Articles of faith and form of covenant, adopted by the First Congregational Church in Lowell, Mass. 25155

Articles of faith and form of covenant, adopted by the South Church in Norwich, Vermont. 2569

Articles of faith, and form of covenant, adopted by the West Church in Andover. 37472

Articles of faith and form of covenant, adopted June 8, 1810. 25132

The articles of faith, and form of covenant, of the Third Congregational Church in Plymouth. 25793

Articles of faith and form of covenant, revised and adopted by the Second Church in Amherst. 27867

The articles of faith and order of the Enon Baptist Church, in Cincinnati. 4992; 20080

Articles of faith and practice of the Baptist Church in Clifton Park. 28521

The articles of faith and the cove-

nant adopted by the Second
Congregational Church in Co-
hassett. 32752

The articles of faith, and the
covenant of Park Street Church,
Boston. 19821

Articles of faith, form of covenant, principles of discipline
and rules of practice adopted
by the church of Christ in
Fitchburg Mass. 20532

Articles of faith: Holy Bible.
32798

The articles of faith of the Boston Park Street Church. 542

The articles of faith, the covenant and rules of discipline of
the First Congregational
Church in Nantucket. 34360

Articles of faith... the General
Conference of Maine. 32797;
34122

Articles of impeachment by the
House of Representatives...
against Samuel Blagge. 25257

Articles of impeachment, preferred by the House of Representatives against Seth Chapman. 21807

Articles of impeachment preferred by the House of Representatives against Walter
Franklin. 21808

The articles of religion of the Protestant Episcopal Church. 25994

Articles of the Endeavour Fire
Company. 32530

Articles of the North Consociation
of Litchfield County. 24190

Articles of the Washington Fire
Company. 4182

Articles of war. 3528; 18383

Articles on the American Education Society. 37507

The artillerist; comprising the
drill without arms. 5143

The artist & tradesman's guide.
15127; 30585; 37508

Arund Rutgers. 40807

As it fell upon a day. 15411;
15412

As the ev'ning star appearing.
17826

As vanquish'd Erin. 19734

...As you like it. 3178; 10232

As you sow, so must you reap.
34800

Asa Bulkley. 30923

Asa Herring. 26374; 35688

Ask why a blush. 151

Asphasia, A tragedy in modern
Greek. 40259

Assays of foreign coins. 26375;
35689

An assemblage of the ordinances
of the corporation. 2039

Assemblée publicque. A une assemblée... convenable pour rep-
resenter le Territoire comme
Delegue dans le Congrès des
Etats Unis. 13323

Assemblée publicque. A une assemblée tres nombreuse, et
tres respectable, des citoyens
democratiques du Comte de
Wayne. 7605

The Assembly's shorter catechism. 11401

Assessment law of Washington.
26376

Assignment... 3022

The assistant to the family religion. 28532; 32750

The assizes. 7843

Association of members of the
Federal Street Society for
Benevolent Purposes. 15517

Association of the Confraternity
of the Rosary. 7847

Astronomia: or Directions for
the ready finding of all the
principal stars in the heavens.
4879

Astronomical calculations for
1823. 7848

Astronomical calendar; or farmers' almanac. 7849

Astronomical calendar, or Western almanac. 11643

An astronomical diary. 157;
158; 27899

An astronomical ephemeris, or
almanac. 7850; 7851; 11644;
19469; 23553; 27900

Astronomical recreations. 16340

At a convocation of the Grand

Lodge of Kentucky. 16193
At a General Assembly of the
state of Connecticut... 32804
At a general meeting of the members of the Mutual Assurance
Society... 9595
At a legal meeting of the Freeholders and other inhabitants of
the Town of Boston. 8126
At a meeting, held March the 4th,
1822. 8142
At a meeting of citizens of Canandaigua. 35476
At a meeting of delegates... 18th
October... 11564
At a... meeting of farmers &
manufacturers. 29326
At a meeting of Salt Manufactur-
ers. 27901
At a meeting of the acting com-
mittee of the Pennsylvania So-
ciety for the Promotion of In-
ternal Improvements. 2713;
25711; 25712
At a meeting of the Directors of
the House of Industry. 28223
At a meeting of the friends of
the present administration.
34402
At a meeting of the merchants,
and other citizens of Belfast.
376
At a meeting of the Overseers of
Harvard University. 16460
At a meeting of "The Pennsylvania
Society for the Promotion of
Internal Improvement." 25713;
25714
At a meeting of the Pennsylvania
Society for the Promotion of
Manufactures and the Mechanic
Arts. 30195; 30196; 31097
At a meeting of the rector and
visitors of the University of
Virginia. 27522
At a meeting of the Republican
members of both branches of
the state of New-York. 11634
At a meeting of the subscribers
to the plan... held at the Indian
Queen, April 2, 1828... 34705
At a meeting of the trustees of
the University. Tuesday, Jan.

1, 1821. 6433
At a meeting of the vestry of the
United Churches of Christ
Church, St. Peter's, and St.
James's. 25754
At a numerous meeting of the
citizens of the village of
Utica. 36989
At a public commencement held
in the chapel of the Univer-
sity, March 16th, 1827. 30825
At a respectable meeting of citi-
zens... to receive the report
of the committee... 40474
At a stated meeting of the Grand
Lodge of Maine, Portland,
July 11, A.D. 1822. 8748
At a very numerous and respect-
able meeting of farmers and
manufacturers... of the city
and county of Philadelphia.
27902
At an adjourned meeting of the
stockholders of the Union Bank
of Maryland. 3508
At General Assembly of the State
of Rhode Island and Providence
Plantations. 2999
At morning's dawn the hunters
rise. 13956
At night when careless hearts repose. 21388
At the General Assembly of...
Rhode Island. 2997-2998;
3000; 6630-6634; 10098-10101;
13938-13941; 17809-17813;
22074-22078; 25933-25936:
30441-30443; 35017-35018;
40260
At the state convention of the
friends of Gen'l Jackson.
32922
Atala y René. Por F.A. de
Chateaubriand. 32655
The Athanasian creed. 35445
Athens; and other poems. 17633
The Atlantic Insurance Company,
and the Merchants Fire Insurance Company of New York,
vs. Samuel Nevins. 25688
The Atlantic souvenir. 19471;
23555; 27903; 32034
Atlas accompanying Greenleaf's

Map and statistical survey of the state of Maine. 38831

An atlas accompanying Worcester's epitome of geography. 37235

Atlas adapto al systema nuevo de geografia. 32478

Atlas classica; or, Select maps of ancient geography. 16143; 28874; 38570

Atlas, exhibiting the prevailing religions... 7691

An atlas of ancient geography. 26168

An atlas of the state of New York. 38007

Atlas of the state of South Carolina. 21461; 25377; 25378

Atlas of the United States. 13408

Atlas on a new plan. 14967

Atlas to accompany Geography for beginners. 27651

The atoning sacrifice. 41592

The atrocities of the pirates. 18000

Attach part of Chicksaw Country to Monroe County. 35690

Attachment to the redeemer's kingdom. 22533

An attempt at a Scriptural statement and defence of the doctrine of the Trinity. 5330

An attempt to answer the important question, What must I do to be saved? 24313

Attempt to demonstrate the existence and superintending providence of an eternal being. 1051

An attempt to demonstrate the practicability of emancipating the slaves of the United States. 21792

An attempt to familiarize the church catechism. 26243

An attempt to induce the people of Georgia, to commence the work of internal improvement. 15133

An attempt to prove that John's baptism was not gospel baptism. 1686

An attempt to reconcile the doctrine of election, regeneration, and salvation. 13212

Attorney general's report upon the resolution for the amendment of the law. 40487

Au clair de la lune. 16390

Auber's opera. 32036

Auburn Artillery by-laws. 37515

Auction of real estate. 9559

Auction sale! A catalogue, of rare and valuable theological & classical books. 17952

Auction system. 40809

The auction system being a series of numbers published in the Federal Gazette. 15134

Auction. Will be sold without reserve, for cash on Thursday, the fifth day of April. 29695

Auctions... [New York] 32039

Auctions. At a large and respectable meeting of citizens, convened at Masonic Hall. 32040

Auditor of State's report. 2584

Auditor's report. Auditor's office, Jackson. 34154

Auditor's report, January 20, 1820. 2585

The Augsburgh Confession. 32041

Augustus Aspinwall. 35691

Auld lang syne. A favorite Scotch song. 15135

Auld lang syne. [Butler] 12033

Auld lang syne. [Carr] 4921

Auld lang syne. [De Ronceray] 20297

Auld lang syne. [King] 1863

Auld lang syne. [Ross] 3057

Auld Robin Gray. 4511

Aunt Mary's tales, for the entertainment and improvement of little boys. 29270; 29271

Aussitôt que je t'aperçois. 13792

Austria. 35195

Auszüge aus Engel's Philosop für die Welt. 8626

An authentic account of the conversion, experience, and happy deaths, of nine girls. 1563

An authentic account of the conversion, experience, and happy deaths of ten boys. 1564

An authentic biography of General La Fayette. 15137; 19476

The authentic confession of Jesse Strang. 30725

Authentic documents relative to the Black River and St. Lawrence Countries. 629; 1791

The authentic history of Isaac Jenkins. 7984

An authentic history of the celebrated horse American Eclipse. 14769

An authentic history of the late war between the United States and Great Britain. 38349

An authentic key to the art of short-hand writing. 15273

An authentic narrative of the loss of the American brig Commerce. 3023; 13955; 37334; 37335; 40283

An authentic narrative of the shipwreck and sufferings of Mrs. Eliza Bradley. 574; 575; 4822; 8169; 11975; 15539; 23920; 37926

An authentic report of a trial before the Supreme Judicial Court of Maine. 21263

An authentic report of the discussion which took place by agreement at Carrick. 15138; 19477

An authentick history of the late war between the United States and Great Britain. 38348

The author's apology for protesting against the Methodist Episcopal government. 39910

The author's defence, by explanations and matters of fact. 17517

The author's jewel. 14124

The authority of a three-fold ministry in the church. 1583

Auto biographical sketches. 38054

Autrittsrede gehalten in Gegenwart des Direktoriums des Theologischen Seminariurus. 30532

Autumn. Manhood--The autumn of life. 32046; 37521

Aux Catholiques des Etats-Unis. 33165

Aux électeurs du premier district congressionel de la Louisiane. 16926; 21236

Aux--nty directed, a sermon. 1786

Les Aventures de Télémaque, Fils d'Ulysse. 5325; 16131; 28866; 38562

Awake sweet harp of Judah! 13140

Awake the loud bugle to hail La Fayette. 16136

Awake the note of war. 15783

Awake ye dull sluggards. 174

Away, away, to the Mountain's brow. 1925

Away with melancholy. 2347; 2348; 17244

...Away with melancholy, with variations for the piano forte. 2214

Away with this pouting and sadness. 9910

The ayah and lady. 10259; 35176

The Ayrshire legatees; or, The Pringle family. 12639

B

The babes in the wood, in verse. 11657; 12123; 20046

Babington's Practical View of Christian Education. 37533

Babylon and infidelity foredoomed of God. 33675

Babylon the great. 19485

Baccalaureate. A discourse to the senior class in the College of New Jersey. 38071

Baccalaurate address, delivered at the annual commencement of the Cincinnati College. 8328

Baccalaureate address, pronounced on the evening of the anniversary commencement of the University of Nashville. 29502

The backslider. 178; 8792; 16241

Bacon & co's. select waltzes.
4518

The bad boy reformed. 37542

The bad wife's looking glass.
14864

The badge; a moral tale for children. 15149

Bailey & Rinker. 26377

Bailey's Franklin almanac.
23574; 27925; 27926; 32066;
32067

Bailey's Rittenhouse almanac.
184

Bailey's Washington almanac.
7867; 7868; 7869; 11662;
11663; 11664; 15153; 19496;
19497; 23575; 23576; 27927;
32068

Baine's history of the late war.
186

Balances--collectors customs and
receivers for land sold.
35692

Balances--collectors of the customs. 30924

Balances due by receivers.
26378

Balances, &c. on the books of
the second auditor. 40810

Balances on books of receipts
and expenditures. 30925

Balances on books of the revenue.
35693

Balances on the books of fourth
auditor. 26379; 30926; 30927

Balances on the books of the register of the treasury. 35694;
40811

Baldwin's fables. 1399

Ballot, state election. 39493

The balloting book, and other
documents relating to military
bounty lands. 21652

The balm of Gilead. 41554

The balm of the Covenant. 33191

The Baltimore almanac. 208;
7884; 11671; 15167

Baltimore and Ohio Railroad
Company. 35695; 40812

Baltimore and Ohio Railroad -
iron. 35696

Baltimore Chamber of Commerce.
35697

The Baltimore collection of sacred musick. 209

The Baltimore directory for 1822
& '23. 9182

The Baltimore vaccine catechism.
18007

Baltimore--vessels sunk for defence of. 26380

The Baltimore Waltz. 1324;
8774

Bancroft's agricultural almanack.
19513; 23595; 27957

The banditt's bride. 3306;
22359; 40521

Bank charter. 31913

The bank dinner, an exposé of
the court party of Kentucky.
16508

Bank of Chilicothe. 30928

Bank of Pennsylvania. 37584; 37585

Bank of the United States. 35698

Bank robbery. Report of the trial of Milligan & Welchman.
4543

Bank United States. 40813

Bankrupt act, 5 Geo. iv. c. 98.
24734

Bankrupt law. 4974

Bankruptcy. Jan. 3, 1826.
26381

Banks and Braes O'Bonnie Doon.
15175

The banks of Allan water. 5633;
5634

Banks of the District of Columbia.
26382; 30929; 35699; 40814

The banks of the Irvine. 30288

The banks of the Ohio. 13044;
13045

Bannister Stone. 35700

Bannockburn; a novel. 9979

Baptism; an authentic narrative.
32100

Baptism not regeneration. 1810

Baptism: Objections in miniature to Antipaedo-Baptist
views. 32101

The Baptist catechism. 220;
7893; 7894; 19514

The Baptist hymn book. 19728

Baptist Missionary Convention.
April 1, 1828. 35701

The Baptist songster. 41566

Barbarossa; a tragedy. 12005

Barbauld's hymns. 310

The Barber of Seville. 10141

Il barbiere di Siviglia. 3062; 22124

Barelegs & Flick, or a dialogue between a great man and an office hunter. 321

Barnabas; or the son of consolation. 32896

Barracks at Carlisle, Penn. 35702

Barracks at New Orleans. 35703

Barracks, store houses, hospitals, &c. 30930

Barrataria. 35704

The barren fig-tree. 13497

Basil; a tragedy. 11665

The basket cotillion, or The Castilian maid. 17095

The basket-maker. 336; 2843; 2844; 19623; 28072

The basket of fragments. 38723

Bason's Country almanack. 337; 4622; 7969; 7970; 11758; 11759; 15278; 15279; 19624

Bastrop's Land Claim. 22674

The Bath waltz, a popular air. 3458

Bath waltz. For the piano forte or harp. 14840

The battle of Aughrim. 15129; 28074

The battle of Borodino. 5288

Battle of King's Mountain. 14105

The Battle of Leipsic. 13957

The battle of Lepanto. 41402

The battle of New Orleans. 22493

The Battle of Prague. 1885; 1886; 1887; 9217; 13037; 16830

The Battle of Tewkesbury. 864

Battle of the Thames. 8624

The Battle of Waterloo. 2579

Der Bauer als Landmesser oder die practische Feldmesskunst. 19146

Be mine, dear maid. 968; 12335; 15413

Be mine tender passion! 3342

Bear and forbear. 31800

The beatitudes. 35141

Beauchamp's trial. 23726

The beauties of Blair. 32394

The beauties of Burke. 32528

The beauties of Chesterfield. 35383; 38132

Beauties of divine truth. 28983

The beauties of harmony. 1951; 33853

The beauties of Henry Kirk White. 31730; 41496

The beauties of history. 40562

The beauties of Johnson. 33723

The beauties of Kirke White. 27633

The beauties of Lord Byron. 23984; 28350; 32542

Beauties of modern history. 356

Beauties of primitive Christianity. 21193

The beauties of psalmody. 811; 28541

The beauties of Shakspeare. 3179; 6772; 6772a; 17944; 30578

The beauties of Sir Walter Scott and Thomas Moore. 23728; 28080; 35117

The beauties of Sterne. 35399

Beauties of the Bible. 10180

Beauties of the British classics. 23729

Beauties of the British poets. 23730

The beauties of the children's friend. 28110

The beauties of the healing art. 22256

The beauties of the late Rev. Dr. Isaac Watts. 7602

Beauties of the New England primer. 2424

Beauties of the souvenirs. 32247; 37734

Beauties of the Waverley novels. 35118

The beautiful grape vine. 28081

The beautiful maid. 1025

The beauty and stability of gospel institutions. 4831

The beauty and usefulness of sacred music in the worship of God. 11394

The beaux stratagem. 8681; 16116

Beaux without belles, or, Ladies we can do without you. 955

The bed of roses.   12673
Bedenklichkeiten über den Plan
    zur Vereinigung der Deutschen
    Ev. Lutherischen Gemeine in
    und bey Philadelphia. 20428
The bee-hive; a musical farce in
    two acts.   25374
Beers' almanac.   368; 369; 370;
    4648; 4649; 4650; 4651; 7986;
    7987; 7988; 7989; 11776;
    11777; 11778; 11779; 11780;
    11781; 11782; 11783; 11784;
    15294; 15295; 15296; 15297;
    15298; 15299; 15300; 15301;
    19645; 19646
Beers' Calender.   371; 4652;
    7990; 7991; 11785; 11786;
    15302; 15303; 15304; 15305
Beers' Carolinas and Georgia al-
    manac.   372; 4653; 7992; 11787;
    15306; 19647; 32261; 37750;
    37751; 37752
Beers' Long-Island almanac.
    7993; 11788; 15307; 15308
Beers' Louisiana and Mississippi
    almanack.   15309; 15310;
    19648; 23733; 28095a; 28096;
    32262; 32263
Beethoven's celebrated polacca.
    7995
Beethoven's Grand waltz. 37753
Beethoven's rondo from his grand
    sinfonia in C.   4656
The beggar's opera. 8805; 12648
Begin the high celestial sham. A
    hymn.   20935
Begone dull care.   12853
"Behold the gentle dew." 1773
Bekäntniss, oder die letzten
    Lebens-Stunden von John Lech-
    ler.   9244
Believe me if all those endearing
    young charms.   14204; 14205;
    18094; 22374
The believers rest.   31639
The believer's confidence; a ser-
    mon.   11321
The believer's pocket companion.
    1136
Bell & Lawrence's almanack.
    11791; 23737
Bell's almanac.   23738
The belle's stratagem, a comedy.

8457; 12277; 20202
Belli Catilinarii et Jugurthini
    historiae.   3100
The bells of St. Petersburg.
    10343; 14206
Beloved physician. A sermon
    occasioned by the death of
    Doct. Andrew F. Warner.
    21331
Belshazzar: a dramatic poem.
    9495; 9496
Beman on intemperance. 37756
Bemerkungen von James Buchan-
    an, Esq. Mitlied des Con-
    gresses von Pennsylvanien.
    32506
Benajah Wolcott. 35705
Bendemeer's stream.   5563
The benefits of affliction. 23741
The benefits of education.   5741
The benefits of the Christian Sab-
    bath.   40563
The benefits resulting to the fam-
    ily of man from the mediation
    of Jesus Christ.   4538
The benevolent lawyers, or vil-
    lainy detected.   12160
Benjamin Freeland.   January 14,
    1828.   35706
Benjamin Simmons. January 28,
    1828.   35707
Benjamin Warner's catalogue of
    books. 4173
Benjamin Wells.   26383
Benjamin Woodworth.   26384
Bennett and Walton's almanac.
    395; 4665; 4666; 8002; 11800;
    15321; 19662; 23746; 23747;
    23752; 28100; 28103a; 32269;
    37762
A bereaved husband's grief. 9146
La bergère délaissée.   8835
Bericht der Verrichtungen der...
    Ev. Lutherischen Conferénz,
    von dem Staat Tennessee. 5270;
    12474; 12475; 16079; 20435;
    24449; 28811
Bericht von der Committee, bes-
    timmt, durch des Haus der
    Representanten. 2684; 2685
The Berkshire agricultural alman-
    ack. 28107; 32276
The Berlin. Arranged for the

piano forte. 14942

The Berlin waltz. 15333

Bertram, or, The castle of St. Aldobrand. 9443; 17082; 29701

Beschäftigungen des Herzens mit Gott. 25914

Betrachtung über den Menschen. 12984; 16760; 21088

Betrachtungen u. Gebete, oder Gedanken und Unterhaltungen des Frommen mit Gott. 24763; 29096; 29097

Better organization of the Quartermaster's Department. 26385

Better to be; A poem. 12480

Between Benjamin Prince, public administrator in the city of New York, appellant, and George Hazleton. 9670

"Beware of imposition." - A Handbill. 19671

Bezaleel Wells. 35708

Die Bibel. 28112; 32281; 37773; 37774

The Bible a code of laws. A sermon. 28087

The Bible above all price. 2671

Bible atlas. 28172; 28173; 28174

The Bible boy. 4702; 11853; 19718; 28175

The Bible-class book. 32366; 32367; 38584; 38585

The Bible class text book. 14916; 14917; 14918; 14919; 14920; 27645

The Bible doctrine of God. 39205

The Bible excellent: A sermon. 5224; 12423

Bible happiness. 19719

Bible history. 28176; 32368

Bible news; or, Sacred truths. 23382; 27705

The Bible of reason. 34860

Bible questions. 34414

The Bible recommended to young people. 19720; 28177

Bible rhymes on the names of all the books. 6113

The Bible rule of church government. 37497

Bible stories with suitable pictures. 457

Bible studies, selected from various sources. 37738

The Bible the Christian's textbook. 28184

The Bible's petition to the children of a Lord's Day school. 19725

Biblia. 32282; 37775

La Biblia sagrada. 15340; 23763; 37776

Biblical dialogues between a father and his family. 10151

A Biblical nomenclature, or vocabulary. 4285

The Biblical reader. 23841

Biblical Repertory. 29240

Bickersteth's Treatise on the Lord's Supper. 19727

Bid me discourse. 15414

A bill, concerning coroners. 25349

A bill, concerning divorces. 25350

A bill, concerning grand and petit jurors. 34127

A bill concerning notaries public. 25351

A bill concerning slaves, free negroes and mulattoes. 7726b

A bill, concerning the Baltimore and Ohio Rail-Road. 37028

A bill concerning the supreme, circuit, and county courts of the Territory of Michigan. 25352

A bill concerning the sureties of John Preston. 11309

A bill, directing the mode of proceeding in chancery. 25353

A bill entitled, An act for the more effectual prevention of crimes and reformation of offenders. 5952

A bill, establishing boards of commissioners. 25354

A bill for an act concerning public roads. 29303

A bill for an act regulating the salaries, fees, and compensation of the several officers and persons therein mentioned. 29304

A bill for an act repealing cer-

A bill, to regulate ferries. 25339

A bill, to regulate taverns. 25340

A bill, to restrain unincorporated banking associations. 25341

Bills and resolutions reported and printed for the Senate of the Commonwealth of Pennsylvania. 25689

The bills of the Senate members. 6409; 17567

Bingham's cotillion for the piano forte. 1800

Biographia Americana. 20600

Biographical and other extracts from the manuscript writings of Barnaby Nixon. 9719

Biographical dictionary, or sketches of the lives of celebrated characters in every age and nation. 25086

Biographical memoir of Doctor Frederick Ridgely. 35198

Biographical memoir of Dr. John Davis. 34193

Biographical memoir of Dr. Samuel Powel Griffitts. 28785

A biographical memoir of Hugh Williamson. 465; 1677; 5642

A biographical memoir of Josiah Goodhue, M.D. 41542

Biographical memoir of Major General Anthony Wayne. 41451

A biographical memoir of Richard Jordan. 28189; 37851

A biographical memoir of Samuel Bard. 5208

A biographical memoir of Wright Post, M.D. 39649

Biographical memoirs of the illustrious Gen. Geo. Washington. 24223

Biographical notice of General Lafayette. 15406

Biographical sketch of Andrew Jackson. 37074; 37075

A biographical sketch of the life of Taulerus. 37501

Biographical sketch of the life of the Hon. William T. Barry. 22416

A biographical sketch of the life of the late Capt. Michael Cresap. 24967

Biographical sketch of the life of the Marquis de La Fayette. 15407

A biographical sketch of the Rev. Andrew Flinn. 466

A biographical sketch of Thomas Jefferson. 33361

A biographical sketch of Tucker Harris, M.D. 5848

Biographical sketches and interesting anecdotes of persons of colour. 25432

Biographical sketches of distinguished American naval heroes in the war of the revolution. 14804

Biographical sketches of eminent lawyers, statesmen, and men of letters. 5776

Biographical sketches of great and good men. 32384; 37852

Biography for boys. 398

The biography of Samuel Whiting. 9434

The biography of the American military and naval heroes of the Revolutionary and late wars. 23825

The biography of the British stage. 15408

Biography of the Hon. Caleb Strong. 571

Biography of the illustrious citizen, General Lafayette. 15409

The biography of the principal American military and naval heroes. 7682; 11455; 14949

Biography of the Rev. Barnabas Bruen. 4712

Biography of the signers to the Declaration of Independence. 467; 3103; 14043; 35099

Bioren's annual compting-house sheet almanack. 4713; 11862

Bioren's Pennsylvania Pocket Remembrancer. 468; 4714; 11863

Bioren's Town and Country Almanack. 469; 4715; 11864

Bird and Abraham Smith. 26881

The bird let loose. The celebrated trio. 4654; 4655

The bird waltz, for the harp or piano forte. 2639; 2640; 2641; 2642; 6372; 9807; 13655; 13656; 13657

The birth of Washington, a poem. 8192

Bishop Hobart. 23828

The bishop's office: a sermon. 29057

Black and whites equal. 3289

The Black Bird. O Lassie, Art Thou Sleeping Yet. 494; 37854

The black book; or, A continuation of travels in the United States. 35075; 35076; 40322

Black dwarf and Old mortality. 6740

Black ey'd Susan. 1948; 8091

Black list: the names of Tories who took part with Great Britain in the revolution. 495

The black velvet bracelet. 32389

The black velvet pelisse. 25634

Blackbeard. A comedy, in four acts. 17898

The Blackbird, being a choice selection of the most popular American, English, Irish, and Scotch songs. 11899; 32390

The Blackbird; consisting of a complete collection of the most admired modern songs. 497; 28193

The Blackbird's nest. 498; 499; 500; 15455; 23830

Blackstone's commentaries. 5832

Blair's lectures on rhetoric. 9362; 37859

Blair's outlines of ancient history. 28196

Blair's outlines of chronology. 20720; 23837; 23838

Blair's outlines of the history of ancient Greece. 23840

Blake's Evening companion. 4743; 8111

Blake's new & complete preceptor for the Spanish guitar and lyre. 4744

Blake's select beauties for the German flute. 4745

The blank book of a small colleger. 15469

The blessed family. 14107

The blessedness of the pious dead. 41603

The blessing of Abraham come on the Gentiles. 18003

The blind Irishman restored to sight. 4746

The blind man & little George. 14108

The blind minstrel. 8066

The blood-red knight. 11910

The bloody buoy, thrown out as a warning to the political pilots of America. 12192; 12193

Bloomingdale Asylum report. 19772

A blow at the root of aristocracy. 2752

Blue Beard, or the fatal effects of curiosity and disobedience. 2722

Blue Beard; or the marshal of France. 6798; 10280

The blue bells of Scotland. 1906; 5732; 5733; 12966; 16744; 21073

The blue bird. 14099

Blue devils; in one act. 8394; 15814

Blue eyed Mary. 515; 4748; 4749; 5002

Blue lights, or The convention. 6733

Blue-stocking Hall. 35105

Blunt's edition of the Nautical almanac, and astronomical ephemeris. 4750; 8117; 11911; 19775; 23848; 28206; 37875

The Board of Health [Salem, Mass.] 22182

Board of trustees, borough of Vincennes. 19147

The boarding house; or Five hours at Brighton. 11766

The boarding school. A poem. 35561

The boarding school; or, Lessons of a preceptress to her pupils. 38611

A boat to Richmond. 29618

The boatswain's mate. 3242
Bodman's oration on the birth of
  our Savior[!] 23850
Body and soul. 19281
A Bohemian walzer. 1871
A bold stroke for a wife. 8299;
  15706
Bonaparte retreat from Moscow.
  3117
Bonaparte; with the Storm at sea;
  Madeline, and other poems.
  519; 1805
Bonaparte's coronation march.
  520
Bonaparte's grand march. 4759;
  4760
The bondage of the seventh of
  Romans contrasted with true
  Christian liberty. 191
Bonie Doon. 4761
The Bonnie boat. 786
The Bonnie house of airly.
  15495
The bonny boat. 2215
Bonny brave Scotland. 17534
A book containing specimens of
  penmanship. 2779
A book for Massachusetts chil-
  dren. 38975
A book for New Hampshire chil-
  dren. 12826; 24842; 38976
Book of animals. 521
The Book of Common Prayer.
  2876; 2877; 6545; 6546; 6547;
  10023; 10024; 10025; 13862;
  13863; 13864; 17705; 17706;
  17707; 17708; 17709; 21985;
  21986; 25845; 25846; 25847;
  25848; 25849; 30357; 30358;
  30359; 30360; 30361; 34895;
  34896; 34897; 34898; 34899;
  34900; 40159; 40160; 40161;
  40162; 40163
Book of cuts, designed for the
  amusement & instruction of
  Young people. 11919
The book of fables. 522
The book of games. 4763; 8123
The book of Job and allegory.
  20839
Book of nature. 523; 524; 4764
The book of nature [Gillespie]
  24691

The book of nature [Good] 24712;
  29040; 33372
The book of nature [Hutton] 9088
The book of pictures. 8124;
  19793
The book of prices adopted by
  the house carpenters of the
  towns of Zanesville & Putnam.
  32412
The book of public worship prepared for the use of the Boston Society of the New Jerusalem. 39775
The Book of Riddles. 525; 4765;
  11920
The book of the boudoir. 39642;
  39643
The book of the church. 22333
The book of versions; or, Guide
  to French translation. 38124
Book-keeping, by single entry.
  11426
Book-keeping, in the true Italian
  form. 12939
Books at auction. 14279
Books published by Wells and
  Lilly. 7626
The boot black, to his generous
  patrons. 4766
The Borough of Bristol has been
  for a number of years an
  agreeable resort for the inhabitants of Philadelphia...
  11921
Bosquejo ligerísmo de la revolución de Méjico. 10128
Boston annual advertiser. 532
"The Boston Bard" to the citizens of Boston. 24143
The Boston Brigade march.
  16520; 16521
Boston cadet's march. 535;
  4789; 8143; 11935; 15514;
  19811
The Boston directory. 536;
  4792; 8145; 11940; 19812;
  23880; 28241; 32432; 37904
The Boston Handel and Haydn
  Society collection of church
  music. 9398; 25250; 38906;
  38907; 38908
Boston Independent Cadets' grand
  march. 33802

Boston Medical Police. 540

The Boston nunnery. 541

Boston pier, or Long-Wharf, Incorporated. 19822

Boston prize poems. 15522

Boston reading lessons for primary schools. 33455

The Boston report and mercantile memorials. 32572; 32573

The Boston Sea Fencibles sheet anchor fund. 11947

Boston Theatre. 4803; 4804

Botanical exercises. 1072; 1073

The botanical garden. 28256

Botanical grammar and dictionary. 33037

Both sides. A letter to the Rev. Thomas Stringfield. 28991

Both sides: Being a correspondence between a priest and a layman. 40451

Both sides of the question. 8873

Botheration; or, A ten year's blunder. 34629

Boundary . . . Georgia and Florida. 26882; 36177; 41062

Boundary line - U.S. and Great Britain. 36178

Boundary on the Pacific Ocean. 26883

Bounding billows. 11955; 19829; 21206; 28774

Bounty lands unfit for cultivation. 26884

Le Bouquet. A much admired waltz. 373

The Bouquet; a poetical offering to lovers of taste. 32453

Bowdoin College...Order of exercises for commencement. 4812

Bowdoin College...Order of exercises for exhibition. 15532; 19832

Bowen's picture of Boston. 37919

Bowie and Kurtz, et al. 41063

The boy's own book. 38194

Boyer's French Dictionary. 8164; 23915; 28263

Boylston medical prize dissertations. 5514

The Boyne water. 23597

The boys & girls must love each other. 20846

The boys of Switzerland. 471; 19735

Bracebridge Hall. 9129; 24961

Bradford County. Democratic corresponding committee. 32952

The braes o' Balquhither. A favorite Scotch ballad. 5153

Brahams' celebrated Polacca. 576

The bramble. 38713

Brambletye House; or, Cavaliers and Roundheads. 26089

The brand plucked out of the fire. 6853

The bravo of Perth: or, Voorn the robber. 15547; 23925

Brazilian waltz. 583

Bread the staff of life. 28272

Breakwater at the capes of Delaware. 26885

Breakwater in Delaware Bay. 22849; 31199; 36179; 36180

The breeze that wafts thee far away. 8775

La Bretonne. A celebrated air. 16756

Breve relacion de la destruccion de las Indias occidentales. 4926; 5790

Brevet rank and pay. 31200

Brian Boroihime, or, the maid of Erin. 30037; 33799

The Brick Church hymns. 14187

The bride; a drama. 32069

The Brides Waltz. 945

The bridesmaid's song & chorus. 23241; 23242; 23243

Bridge documents. 4834

A bridle for devils. 12491

A brief account of an emigrant from the county of Bristol. 37939

A brief account of the construction, management, & discipline &c. &c. of the New York State Prison. 25820

Brief account of the dreadful occurrence at the laying of the corner stone of the Methodist Church in North Bennet Street. 32472

A brief account of the execution of the six militia men. 11986; 32473

A brief account of the life of Emanuel Swedenborg. 28275

A brief account of the lives of the three brothers, Israel Thayer, jr., Nelson and Isaac Thayer. 19859

A brief account of the origin and progress of the divisions in the First Presbyterian Church in the city of Troy. 28276

A brief account of the religious experience, sickness and death of the late pious Miss Mary M. Tooker. 35539

A brief account of the rise, progress and present state of the theological seminary of the Presbyterian Church in the United States. 10014

A brief account of the sickness and death of Hannah Quinby. 4836

A brief address concluding the ceremonies at the annnversary meeting of the Washington Medical Society. 41597

Brief address to the Roman Catholic congregation worshipping at St. Mary's. 8262

Brief and correct account of an earthquake which happened in South America. 585; 1357

A brief but authentic sketch of the leading events in the life of Marquis La Fayette. 15551

A brief concordance to the Holy Scriptures. 4851; 8189; 28300; 37958

A brief confutation of the errors of the Church of Rome. 40125

Brief consideration on the present system of Methodist Episcopal government. 15552

A brief defense of the Bible of the Old and New Testament, against infidelity. 2285

A brief description of the property belonging to the Lycoming Coal Company. 33932

A brief essay on the best means

of promoting the interest of public education. 25051

A brief essay on the causes of dry-rot in public and private ships. 37712

A brief essay, towards an apology for a play actor. 20425

A brief examination of Asa Rand's book, called "A Word in Season." 5665

A brief examination of Col. James Monroe's claims against the United States. 27492

A brief examination of Rev. Mr. Sullivan's reply to the review of his remarks upon a sermon. 35060

A brief examination of the authority conferred by law on brevet commissions. 19860

Brief explanation of the principal terms made use of in astronomy. 16317

A brief explication of the Assembly's shorter catechism. 12006

A brief exposition of the case of Elbert Anderson. 23520

A brief exposition of the claim of Ebenezer Cooley. 28593

A brief exposition of the fanaticism, false doctrines, and absurdities of the people called Shakers. 8177

A brief exposition of the views of John L. Sullivan. 8381

A brief exposure of Rev. Mr. Robinson's evasion, perversions, and general unfairness in controversy. 35439

Brief hints to parents, on the subject of education. 4837; 11987; 15553; 15682; 34208

A brief history of reform. 37940

A brief history of the Evangelical Missionary Society of Massachusetts. 1134

A brief history of the First Presbyterian Church & Society in Utica. 41353

A brief history of the formation of the North Church in Hartford, Connecticut. 29156

A brief history of the life and services of Ichabod Perry. 34729

A brief history of the Presbyterian church in the state of Indiana. 32980

A brief history of the rise, progress, and termination of the proceedings of the Synod of Kentucky. 13838

A brief history of the society. [Massachusetts Evangelical Missionary Society] 2175

A brief inquiry into some of the objections urged against the election of Andrew Jackson. 37291

A brief inquiry into the origin and principles of free masonry. 1453; 1454

A brief memoir concerning Abel Thomas. 15554

A brief memoir of Andrew Underhill. 11988

Brief memoir of Krishna-Pal. 19184

Brief memoir of Solomon Underhill. 28277

A brief memoir of the late Thomas Bateman. 8178

A brief memoir of the life and conversion of Mahomed Ali Bey. 28278

A brief memoir of the life of Dr. Benjamin Franklin. 15555

Brief memoir of the life of William Penn. 4140; 7548

A brief narrative of events which transpired in the church and society in North Granville. 11989; 14001

A brief narrative of the captivity and sufferings of Lt. Nathan'l Segar. 22235

A brief narrative of the most distressing shipwrecks, and the sufferings of their crews. 12661

Brief notice of an "Account of the true nature and object of the late Protestant Episcopal Clerical Association." 38998

Brief notices of the principal events in the public life of Governor Clarke. 586

The brief of his Holiness Pope Leo XII. 25089

Brief of the case of Beverley Chew, William Emerson, and the curator of E. Lorrain. 15556

Brief of the case of Caricaburu, Arieta & Company, merchants of the Havanna. 4339

A brief oratorical treatise on astronomy and natural philosophy. 38892

A brief outline of the evidences of the Christian religion. 19390; 23447; 31922; 37411

A brief outline of the mode of instruction pursued by the Rev. John M. Mason. 34045

A brief refutation of the slanders published in the Coffin hand bill. 32929

The brief remarker on the ways of man. 3101; 6710; 14039

Brief remarks addressed to a Catholic layman. 8179; 8945

Brief remarks on the atonement and mediation of Jesus Christ. 34560

Brief remarks on the rail roads, proposed in Massachusetts. 32275

Brief remarks upon Rev. Thomas Andros's strictures on the review of his essay. 10439

Brief remarks upon the carnal and spiritual state of man. 31936

A brief reply to a ludicrous pamphlet. 5612

Brief review of a sermon entitled Trinitarians rational. 15557

A brief review of Doctor Bond's "Appeal to the Methodists." 30606

A brief review of the origin, progress and administration of the Bank of the U. S. 8180

A brief review of the past sixty years. 15558

A brief review on a debate on

Christian baptism. 13903

A brief sketch of the birth, life and sufferings of Capt. Francis Duclos. 16008

A brief sketch of the causes and treatment of disease. 6968

Brief sketch of the characters and sufferings of the Pilgrims. 587

A brief sketch of the first settlement of the country of Schoharie. 12008

A brief sketch of the indictment, trial, and conviction of Stephen and Jesse Boorn. 4141

A brief sketch of the last hours of the Rev. Solomon Allen. 8181

A brief sketch of the life and character of Mrs. Elizabeth Adams. 40568

Brief sketch of the life, character and services of Major General Andrew Jackson. 33545

A brief sketch of the life of Horace Carter. 19861

A brief sketch of the military operations on the Delaware during the late war. 588

A brief sketch of the occurrences on board the Brig Crawford. 28279

A brief sketch of the property belonging to the North American Coal Company. 28280; 30069; 31870

A brief sketch of the revival of religion in Boston. 23583

A brief statement of certain controversies mentioned and alluded to throughout the Rev. D. Elliott's letters. 32211

A brief statement of facts relating to difficulties in Killingworth, Conn. 32474

A brief statement of the proceedings of the citizens of Utica. 36990

A brief summary of Baptist sentiments and practice. 32475

A brief summary of Christian doctrine and a form of cove-

nant adopted by the First Church in Dedham. 8522

A brief summary of Christian doctrine and a form of covenant adopted by the First Church in Hartford. 8956

A brief summary of Christian doctrine, and a form of covenant, adopted by the Third Church in Berlin. 8007

A brief summary, of some of the principal incidents, relative to the life of Ursula Newman. 39146

A brief summary of the history and doctrine of the Holy Scriptures. 2272; 6058

A brief summary of the sacred history, and Christian doctrine. 33197

A brief summary of the trial of three brothers, Israel Thayer, jr., Isaac Thayer, & Nelson Thayer. 19862

A brief system of Sabbath School instruction. 23556

A brief topographical and statistical manual of the state of New-York. 8855

A brief view of Christian baptism. 19863

A brief view of Cumberland College. 38313

Brief view of the American Bible Society. 11590; 15074

A brief view of the American Education Society. 23479

A brief view of the church. 15527

A brief view of the formation, government and discipline, of the Church of God. 41570

A brief view of the government of the Methodist E. Church. 32476

A brief view of the law relating to transactions between principals and factors or agents. 19864

A brief view of the policy of the founders of the colonies. 32574

A brief view of the present relations between the government

and people of the United States
and the Indians.　37941
A brief view of the writ ne exeat
regno.　4640
A brief vindication of the stage.
20426
Brief von der Correspondirenden
Committie von Lancaster
County.　13042
Brigade orders.　17474; 21725
Bright be thy dreams.　8067;
8068
Bright star of evening!　18148
Bright sun I adore thee.　12871
Brignal banks.　29718
Bristol march.　22257
The Bristol waltz.　1026
British Colonial trade.　26886;
26887
The British perfumer.　9271
The British poets.　4838
Broad grins of Rochester.　36998
The broken harp.　18095
The broken hyacinth.　35177
The broken sword.　24354
The broken vow.　15140
The Brooklyn directory.　23932
The Brooklyn waltz.　20194
The broom of Cowdenknows.　5564
The brother and sister. A petit
opera.　8551
Brother and sister. The cele-
brated Echo song.　472
The brothers; a comedy.　15901
The brothers, or consequences.
11996
Brown University. Commencement.
604
The Browne family.　37971
Bruce, David & George. New
York, 1821. [Specimen of
printing types.]　4860
Bruce's address to his army.
626; 6379; 13736
Brunswick Waltz.　608
The Brussel's waltz.　9453
Brutus; or, The fall of Tarquin.
6398; 30157
The buccaneers: a romance of
our own count[r]y.　29388;
29389; 29390
Büchlein des Hans Frumann,
welcher von Himmel und

Hölle zeuget.　24649
A budget of blunders.　12990
A budget of scraps.　13087
Buds & flowers.　3192; 14100
Buffalo in 1825.　19506; 19894
Bugle andante.　1997
The bugle call.　16861
Building the walls| of Zion.
33434
Bulfinch on penitentiaries.
31201
Bull of his Holiness Leo XII.
25090; 25091
Bulle de sa Sainteté Léon XII.
25092
A "Bunker Hill" contest, A.D.
1826.　25721
Bunyan's Grace abounding to the
chief of sinners.　32515
Bunyan's Pilgrim's progress,
from this world to that which
is to come, exhibited in meta-
morphosis.　4870; 23695
Burden's Plough.　1634
A burletta of fun - frolic, - and
flash.　17184; 17185
Burlington arcade.　12025
The Burman slave girl.　4135;
37055
Burning frigate Philadelphia at
Tripoli.　26888
Burns' Cotter's Saturday night.
23974
Burns' select works.　628
Business to be acted upon [U.S.
Congress]　26889; 31202;
31203; 36181
Die Busse erklärt und aubefohlen
Ein ernstlicher Ruf an das Ge-
wissen eines jeden Menschen.
30798
Busstags predigt am 20. August
1820.　2354
The busy body, a comedy.　8300
But think me not so foolish a
maid.　16581; 16582
Butler's catechism.　28340
The butterfly. A duett.　22179;
22180
The Butterfly, Cottilions.　636
The butterfly's ball and the grass-
hopper's feast.　8228
Buy a broom. A celebrated Ba-

varian song. 19911

Buzzard's and Barnstable Bay canal. 26890

By a murmuring brook. 18096

By Albion K. Parris, Governor of the State of Maine: a proclamation. 9333; 9334; 16993; 16994

By authority. An act for the relief of the poor. 16658

By authority. Infantry tactics. 22850

By his Excellency, Gideon Tomlinson, Governor of the State of Connecticut. A proclamation. 32805

By his Excellency John Brooks... A proclamation. 2159; 5975; 5977; 5976; 9402; 9403; 13248

By his Excellency Jonas Galusha, Esquire, Governor, Captain-General & Commander in Chief, in & over the State of Vermont, a proclamation. 4088

By His Excellency Levi Lincoln, Governor of the Commonwealth of Massachusetts, A Proclamation. 21359; 25258; 25259; 29663; 29664; 34053; 39494

By His Excellency Oliver Wolcott, Governor and Commander in chief in and over the State of Connecticut..do hereby appoint, Friday. 5061

By his excellency Oliver Wolcott, Governor and commander in chief in and over the state of Connecticut. A proclamation. 24196

By his Excellency Richard Skinner, Captain-General, Governor, and Commander in Chief, in and over the State of Vermont, A proclamation. 4089; 7514

By His Excellency William Eustis ...A proclamation. 13249

By His Honour Marcus Morton. 21360

By Lewis Cass, Governor in and over the territory of Michigan, a proclamation. 39581

By the Governor a proclamation for a day of thanksgiving. 9628

By the Governor a proclamation for a fast. 2431; 9629; 17320

By the Governor of the State of Maine. A proclamation...a day of humiliation and prayer. 5914

By the governor of the state of Maine. A proclamation for a day of public thanksgiving. 33986

By the President of the United States of America. A proclamation. 14498; 22851; 36182; 36183; 41064; 41065; 41066; 41067

By the President of the United States of America, To all and singular to whom these presents shall come, greeting. 41068

By the simplicity of Venus doves. 15415; 15416

By virtue of an order of the Orphans' court for the said County of New-Castle. 17311

By William D. Williamson, President of the Senate and officiating Governor of the state: a proclamation. 5915

By William P. Duval, Governor of the Territory of Florida. Proclamation. 16161

Bye-laws, adopted June, 1829. [Freemasons--North Carolina] 38664

Bye-laws and orders of the Town of Danvers. 953

Bye-laws for the town of New-Bedford. 9612

Bye-laws of Brookville Harmony Lodge. 33258

Bye-laws of Otsego Medical Society. 6356

Bye-laws of the Groton Work House. 8902

Bye-laws of the Medical Society of the County of Genesee. 13282

Bye[!]-laws of the Medical Society of the County of Orange [N.Y.] 39543

Bye-laws of the Presbyterian Church in the Borough of Carlisle. 15681

Bye-laws of the town of Wiscasset.   11463

Bye-laws of Transit Lodge. 16226

Byerly's new American spelling
book.   637; 638; 8231; 19912;
28348

By-laws [B. and O. Railroad Co.]
27951

By-laws [Freemasons. Lebanon,
Pa.]   1313

By-laws [Freemasons. Tallahas-
see.]   28953

By-laws and ordinances of the
City of Detroit.   20300

By-laws and ordinances of the city
of Pittsburgh.   34812

By-laws and regulations [Citizens
Fire Society. Boston] 15768

By-laws and regulations of the
Portland Athenaeum. 30308

By-laws and regulations of the
twelfth Medical Society of Ohio.
21382; 22528

By-laws and regulations ordained
and established by the governors of the New-York hospital.
3263; 26101

By-laws and Resolutions of the
most worshipful Grand Lodge
[Freemasons. Ohio.] 1310

By-laws, and rules and regulations of the Baltimore and Ohio
Rail Road Company. 37571

The by-laws and rules and regulations of the Charleston Library
Society. 32646

By-laws and rules of order of
Columbia Lodge.   1288

By-laws and rules of the Bank of
Montpelier. 23601

By-laws and standing resolutions
of the Guardians of the Poor.
6445

By-laws and system of education,
established at Augusta College.
32042

By-laws for the government of the
Board of trustees of the Northern Dispensary.   39831

By-laws for the government of the
Natchez Royal Arch Chapter.
12598

By-laws for the government of the

poor, and alms house of Baltimore.   23589

By-laws for the town [Charles-
town, Mass.]   722

By-laws for the town of New-
Bedford.   6191

By-laws of Ancient Landmark
Lodge, Portland.   24602

By-laws of Annapolis Lodge.
28932

By-laws of Cassia lodge. 16200

The by-laws of Clinton Lodge.
24611

By-laws of Columbia Holy Royal
Arch Chapter.   28950

By-laws of Columbia Mark Lodge,
of the City of Philadelphia.
1315; 8762; 38670

By-laws of Concord Chapter of
Royal Arch Masons. 24605

By-laws of Concordia Lodge [Bal-
timore]   5372

By-laws of Concordia Lodge [Phil-
adelphia]   8763

By-laws of Concordia Royal Arch
Chapter.   12594

The by-laws of constitutional form
of government of the Episcopal
Church of St. Philip's in the
city of Charleston.   12104

By-laws of Corinthian Lodge.
8750

By-laws of Darius chapter.
24598

By-laws of Fire Company, No. 1
[Rochester]   30474

By-laws of Franklin Chapter No.
2.   20595

By-laws of Franklin Lodge.
24612

By-laws of Golden Rule Lodge.
24597

By-laws of Hibernia Lodge.
12605

By-laws of Hoffman Lodge.
38660

By-laws of holy and undivided
trinity encampment held at
Harrisburg, Pennsylvania.
31855

The by-laws of Libanus Lodge.
12586

By-laws of Lodge No. 51, held

in the City of Philadelphia.
5397

By-laws of Lodge No. 69, held in
the Borough of Chester. 20592

By-laws of Marshall Lodge. 8747

By-laws of Miami Lodge. 16221

By-laws of Missouri Royal Arch
Chapter, St. Louis. 8755

The by-laws of Mount Nebo Lodge.
12612

By-laws of Phoenix Lodge. 16217

By-laws of St. Alban's Lodge.
5374

By-laws of St. Andrew's Lodge.
24583

The by-laws of Solar Lodge.
8735

By-laws of Solomon's Lodge.
8764

By-laws of the Board of managers
of the American Colonization
Society. 27827

By-laws of the Canandaigua Fire
Company. 32566

By-laws of the city of New
Haven. 9644

The by-laws of the city of Norwich. 9738

By-laws of the Commercial Bank
of Pennsylvania. 20150

By-laws of the company of artillery at present under the command of Capt. Wm. Cumber-
son. 25544

By-laws of the Dutchess Medical
Society. 17087

By-laws of the East India Marine
Hall Corporation. 24391

By-laws of the First Company,
Washington Guards. 39789

By-laws of the First Congregational Church in the city of New
York. 2518

By-laws of the Free School Society of New York. 22007

By-laws of the Kingston Union
Lodge. 12615

By-laws of the Lechmere-Point
Library Association. 9246

By-laws of the Light Infantry Company of Winslow Blues. 548

By-laws of the Manufacturers'
Bank. 21946

By-laws of the Massachusetts
General Hospital. 5985

By-laws of the Medical Society
of South Carolina. 25295

By-laws of the Medical Society
of the County of Albany. 6007;
34097

By-laws of the Medical Society
of the County of Washington.
17090

By-laws of the New York Institution for the Instruction of
the Deaf and Dumb. 39828

By-laws of the Oneida Medical
Society. 9788

By-laws of the Philadelphia Saving Fund Society. 6456; 21877

By-laws of the Portland Mutual
Fire Insurance Company.
34852

By-laws of the Portland Rifle
Company. 40130

By laws of the proprietors of
Portland Library. 6514; 25812

By-laws of the Providence Forc-
ing Stationary Engine Co.
34933

By-laws of the Public School Society of New York. 25877

By-laws of the Quincy Company
of Firemen. 25889

By-laws of the Richmond Fayette
Light Artillery. 37039

By-laws of the Salem Charitable
Marine Society. 17886; 22189
26007

By laws of the South Carolina
Canal and Railroad. 35361;
35362

The by-laws of the town of Hallowell. 38898

By-laws of the town of Marietta.
5935

By-laws of the town of Portland.
17675

By-laws of the town of Saco.
22173

The by-laws of the town of Salem.
17881

By-laws of the trustees of the
Public School Society of New-
York. 40201

By-laws of the trustees of the

Sailor's Snug Harbor in the city of New York. 13575

By-laws of Utica Encampment. 16215

By-laws of Warren Mark Lodge of Baltimore. 5373

By-laws of West-Chester Lodge. 20586

By-laws of Windsor Mark Lodge. 24630

By-laws, rules, and regulations [Cincinnati Royal Arch Chapter] 24619

By-laws, rules and regulations [Kensington Bank] 25025

By-laws, rules and regulations [Schuylkill Permanent Bridge Company] 10189

By-laws, rules and regulations of the Medical Society of New-Jersey. 2199

By-laws; with rules and regulations for the government of the Asylum for the Insane in Charlestown. 4960

C

C. Brown's, New-York State almanac. 23985; 28351; 28352

C. Cornelii Taciti Historiarum libri quinque. 14254

C. Crispi Sallustii De Catilinae conjuratione belloque jugurthino historiae. 6707

C. Crispi Sallustii opera. 6708; 22194; 22195; 22196

C. Julii quae extant interpretatione et notis illustravit Johannes Godvinus. 643; 28357; 38022

The Cabal; or, A peep into Jacksonism. 32543

The cabin boy. 32545

Cabinet. 38020

The cabinet; a comic opera. 28701; 32977

The cabinet maker's guide. 28353

Cabinet of curiosities. 8860

The cabinet of Momus. 28354

The cabinet of useful arts and manufactures. 23985a; 28355

The cabinet; or, Philosopher's masterpiece. 15622; 32887; 37292

The cabinet, or Works of darkness brought to light. 15623; 19920; 19921

Cadets at West Point. 36185

Cadets. Letter from the Secretary of War. 36184

Cadets march. 4897

Cadets' visit to Quincy. 4403

Cadwallader Wallace. 31204

Caii Julii Caesaris Commentarii. 4898; 38023

Cain, a mystery. 8233

Caius Gracchus; a tragedy. 16829

Caleb Stark. 26891

The Caledonian hunt. 4899; 21167

The calendar of nature. 11552

Calendar of the festivals and lunar months of every year observed by the Israelites. 35250

Der calender eines Christen. 32551; 38025

Calender für den Westlichen Bürger und Landmann. 38026

A call from the ocean. 26247

A call, to come over to the help of the Lord. 12638

A call to the unconverted. 4633; 7973; 7974; 19631; 19632; 19633; 23716; 23717; 23718; 28075; 37726

A calm address to the believers and advocate of endless misery. 6478

A calm and conciliatory review of Swedenborgianism. 648; 2568

A calm review, of the spirit, means and incidents of the late "Oneida Revival." 28362

Calthorpe; or, Fallen fortunes. 5423

Calumny refuted, or, Plain facts versus misrepresentations. 15627

Calumny refuted. The unexpected and very singular attack upon Mr. Richardson...has been promptly met. 35031

torial reign of the Son of God.
4909

A candid review of ten letters,
containing reasons for not embracing the doctrine of universal salvation. 28377

A candid statement of facts, relative to the difficulties between
the Pacific Congregational
Church, in Providence, R.I.,
and those brethren who with-
drew. 13887

A candid statement of the reasons
which induce the Baptists to
differ in opinion and practice.
3082

A candid view of the presidential
question. 33747

The candidate for confirmation instructed. 24868; 38999

The Candle, or An answer to the
Stand. 667

Caniadau sion, sef casgliad o
hymnau a salmau. 31677

Canine biography. 668

The canon of the Old and New
Testaments ascertained. 23448

Canons for the government of the
Protestant Episcopal Church.
21987; 40164

Canton March. 29881

Capriccio for the piano forte.
16757

Captain Deem's march. 15639

Captain Harper's grand march.
21389

Capt. J. G. Watmough's kent bugle
slow march. 16724

Captain James. 669

Captain James Page's kent bugle
military slow march. 9154

Captain John Burnham. 41071

Capt. Kidd. 670

Captain Morgan; or, The conspiracy unveiled. 30755

Capt'n Mulligan. A favorite Irish
dance. 12053

Capt. Partridge's lecture on education. 2661; 34650

Capt. Partridge's lecture on national defence. 6391; 6392

Captains of the Army of the
United States. 26898

Captive African slaves. 26899

The captive in Ceylon. 28379

A captive once said to a linnet.
671; 4911; 4912

The captivity and sufferings of
Mrs. Mary Velnet. 32568

Carbonaro; a Piedmontese tale.
39286

A card. 31689

Carding & cloth dressing. 5852

A careful and free inquiry into
the true nature and tendency
of the religious principles of
the Society of Friends. 15583

A careful and strict enquiry into
the modern prevailing notions
of that freedom of will. 33049

The careless sinner awakened.
1033

Carey Owen. An Irish air.
21982

Cargoes of slave ships Constitution, Louisa, &c. 26900

The Carib chief: a tragedy.
3503

Carl Gock's neuestes selbstlehr-
endes Rechenbuch. 12691

Carl Gock's Verläumdungen, oder,
Die rechtfertigung der hoch-
deutschen Lutherischen und
Reformirten Synoden. 12709

Carmina sacra. 14830

The carnival of Venice. 9716

The Caroline waltz. 13008

Carolinian herald of liberty, religious and political. 5575

The Carolinian spelling book.
28891

Caroliniensis. 18251

Caron de Beaumarchais. 36188

Carpenter's book of prices.
38073

The carpenter's new guide. 30060

Carr's canzonetts. 15683

The carrier of The Philadelphia
Album respectfully present to
its patrons the following New
Year address. 30218

The carrier of the Poughkeepsie
Journal to his patrons. 25819

The carrier pigeon. 2331; 9538;
13384; 17218; 17219; 17220;
21514

The carrier's address of the
"Montgomery Republican."
39627

The carrier's address of The National Advocate. 39694

The carrier's address to the
friends and patrons of the Raleigh Star. 20539

The carrier's address to the patrons of Mrs. Colvin's Messenger. 37320

Carrier's address to the patrons of the Albany Argus. 11563

Carrier's address, to the patrons of The Democrat. 38366

Carrier's address, to the patrons of the Indiana Intelligencer.
24949

The carrier's address to the patrons of the Indiana Oracle.
16663

Carrier's address to the patrons of the Martinsburg Gazette.
25234

The carrier's address to the patrons of the Patriot & Chronicle. 39973

The carrier's address, to the Patrons of the Statesman and Gazette. 35389

The carrier's address to the patrons of the "Washington Republican." 37092

Carrier's address, to the patrons of the Western Register. 41484

The carrier's address to the patrons of The York Recorder.
41615

The carrier's Christmas present, to the patrons and friends of the Old Dominion. 30113

Carrier's New Year Address
[Essex Register] 1124; 5265

Carriers' New Year Address
[Salem Gazette] 6700; 10175

Carrier's New Year Address
[Salem Observer] 22192

Carrier's New Year's address of the Rhode Island Republican.
10107

The carrier's New-Year's address to the patrons of The Christian Intelligencer. 15756

Carrier's verse, to his patrons.
12073

Carriers addresses. 6193

The carriers of the Palladium to its patrons. 2412

The Carrollton march. 32839

Carta de Benigno Morales á
Felix Megia. 21513

Cartas americanas. 14779

Cartas de Heloysa y Abelardo.
15008

Cartas marruecas y poesias selectas. 28356

Cartilla para los gefes y los pueblos en America. 12074

The case in question 'Doherty's heirs and others vs. Blake & Cumings. 32614

Case of Berger. 4927

Case of divorce of Andrew Ure.
695

The case of Edmund Shotwell and others. 32615

Case of Francis Larche. 36189

The case of George W. Niven.
8290

The case of Gibbons against Ogden. 19257

Case of Henry Hitchcock. 26901

Case of Henry Lee. 36190

The case of John I. Barr, vs.
Daniel Lee. 8291

Case of Messrs. Boude, Logan, and others. 5877

The case of Nancy Linton. 30747

The case of Robert M. Goodwin.
6712

Case of Russell Jarvis. 36191

Case of the Appelant (Debt)
Court for trial of Impeachments and Correction of Errors. 9671

The case of the Episcopal
Churches in the United States considered. 28417

The case of the proprietors of East New Jersey. 19778

The case of the public printer.
32884

Case of the ship James Birckhead. 37215

The case of the six militia men fairly stated. 32948

The case of the six mutineers.
32939; 32940; 32941
Case of three remarkable tumors
extirpated from the nose.
22492
Case of tumor at the angle of the
jaw. 37719
Cases argued and determined in
the Supreme court of North
Carolina. 39856
Cases decided in the Supreme
Court of Ohio. 25622; 34598
Cases determined in the Courts
of equity. 16336
Cases... in the High court of chan-
cery. 16335; 33407; 38812
Cases of cures performed by the
use of Swaim's Panacea.
30748; 40581
Cases selected from the decisions
of the Court of Appeals of Ken-
tucky. 16783
Cash duties, warehouse system.
41072
Cash for chickens. 23317
The casket: a Christmas and
New Year's present. 32616
The Castilian. 40688
The Castilian maid. 12077;
12078; 14939
The Castilian rondo. 12668
The Castle Garden march. 20000;
20001
The Castle of Otranto. 14817
The castle spectre. 9202; 33855
Castler Crosier. 28273
The cat. 32618
Catalog of original pictures and
engravings. 28640
Catalog of the teachers and pu-
pils of the Young Ladies Semi-
nary. 24761
Catalogo de la libreria Francese
Spagnoula ed Italiana. 15331
Catálogo de los profesores y
alumnos del Instituto de educa-
cion culta de Mount Pleasant.
39651
Catalogo ragionato de' libri, che
si trovano attualmente nel ne-
gozio de Lorenzo e Carlo da
Ponte. 12321
Catalogue. [Apprentices' Library.

New York.] 2520
Catalogue [Bennington Academy]
37763
Catalogue [Brown University Med-
ical School] 4854
Catalogue [Cazenoria Seminary]
38097
Catalogue [Franklin Circulating
Library] 1282
Catalogue [Gilmanton Academy]
1392
Catalogue [Monson Academy]
39625
Catalogue instructors and pupils
Belleville Seminary. 31850
Catalogue of a cabinet of ma-
teria medica. 25963
Catalogue of a general assort-
ment of books. 15696
Catalogue of a private library
[Edward Pennington's] 24577
A catalogue of a select portion
of the very extensive and val-
uable stock of books. 12617
Catalogue of a valuable collec-
tion of books. 23998
Catalogue of a valuable private
library. 5501
Catalogue of additions [M. Rob-
inson's Library] 13886;
22004; 29558; 40197
Catalogue of American indigenous
trees. 2870
A catalogue of American miner-
als. 22115
Catalogue of an exhibition of por-
traits painted by the late Gil-
bert Stuart. 32620
A catalogue of an extensive col-
lection of books... for sale by
Collins & Co. 15812
Catalogue of an extensive collec-
tion of books... for sale by H.
C. Carey & I. Lea. 19943;
19944
A catalogue of an extensive col-
lection of books... for sale by
W. P. Bason. 15277
Catalogue of books [Boston Medi-
cal Library] 11945
Catalogue of books [Charlestown
(Mass.) Union Library] 723
Catalogue of books [Door & How-

land] 38410

Catalogue of books [Hale Donation Library] 16378

Catalogue of books added to the
Boston Athenaeum. 37898

Catalogue of books, amounting, at
retail prices, to over 100,000
dollars. 7985

Catalogue of books at auction
November 25 (23) 1825. 20235

Catalogue of books, belonging to
Merrell & Hastings' Circulating Library. 13305

A catalogue of books belonging to
Middlesex Law Library Association. 34135

Catalogue of books belonging to
New-Bedford Library. 6192

Catalogue of books, belonging to
New-Bedford Social Library.
29919

Catalogue of books belonging to
the Apprentices' Library Company of Philadelphia. 11630

Catalogue of books, belonging to
the Brooklyn Apprentices' Library Association. 23931;
32484

A catalogue of books, belonging
to the Brothers', Linonian,
and Moral Libraries. Yale
College. 23394

Catalogue of books belonging to
the Calliopean Society, Yale
College. 19346; 37269

Catalogue of books belonging to
the Essex Southern District
Medical Society. 16072

Catalogue of books belonging to
the Hartford Library Company.
33490

Catalogue of books belonging to
the Law Library Company of
Philadelphia. 13071

Catalogue of books belonging to
the Library Company of Sag
Harbor. 7726a

Catalogue of books belonging to
the library of Amherst College. 27861

A catalogue of books belonging to
the library of Christ Church.
13747

Catalogue of books belonging to
the library of the Baltimore
Athenaeum. 27955

Catalogue of books belonging to
the library of the Dialectic
Society at Chapel-Hill. 30089

Catalogue of books belonging to
the library of the Philanthropic Society at the University of
North Carolina. 39879

Catalogue of books belonging to
the library of the Philological
Society of Middlebury College.
13333; 17154

Catalogue of books belonging to
the library of the Philological
Society of Nassau-Hall. 34888

Catalogue of books, belonging to
the library of the University
of Pennsylvania. 40018

Catalogue of books belonging to
the Linonian Brothers' and
Moral libraries. 11496

Catalogue of books belonging to
the Linonian Society, Yale
College. 41612

A catalogue of books, belonging
to the Massachusetts Medical
Society. 9427

Catalogue of books belonging to
the Princeton Library Company.
21974

Catalogue of books belonging to
the Society of Brothers in
Unity. Yale College. 41609

Catalogue of books belonging to
the Washington Circulating Library. 41438

Catalogue of books, comprising
the stock in trade of Howe &
Spalding. 16601

Catalogue of books, &c. for the
use of Sunday schools. 1530

Catalogue of books, &c. published by the American Sunday-
School Union. 37451

Catalogue of books for sale
[Cushing and Appleton] 20238

Catalogue of books for sale
[Whipple] 4265

Catalogue of books for sale by
Samuel T. Armstrong. 144

A catalogue of books, imported

in the Electra.   7570

Catalogue of books in Social Library.   11948

Catalogue of books in the Albany Library.   4443; 31917

Catalogue of books in the Boston Atheneum[!]   28236

Catalogue of books in the Boston Library.   15519

Catalogue of books in the Boylston Medical Library.   16463

Catalogue of books in the Brooklyn Circulating Library.   4841

Catalogue of books in the library [Dartmouth College]   957

Catalogue of books in the library of Brown University.   23948

Catalogue of books in the library of the First Society of Unitarian Christians in ... Philadelphia.   9893

A catalogue of books in the Library of the Military Academy at West Point.   19109

Catalogue of books in the library of the Procellian Club.   29167

Catalogue of books in the library of the United Fraternity at Dartmouth College.   958

Catalogue of books in the library of Williams College.   7675; 37199

Catalogue of books in the library of Yale College.   14990

A catalogue of books in the Maryland State Library.   29637

A catalogue of books in the New-Haven Social Library.   9647

A catalogue of books, in the Ohio State Library.   25623; 34599

Catalogue of books in the Portland Athenaeum.   34848

Catalogue of books in the Portsmouth Athenaeum.   30313

Catalogue of books in the Sabbath school library, of the Fourth Presbyterian Church, Washington.   4183

Catalogue of books in the state library [Ohio]   13620

Catalogue of books in the United Fraternity Library.   15931

A catalogue of books in the vari-ous departments of ancient and modern literature.   8554

Catalogue of books in the Washington Library.   11349

A catalogue of books, including two private libraries now on sale.   8583

A catalogue of books of the stock of the late firm of Thomas Dobson & Son.   12383

A catalogue of books on sale, by Pishey Thompson.   10443; 18189; 22457; 35502

Catalogue of books, presented by the committee... received by the general meeting of the Albemarle Library Society.   11567

Catalogue of books published, and for sale by, the American Sunday School Union.   19416

A catalogue of books... published by Mathew Carey.   8263

A catalogue of books recently imported.   7571

Catalogue of books, stationery, etc.   24921

Catalogue of books to be sold at M. Poor's.   17659

Catalogue of books, to be sold at public auction.   19500

Catalogue of books to be sold to booksellers only.   20789

Catalogue of Boxford Academy.   37921

Catalogue of Columbia College.   24166

Catalogue of Dana's Circulating Library.   32886

Catalogue of Davis & Force's Washington circulating library.   966; 967; 5157

Catalogue of domestic goods to be sold by auction.   24739

Catalogue of duplicates in the library.   16464

Catalogue of elegant cabinet furniture.   28641

Catalogue of extensive and valuable collection of metalick fossils.   10450

Catalogue of fruit and ornamental trees.   10012; 13850

Catalogue of fruit trees   [Albany

Nursery] 28316; 31920

Catalogue of fruit trees [Brighton Nursery] 37213

Catalogue of garden & flower-seeds. 2674

Catalogue of green-house plants. 25063

Catalogue of H. C. Sleight's circulating library. 17996

Catalogue of Hamilton College Library. 24785

Catalogue of instructers [!] and scholars in the English High School. 19813

Catalogue of kitchen-garden, field and flower seeds, bulbous roots, &c. Sold by G. Thorburn. 3434; 6969; 10449; 18195; 30796

Catalogue of kitchen garden, herb, tree, field and flower seeds, bulbous flower roots, agricultural books, &c. for sale at the office of the New England Farmer. 30496; 35082; 40331

Catalogue of Latin, Greek, & Hebrew books, lately received from Germany. 20231; 20232

Catalogue of Latin, Greek, French, & English classics. 20230

Catalogue of Latin, Greek, Hebrew, French, German & Italian books, just received on consignment from Europe. 38634

Catalogue of law books, for sale by F. Lucas, Jr. 21267

Catalogue of law books for sale by M. Carey & Sons. 4917

Catalogue of maps & geographical works, published and for sale by John Melish. 9455

Catalogue of maps and geographical works published by H. S. Tanner. 40602

A catalogue of minerals, contained in the cabinet of the late Benjamin DeWitt. 1018

Catalogue of minerals, found in the State of Vermont. 16381

A catalogue of... miscellaneous books, for sale at O. A. Roor-

bach's. 35068

Catalogue of Monitorial School, No. 2. 34851

A catalogue of music and musical instruments. 2648

Catalogue of music published and sold by E. Riley. 3020; 10113

Catalogue of new and valuable French books, and London publications. 12210

Catalogue of officers, system of education, and laws of Madison College. 29588

A catalogue of ornamental trees ... for sale by Michael Floy. 12563

Catalogue of paintings... exhibited by the American Academy of the Fine Arts. 4463; 7789; 15073; 30034; 34528; 37427

Catalogue of paintings, prints, and medals, in the Hartford Gallery of Fine Arts. 20824

Catalogue of pictures in the gallery of paintings. 38082

Catalogue of pictures in the third exhibition [Boston Athenaeum] 37899

A catalogue of plants collected in a journey to and from the Rocky mountains. 1778

A catalogue of plants growing without cultivation in the vicinity of Amherst College. 38990

Catalogue of prints... to be sold at Columbian Hall. 32619

A catalogue of rare and curious books. 20132

Catalogue of Sanderson Academy. 40354

Catalogue of scholars at the Public Latin School. 11943

A catalogue of school and classical books. 33548

Catalogue of subjects contained in the Hubard Gallery. 1689

Catalogue of teas, imported in the ship New Jersey. 31856

Catalogue of that part of the late Dr. Bentley's library, not bequeathed to literary institu-

21706

Catalogue of the faculty and students of Vermont Medical Institution.   7515

A catalogue of the first exhibition of paintings, in the Athenaeum gallery.   28237

A catalogue of the fraternity of Phi Beta Kappa Alpha of Massachusetts. Harvard University.   13740; 25732; 40037

A catalogue of the fraternity of Phi Beta Kappa Alpha of New-York, Union College.   30210

Catalogue of the Gardiner Lyceum.   12645

Catalogue of the graduates of Yale College.   31829

Catalogue of the Hallowell Circulating Library.   1494

Catalogue of the honorary and immediate members of the Peucinian Society, of Bowdoin College.   23913

Catalogue of the honorary and immediate members of the Porcellian Club, of Harvard University.   8963

Catalogue of the instructers and scholars of the Boston English High School.   23881

Catalogue of the instructers [sic] visiters [sic] and pupils of the Lexington Female Academy.   9265

Catalogue of the Ladies' Circulating Library, Boston.   39242

A catalogue of the library belonging to the General Theological Seminary.   17411

Catalogue of the library of Bowdoin College.   4813

Catalogue of the library of M. Carey.   8264

Catalogue of the library of the American Philosophical Society.   15088

Catalogue of the library of the Athenaean Society, Bowdoin College.   8160

A catalogue of the library of the Department of State.   22853

A catalogue of the Library of the First Church in Salem.   40348

Catalogue of the library of the late Rev. Paschal N. Strong.   26151

Catalogue of the library of the law school of Harvard University.   24802

Catalogue of the library of the Medical School of Maine, at Bowdoin College.   11965; 19838

Catalogue of the library of the Peucinian Society, Bowdoin College.   11967; 37918

Catalogue of the library of the Pennsylvania Society for the Advancement of Chrisitianity in Pennsylvania.   13877

A catalogue of the library of the state of Virginia.   37029; 41382

Catalogue of the library of the University of Virginia.   37040

Catalogue of the library of the West Parish Association in Boston.   23901

Catalogue of the Litchfield Law School.   33869

Catalogue of the matriculated students of Jefferson Medical College.   39136

A catalogue of the medical library belonging to the Philadelphia almshouse.   17603

Catalogue of the medical library of the Pennsylvania Hospital.   21844; 40012

Catalogue, of the members and books of the Erodelphian Society, in Miami University.   39579

A catalogue of the members of Harvard University Hasty Pudding Club.   38929

Catalogue of the members of the Adelphic Society, instituted in Union College.   3511

Catalogue of the members of the Boylston Medical Society of Harvard University.   20835

Catalogue of the members of the

class graduating at Union College. 35582

Catalogue of the members of the
Connecticut Alpha of the Phi
Beta Kappa. 6443

Catalogue of the members of the
female seminary, under the
care of Mr. Emerson. 8232

Catalogue of the members of the
First Presbyterian Church in
Rochester. 40306

A catalogue of the members of the
Merrimack County Agricultural Society. 39564

Catalogue of the members of the
New Hampshire Alpha of the
Phi Beta Kappa Society. 9886

Catalogue of the members of the
New Haven Female Seminary.
17339

A catalogue of the members of
the North Church in Salem.
30516

Catalogue of the members of the
Philomathean Society, instituted in Union College. 3512

Catalogue of the members of the
Society of Social Friends,
Dartmouth College. 8508

Catalogue of the Mercantile Library of Philadelphia. 13301;
34765

Catalogue of the mineralogical
collection, belonging to the
Literary and Historical Society of Quebec. 39299

A catalogue of the minerals,
which have been discovered in
the state of New York. 19232

Catalogue of the Mount Pleasant
classical institution, Amherst,
Mass. 39652

A catalogue of the names and
places of residence of the
members of the Third Baptist
Church in Boston. 11952

Catalogue of the New Haven Gymnasium. 34450

Catalogue of the Newburyport Sabbath School Library. 25586

Catalogue of the officers and
cadets of the American Literary, Scientific and Mili-

tary Academy. 6315; 6316;
9739; 13605; 17453; 25609;
25610; 30095; 34587

A catalogue of the officers and
members of Boscawen Acad-
emy. 32413

Catalogue of the officers and
members of the Adams Fe-
male Academy. 27779

A catalogue of the officers and
members of the Massachusetts
Peace Society. 2176

Catalogue of the officers and
members of the Pinkerton
Academy. 30272

Catalogue of the officers and students [Berkshire Medical In-
stitution] 8006

Catalogue of the officers and students [Warren Academy]
11346

Catalogue of the officers and students in the Medical College
of Ohio. 25293; 29714;
34096; 39542

Catalogue of the officers and students in Yale College. 14991;
23389; 31830; 41604; 41605

Catalogue of the officers and students of Bowdoin College. 565;
4814; 8154; 8155; 11959;
11960; 15533; 15534; 19833;
19834; 23911; 23912; 28259;
32456; 32457; 37917

Catalogue of the officers and students of Bradford Academy.
573; 8167; 23919; 28265;
37924

Catalogue of the officers and students of Brown University.
8197; 15577; 15578; 19882;
32496; 32497; 37968

Catalogue of the officers and students of Castleton Medical
College. 32617

Catalogue of the officers and students of China Academy. 8337;
32672

Catalogue of the officers and students of Concord Academy.
20158

Catalogue of the officers and students of Dartmouth College.

956; 5145; 8505; 12324; 15929; 20260; 24295; 28662; 32891

Catalogue of the officers and students of Dickinson College. 12374; 37296

Catalogue of the officers and students of Farmington Academy. 38554

Catalogue of the officers and students of Gardiner Lyceum. 16251

Catalogue of the officers and students of Hamilton College. 5528; 5529; 8923; 12749; 20793; 24786

Catalogue of the officers and students of Hampden Sydney College. 8927

A catalogue of the officers and students of Harvard University. 29160; 33492; 38926

Catalogue of the officers and students of Lexington Academy. 13102

Catalogue of the officers and students of Maine Wesleyan Seminary. 29609; 39417

Catalogue of the officers and students of Miami University. 39578

Catalogue of the officers and students of Middlebury College. 9480; 13329; 17153; 21453; 25364; 29751; 34134

Catalogue of the officers and students of Nassau Hall. 10017; 13854; 21976

Catalogue of the officers and students of New-Hampton Academy. 9643

Catalogue of the officers and students of Phillips Exeter Academy. 2762; 6475; 13769; 17625; 25766; 34784; 40068

Catalogue of the officers and students of Rutgers Medical Faculty, Geneva College. 33338; 33339

Catalogue of the officers and students of the Academical and Theological Institution, New Hampton. 39758

Catalogue of the officers and students of the Collegiate institution, Amherst, Mass. 7810; 11616

Catalogue of the officers and students of the Columbian College in the District of Columbia. 20137

Catalogue of the officers and students of the Miami University. 25330; 29742; 34125

Catalogue of the officers and students of the Mount Pleasant classical institution, Amherst, Mass. 39653

Catalogue of the officers and students of the Theological Seminary at Auburn. 19472; 23557; 26195; 27905; 32037; 37516

Catalogue of the officers and students of the Theological Seminary, Princeton, N. J. 2872; 30343

Catalogue of the officers and students of the university in Cambridge. 1532; 1533; 5552; 8958; 12783; 16462; 20826; 24803

Catalogue of the officers and students of the University of Vermont. 11295; 11296; 11297; 14778; 23156

Catalogue of the officers and students of the Wesleyan Academy, Wilbraham, Mass. 27644; 31749; 37138; 41517

A catalogue of the officers and students of Transylvania University. 6992; 10470; 14309; 18229; 22499; 26233

Catalogue of the officers and students of Union College. 3510; 14332; 18264

Catalogue of the officers and students of Waterville College. 12202; 15804; 20116; 24155

Catalogue of the officers and students of Williams College. 14931; 19297; 23335; 27070; 31766; 37200; 41545

Catalogue of the officers and students of Woodman Sandbornton Academy. 31804

Catalogue of the officers and students of Yale College. 4390; 7719; 11492

Catalogue of the officers, graduates and students [Maine Charity School] 9350

A catalogue of the officers, instructers, and students of Hopkinton Academy. 29253; 33588; 39027

A catalogue of the officers, instructers and students of Pembroke Academy. 25681

A catalogue of the officers, teachers, & graduates of Transylvania University. 26234

Catalogue of the organic remains. 25405

Catalogue of the Philadelphia Circulating Library. 17608

Catalogue of the Portsmouth, N. H. North Parish Library. 25814; 30314

A catalogue of the principal articles contained in the Boston Museum. 8147

Catalogue of the professors and students of the Theological Seminary, Andover. 121; 7815; 11621; 15105; 19435; 23522

Catalogue of the regents of the University; and faculty, fellows and students of the College of Physicians and Surgeons of the State of New York. 30039

A catalogue of the scholars in the Public Latin School. 23892; 28247; 32443

Catalogue of the second annual exhibition in Peale's Baltimore Museum. 13687

A catalogue of the second exhibition of paintings, in the Athenaeum Gallery. 32425-32427

Catalogue of the senior class [Union College] 30864

Catalogue of the Shakespeare Circulating Library. 3183

Catalogue of the Society of Social Friends. 24298

Catalogue of the splendid and valuable private library of the late Rev. John B. Romeyn. 22122

A catalogue of the subjects contained in the Hubard gallery. 16606; 20968; 20969

Catalogue of the teachers and pupils of Byfield Seminary. 4891

Catalogue of the teachers and pupils of the Chauncy Hall School, Boston. 37901

Catalogue of the teachers and pupils of the female seminary and collateral school in Wethersfield, Ct. 27624

Catalogue of the teachers and scholars of the Young Ladies' High School, Boston. 37912

A catalogue of the trustees and faculty of Transylvania University. 35552

Catalogue of the trustees, faculty and students, of the Charleston College. 15725; 20125; 38110

Catalogue of the trustees, instructers [!] and pupils of Bridgewater Academy. 11985

Catalogue of the trustees, faculty & students of Geneva College. 29006

Catalogue of the trustees, instructers and students of Amherst Academy. 11615; 23513

Catalogue of the trustees, instructers [sic] and students of Fredonia Academy. 28916; 33247

Catalogue of the trustees, instructors and students of Hopkins Academy, Hadley. 1665

Catalogue of the trustees, instructers and students of New-Salem Academy. 29959; 34466; 39777; 39778

Catalogue of the trustees, instructors and students of Phillips Academy, Andover. 2760; 7814; 25765; 40067

Catalogue of the trustees, instructors, and students of Plainfield Academy, Plainfield, (Con.). 34819

Catalogue of the trustees, instructors, and students of Westfield Academy. 19252

Catalogue of the trustees, teachers and pupils, of the Ontario Female Seminary. 30123

Catalogue of the Union Circulating Library. 18263

Catalogue of the Waverly Circulating Library. 37106

Catalogue of theological & miscellaneous books. 19275

Catalogue of theological books for sale by A. Finley. 8704

A catalogue of those who have been members of the Theological Seminary, of the Presbyterian Church. 10015

Catalogue of those who have been educated at the Theological Seminary in Andover. 4480

A catalogue of valuable works in theology, jurisprudence, and philology. 20133

Catalogue of vocal and instrumental music. 19300

Catalogue. President Jefferson's library. 39131

Catalogue Senatus Academici, eorum qui munero et officia gesserunt, quique alicujus gradus laurea donati sunt in Universitate Brownensi. 28307

Catalogus bibliothecae. Collegii Alleghaniensis. 11574

Catalogus collegii Neo-Caesariensis. Rerumpublicarum foederatum americae summae potestatis. 6538; 17698; 30345

Catalogus per triennium eorum qui officia gerunt, quique alicujus gradus laurea donati sunt, in Collegio Watervillensi. 20117

Catalogus senatus academici [Amherst College] 31996

Catalogus senatus academici [Bowdoin College] 8156; 19835; 32458

Catalogus senatus academici [Hamilton College] 20794

Catalogus senatus academici [Harvard University] 5553; 16465; 29161

Catalogus Senatus Academici [Middlebury College] 2256;

13330; 25365; 39593

Catalogus senatus academici [Transylvania University] 14310; 10471; 18230

Catalogus senatus academici [Union College] 22541; 35583

Catalogus senatus academici [Williams College] 14932; 27671; 41546

Catalogus Senatus Academici [Yale University] 4353; 27719; 41606

Catalogus Senatus Academici Collegii Dartmuthensi. 8506; 20261; 32892

Catalogus Senatus Facultatis [Harvard University] 5554

Catalogus Universitatis Brownensis. 603; 12011

The cataract of the Ganges. 17186; 17187; 17188

Catechesis religionis Christianae brevior Hebraice versa publiceque oblata 1689. 6769

A catechetical and practical grammar, of the English language. 37178

A catechism and confession of faith, approved of and agreed unto by the general assembly of the patriarchs, prophets and apostles, Christ himself. 4609; 32210

A catechism: compiled and recommended by the Worcester Association of Ministers. 4337; 7711

Catechism exhibiting in questions and answers the fundamental doctrines and duties of the Christian religion. 33020

Catechism for a young child. 28420

A catechism for the deist. 38083

Catechism for the instruction and direction of young communicants. 8400

A catechism for the use of children. 13684

A catechism for the use of the New Jerusalem Church. 24664

A catechism for young children.

12346

Catechism number three. 39000

Catechism of animated nature. 5991

Catechism of astronomy. 9118; 12932

Catechism of botany, containing a description of the most familiar and interesting plants. 16674; 24957; 39099

Catechism of botany or an easy introduction to the vegetable kingdom. 2188; 5992

A catechism of classical biography. 9119

A catechism of English grammar with parsing exercises. 28294

A catechism of English grammar with practical exercises. 12571

Catechism of general knowledge. 5993

Catechism of geography. 5994

A catechism of Grecian antiquities. 9120; 16675; 29333

Catechism of Grecian history. 12933; 16676

The catechism of health. 5995

Catechism of Jewish antiquities. 9121; 16677

A catechism of mythology. 9122; 16678; 39100

A catechism of natural theology. 39847

The catechism of nature for the use of children. 2115

Catechism of practical chemistry. 9123; 21029; 39101

A catechism of Roman antiquities. 9124; 29334

A catechism of Roman history. 12934; 16679

A catechism of scripture doctrine. 4232; 11382; 27593

A catechism of scripture history. 37945

Catechism of the Bible. 5996

A catechism of the Christian doctrine. 28424

The Catechism of the Council of Trent. 38084

Catechism of the diocese of Bardstown. 20266

A catechism of the history of England. 16680

Catechism of the history of New Hampshire. 38531

The catechism of the Protestant Episcopal Church. 17710; 17711

A catechism of the Roman Catholic faith. 24036

The catechism of the Wesleyan Methodists. 27605; 27606

A catechism of universal history. 9125; 16681; 24958; 39102

Catechism of universal history for the use of schools and families. 5997

A catechism on botany. 9126

A catechism on the principal parables of the New Testament. 29520

A Catechism; or, Compendium of Christian doctrine and practice. 4525; 15156; 27935

A Catechism; or, Short abridgement of Christian doctrine. 699

Catéchisme de l'Eglise Protestante Episcopale des Etats Unis d'Amerique. 21988

Catechisme de la Louisiane. 38085

Catechisms in a series of numbers. 9127

The catechisms of the Wesleyan Methodists. 41475

Catechisms on practical chemistry. 9128

Catechismus, oder: Kurzer Unterricht Christlicher Lehre. 8293; 24035; 24825; 25911; 25912; 28421; 38958

Catechismus religionis, juxta usum ecclesiae episcopalis reformatae in republica foederata Americana. 2878

The catechist. 5502; 28422

Cat-fight; a mock heroic poem. 16972

Catharine and Petruchio. 3180

Catharine Brown, the coverted Cherokee. 698

Catharine Stearns and George

Blake. 31207

The Catholic Christian instructed, in the Sacraments. 703; 15707

The Catholic doctrine of the blessed Eucharist. 8212

The Catholic faith, ever the same. 9752

The Catholic manual. 20002

The Catholic school book. 15109

Catholic worship and piety, explained. 4606

Catholics, attend! 20006

Cato to the people of the state of New York. 18198

Cattle show and fair, for the exhibition and sale of all kinds of live stock. 15702

Cattle-show, exhibition, Brighton. 5989

Cattle show, ploughing match, and exhibition of manufactures, at Topsfield. 20422

Caucus calumny refuted. 15703

The cause and cure of infidelity. 13476

Cause, evils and remedy of intemperance. 35151

The cause of education in Tennessee. 25114

The cause of the Greeks. 15292; 28084

Cause of the people. 38093

The causes, evils and the remedy of intemperance. 30388

Causes for trial and argument, at the December term, A.D. 1822. 9617

Causes for trial and argument, before the Honorable Nicholas Ridgely. 20010

Causes of an unsuccessful ministry. 40509

The causes of our fear, and the grounds of our encouragement. 1089

Causes of the progress of liberal Christianity in New England. 23505; 27847

Caution to banks, merchants, &c. 14006

Cautions against the use of tobacco. 30219; 30220

Cautions to seamen and other

voyagers. 6353

Cautions to young persons concerning health. 11351

The cavalier; a romance. 8001

Cavalry exercie [sic]. 15704

Cavalry tactics: comprising the modern mode of discipline. 8503

Cavalry tactics. Letter from the Secretary of War. 31208

A caveat; or, Considerations against the admission of Missouri, with slavery, into the Union. 701

The Cayuga County agricultural almanack. 8298

Cease sweet girl. 22117

Cecil's sixty curious, interesting and authentic narratives. 20938

The celebrated air Love has eyes. 11870

The celebrated cavatina Di tanti palpiti. 10142; 13990

The celebrated echo song. 473

The celebrated Hanseatic quick step march. 20013

The celebrated horse, Sir Archie, will stand. 27868

The celebrated horse Whip will stand the ensuing season... 32533

Celebrated horse Young Emperor ... 11440

Celebrated march for the piano forte. 1383

The celebrated Missionary hymn. 20014

The celebrated overture to La dame blanche. 19783

The celebrated overture to Tancredi. 6669

The celebrated overture to the Caravan. 1456

The celebrated overture to the opera of Tancred. 22125

The celebrated piano forte song. 10143

The celebrated quarrel & reconciliation waltzes. 6129

The celebrated race horse Muckle John. 40293

The celebrated selection of beauties for the flute. 13588

The celebrated Spanish serenade Isabel. 19736

Celebrated speeches of Chatham, Burke & Erskine. 21914

The celebrated Washington waltz. 37056

Celebration at Flushing of the birth-day of Linnaeus. 16910

Celebration of freedom. 4931

Celebration of the fiftieth anniversary of American independence. 23888

Celebration of the forty-ninth anniversary of American independence. 19819

Celebration of the passage of the first boat from the grand canal into the Hudson. 12083

The celestial magnet. 3237

La centerentola, or, The triumph of goodness. 25967

La Centerentola waltz. 3411

Census for 1820. 7202

Census of 1820. 14998a

Census of Maryland, for 1820. 13227

A census of the new buildings erected in this city. 20808

A century discourse, preached at Little-Compton, R. I. 25649

A century sermon, being the substance of a discourse delivered in Hebron. 40081

Century sermon, delivered at Danbury January 1, A. D. 1801. 35053

Century sermon preached at Foxborough, October 24, 1828. 40082

Century sermons. Two discourses, delivered at Bellingham, (Mass.) in the year 1822. 8709

Cephas L. Rockwood. 31209

Ceremonies and oration at laying the corner stone of the City Hall of the City of Washington. 4179

Ceremonies on laying the corner stone of Trinity Church in the city of Washington. 37093

Ceremonies on laying the foundation stone of Freemasons' Hall in the city of Washington. 24587

Certificates, &c. The following are the certificates of the County surveyors. 24048

Certificates of further credits for land. 26902

Certificates of the singular efficacy of those... medicines, prepared by W. T. Conway. 863

La Cesarine. 15323

C'est L'amour. 12085; 12086; 13909; 20240

Chad Miller. 31210

Chahta holisso a tukla. 31821

Chahta uba isht taloa. 41599

Chain of reason. 38414

The challenge accepted. 7730

The champion of freedom. 16750; 16751

The chancellor's memorial to the General Assembly of Maryland. 19768

Chancery cases argued and determined in the Court of Appeals of South Carolina. 30664

The chancery practice of the state of New York. 39650

Change of stations of troops U. S. 36192

Changing scenes. 20019

The chaplet of Comus. 713

Chapman's tables of interest. 4951

A chapter of modern chronicles. 30521

Character and claims of the Protestant Episcopal Church. 2891

Character and prospects of the real Christian. 32531

Character and reward of a good servant. 20398

The character and reward of the righteous. 24122

The character and suffering of the Pilgrims. 1703; 5657

The character and use of the Scriptures. 15720

Character and work of a gospel minister. 28332

Character essential to success in life. 3390; 6939; 18156; 40613

The character of an officer, and duty of soldier. 4306

Character of Jesus Christ. 30689

Character of John the Baptist. 20994

Character of Tanner's American Atlas. 18142

The character of the Christian mysteries. 41399

Character of the Puritans. 24742

The character, trials, and security of the church. 35417

The characteristic of homoeopathia. 20779

Characteristics of the minister's work. 35043

The characteristics of the present age. 37879

Der Charakter und Werth von Washingtons hinterlassenen Schriften, sowie der Plan zu deren herausgabe. 30681

Charfreytags Gedanken, oder das Leiden Christi in Reimem gesezt. 5904

Charge addressed to the graduates at the medical commencement of the Columbian College [Staughton] 40529

A charge delivered to the clergy of the Protestant Episcopal Church in the Diocess of Maryland. 9189

A charge delivered to the graduating class of the Columbian College, D.C. [Sewall] 35152

A charge delivered to the Grand jury of the Circuit court. 3346

A charge, delivered to the grand jury of the United States for the Louisiana district. 5182

The charge of the Hon. Chief Justice Mellen. 2226

Charge to Rev. Jacob J. Janeway. 32493

A charge to the clergy of the Protestant Episcopal Church... delivered in St. Pauls Church. 23312

A charge to the clergy of the Protestant Episcopal Church in the commonwealth of Pennsylvania. 39928

A charge to the clergy of the Protestant Episcopal Church in the state of Connecticut. 4857

A charge to the clergy of the Protestant Episcopal Church in the state of New-Jersey. 38303

Charges against the Creek agent. 36193

Charges and specifications against Brevet Major Samuel Miller. 8313

Charges, preferred by John White. 23310

Charitable exertions an evidence of a gracious state. 22363

The Charitable Fire Society, Incorporated. 1041

Charity at home. 17819

Charity hospital of New-Orleans. 39327

A charity sermon on the late fire at Savannah. 1878

Charity to poor children. 9001

La Charlatanisme, comedie-vaudeville. 35129

Charles A. Burnett. 31211

Charles Anderson and Arthur Jones. 26903

Charles Ashton; the boy that would be a soldier. 12100

Charles Lorraine: or, The young soldier. 14109

Charles Noble. 26904

Charles the Second; or, The merry monarch. 39980

Charless' Missouri almanac. 719; 4956; 8314; 12101; 15721; 20030; 24058; 28438; 32641

Charless' Missouri and Illinois almanac. 38108

The Charleston almanack. 24061

Charlestown fire. 38116

Charlestown Union Library, Subscription list. 4962

Charlie is my darling. 8322; 8323; 8324; 8325

Charlotte Temple. 3070; 17866; 17867; 22150; 25975; 25976; 25977; 30486; 30487; 30488;

35073; 40321

Charlotte's daughter. 35074

Charmant Ruisseau. 20036

Les charmes de New York. 32407

The charming portrait. 3287;
6840

The charms of melody. 15155

A chart of chronology. 23839

Chart of Portland Harbour. 21497

The charter [Philadelphia Seventh
Presbyterian Church] 9901

The charter [Providence Association of Mechanics...] 2907

Charter. An act relative to the
City of Detroit. 28695

Charter and bye-laws of the independent troop of horses. 19938

Charter and by-laws of Kaal Kadosh Mikve Israel. 17613

Charter and by-laws of St.
Philip's Church. 21875

Charter and by-laws of the Athenaeum of Philadelphia. 159;
2741

Charter and by-laws of the city of
Burlington. 15600

The charter and by-laws of the
fire department of the city of
Troy. 40684

Charter and by-laws of the First
Universalist Society. 34932

The charter and by-laws of the
General Society of Mechanics
and Tradesmen of the city of
New York. 12653

Charter and by-laws of the New-
Bedford Institution for Savings.
21602; 21603

Charter and by-laws of the New
York Chamber of Commerce.
34494

The charter and by-laws of the
New-York dispensary. 6266

Charter and by-laws of the Ohio
Insurance Company. 25628

Charter and by-laws of the Philadelphia Museum Company.
34766

The charter and by-laws of Webb
Encampment. 5379

Charter and constitution of the
Windham County Agricultural Society. 7683

The charter and laws of Hampden
Sydney College. 16388

Charter and ordinances of the village [Cooperstown] 38282

The charter and renewal of the
charter of the Bank of Orleans.
11678

The charter and stockholders' by-
laws of the Cincinnati Insurance
Company. 38177

Charter, as amended [Jefferson
Benevolent Institution of Pennsylvania.] 9145

The charter, articles of agreement, and by-laws, rules and
regulations of the Providence
Association of Mechanics and
Manufacturers. 30380

The charter; being a plain statement of facts, in relation to an
application to the legislature of
Pennsylvania. 31967

Charter, bye-laws, and catalogue
of books, of the Charlestown
Social Library. 24068

Charter, by-laws and ordinances,
of the corporation of the rector,
churchwardens and vestrymen,
of St. Stephen's Church. 21876

Charter, by-laws, and regulations
of the High School of New-
York. 20883

Charter, by-laws, &c., of the
Louisville and Portland Canal
Company. 21259

Charter, by-laws, regulations
[New Haven Hospital] 25520

The charter, by-laws, regulations,
and policy, of the New Hampshire Medical Society. 9638

Charter, constitution and bye-
laws of the Lyceum of Natural
History. 13558; 25566

Charter, constitution, and by-laws
of the New-York Mechanic and
Scientific Institution. 9700;
13567

The charter, constitution, and
circular of the Rhode-Island
Historical Society. 10105

The charter granted July 22,
1686 [Albany, N.Y.] 23442

Charter, laws and ordinances of

the corporation of the borough of Carlisle. 15680

Charter, laws, and regulations of the Corporation for the Relief of the Widows and Children of the Clergy. 28604

Charter of incorporation, constitution and by-laws of the Franklin Institute of the State of Pennsylvania. 16182

Charter of M'Kim's School. 5889

Charter of Newport, R. I. Trinity Church. 13584

The charter of the city of Boston. 28224

The charter of the Commercial Bank of Cincinnati. 38175

Charter of the First Congregational Society of the Unitarian Christians. 30868

The charter of the Mechanics and Manufacturers Bank, in Providence. 29710

The charter of the Monroe Academy. 29786

Charter of the Narragansett Bay Company. 34361

Charter of the Pennsylvania Bank. 38055

Charter of the Polytechny, adopted October 17, 1829. 38139

Charter of the Providence Mechanic Banks. 34934

Charter of the Providence Washington Insurance Company. 2911

Charter of the Theological Seminary of the Presbyterian Church. 30344

Charter of the town of Alexandria. 4446

Charter of the trustees of the Fire Association of Philadelphia. 24536

The charter of the village of Geneva, 20646

The charter of Trinity Church. 29886

The charter of Webb Encampment of Knights of Templar. 33261

The charter, regulations, and by-laws, of the Philadelphia College of Pharmacy. 25738

Charter, with the revised code of laws [Alexandria, Va.] 27802

Charters, statutes and by-laws of the University of Pennsylvania. 25718

Charts and nautical books, published by Edmund M. Blunt. 1662

Charts, pilots, nautical books, instruments and stationery. 10179

A check to Arianism. 27753

Checks to antinomianism. 1251

Cheer up! pull away. 14907

Cheery cheek'd Patty. 15731

Chelys Hesperia. 23349

The chemical catechism. 6375

Chemical instructor. 8586; 24394; 33038

Cherokee and Creek boundary. 41073

Cherokee Council to Col. H. Montgomery. 36194

Cherokee government. 36195

Cherokee hymns. 37580; 37915

Cherokee Indians. Memorial of John Ross. 41074; 41075

Cherokee lands--North Carolina. 36196

Cherry-cheek'd Patty. 10114; 12116

The Cherry orchard. 1076

Cherry ripe. 1668; 20950; 20951; 20952

Chesapeake and Delaware Canal Company. 41076

Chesapeake and Ohio Canal. 26905; 26906; 26907; 31212; 36197; 36198; 36199; 36200; 36201; 36202; 41077; 41078; 41079

Chester County Cabinet of Natural Science. 38130

Chesterfield travestie. 4975

Chesterfield's advice to his son. 20041

Chichasaw Treaty. 35169

The chieftain. A favorite ballad. 12121; 12122; 15736

Child of mortality. 15548

The child of want and misery. 15738

The child's arithmetick. 24564;
28902
The child's assistant in acquiring
useful and practical knowledge.
38136
The Child's Assistant in the art of
reading. 18163; 26185
The child's assistant to a knowledge
of the geography and history of
Vermont. 29115; 38893
The child's botany. 33385; 38786
The child's catechism. 17030
The child's companion [Bingham]
11860
The Child's companion [Lewis]
33852
The child's first alphabet of Bible
names. 28458
Child's first book. 8185; 15741;
28295; 37955
The child's first spelling book.
19194; 41436
The child's instructor. 8336; 32669
The child's instructor and moral
primer. 1449; 8335; 20048
The child's instructor consisting
of easy lessons for children.
33065
The child's instructor; or, Second
book for primary schools.
39245
The child's manual. 39920
The child's monitor. 8439
The child's own story book.
20049; 21378
The child's picture-book. 734
The child's port folio. 12124
The child's prayer book. 30145
The child's primer. 33812
The child's remembrancer. 20050
The child's scriptural catechism.
15160; 27942
The Children in the wood. 15740;
28456; 32670; 32671; 38135
The children of the Abbey. 3038;
10131; 25960; 30473; 35061;
40304
The children of the Hartz moun-
tains. 26072; 35178
Children's amusements. 732; 8334
The children's catechism. 6139;
13422; 29828
The children's companion. 20047;

28457
The children's friend. 4977
Children's magazine. 4978
Chili/and Peru in 1824. 15319
Chillicothe almanac. 735; 4979
China... with remarks on the
European embassies to China.
14816
Chipola Canal Company. 36203;
36204
Chit chat. 9539
The chivalrous knight of France.
17096
A choice collection of new cot-
tillions. 16725
A choice collection of patriotic
and comic songs. 32675
A choice collection of riddles &
charades. 34944; 40204
The choice...containing psalms
and hymns. 1040
Choice Emblems, for the improvement and pastime of
youth. 737; 14989
Choice hymns for social and private devotion. 39036
Choice pleasures for youth.
28461
Choice reading for Sabbath School
children. 39415
A choice selection of hymns and
spiritual songs; designed to
aid in the devotions of prayer,
conference and camp-meetings.
12125; 20052; 24084; 28462;
28463; 32676; 38141; 38142;
32677; 32678; 39985
A choice selection of hymns, and
spiritual songs, for the use of
Christians. 33060
A choice selection of the latest
social and camp-meeting hymns
and spiritual songs. 22288
Choix d'anecdotes, on faits me-
meorables, saillies et bons-
mots. 12207
Choral Harmonie. Enthaltend
Kirchen-Melodien, die bei allen Religious Verfassungen
gebräuchlick. 8821
Choral harmony: being a selection of the most approved anthems, choruses, and other

pieces of sacred music. 34046

The Chorister. 687

Christ against Kneeland. 17626

Christ blesses little children. 33803

Christ Church Academy, at Cow Neck, Long-Island. 20053

Christ crucified, the characteristick of apostolick preaching. 20749

Christ formed in the soul. 1034

Christ Hagonthahninoh Nonodagahyot. 37777

Christ knocking at the door of sinners' hearts. 20534

Christ the glory of the temple. 18021

Christ the son of God before He was made flesh. 4277

Christ the true light. 28765

Christian almanack. 739; 4983; 4984; 4985; 4986; 8339; 8340; 8341; 8342; 8344; 12126; 12127; 12128; 12129; 12130; 12131; 15743; 15744; 15745; 15746; 15747; 15748; 15749; 15750; 15751; 15752; 20055; 20056; 20057; 20058; 20059; 20060; 20061; 20062; 20063; 24088; 24089; 24090; 28466; 28467; 32680; 32681; 32682; 38145

The Christian almanack, for Alabama and Tennessee. 24086

The Christian almanack, for Connecticut. 24087; 28464; 28465; 32679; 38143; 38144

The Christian almanack for Georgia. 38146

The Christian almanack for Illinois. 24091

The Christian almanack for Kentucky. 32683; 38147

The Christian almanack, for Maryland. 24092; 28468; 32684; 38148

The Christian almanack for Mississippi. 38149

The Christian almanack for Missouri. 28469

The Christian almanack for New England. 28470; 32685; 32686; 38150; 38151

The Christian almanack, for New-Jersey. 24093

The Christian almanack, for New-York. 24094; 24095; 28471; 32687; 32688; 38152; 38153

The Christian almanack for North Carolina. 28472; 32689; 38154

The Christian almanack, for Ohio. 28473; 32690; 38155

The Christian almanack, for Pennsylvania. 28474; 28475; 32691; 32692; 38156; 38157; 38158

The Christian almanack for Rhode Island. 32693

The Christian almanack, for South Carolina. 24096; 28478; 32694; 32695; 38159

The Christian almanack, for Tennessee. 32696

The Christian almanack, for the state of Connecticut. 32697

The Christian almanack, for the state of New-York. 28476

The Christian almanack, for the United States. 28477

The Christian almanack, for the western district. 24097; 28479; 32698; 38160

The Christian almanack, for Virginia. 32699; 38161

The Christian almanack; New England religious, astronomical diary. 738

The Christian almoner. 5577

The Christian and civic economy of large towns. 4940

The Christian and farmers' almanack. 8343; 12132; 15753; 20064; 24098; 28480; 32700; 38162

The Christian and miscellaneous port folio. 12373

The Christian armour. 25314

Christian atonement. 24099

Christian baptism according to the authority of the Scriptures. 32701

Christian baptism; or, A discourse on Acts II. 40355

The Christian bishop approving himself unto God. 29234

Christian brethren's discipline. 20065

The Christian calendar and New
England farmer's almanack.
15754; 20066; 24100; 28481;
28482; 28483; 32702
Christian character. A sermon,
preached at Hawk's Church.
33602
Christian character exemplified,
in the life of Adeline Marble.
9469
The Christian character exemplified. Taken from the papers
of Margaret Magdalen Al-
thens. 87
Christian charity explained. 39119
The Christian comforter. 740
Christian communion. 8604;
20378; 20379; 20380; 20381
The Christian contemplated.
24977; 33702
The Christian course, a sermon.
41453
Christian deportment. 35044
A Christian described, and his
right proved and vindicated.
2617
A Christian directory, guiding
men to their eternal salvation.
2656; 2657
The Christian doctrine and ordinances. 35487
The Christian drummer. 741;
31973
The Christian duty of Christian
women. 20750
The Christian economy. 15755
Christian essays. 41522
A Christian exhortation to sailors.
38163
Christian experience and letters.
866
Christian experience of Rev. An-
drew Fuller. 1337
The Christian experiences, gospel labours, and writings.
8467
The Christian faith in our Lord
Jesus Christ, plainly asserted.
20067
Christian faithfulness and zeal es-
sential to the preservation of
the church. 29065
The Christian farmer's almanack.

32703
The Christian father's present to
his children. 21043; 24970;
29350; 29351
Christian fellowship. 39120;
39121
Christian freedom. 32704
The Christian guide to a right
understanding. 26200
The Christian healer. 37844
The Christian hymn-book [Gard-
ner] 24660; 38724
The Christian Hymn Book [Stone]
40541
Christian hymns adapted to the
worship of God our Saviour.
11937; 12133
Christian hymns. Sufferings of
Christ. 20068
The Christian Indian. 20069
Christian instruction. 4281
The Christian liturgy and book
of common prayer. 28423
The Christian manual, a treatise
on Christian perfection. 39565
Christian martyrs. 33014
The Christian melodist. 33151
A Christian memento. 15757;
38164
The Christian minister's affec-
tionate advice to a married
couple. 353; 4641; 15290;
19638; 23722
The Christian minister's last
honor. 20293
The Christian minister's valedic-
tory. 7972
The Christian ministry. 19729
The Christian missions. 19887
Christian mourning. 29473
Christian offices for the use of
families and individuals.
31825
Christian parent's assistant.
38078
The Christian pastor's manual.
28299
Christian patriotism. 24648
The Christian perfection. 21428
Christian perseverance. 37162
The Christian philosopher.
24349; 28702; 38385
Christian piety and knowledge.

29814

The Christian Pilgrim. 620; 621; 20070

The Christian principle in relation to pauperism. 24101

Christian psalmody. 4334; 7710; 23383

The Christian Quaker. 17547

The Christian register and almanack. 742; 8345; 8346; 12134; 15758; 20071; 24102

Christian researches in Syria and the holy land. 25009

Christian revolutioner in the similitude of David with his sling and five stones. 30480

Christian sincerity. 30462

The Christian soldier. A sermon. 12644

The Christian soldier, or Heaven taken by storm. 19205

Christian sympathy. 20913

The Christian traveller. 34967

The Christian world unmasked. 8009; 19668

Christian zeal. 37972

The Christian's companion. 38875

The Christian's consolations against the fears of death. 4377; 16003; 24364

Christian's daily companion. 31784

The Christian's duty in perilous times. 39707

The Christian's duty in relation to the contraction and payment of debts. 32031

The Christian's gain. 8537

The Christian's guide to heaven. 24103; 38086

The Christian's inheritance. 774; 12161; 32726

The Christian's instructor. 20946

The Christian's instructor instructed. 29489

The Christian's knowledge of Christ a sourse [!] of confidence and consolation. 3034

The Christian's manual. 17130; 25316; 29732

The Christian's motto. 20072

The Christian's pocket companion [Courtney] 28612

The Christian's pocket-companion [Royce] 24903; 25979

The Christian's pocket-companion and daily assistant. 22294

The Christian's treasure. 20073

Christians should support and defend the truth. 32378

Christians weapons not carnal. 25369

Christianity abstracted from signs. 459

Christianity an internal and practical principle. 744; 12135

Christianity and infidelity contrasted. 745; 15760

Christianity and literature: in a series of discourses. 23578

Christliche Morgen und Abend Gebäter, auf alle Tage in der Wochen. 1482

Christlicher Unterricht der Religion. 746; 24828

Christliches Gebet-Büchlein. 1479; 1480; 1481; 29102

Christliches Hand-Buchlein. 8690

A Christmas at Brighton. 8347

The Christmas gift. 35540

Christmas holidays. 28485

Christmas hymn. 9077

A Christmas sermon in the Universalist meeting house, Watertown, Mass. 35425

Christmas tales. 28486

Christ's sudden and certain appearance to judgment. 14784; 23167; 27512

Christ's triumphant entry into Jerusalem. 747

Christ's warning to the churches. 13053

A chronicle of the conquest of Granada. 39103

Chronicles of the Canongate. 14058; 30540; 30541; 30542; 35119; 35120

Chronicles of Turkeytown. 40464

A chronological compendium of the history of the United States. 30149

Chronological compendium, or History in miniature, of the most noted revolutions, wars, discoveries, calamities and events. 8348

A chronological history of New
England. 25833

A Chronological Register of Boscawen (N. H.) 2865; 13845

The Church Catechism. 1628;
4989; 24869; 28492; 29235

The church, in the first of persecution. 32854

A church in the house. 33527

A church manual for the communicants. 40046

Church manual for the members
of the First Presbyterian
Church, Elizabeth-town, N.J.
16966

Church manual for the members
of the First Presbyterian
Church, Newark, N. J. 29123

Church manual for the members
of the Presbyterian Church,
Morris-Town, N. J. 11748;
32216

Church manual, No. 4, for the
communicants of the Laight St.
Presbyterian Church, city of
New York. 34544

The Church obligated to support
its ministers. 23749

The church of Christ; a sermon.
5459

The Church of Christ, and way
of Salvation universal. 9203

The church of Christ independent
of the synod of Dordrecht.
11613

The church of the redeemed.
1781

The church perfect and entire.
20222

Church poetry. 13423

The churchman. 32708

The Churchman's almanac.
38169; 38170

The Churchman's profession of
his faith and practice. 5599;
5600; 20914; 38171

The Churchman's reasons for
bringing his children to baptism. 12138; 38172

The churchman's reasons for his
profession. 20076

Churchwardens--Elizabeth City
parish, Virginia. 41080; 41081

A chymical examination of the
mineral water of Schooley's
Mountain [N. J.] 34168; 34169

The Cincinnati directory. 20081;
38176

Cincinnati in 1826. 28729

Cinderella. 2723; 2724; 9882;
17594; 21863; 32714; 40027

The circassian rondo. 5623

The Circassian waltz. 12147

The circle of anecdote and wit.
12208; 20128

Circular. Abstract from a report of a committee, accepted
in Grand Lodge. 8751

The circular address of the im-
porting committee, of the Agricultural Society. 14169

Circular. A meeting of a few individuals, who have received
their education at Harvard
College. 29162

Circular and address of the National institution for promoting
industry. 2392

Circular and catalogue of the faculty and students of the College
of Physicians & Surgeons. 8389;
20461; 24479; 30040; 33117;
38527

A circular and the by-laws of
the Vermont Mutual Fire Insurance Company. 41374

Circular, announcing his [Samuel
Brewer] partnership as drug-
gist. 31851

Circular asking Isaac G. Beece
to become agent for the Portland Gazette. 15028

Circular. A view of the most
important subjects before Congress. 18240

Circular, Baltimore. May, 1824.
15938

Circular. Boston, June 29, 1824.
18032

Circular. [Boston Committee
Music Society] 23876

Circular, Boston, November 1,
1823. 12148

Circular, Chillicothe, May 12,
1827. 28459

Circular. Committee Room, Albany, October 22d, 1824. 15695

Circular. Concerning the Rhode Island Coal Company. 30566

Circular. [Democratic Party. Kentucky] 15958

Circular. Frankfort, February 17th, 1820. 2628

Circular. General Protestant Episcopal Sunday School Union. 27640

Circular. Hall of the Academy of Natural Sciences of Philadelphia. 11521

Circular. [Hampden Sydney College] 8928

Circular letter addressed to Lemuel Shaw. 14838

Circular letter addressed to the trustees of the University of Pennsylvania. 19621

Circular letter [Benedict] 385

Circular letter [Carey] 25715

Circular letter [Freemasons. Michigan] 28938

Circular letter from the Columbia Institute. 28553

Circular letter from a committee appointed by the Legislature of Kentucky. 7962

Circular letter of November 1824 regarding the prospectus of a work by Dr. Thos. Ewell. 16089

Circular letter of the Grand Lodge of the state of New York. 12603

Circular letter of the Meredith Baptist Association. 32153

Circular letter on the system of committing to jail prisoners for trial. 28390

Circular letter submitting a plan to the historical society of Pennsylvania. 24001

Circular letter, to solicit subscriptions. 11933

Circular letter to the bishops. 6271

Circular letter to the members of the Methodist Episcopal Church. 13314

A circular letter to the practitioners of physic and surgery in the state of New-York. 38180

Circular. Linnaean Botanic Garden and Nurseries. 34886

Circular. Medical College of Ohio. 2198

Circular. Medical lectures. 12014

Circular. Medical lectures in Brown University. 8200

Circular, Nashville. April 25, 1827. 29341

Circular. New York. July 12, Aug. 15, 1821. 4462

Circular. New-York, 13th January, 1827. 30499

Circular [Northfield Academy] 39881

Circular--No. IV. To the voters of the second Congressional district of Tennessee. 37504

Circular no. 3 [Democratic Party. Pennsylvania] 1007

Circular no. III; to the American members, and patrons of the institution. 7788

Circular of Mr. Lea to his constituents. 33827

Circular of the Apprentices' Library Company of Baltimore. 7886

Circular of the board of managers of the Theological School. 10043

Circular of the Central Committee. 1003

Circular of the Education Society, to its members. 22318

Circular of Thos. P. Moore. 6109

Circular. On instituting a society for the promotion of a taste for music in Boston. 26158

Circular on steam mills and distilleries. 33066

Circular on tariff duties. 29957

Circular on the cultivation of cotton. 8471

Circular. Plan of the Fairfield Literary and Theological Seminary. 28836

Circular respecting the Bunker Hill monument. 15589

Circular signed Yale College July
1, 1829.   37446

Circular.   Sir.   You must know,
that it is above ten years since
I left the District of Columbia.
3247; 6810

Circular.   State of New York,
Secretary's Office.   17368

Circular stating the objects of the
[American Unitarian] Association.   23506

Circular, stating the political
principles of the editors.
15056

Circular.   Steubenville, 6th Oct.
1826.   24717

Circular.   Studies.   [Hampden
Sydney College]   16389

Circular.   The Jackson Republican
committee of Rochester.   32942

Circular.   The medical department
of The Columbian College.
20138

Circular.   The Subscribers having
formed a connexion in the business of Land-agents.   2917

Circular.   The subscribers propose to open a school for boys.
37366

Circular.   The undersigned, committees appointed by the towns
of Wiscasset and Alma.   14955

Circular, to be sent to every one
who is indebted by John Binns.
37850

Circular to district attorneys,
clerks and marshals.   7203

Circular.   To editors and printers
of public journals throughout
the United States.   30047

Circular... to solicit subscriptions
for the relief of Thomas Jefferson.   25872

Circular.   To the citizens of the
senatorial district embracing
Knox, Daviess and Martin counties.   24464

Circular to the collectors.   26908

Circular.   To the electors of the
twelfth congressional district
of Kentucky.   29197

Circular to the freemen of the
tenth Congressional district in

North Carolina.   29523

A circular to the friends of the
education of the poor.   15764

Circular to the members of the
Protestant Episcopal Church.
28999

Circular to the officers of the
Bible Societies.   39875

Circular.   To the people of Fayette, Woodford and Clark
Counties.   28506

Circular.   To the people of Kentucky.   32464

Circular.   To the people of the
state of Mississippi.   41567

Circular.   To the voters of the
Second Congressional District.
29461

Circular.   To the voters of the
senatorial district. 29069

Circular.   Vindication of Mrs.
Judson.   11934

Circular.   Washington, May 15,
1826.   24987

Circular.   Washington, July 19,
1828.   34595

Circular.   Washington City, March
3, 1821.   4623

Circular.   Washington City, 19th
May, 1824.   16723

Circular with a catalogue of students.   27799

Circulating kalendar.   18084

A circumstantial account of the
occurrences that took place
during the cruise of the ship
Louisa.   1342

A circumstantial estimate of the
cost of a railway.   32715

Circumstantial evidence.   4668

Circus.   In the rear of Maj.
Barton's Hotel.   12149

Circus.   Messrs. Pepin & Barnet.
13725

Circus.   Mr. Pepin, manager of
the circus, on his way to St.
Louis.   27750

Circus.   Monday evening, March
9, 1829.   38181

The cities of the plain.   28835;
33116

The citizen, a farce.   13426;
17250

The Citizen's and farmers almanac. 753-757; 4995; 4996; 8353;
8354; 12150; 12151; 15765;
15766; 20082-20084; 24109;
24110; 28498; 32716; 38182
The citizen's and farmers' little
messenger. 28499
The citizens' and farmers' yearly
messenger. 15767; 20085;
24111; 28500; 32717; 38183-
38185
Citizens of Georgia - claim on
Creek Indians. 36205; 36206
Citizens of Newburyport. 26909
Citizens of the South-End! 15498
Citizens rights and free trade. 965
City affairs. 35150
City charter proposed for the adoption of the freemen of Providence. 40192
City of Albany. At a numerous and
respectable meeting of the Republican Citizens. 997
City of Boston. In common council. 28225; 32415; 32416;
37887; 37888
City of Boston. Report of the committee...on the memorial of
the warden and inspectors of
Ward No. 9. 32417
City of Boston. Selectmen's room.
8139
City of Boston. The committee of
the city council on the subject of
lands lying north of the County
Court-House. 28226
City of Boston. The Committee,
to whom was referred the con-
sideration of the expedience of
introducting [!] the system of
monitorial instruction into the
primary schools. 28227
City of New York as laid out by the
commissioners. 6587
City of New York - ss Mordecai
M. Noah. 34559
City of Portland. 39706
The city of the sun. 38186
City of Washington affairs. 124
City ordinances. City of Boston.
8127
City railways. 40220
City reformation prescribed and

demanded by the Holy Bible.
12152
Civil and military history of An-
drew Jackson. 20086
The civil and political history of
the state of Tennessee. 12799
Civil government an ordinance of
God. 24417
Civil government of the State of
New Hampshire. 13501; 21616
Civilization of the Indians. 26910
The claim of Amasa Stetson. 22372
Claim of Maryland for interest.
36207
The claim of Richard W. Meade
upon the United States. 20088
Claim of the Marquis de Maison
Rouge. 22854; 36208
Claim of the state of Pennsylvania.
36209
The claim of the western naviga-
tion of the city of Baltimore.
38075
The claim of William Vans.
19123; 19124
Claimants under first article of
the Treaty of Ghent. 41082
Claimants under the Florida
Treaty. 26911
Claims and titles to land in West
Florida. 26912
Claims of citizens of Florida.
41083
The claims of citizens of the United
States on Denmark. 24269
The claims of classical learning
examined. 17870
The claims of education socie-
ties. 37531
The claims of Free-Masonry.
29422
Claims of James Monroe. 41084
The claims of past and future
generations of rulers.
22350
The claims of Puritanism. 24341
The claims of seamen. 31729
Claims of Sunday schools upon
churchmen. 32718; 37293
The claims of the citizens of the
United States of America on
the governments of Naples,
Holland and France. 24455

The claims of the citizens of the
United States on Denmark.
24268

The claims of the Delaware &
Raritan Canal Company. 24112

The claims of the Episcopal
Church. 39655

The claims of the orphan, a sermon. 1629

Claims on Spain. 41085

Claims on the United States.
15102

Claims under eleventh article of
Treaty with Spain. 36210

The clandestine marriage. 8390

Clara, comédie en un acte.
34022

Clara, or The reform. 759

Clare de Kitchen. 3004

Clari; or, The maid of Milan.
13683

Clarissimo... Armigero, Univers-
atatis Transylvaniensis. 6993;
10472; 14311; 18231; 22500

The class book of American literature. 24645; 24646

A classical dictionary. 9254;
21190; 29475

A classical French reader. 20863

The classical, mathematical, and
English Institute. 39984

The classical reader. 24743;
33424; 38833

Clay and slavery!! 15780

A clear view of the state of the
Roman Catholic succursal
church. 8362

Cleland's statistical view of Glasgow. 781

Clementi's grand waltz. 12166

Clementi's second waltz. 782

La Clementina. 783

The Clergyman's almanack. 784;
5001

The clergyman's companion.
33568

The clergyman's daughter. 4271

The Clergyman's minor almanack.
785

Clerical and ecclesiastical bigot-
ry and intolerance. 15287

Clerical discipline, exemplified
by the Franklin Association.

8702

The clerk and magistrate's assistant. 8366

Clerks... Department of State.
26913; 31213; 36212; 41088

Clerks... Navy Department.
26914; 31215; 36211; 41089

Clerks... Post Office. 26915;
36213; 41086

Clerks.. Treasury Department.
31216; 41087

Clerks... War Department. 26916;
31214; 36214; 41090

Clinton and Economy forever! 63

Clinton's triumph. 18162

Clio. 9874; 30202

The clock of time. 6352

The closet. 32740

The closet companion. 19897

A cloud of witnesses, for the
royal prerogatives of Jesus
Christ. 15790

The clubs of London. 34019

The cluster of spiritual songs.
39558

The Clyde reel. 20209

Coach line for Philadelphia. 798

Coalition Consummated. 64

Coasting trade through Delaware
Bay. 36215

Cobb's abridgment of J. Walker's
critical pronouncing dictionary.
31642; 37063; 41411; 41412

Cobb's spelling book. 27735;
32744; 32745; 38208; 38209

Cock Robin's courtship and marriage. 15798; 20108a; 24137

Cock Robin's death and burial.
801

Cockney warriors at the battle of
Aldgate. 959

Code of procedure, for giving effect to the penal code. 21250;
21251

Code of reform and prison discipline. 25123

Code of 1650. 843; 8423; 20164;
32803

Codification. Speech of the Hon.
John L. Wilson. 31781

Le coiffeur et le perruquier.
35130

Coinage at the mint U.S. 41091

Colbert [Carey] 24002; 28391; 28392; 28393; 28394; 28395

Colburn's first lessons. 24151; 28535; 28536; 32754; 32755; 32756; 32757; 32758; 32759; 32760; 32761; 38212

The cold wave my love lies under. 4508

Coleccion de ejercicios facultativos para la uniforme instruccion de la tropa del Real cuerpo de artillería. 31570

Cole's selection of favourite cotillions. 812; 15807; 15808

Cole's collection of favourite Scotch & Irish airs. 15805

The collateral Bible. 15341; 23764

Collectanea graeca majora. 38324

Collectanea graeca minora. 5135; 12317; 20249; 20250

Collectanea, or Miscellaneous observations. 20543

Collectanea: or Select poems. 14202

Collectenae. No. 1. 15810

Collection d'operas et vaudevilles. 32766

A collection of admired duetts for two German flutes. 8388

A collection of affidavits and certificates relative to the wonderful cure of Mrs. Ann Mattingly. 17080

A collection of astronomical definitions. 5022

A collection of cases over-ruled. 5498

Collection of church music. 12761; 29133

Collection of cottillions. 6724

A collection of dialogues and phrases in German and English. 15005

A collection of discourses. [Stanford] 3302

A collection of discourses on various subjects. 28504

A collection of epistles from the yearly meeting of Friends in London. 5407

A collection of essays and tracts in theology. 14177

Collection of facts and documents relating to ecclesiastical affairs. 28547

A collection of favorite songs arranged for the Spanish guitar. 29796

A collection of forms, adapted to the use of justices of the peace. 15811

A collection of forms used by the clerks of the courts. 25957

A collection of fugitive poems. 15776

A collection of hymns for the Methodist Society. 29734

Collection of hymns for the use of native Christians of the Iroquois. 29377

A collection of hymns for the use of the Methodist Episcopal Church. 6029; 11396; 13312; 17131; 23288; 25319; 25320; 34115; 39569

A collection of interesting tracts. 21432

A collection of juvenile waltzes. 815

Collection of music arranged for the Spanish guitar. 3461

A collection of new receipts and approved cures for man and beast. 27939

A collection of psalm, hymn, & chant tunes. 13865

Collection of psalms & hymns for social and private worship. 780; 816; 8361; 11953; 12205; 17942; 24126; 28548

A collection of sacred music. 4924; 5537

A collection of some of the most interesting narratives of Indian warfare. 6027

Collection of specimen sheets. 15584

A collection of sundry books, epistles and papers written by James Nayler. 39704

A collection of the forms and entries, which occur in practice, in the courts of King's bench. 32018

A collection of the laws relative to the Chesapeake and Dela-

ware Canal. 12117
A collection of the miscellaneous
writings of Professor Frisbie.
12629
Collection of the ordinances of
the City of Charleston. 12102;
24059
A collection of the promises of
scriptures. 775
A collection of theoretical and
practical observations on medi-
cine. 26167
A collection of tracts, on several
subjects. 21226
A collection of useful, interesting
and remarkable events. 20292
Collections [New Hampshire His-
torical Society] 17335
Collections of the Massachusetts
Historical Society. 9425; 13262
Collections of the New-York His-
torical Society. 6272; 25575;
39825
Collections of the Rhode-Island
Historical Society. 30445
The College cadets march. 4158
The collegians. 38842
The Collell claim in Mobile.
32767
Colloquy on the immortality of
the soul. 38918
Colmena Española o, Piezas es-
cogidas de varios autores Es-
pañoles. 22193
Colombia: its present state.
20787
Colonel Chambers. 26917
Colonel Croghan's march. 12211
Col. Gibbens march. 12022
Col. Pickering's observations in-
troductory to reading the Decla-
ration of independence. 13773
Col. Pipkin's regiment Tennessee
Militia. 36216
Col. Pluck's Grand March.
15823
Colonel Wm. Steuart's march and
quick step. 21146
The Colonists. 27736
Colonization of free people of
colour. 31217
Colonization society. 11595;
36217

Columbia and Greene County
preacher. 20134
Columbia College exhibition.
15828
Columbia County almanack. 28552;
38228
Columbia, land of liberty. 582
Columbia mia venite qua! 6120
The Columbiad. 19607
The Columbian almanack. 12215;
24173; 28555; 32775; 38229a
The Columbian arithmetick.
27739
The Columbian calender, or New
York and Vermont almanack.
823; 12216; 15830; 20135;
24174; 28557; 32776; 32777;
32778; 32779; 32780; 38230;
38231
The Columbian citizens' almanac.
38232
The Columbian class book. 16947;
21262; 29546; 39328
Columbian College in the District
of Columbia. 5035; 16272;
20139; 24170
Columbian dollars. 19904
The Columbian family and pulpit
Bible. 8011
The Columbian orator. 4711;
11861; 28185; 32381
The Columbian reader. 5183
The Columbian riddler. 826;
20142
The Columbian spelling book
[Cole] 12203; 15809
The Columbian spelling-book
[Crandall] 910; 911; 5107;
8462; 20215; 38300
The Columbian tragedy. 8403
The Columbian waltz. 13104
The Columbus almanack. 828;
5038; 20143; 24175; 32782;
32783; 38233
The Columbus magazine almanac.
24176; 28559; 38234
Columbus; or, A world discov-
ered. 13412
Columbus, or The discovery of
America. 664
Come chace that starting tear
away. 11871
Come down to the lattice. 21390

Come dwell with me. 1926

Come haste to the wedding. 5041

Come honor the brave! 15831

Come listen to my song. 38238

Come live with me and be my love. 11872

Come my gallant soldier come. 474

... Come, oh come with me. 2356

Come rest in this bosom. 2216; 2317; 6496; 6497; 6498; 6499; 6501; 9964; 9965; 9966; 13799; 13800; 13801; 21922; 21923

Come sound his praise abroad. 829

Come strike the silver string. 17956

Come take the harp. 3322

Come where the jessamine sweetens the gale. 3323

The comedies of Aristophanes. 19457

The comic adventures of Old Mother Hubbard and her dog. 8407; 20144; 25431

Coming out, and The field of forty footsteps. 34846

Comin' thro' the Rye. 20145; 24179

Comly's primer. 15833; 24181; 32787

The commander in chief deems it unnecessary under existing circumstances, again to order the court martial for the trial of Maj. General Samuel L. Winston, to reassemble. 25393

The commander in chief of the militia of the state of Mississippi, intending as far as practicable, to review the various Regiments composing the same. 34157; 39609

The commandments and sacraments explained in fifty-two discourses. 5636

Commencement [Brown University] 8198; 19883

Commencement [Dartmouth College] 5146; 20262; 38331

Commencement exercises of the Collegiate Institution. [Amherst] 15100

Commencement. Middlebury College. 2257

Commencent of the Columbian College. 20140; 24171

Commencement of the Miami University. 25331

Commencement of the Ohio Canal. 20148

Commencement. University of Pennsylvania. 34712

Commencement. University of Vermont. 41376

Commencement, Williams College. 19298; 31767; 37201; 41547

Commendation and reproof of Unitarians. 37561

Commentaries on American law. 25026; 37765

Commentaries on the laws of England. 8093; 19760; 28194

A commentary on the book of Psalms. 9061

A commentary on the Epistle to the Hebrews. 30733

A commentary on the new system of naval architecture. 14238

A commentary on the Roman and the Spanish statute of frauds. 39840

Comments on the memorial from Williams College. 18069

Commerce and navigation of the United States. 26918; 36218; 41092

Commerce of southern America. 9117

Commercial and manufacturing directory. 38240

Commercial and notorial precedents. 9528

Commercial directory. 12218

Commercial formalities of Rio de Janeiro. 34087

Commercial Gazette extra. 35007

Commercial line of steam-boats. 12219

Commercial relation with Colombia. 26919

Commission under the Treaty of Ghent. 36219

Commissioner of Public Buildings. May 5, 1826. 26920

Commissioners sale. 38241

Commissioners under the Treaty of Ghent. 26921

The committee appointed at the general meeting held at Green Street, Philadelphia. 28973

The committee appointed to consider and report what measures are necessary in relation to imprisonment for debt. 5967

The committee of both houses of the legislature, to whom... was referred a message of His Excellency the Governor. 9405; 9406

The committee of both Houses to whom were referred the petitions of the trustees of Amherst College and of Williams College. 29674

The Committee of both Houses, who were appointed to consider "what measures it may be proper for the Legislature of this Commonwealth to adopt..." 2148

The Committee of Claims, to whom was referred the petition of Matthew M'Nair. 10807

The committee of general correspondence for the state of Missouri, appointed by the friends of Andrew Jackson. 32931

The Committee on Roads and Canals, to which was recommitted, the Bill to aid the state of Illinois. 26922

The Committee on so much of the Governor's message as relates to paupers. 2432

The Committee on the Public Lands, to which was referred the bill from the Senate, entitled "An act to extend the time for locating Virginia military land warrants." 26923

Committee to inquire into the cause of the increase of pauperism. 10411

The Committee, to whom was referred, at the last session of the General Court, the consideration of the pauper laws. 5968

The committee to whom was referred so much of the governor's message as relates to the boundary line. 25255

The Committee, to whom was referred the message of His Excellency the Governor of 20th January. 25256

The committee, to whom was referred the report of the committee of both houses on railways and canals. 39494

The committees vindicated. 8411

The Common almanac for 1823. 8412

Common benefits not the purchase of Christ. 20329

Common objections to Christianity. 41560

Common place book upon the plan recommended and practiced by John Locke. 7559

The common school manual. 28066; 28067

Common schools. 24183

Common sense addresses to the citizens of the southern states. 32575; 32576; 32577; 32578; 38056; 38057

Common sense and genius. 8069

The communicant's companion. 1574; 20860; 24833; 33528

The communicant's spiritual companion. 5562

Communication across the Isthmus of Panama. 31218

Communication, addressed to Friends. 12621

A communication from a committee of the Common council of Alexandria. 19392

Communication from the Brookfield Association. 5044

Communication from the chairman of the Board of health. 38109

Communication from the Chesapeake and Delaware Canal Company. 12118

Communication from the Comptrollers [N. Y.] 2482; 29988

Communication from the delegate of Florida. 36220

Communication from the executive of Delaware. 12355

A communication from the executive [Md.] 34027; 37301; 37302; 39442; 39443; 39444; 39445; 39446

Communication from the Governor [Pennsylvania] 30169

Communication from the Governor of Ohio. 39901

Communication from the Governor to the Legislature of Maryland. 25235

A communication from the president of the Chesapeake and Ohio Canal Company. 39447

A communication from the regents of the University. 25570

A communication from the Register in chancery. 37303

Communication from the Secretary of State [N. Y.] 9672

Communication from the Secretary of the Navy, to the Chairman of the Committee on Naval Expenditures. 3634

A communication from the Secretary of the territory [Mich.] 29746

Communication from the Secretary of the Treasury. 18678

Communication from the Treasurer of the Western Shore [Md.] 25236; 37304; 39448

Communication from the Trustee of the state to the General Assembly [Md.] 25237

Communication from the trustees of Nashoba. 32788

Communication of E. F. Chambers. 21340

A communication of the ecclesiastical council. 15561

Communication of the Society of Friends. 5405; 8779

Communication of the treasurer of the Western Shore [Md.] 25238

A communication on the improvement of government. 16665

Communication on the language, manners and customs of the Berbers. 17948

Communication to Stephen Allen. 12428

Communication. To the editors. 40390

Communications from the governor. 30170

Communications from the President and directors of the Literary Fund. 13790

Communications of Daniel Rose and Joel Miller. 39391

The communion of all saints demonstrated. 7786

The communion of saints. A discourse. 5413

A companion for the Book of common prayer. 29236; 29237

A companion for the festivals and fasts of the Protestant Episcopal Church. 16556

A companion to the American Museum. 11602

Company discipline. On the basis of infantry regulations. 623

Company orders. [New England Guards] 9620; 21606; 25498

Company orders. For parade duty. 17069

Comparative calculations, and remarks on internal improvements. 5045

Comparative statement of duties. 18679; 18680; 36221

Comparative statement of present duties. 14499

A comparative view and exhibition of reasons, opposed to the adoption of the new constitution. 8413

A comparative view of the existing tariff of duties. 832

A comparative view of the grounds of the Catholic, and Protestant churches. 1252

Comparative view of the heights of the principal mountains. 2341

A comparative view of the sensorial and nervous system in men and animals. 11345

Comparative view of the sermons of William Penn, Robert Barclay, and other primitive Friends, with those, lately published, of Elias Hicks. 20151

A comparative view of the systems of Pestalozzi and Lancaster. 19880

A comparison of the apostolic age with the present. 28088

A compend of ecclesiastical history. 34040

A compend of English grammar [Greene] 24738

A compend of English grammar [Michener] 17140

A compend of history from earliest times. 4258; 7641; 11405; 14884; 23307; 27628; 37159; 41490; 41491

Compendio de la historia de los Estados Unidos de America. 20152

A compendious abstract of the history of the Church of Christ. 20619

A compendious Hebrew and English lexicon. 24973

A compendious history of New-England. 2342; 2645

A compendious introduction to the study of the Bible. 29255

A compendious narrative, elucidating the character, disposition and conduct of Mary Dyer. 16027; 24389; 24390

A compendious system of elementary geometry. 8239

A compendious system of English grammar. 34798

A compendious system of geography. 11427

Compendious system of Greek grammar. 16118; 19254

A compendious system of midwifery. 15969; 24338; 32971

A compendious treatise on the use of globes & maps. 5792

A compendious trial of the Rev. William Hogan. 8414

Compendium of agriculture. 16006

A compendium of arithmetic. 3244

A compendium of cattle medicine. 14894

A compendium of church discipline. 19579

A compendium of English grammar. [Chessman] 4969

A compendium of English grammar [Kirkham] 13024; 39209

A compendium of general history. 37134

A compendium of geography. 25980

A compendium of grammar. 5493; 5494

Compendium of operative midwifery. 33502

A compendium of physiological and systematic botany. 3365

A compendium of picturesque anatomy. 30634

A compendium of the common law in force in Kentucky. 9076

A compendium of the course of chemical instruction in the medical department of the University of Pennsylvania. 29136; 33477

A compendium of the flora of the northern and middle states. 26227

A compendium of the law of evidence. 17540

A compendium of the minutes of the Warren Baptist Association. 19581

Compendium of the order of the burial service. 28562; 29363

A compendium of the system of divine truth. 15701; 24041

A compendium of the travels of the children of Israel. 14905

A compendium of the true Christian religion. 33551

Compendium of Universalism. 14294

Compensate registers and receivers. 36222

Compensation of collectors. 36223

Compensation to surveyor general. 31219

A compilation and digest of the

road laws. 34674

A compilation for the use of the members of the Protestant Episcopal Church. 10027

Compilation of articles relating to the culture and manufacture of hemp. 38524

A compilation of hymns, adapted to public and social divine worship. 38917

A compilation of laws [Ohio] 21726

A compilation of the laws of the state of Georgia. 5441

Compilation of the ordinances, of the common council of the town of Dayton. 24312

The complaint; or night-thoughts. 4357; 14996; 19350; 19351; 23395; 23396; 27725; 37279; 41618

A complete analysis of the several acts and chapters embraced in the revised statutes. 34495

Complete and authentic history of the battle of Bunker Hill. 19844

The complete art of boxing. 38242

A complete dictionary of music. 28333

Complete directions for parsing the English language. 25072

A complete genealogical, historical, chronological, and geographical atlas. 1912; 1913; 5801

A complete German grammar. 32057; 37539

A complete historical, chronological, and geographical American atlas. 8252; 12055; 28386

A complete history of Marquis de Lafayette. 20153

A complete history of the late American war with Great Britain. 18012

A complete history of the Marquis de Lafayette. 20154; 24184

A complete history of the United States of America. 4880; 4881; 8225

A complete index to Wentworth's

System of pleading. 11395

A complete key to Smiley's New federal calculator. 22291; 35223

A complete key to the revised impression of Bennett's practical arithmetic. 15320

A complete key to the teachers' assistant. 21280a

Complete measurer. 1826

The complete New-England almanac. 38243

A complete preceptor for the clarionet. 833; 12222

Complete preceptor for the German flute. 20738

A complete refutation of the Reply of Mr. Joseph Harvey. 2646

A complete set of improved lunar tables. 4186

A complete system of stenography. 7551

A complete system of stenography, or short-hand writing. 12388

The Complete Vermont Almanac. 32789

The complete vocal instructor. 29023; 33357

The complete works of Henry Kirke White. 41497

Compontimenti poetici d'un Italiano profugo in America. 40381

Composure in death. 6854

Comptroller General South Carolina. 36224

Comptroller's statement [N. C.] 25601; 30071

A concatenation of speeches, memoirs, deeds. 15837

Concern for the honor of the craft the duty of every Mason. 12004

Concerning the earths in the solar system. 35446

A concert, at the Rev. Dr. Porter's meeting-house. 10155

Concert in commemoration of the inauguration of the President. 5037

Concert January 11th, 1825.

19446

Concert of sacred music at Stoddard's Hall. 20156

Concert of sacred music. On Tuesday evening, Febr'y 24, 1829. 37980

Concert of sacred music, on Tuesday evening, March 25, 1823 in St. Matthew's church. 13541

Concert of sacred music, to be performed at the Universalist meeting-house, in Roxbury. 14007

Concert, this evening, Dec. 14th, 1824. 15116

Concert this evening, May 12, 1825. 19448

Concia ad clerum; a sermon at the opening of the General Synod of the Reformed Dutch Church. 13338

Concio ad clerum. A sermon delivered in the chapel of Yale College. 35472

Concio ad clerum. A sketch of the present condition and prospects of the Christian Church. 5486

Concise account of the conversion of a young man. 834

A concise and brief journal of the late war with Great-Britain. 38745

A concise and easy method of preserving objects of natural history. 37984

A concise answer, to the general inquiry, who, or what are the Shakers. 13184; 21287; 21288; 25179; 25180; 39376

Concise decimal tables for facilitating arithmetical calculations. 20091

Concise grammar of the English language. 20788

A concise history of England. 40676

A concise history of the united persecutions against the Church of Christ. 33323

A concise narrative of a tour, through some parts of England.

5047

A concise narrative of General Jackson's first invasion of Florida. 31581; 31582; 31583; 36996; 36997

A concise narrative of the rise and progress of the East Tennessee Missionary Society. 16030

A concise natural history of birds. 835; 15838

A concise statement of the proceedings of the Baptist Church of Leverett. 15839

A concise system of grammatical punctuation. 1448; 8887; 38830

A concise view of some of the facts and arguments, respecting another bridge to South Boston. 17954

A concise view of the critical situation, and future prospects of the slave-holding states. 22227; 22228

A concise view of the United States. 17524

The conclave. 20157

A concordance to the Holy Scriptures. 28301; 37959

A condensed geography and history of the western states. 33201

The condition of Greece. 34140

The condition of the Cumberland Road. 36225

Conditions of sale of store lots. 20159

The condottier, a poem. 5049

Conduct of General Jackson to the Kentucky troops. 31818

Conduct of George M'Duffie. 8482

The conduct of the understanding. 13130; 21240

Condy Raguet. 36226

The confederacy. 14766

Conference hymns [Bennet] 11795

Conference hymns [Greene] 33416

The conference meeting hymn book. 34014; 34015

A conference on society and manners in Massachusetts. 836

Considerations on the impropriety and inexpediency of renewing the Missouri question. 679

Considerations on the Indian trade. 5067

Considerations on the practicability and importance of opening a navigation to the interior of the state. 8540

Considerations on the principal events of the French revolution. 6850

Considerations on the proposed canal to connect the rivers Delaware and Raritan. 20178

Considerations on the propriety and necessity of annexing the province of Texas. 38260

Considerations on the purity of the principles of William H. Crawford. 12156

Considerations suggested by the establishment of a second college in Connecticut. 15849

Considerations tending to render the policy questionable of plans for liquidating, within the next four years, the six per cent. stocks of the United States. 25068

Considerations upon the art of mining. 5745

Considerations upon the expediency of abolishing damages on protested bills of exchange. 39378

Considerations which demand the attention of farmers. 32816

Consolation in death, a sermon. 893; 38293

Consolation to bereaved parents. 20179

The consolations of gospel truth. 13778; 17643

Console moi, divine mélodie. 5473

Consolidating revenue laws. 26926

Consolidation. An account of parties in the United States. 15861

A conspectus of the pharmacopoeias of the London, Edin-

burgh and Dublin colleges of physicians. 22460

Conspiracy of the Spaniards against Venice. 35092a

Constitucion de la Republica de Colombia. 8399

Constitution. [American Medical Academy] 15086

Constitution. [Cincinnati Medical Chirurgical Society] 752

Constitution. [Columbian Light Infantry] 5036

Constitution. [Connecticut Protestant Episcopal Church] 6550

Constitution. [Haydn Society of Philadelphia] 5566

Constitution. [Plymouth Bible Society] 17652

Constitution. [Worcester Auxiliary Unitarian Association] 19482

Constitution. [Young Ladies' Missionary Society of Philadelphia] 15000

Constitution. [Young Men's Baptist Education Society. Providence] 10048

Constitution; act of incorporation. [Ohio. Theological Seminary.] 18175

The constitution, act of incorporation, and statutes of the General Theological Seminary. 9698; 39822

Constitution adopted Nov. 27, 1821. [Kappa Lambda Society] 16759

Constitution amended; or items submitted to the consideration of the people of the State of New York. 6323

Constitution. American Academy of Language and Belles Lettres. 89

Constitution and abstract of principles approved by the Alabama Baptist Association. 37593

Constitution and act of incorporation of the Pennsylvania Society for Promoting the Abolition of Slavery. 2710

Constitution and address of the

Bible Association of Friends in America. 37841

The Constitution and address on the formation of an Education society. 33900

Constitution and articles of association, adopted for the government and regulation of the troops of horses. 12326

Constitution and by-laws... [Albany Horticultural Society] 37405

Constitution & by-laws. [America Beneficial Society] 88

Constitution and by-laws. [College of Apothecaries of Philadelphia] 5024

Constitution and by-laws [Diligent Fire Company, Philadelphia] 1028

Constitution and by-laws [New York Athenaeum] 21676

Constitution and by-laws [Pennsylvania Fire Company] 2707

Constitution and by-laws [Philadelphia Chebra Bikur Cholim] 17607

The constitution and by-laws [Saratoga Society for Promoting Agriculture] 3108

Constitution and by-laws. [Society of Teachers. Baltimore] 6821

The constitution and by-laws. [United Beneficial Society of Baltimore] 14335

Constitution and by-laws. [United States Beneficial Society of Philadelphia] 19108

Constitution and by-laws and act of incorporation of the Hillsborough Society, for the Promotion of Agriculture. 5587

Constitution and by-laws, &c. of the Female Orphan Asylum. 34849

Constitution and by-laws, of a classical and belles lettres academy. 8193

Constitution and by-laws of the Agricultural Society of the County of Essex. 11550

Constitution and by-laws of the

associated members of the Bar of Philadelphia. 6450

The constitution and by-laws of the Beneficial Society of Journeyman Hatters of Brooklyn. 19659

The constitution and by-laws of the Boston Debating Society. 11939

Constitution and by-laws of the Charleston Infant School Society. 38112

Constitution and by-laws of the Cincinnati Benefit Society. 12143

Constitution and by-laws of the College of Natural History of U. V. M. 27508

Constitution and by-laws of the Fame Hose Company. 33119

Constitution and by-laws of the Female Union Beneficial Society of Philadelphia. 1218

Constitution and by-laws of the fire department of the City of New York. 25535

The constitution and by-laws of the Franklin Beneficial Association. 38626

Constitution and by-laws of the Franklin Debating Society. 38627

Constitution and by-laws of the Galilean Society. 25749

Constitution and by-laws of the Grand Lodge of Missouri. 5387; 28940

Constitution and by-laws of the Grand Lodge of the District of Columbia. 33256

Constitution and by-laws of the Grand Lodge of the state of Connecticut. 20566

Constitution, and by-laws, of the Grand Lodge of the state of Illinois. 24592

Constitution and by-laws of the Grand Lodge of the state of Rhode Island. 24623

Constitution and by-laws of the Hebra Biker Houlam. 38954

Constitution and by-laws of the Hillsborough County Confer-

Constitution and by-laws of the
United Hebrew Beneficent Society of Philadelphia. 40711

Constitution and by-laws of the
Worcester County Institution for
Savings. 37248

Constitution and canons of the
Protestant Episcopal Church in
the state of New-York. 34912

Constitution and circular of the
American Unitarian Association.
19424

Constitution and documents [Amer-
ican Society for Meliorating
the Condition of the Jews] 7805

Constitution and exercise of the
Boston Sea Fencibles. 8149

Constitution and extract from report of the Fatherless and
Widows' Society. 16120

Constitution and form of government for the state of Mississippi. 6069; 9506

Constitution and laws. [Boston
Marine Society] 539

Constitution and laws of Rensselaer School. 25922

Constitution and laws of the Franklin Fire Club. 5139; 38628

Constitution and laws of the Society for Religious Inquiry, of
the University of Vermont.
31610

Constitution and list of members.
[Pennsylvania Prison Society]
6432

Constitution and minutes of the
Massachusetts Baptist Convention. 15205

Constitution and officers of the
Bible and Common Prayer Book
Society. 8048

Constitution and proceedings of the
Doctrinal Tract and Book Society. 38400

The constitution and regulations of
the Grand Royal Arch Chapter
of the state of New York.
38661

Constitution and regulations of the
Royal Arch Grand Chapter of
the state of Alabama. 28921

The constitution and regulations of

the Society of Ancient Masons,
in Virginia. 5573

Constitution and rules, for the
government of the Library
Company of Reading. 6593

Constitution and rules of the Baltimore Female Union Society.
210

Constitution and rules of the New-
York Female Union Society.
2529

The constitution and rules of the
St. Andrew's Society of Baltimore. 22177

The constitution and seventh annual report. [Female Auxiliary
Bible Society of Newark] 12526

Constitution and sixth annual report. [Female Bible Society
of Boston] 1214

The constitution and standards of
the Associate Reformed Church.
27894; 27895

Constitution and subscribers'
names of the Female Benevolent Society. 8585

The Constitution as amended.
[New York] 13546

Constitution.   Associated Mechanics and Manufacturers. 155

Constitution.   Baltimore, First
Philosophical and Evangelical
Association. 19510

The constitution.   Baltimore Vaccine Society for Exterminating
the Small Pox. 7888

Constitution.   Bible Society of
Grafton County. 32369

The constitution, by-laws and
rules, of the Brooklyn Sabbath
Union School Society. 28289

Constitution, canons and regulations of the Protestant Episcopal Church in the state of Pennsylvania. 21996; 40181

Constitution, circular, &c. of the
Baptist General Tract Society.
15178

Constitution, Connecticut Baptist
Education Society. 32812

The constitution, containing the
confession of faith. [Presby-
terian Church] 6523

Constitution de L'Etat du Missouri. 2295

Die Constitution der Vereinigten Staaten von America. 12244

Constitution des theologischen Seminariums der Evangelisch-Lutherischen Kirche. 24684

Constitution, &c. of the Charleston Catholic Book Society. 5256

Constitution, government and digest of the laws of Liberia. 21211

Constitution, laws and regulations, for the government of the Grand Lodge of Alabama. 33252

Constitution made and established at a general convention of delegates, at New Echota. 28449

The constitution, medical police. [Medical Society of Augusta, Georgia] 13281

Constitution, names of members and government of the corps. [Boston City Guards] 8355

Constitution. Newton Temperance Society and Lyceum. 39843

Constitution of a Society for Detecting Horse Thieves. 22314

Constitution of Augusta Unitarian Society. 23559

The constitution of Coahuila and Texas. 38204

Constitution of Grand Royal Arch Chapter of Virginia. 1321

The constitution of man, considered in relation to external objects. 32785; 38235

The constitution of '76. 24209; 28586

The constitution of the Active Fire-Club. 10173

Constitution of the Agricultural Society of Hamilton County. 27791

Constitution of the American Home Missionary Society. 23485

The constitution of the American Institute of 1770. 19409

Constitution of the American So-

ciety for Meliorating the Condition of the Jews. 108

Constitution of The American Sunday School Union. 23496

Constitution of the American Tract Society. 11607

The constitution of the Ancient and Honourable Fraternity of Free and Accepted Masons. [N. Y.] 28946

The constitution of the associated churches in the southern district of the county of Litchfield. 38249

Constitution of the Association of Traders and others, in Boston. 32424

Constitution of the Auxiliary Bible Society of Burlington. 37522

Constitution of the Auxiliary Bible Society of Knox county, Indiana. 19478

Constitution of the Auxiliary Bible Society of the county of Clinton. 7854

Constitution of the Baltimore Chamber of Commerce. 15168

Constitution of the Baltimore Female Society for the Relief of the Indigent Sick. 19509

The constitution of the Baptist Auxiliary Education Society of the Young Men of Boston. 15176; 32102

Constitution of the Baptist State Convention in Alabama. 11682

Constitution of the Boston Debating Society. 4791

Constitution of the Boston Fire Club. 19815

Constitution of the Boston Light Infantry. 8146

The constitution of the Boston Mechanics' Institution. 28245

Constitution of the Boston Monitorial School. 15520

Constitution of the Boston Sunday School Society. 28250

Constitution of the Branch Bible Society of Brooklyn. 19853

Constitution of the Charlestown Light Infantry Company. 39495

Constitution of the Church Scholarship Society. 28493

Constitution of the City Guards. [Mass.] 39496

The constitution of the Claremont Theological Scholarship Society. 24113

Constitution of the Colonization Society of Kentucky. 39191

Constitution of the Columbia Typographical Society. 5031; 24168

Constitution of the Columbian Artillery Company. 28556

Constitution of the Connecticut Medical Society. 15847

Constitution of the Conservative Fire Society. 23878

Constitution of the Domestick Missionary Society of Rhode Island. 33003

Constitution of the Dorcas Society. 38408

Constitution of the Dorchester Female Tract Society. 12533

Constitution of the Downingtown Society for the Acquisition and Promotion of Natural Knowledge. 1045

Constitution of the Education Society in the Eastern part of Vermont. 104

Constitution of the Episcopal Missionary Association of Zion Church. 1108

Constitution of the Evangelical Lutheran General Synod of the U.S. 1128

Constitution of the Fatherless and Widows' Society. 28242

Constitution of the Federal Street Young Men's Tract Society. 38558

The constitution of the Female Hebrew Benevolent Society of Philadelphia. 20505

Constitution of the Female Philantropick [!] Society. 12531

Constitution of the Female Society of Boston. 8696

Constitution of the Free Produce Society of Pennsylvania. 28918

Constitution of the General Convention of State Grand Chapter. 38679

Constitution of the General Society of Mechanics of New-Haven. 38737

The constitution of the General Theological Seminary. 9699

Constitution of the Grand Chapter of the State of Alabama. 12583

Constitution of the grand encampment of Knights Templar of Massachusetts. 16205

Constitution of the Grand Encampment of Knights Templars... of New York. 1296

Constitution of the Grand Holy Royal Arch Chapter of Pennsylvania. 16222

Constitution of the Grand Lodge of Alabama. 5370

Constitution of the Grand Lodge of Delaware. 1287

Constitution of the Grand Lodge of Georgia. 1290

Constitution of the Grand Lodge of Maryland. 12593

Constitution of the Grand Lodge of Michigan. 24607

Constitution of the Grand Lodge of the District of Columbia. 8738

Constitution of the Grand Lodge of the state of Georgia. 28925

Constitution of the Grand Lodge of the state of New-York. 8758; 16212

Constitution of the Grand Royal Arch Chapter of the state of Maryland. 16201

Constitution of the Grand Royal Arch Chapter of Virginia. 38684

Constitution of the Harmony Fire Company. 30234

Constitution of the Haverhill South Parish, Sabbath School Union. 20840

Constitution of the Hebrew Congregation of Kaal Kadosh Beth-Elohim. 721

Constitution of the Hebrew Female Benevolent Society of N.Y. 1555

Constitution of the Independent Volunteers. 1746

Constitution of the Indigent Widows'

and Single Women's Society of Philadelphia. 33657

The constitution of the Infant School of the city of Albany. 37406

Constitution of the Infant School Society of the Northern Liberties and Kensington. 33664

Constitution of the Kappa Lambda Society of Hippocrates. 5740

Constitution of the Killingly Auxiliary Bible Society. 9201

Constitution of the Ladies' Charitable Mission Society. 1896

The constitution of the Ladies' Society of Columbia. 13040

Constitution of the light infantry company of Winslow Blues. 11461

Constitution of the Marine Bible Society of Boston. 39430

Constitution of the Maryland Auxiliary Bible Society. 5962

Constitution of the Maryland Society for Promoting Internal Improvement. 21350

Constitution of the Massachusetts Charitable Fire Society. 17065

Constitution of the Massachusetts Charitable Mechanic Association. 29689; 39517

Constitution of the Massachusetts Rail Road Association; 39524; 39525

Constitution of the Massachusetts Society for Promoting Christian Knowledge. 5988

Constitution of the Mechanics' Society of Detroit. 20301

Constitution of the Medical Society of the District of Columbia. 2204

The constitution of the Methodist Mutual Benefit Society. 13319

The constitution of the Mexican United States. 39576

The constitution of the Middlesex County Bible Society. 25367

The constitution of the Middling Interest Association. 9482

Constitution of the Missionary Society of New Hampshire. 39753

Constitution of the Missionary Society of New Jersey. 21642

Constitution of the Missionary Society of the First Presbyterian Church, Brooklyn. 37947

The constitution of the Missionary Society of the Mississippi Presbytery. 2856

Constitution of the Mozart Association. 21534

Constitution of the Musical Fund Society of Philadelphia. 2379; 9594

Constitution of the Musical Institute of the City of New-York. 34358

Constitution of the Natchez Fencibles. 29885

Constitution of the New England Guards. 17314

Constitution of the New-England Society, Augusta, Ga. 25503

The constitution of the New Hampshire Baptist Sabbath School Union. 39754

Constitution of the New Hampshire Branch of the American Education Society. 27832; 29946

Constitution of the New Hampshire Militia. 17336

Constitution of the New Hampshire Society for the Promotion of Temperance. 34449

Constitution of the New York Baptist Missionary Society. 17403

Constitution of the Newburyport Debating Society. 13581

The constitution of the Northwestern Branch of the American Society for Educating Pious Youth. 105

Constitution of the Oliver-street Baptist Foreign Mission Society. 21742

Constitution of the Park-Street Association of Ladies for Foreign Missions. 23891

Constitution of the Pennsylvania Horticultural Society. 30193

Constitution of the Pennsylvania

Conversation-Lexicon. 38263

The conversation of our Saviour with Nicodemus. 9140

Conversations on anatomy. 35057

Conversations on arithmetic. 13691

Conversations on baptism. 28770; 33054; 33055

Conversations on chemistry. 2098; 9359; 16762; 25223; 34010; 39427

Conversations on common things. 15983; 24356; 32990; 38398

Conversations on English grammar. 5696; 5697; 9109; 9110; 16666; 21019; 24951; 33666; 33667

Conversations on etymology. 9111; 16667

Conversations on infant baptism. 1796; 5720; 21057; 39138

Conversations on mineralogy. 11289

Conversations on natural history. 862

Conversations on natural philosophy. 506; 2099; 2100; 5931; 5932; 13215; 17017; 21325; 23842; 25224; 25225; 28197; 29621; 34011; 39428

Conversations on political economy. 505; 2101; 34012; 39429

Conversations on some leading points in natural philosophy. 33011

Conversations on the animal economy. 40217

Conversations on the Bible. [Abbott] 37349

Conversations on the Bible. [Hall] 5518; 5519; 29116

Conversations on the Sandwich Island mission. 38264

Conversations on the science of the human mind. 20400

Conversations reconsidered. 38265

Conversations with a young traveller. 34044

The conversion and edifying death of Andrew Dunn. 33604

Conversion and happy deaths of nine girls. 3011

The conversion of Augustine. 10037

The conversion of mariners. 4949

Conversion of Mrs. Eleanor Emerson. 12445; 12446; 24421

The conversion of President Edwards. 33050

The conversion of sinners superior to that of miracles. 2631

The conversion of the Jews. 12489

The cook's oracle. 9213; 13028; 20186

Co-operation in evangelizing the world. 12029

The Copenhagen waltz. 5080; 5795; 12989; 13054; 15870

Copia eines briefs. 869

Copies of the bill of complaint, answers and decretal order in the suit instituted by Adam Hoops. 870

Copy of a letter addressed to each member of Congress. 16476

Copy of a letter from Mary Peisley. 21590

Copy of a letter from Phillis. 32836

Copy of a letter written by John Mott. 37319

Copy of a memorial from the trustees of the College of Physicians and Surgeons. 34532

Copy of deed of trust. [Philadelphia Cemetery] 30222; 30223

A copy of the acts and doings respecting the De Forest fund, at Yale College. 14992

A copy of the deed from a committee of the town of Augusta. 16995

Copy of the record of the trial of Selden Braynard. 871; 28271

Copy of the records of Charlestown. 15729

A copy of writings left by Miss Clarissa Wight. 4282

The coquette. 5253; 16169; 33215; 33216; 38612

Cora; or, The genius of America. 32837

Corderius americanus. 34083

Corinthian waltz. 16862

Coriolanus; or, The Roman matron. 10233; 14088

Cornelii Schrevelii Lexicon Manuale. 35110a

The coronation; or Hypocrisy exposed. 8222

The coronation, or, The merry days of King Arthur. 8447; 8448

Corporation of Baltimore. Report. 36240

Corporation of Washington. Memorial. 36241

Corporations--Washington, Georgetown, and Alexandria. 36242

A correct account of the dying confession and execution of James Reynolds. 22152

A correct copy of the trial and sentence of Richard Johnson. 38283

A correct report of the trial of Josef Perez. 12264

A correct statement and review of the trial of Joseph T. Buckingham. 8449

A correct view of the controversy between the Congregational Association of South Carolina and the Rev. L. D. Parks. 8450

Corrections to the papers on the coast survey. 24811

Correspondence and documents [Bank of the United States] 218

The correspondence and documents relating to the proposals for five millions. 8451

Correspondence between a mother and her daughter. 6937

A correspondence between Charles Ludlow and the United States Navy Department. 9306

Correspondence between Dr. Charles Caldwell... and Dr. James Fishback. 23987

Correspondence between General Jackson and Mr. Monroe. 16689

Correspondence between J. & D. Hinsdale, and the agents of the Eagle Bank. 24851

Correspondence between Jasper Lynch and Mr. Samuel B. Griswold. 16953

Correspondence between John Adams and Wm. Cunningham. 18

Correspondence between John C. Spencer, Esq. and James Hillhouse. 10321

Correspondence between John Quincy Adams, ... and several citizens of Massachusetts. 37361; 37362; 37363; 37364

Correspondence between Mr. --, a member of - College, and the Rev. --. 873; 6202

Correspondence between Mr. Granville Sharp Pattison and Dr. N. Chapman. 715; 4376; 4952; 4953

Correspondence between Senhor Jose Silvestre Rebello and citizen Antonio Gonsalves da Cruz. 15898; 17762

Correspondence between the agent of the Commonwealth and His Excellency the Governor. 25261

Correspondence between the committee of the Trinitarian Society and the committee of the First Society in Castine. 35560

Correspondence between the eastern Federalists and John Quincy Adams. 38284

Correspondence between the First Congregational Society in Eastport and Rev. Wakefield Gale. 38440

Correspondence between the Hon. John Adams... and the late Wm. Cunningham, esq. 11528

Correspondence between the late Commodore Stephen Decatur, and Commodore J. Barron. 975; 976; 977; 978

Correspondence between the Rev. John H. Rice, D.D. and James M. Garnett. 35026

A correspondence between the Rev. Messrs. Lowe and Walton. 2022

Correspondence between the treasurer of the W. shore of Maryland, and the third auditor of the United States. 29638

A correspondence between the trustees of the New-York Free School, and the trustees of the Bethel Free School. 13891

Correspondence of Lord Byron, with a friend. 19914

The correspondence published by Professor Mitchell. 22029

Correspondence relative to the emigration to Hayti, of the free people of colour. 15970

Correspondence relative to the prospects of Christianity. 15877

Correspondence respecting French aliens. 39449

Correspondence respecting two publications which appeared in the Raleigh Register. 22030

Correspondence - Secretary of War and General Jackson. 36243

Correspondence which led to the duel. 331

Correspondence with Brazilian government. 36244

Correspondence with William Woodville. 8465

Correspondencia de Abelardo y Eloisa. 23405

Cortez: or, The conquest of Mexico. 17647

Cosmetic doctor. 6600

The cossack. 12267; 12268; 12537; 16134; 29129

Cost per mile - road to New Orleans. 26932

Cotillions. 12273

The cottage boy. 5089

Cottage economy. 15794

The cottage girl. 394; 877; 15318; 28605

The cottage in the grove. 1654

The cottage in the woods. 38285

The cottage minstrel. 28606

The cottage reel. 20522

Cottage rondo. 9043

The cottager's joy. 13794

The cottager's wife. 878

Cottom's new Virginia & North Carolina almanack. 8455;

24225; 28609; 32842

Cottom's Virginia almanack. 15880; 24226

Cottom's Virginia and North-Carolina almanack. 880; 5090; 8456; 15881; 24227; 28610; 32843; 38286

Cotton and hemp for sails and cordage. 41097

Cotton cordage and canvass. 26933

The Council of Caiaphas. 12716

The council of dogs. 5091

Counsels and cautions for youth. 40648

Counter memorial of sundry citizens of the District of Columbia. 26934

Counter report relative to the Susquehannah Canal wing-dam. 9372

A countercheck to Shakerism. 15574

Counterpart to "A strange thing." 32844

The counting-house almanac. 5092

The counting-house tabular tariff sheet. 32218

A country clown. 37935

Country dances. 12275

The country girl. 11491

Country neighbours. 624

Country school-master and his nephew. 882

Courage in doing good. 11658

Courageous minister. 27691

A course of critical lectures, or A system of theology. 22454

The course of examination and questions propounded in the several schools of the University of Virginia. 37041

A course of examinations on anatomy. 15840

A course of fifteen lectures on medical botany. 40300

Course of Hebrew study. 3361

Course of instruction for under-graduates in Harvard College. 1534; 5555; 8959

Course of lectures for Sunday evenings. 24230; 38290

The course of lectures in this

college, for the ensuing winter
session [Geneva College]
40335

A course of mathematics.   9087;
20989; 24933

Course of popular lectures.
38334

Course of studies designed for the
private med. school.   1678

Course of study [Williams Col-
lege]   14934

Course of study preparatory to
the Bar or the Senate.   14844

Course of study for candidates
for the ministry.   25326

The course of time.   34829;
34830; 34831; 34832; 34833;
34834; 40101; 40102; 40103

Court Assembly - March Term,
1823.   12276

Court martial - Colonel Chambers.   26935

Court of appeals.   William M.
Crowell, and others.   17342

Court of impeachment for the trial of James Prescott.   5969

Courts in Michigan.   26936

The cousins.   24909

The covenant and declaration of
faith of the Second Church of
Christ in Dorchester.   33004

The covenant, doctrinal articles,
and articles of discipline;
adopted by the church, in Foxborough.   1269

Covenant of the Bethel Baptist
Church.   2521

Covenants of the Congregational
Church of Christ in Buston.
15614

Cowden Broom.   5094

Cramer's Deutscher Pittsburgher
calender.   907

Cramer's magazine almanack.
908; 5105; 8460; 12281; 15889;
20213; 24237; 28615; 32847;
38298

Cramer's Pittsburgh almanack.
909; 5106; 8461; 12282; 15890;
20214; 24238; 28616; 32848;
38299

Cread Glover.   41098

The creation, a sacred oratorio.

16398; 29178

Creation versified.   8464

Creed and covenant of the First
Congregational Church, Brown-
field, Maine.   23952

Creed Glover.   41099

Creek Indian broke.   36245

Creek Indians.   41100

Creek treaty.   36246

The Creekiad.   34807

Creeks removed west of the Mississippi.   36247

The cries of London.   914; 15893

Cries of New-York.   8466

The criminal recorder.   11404;
15894

The criminality of intemperance.
14826

The crisis.   A sermon preached
at Hallowell.   16293

The crisis; a solemn appeal to
the President.   12056; 12057

Crisis in the affairs of the Domestic and Foreign Missionary
Society.   38302

The crisis, [No. 1 and 2] or
Thoughts on Slavery.   1588; 1589

The crisis; or, An attempt to
show from prophecy, illustrated
by the signs of the times, the
prospects and the duties of the
Church of Christ.   28594

The crisis: or, Essays on the
usurpations of the federal government.   30851

The critic.   10254; 17962

A critical and historical review
of Fox's Book of martyrs.
19439

A critical orthography, and easy
guide to pronounciation of the
English language.   15710

A critical pronouncing dictionary.
4146; 4147; 7555; 7556; 11326;
11328; 11329; 14810; 14811;
19168; 19171; 23194; 31643;
31645; 31646; 31647; 31648;
37066; 37067; 37068; 41414

Critical pronouncing spelling-
book.   4874; 12023; 19900;
23968; 38000

A critical review of Noah Webster's spelling-book.   32746

Dartmouth College and the state of New Hampshire. 32895

The dashing white sergeant. 475; 19737; 19738; 19739

The daughter of a genius. 16563

Daughters of Eve. 24299

David Cusick's sketches of ancient history. 28645; 32871

David Rogers and son. 41103

Davidson's Latin grammar. 28664

Davis & M'Carty's agricultural almanac. 8511

Davis & M'Carty's Magazine Almanac. 8512

The dawning of music in Kentucky. 1557

A day after the fair. 35354

The day after the wedding. 12992; 16773

A day at Fonthill Abbey. 12341

A day in Turkey. 971

The day of adversity. 20274

The day of doom. 37175

Day of judgement. 972

The day of marriage. 973

Day's New-York miniature almanac. 5160; 8517

Day's New-York pocket almanac. 12342; 15945; 20275; 24311; 28671; 32909; 38352

Days of absence. 22143

Dazee, or, The re-captured negro. 10260

Dazel's Collectanea Graeca minora. 15919

De bello Gallico. 15624

De Lisle; or, The sensitive man. 32916; 32917

De oratore. 8351

De Vere; or, The man of independence. 31658

De viris illustribus urbis Romae. 13103

Dead alive. 9777

The dead shot. 614

Deaf and dumb, an historical drama. 9034

Deaf and dumb. Dec. 22, 1825. 22857

Deaf and dumb, from the Columbian Observer. 8518

Deaf and dumb. Memorial of the trustees of the Kentucky Institution. 26946

Deaf and dumb school. 7823

The deaf lover. 13781; 21909

Deafness and other diseases. 49; 4428

Dear harp of my country. 6871

Dear Kate thy charms were like the rose. 9520

Dear Sir, [Circular letter requesting votes] 17127

Dear Sir agreeably to your request, I have prepared a list. 4114

Dear sir, having consented, by the advice of my friends, to become a candidate. 27755

Dear Sir--Having opened a medicine store, in this place. 29581

Dear Sir: I have submitted a claim to Congress... 20279

Dear Sir, I shall need no apology for addressing you. 674

Dear Sir, Jonas Galusha, President of the Society. 4094

Dear Sir, On a review of your letters and those of Isaac H. Bronson. 28286

Dear Sir, Pursuant to the order of the Legislature of the state of New-York. 2515

Dear sir, Your attention is respectfully requested to an association of scholars. 673

Dear wanderer. 3216

Dear woman, lovely woman. 16495

Dearest eyes. 5163

Dearest lassie. 16137

Dearest sweetest bonny lassie! 962; 15950

Death a gain to the Christian. 15826

Death, a vision; or, The solemn departure of saints and sinners. 39360

Death abolished. 15531

Death; an essay in verse. 28795

The death and burial of Cock Robin. 802; 8373; 15799; 20108; 24138

The death and resurrection of the believer. 10320

Death and the lady. 38355

The death-bed confessions of Lady Guernsey. 12734

Death-bed confessions of the late Countess of Guernsey. 8905; 12735

The death bed of a free-thinker. 8521

The death bed of a medical student. 5164

Death-bed scenes, and pastoral conversations. 37087

Death, judgment, and eternity. 35111

The death of Abel. 20665; 38752

The death of Christ. 24384

The death of Crazy Jane. 974

The death of death in the death of Christ. 30137

The death of good men. 40566

The death of Life in London. 12722

Death of officers on the Gulf frontier. 36253

Death of Sam Patch. 38356

Death, the believer's gain. 1355

Death's doings. 32881

Debate, in the Senate of New-York. 5471

A debate on Christian baptism. 8241; 15630

Debate on Mr. Fisher's resolutions. 17439

Debate on the bill declaring the qualifications of electors. 17475

Debate on the bill directing a prosecution against the several banks. 39857

Debate on the bill establishing free schools. 35019

Debate on the convention question in the House of Commons. 9727

Debate on the evidences of Christianity. 39945; 39946; 39947

Debate on the revenue. 33726

Debate on the Spanish Treaty. 2996

Debate on the tariff. 33999

Debates in the Congress of the United States. 12349

Debates in the House of Dele-

gates of Virginia. 41383

The debates, resolutions, and other proceedings, in convention, on the adoption of the federal constitution. 28775

The debates, resolutions, and other proceedings, of the convention of delegates, assembled at Portland on the 11th, and continued until the 29th day of October, 1819. 2073

The debt of nations to Christianity. 33693

The decency and order of divine worship. 17198

Decimal interest table. 33491

Decimal tables of interest. 10069

Decision and perseverance recommended. 6689

The decision of the bishops who united in the consecration of the Rev. Henry U. Onderdonk. 30371

Decision of the Supreme court of the U. States, given at the February term 1823. 14500

The decision; or, Religion must be all, or is nothing. 12997; 12998; 16776; 25023; 29402; 29403; 33754; 33755; 39180

Decisions of the court of appeals of Kentucky. 5755; 13001

The decisions of the Supreme Court of the state of Missouri. 39614

A declaration and protest of the wardens and vestry of Christ Church, Cincinnati. 12144

The declaration, constitution, and bill of rights [Methodist Societies] 25327

Declaration del pueblo de Tejas, reunido en convención general. 22441

The declaration of faith, compact and platform, adopted by the First Universalist Church of Christ in Roxbury. 10156

Declaration of faith of the regular Baptist Church of Christ, in Marietta, Ohio. 13216

The Declaration of independence of the United States. 3491;

10810

A declaration of Ohio Yearly
Meeting. 33297; 38700

The declaration of rights and the
constitution of Maryland. 17034

A declaration of the articles of
faith of the First Baptist
Church of Christ in Roxbury.
10154

A declaration of the Christian
faith and doctrine, of the Society of Friends. 28905

A declaration of the faith of the
Baptist Church in Brookline.
37945a

A declaration of the Yearly Meeting of Friends, held in Philadelphia. 8786; 33300; 33301

La découverte des sources du
Mississippi et de la rivière
Sanglante. 15314

The decoy. 980

Decree of the Circuit Court on
the United States, in the case
of the ship Argonaut. 14501

A dedication anthem. 25612

Dedication of the Second Parish
Meeting House in Saco. 30506

Dedication to the members of the
Third Baptist Church in Baltimore. 2616

A dedicatory discourse, delivered
in Zion Chapel. 20295

The deed of gift. 11481

Deed of the lands of Nashoba,
West Tennessee. 31823

Deeds and other documents relating to the several pieces of
land. 11529

Deep Creek and Castleman Sum-
mits. 26947

Deep in a hollow glen! 9058

Deep in my breast. 12265; 15878

A defence. 29830

Defence against the charges exhibited by his prosecutors in
Baltimore city station. 31756

A defence before the Christian
public. 35191

A defence of "Baptism a term of
communion." 1869

A defence of Catholic principles.
5467; 29038

A defence of Col. William Lovetruth Bluster. 22290

A defence of direct taxes. 8265

Defence of Dr. Woods. 981

A defence of Freemasonry.
34865

Defence of Gen. Henry Dearborn.
15949

A defence of lay-teaching. 12350;
12351

A defence of "our fathers," and
of the original organization of
the Methodist Episcopal
Church. 28794; 33076; 33077

A defence of the agency of the
Pulteney estate. 7009

A defence of the American Sunday School Union. 33461

Defence of the Christian doctrines of the Society of
Friends. 20281

A defence of the Christian religion. 15886

Defence of the divinity of Jesus
Christ. 21297

A defence of the drama containing Mansel's free thoughts.
23986; 24318

A defence of the Elkhorn Association. 8706

A defence of the experiments to
determine the comparative
value of the principal varieties
of fuel. 32511

Defence of the Exposition of the
Middling Interest. 8523

A defence of the national administration. 37113

Defence of the Third article of
the Massachusetts Declaration.
2658

A defence of the Trinitarian system. 8954

A defence of the truth. 39350

Defence of the Vindication of the
Catholic doctrine. 12328

A defence of Thomas B. Reed.
33481

A defence of truth, and Free-
Masonry exposed. 28676

Defense against accusations of
Huntsville Democrat. 29562

A defense of the Protestant Episcopal Church, against the charges of enmity. 33324

Deficiencies and danger of the novice. 7718

The defining spelling book. 10291

Definitions and elementary observations in astronomy. 8909

Definitive statement, on the part of the United States, of the case referred, in pursuance of the convention of 29th September, 1827. 41104

The deformed transformed. 15615

Deism refuted. 1672

Delaware. 38571

Delaware and Hudson Canal. 36254

The Delaware and Maryland almanac. 8531; 12359; 15956; 20288; 24327; 28683; 32919; 38365

Delaware and Raritan Canal. 20289; 20290

Delaware and Rariton [sic] Canal. 24329

Delectus sententiarum graecarum. 31572

Delia's birth-day. 6869

A delineation of the characteristic features of a revival. 28284

Delinquency, no fable. 995

Democedes. 28274

Democratic convention. 34400

Democratic nominations for president. 15843a

A demonstration of the right to the navigation of the waters of New York. 6918

The demurrer. 33535

A denial of certain charges made against the Protestant Episcopal Church. 34901

Dension Douglass. 36255

Department of medicine. [Pennsylvania University] 17587

El derecho del hombre, para el uso y provecho del genero humano. 6364; 9801

A descant on the universal plan, corrected. 13689

A descant on Universalism. 9832; 9833; 13690

A description and general view

of Elisha Hale's horizontal water wheel. 1489

A description and practical application of Bolles's trigonometer. 15490

Description and use of a diagram of navigation. 11354

The description and use of Bartlett's celestial planisphere. 19616; 23711

A description, by John Baker, of the mode of spaying sows. 7870

Description of a direct route for the Erie Canal. 10063; 34956

Description of a land-tortoise. 24792a

Description of a new species of Cephalopode. 16886

Description of a plan for navigating the rapids in rivers. 12154

Description of a small muscle at the internal commissure of the eyelids. 16590

Description of an Egyptian mummy. 7586; 14831; 19191

Description of an hermaphrodite Orang outang. 24792

A description of Bridgeman's Rotary railway. 37936

A description of Brunswick Maine. 2918; 13898

Description of Dunlap's painting of Christ. 1056

Description of Haviland's design for the new penitentiary. 5561

A description of his painting [Trumbull] 3492

A description of Ithiel Town's improvement in the construction of wood and iron bridges. 6983; 22489

Description of new species of North American insects. 40358

Description of several species of the Linnaean genus Raia. 16887

Description of six new species of the genus Unio. 29460; 33833

Description of some of the medals struck in relation to important events in North America. 6004

A description of the American marine rail-way. 30738

Description of the antiquities discovered in Ohio. 164

The description of the city of New-York. 29135

Description of the Court of Death. 1010

Description of the distinct, confluent and inoculated small pox. 38579

Description of the Eastern Penitentiary. 40446

Description of the eruption of Long Lake and Mud Lake in Vermont. 24385

A description of the etiquette at Washington City. 38272

Description of the four pictures, from subjects of the revolution. 30844

Description of the Great Western Canal. 8541

Description of the hall of the House of Representatives. 13406

Description of the Incas of Peru. 28692

A description of the island of St. Michael. 4220; 7611

Description of the panorama of the palace and gardens of Versailles. 4079; 8542

Description of the panorama of the superb city of Mexico. 32522

A description of the scenery and incidents in the picturesque and beautiful spectacle called, Peter Wilkins. 32964

Description of the scenery and principal incidents... in three acts, called the AEthiop. 38369

A description of the Thames tunnel. 28693

Description of the view of the city and lake of Geneva. 37994

A description of Trenton Falls. 30589; 35173; 35174

Description of two new species of the genus Batsachoid. 16888

Descriptions of insects. 14048

Descriptions of some new terrestrial and fluviatile shells. 40359

Descriptions of ten species of South American birds. 19790

Descriptive catalogue of a collection of rare minerals. 38370

Descriptive catalogue of Original Cabinet Paintings. 1011

A descriptive, diagnostic and practical essay on disorders of the digestive organs. 12746

El desengaño del hombre. 10051

The deserted boy. 21712

The deserter, a musical drama. 12369

The deserter. Written expressly for Miss Paton. 345

Desertions from French ships. 26948

Desertions from the Army. 26949; 26950; 26951

The design and importance of the Education Society. 20283

The design and tendency of Christianity to diminish the miseries. 17832

The design and use of the book of Psalms. 8862

The design of baptism. 38120

The design of the Lord's supper. 24336

Designs of paintings. 26952

Desilver's Philadelphia directory. 32965; 38371

Desilver's United States almanac. 20299; 32966; 32967

Desilver's United States' Register. 38372

The desires of the deity. 15968

Desmond's song. 19740

The desolations and the restoration of Zion. 360; 361

Destruction of Frigate Philadelphia. 31228

The destruction of Jerusalem [Holford] 1648; 1649; 20927

Destruction of Jerusalem [Josephus] 33735

The destructive influence of sinners. 12165

A desultory examination of the re-

38383

A dialogue, on the effectual means of separating Free Masonry from the Church of Christ. 35392

A dialogue on the geography of the United States. 17116

A dialogue on the penitentiary system. 1024

The dialogues of devils. 29572

Dialogues on atonement. 20309

Dialogues on domestic and rural economy. 325

Dialogues on the nature, design, and evidence of the theological writings. 5008

Dialogues on the Ten Commandments. 38384

Diary of an ennuyée. 24974

Diccionario de las musas. 29039

Diccionario filosofico. 23181

Diccionario nuevo de las dos lenguas. 13582

A dictionary of arts and sciences. 5499

A dictionary of chemistry. 7496

A dictionary of practical surgery. 8443; 12257

A dictionary of select and popular quotations. 16964; 32983

A dictionary of the Holy Bible. 13222; 15573; 37960

A dictionary of the New Testament. 28101

A dictionary of the proper names in the New Testament. 33022; 38434

The differences among professors of Christianity. 5578

Differences between Quakerism & Christianity. 12375

The differential and integral calculus. 35086

The difficulties and temptations which attend the preaching of the gospel. 2264; 2265

The difficulties of infidelity. 20452; 38519; 38520

The difficulties of Protestantism. 1253; 38593

The difficulties of Romanism. 38521

Difficulties of the ministry.

14880

A digest, compiled from the records of the General Assembly of the Presbyterian Church. 2848

Digest of accounts of manufacturing establishments in the United States. 14502

A digest of cases adjudged in the circuit court of the United States. 11402

A digest of cases reported in the Constitutional Court. 18053

A digest of Martin's reports. 25145

A digest of reported cases, argued & determined in the Supreme judicial court of Mass. 19730

A digest of reports in equity. 8925; 8926

A digest of the acts of Assembly of Pennsylvania. 40681

A digest of the cases decided and reported to the supreme court of judicature [N. Y.] 21654

Digest of the cases decided in the supreme judicial court of the commonwealth of Massachusetts. 21431

A digest of the commercial regulations of the different foreign nations. 18681

A digest of the decisions of the Supreme Court of the United States. 7206; 41488

A digest of the English statutes of force in the state of Georgia. 24674

A digest of the law of actions and trials at nisi prius. 1116

A digest of the law of partnership. 9525; 9526; 17196

A digest of the law relative to pleading and guidance. 15117

A digest of the laws of England. 12293; 15836; 24186; 28627

A digest of the laws of Georgia. 8813

Digest of the laws of New York. 39791

Digest of the laws of Pennsylvania. 17737

A digest of the laws of South
Carolina. 9134

A digest of the laws of the corporation of the city of Washington. 12021

A digest of the laws of the state
of Alabama. 11558

A digest of the laws of the state
of Connecticut. 10388

Digest of the laws of the state of
Georgia. 1373

A digest of the laws of the United
States. 7207; 29053

Digest of the laws, rules, and
regulations, for the government of the Grand Lodge of
Kentucky. 24595

A digest of the nisi prius reports.
13211

A digest of the ordinances of the
corporation of the city of
Philadelphia. 9301; 34742

A digest of the probate laws of
Massachusetts. 17691

A digest of the reported cases
adjudged in the several courts
held in Pennsylvania. 39992

A digest of the reported cases on
points of practice and pleading
in the courts of equity. 37937

A digest of the rules of the supreme court of the Territory
of Michigan. 6036

A digest of the statute law of
North Carolina. 18161

A digest of the statute of Kentucky. 9196

A digested index of the laws of
the corporation of the city of
Washington. 38888

A digested index of the reported
cases adjudged in the courts
of North Carolina. 24815

A digested index of the reports
of the Supreme Court [N. Y.]
8350

A digested index to the crown
law. 14297; 35536

A digested index to the nineteen
volumes of Mr. Vesey's reports. 8547

A digested index to the Virginia

reports. 20786

The dignity of Christ's character. 16607

La diligence. 9437

Dilworth's book-keepers' assistant. 8548

Dinarbas, a tale. 25046

Dinner to Mathew Carey, esq.
32985

The Diorama. 38797

The diplomacy of the United
States. 25164; 33933

Diplomatic code of the U.S.
28776

The diplomatic correspondence
of the American Revolution.
41105

Directions for a devout and de-
cent behaviour in the public
worship of God. 5186;
24522

Directions for Buzzard's Bay
and New-Bedford. 6781

Directions for forming and conducting Sunday schools.
37452

Directions for persons just com-
mencing a religious life.
38393

Directions for the cultivation of
certain medical plants. 40421

Directions for the rearing of
silk worms. 34706

Directions for transferring prints
to the surface of wood.
28707

Directions for using the arms
known by the name of Hall's
rifle. 19465

Directions for using the medicines, &c. 180

Directions how to stock and use
Gideon Davis's improved bar-
share. 38344

Directions to applicants for grants
of land. 15979

A directory for the village of
Buffalo. 32987

A directory for the village of
Rochester. 28708

Directory and stranger's guide
for the city of Charleston.
8552; 15980

A directory for the public offices. 1262

Directory, or Guide to the residences and places of business. 32988

A dirge: on the death of our illustrious 2d and 3d Presidents. 24906

Disbursements to the Indians. 31229

Discipline militia. 31230

The discipline of Friends. 12626

The discipline of the Methodist Society. 6034; 17417

Discipline of the yearly meeting of Friends. 5404; 24640

The disclosure. 15981

A disclosure of facts, in consequence of a decree for alimony. 20785

Disclosure of the real parties to the purchase and sale of the Tradesman's Bank. 23700; 37699

The discouragements and encouragements of the gospel ministry. 10126

Discours addressé à la Legislature en refutation du Kappart de Mr. Livingston. 25146

Discours prononcé dans la chambre des représentans de l'état de Louisiane. 15933

Discours, sur la charité. 6491

The discourse. [The sermon.] 21294

A discourse adapted to the character of Washington. 17236

A discourse, addressed to Christians. 40403

A discourse addressed to religious people. 34715

A discourse addressed to the New-Hampshire Auxiliary Colonization Society. 20253

A discourse addressed to the Norfolk Auxiliary Society. 20409

A discourse; "Addressed to those who make a moderate use of ardent spirits." 38099

A discourse against transsubstantiation. 40652

A discourse at the funeral of Mrs. Emily Jewett. 17892; 26015

A discourse before the Society for the propagating the Gospel among the Indians. 2023

A discourse commemorative of the talents, virtues and services of the late De Witt Clinton. 32802

A discourse concerning meekness. 33529

A discourse concerning the divine providence. 14106

A discourse concerning the influence of America on the mind. 12928

A discourse, concerning the inventions of men in the worship of God. 33775

Discourse, December 27, 1825, before Macon Lodge. 25001

A discourse, delivered at Acworth. 38271

A discourse, delivered at Brunswick [Maine] 920

A discourse delivered at Concord. 19865

A discourse, delivered at Danvers. 12447

A discourse delivered at Dedham. 3008

A discourse delivered at Hamilton Centre. 35381

A discourse delivered at Kennebunk. 28890

A discourse, delivered at Lancaster. 35488

A discourse delivered at Marblehead. 8950

A discourse delivered at Maryville. 8942

A discourse delivered at Methuen. 25999

A discourse, delivered at Northhampton, N. H. 5403; 8772

A discourse delivered at North Bridgewater. 10358

A discourse, delivered at Nottingham-West. 12136

A discourse delivered at Plymouth, Dec. 20, 1828. 38823

A discourse, delivered at Ply-

mouth.   December 22, 1820.
7609; 7610; 23270; 27582

A discourse delivered at Schen-
ectady, July 25, A.D. 1826.
27727

A discourse delivered at Schenec-
tady, July 22d, A.D. 1823.
12185; 12186; 12187

A discourse delivered at St.
Johnsbury. 10277

A discourse, delivered at Shrewsbury. 7781

Discourse delivered at Stafford.
25047

A discourse, delivered at the annual meeting of the Hartford
Evangelical Tract Society.
1348

A discourse delivered at the anniversary of the New-York Female Auxiliary Bible Society.
12015

A discourse, delivered at the
Brick Church in Canandaigua.
24399

A discourse, delivered at the
celebration of the nativity of
St. John the Baptist. 4318

Discourse, delivered at the con-
secreation of the synagogue, of
the Hebrew Congregation, Mik-
va Israel. 986

Discourse delivered at the constitution of Rising-Star Lodge.
27608

A discourse, delivered at the
council-house, Detroit. 17209

A discourse, delivered at the
dedication of the American
Asylum. 5419

A discourse, delivered at the dedication of the Brick Church in
Buffalo. 28759

A discourse, delivered at the dedication of the First Universalist Meetinghouse in Westminster. 10494

A discourse delivered at the dedication of the Stone Church of
the First Parish in Portland.
25594

A discourse delivered at the dedication of Westminster Church

in Providence. 38530

A discourse, delivered at the
evening meeting, of the First
Universalist Society, in Portland. 10362

A discourse delivered at the installation of the Rev. Mellish
Irving Motte. 32633; 32634;
38103

A discourse delivered at the opening of St. Mary's Church.
27541

A discourse delivered at the opening of the Christian meetinghouse in Boston. 24129

Discourse delivered at the opening of the general assembly
of the Presbyterian Church.
38464

A discourse delivered at the ordination of the Rev. Calum
Monroe. 15948

A discourse delivered at the ordination of the Rev. Frederick
A. Farley. 32631; 32632

A discourse delivered at the ordination of the Rev. William
O. Grant. 15734

A discourse delivered at the organization of the Trinitarian
Congregational Church. 5662

A discourse delivered at the Universalist Church, in Lombard
Street. 32078

A discourse delivered at the Universalist Church, in the city
of Hudson. 6479; 9926-9928;
21894; 27752

A discourse delivered at the Universalist Meeting House, in
Charlestown. 14322

Discourse delivered at the Universalist Meeting-House, in
Barre, Vt. 25658

A discourse, delivered at Trinity Church, Cornish. 21192

A discourse delivered at Uxbridge, Mass. 9040

A discourse, delivered at Waits-
field. 24049

A discourse delivered at Westhampton. 40686

A discourse delivered at Worcester. 20687

A discourse, delivered before Constellation Lodge. 38353

A discourse delivered before the African Society. 8951

A discourse delivered before the Amelia Washington Lodge. 28589

A discourse delivered before the Associated Lodges. 12900

A discourse delivered before the Bible Society. 2619

A discourse, delivered before the Charitable Society of Plymouth. 10460

A discourse delivered before the Convention of Congregational ministers. 212

A discourse delivered before the Female Samaritan Society. 5161

A discourse, delivered before the First Universalist Society in Warner. 7967

A discourse delivered before the General assembly of the Presbyterian Church. 3006

A discourse delivered before the Hillsborough Agricultural Society. 8584

A discourse delivered before the Historical Society of the state of Pennsylvania. 31588

A discourse, delivered before the Honourable Legislature of Vermont. 9276

A discourse, delivered before the Legislature of Vermont [Fisk] 24540; 28886

A discourse, delivered before the Legislature of Vermont [Woodman] 37229

A discourse delivered before the Masonic fraternity, assembled at Brownville. 10246

A discourse delivered before the Masonic Society, at Chapel-Hill. 29252

A discourse delivered before the New England Society. 14882

A discourse delivered before the New York Protestant Episcopal Missionary Society. 24372

A discourse delivered before the Second Congregational Society in Marblehead. 37717

A discourse delivered before the Second Congregational Society in Worcester. 27956

A discourse delivered before the Society for Propagating the Gospel Among the Indians and others. 12775

A discourse delivered before the Society for the Commemoration of the Landing of William Penn. 21018

A discourse delivered before the Society for the Promotion of Christian Education. 19855

A discourse delivered before the trustees, faculty, and students of Rutgers College. 40386

A discourse, delivered before the Universalist Society, in Portland. 1692

A discourse, delivered before the Western Conference of Lutheran Ministers. 33867

A discourse, delivered before the Worcester Auxiliary Society. 15172

A discourse delivered by appointment of the general synod of the Reformed Dutch Church. 17157

A discourse delivered Dec. 3, 1824. 17740

A discourse delivered February 26, 1828. 37221

A discourse delivered in Bedford. 33228

A discourse, delivered in Belfast. 5414

A discourse, delivered in Boston. 23714

A discourse delivered in Bristol. 5928

A discourse delivered in Charleston [S. C.] before the Reformed Society of Israelites. 28385

A discourse, delivered in Charleston [S. C.] on the 21st of Nov. 1825. 20807

A discourse, delivered in Danvers. 3356

A discourse delivered in Farmington. 12399

A discourse delivered in Haverhill. 11761

A discourse delivered in Hollis
Street Church. 30266

A discourse, delivered in Ipswich. 28654

A discourse, delivered in Princeton. 12769

A discourse delivered in Quincy.
27639

A discourse delivered in St.
Paul's Church. 4300

A discourse delivered in Saxton's
Village. 15853

Discourse delivered in Stephen-
town. 367; 37757

A discourse, delivered in the Baptist church at Paris, Kentucky. 38729

Discourse delivered in the Baptist Church, Georgetown,
S.C. 8249

A discourse, delivered in the
Baptist meeting house at Deerfield. 23707

A discourse delivered in the Central Universalist Church.
37171

Discourse delivered in the chapel
of Nassau-hall. 21457

A discourse, delivered in the Circular Church, Charleston.
25084

A discourse delivered in the city
of Edinburgh. 33196

A discourse delivered in the city
of Mobile. 41431

A discourse, delivered in the
East parish in Bradford. 6438

A discourse, delivered in the
First Presbyterian Church, in
Rochester. 25682

A discourse delivered in the
meeting-house of the First
Parish in Malden, Mass.
32747

A discourse, delivered in the
Middle Dutch Church in Cedar-
Street. 20308

A discourse, delivered in the
North Church, in Salem.
37932

A discourse, delivered in the
Presbyterian Church, at
Ballston, N.Y. 38963

A discourse, delivered in the
Presbyterian Church in
Cedar-Street. 22146

A discourse, delivered in the
Presbyterian Church in Frederick. 21140

A discourse, delivered in the
Representative's chamber.
in Concord. 365

A discourse delivered in the Second Baptist meeting-house in
Boston. 15157

A discourse delivered in the Second Presbyterian Church, Cincinnati. 35069

A discourse delivered in the
Stone Church, Summer-street.
13025

A discourse delivered in the Universalist Chapel, Portland.
26148

A discourse, delivered in the
Universalist meeting-house, in
Charlestown. 7019

A discourse delivered in the
West Church in Boston. 2024

A discourse delivered in Trinity
Church, New-York. 22206

A discourse delivered in Wells-
burgh. 1032

A discourse delivered Jan. 18,
1794. 10314

A discourse, delivered June 4,
1823. 13904

A discourse delivered June 10,
1827. 30625

A discourse, delivered November
3, 1819. 1256

A discourse, delivered November
24, 1819. 2720

A discourse delivered October 13,
1813. 24427

A discourse delivered on the 4th
of July, 1828. 35065

A discourse, delivered on the
fourth of July, 1825. 20773

A discourse delivered on the 4th
of July, 1824. 17676

A discourse delivered on the oc-

casion of the annual Thanksgiving in Massachusetts. 39322

A discourse delivered on the
Sabbath after the decease of
the Hon. Timothy Pickering.
41348

A discourse delivered on the
17th of March, 1828. 33850

A discourse, delivered on the
twenty-fourth of October, 1826.
27625

A discourse, delivered to the
First Society in Mendon.
28722; 33001

A discourse, delivered upon the
occasion of the death of David
Acheson. 24983

A discourse designed as an exposition and refutation of the
reasons assigned in a pamphlet. 8614

A discourse exposing Robert
Owen's system. 25178

A discourse; Human standards in-
jurious to personal religion.
39055

Discourse in commemoration of
the lives and services of John
Adams and Thomas Jefferson.
27583

A discourse in the North Meeting-House in Bridgewater.
5663

A discourse, in which the doctrine of the Trinity is examined. 16159

A discourse...landing of William
Penn. 4253

A discourse occasioned by the
death of Col. James Morrison.
12860

A discourse, occasioned by the
death of Edward P. Simons.
12811

A discourse occasioned by the
death of Miss Harriet Bennet.
29265

A discourse, occasioned by the
death of Mr. Caleb Hathaway.
11623

Discourse occasioned by the
death of Mr. Frederick Lock-
wood. 19202

A discourse occasioned by the
death of Rev'd James M'Chord.
4737

A discourse occasioned by the
death of the Hon. Samuel
Tobey. 15110

A discourse of a serious, moral,
and historical nature. 13888

Discourse of church government.
17678

Discourse of his Eminence Car-
dinal Chiaramonti. 9948

A discourse of the genius and
character of the Rev. Horace
Holley. 32548

A discourse on a new system of
society. 21761; 21762

A discourse on being born again.
28049

A discourse on Christian duty.
21082

A discourse on Christian liberty.
20278

A discourse on denying the Lord
Jesus. 31739; 31740; 31741;
31742

A discourse on divinity. 29215

A discourse on education. 29420

A discourse on gospel discipline.
6688

A discourse on human depravity.
22250

A discourse on intemperance.
33010

A discourse on medical education. 8375

A discourse on ministerial fidelity. 29209; 29210

A discourse on opening the new
building in the House of Refuge. 26127

A discourse on pastoral duty.
8397

A discourse on popular education.
25312

A discourse on predestination.
5610

A discourse on regeneration.
37166; 37167; 37168; 37169

Discourse on religion and doctrines. 41569

A discourse on religious innova-
tions. 16814

Discourse on Romans IX.
5187

A discourse on some general outlines of law. 2764

A discourse on some points of
difference between the sheriff's
office. 40577

Discourse on sovereignty of God.
37702

A discourse on the beneficial re-
sults consequent on the progress of liberal opinions. 29199

A discourse on the character and
public services of DeWitt Clinton. 40243

A discourse on the character and
scientific attainments of DeWitt
Clinton. 34170

A discourse on the character and
services of Thomas Jefferson.
25406

A discourse on the character and
work, and the death and resurrection of the two witnesses.
18243

A discourse on the character
proper to a Christian society.
12209

A discourse on the death of the
Honourable Thomas Jefferson
and John Adams. 26128

A discourse on the doctrine of
the Trinity. 29730

Discourse on the duties of church
members. 40439

A discourse on the duty of Christians. 35369

A discourse on the early history
of Pennsylvania. 5213

A discourse on the evidences of
revealed religion. 4942; 24051;
24052; 27734

A discourse on the future blessedness of the sons of God.
16978

A discourse on the genius &
character of the Rev. H. Holley. 19923

A discourse on the good and evil
principles of human nature.
28672

A discourse, on the importance
of character and education.
12729

A discourse on the importance of
classical learning. 38725

A discourse, on the intemperate
use of spirituous liquor.
30402

A discourse on the life and character of DeWitt Clinton. 33793

A discourse on the life and character of Samuel Bard. 6086

A discourse on the life and character of Thomas Addis Emmit.
34171

A discourse on the limited influence of the Gospel. 41508

A discourse on the lives and
characters of Thomas Jefferson and John Adams. 27682

A discourse on the nativity of
Christ. 19173

A discourse, on the nature of the
instrumentality which God exercises. 28524

A discourse on the object and
utility of the Rhode Island
Medical Society. 14191

A discourse on the occasion of
forming the African Mission
School Society. 37057

A discourse on the official relations of New Testament elders.
24376

A discourse on the paramount
importance of spiritual things.
32989

A discourse on the present state
and duty of the church. 15479

A discourse on the principles of
action in religious bodies.
24130

Discourse on the progress of
medical science. 5939

A discourse on the proper character of religious institutions.
20130

A discourse on the proper subjects of Christian baptism.
37502

A discourse on the proper test of
the Christian character. 15820

A discourse on the prospects of
letters and taste in Virginia.
33483

A discourse on the reciprocal duties of a minister and his people. 34198

A discourse on the religion of the Indian tribes. 1782

A discourse on the settlement and progress of New England. 6513

A discourse on the shortness and calamities of human life. 13246

A discourse on the sins of the tongue. 41616; 41617

A discourse on the sovereignty of God. 37703

A discourse on the state and prospects of American literature. 6087

A discourse on the subject of intemperance. 38714

A discourse on the urim and thummim. 3303

A discourse on the value and importance of a learned & efficient ministry. 39656

A discourse on the western autumnal disease. 27510

A discourse or lecture on the subject of civilizing the Indians. 24294

A discourse preached at Plympton. 6363

A discourse, preached at the dedication of the Bethlemen Church. 29447

A discourse preached at the dedication of the First Congregational Unitarian Church. 33314

A discourse, preached at the dedication of the Second Congregational Unitarian Church. 24050; 28431; 28432

Discourse preached at the opening of the Synod of the Evangelical Lutheran Church. 38945

A discourse, preached before the Society for Propagating the Gospel. 7014

A discourse, preached in Plymouth. 12996

A discourse preached in the Center Church, in New Haven. 32060

A discourse, preached in the First Congregational Unitarian Church. 38716

A discourse preached in Winthrop. 6974; 14287

A discourse pronounced at the request of the Essex Historical Society. 35420

A discourse, pronounced before His Excellency John Brooks. 14277

A discourse, pronounced before His Excellency William Eustis. 17949; 17950

A discourse pronounced before the Phi Beta Kappa Society, at Brunswick. 31660

A discourse pronounced before the Phi Beta Kappa Society, at the anniversary celebration. 26146

A discourse pronounced upon the inauguration of the author, as Dane professor. 40553

A discourse read before the Essex Agricultural Society. 2770

A discourse the substance of which was delivered at the annual general meeting of the Baptist Missionary Society. 8723

A discourse, the substance of which was delivered in Woodbridge. 8205

Discourse to the students of Phillips Exeter Academy. 20885

A discourse upon the duration of future punishments. 14010

A discourse upon the essential doctrines of the Gospel. 7717

Discourses and dissertations on the scriptural doctrines. 21296

Discourses delivered at the Royal Academy. 6628

Discourses, delivered in the College of New Jersey. 8881

Discourses, delivered to the members of Blandford Lodge. 26029

Discourses in various subjects. 38188

chemistry. 38266

A dissertation, read before the Massachusetts Medical Society. 29760

Dissertation second. 2796

Dissertations on cynanche trachealis. 14249

Dissertations on the importance and best method of studying the original languages of the Bible. 6911

Dissertations on the questions which arise from the contrariety of the positive laws. 33885

Dissertations on the regenerate life. 12380

Dissertations on the unity of God. 32705

Dissertations upon several fundamental articles of Christian theology. 23560

A dissuasive from controversy respecting the mode of baptism. 32252

The distinctive character and claims of Christianity. 18250

Distress me with these tears no more. 3217

Distressing calamity. 5188

The distrest mother. 10059

The distribution of the Bible. 23544

Distribution of the laws. 36257

District of Columbia. Memorial. 36258

District tonnage of the United States. 26954; 36259; 41107

Diversions of Hollycot. 39155

A divertimento di ballo. 12805

Divertimento, for the piano forte. 17854; 21393

The diverting amusement of the house that Jack built. 5189

The diverting history of John Bull. 30155

Dividing line--Florida and Georgia. 36260

Dividing line--Georgia and Florida. 36261; 41108

Divine & moral songs for children. 31678

The divine authority of the Chris-

tian revelation acknowledged. 38396

Divine breathings. 3203

Divine communications. 9793

Divine favors that call for gratitude. 25315

Divine love, the source of all Christian virtue. 34963

Divine providence and human agency. 24644

The divine purpose; displayed. 21373; 29700; 34086

Divine revelation. 38397

Divine songs. 4193; 4196; 11358; 11359; 14845; 19206; 23232; 27572; 31679

Divine soverignty displayed. 2185

The divine unity the doctrine of the Bible. 32460

The divinity of Christ [Johnson] 9153

The divinity of Christ [Kean] 5742; 5743

Do I do I don't do nothing. 20317

Do I grow in grace? 20321

Docks for repairing ships of war. 26955

Doctor Bolus. 32996

Doctor Eliakim Crosby. 36262

Dr. Fullerton having returned to Princeton. 28984

Dr. Griffin's letter. 38840

Dr. J. W.'s last legacy. 31757

Doctor Johann Habermanns Christliches Gebät-Büchlein. 5512; 38876

Dr. John Williams' last legacy. 27661; 27662; 27663; 31758; 41539

Dr. L. has the honour to inform the physicians. 39310

Doctor Lee's patent New-London bilious pills. 1928

Dr. M'Nairy's circular. 33960

Dr. Marryat's therapeutics. 34018

Dr. Martin Luther's Kleiner Katechismus. 39340

Dr. Moore. 14150

Dr. Moore's Essence of life. 27643

Dr. Nichols' Paraphrase on the Daily Morning and Evening Prayer. 6296

Dr. Samuel K. Jenning's protests and argument. 29361

Dr. Thomas Anderson Treasurer. 16901

Dr. Watts, an anti-trinitarian. 7679

Dr. Watts' Catechism. 19207

Dr. Watts' Divine & Moral songs. 4192

Dr. Watts' divine songs. 4194; 4195; 4197; 4198; 14846; 31680

Dr. Watts' Historical catechism. 4200

Dr. Watts' plain and easy catechism for children. 14851; 31681

Dr. Watt's preface to the Psalms. 22052; 25915

Dr. Wilson, from the Committee. 17585

The doctrinal articles, the covenant, and articles of order and discipline adopted by the church. 25874

A doctrinal catechism. 33422

A doctrinal circular address. 24477

A doctrinal epistle. 16529

The doctrine of baptism. 28684; 28685

Doctrine of Christian baptism. 4545; 5505

The doctrine of Christian perfection. 5190; 8555; 25165

The doctrine of constructive larceny. 21536

The doctrine of election illustrated. 10064; 26124; 35378

The doctrine of incest stated. 25170; 29561

The doctrine of life for the New Jerusalem. 6926

Doctrine of possibility of apostacy, proved. 40154

The doctrine of pronouns applied to Christ's testimony of himself. 31810

The doctrine of religious experience. 37709

The doctrine of salvation by faith proved. 4997; 32722

The doctrine of St. Paul. 13772

The doctrine of the atonement explained. 20928

The doctrine of the immediate happiness. 12883

The doctrine of the New Jerusalem. 3372; 6927; 35447; 40585; 40586

The doctrine of the sacraments. 37713

The doctrine of the saints' perseverance. 3505

The doctrine of the Scriptures respecting regeneration. 39849

The doctrine of the Trinity proved. 8883

The doctrine of the Trinity, stated, and defended. 9062

The doctrine of the universal agency of Good. 31699

The doctrine of universal salvation. 24232

The doctrines and discipline of the African Methodist Episcopal Church. 43

The doctrines and discipline of the Methodist Episcopal Church. 2249; 6030; 17132; 21433; 25321; 39570

Doctrines and duties of the Christian religion. 27845

Doctrines of faith and form of covenant. 14305

The doctrines of Friends. 19625; 19626; 37722

The doctrines of the church. A sermon. 2315

The doctrines of the church vindicated. 25902

Document accompanying the message of [the governor] 37305; 39450; 39451; 39452; 39453; 39454; 39455; 39456; 39457; 39458; 39459; 39460; 39461

Document relating to bill number fifty-eight. 36263

Document submitted by Mr. Holmes. 10811

Document to accompany the joint resolution authorizing the delivery of rifles. 26956

Dreadful riot on Negro Hill!
28732
The dreams of Pindus. 38191
Drey Predigten des Sel. Dr. Martin Luthers. 13164
Drey wunderbare neue Geschichten oder Lieder. 33012
Drink to me only with thine eyes.
8570
Drops of brandy. 12400
The drowsiad. 38421
The druggists manual. 25739
The drum. A favorite song.
19987
The Drummer's assistant 2021;
13157
The drunkard's looking glass.
31700
The drunkard's progress. 20339;
23696
The drunken sailor. 21391
Drunkenness excludes from heaven.
29564
Dry docks. January 25, 1828.
36267; 36268
Dry docks - Portsmouth, N.H.
31237; 31238
The Dublin mail. 8573
The duel, or, My two nephews.
13686
Duelling, under any circumstances,
The extreme of folly. 11969
Duelling incompatible with true
honor. 1798
The duenna, an opera. 10255
A duett for two performers. 1907;
1909
Duff Green, Esq. - mail contract.
31239
Dufief's Nature displayed. 20343
Duke Christian of Luneburg.
17674
The Duke of York's march. 5210
Dulce domum.   577; 8172
Dunallan; or, Know what you
judge. 29404; 33756; 33757;
33758
Duncan Gray. A Scotch air.
12405
Duncan McArthur. 36269
Duncan's reel. 15470
The duplicate letters, the fisheries and the Mississippi. 7740;

11530; 11531
Duplicity exposed. 12409
Durang's hornpipe. 12410
Durazzo; a tragedy.   12796;
24822
Dussek's favorite sonata.
5215; 12412
Dutchess County almanac. 1061;
5218; 35431
The Dutchess County farmer's
almanac. 1062; 5219; 5220;
8579; 12415; 16021; 20352a;
20353; 24381; 24382; 28745;
28746
Duties and responsibility of the
Christian ministry. 40467
Duties and responsibilities of the
professional office in theological seminaries. 35452
The duties of an American citizen.   23237; 23238
The duties of children.   4943;
4944; 8309
Duties of congregations to their
pastors. 27666
The duties of parents. 15173
Duties of the rich. 31805
The duties of the watchman upon
the walls of Zion. 10045
Duties on importations--regulations. 41109
Duties on imported teas. 36270
Duties on imports. 31240; 36271
Duties on merchandise, tonnage.
36272
Duties on teas.   36273
Duties on the inland frontier.
31241
Duties on woollen goods. 31242;
36274
Duties on woollens. 964; 28667
Duties received, outstanding bonds,
&c. 41110
The duties, trials and rewards of
the gospel ministry. 17598
The duty and benefit of a daily
perusal of the Holy Scriptures.
29844; 34223
Duty and privilege of Christians
to devote their all to spreading
the gospel. 28371; 32561
The duty and reward of honouring
God. 10134

The duty and the interest of contributing liberally to the promotion of religious and benevolent institutions. 12288

Duty of a Christian minister explained. 3292

The duty of caring for the souls of relatives. 2979

The duty of Christian freemen to elect Christian rulers. 33064

The duty of Christians to pray for ministers. 9220

The duty of Christians to pray for the missionary cause. 30303

The duty of Christians to the Jews. 12898

The duty of Christians toward the heathen. 11288

The duty of distinction in preaching. 20544

Duty of fasting and prayer. 12153

The duty of fulfilling all righteousness. 8162

Duty of honoring parents. 38456

The duty of honouring God with our substance. 1093

The duty of living for the good of posterity. 4950

The duty of observing the Sabbath. 5826

The duty of praising God for national blessings. 5127

The duty of praying for all that are in authority. 20335

The duty of public usefulness. 13117

The duty of religious toleration. 9737

The duty of spreading the gospel. 78

The duty of supporting the Christian ministry. 27558

The duty of supporting the gospel ministry. 11796

The duty of the clergy, with respect to inculcating the doctrine of the Trinity. 39001

The duty of the people of God to excite others. 32236

Duty on imported salt. 31243; 31244

Dyer's New-York selection of sacred music. 33027; 33028

Dyer's Philadelphia selection of sacred music. 33029; 33030; 33031

Dyer's second edition of a selection of upwards of sixty favourite and approved anthems. 8581; 12417

Dyer's selection of the most celebrated and popular chorusses. 38439

The dying address of the three Thayers. 20360

Dying believer committing his soul to Christ. 17833

The dying peasant, and other poems. 24027

The dying thought of the Rev. Richard Baxter. 19634

The dying words of Charrilla Saben. 3084

E

E. Huntington's Complete alphabetical sets. 1711

E Pluribus Unum. British cruelty, oppression, and murder. 16394

Each sorrow repelling. 23244

The Eagle Creek Baptist Association. 28020

Earl Moira's welcome to Scotland. 14051

Early impressions. 33033

Early instruction recommended in the life of Catherine Haldane. 1485; 1486; 1487; 1488

Early lays. 30613

Early lessons. 5228; 12429; 20370; 28761

Early piety; or Memoirs of children. 4871; 8582; 15596; 28749

Early piety recommended in a sermon. 5827

Early piety, recommended in the history of Miss Dinah Doudney. 1459; 12726

An earnest appeal to the friends of reform. 32824

An earnest appeal to the public.

18194

The earthquake. 5421; 5422

East-Haven register. 15987

The East-India Marine Society of Salem. 6699

The East Indian. 21502

East Tennessee almanac. 24392

Eastern lands. 1070

An easy and correct method of cutting men's garments. 12155

An easy entrance into the sacred language. 17873

An easy grammar of geography [Willetts] 4287; 11428; 19284; 27657; 27658; 27659; 27660; 37188

An easy grammar of geography [Phillips] 2758

Easy grammar of natural and experimental philosophy. 6473; 17622; 40060

The easy instructor. 1975; 33870

An easy introduction to the game of chess. 16032

An easy introduction to the study of geography. 14135; 17998; 22292; 35224

An easy introduction to the knowledge of nature. 7007

An easy lesson for the pianoforte or harp. 1522; 5542

Easy lessons for young children. 3253

Easy lessons in geography and history. 19395; 27806; 37421

Easy lessons in geometry. 39010

Easy lessons in reading. 13075; 21178; 21179; 21180; 25074; 29463; 29464; 29465; 39255; 39256

Easy lessons of Scripture history. 18241

Easy method of learning the elements of the French pronunciation. 5225; 20366

An easy method of learning the Roman history 1469

An easy mode of conjugating. 147

The easy reader. 33307

Easy reading lessons for children. 307

Ebeneezer Cooley. 36275

Eberhard Ludwin Gruvers Grund-

forschende Fragen. 8904

Ebor nova. 20628

Écarte. or, The salons of Paris. 40273

Ecce Homo! 29244

Ecce signum! 20368; 20809

Eccentric and concentric solar cycles. 25646

Eccentric biography. 20369

Ecclesiastical affairs. 24516

Ecclesiastical annals and evangelical fragments. 33089

Ecclesiastical government. 3030

An ecclesiastical history, ancient and modern. 6123; 6124; 6125; 6126

An ecclesiastical history, from the commencement of the Christian era. 3085

The ecclesiastical history of Eusebius Pamphilus. 12466

An ecclesiastical memoir of Essex Street Religious Society, Boston. 11941; 14028

Ecclesiastical peace recommended. 27763

Ecclesiastical proceedings in the case of Mr. Donald McCrimmon. 29574

An ecclesiastical register of New-Hampshire. 5292

The echo duet. 578

The eclectic and general dispensatory. 28758

L'economia della vita umana, di Dodsley. 15994

The economical hydrostatic lift. 9198

The economist. 16041

The economy and policy of a Christian education. 12774

The economy of human life. 20328; 28720; 28721

The economy of the eyes. 16815

Economy of the kitchen-garden. 37211

The Eden of hope. 40483

Edge-hill. 33513

Editorial notice. 18061

Edmund and Margaret. 8597

Edmund Brooke. 26962; 26963; 36276; 36277

Edmund's lyre. 24404

Education. 32579; 38058

Education in the city of New York. 8598

Edward Bates against Thomas H. Benton. 32231

Edward Cary. 36278; 41111

Edward Duncombe. 33047

Edward Lee. 26964

Edward Mansfield. 30591

Edward the Sunday scholar. 20973

Edward Wood. 31245

Edwin: a tale. 11510

Edwin and Henry. 16048; 20385

Efectos de las facciones en los gobiernos nacientes. 37018

Effects of drunkenness. 11386

Effects of education. 32392

The effects of intemperance. 30258

The effectual preacher. 14997

An efficacious method of acquiring...knowledge. 16383

An effort to make all things according to the pattern shewed in the Mount. 29028; 29029

Effusions of the Heart. 3162

Egypt. 20386

Egyptian mummy. 16049

Eight sermons addressed to children. 38427

Eighteen sermons [Freeman] 38633

Eighteen sermons [Gurney] 1473

Eighteen sermons [Whitefield] 4273; 23315

1828. Address to the patrons. 31987

The eighteenth annual report of the board of trustees of the New York Protestant Episcopal Tract Society. 34923

Eighteenth concert of the Musical Fund Society of Philadelphia. 39686

Eighth and ninth letters to the Rev. Samuel Miller. 10315

Eighth anniversary of the American Bible Society. 15075

Eighth annual meeting of the Baptist Education Society of the State of New York. 19515

The eighth annual report for the year 1824, of the managers of the Indigent Widows' and Single Women's Society. 21015

The eighth annual report of the American Society for Colonizing the Free People of Colour. 19405

The eighth annual report, of the Asbury Sunday School Society. 19463

The eighth annual report of the Association for the Relief of Respectable Aged Indigent Females. 4504

The eighth annual report of the board of directors [Massachusetts Domestic Missionary Society] 25275

The eighth annual report of the board of managers of the Charleston Protestant Episcopal Sunday School Society. 28444

The eighth annual report of the board of managers of the general convention of the Baptist denomination. 7946

Eighth annual report of the board of managers of the Kentucky Bible Society. 16792

The eighth annual report of the Board of Managers of the New York Protestant Episcopal Missionary Society. 17418

Eighth annual report of the Committee of finance. 529

Eighth annual report of the controllers of the public schools. 25691

Eighth annual report of the directors of the American Education Society. 11598

Eighth annual report of the directors of the Boston Society for the Religious and Moral Instruction of the Poor. 15524

Eighth annual report of the directors of the New York Institution for the Instruction of the Deaf and Dumb. 30046

The eighth annual report of the Female Missionary Society of the Western District, N.Y. 16128

The eighth annual report of the Long Island Bible Society. 13134

The eighth annual report of the New York Religious Tract Society. 2538

The eighth annual report of the Ohio Bible Society. 2594

Eighth annual report of the Philadelphia Orphan Society. 13750

Eighth annual report of the Presbyterian Education Society. 25828

Eighth annual report of the president and directors of the Board of Public Works. 19151

Eighth annual report of the trustees of the New Hampshire Baptist Domestic Mission Society. 28005

Eighth annual report of the Vermont Bible Society. 4093

Eighth annual report of the Washington Orphan Asylum Society. 19200

Eighth concert. 21580

The eighth of January. 40457

Eighth general report of the president and directors of the Chesapeake and Delaware Canal Co. 28450

Eighth report of the American Bible Society. 15076; 15077

Eighth report of the directors of the Western Education Society. 27614

Eighth report of the Female Bible Society of Philadelphia. 8693

The eighth report of the Massachusetts Peace Society. 17072

The eighth report of the New York Female Union Society. 17409

The eighth report of the United Foreign Missionary Society. 22545

Eighth report of the Vermont Colonization Society. 31605

The eighth report of the Young Men's Bible Society. 37283

The eighth set, of new cotillions. 1084

Eighth supplement to Volume II... catalogue of books, belonging to the Library Company of Philadelphia. 40050

Ein Rede, in der Form einer Predigt, über die Lehre von dem Daseyn eines Gottes. 12550

Eine beschreibung von dem leben und medicinischen erfindungen von Samuel Thomson. 35509

Eine Predigt, Gehalten den 5th Februar, 1820. 1125

Eine Predigt, gehalten vor den General-Synode der Deutschen Reformarten Kirche. 1558

Eine Predigt über Apost. Geschichte Cap. 26. 1050

Eine Predigt von L. S. Everett. 33104

Eine Sammlung auserlesenen Geschichten, zum Gebrauch der Jugend. 29196

Eine Sammlung auserlesener Rezepte heilsamer Mittel bey Krankheiten der Menschen und des Viehes zu gebrauchen. 24243

Eine Sammlung von neuen Recepten und bewahrten Curen. 27940

Eines Christen reise nach der seligon ewigkeit. 32516

Einige Erklärungen der Methodistischen Lehrsäze. 8607

Eintritts Rede gehalten in Gegenwort der Verwalter uber die deutsche Reformirke Theologische Schulanstalt. 21375

The ejectment law of Maryland. 9316f

Elbert Anderson. 26965

The elder's death-bed. 5239

Eleanor Simpson. 36279

Electing love. 3068

Election day. 28771

Election laws of the state of Maryland. 2119

Election in Michigan. 26966

The election No. 1. 8608

The election of president in the House of Representatives. 16174; 20389

The election of President of the United States, considered. 12631

An election sermon. 12319; 32883;

Election to life eternal. 4532; 11667

Electors of Essex South District.
16050
Electors of Knox. 12020
Electro-magnatism. 29064
Elegant extracts. 21141; 25052;
25053; 25054
Elegant lessons. 4276; 19269
Les elegante quadrilles. 20390
Elegiac stanzas. 9932
An elegy. On his family vault.
15989
Elegy on the death of Commo-
dore Stephen Decatur. 4378
Élemens de la grammaire fran-
çaise. 5821
Elementa Linguae Graeca. 1765
Elementary analysis of some
principal phenomena of oral
language. 15263
Elementary catechism on the con-
stitution. 35385
An elementary compendium of
physiology. 16982
An elementary course of Bible
theology. 26144
An elementary course of civil
engineering. 30576; 35156
Elementary discourses. 8214;
28324
Elementary exercises for the deaf
and dumb. 4429
Elementary exercises in geography. 1472; 20772; 29098;
33447
Elementary practices for singing.
9911
The elementary reader. 19270
The elementary spelling book.
41460; 41461; 41462; 41463;
41464
An elementary system of physiology. 19796
Elementary treatise on algebra.
17875; 25995
An elementary treatise on arithmetic [Lacroix] 5784; 21143
An elementary treatise on arithmetic [Ryan] 30503
An elementary treatise on astronomy [Farrar] 28856
An elementary treatise on astronomy [Gummere] 8907
An elementary treatise on conic

sections. 16022
Elementary treatise on estates.
2863; 34879
An elementary treatise on logic.
14328
An elementary treatise on mechanics. 20489
An elementary treatise on mineralogy and geology. 8364
An elementary treatise on plane
and spherical trigonometry.
1893; 27744
An elementary treatise on plane
trigonometry. 22311; 40471
An elementary treatise on the application of trigonometry to
orthographic and stereograph-
ic projection. 8684; 20490;
33150
Elementos de la lengua castellana. 4084; 19127; 31593
Elementos de quimica. 24310
Elements de la grammaire française. 25107
Elements of agricultural chemistry. 5158
Elements of algebra. 21144
Elements of analytic trigonometry. 24812
The elements of arithmetic. 13677
Elements of arithmetic, theoretical and practical. 16479;
24813; 33497; 38932
Elements of arithmetic, translated from the French of M.
Bezout. 15337
Elements of arithmetick, by ques-
tion and answer. 17837; 17838;
30472
The elements of astronomy [Tree-
by] 14314; 26237
Elements of astronomy [Wilbur]
41518
Elements of astronomy [Wilkins]
11424; 14922; 23327; 27648;
37181; 41521
Elements of botany. 28068
The elements of chemical science. 1417
Elements of chemistry [Fyfe]
28986
Elements of chemistry [Turner]
35570; 40695

38095
Elements of natural philosophy. 28881
The elements of numbers. 6355; 13648; 39942
Elements of operative surgery. 40608
Elements of ornamental literature. 24672
Elements of orthography. 4448
Elements of penmanship. 4638; 19636
Elements of phrenology. [Caldwell] 15625; 28359
Elements of phrenology [Combe] 24177
Elements of physics. 37506
Elements of physiology. 6641; 13949; 22090; 22091
The elements of pleas in equity. 15289
The elements of political economy. 13906
Elements of surgery. 12393
Elements of technology. 37847
Elements of the Chaldee language. 12778
Elements of the English language. 799
Elements of the etiology and philosophy of epidemics. 18010
Elements of the French language. 20392
Elements of the game of chess. 29494
Elements of the geometry of planes and solids. 33498
Elements of the grammar of the English language. 8609
Elements of the philosophy of the human mind. 6894; 6895; 10351; 10352; 30711
Elements of the theory and practice of physic. 38835
Elements of therapeutics and materia medica. 4954; 12098; 22092; 28435
Eleonora, or, The young Christian. 10038
The eleven sermons which were preached by the Rev. Hosea Ballou. 7873
Eleventh anniversary of the

American Bible Society. 27821
Eleventh annual exhibition of the Pennsylvania Academy of the Fine Arts. 9863
Eleventh annual meeting of the Baptist Education Society. 32103
Eleventh annual report [Philadelphia Orphan Society] 25748
The eleventh annual report, for the year 1827 of the managers of the Indigent Widows' and Single Women's Society. 33658
The eleventh annual report of the American Society for Colonizing the Free People of Colour. 31954
Eleventh annual report of the American Tract Society. 19420
Eleventh annual report of the Bible Society of Virginia. 15397
Eleventh annual report of the Board of Directors of the Princeton Theological Seminary. 13853
Eleventh annual report of the Board of Directors of the Washington County Bible Society. 14835
The eleventh annual report of the board of managers of the New-York Protestant Episcopal Missionary Society. 30051
The eleventh annual report of the Board of managers of the New York Protestant Episcopal Sunday School Society. 34547
Eleventh annual report of the controllers of the public schools. 39993
Eleventh annual report of the directors of the American Education Society. 27829
Eleventh annual report of the directors of the Boston Society for the Religious and Moral Instruction of the Poor. 28249
The eleventh annual report of the Female Missionary Society of the Western District, N. Y. 28861

The eleventh annual report of the
Long Island Bible Society.
25134

Eleventh annual report of the
managers of the Marine Bible
Society of New-York. 29624

Eleventh annual report of the
New York Female Auxiliary
Bible Society. 30042

The eleventh annual report of the
New York Female Union So-
ciety. 30043

Eleventh annual report of the New
York Religious Tract Society.
13574

The eleventh annual report of the
New York Sunday School Union
Society. 30056

Eleventh annual report of the receipts and expenditures of the
City of Boston. 11922

Eleventh annual report on the state
of the Asylum. 34758

The eleventh hour. 28531

Eleventh report of the American
Bible Society. 27822

Eleventh report of the Connecticut Reserve Bible Society.
20175

Eleventh report of the directors
of the American Asylum at
Hartford. 27837

The eleventh report of the Female Bible Society of Philadelphia. 20503

Eleventh report of the New Hampshire Bible Society. 9637

Eleventh report of the New Jersey
Bible Society. 9656

Eleventh report of the Rutland
and Stamford Auxiliary Bible
Society. 14025

The eleventh, twelfth and thirteenth annual reports of the
Board of Public Works. 41384

Eli and his children. 20437

Elia. Essays. 33813; 33814

Elijah Carr. 36280

Elijah L. Clarke. 31246

Eliphalet Loud. 26967

Elixir institutorum, vel consider-
ationes tempestivae, morales
et religiosae. 12378

The elixir of moonshine. 8359

Eliza. 12269

Elizabeth C., or, Early piety.
35517

Elizabeth de Bruce. 29374

Elizabeth Keazy. 26968

Elizabeth Kramer. 26969

Elizabeth Lewis. 26970

Elizabeth Mays. 36281; 41112

Elizabeth Morgan. 26971

Elizabeth, or The exiles of Si-
beria. 879; 8453; 12274;
28607; 28608; 32841

Elizabeth Shaw. 31247; 36282

Ella Rosenberg; a melo-drama.
13000

Ellen; a pleasing instance of
early piety. 12437

Ellen a tale - in three parts.
5941

Ellen Aureen. 6091; 13370;
17191; 17192

Ellen Dix. 41113

Ellen: or, The disinterested girl.
20395; 28773

Ellen's love. 6519

Elliner, and other poems. 26205

Elliot's annual calendar. 28777;
33057; 33056

Elliot's sheet almanac 1829.
33058

Elliot's soliloquy. 16150

Elliot's Washington pocket almanac. 5241; 12438; 16051;
20397; 24413; 28778; 38458

Elliot's Washington sheet almanac. 1088; 12439

Elnathan, a narrative. 24418;
28781

The elocutionist. 37694

Eloquence of the United States.
31773; 41556

Elspeth Sutherland; or, The effects of faith. 33061

Elvington Roberts. 36283

Ely's Pocket companion. 8617

Emblems and fables. 4351

The Emerald isle. 5248; 12443

Emerson's first part. 38467

Emigrant, or, History of Mr.
and Mrs. L. 12451

Emigrating Indians. 36284;
36285

The English in France. 40071

English joint stock companies. 24006

English life; or Manners at home. 20416

The English orthographical expositor. 1784; 12945; 21051; 33700

The English physician. 24252

The English practice. 10220

The English reader. 2362; 2363; 2364; 2365; 2366; 2367; 2368; 2369; 2370; 2371; 2372; 2373; 6155; 6156; 6157; 6158; 6159; 6160; 6161; 6162; 6163; 6164; 6165; 9581; 9582; 9583; 9584; 9585; 9586; 13441; 13442; 13443; 13444; 13445; 13446; 13447; 13448; 13449; 13450; 13451; 13452; 13453; 13454; 17265; 17266; 17267; 17268; 17269; 17270; 17271; 17272; 17273; 17274; 21554; 21555; 21556; 21557; 21558; 21559; 21560; 21561; 21562; 21563; 21564; 21565; 21565; 21567; 21568; 21570; 21571; 21572; 25446; 25449; 25451; 25452; 25453; 25456; 25457; 25458; 25459; 25460; 25461; 25462; 25463; 25464; 25465; 25466; 25467; 29852; 29853; 29854; 29855; 29856; 29857; 29858; 29859; 29860; 29861; 29862; 29863; 39665; 39666; 39667; 39668; 39670; 39671; 39673; 39674; 39675; 39676; 34231; 34232; 34233; 34234; 34235; 34236; 34237; 34238; 34240; 34241; 34242; 34243

The English spelling-book; containing the rudiments of the English language. 11801; 19665; 23756

An English spelling book; or, An introduction to the art of reading. 9936

An English spelling-book with reading lessons. 6166; 9587; 13455; 39677

English synonymes explained. 24236

The English teacher. 17276

An Englishman's sketch-book. 32401

Englishmen in India. 5259

Engravings and descriptions of a great part of the apparatus used in the chemical course. 24791

Enlargement of the Erie Canal. 28796

Ennion William's highly improved commercial tables. 14924

Ennion William's reply to John Rowlett's "Caution to Banks." 14925

An enquiry concerning the grant of the legislature. 37982

An enquiry into the duties of the female sex. 1395; 20680

An enquiry into the origin and tendency of political institutions. 10166

Ensayo politico. 13973

The entail. 12640; 12641

The entertaining and interesting story of Alibaba. 20417

The entertaining and marvellous repository. 28797

The entertaining history of Jobson & Nell. 1106

Entertaining pieces. 1107

An entire new work, just published. 28660

Epeögraphy; or, Notations of orthoëpy. 39424

Ephraim Sutton. 26975

An epick poem in commemoration of Gen. Andrew Jackson's victory. 28791

The Epicurean, a tale. 29789; 29790; 29791

Episcopacy and confirmation. 12457; 38482

The Episcopal church not Calvinistick. 28620

The Episcopal manual. 11444; 11445; 41558

Epistel und Weissagung von Gottgesandt. 11654

An epistle and testimony from the yearly meeting of Friends. 12625; 33294

An epistle from Indiana Yearly Meeting. 33288a

Epistle from the Marquis de La Fayette. 16845

Epistle from the Ohio Yearly Meeting. 1330

The epistle from the yearly meeting, held in London. 8782; 8783; 12623; 16235; 20608; 20609; 24638; 27740; 28965; 33292; 38693

An epistle from the yearly meeting held in Philadelphia. 5411;

An epistle from the yearly meeting of Friends for New England. 33293

Epistle from the yearly meeting of Friends held in New York. 38699

An epistle from the Yearly Meeting of Friends, held in Philadelphia. 28977; 33303; 38701; 38702

An epistle of love. 25120; 29515

The epistle of Paul. 4671

The epistle of St. Paul. 15342

An epistle of tender caution against stumbling at the faults of others. 17907

Epistle of the Yearly Meeting of Friends of North Carolina. 33296

An epistle to Friends of the New York yearly meeting. 37222

An epistle to Friends of the Quarterly & Monthly Meetings. 28978

Epistle to Friends within the compass of Ohio and Indiana Yearly Meeting. 33304; 33305

An epistle to Friends within the compass of Philadelphia Yearly Meeting. 34209

Epistle to Joseph T. Buckingham. 24144

An epistle to the members of the religious society of Friends, belonging to the Yearly Meeting of Pennsylvania. 28969; 33289

An epistle to the national meeting of Friends, in Dublin. 9937

An epistle to the quarterly & monthly meetings of Friends. 37234

An epistle to the Quarterly, Monthly, and Preparative meeting of Friends, within the compass of Ohio Yearly Meeting. 33298; 33299

Epistles and testimonies issued by the yearly meetings of Friends, in North America. 33295

Epistles received by the yearly meeting of women Friends, held in New York. 20614

Epistles written by George Fox. 33224

An Epithalamium, a duett. 1111

Epitome historiae Graecae. 10285; 35206

Epitome Historiae Sacrae. 5260; 5822; 9266; 21208; 21209; 25108; 39292

An epitome of ancient and modern history. 10491

An epitome of Christian doctrine. 1112; 17222; 33080

Epitome of chymical philosophy. 20255

Epitome of English grammar. 24846

An epitome of general ecclesiastical history. 29627; 39432; 34020

An epitome of geography. 27703; 37238

An epitome of Grecian antiquities. 28520

An epitome of history. 37239

An epitome of infantry and cavalry discipline. 37869

Epitome of Mr. Maffit's discourse. 9327

An epitome of modern geography. 4332

An epitome of polite literature. 8629

An epitome of Sacred history. 1113; 25985; 38483

An epitome of systematic theology. 40454

An epitome of the English language. 13456

An epitome of the improved Pestalozzian system of education. 21283

An epitome of the physiology, general anatomy, and pathology of Bichot. 38960

Epitre au Roi de France, sur le non-payemem[!] de l'indemnité de St-Domingue. 40091

The equality of mankind. 4257

Erastus Granger. 41115; 41116

Erbauliche Aufsätze. 20419

Erbauliche Lieder-Sammlung zum Gottesdienstlichen Gebrauch. 24446

Erbauliches Gebät-buch und Unterhaltungen mit Gott. 8630; 20420

Erie & junction canal directory. 35170

"Erie Canal Transportation Company." 16067

The Erie organ. 39346

Erlaeuterung der frey-maurerey. 34195

Erläuterungs-Spiegel. 29205

Ermina. 30592

Die ernste Christenpflicht. 24438

The errand-boy. 6786

Errata of the Protestant Bible. 19183

Errata; or, The works of Will Adams. 13472

Error refuted. 17807; 30438

Errors in education. 33229; 33230

The errors of Anna Braithwaite. 16069

Errors of youth. 1114

Erskine's Remarks on the internal evidence for the truth. 12459

Erweckung an das Herz der Jugend. 19243

Erzählung von etlichen blutigen Thaten des General Jackson. 33083

Escalala: an American tale. 15288

Eskah, a tragedy. 38321

The Eskdale herd-boy. 35415

L'espérance. 18179; 22447

Espiritu de los estatutos y reglamento de la orden francmasonica. 8292

El espiritu del despotismo, tra-ducido del ingles y dedicado al Simon Bolivar. 7961

Esplicacion practica de la naturaleza de la hernia. 16613

Esposicion de los sentimientos de los funcionarios publicos. 31854

Essai sur l'homme, traduit par Charles Le Brun. 13811

An essay concerning human understanding. 16930; 21241

An essay concerning the Free agency of man. 344

An essay concerning tussis convulsiva. 11352

An essay in a course of lectures on abstracts of title. 13844; 34880

An essay, in three parts. 20099

An essay in which the doctrine of a positive divine efficiency exciting the will of men to sin. 125

An essay, intended to establish a standard for an universal system of stenography. 26183

Essay on a national bankrupt law. 21243

An essay on a uniform orthography for the Indian languages. 2769

An essay on anger. 12523; 38556

An essay on commonwealth, or plain remarks on the cause of the misery. 16070

An essay on commonwealth's Part 1. 8634

An essay on communion. 17128

An essay on diseases of the internal ear. 40346

An essay on duelling. 39129

An essay on education. 12828

An essay on elocution. 16026; 33026; 38438

An essay on English education. 16761

An essay on equity in Pennsylvania. 25067

Essay on expansibility. 33572

An essay on faith. 12458; 24439; 38486

Essay on flax husbandry. 6502

Essay on free trade. 24007;

28396

An essay on fundamentals in religion. 20540

Essay on impost duties. 4955; 28437; 38107

An essay on infant cultivation. 32058

An essay on inland navigation. 38488

Essay on language. 19939

An essay on man. 2815; 2816; 2817; 2818; 2819; 2820; 6506; 6507; 9976; 13812; 13813; 13814; 17664; 17665; 17666; 17667; 17668; 17669; 21932; 21933; 21934; 21935; 30297; 30298; 34840; 34841; 34841a; 40114

An essay on medical jurisprudence. 19231

An essay on morbid sensibility of the stomach and bowels. 29367; 33720

An essay on penal law in Pennsylvania. 28748

An essay on pleading. 28812

Essay on repentance. 1117

An essay on salt. 14770

An essay on secret prayer. 20418

An essay on sheep. 16356

An essay on Suspended animation. 12047; 12204

An essay on terms of communion. 8184

An essay on the art of boring the earth. 24441

An essay on the baptism of John. 193

An essay on the bombyx mori. 26061

An essay on the causes which prevent the progress and usefulness of medical science in the United States. 2599

An essay on the certainty of medicine. 12044; 32544

An essay on the character & writings of Saint Paul. 25418

Essay on the character of man. 20421

An essay on the chemistry of animated matter. 8622

An essay on the church. 29383; 39163

An essay on the composition of a sermon. 12164

An essay on the dangers of interments in cities. 17631

An essay on the devastation of the gums. 9218

An essay on the disease of Yellow Fever. 213; 4540

An essay on the diseases of the jaws. 33801

An essay on the disorders and treatment of the teeth. 9815

An essay on the doctrine of contracts. 1118; 4098; 23159; 27509

An essay on the doctrine of the Trinity. 4172

An essay on the doctrine of the two natures of Christ. 12463; 12464; 16071

An essay on the doctrines of foreknowledge. 33096

Essay on the establishment of a Chancery Jurisdiction in Massachusetts. 4342

An essay on the evils of popular ignorance. 5354; 5355

Essay on the expediency and practicability of improving or creating home markets. 30801; 40650

An essay on the geology of the Hudson River. 50

An essay on the history, causes, and treatment of typhus fever. 39386

An essay on the importance and the best mode of converting grain into spirit. 12465

An essay on the importance of considering the subject of religion. 28900; 33217

The essay on "The influence of a moral life on our judgement in matters of faith." 14923

An essay on the invalidity of Presbyterian ordination. 38267

Essay on the kingdom of Christ. 19794

An essay on the late institution

of the American Society for Colonizing the Free People of Colour. 1119

An essay on the law of bailments. 33733

An essay on the law of contracts. 8338

An essay on the law of mortgages. 16858

An essay on the law of patents. 8698

An essay on the learning of contingent remainders and executory devises. 24512

An essay on the Lord's Supper. 16342; 29075

An essay, on the manufacture of straw bonnets. 22358

An essay on the medicinal properties of the Aralia pinosa. 872

An essay on the natural equality of men. 602

An essay on the nature and discipline of a Christian church. 11490

An essay on the nature and immutability of truth. 19641

An essay on the nature and treatment of that state of disorder generally called dropsy. 4263

An essay, on the new heaven and earth. 5772

An essay on the non-existence of malaria. 39156

Essay on the origin of the federal government. 2031

Essay on the penal law of Pennsylvania. 30857

An essay on the policy of appropriations. 23456

An essay on the powers and faculties of the human mind. 37729

An essay, on the probation of fallen men. 31777

An essay on the question whether there be two electrical fluids or one. 16408

An essay on the remote and proximate causes of phthisis pulmonalis. 20790

An essay on the right of a state to tax a body corporate. 27874

An essay on the sciences of bone setting. 40589

An essay on the Scripture doctrine of atonement. 8215

An essay on the structure, functions, and diseases of the nervous system. 33017

An essay on the study and pronunciation of the Greek and Latin languages. 19267

An essay on the temperature of the interior of the earth. 32838

An essay on the ultimate principles of chemistry. 31585

Essay on the warehousing system. 33084

An essay on toleration. 25632

An essay on venereal diseases. 19982

Essay to do good. 17075

An essay to vindicate the cause of truth. 1904

Essay upon the influence of the imagination on the nervous system. 34862

Essay upon the law of contracts. 9989; 21960

An essay upon the learning of devises. 9990

An essay upon the Sabbath. 39251

The essayist, or Literary cabinet. 24442

Essays and dissertations in Biblical literature. 38489

Essays and letters, by Dr. B. Franklin. 5363; 8726

Essays and letters on the world. 913

Essays and miscellaneous writings of Walter Nichols. 25595

Essays and poems. 20690

Essays, and sketches of life and character. 1120; 3078

Essays and The bee. 1401

Essays at poetry. 32035

Essays by Cowley and Shenstone. 890

Essays by Lords Bacon and Clarendon. 179

Essays chemical, electrical, &

galvanic. 20812

Essays from the manuscripts of Celinda S. Reynolds. 40258

Essays, historical, moral, political and agricultural. 34009; 39426

Essays in a series of letters. 24561

Essays, mathematical and physical. 9358

Essays, moral and entertaining. 760; 761

Essays, moral, economical and political. 32059

Essays of Howard on domestic economy. 2557

The essays of Philanthropos. 21145; 29442

Essays on banking. 794; 38202

Essays on Christian baptism. 38687

Essays on education. 19614

Essays on fevers. 13348

Essays on holiness. 25157

Essays on intemperance. 32217

Essays on men and manners. 3199

Essays on peace & war. 29443; 33808

Essays on penitentiary discipline. 38059

Essays on phrenology. 8405

Essays on political economy. 8269

Essays on Present Crisis. 1137

Essays on slavery. 27511

Essays on some of the first principles of metaphysicks. 15604

Essays on the autumnal and winter epidemics. 38268

Essays on the distinguishing traits of Christian character. 10326; 22355; 40513

Essays on the evidences, doctrines, and practical operation, of Christianity. 38873

Essays on the geology and organic remains of a part of the Atlantic frontier. 39646

Essays on the human mind. 9275

Essays on the means of regeneration. 40618

Essays on the most important subjects in religion. 6734; 10191

Essays on the nature and principles of taste. 73; 4449

Essays on the nature and uses of the various evidences. 19140

Essays on the observance of a Sabbath. 9252

Essays on the philosophy of instruction. 41527

Essays on the present crisis. 28800; 38505

Essays on the public charities. 32581; 32582; 32583; 38060

Essays on various subjects connected with midwifery. 12367

Essays on various subjects of medical science. 16592

Essays on various subjects of taste. 10492

Essays, poems and plays. 20691

Essays tending to prove the ruinous effects of the policy of the United States. 24008

Essays to do good. 2182; 9435; 9436; 13270

Essays upon French spoliations. 1238; 24545

Essays upon popular education. 24031

Essays upon the history, organization and tendency of Free Masonry. 33085

Essays upon the origin, perpetuity, change, and proper observance, of the Sabbath. 39052

The essential doctrines of the gospel. A sermon by J. H. Fairchild. 38525

The essential doctrines of the Gospel: an introductory sermon delivered in the Presbyterian Church in Vandewater-st. 12300

The essentials of English grammar. 40077

The essentials of religion. 28704

Essex Agricultural Society. Account of premiums. 38490

Essex Cattle Show. 5263

Essex Historical Society. 5264

Essex Jackson Meeting. 32930

Esther. 28801

Estimate of appropriations.
26976; 36288; 41117; 41118
Estimate of the comparative ex-
penses of the army. 7212
An estimate of the revenue which
may be derived from the Mor-
ris Canal. 28108
Estimates of appropriations.
31250; 36289
Estractos de los mas celebres
escritores Españoles. 28628
Etchings from the religious world.
33531
The eternal principle of life and
light. 28802
Eternal salvation of his people.
41434
The ethereal physician. 12009
Ethic strains on subjects sublime
and beautiful. 6326
The Ethiopian manifesto. 41620
Etymological dictionary. 5506;
24753
Ka Euanelio A Ioane. 37806
Ka Euanelio A Marako: 37807
Euclid's elements of geometry.
8638
Eugene and Lolotte. 33343
Eugenia, or Early scenes in Cum-
berland. 13220
Eulogies on J. Adams, T. Jeffer-
son, La Fayette. 24445
Eulogium commemorative of
Jason O. B. Lawrence. 16697
An Eulogium, in commemoration
of His Excellency William W.
Bibb. 1622
Eulogium in commemoration of
the Honourable William Tilgh-
man. 28744
Eulogium of Thomas Jefferson and
John Adams. 27649
Eulogium on Adams and Jefferson.
24559
Eulogium, on Col. Wm. A.
Trimble. 8922
An eulogium on De Witt Clinton.
34003
An eulogium on Dr. Samuel Wil-
son. 29826
An eulogium on Nathan Smith.
39230
An eulogium on the late Hon.

Theodore Gaillard. 39246
An eulogium on the late Thos.
Jefferson & Jno. Adams.
24796
Eulogium on the late Wright Post.
35230
Eulogium on the life and charac-
ter of the Rev. Henry Hol-
combe. 17806
Eulogium on Thomas Jefferson.
28183
An eulogium, pronounced by the
Hon. James Strong. 10364
Eulogium to the memory of Dr.
Samuel Wilson. 28677
An eulogium, to the memory of
James Tilton. 13182
Eulogium to the memory of the il-
lustrious patriots. 24069
An eulogium upon the Hon. Wil-
liam Tilghman. 28186
Eulogium upon the Rev. John F.
Grier. 40021
Eulogy before Columbian Lodge.
1793
Eulogy delivered at Belfast.
24986
Eulogy, delivered in the chapel
of Brown University. 6684
A eulogy, delivered in the chapel
of Williams College, Novem-
ber 6, 1823. 32870
A eulogy, delivered in the chapel
of Williams College, on ac-
count of the lamented death of
Harry Ware. 35153
Eulogy of the life and character
of John H. Livingston. 23146
An eulogy on Alexander Metcalf
Fisher. 9211
Eulogy on Gen. Chs. Cotesworth
Pinckney. 20629
Eulogy on John Adams and Thom-
as Jefferson, delivered August
2, 1826. 26062
An eulogy on John Adams and
Thomas Jefferson, pronounced
August 10, 1826. 26117
An eulogy on John Adams, and
Thomas Jefferson; pronounced
by request of the Common
council of Albany. 24371
Eulogy on John Adams and Thom-

discourses. 40225

The evidences of Christianity stated in a popular and practical manner. 41559

Evidences of piety. 15491

Evidences of revealed religion. 30794

Evidences of the divinity of Jesus Christ. 940

The evidences, on which the general system of the final restitution of all fallen intelligences, is founded. 1873

Evils and cure of intemperance. 40285

Evils of intemperance. A sermon preached at Hallowell. 5458

The evils of intemperance, and the duty of the temperate. 37500

The evils of intemperance, exemplified in poetry and prose. 38510; 38511

Evils of quarantine laws. 16977

Evils which threaten our country. 41435

An examination, by the Layman. 39252

Examination--land offices. 36290

An examination of a pamphlet. 1146; 16091

Examination of a report by the committee on incorporations. 39373

An examination of a review of Dr. Taylor's sermon. 38515

Examination of a tract on the alteration of the tariff. 15657; 15658; 15659

An examination of an epistle issued by a meeting of the followers of Elias Hicks. 28967

An examination of certain proceedings of the board of superintendents, of the Theological Seminary of the Reformed Dutch Church. 36995

An examination of charges against the American missionaries at the Sandwich Islands. 28813

An examination of Commodore Porter's Exposition. 20207

An examination of essays on fevers. 15835

Examination of Joseph Antoine, Johan Fransoeis Wohlfahrt and Joanna Wohlfahrt. 33105

An examination of Miss Wright's System of knowledge. 39351

An examination of Mr. Calhoun's economy. 12076

An examination of Mr. Dufief's philosophical notions. 21320

An examination of some of the provisions of the "Act, to create a fund for the benefit of the creditors. 38516

Examination of some principles and rules of conduct in religious matters. 15006

Examination of subjects who are in the House of Refuge. 22320

An examination of the charge, prepared by Gen. Jackson. 28824

Examination of the Charleston (S. C.) memorial. 28397

An examination of the civil administration of Governor Jackson in Florida. 33106; 33107

Examination of the controversy between Georgia and the Creeks. 20448

An examination of the controversy between the Greek deputies and two mercantile houses of New York. 24370; 28736

Examination of the decision of the commissioners under the fourth article of the Treaty of Ghent. 41427

An examination of the divine testimony concerning the character of the son of God. 16345

An examination of the doctrine of predestination. 32094

An examination of the line of the Great Erie Canal. 8650

Examination of the Muscle Shoals. 26977

Examination of the New system of society. 24538

An examination of the new tariff. 4901

An examination of the principles of peace and war. 5333

An examination of the question

"Whether a man may marry his deceased wife's sister?" 28825

An examination of the reasons alleged by a Protestant, for protesting against the doctrine of the Catholic Church. 28826

An examination of the reasons, why the present system of auctions ought to be abolished. 33108; 38517

Examination of the relations between the Cherokees and the government of the United States. 38518

An examination of the "Remarks" on Considerations suggested by the establishment of a second college in Connecticut. 19503; 23304

An examination of the remarks on the report of the commissioners appointed by the Legislature of New York. 23404

An examination of the Report of a Committee of the citizens of Boston. 33179

An examination of the strictures in the New England Journal. 13349

An examination of the strictures upon the American Education Society. 40569

An examination of the substance of a discourse on the unpardonable sin. 8648

Examinations in anatomy. 39023

An example from the Holy Scriptures. 39066

Example of the first preachers of the gospel considered. 27764

Examples of piety. 30797

Examples of questions. 38899

The excellence and influence of the female character. 22356

The excellence of liberality. 34596

The excellence of the female character; a sermon. 22357

The excellency of the female character vindicated. 32462

The excellency of the Scriptures. 13884

Excerpta ex auctoribus classicis. 946

Excerpta ex scriptis Publii Ovidii Nasonis. 30135

Excerpta ex scriptoribus scholasticis. 16092

Excerpta quaedame scriptoribus Latinis probatioribus. 31707

Excise on domestic spirits. 26978

The exclusive system. 31640; 37061

Excommunication of Mrs. Maria Townsend. 13362

An excursion of the dog-cart. 8651

Excursions on the River Connecticut. 24465

Excuses for the neglect| of the communion considered. 37710

Execution of Powars for the murder of Timothy Kennedy. 4379

Execution of Samuel Clisby and Gilbert Close. 8652

Execution of Stephen Merrill Clark. 5281

The Executioner. 3044

Executive communication to the General Assembly of Maryland. 2120; 5954

The executive proceedings of the Senate of the U. S. 26979

Executors and administrators instructor. 37952

Executors of John Kerlin, et al. 26980

Executors' sale. 29195

Exempla minora. 5282; 12484

Exercise in orthography. 24466

Exercises at the annual examination of the Theological Seminary, Andover. 4481; 7816; 11622

Exercises at the annual exhibition. Sept. 27, 1820. 122

Exercises at the installation of the Rev. J. P. Geortner. 29181

Exercises for the piano forte. 34103

Exercises in geography. 538; 1147

Exercises in grammar. 38922

Exercises in history, chronology,

and biography. 10152

Exercises in mensuration. 24467

Exercises in reading and recitations. 11746; 19603; 19604; 32207; 32208

Exercises in writing French. 38616

Exercises on the syntax of the Greek language. 21592

Exercises on the terrestrial globe. 27706

An exhibit of the losses sustained at the office of discount and deposit, Baltimore. 12485

Exhibit of the shocking oppression and injustice suffered for sixteen months by John Randel, Jun. 19950; 19951; 19952

Exhibiting for the benefit of the Massachusetts General Hospital. 5283

Exhibition at Milton Academy, August 23, 1820. 2277

Exhibition, by a part of the junior class, in the chapel of Brown University. 19884

Exhibition, in the chapel [Brown University] 4853; 8199; 12012

An exhibition of Calvinism. 24468

Exhibition of rare old paintings at the Athenaeum. 37900

Exhibition of the Adelphic Union Society. Williams College. 31770; 37204; 41551

An exhibition of the Dismal Swamp Canal. 20315

Exhibition of the Junior class. Williams College. 37202

An exhibition of Unitarianism. 16093; 20449

An exhortation to all professing the Christian name. 29823

An exhortation to the frequent reception to the Holy Sacrament. 8653

The exile; a comedy. 10096

Exile of Erin. 12486

Exiles of Eden. 20450

Eximiae latinorum sententiae. 15660

The expedition of Humphrey Clinker. 40469a

The expedition of Orsua. 6832

Expedition up the Missouri. 26981

An expeditious method of learning the Latin language. 33688

Expenditure, artillery school. 31251

Expenditure, naval appropriation. 26982; 31252

Expenditure of appropriations. 26983

Expenditures at national armories. 31253

Expenditures in the Department of State. 36293

Expenditures--internal improvements. 26984

Expenditures - Military Academy at West Point. 36291

Expenditures of public departments. 36294

Expenditures - public buildings. 31254; 36292

Expenses of Naval courts martial. 26985

Expenses of the town of Malden. 17011

Expenses of the town of Salem. 3090; 6695; 10170; 17882; 22183

Expenses of Winnebago deputation. 41119

The experience and gospel labours of the Rev. Benjamin Abbott. 4; 1229; 19357

Experience by a Green Mountain girl. 5284

The experience, Christian and ministerial of Reuben Peaslee. 9831

The experience of a clergyman. 33110

The experience of Sampson Maynard. 34088

The experience of William Keith. 25016

The experienced American housekeeper, or Domestic cookery. 12487; 30492; 40327

The experiences of several eminent Methodist preachers. 7629

An experimental enquiry into the medical properties of the

Aralie spinosa. 26150

An experimental inquiry into the botanical history, chemical properties and medicinal virtues of the Spirea tomentosa of Linneus. 6001

An experimental inquiry of the general nature of inflammation. 5558

Experimental observations on the operation of lithotomy. 2668

An experimental treatise on optics. 24508

Experiments on anthracite. 23145

Experiments on rail roads, in England. 37572

Experiments on the power of the veins. 9240

Experiments to ascertain the length of the seconds pendulum, at Columbia College. 14027

Experiments to determine the comparative quantities of heat. 23963

Experiments to determine the comparative value of the principal varieties of fuel. 28317

Experiments to establish a peculiar physico-organic action. 40657

Expert letter-writer. 24469

An explanation of some canon laws. 1154

An explanation of the Apocalypse. 22310

An explanation of the church catechism. 20451

Explanation of the salutation of the cross. 13634

An explanation of the views of the Society for Employing the Female Poor. 22315; 26096

Explanation of the views of the Society for Employing the Poor. 546; 1351; 3255

Explanations of an engraved plan for an establishment for the reception of individuals in a state of mental derangement. 40281

Explanations of the ground plan of the University of Virginia. 16709

The explanatory and pronouncing French word book. 25758; 40061

Explanatory notes upon the New Testament. 7630

The explanatory reader. 19286; 41538

Explanatory remarks and observations on the subject of fire insurance. 6024; 13303

Explicit avowal of nothingarianism. 14927

Exploration of the Northwest Coast. 26986

Explore South Seas. 36295

Explore the southern polar regions. 36296

Exports with benefit of drawback. 26987

An exposé of some of the misrepresentations contained in a pamphlet, entitled A letter from a Friend in America. 24470; 24471

An exposé of the causes of intemperate drinking. 1577

An exposé of the relief system. 19277

An exposé of the rise and proceedings of the American Bible Society. 1149

Exposicion de los sentimientos de los funcionarios publicos. 28208

Exposition and protest, reported by the special committee of the House of Representatives. 40488

An exposition of certain newspaper publications. 23949

An exposition of facts connected with the late prosecutions in the Methodist Episcopal Church. 33111

An exposition of facts, in a letter to Stephen Gould. 11757

An exposition of I Tim. III. 16. 21103

An exposition of modern scepticism. 38754

An exposition of some of the evils arising from the auction

system. 5285; 9701

An exposition of some of the reasons why measures should be taken for the construction of a canal round the falls of the river Ohio. 18144

An exposition of the Book of common prayer. 24565

An exposition of the case of the Africans. 6085

Exposition of the causes which led to the late controversy between General William Lytle and James W. Gazlay. 8104; 8105

An exposition of the conduct of the two houses of G. G. & S. Howland and Le Roy. 23719

An exposition of the dangers of interment in cities. 13675

Exposition of the doctrine of the Catholic Church. 4375; 23855; 37884

An exposition of the doctrines of Calvinism. 39359

An exposition of the facts and circumstances which justified the expedition to Foxardo. 21939

An exposition of the faith of the Religious Society of Friends. 12479; 24452; 33097; 38504

An exposition of the historical writings of the New Testament. 33763

An exposition of the late general election in New-York. 24472

An exposition of the misrepresentations contained in a publication issued by Robert Potter. 19913

An exposition of the natural system of the nerves of the human body. 19653

An exposition of the Old and New Testament. 29198; 33530

An exposition of the penitentiary system. 4645

An exposition of the political character and principles of John Quincy Adams. 29328; 33669

An exposition of the political conduct and principles of J. Q. Adams. 29329; 29330

An exposition of the practicabil-

ity of constructing a great central canal. 28827

An exposition of the principles and views of the middling interest in the city of Boston. 8654

An exposition of the principles on which the system of infant education is conducted. 28828; 28829

An exposition of the relationship existing between Jacob Martin, formerly of South Carolina and Elizabeth Pennington. 22397

An exposition of the situation, character, and interests of the American republic. 8898

Exposition of the system of instruction and disciplined pursued in the University of Vermont. 41377

Exposition of the titles to the lands in Florida. 33112

An exposition, relating to some of the proceedings of the Ohio Presbytery. 23286

Expositor and philanthropist. 8655

Expository remarks on the discipline of the primitive churches. 1338

An exposure of the folly and falsehood of George C. Light. 38034

Exposure of the misrepresentations contained in a professed report of the trial /of Mr. John N. Maffitt. 13186

An expostulatory address to the members of the Methodist Society, in Ireland. 4148

Extend Cumberland Road. 36297

The Extinguisher. 1150

Extract from a report written by an officer of the United States' Army. 1151

Extract from an address delivered on the morning of May 31, 1826. 27552

An extract from Baxter's Aphorisms on justification. 11764

Extract from "Cursory views of

the liberal and restrictive systems of Political Economy." 24009

Extract from the address of the Rt. Rev. Bishop Hobart. 2902

Extract from The advice of William Penn, to his children. 6403

An extract from the journal of John Nelson. 6184; 17303

Extract from the journal of the Ohio annual conference of the Methodist E. Churches. 39573

Extract from the minutes of Indiana Yearly Meeting. 24637

Extract from the Proceedings of Grand Lodge of the most ancient and honorable fraternity of Free and Accepted Masons, of the state of Indiana. 5377; 8741

Extract from the proceedings of the Grand Lodge of free and accepted Masons of the state of Louisiana. 28930; 38644

Extract from the Proceedings of the Grand Royal Arch Chapter of the state of Ohio. 1309; 12609; 20589

Extract from the proceedings of the most worshipful Grand Lodge of the Ancient and honorable fraternity of free and accepted Masons, in the state of Ohio. 5394; 8760; 12608; 16220; 20588

An extract from the report of the directors of Massachusetts State Prison. 29665

Extract of a letter from **** **** to a friend in New Jersey. 32232

Extract of a letter from a young Greek. 30227; 30228

Extract of a letter from Francis Adams. 22860

An extract of my pamphlet. 40270

An extract of the Christian's pattern. 1739; 1740; 21006; 35496

Extract of the minutes of the proceedings had by the Committee appointed by the six resp. Lodges of New-Orleans. 4380

Extract of the proceedings of the Grand Lodge of the Most ancient fraternity of Free and accepted Masons of the state of Louisiana. 1297; 5381; 16195; 24599

Extractos de los mas celebres escritores y poetas españoles en dos partes. 8475

Extracts concerning the importance of religion. 1152

Extracts, etc. from the minutes of Indiana Yearly Meeting. 28964; 33290

Extracts from a discourse delivered in St. Louis. 37927

Extracts from a journal, written on the coasts of Chili, Peru, and Mexico. 16379; 16380

Extracts from a sermon in London, on the 22d Jany. 1826. 24959

Extracts from a sermon, preached at Goffstown, New Hampshire. 16449

Extracts from a Unitarian catechism. 16094

Extracts from a work by the learned and celebrated President Edwards. 20375

Extracts from an act to provide against infectious & pestilential diseases. 25536

Extracts from an address before the Rutland County Foreign Missionary Society. 25065

Extracts from an address of the subscribers. 21848

Extracts from an article in the North American Review. 18067

Extracts from Dr. Benjamin Rush's inquiry into the effects of ardent spirits. 14017; 30493

Extracts from Godolphin, Sea laws. 24474

Extracts from legal opinions. 28830

Extracts from letters and other pieces written by Margeret

Jackson. 21039

Extracts from Letters written by the late Henry Pendleton Smith. 3243

Extracts from the act of assembly, incorporating the Fire Association of Philadelphia. 38576

Extracts from the American slave code. 40045

Extracts from the bye-laws of the company, together with some statements respecting oil gas, lately received from the Liverpool company. 11942

Extracts from the Correspondence of the American Bible Society. 94

Extracts from the Crisis. 12058; 12059

Extracts from the diary and letters of Miss Lucy Howard. 24901

Extracts from the eighteenth and nineteenth reports of the directors of the African Institution. 23434

Extracts from the epistles of the yearly meeting in London. 5408

Extracts from the journals kept by the Rev. Thomas Smith. 6814

Extracts from the letters of Elizabeth, Lucy and Judith Ussher. 41352

Extracts from The medical ethics. 6435; 40022

Extracts from the Memoirs of Caroline E. Smelt. 4132; 6989; 14134

Extracts from the minutes [Methodist Society.] 29741; 39574

Extracts from the minutes of Indiana yearly meeting. 20606

Extracts from the minutes of Ohio yearly meeting. 5409; 20613; 24641

Extracts from the minutes of our Yearly Meeting, held in Baltimore. 33287; 38691

Extracts from the minutes of

our yearly meeting held in Philadelphia. 1332; 8787

Extracts from the minutes of the Associate Synod of North America. 153; 6531; 6532; 11507; 13837

Extracts from the minutes of the Congregational Churches in Rhode Island Consociation. 24194

Extracts from the minutes of the General Assembly of the Presbyterian Church. 2849; 2850; 6524

Extracts from the minutes of the General Association of Massachusetts. 839; 8418; 12232; 15846; 20162; 24191

Extracts from the minutes of the General Association of New Hampshire. 5954; 8419; 15841a; 24193

Extracts from the minutes of the General Convention of the Congregational and Presbyterian ministers in Vermont. 5055; 5056; 8420; 12235; 15842a; 20163; 24195; 28573; 38253

Extracts from the minutes of the Mississippi Presbytery. 17688; 21966; 30330; 40143

Extracts from the minutes of the New-York yearly conference of the Methodist Society. 21438

Extracts from the minutes of the Presbytery of Oneida. 2857

Extracts from the minutes of the proceedings of the Associate Reformed Synod, of New York. 7845; 15130; 37511

Extracts from the minutes of the proceedings of the Associate-Reformed-Synod of the West. 15131; 27897; 37512

Extracts from the minutes of the proceedings of the eighteenth general synod of the Associate-Reformed Church in North America. 4503

Extracts from the minutes of the Proceedings of the nineteenth General Synod of the Associate-Reformed Church in North America. 7844

Extracts from the minutes of the proceedings of the seventeenth general synod of the Associate-Reformed Church in North America. 154

Extracts from the minutes of the Synod and Ministerium of the Evangelical Lutheran Church, in the state of New-York. 20430

Extracts from the minutes of the Synod of Philadelphia. 13839

Extracts from the minutes of the Synod of Pittsburgh. 6534

Extracts from the minutes of the synod of the Evangelical Lutheran Church, in the state of New-York. 8640; 12472

Extracts from the minutes of the XXX session of the synod and ministerium of the Evangelical Lutheran Church, in the state of New-York. 20431

Extracts from the minutes of the XXXII session of the synod and ministerium of the Evangelical Lutheran Church in the state of New York. 28805

Extracts from the minutes of the 25th General Convention of Congregational and Presbyterian ministers in Vermont. 842

Extracts from the minutes of the yearly conference of the Methodist Society. 17138

Extracts from the minutes of the Yearly Meeting of Friends, held in Philadelphia. 28970; 33302; 38703

Extracts from the North American Review. 23473

Extracts from the papers of Edwin Price. 2866

Extracts from the proceedings of the General Grand Chapter of the United States of America. 38675

Extracts from the proceedings of the Grand Chapter of the state of New York. 12606; 16216; 20584; 20585; 24613; 28944; 38662

Extracts from the proceedings of the Grand Chapter of the state of Vermont. 20597; 24628; 28955

Extracts from the proceedings of the Grand encampment of the state of New York. 24614

Extracts from the proceedings of the Grand Lodge of the state of Mississippi. 38653

Extracts from the proceedings of the Grand Royal Arch Chapter of the state of Ohio. 5395

Extracts from the proceedings of the Grand Royal Arch Chapter of the state of Vermont. 33279; 38681

Extracts from the Proceedings of the most worshipful Grand Lodge of the ancient and honourable fraternity of free and accepted Masons in the state of Ohio. 1311

Extracts from the projected penal code. 13119; 13145

Extracts from the report and records of the Merrimack Bible Society. 39563

Extracts from the Report of the Board of Missions to the General Assembly of the Presbyterian Church. 6525; 6526

Extracts from the Report of the Reverend Samuel Bacon. 181

Extracts from the "Rules and regulations for the Field Exercise and Maneuvers of the Infantry of the United States." 13250

Extracts from the rules and regulations of the Cumberland bar. 38310

Extracts from the writings of Daniel Phillips and William Penn. 21883

Extracts from the writings of Francis Fenelon. 28867

Extracts from the writings of Lady Guion. 1475

Extracts from the writings of primitive Friends. 12628; 16237

Extracts from the writings of the early members of the Society of Friends. 19627

Extracts from various writers on cattle. 34563

Extracts, literary, moral, and religious. 29144

Extracts of a letter on the mode of choosing the President. 22326

Extracts of Ohio Yearly Meeting. 1331

Extracts on silent worship. 38690

Extrait mythologique. 5783

Extraordinary circumstances. 1153

The extraordinary life and adventures of Robin Hood. 6656; 13969; 30469; 35059

Eye infirmary. 25273; 25274

The eye of affection. 20845

Ezekiel's vision. 38011

F

Fables amusantes. 6437; 34725; 40028

Fables choisies, à l'Usage des enfans. 12091; 24046

Fables for the Holy alliance. 13376

Fables for young ladies. 1155

Fables in prose. 16301

Fables in rhyme. 18158; 22431

Fables of Aesop and others. 42; 4414; 23432; 23433; 27788; 31904

The fabrication of the Pentateuch proved. 38522

Fabulas en verso castellano. 26013

Fabulas literarias. 24956

Facilitated carrying. 20453

Facts and arguments in favour of adopting railways in preference to canals. 20454; 20455

Facts and documents confirmatory of the credibility of the debate on baptism. 32559

Facts and documents in relation to Harvard College. 39016

Facts and documents, relating to ...a council, holden at Rehoboth. 26201; 26202; 26203

Facts and elucidations as connected with the management of the patriotic bank. 38358

Facts and observations illustrative of the rise and progress of the present state of Society in New York. 8592

Facts and observations; illustrative of the past and present situation, and future prospects of the U. S. 8270-71a; 13758

Facts and observations illustrative of transactions in the Society of Friends. 13758

Facts and observations in relation to the origin and completion of the Erie canal. 20456; 28831

Facts and observations on liver complaints. 1161; 8660

Facts and observations on the culture of vines. 4966; 8330

Facts and observations on the merits of the memorial of the president and directors of the first Great South-Western Turn-Pike Road Company. 38462

Facts and observations respecting the doings of the First [sic] church in Boxford. 19841

Facts and opinions respecting Mr. John Quincy Adams. 33113

Facts are the theme. 28832

Facts concerning the six militia men and General Jackson. 20457; 38523

Facts connected with the application for the power to improve the navigation of Connecticut River. 24476

Facts for the consideration of ship-builders. 31962

Facts illustrative of the character of the anthracite, or Lehigh coal. 16880; 21187; 21188; 29471

Facts in refutation of the aspersions against the character and memory, of Col. Wm. Stephens Smith. 18020

Facts in relation to Mrs. Leigh's system of curing stammering. 25082

Facts in relation to the introduction of gas light into the city of Philadelphia. 17611

Facts, observations, and practical illustrations, relative to puerperal fever. 11636; 23541; 23542

Facts relating to the improvement of Connecticut River. 28833

Facts stated that the truth may not be blamed. 13016

The fair American. 13631

A fair and candid examination of the sentiments of the antipedobaptists. 5286

Fair and candid exposition of the doctrine of Universalism. 14963

A fair and full view of the votes of John Andrew Shulze. 12490

A fair and just comparison of the lives of the two candidates. 16096; 33114

Fair Ellen. 15542

Fair Lucretia's garland. 28834

The Fair one with golden locks. 1156

The fair penitent. 17865

Fair play on both sides. 8656

The fair reasoner. 16294

The fairies. 21036

Fairy legends and traditions of the south of Ireland. 28621; 32853

The fairy's song. 20730; 20731

Faith and love towards the Saviour of sinners. 20462

Faith and works inseparable. 34738

Faith, hope, and charity; a sermon. 2300; 2301

Faith in Jesus Christ. 8659; 16099

The faith once delivered to the saints. 11775; 15293; 19425; 23507; 27849

The faith of the Dutch Church. 12493

The faith of the people called Quakers. 35569

Faith, the guide and support of the believer. 38474

The faithful dog. 1159; 28837

The faithful little girl. 28837a; 38528

The faithful minister's monument. 19292

A faithful representation of the interior of the House of Lords. 1160

The faithful servant of Christ, and his glorious reward. 2262; 2263

The faithful servant of God exemplified. 10226

Faithless Emma. 3325

The fall of Babylon. 24480; 33118

The fall of Iturbide. 14230

The fall of Jerusalem. 2271

The fall of Paris. 1162

Fallen is thy throne. 2116

A false position exposed. 8661

False stories corrected. 8661a

False teachers. 11415

Falsehood and forgery detected and exposed. 12364

Falsehood & persecution exposed. 998

Falsehood and slander exposed. 32934

Fame and fancy, or Voltaire improved. 24131

Familiar description of beasts. 33120

Familiar description of birds. 24481; 33121

Familiar dialogues. 2969; 38529

A familiar exposition of the catechism, adapted to the use of the Protestant Episcopal Church. 25867

Familiar illustrations of the principal evidences and design of Christianity. 33450

Familiar instructions for the public worship of Almighty God. 20464

Familiar instructions in the faith and morality of the Catholic Church. 38319

Familiar lectures on botany.

40034

Familiar letters between a mother
and her daughter at school.
30762

Familiar letters on sacraments.
12564; 16162

Familiar sermons. 22024

Familiar spelling book. 22485;
26223; 40660

The family adviser. 32742

The family altar. 35085

Family and private prayers.
11803; 11804

The family Bible. 23341

The family dentist. 8712

Family dialogues. 33605

The family directory, in the art
of dyeing. 23929

The family dyer. 24947

Family instruction and government. 27664

Family instructor. 1164

Family Jars, a musical farce.
1165; 25158

The family mansion. 3387

Family maxims. 33772

The family monitor. 39122;
39123; 39124

The family physician [Benezet]
23742

Family physician [Ewell] 24463

A family prayer-book containing
forms of morning and evening
prayers. 4843; 11992; 19867;
23934; 37950

The family prayer-book; or, The
Book of Common Prayer.
13866; 13867

Family prayers for each morning
and evening in the week.
14250

The family receipt book. 20465

Family receipts. 20466

Family record of Aaron and Lydia
Cilley. 5290

Family worship extracted from a
letter. 1036

Fancy dipp'd her pen in dew.
14888; 19263

Fancy's vision. 12988

Fanny. 5521

Fanny, continued. 778

Fanny the maid of the dee.

21493

Fanshawe, a tale. 33508

Fantaisie, avec sept. variations.
9179

Fantaisie, in which is introduced
the favorite Scotch air of
They're a' noddin. 18149

Fantaisie sur un air ecossais
pour le piano forte. 1067

A fantasia for the piano forte.
2332

Fantasie. 22424

Fantasie and variations on a
theme from the opera of Don
Juan. 11912

Fantasie for the flute. 1504

Far far from me my lover flies.
19741

Far, far o'er hill and dell.
18041; 18042; 22323; 22324

Fare thee well! 6131

Fare thee well thou lovely one!
6372

The farewell. 17298; 21586

Farewell! A discourse, delivered at Phillipston. 4621

The farewell address of Elisha
Tyson. 18260

Farewell address to the people of
the United States. 27561

Farewell ball. Yale College,
1829. 41611

Farewell but whenever you welcome the hour. 10344; 16765

A farewell discourse, addressed
to the Church and Society of
the First Parish in Saco.
32749

A farewell discourse, delivered
before the Baptist Church in
Warren, R.I. 729

A farewell discourse, preached
in the First Presbyterian
Church, Columbia, S.C.
16510

A farewell discourse, preached
to the Congregational Church
and Society in Leverett. 7716

A farewell discourse preached
to the First Congregational Society in Eastport. 4705

Farewell discourse to his people,
delivered at Norfolk, Conn.

38475

Farewell hymn on leaving the old meeting house in Quincy. 33122

Farewell letters to a few friends in Britain and America. 7563; 11336

A farewell. Philadelphia, Oct. 28, 1828. 32584

A farewell sermon addressed to the First Presbyterian Church and Society in Newburyport. 947; 5136

A farewell sermon, delivered at Bethel. 34178

Farewell sermon, delivered before the Congregational Church and Society in Newport (N. H.) 14881

A farewell sermon, delivered in the Brick meeting house, Thomaston. 38402

A farewell sermon delivered to the church and congregation at Lexington, N. Y. 24798a

The farewell sermon, delivered to the Presbyterian Church and Society in Dracut. 30560

Farewell sermon of Rev. Jacob T. Field. 28872

The farewell sermon of Rev. Samuel Johnson. 33722

A farewell sermon, preached in Trinity Church, Southwark. 24964

A farewell sermon preached October 25th, 1829. 38459

Farewell sermon to the people of Windham, N. H. 29145

Farewell! thou coast of glory. 17855

Farewell to my harp. 24891

Farewell to thee Araby's daughter. 16818

Farewell to time. 37257

The farm house. 20467

The farm yard journal. 37390

The farmer. 17487

The farmer's accountant and instructions for overseers. 35436

The farmer's almanac. 1170; 1171; 1172; 1173; 1174; 1175;

1176; 1177; 1178; 1179; 1180; 1181; 1182; 1183; 1184; 1185; 1186; 1187; 1188; 1189; 1190; 5293; 5294; 5295; 5296; 5297; 5298; 5299; 5300; 5301; 5302; 5303; 5304; 5305; 5306; 5307; 5308; 8664; 8665; 8666; 8667; 8668; 8669; 8670; 8671; 8672; 8673; 8674; 12495; 12496; 12497; 12498; 12499; 12500; 12501; 12502; 12503; 12504; 12505; 12506; 12507; 12508; 12509; 12510; 12511; 12512; 12513; 16100; 16101; 16102; 16103; 16104; 16105; 16106; 16107; 20468; 20469; 20470; 20471; 20472; 20473; 20474; 20475; 20476; 24483; 24484; 24485; 24486; 24487; 24488; 24489; 24490; 24491; 24492; 24493; 24494; 28839; 28840; 28841; 28842; 28843; 28844; 28845; 28846; 28847; 28848; 28849; 33124; 33125; 33126; 33127; 33128; 33129; 33130; 33131; 33132; 33133; 33134; 33135; 33136; 33137; 33138; 33139; 33140; 38534; 38535; 38536; 38537; 38538; 38539; 38540; 38541; 38542; 38543; 38544

Farmer's and Mechanic's almanac. 1191; 12514; 20477; 20478; 24495; 24496; 24497; 38545

The farmer's and mechanics' assistant. 16331

The farmer's and mechanic's guide. 38546

The farmers' and mechanics' practical arithmetic. 9811

Farmers and merchants almanac. 38547

The farmers' and planters' almanac. 28850; 33141; 38548

The farmer's assistant. 2551

The farmer's calendar or Ontario almanac. 38549

Farmer's calendar, or the Buffalo almanack. 16108; 24498

The Farmer's Calendar; or, Utica almanack. 1192; 1193; 1194; 5309; 5310; 8675; 12515;

16109; 20479; 20480; 24499;
24500; 28851; 33142
The farmer's calendar, or Watertown almanack. 5311; 8676
Farmer's calendar; or, Western
almanack. 16110; 16111;
16112; 20481; 20482; 24501;
28852; 28853; 33143
The farmer's daughter. 8576
The farmer's diary; or, Beers'
Ontario almanack. 1195; 1196;
5312; 8677; 12516; 24502
The Farmer's diary; or, Bemis's
Ontario almanack. 1197
Farmer's diary; or Catskill almanack. 1198; 1199; 5313;
12516a; 33144; 38550
Farmer's diary; or Newburgh almanack. 1200
The farmer's diary, or Ontario
almanack. 8678; 12517; 16113;
20483; 20484; 24503; 28854;
33145; 33146; 38551
The farmer's friend. 38553
The farmer's instructor. 12518;
16114
A farmer's letters. 33147
Farmer's library. 21166; 25066;
33819
Farmer's manual. 4882
The Farmer's materia medica.
21429
Farmer's, Mechanic's and Gentle-
man's almanac. 1201; 5314;
8679; 12519; 16115; 20485;
20486; 24504; 28855; 33148;
38552
The Farmer's pocket almanack.
1202; 5315
The Farmers' Register and Mary-
land Herald Extra. 36298
The Farmer's wife. 476
Farmers of Middlesex. 33149
Farmers tickett. 34387
Farmington canal. 28190
The farmyard journal. 7755;
31911
Farrow and Harris. 36299;
36300; 36301
The fasciculus of wit. 15565
The fashionable American letter
writer. 12520; 24509; 33152
The fashionable letter center.

8685
The fashionable letter writer.
16119; 33153
The fashionable tour. 8513;
20271; 33154
Fast sermon [Colman] 5028
A fast sermon, on the national
profanation of the Sabbath.
23340
The fatal dowry. 25281
The fatal effects of ardent spir-
its. 2826
The fatal effects of indifference.
5873
The fatal ladder. 33155
The fatal looking-glass. 35164
Father Clement, a Roman-Cath-
olic story. 29405; 29406;
39181
Father Rowland, a North Ameri-
can tale. 40089
Father thy word is past. 9206
A father's gift to his son. 5316
A father's legacy to his daugh-
ters. 5500; 12723; 29079
A father's letters to his son.
37697
A father's reasons for baptizing
his infant child. 3; 11518;
15009
A father's reasons for Christian-
ity. 28857
A father's serious advice to his
children. 161; 162; 163
The fathers of New England. 6690
Fauna Americana. 20815
A favorite air [Kelly] 21093;
21094
A favorite air by Rousseau. 6673
A favorite air. With variations
for the piano forte. 13055
A favorite allegretto. 12669
The favorite Bath waltz. 5317;
16121; 20491
A favorite cotillion. 20853
The favorite dances in Tom and
Jerry. 2219; 16122
The favorite Flemish rondo. 6383
A favorite Irish air. 21169
A favorite march. [Evans]
12478
A favorite march by Mozart.
2349; 13417

Favorite march in the Cataract of the Ganges. 1207; 20494

The favorite masquerade song. 3343

The favorite new martial air. 13893

The favorite of nature. 9188

A favorite overture for the piano forte. 13057; 13058

The favorite overture to Blaise and Babet. 5180

The favorite overture to Iphigenie. 12689

The favorite overture to The caliph of Bagdad. 19782

The favorite overture to the new musical farce of Belles without beaux. 7573; 14822

The favorite overture to the opera of John of Paris. 19784

The favorite Pas de deux in cherry and fair star. 20495

A favorite pollacca [Blayney] 11907

A favorite pollacca [Carayo] 15640

A favorite pot pourri for the harp. 5176; 5177; 5178

The favorite Russian air of Ne'er can the rose. 17097

The favorite Scotch air Auld lang syne. 3056; 6668

The favorite Scottish melody. 37495

A favorite set of cotillions. 15322

The favorite song Arbre charmant. 16358

A favorite Spanish dance. 15905

The favorite Swiss waltz. 5318; 9542

Favorite variations for two performers on a piano forte. 1283

The favorite Vienna waltz. 5319

A favorite waltz, composed by Mozart. 2350; 2351; 6132; 9564; 9565; 9566; 13418

A favorite waltz. For pianoforte and tambourine. 3316; 6863

Favorite waltz, from the Barber of Seville. 3060

Favorite waltz. No. 1. The subject from the Opera of Zampa. 1576

A favorite waltz, with variations for the piano forte, composed and dedicated to Miss Mary Livingston Greenleaf. 1713

Favorite waltzes. 15871

The favourite dance in Tom and Jerry. 2218; 20492; 21392

A favourite duett for two performers. 9222

A favourite fandango. 13056

A favourite Irish air. 21168

Favourite Laudler waltz. 374

A favourite lesson for the harpsichord or piano forte. 67

Favourite mad song. 1208

Favourite march in The cataract of the Ganges. 20493; 20798

The favourite movement in the overture to Macbeth. 19189

A favourite ode in celebration of the Fourth of July. 5704

The favourite Russian air. 6873

The favourite Spanish dance. 20672

Favourite Swiss waltz. 16123

Fayette election August, 1822. 8689

A feast for the hungry. 24156

Feast of knowledge. 7874

The feast of reason. 1210

Feast of roses. 4719

The feast of wit; or, A collection of choice anecdotes. 20498

The feast of wit, or Frolic of laughter. 5046

The feast of Zion. 40436

The federal calculator. 24816; 35221

Federal remonstrance. 16126

Federal republican meeting. 12524

The Federalist, on the new Constitution. 24513; 24514

Feeble means produce great effects. 20499

Fellenberg School. 24515

Fellow citizens [Brown] 37961

Fellow-citizens, a large proportion of the inhabitants of Wayne County. 11370

Fellow citizens, in presenting myself as a candidate to the

citizens of the first congressional district. 10011

Fellow citizens of Jefferson and
Oldham Counties. 30682

Fellow citizens of Johnson, Alexander, & Union counties.
33171

Fellow citizens of the first congressional district. 8543

Fellow-citizens of the state of Illinois. 33019

Fellow citizens of the state of
Maine. 1584

Fellow-citizens read this. 31776

Fellow Citizens! The important
Day has arrived. 1212

Fellow soldiers... 2076

Fellowship and charity co-exten-
sive. 15605

Female Classical Seminary.
20504

Female education. A discourse,
delivered at the dedication of
the Seminary Hall in Saugus.
8620; 8621; 12449

Female education: an address
delivered in Trinity Church,
Newark. 25821

Female influence. 12534

The female labourer in the vineyard. 29200

Female policy detected. 4162;
19181

Female quixotism. 22439; 40625;
40626

The female speaker. 15259

The female Sunday school teacher. 9452; 13287

The female wanderer. 1219;
16130; 26129; 26130; 40523

Der Fertige Rechner. 33167

Fessenden and Co.'s encyclopedia.
23944

La festa de la rosa. 14908

Feurige Kohlen der aufsteigenden
Liebesflammen im Lustspiel
der Weisheit. 24527

A few considerations in relation
to the choice of president.
8699

A few crumbs of history. 12540

A few days in Athens. 20264

A few hints, on monarchy & re-

publicanism. 20514

A few historical facts. 8114

A few historical sketches of
those that have held or borne
testimony. 32529

A few imperfect rhymes on the
sovereignty of Jehovah. 10297

A few notes on certain passages
respecting the law of nations.
12481

A few observations and remarks
on that part of the executive
message relating to the Onondaga salt springs. 20515

A few plain and candid objections,
to the committee appointed by
the Rev. J.M. Hanson. 29419

A few reflections upon the fancy
ball. 33170

A few remarks, on the late attempt of the clergy of this
city, to enforce the Sunday
laws. 5329

A few serious questions for reason and conscience to decide.
19332

A few strictures on an extract
said to be taken from the
"Christian Disciple." 1228

A few thoughts (of an aged layman,) respecting Jesus Christ.
16184

A few words on the crisis.
15564

Fifteenth annual exhibition of the
Pennsylvania Academy of the
Fine Arts. 25703

15th Annual report. [Public
School Society of New York]
2913

Fifteenth annual report of the
American Tract Society.
37455

The fifteenth annual report of
the Association for the Relief
of Respectable, Aged, Indigent Females. 32033

Fifteenth annual report of the
Auxiliary Foreign Mission Society, of Franklin County.
27913

The fifteenth annual report of the
Cincinnati Miami Bible Society.

38178
Fifteenth annual report of the re-
ceipts & expenditures of the
city of Boston. 28229
Fifteenth annual report of the
trustees of the Society of the
Protestant Episcopal Church
for the Advancement of Chris-
tianity in Pennsylvania. 30374
The fifteenth report of the Bible
Society of Philadelphia. 11855
The fifteenth report of the Board
of Trustees of the Protestant
Episcopal Society for the Ad-
vancement of Christianity in
South Carolina. 22001
15th report of the New-Hampshire
Bible Society. 25517
Fifteenth report of the Vermont
Bible Society. 31604
Fifth annual convocation of the
Grand Royal Arch Chapter of
North Carolina. 28948
Fifth annual meeting of the Bap-
tist Education Society, of the
state of New-York. 7895
The fifth annual meeting of the
Bible Society of Northampton
County. 15395
The fifth annual meeting of the
Palestine Missionary Society.
25652
Fifth annual meeting of the Rich-
mond and Manchester Coloniza-
tion Society. 35038
Fifth annual report, Committee of
Management, of the Tract As-
sociation of the Society of
Friends. 10469
The fifth annual report, for the
year 1821, of The Managers
of the Indigent Widows and
Single Women's Society. 9107
Fifth annual report of the Ameri-
can Society for Colonizing the
Free People of Colour. 7794
Fifth annual report of the Auxil-
iary Foreign Mission Society of
Hartford County. 32051
Fifth annual report of the Board
of Directors of the Massachu-
setts Domestic Missionary So-
ciety. 13259

Fifth annual report of the board
of managers of the Charleston
Port Society. 32647
The fifth annual report of the
board of managers of the
Charleston Protestant Episco-
pal Sunday School Society.
15727
The fifth annual report of the
Board of Managers of the Ken-
tucky Bible Society. 5758
The fifth annual report of the
board of managers of the New
York Protestant Episcopal
Missionary Society. 6282
The fifth annual report of the
Board of Trustees of the New
Hampshire Baptist Domestick
Mission Society. 17332
Fifth annual report of the Boston
Society for the Moral and Religious Instruction of the Poor.
4801; 4802
Fifth annual report of the Charleston Bethel Union. 28440
Fifth annual report of the controllers of the public schools
of the first school district of
the state of Pennsylvania.
13698; 13699
Fifth annual report of the directors of New-York Institution
for the Instruction of the Deaf
and Dumb. 6276; 17414
The fifth annual report of the directors of the New York Evangelical Missionary Society.
6267
The fifth annual report of the
executive board of the Mississippi Baptist Missionary Society. 7919
Fifth annual report of the Female Tract Society of the City
of New-York. 28862
The fifth annual report of the
Herkimer Bible Society. 9004
The fifth annual report of the
Long Island Bible Society.
2006
The fifth annual report of the
managers of the Auxiliary
New-York Bible and Common

Prayer Book Society. 4514

Fifth annual report of the managers of the Marine Bible Society of New York. 5928

Fifth annual report of the managers of the New York Asylum for Lying-in Women. 37328

Fifth annual report of the Massachusetts Peace Society. 2178

Fifth annual report of the Missionary Society of the Methodist Episcopal Church. 17136

The fifth annual report of the Missionary Society of the Reformed Dutch Church. 30414

The fifth annual report of the Mississippi Baptist State Convention. 28001

Fifth annual report of the New York Female Auxiliary Bible Society. 6269

Fifth annual report of the New-York Sunday School Union Society. 6287

Fifth annual report of the Philadelphia Orphan Society. 2744

The fifth annual report of the Providence Female Tract and School Society. 2908

Fifth annual report of the Provident Society for Employing the Poor. 40199

The fifth annual report of the Society for Promoting Religious Instruction in the Isle of Shoals. 26097

Fifth annual report of the surgeons of the Massachusetts Charitable Eye and Ear Infirmary. 39516

Fifth annual report of the trustees of the Female Missionary Society of the Western District. 5324

Fifth annual report of the trustees of the High-School Society of New-York. 38972

Fifth annual report of the Young Men's Missionary Society of New York. 4365

Fifth annual report to the Legislature, by the Pennsylvania Institute for the Deaf and

Dumb. 21845; 25708

Fifth general report of the president and directors of the Chesapeake and Delaware Canal Company. 15733

The fifth report of the Albany Sunday School Union Society. 11566

Fifth report of the American Bible Society. 4465

The fifth report of the American Sunday-School Union. 37453; 37454

Fifth report of the Bible Society in the county of Middlesex. 450

Fifth report of the board of directors of the Presbyterian Education Society. 13849

The fifth report of the Connecticut Society Auxiliary to the Baptist Board of Foreign Missions. 853

Fifth report of the directors of the American Asylum at Hartford. 4476

Fifth report of the directors of the American Education Society. 103

The fifth report of the Philadelphia Sunday and Adult School Union. 6462; 9904

Fifth report of the Society for the Prevention of Pauperism in the City of New-York. 6818

Fifth report of the South Carolina Domestic Missionary Society. 38407

The fifth report of the United Foreign Missionary Society. 10507

The fifth report of the Young Men's Bible Society of Baltimore. 23397

Fiftieth anniversary of American independence. 26003

The Fifty Associates. 12544

$50 reward. Negro Washington eloped from my farm. 19464

50 dollars reward. Ran away from the subscriber, living in Prince George's County.

24369

Fifty reasons or, motives why the Roman Catholic apostolic religion ought to be preferred to all the sects. 26259

Fifty-eighth anniversary. Minutes of the Warren Baptist Association. 19582

Fifty-one substantial reasons against any modification whatever of the existing tariff. 15661

Fifty-sixth anniversary. Minutes of the Warren Baptist Association. 11726

Fifty-seventh anniversary. Minutes of the Warren Baptist Association. 15238

La figlia dell'aria. 24657

Figurative instruction, ancient and divine. 21786

Filial affection. 3113

Fin ch'han dal vino! 29130

Final appeal to the Christian public in defence of the "Precepts of Jesus." 34952

A final reply to the numerous slanders, circulated by Nathaniel Chapman. 6396; 6397

Final report of the Committee of both branches of the City Council of Boston. 23856

Final restoration demonstrated from the Scriptures of truth. 5752

The final tendency of the religious disputes of the present day. 41577

Finances. Annual report of the Secretary of the Treasury. 41121

Finances - Chesapeake and Ohio Canal Company. 41120

Finances of the canal fund of the state of New York. 40651

Fine arts. 34203

A finishing stroke to the high claims of ecclesiastical sovereignty. 30607

Die Finsterniss in der freyen Kirche von America. 12488

Fire and water. 4644

Fire engines. 32834

Fire in the library. 26988

The fire worshipper. 4509

Fireside stories. 28878

The firm of Pratt & Meech was dissolved. 25297

The first and accurate account of one of the American colonists. 7661

The first and second annual reports of the Board of Delegates, from the Male Sunday Schools of Baltimore. 2090

First anniversary report of the directors of the Young Men's Auxiliary Education Society of the City of New York. 27728

The first annual address, delivered before the Hartford Peace Society. 39297

The first annual report of the acting committee of the Society for the Promotion of Internal Improvement in the Commonwealth of Pennsylvania. 25716

First annual report of the Albany Institute. 19388

First annual report of the American Seamen's Friends Society. 37447

First annual report of the American Society for Promoting the Civilization and General Improvement of the Indian Tribes. 15090

First annual report of the American Tract Society. 23502

The first annual report of the Auxiliary Foreign Mission Society of Cincinnati. 27911

First annual report of the Auxiliary Foreign Mission Society of New-York. 32053

First annual report of the Baptist General Tract Society. 19517

First annual report of the Bible Society of Queen Ann's Parish. 11856

First annual report, of the board of attending and consulting physicians and surgeons, of the Dexter Asylum. 40195

The first annual report of the

board of managers of the Boston Mechanics' Institution. 332439

First annual report of the Board of Managers of the Charleston Port Society. 15726

First annual report of the board of managers of the Fayette County, Kentucky Bible Society. 33157

The first annual report of the board of managers of the Female Episcopal Bible, Prayer Book and Tract Society of Charleston. 33164

First annual report of the board of managers of the Missionary Conference Society. 21436

First annual report of the Board of Managers of the Prison Discipline Society. 30347; 30348

First annual report of the board of trustees of the Manual Labour Academy of Pennsylvania. 40052; 40053

First annual report of the board of trustees of the New-York Protestant Episcopal Press. 39833

First annual report of the board of trustees of the Norfolk County Bible Society. 39851

First annual report of the Charitable Society of Windham County. 718

First annual report of the directors of the Connecticut Branch of the American Education Society. 27830

First annual report of the Directors to the stockholders of the Baltimore & Ohio Railroad Co. 27952

First annual report of the Eastern Auxiliary Foreign Mission Society of Rockingham County, New-Hampshire. 24393

First annual report of the executive committee of the American Society for the Promotion of Temperance. 31966

First annual report of the executive committee of the American Unitarian Association. 23508

First annual report of the executive committee of the board of managers of the General Protestant Episcopal Sunday School Union. 29000

The first annual report of the Female Bible, Missionary and Tract Society, of New-Utrecht. 24518

First annual report of the Female Sunday School Society of St. James's Church. 8697

First annual report of the General Union for Promoting the Observance of the Christian Sabbath. 38740

The first annual report of the Genesee Conference Missionary Society. 13315

The first annual report of the Harmony Auxiliary Bible Society. 12771

First annual report of the Hartford County Sabbath School Union. 33489

The first annual report of the Homily Society of St. Paul's Church. 13753

The first annual report of the House of Refuge of Philadelphia. 40049

First annual report of the Indiana Sabbath School Union. 29319

First annual report of the Infant School Society of Boston. 39091

First annual report of the Infant School Society of Philadelphia. 33665

First annual report of the Infant School Society of the Northern Liberties and Kensington. 39094

First annual report of the Juvenile Female Auxiliary Tract Society of Trinity Church, Baltimore. 12978

First annual report of the Juvenile Finleyan Missionary Mite Society of Baltimore. 12979

First annual report of the Maine

Sabbatch School Union. 29608

First annual report of the managers of the Society for the
Reformation of Juvenile Delinquents in the City of New
York.   22321

First annual report of the Marine
Bible Society of Boston. 5937

First annual report of the Missionary Society for the County
of Rensselaer.   17173

First annual report of the New
Hampshire Baptist Sabbath
School Union.   39755

First annual report of the New
Hampshire Branch of the
American Education Soceity.
29947

The first annual report of the
New-York City Tract Society.
34531

First annual report of the New
York Eye Infirmary. 9695

First annual report of the Pennsylvania Branch of the American Tract Society. 31985

First annual report of the president and directors of the
Chesapeake and Ohio Canal
Company.   38126; 38127;
38128

First annual report of the proceedings of the Franklin Institute.   20555

First annual report of the Raleigh
Peace Society. 2935

The first annual report of the Religious Society of the city of
Washington. 2980

First annual report of the Society
for the Encouragement of Faithful Domestic Servants in New-
York. 26099

First annual report of the superintendent of public instruction
to the legislature of Maryland.
34028

First annual report of the trustees of the High-School Society,
in the city of New York. 20884

First annual report of the United
Auxiliary Missionary Soceity.
18265

First annual report of the Vermont Sabbath School Union.
27506

First annual report of the Young
Men's Missionary Society of
New-York.   19356

First annual report of the Young
Men's Temperance Society of
Philadelphia.   41624

First biennial report of the trustees and instructer of the
Monitorial School, Boston.
23883

First book for a little child just
beginning to learn its letters.
12548

A First Book for children. 6167

A first book for the use of the
teachers. 25636

The first book, or spelling lessons for primary schools.
24537; 25080

First catalogues and circulars of
the Botanical Garden of Transylvania University. 18232

First catechism for children.
17623; 21885; 25759; 25760;
30247

First Church in Salem.   30514

First commencement of the Columbian College.   16273

The first companion to the Royal
patent chiroplast or hand directors. 1998

The first day of the week.   28879;
33176

First drill for recruits. 38577

First elements of the French language. 17600

First exhibition of the Washington College Athenaeum. 31670

The first floor: a farce. 15792

First fruit and lump, root and
branch. 9075

The first jubilee of American Independence. 25584

First lessons in arithmetic. 8379;
12200; 20112

First lessons in English grammar.   31812

First lessons in geography and
astronomy. 8485; 12303; 20224;
20225; 20226; 24256; 24257;

24258; 24259; 28633; 32866; 38316

First lessons in intellectual philosophy. 37862

First lessons in Latin. 38199

First lessons in practical geometry. 38730

First lessons in the history of the United States. 14276; 22445; 35484

First letter of W.W. Potter, to the committee of the Philadelphia Medical Society. 34858

The first lines of arithmetic. 17125

The first lines of English grammar. 12000; 15571; 23940

First lines of the practice of physic. 8477

The first lines of the practice of surgery. 8444; 32832; 32833

First night of Paul Pry... 23896

The first of April. 28880

First, or Mother's catechism. 17624

First principles of English spelling and reading. 30648

First principles of the differential and integral calculus or the doctrine of fluxions. 15338

First principles, or Hints to suit the times. 4846

First quarterly report of diseases treated at the New-York City Dispensary. 25569

First report of the American Bible Class Society. 31947

The first report of the American Home Missionary Society. 27835

The first report of the American Society for Meliorating the Condition of the Jews. 11605

First report of the American Sunday School Union. 19417; 19418

First report of the Bank for Savings. 216

The first report of the Bible Society of Washington City. 41440

The first report of the board of directors of the Charleston

Infant School Society. 38113; 39092

The first report of the board of managers of the Pennsylvania Colonization Society. 30190

First report of the Brooklyn Female Bible Society. 23933

First report of the Charleston Bethel Union. 8319

First report of the Charleston Sunday School Union Society. 12105

First report of the Committee of the Philadelphia Medical Society. 34764

First report of the directors of the Auxiliary Education Society of the Young Men of Boston. 170; 171

First report of the directors of the Penitent Female's Refuge. 2678

First report of the Female Missionary Society, of the First Presbyterian Church of Brooklyn. 15562

First report of the managers of the Episcopal Missionary Association of Zion Church. 6288

First report of the New-York Bethel Union. 9694

The first report of the New York Bible Society. 2522

First report of the New-York Colonization Society. 13565

First report of the Pennsylvania Canal Commissioners. 30171

First report of the Provident Society for the Employment of the Poor. 22005

First report of the St. Lawrence Domestic Missionary Society. 40344

First report of the South-Carolina Domestic Missionary Society. 22331

First report of the trustees of Oneida Academy. 34613

First report of the United Domestic Missionary Society. 14336

First report of the Vermont Colonization Society. 4095

The first report of the Western
Domestic Missionary Society.
31716

The first report of the Western
Sunday School Union. 27618;
27619

The first report of the Young
Men's Missionary Society, of
the Reformed Dutch Church
in Brooklyn. 28288

The first report on the state of
education in Pennsylvania.
34709

The first rose of summer. 13385

First semi-annual convocation of
the Grand Royal Arch Chapter
of the state of Alabma. 16187

First semi-annual report, to the
president and directors of the
South Carolina Canal and Rail-
road Company. 35363

First session. Sconcia's new system of instruction as a science.
26024

The first set of cotillions. 1232

The first settlers of New-England.
8333; 32668; 38133

The first settlers of Virginia.
20270

The first seventeen chapters of
the ordinances of the illustrious university. 15403

First spelling book. 29398

First statement on the part of
Great Britain. 38813

The first supplement to the catalogue of the library belonging
to the General Theological
Seminary. 25573

Fish out of water. 29553

The fisherman and his boy.
33181

Fishers hornpipe. 16151

Fishkill Landing Bible Society.
33182

The five apprentices. 32074

Five books of the history of C.
Cornelius Tacitus. 26166

Five dissertations on fever.
12566

Five hundred progressive exercises in parsing. 28980;
33308

Five hundred questions deduced
from Goldsmith's history of
England. 9

Five letters on Atonement. 8711;
10316

Five pebbles from the brook.
16065

Five pretty stories for little boys
and girls. 38589

Five sermons against popery.
30561

Five South American waltzes.
12555

Five thousand receipts in all the
domestic and useful arts.
21281; 29577; 39367

Five waltzes for the piano forte.
1239

Fixing the time of adjournment.
26989

Flageolet instructor. 1240

Flauto traversiere. 25953

Fleurette and other rhymes.
33937

Fleury's short historical catechism. 1255

Fleuve du Tage. A favorite
French air. 1858; 6500; 9967;
9968; 9969; 13802

Flirtation: a novel. 32536

The floating beacon. 195; 16152

Flora McDonald. 9183

A flora of North America. 333;
4620

A flora of the northern and middle sections of the United
States. 18224

Flora-day. 16160

Flora's dictionary. 38600

Flora's wreath. 2191

Florida Indians. 26990; 26991;
31255; 36302

The Florida pirate. 12560;
33204

Florida, resolutions. 36303

Florula Bostoniensis. 461; 15401

Florula cestrica. 24292; 24293

Flow, flow, Cubana! 5635

Flow on thou shining river. 3326;
6874; 6875; 22375

Flowers of ancient history. 7729

The flowers of autumn. 33205

Flowers of song. 17217

Flowers of wit. 21111
Floyd S. Bailey, esq. I received
    your letter. 20723
Flute instructor. 33208
Flute melodies. 8967
Fly to the desert. 5761
The flying pen. 16148
Folgendes ist der vierte Theil
    von meinem armen Lebens-
    Lauf. 30523
Follow, follow, thro' the Sea.
    477; 21335; 21336; 21337
The following address, written
    by one of the trustees of the
    proposed new college. 25797
The following appointments have
    been made in the Army. 7042
The following discourse, being an
    humble attempt to vindicate
    the ways of God to man.
    40430
The following facts in relation to
    J. Kunkle. 28079
The following important letter
    was addressed to the Hon.
    Henry Baldwin. 1259
The following is a specimen of
    the lexicography of Webster's
    dictionary. 27588
The following is the substance of
    a trial of Messrs. William &
    P. C. Smith. 17535
The following letter from Mr.
    Sloane, a member of Congress
    from Ohio and accompanying
    comments, are taken from the
    Richmond Whig. 35219
The following narrative of the ex-
    ercise and experience, togeth-
    er with a remarkable vision of
    an Indian woman. 4295
The following of Christ. 16651;
    35497
The following order of proces-
    sion, etc. will be observed on
    the occasion of laying the cor-
    ner stone of the Episcopal
    Church of St. John. 24028
The following order of procession,
    will be observed by the Ma-
    sonic Fraternity, in dedicating
    the New Masonic Hall, in Hag-
    erstown. 16199

The following prospectus for
    printing by subscription. 27532
The following report, made by
    the president of the Bank of
    Columbia. 23599
The following report, which is to
    be submitted to a town meet-
    ing is now printed. 25798
The following resolution was
    adopted at a meeting of the
    friends of Gen. Jackson in
    this county. 29342
The following uniform is hereby
    prescribed for the Generals
    of Divisions. 6071
The following uniform is hereby
    prescribed for the Regimental
    field, and Staff Officers, of
    the Militia of this state. 6070
The folly of finery. 28894
The footsteps of virtue. 16166
For Albany at 6 o'clock A.M.
    30090
For missionaries after the apos-
    tolical school. 21031
For the benefit of coasters and
    seafaring gentlemen. 4658
For the benefit of Mr. Finn.
    28251
For the oracles of God. 12935;
    12936; 16682; 21032
For the year 1820. Annual re-
    port of the British Charitable
    Society. 591
For thee alone my Mona dear.
    5545
The foray. 769; 776; 4275
The force of prejudice. 12565
The force of truth. 22210; 22211;
    22212; 30537; 30538; 30539
Foreign commerce. 31256; 31257
Foreign missions. 31258
Foreign wool imported. 31259
A foreigner's opinion of England.
    8843
The forest of Rosenwald. 6900;
    6901
The forest rose. 23376
The forest sanctuary. 29191
The foresters. [Rawlings] 22036
The foresters. [Wilson] 23347;
    23348
Forgery defeated. 10052

dence and authority of the Christian system. 5115

Four short sermons, the first of which relates to the death of Commodore Decatur. 1268

The four sisters. 876; 5085; 5086; 5087; 5088

Four views of Fairmount waterworks. 39268

The fourteenth anniversary of the Hudson River Association. 37650

Fourteenth annual report of the American Tract Society. 31971

The fourteenth annual report of the Association for the Relief of Respectable, Aged, Indigent Females. 27898

The fourteenth annual report of the board of managers of the Auxiliary New York Bible and Common Prayer Book Society. 37527

The fourteenth annual report of the board of trustees of the New York Protestant Episcopal Tract Society. 17725

Fourteenth annual report of the Massachusetts Society for the Suppression of Intemperance. 29694

Fourteenth annual report of the Philadelphia Orphan Society. 39937

Fourteenth annual report of the receipts & expenditures of the City of Boston. 23857

Fourteenth annual report of the trustees of the Society of the Protestant Episcopal Church for the Advancement of Christianity in Pennsylvania. 25866

14th concert. 29875

Fourteenth report of the Bible Society of Philadelphia. 8050

The fourteenth report of the board of trustees of the Protestant Episcopal Society for the Advancement of Christianity in South-Carolina. 17723

The fourteenth report of the Female Bible Society of Philadelphia. 33162

Fourteenth report of the New Hampshire Bible Society. 21626

Fourteenth report of the Vermont Bible Society. 27504

Fourth and fifth letters to the Rev. Samuel Miller. 6835

Fourth anniversary of the Baptist State Convention in Alabama. 27968

Fourth annual common school report. 21655

Fourth annual convocation of the Grand Royal Arch Chapter of North Carolina. 24615; 24616

Fourth annual meeting of the Baptist Education Society. 4544

Fourth annual meeting of the Berkshire Bible Society. 4669

The fourth annual report of the American Society for Colonizing the Free People of Colour of the United States. 4467

Fourth annual report of the American Tract Society. 37456

Fourth annual report of the Auxiliary Foreign Mission Society. 32049

Fourth annual report of the board of managers of the Charleston Port Society. 28443

The fourth annual report of the board of managers of the Charleston Protestant Episcopal Sunday School Society. 12103

The fourth annual report of the board of managers of the New York Protestant Episcopal Sunday School Society. 6283

Fourth annual report of the board of managers of the Prison Discipline Society. 40156

Fourth annual report of the board of managers of the Protestant Episcopal Female Tract Society of Baltimore. 6561

The fourth annual report of the Board of Trustees of the New Hampshire Baptist Domestick Mission Society. 13508

Fourth annual report of the Boston Society for the Moral and Religious Instruction of the Poor. 547

Fourth annual report of the controllers of the public schools of the first school district of the State of Pennsylvania. 9842

The fourth annual report of the directors of the New-York Evangelical Missionary Society. 2526

Fourth annual report of the directors of the Penitent Female's Refuge. 13916

The fourth annual report of the Female Missionary Society of the Western District. 1216

The fourth annual report of the managers of the Auxiliary New-York Bible and Common Prayer Book Society. 172

Fourth annual report of the managers of the New York Asylum for Lying-in Women. 30036

The fourth annual report of the managers of the Society for the Prevention of Pauperism. 6819

Fourth annual report of the managers of the Society for the Reformation of Juvenile Delinquents. 40478

Fourth annual report of the Marine Bible Society of New York. 2106

Fourth annual report of the Massachusetts Domestic Missionary Society. 9422

Fourth annual report of the Massachusetts Peace Society. 2177

Fourth annual report of the Massachusetts Sabbath School Union. 39528

The fourth annual report of the Missionary Society of the Methodist Episcopal Church. 13316

Fourth annual report of the New Hampshire Auxiliary Colonization Society. 34445

The fourth annual report of the New York Protestant Episcopal Missionary Society. 2535

The fourth annual report of the Providence Religious Tract Society. 40198

Fourth annual report of the Provi-dent Society for Employing the Poor. 34936

The fourth annual report of the Religious Tract Society of Baltimore. 2970

The fourth annual report of the Rhode-Island Sunday School Union. 40267

Fourth annual report of the Seamen's Union Bethel Society of Baltimore. 30557

Fourth annual report of the standing committee of the Protestant Episcopal Missionary Society in Charleston. 13882

Fourth annual report of the surgeons of the Massachusetts Charitable Eye and Ear Infirmary. 34075

Fourth annual report of the trustees of the High-School Society, of New York. 33542

Fourth annual report of the Vermont Sabbath School Union. 41375

Fourth annual report read at the anniversary of the Society [Charleston Bethel Union] 24062

Fourth annual report to the American Unitarian Association. 37459

Fourth annual report Union Board of Delegates. 10503

Fourth appendix to M. Carey's catalogue. 32585

Fourth auditor's balances. 41122

The fourth class book. 33220; 38615

Fourth memorial of Joseph W. Brackett and Samuel Leggett. 11972

The Fourth of July anticipated. 11753

Fourth of July 1829. Laying the cornerstone of one of the eastern locks of the Chesapeake and Ohio Canal. 38129

Fourth of July, 1821. Order of performances at the North Meeting House. 6696

Fourth of July. Order of performances at the North Meet-

ing House, July 4, 1825.
22184
Fourth report of the American
Bible Society. 95
The fourth report of the Amer-
ican Sunday School Union.
31968; 31969
The fourth report of the Balti-
more Female Union Society.
4537
Fourth report of the Bank for
Savings in the City of New
York. 11677
Fourth report of the Board of Di-
rectors of the Presbyterian
Education Society. 10008
Fourth report of the directors of
the American asylum, at
Hartford. 93
The fourth report of the General
Baptist Missionary Society.
5430
Fourth report of the New-York
Bethel Union. 21679
The fourth report of the New-
York Female Union Society.
2530
Fourth report of the New York
Sunday School Union Society.
2546
The fourth report of the Philadel-
phia Sunday and Adult School
Union. 6463
The fourth report of the United
Foreign Missionary Society.
7032
Fourth report of the Washington
Asylum Society. 4184
Fourth supplement of volume II
[Library Company of Philadel-
phia] 1958
The fox and the grapes. 20298
Foxe's book of martyrs. 33225;
38620
Fra tante angoscie e palpiti.
13059
Fragen und Antworten über die
Christliche Lehre. 20545
Fragments: From the celebrated
Opera of Norma. 381
Frances & James; or, Examine
yourselves. 28906
Frances Felix. 36305

Frances, the orphan girl. 33226
Francis Berrian, or The Mexican
Patriot. 24552
Francis Comparet. 41123
Francis Henderson. 31263; 36306
Francis Larche. 26997; 26998;
36307
Francis Preston. 26999; 36308
Francis Tennill. 41124
Francis Valle et al. 27000;
36309
Frank; or, Who's the croaker?
1272
Frank, a sequel to Frank in ear-
ly lessons. 8593; 8594
The Frankfort waltz. 13320
Franking privilege to post mas-
ters. 27001
The Franklin almanac. 1279;
1280; 5361; 5362; 8727; 8728;
12578; 12579; 16178; 16179;
16180; 16181; 20552; 20553;
20554; 24572; 24573; 24574;
28908; 28909; 28910; 28911;
28912; 33238; 33239; 33240;
33241; 33242; 38622; 38623;
38624; 38625
Die Franklin Harmonie. 6671
The Franklin Institute of the
State of Pennsylvania. 20558
The Franklin Magazine almanac.
1281; 5366; 8729
The Franklin miscellany. 28907
The Franklin primer. 24575;
28914
The Franklin spelling book 8730
Franklin's letters to his kins-
folk. 8546
Franklin's Way to wealth. 1276
Fraud in the resale of public
lands. 27002
Frauds upon the revenue. 41125
Frederick Brainerd Bridgman, a
modern pioneer missionary.
30767
Frederick D. Tschiffely. 27003
Frederick de Algeroy, the hero
of Camden Plains. 20636
Frederick Onstine. 31264; 36310
The Fredoniad. 28792
The Fredonian waltz. 23331
Free inquiry recommended on
the subject of Freemasonry.

38413
A free letter. 15280
Free man's companion. 28917
Free masonry. 37079
Free negroes and mulattoes. 5971;
  9407
Free Negroes--District of Colum-
  bia. 31265
Free thoughts on faith. 20396
Freedom on the battle storm.
  16522
The freeman's almanack. 24578;
  24579; 28919; 28920; 33250;
  33251; 38635; 38636
The Freeman's almanack, or
  Complete farmer's calendar.
  8731; 12581; 16185; 20561
The Freeman's almanack, or
  Farmer's calendar. 8732;
  12582; 16186; 20562
The Free-Mason almanac. 20563
The freemason's monitor. 7607
Freemasonry, a covenant with
  death. 35097
Free-masonry an honorable insti-
  tution. 28665
Freemen of Rhode-Island! read,
  reflect and decide!! 5402
The Free will Baptist register
  and saint's annual visiter.
  16230; 28959; 33283; 38685
The Freewill Baptist register,
  and saint's visiter. 20599;
  24632
Der Freischütz. 4213; 33284;
  38686
The French accidence. 33221;
  33222
French and other spoliations.
  31266; 31267
The French cook. 35579
The French genders taught in six
  fables. 24718
A French grammar. 11517
French manual for the use of beginners. 24228
The French phrase book. 34777;
  40062
The French practice of medicine.
  37754
French spoliations. 24633; 28960;
  41126
Fretwell Hall. 20601

Die Freymaurerey, oder Offen-
  barung aller Geheimnisse.
  39140
Friend of my soul. 2319; 9799;
  17098; 17502
The friend of peace. 11484
Friend of youth. 11485; 14979
The friend to health. 23995
The friendless boy. 20602
Friendly advice to the unlearned.
  1325
A friendly alarm to a thoughtless
  sinner. 2971
Friendly Creek Indians. 31268
A friendly epistle to the Rev.
  Hooper Cumming. 16232
The friendly instructor. 8953
A friendly letter to a member of
  the Episcopal Church in Mary-
  land. 8777; 10505
Friendly letter to parents and
  heads of families. 28962
The Friends' almanac. 20603;
  20604; 24635; 24636
Friendship. An admired song.
  20121
From flowers which we twine for
  the temple of love. 11873;
  15417
From her whose ev'ry smile is
  love. 13762
From motives of deep interest in
  the beloved children and grand-
  children of my dear departed
  husband. 30630
From our Yearly-meeting, held
  in New York [Society of
  Friends] 1329
From our yearly meeting of wo-
  men Friends held in New
  York. 38698
From the Baltimore Morning
  Chronicle. 16239
From the Biblical Repertory.
  39004
From the Cincinnati Gazette.
  16240
From the Franklin Journal.
  37001
From the New York Statesman.
  15862
From the State Department.
  22862

Frost's astronomical calculations.
24647

The frugal housewife. 38134

Fruit and flowers. 28981

The fruits of education. 32555

Fruits of enterprize exhibited in
the travels of Belzoni. 12630;
15132; 31783

The Fudge family in Washington.
138

Fugitive poems. 33730

Fugitive poetry. 41553

Fugitive slaves. 36311

Fugitives from the United States
to Mexico. 36312

A full and authentic report of the
debates in Faneuil Hall. 8128;
8129

A full length portrait of Calvinism. 23908

Full report of the trial of Wm. F.
Hooe. 24650

Fulminea defensio violati populi
juris. 30477

Fulton--No. IV. 19953; 19954

Fulton--No. VI. 19955

Fundamental rules and regulations
of the stockholders in the New
Theatre in the city of Philadelphia. 9897

Funeral address delivered at the
Second Independent Church
Charleston: (S.C.) at the interment of Edward Peter Simons. 12686

A funeral address, delivered at
the interment of the Hon. John
Nicholas. 765

A funeral discourse commemorative of William Swinton Bennett.
16882

A funeral discourse, delivered in
the First Presbyterian Church,
Alexandria, August 27, 1820.
1529

Funeral discourse, occasioned by
the death of Mr. Nathan Warner. 38106

Funeral eulogy, on the characters
of Thomas Jefferson and John
Adams. 26138

Funeral honors by the town of
Salem. 26004

Funeral honors. Washington,
Miss. 27564

Funeral invitation. Yourself and
family are respectfully invited
to attend the funeral of Maria
Louisa. 31788

Funeral of the national administration. 38715

Funeral oration of the Emperor
Napoleon. 12632

A funeral oration on the death of
Thomas Jefferson. 26258

A funeral sermon, death of the
Hon. Charles Miller and
George Butler. 5576

A funeral sermon, delivered at
Mason, N.H., December 10,
1826. 24844; 29211

A funeral sermon occasioned by
the death of Master John
White. 17231

Funeral sermon occasioned by
the death of Miss Lephe Blanding. 18188

Funeral sermon, occasioned by
the death of Mr. Henry Miner.
35444

Funeral sermon, occasioned by
the death of the Rev. John
Summerfield. 21430

A funeral sermon occasioned by
the death of the Rev. Philip
Melancthon Whelpley. 18074

A funeral sermon, occasioned by
the death of the Rev. Urban
Cooper. 24549

A funeral sermon occasioned by
the decease of Mr. Daniel
Hutchinson. 33000

The funeral sermon of Rev. Christopher S. Morring. 25083

Funeral sermon of the Rev. Benjamin Ogburn. 29472

A funeral sermon on the death of
Captain Abikah Harding.
25039

A funeral sermon on the death of
John Adams and Thomas Jefferson. 25117

Funeral sermon on the death of
the Rev. Elisha B. Cook.
13960

A funeral sermon, on the death

of the Rev. Samuel Parker.
3300

Funeral sermon on the late Hon.
Christopher Gore. 29076

A funeral sermon preached on the
death of Col. Richard Dallam.
797

A funeral sermon, preached on
the first Sabbath in April,
1824, in the First Baptist
Church, Baltimore, Maryland.
16142

A funeral sermon, preached on
the occasion of the death of
Mrs. Hannah Miller. 34141

Funeral sermons preached at
Kings Chapel, Boston. 1284

Funeral solemnities at Dedham,
July 31, 1826. 24317

Funeral thoughts, excited by the
death of John Adams and Thos.
Jefferson. 24651

The furious priest reproved.
11669

Furs. The subscribers will pay
twenty cents in cash, or
twenty-five cents in goods.
8474

A further defence of Colonel William Lovetruth Bluster. 26085

Further remarks on the memorial of the officers of Harvard
College. 16949

Further remarks on the precedent
offered by the decision of the
Board in the case of the
Barque Richards. 15171

The Fusilears. 1343

Future punishment. 25835

Future rewards and punishments.
A sermon preached at the funeral of Moses C. Welch.
17456

Future rewards and punishments.
The substance of a discourse
before the New-England conference of Methodist ministers.
12552; 12553; 20526

G

G. T. Beyer. 36313

G. W. Perpall. 31269

Gabriel Godfroy. 41127; 41128

Gabriel W. Perpall. 27004

Gaiatonsera ionteweienstagwa ong-
we gawennontakon. 4290

Gaieties and gravities. 22297

Gaily sounds the castanet. 11874

Gainoh ne nenodowohgh neuwahn-
uhdah. 41619

Galanthe, the angel of the ruby
tower. 33437

The galaxy of wit. 24653;
28989

Gales's North-Carolina almanack.
1344; 5418; 8796; 12636;
16245; 20620; 24654; 28990;
33315; 38719

The gallant troubadour. 1346;
1347; 20621; 20622; 20623

Gallery of paintings. Descriptive
catalogue of original cabinet
paintings. 1349

Gallery of pictures... at Doggett's
repository. 20625

The gamester; a tragedy in five
acts. 2312; 21500

The gamesters; or, Ruins of in-
nocence. 35485

The gamut and time table. 16141;
20517; 33174

Ein ganz Neues Würfel-Buch ohne
Tabelle. 38721

The garden enclosed. 25667

A garden form'd by nature wild.
13688; 17543

The Garden Gate, and My Grandmother. 1356

Garden seeds, raised at Alfred,
Me. 7707

The gardener's calendar. 30696

The gardener's daughter. 33321

The garland: a collection of
juvenile poems. 21164

The garland for 1830 designed as
a Christmas and New Year's
present. 38726

The garland of flora. 38399

The garland of love. 5625; 9050;
12863

Garry Owen. 38445

Gaspard l'Avisé, comédie-anec-
dote, en un acte. 34948
Gaston de Blondeville. 25891;
25892
The gathering of the clans. 11652;
11653
Gay's chair. 1365
A gazetteer of Massachusetts.
35374
A gazetteer of the New England.
38966
A gazetteer of the state of Geor-
gia. 30590; 40405
A gazetteer of the state of New-
Hampshire. 12494
A gazetteer of the state of New-
York. 18063
A gazetteer of the state of Ver-
mont. 18190
Gazetteer of the states of Illinois
and Missouri. 11769
Gebel Teir. 40693
Geburts- und Taufschein. 1366;
5426; 8807
Gedanken eines Nachfolgers Jesu
über Christlichen Umgang.
38731
Gedanken uber die Bestimung des
Menschen, besonders in Hin-
sicht der gegenwärtigen Zeit.
16443
Geistliche Lieder... Erste und
zweyte Sammlung. 35102
Geistlicher Irrgarten. 24662
Geistliches Blumen-Gärtlein in-
niger Seelen. 14271
Das gëldene ABC für Jedermann.
21158
Das gemeinnützige Haus-Arze-
neybuch. 26020; 40361
Der gemeinnützige Landwirth-
schafts Calender. 1367; 5429;
8810; 12652; 16259; 20637;
24663; 28996; 33327; 38733
Gemeinschaftliches Gesangbuch,
zum gotteslienstlichen Gebrauch
der Lutherischen und Reformirten Gemeinden in Nord-
America. 28997; 33328;
33329
Gems in the mine. 33059
A genealogical memoir of the
family by the name of Farmer.

33123
A genealogical register, being a
record of the descendants of
Col. William Bond. 23853
A genealogical register of the
first settlers of New England.
38532
A genealogy of the families who
have settled in the North parish of Bridgewater. 15694
The genera of North American
birds. 32409
A general abridgment and digest
of American law. 12320
General abstract of the bill of
mortality for the city of Bos-
ton. 11923; 32418; 37889
General anatomy. 8052
Gen. Andrew Jackson and the
Rev. Ezra Stiles Ely. 1368;
33330
General Assembly of Ohio.
36314
A general atlas containing distinct maps of all the known
countries in the world. 1369;
13160; 20638
A general atlas containing fifty-
two maps and charts. 1370
General atlas, pub. by P. Potter.
2836
General Bolivar's grand march.
5431
General Bolivar's march. 20639
General Bolivar's waltz. 21394
General Bozzari's Greek march.
8811
General catalogue of the Theological seminary, Andover.
15106; 27870
General catalogue of the Theological Seminary, Bangor.
27958
General catalogue of the Theological seminary, Princeton.
40153
General catalogue to Robinson's
Circulating Library. 13972
The general character, present
and future prospects of the
people of Ohio. 27904
The general class-book. 37185;
41528

General collection of maps, charts, views, &c. 16260

General Congress, July Fourth, 1776. 14506

A general court martial whereof Major-General Alden Blossom is president. 16992

A general digest of the acts of the Legislature of Louisiana. 33907

General directions for collecting and preserving articles in the various departments of natural history. 40196

General Grand Royal Arch constitution for the United States of America. 28923

A general guide for practicing physicians. 13127; 13128

Gen. Harper's speech to the citizens of Baltimore. 16447

Gen. Harrison's address. 33485

A general history of birds and quadrupeds. 15336

A general history of Connecticut. 40032

General index to the laws of the United States of America. 36315

General index to the sixth and seventh volumes of the laws of Pennsylvania. 13700

A general instructor, or the office, duty, and authority of Justices of the Peace. 572

General Jackson's conduct in the Seminole war. 34723

Gen. Jackson's letter to Carter Beverley. 28314

Gen. Jackson's negro speculations. 33082

Gen. Jackson's waltz. 17099

General La Fayette. 16262

General LaFayette bugle waltz. 16726

General Lafayette. Centinel Office, 12 o'clock August 19, 1824. 16261

Gen. La Fayette. The members of the Corporation of Annapolis are invited to assemble... 15112

General La Fayette. To have been a partaker with Washington in the perils and glory of our great conflict for freedom, is a passport to our hearts. 20640

General LaFayette's grand march. [Fest] 16138

Gen. LaFayette's grand march. [Getze] 16280

Gen. LaFayette's grand march. [Hewitt] 16523

Genl. LaFayette's grand march & quick step. [Meetz] 17094

Genl. LaFayette's grand march and quick step. [Meineke] 17100

Genl. LaFayette's light infantry march. 16332

General LaFayette's march. 23336

Genl. LaFayette's reception march. 17829

Genl. LaFayette's trumpet march & quick step. 16504

General LaFayette's waltz. Arranged for the piano forte. 17808

Genl. LaFayette's waltz. Respectfully dedicated to him by H. N. Gilles. 16289

General laws of Massachusetts. 17050; 29666

General laws of the state of New York. 17373; 21656; 25547

General list of the State of Vermont, 1824. 19130

Genl. Lyman's grand march. 15598

Gen. Metcalffe. To the people of Kentucky. 33331

General Moses Hazen. 27005

General order issued, dated January 21, 1822, prescribing a uniform for the officers of infantry. 25506

General orders, regarding uniform dress. 8426

A general outline of the United States. 16263; 20641

General plan of education appointed for the South Carolina Society's Female Academy. 30671

General plan of education appointed for the South Carolina
Society's Male Academy. 30672
The general principles of English
grammar.   6599
A general prospectus of the
course of instruction, laws and
government, of the Female
Seminary in Meeting Street.
28441
General Quiroga's constitutional
march.   20642
General regulations for the army.
7214; 22863
General regulations for the gentlemen of the bar in the state of
New-Hampshire. 5432
A general report... treasurer of
the Western Shore. 21341;
29639; 34029; 39462
General return of the Army of
the United States. 10819;
10820
General return, of the Boston
Fire Department.   28230
General Stevens; or, The fancy
ball.   31930
General Thomas Flournoy. 31270
A general view of the contents of
the Old and New Testaments.
38190
A general view of the manners,
customs, and curiosities of
nations. 9916; 21886
A general view of the progress of
metaphysical, ethical, and po-
litical philosophy. 10353
A general view of the rise, prog-
ress, and brilliant achievements
of the American Navy. 33335
General Washington's letters to the
Marquis de Chastellux. 23221
General Washington's march. 1371
General Welfare: an investiga-
tion of the powers vested in
the Congress.   35379
General Winder's march. 16264
Gen. Winfield Scott. 41129
Generals of the Army. 41130
The generous chief.   13272
The genius of masonry.   1874;
33794
The genius of oblivion.   12744

Genté é qui l'uccellatore. 6133
Gentle airs.   12759
The gentleman and gardener's
kalendar. 6970
The Gentleman's amusement.
16269
The gentleman's annual pocket
remembrancer. 5435
The gentleman's medical vade-
mecum and traveling compan-
ion. 16979
The gentleman's new Pocket far-
rier.   2139; 21355; 34047
The gentleman's pocket-farrier.
12660
The gentlemen's amusement.
16270
The genuine works of Flavius
Josephus. 5734; 5735; 5736;
12967; 12968; 12969; 16747;
21076; 21077; 33736; 33737
Geographica classica. 635; 4885
Geographical and astronomical
definitions and explanations.
5276
Geographical botany of the United
States. 32250
A geographical, chronological,
and historical atlas, on a new
and improved plan.   23843
A geographical description of the
United States. 9456; 25301;
25302
A geographical description of the
world. 9457
Geographical dictionary, or uni-
versal gazetteer.   14977
Geographical exercises [Hilles]
38981
Geographical exercises; contain-
ing 10,000 questions for prac-
tical examinations. 16455
Geographical exercises... for the
use of West-town Boarding
School.   24671; 27688
A geographical present. 41364
The geographical primer. 16271
Geographical questions. 8900
Geographical, statistical and his-
torical map of Indiana. 1372
Geographical tickets, designed to
accompany & follow the study
of Worcester's geography.

20404

A geographical view of Greece. 17235

A geographical view of the United States. 29050; 38743; 38744

A geographical view of the world. 25761; 25762; 30248; 30249; 30250; 30251; 30252; 30253; 34778; 34779; 40063

Geography for beginners. 27652; 41524

A geography for schools. 8572

Geography, for the use of schools and private students. 1145

Geography illustrated on a popular plan. 40064

Geography made easy, being a new abridgment of the American universal geography. 2343

A geography of New Hampshire. 41419

Geography of the Bible. 37414

Geography; or, A description of the world. 15; 4397; 11526; 19367; 23413; 27774; 31884

Geological and agricultural survey of Rensselaer county. 8587

A geological and agricultural survey of the district adjoining the Erie canal. 16033

Geological essay on the Tertiary formations in America. 12546

Geological essays; or, an Enquiry into some of the geological phenomena to be found in various parts of America. 1547

A geological nomenclature for North America. 33039

A geological survey of the County of Albany. 60; 7768

Geological survey of the environs of Philadelphia. 26246

A geometric system for the measurement of the area of a circle. 24965

George and William Bangs. 36316

George Barnwell, a novel, founded on fact. 26162; 35442

George Barnwell, or The London merchant. 9272; 16907

George Blenkenship. 36317

George Johnston and others. 27006; 36318

George Mason. 38598

George Merchant. 27007

George Mills. 29007

George P. Frost. 36319

George Washington. LaFayette's first grand waltz. 19770

George Wilson. 31272

George Wilson and his friend. 20651

The Georgetown United Blues slow march. 21163

Georgia, a poem. 616

Georgia and Florida. 36321

The Georgia and South-Carolina almanack. 1376; 5448; 8819; 8820; 12663; 20664; 24681; 29016; 38750

Georgia and the general government. 24675

The Georgia delegation to the Secretary of War. 24682

Georgia lands occupied by the Cherokee Indians. 36322

Georgia militia claims. 31271

Georgia. Report adopted by the Legislature. 36320

Georgia resolutions. 24676

The Georgian maid. 4720

Geraldine, or Modes of faith and practice. 5888; 16974

Gerard and Hypolite Chretien. 22864

German air. 12854

The German alphabet. 8822

German popular stories. 24752; 33441

German waltz. 5450; 6405

Il. Germoglio. Rondo. 8823

Germs of thought. 7689

Gertrude of Wyoming. 659

Gesänge bey der Antrittspredigt unsers vielgebieten Lehrers. 8534

Gesungen mit Musik am Christag. 16441

Giddy Gertrude; a story for little girls. 1379

Gideon's three hundred men. 26012

The gift of friendship. 38756

Gift to good children. 3295

Gil Blas. 25095

Gilbert Ainslie; or, The Moss-side family. 10039

Gilbert C. Russell. 27008

Giles Egerton. 31273

Giles Scroggins' ghost. 10070

Gilley's improved primer. 24693

Giovanni Sbogarro. 2558

The gipsy babes. 30593

Giuseppino, an occidental story. 8170

Give me again that look of love. 7543

The giver more blessed than the receiver. 12452

A glance at Dean's 120 reasons for being a Universalist. 37070

A glance at the times. 29027

The glass of whiskey. 20682

Gleanings: consisting of extracts from the writings of Edward Rushton. 40330

Gleanings of religion. 38074

Gloomy winter's now awa. 14144

The glory and importance of the Gospel. 25287

The glory of Christ given to the ministry. 33958

The glory of the latter house. 35089a

A glossary to Say's Entomology. 22203

Go it, Jerry. 28540

"Go let me weep." 9544; 13387

Go my love. A rondo. 19742; 19743

Go then--'tis vain. 8072; 8073

Go youth beloved. 8074

Gobinet's instruction of youth in Christian piety. 1397

God is there! A sacred melody. 11982

The God of the Jews and Christians. 33364

God save America. 8808; 12650

"God shall send them strong delusion." 197

God the author of all things. 37562

God the proper object of gratitude. 19493

God the Saviour of all men. 29705

God's blessing on His own institutions. 41614

God's government and consolation of his people. 16247

God's praises sung. 2672

God's presence and blessing in his house. 12313

God's revenge against adultery. 37128

God's revenge against duelling. 4233; 7617a; 31701

God's revenge against gambling. 11387

God's revenge against murder. 14865

God's ways, not as our ways. 5084

Godfrey Hall: or, Prudence and principle. 29030

Godliness the nation's hope. 37259

The golden calf. 7875

The golden casket. 33354

Golden opportunities! J. B. Yates & A. M'Intyre, managers of the Delaware State Lottery. 22112

A golden treasury for the children of God. 4751; 4752; 4753; 4754; 23851

The golden violet. 29451

Goldsmith's Natural history. 24704; 33366; 33367; 38768

Goldsmith's Roman history. 1403; 1404; 20694a; 24705; 24706; 24707; 33368

Good and bad Luck. 1409

The good and faithful servant approved and honoured by his Divine Master. 24213

The good boy. 20699

The good boy's soliloquy. 1410; 8854

The good child's little hymn book. 38771

Good child's soliloquy. 31974

Good counsel; or, The advantages of useful employment in early life. 20700

Good examples for boys. 20701

Good examples for children. 33373

The good girl. 20702

The good girl's soliloquy. 1411

The good grandmother and her offspring. 5609

A good hope in death. 11472

Good Jackson times. 20703

A good joke. 20704

The Good man. 3422

Good men the protection and ornament of a community. 25656

The good minister. 7673

The Good-natured little boy. 16319; 20705; 24714

Good news from a far country. 34626

The good pastor. 24913

Good reasons for not being a Baptist. 912

Good reasons for not being a Congregationalist. 963

A good wife; or, The character of Elizabeth Markum. 1412a

The goodness of Providence, illustrated in several interesting cases. 16320

The gooseberry bush. 33394

Goslington Shadow. 20200; 20201

The Gospel according to Mathew, translated into the Cherokee language. 37778

The gospel according to Paul. A sermon. 37744

The gospel according to Saint Luke, translated into the Mohawk tongue. 28113

The Gospel an antidote to affliction and death. 79

The Gospel call. 17953

Gospel Communion. 731

The Gospel hymn-book. 38476

The Gospel, its own witness to the conscience. 20354; 24386; 24387

The Gospel Mason, or the beauty of unity. 5750

Gospel melodies. 5470

Gospel melodies, and other occasional poems. 13424

The gospel minister's farewell. 507

The Gospel ministry a display of divine benevolence. 20823

The gospel of a joyful sound. 12813

The gospel of Christ, its effi-ciency and the conversation becoming it. 23953

The Gospel preached to the poor. 14986

A gospel salutation in true Christian love. 27637; 31736

Gospel sonnets. 1899

The Gospel, the only medium of salvation. 21069

The Gospel the wisdom of God. 30690

Gospel to be preached boldly. 1094

Gospel truth accurately stated and illustrated. 28302

The gospel worthy of all acceptation. 1339

The gossip. 12159; 15775

Gotham and the Gothamites. 12971

Gott gewidwete Dank-Empfindungen bey der Ecksteinlegung der zu erbauenden Reformirten Salems¦ Kirche nahe bey Hägerstaun. 8865; 10075

Gott ist die Liebe. 29438

Gott ist die reinste liebe. 8591

The governess. 30594

Government of Florida. 27009

The government of God desirable. 28089

The government of God universal. 30324

Govr. Brook's grand march. 1436

Governor Eustis's march. 16367

Governor Eustis's quick step. 16368

Gov. Gibbs' march and quick step. 3193; 6776

Governor Joseph C. Yates grand march. 9454

Governor Knight's march. 3194

Governor Lewis's waltz. 1582

The governor of Florida. 33397

Governor Worthington's speech on the Maryland test act. 19336

The Governor's communication of the 4th February, 1823. 13229

Governor's election. The Occupant laws. 32926

Governor's letter transmitting a report of the Joint Committee of both houses of the general assembly of Ohio. 6333

Governor's message [Maine] 13196

Governor's message [Mississippi] 34156

Governor's message. [New Hampshire] 2433

Governor's message delivered to the legislature of Pennsylvania. 9843

Governor's message. Fellow-Citizens of the Senate, and House of Representatives. [Mississippi] 39608

Governor's message. Fellow-citizens of the Senate and of the House of Representatives. [Kentucky] 5756

Governor's message. General Assembly May Session. 8429

Governor's message. Gentlemen of the Senate, and of the House of Representatives December 6th, 1826. 25624

Governor's message in reply to the resolutions adopted in the House of Representatives on the motion of Mr. Breckinridge. 21106

Governor's message. Nov. 21, 1826. 23439

Governor's message relative to the Salem Mozart Association. 29668

The Governor's message, respecting fines and forfeitures. 13230

Governor's message to the General Assembly of Ohio. 17476

Governor's message to the General Assembly of the State of Georgia. 20655; 20656; 20657

Governor's message to the House of Representatives, January 9, 1829. State of Maine. 39393

Governor's message to the Senate and House of Representatives of the Commonwealth of Pennsylvania. 13701

Governor's message, to the Senate and House of Representatives of the state of Ohio. 21727

Governor's message transmitting

accounts of the commissioners and engineer on the Western Railway. 34056

Governor's message, transmitting the report of the canal engineer, on the subject of a canal at the Falls of Ohio. 17477

Governor's message, with accompanying documents, relative to the probable trade of the proposed Delaware and Raritan Canal. 39762

Governor's speech. Communication of Gov. Enoch Lincoln. 33974

Governor's speech. Gentlemen of the Council. 31598; 37004

Grace and truth. 5884

The Grace of God manifested in the experience of Eliza Nares. 8867; 12712

Graduate price of public lands. 36323

Graham Hamilton. 9229

Gramachree Molly. 5475

Gramàtica completa de la lingua inglesa. 22360

Gramática de la lengua castellana. 15899

Gramática inglesa, reducida a veinte y dos lecciones. 31569

Grammaire Française. 1938; 33842

A grammar, in which the orthography, etymology, syntax and prosody of Latin language are minutely detailed. 10410

Grammar made easy and interesting; or, A practical grammar of the English language. 33525

A grammar of astronomy. 22488; 26228

A grammar of botany. 10296

A grammar of chemistry, adapted to the use of schools and private students. 20155

Grammar of chemistry, on the plan of the Rev. David Blair. 8415

A grammar of chemistry. By the Rev. D. Blair. 13767; 30254

A grammar of composition. 14019

A grammar of logic and intellectual philosophy. 9136

A grammar of natural and experimental philosophy. 9917; 9918; 9919; 25763

A grammar of rhetoric, and polite literature. 1780; 5710; 24975

A grammar of the English language. 4941

A grammar of the French language [Berard] 23759

A grammar of the French language [Wanostrocht] 7567; 19180; 23205; 31656; 41423

A grammar of the French tongue. 9883; 40029

A grammar of the Greek language; originally composed for the college-school at Gloucester. 1766; 33402

A grammar of the Greek language; translated from the French. 19901

Grammar of the Hebrew language. 35432

A grammar of the Italian language. 37537

Grammar of the language of the Lenni Lenape or Delaware Indians. 31846

A grammar of the Latin language. 41633

A grammar of the Massachusetts Indian language. 8611

A grammar of the Modern Greek language. 34413

A grammar of the Spanish language. 9171; 21079; 29385; 39168

Grammar simplified. 1450; 5496; 8888; 16341; 24741; 29073; 33420; 33421

Grammatical exercises; being a plain and concise method of teaching English grammar. 8791

Grammatical exercises, on the moods, tenses, and syntax of the Latin language. 14009

The grammatical key. 7665; 11422

Grammatical questions adapted to Murray's Grammar. 1422; 11974

A grammatical system of the English language. 7770; 7771; 19391

Grammatical tables. 11981

Granby. A novel. 25115

Grand & splendid bobolition of slavery. 7749

Grand Annual Communication at Lexington. 1294

Grand artillery march. 19988

Grand Austerlitz march. 20799

Grand bobalition or great anniversary fussible. 5476

The Grand Canal celebration ball. 23332

The Grand Canal march. 16288; 20733

The Grand Canal waltz. 13954

Grand cavalry march. 1864

Grand celebration ob de bobalition ob African slavery!!! 20734

Grand Chapter of Massachusetts. 1304

Grand dinner. 20735

Grand Lodge de L'état de la Louisiane. 16196

Grand lodge of free and accepted Masons of Massachusetts. 1303; 8752; 12595; 20577; 28937

Grand Lodge of Free and Accepted Masons of the state of Maine. 28931

Grand Lodge of Kentucky, Friday, August 30th, 5822. 8742

Grand Lodge of Pennsylvania quarterly communication. 24621; 24622

Grand Lodge of the District of Columbia. At the annual communication of the Grand Lodge. 38639

Grand Lodge of the most ancient and honourable fraternity of free and accepted Masons of Pennsylvania. 1314; 5396; 8761

Grand Lodge of the most ancient and honorable fraternity of Free and Accepted Masons of the Commonwealth of Massachusetts. 5384; 33265

Grand Lodge of the Most Ancient
and Honorable Fraternity of
Free and Accepted Masons, of
the State of Maine. 8749; 12591;
16198; 20575; 24601; 33262;
38645;

Grand lodge of the most Ancient
and honorable society of Free
and accepted Masons, of the
State of Maine. 1298

Grand march & quick step of the
5 Regt.   16771

Grand march for the piano forte.
[Barber] 32204

Grand march for the piano forte.
[Klemm]   16819

Grand march from the opera of
Tancredi. 22128; 22129; 22130

Grand march in Bastile and
Turkish march. 20393

The grand march in Pizzarro.
9184

Grand march.   Performed at the
ceremony of completing the
battle monument in Baltimore.
8836

Grand march, waltz & rondo.
12266

Grand minuet.   12829

Grand oratorios, for the benefit
of the Philadelphia orphan
asylum.   1423

Grand quick step.   4211; 19217

Grand Royal Arch Chapter of
Maine.   5383

Grand Royal Arch Chapter of Massachusetts. 5385; 8753; 12596;
16206; 20578; 24604; 28935;
28936; 33266; 38650; 38651

The Grand Royal Arch Constitution
for the State of North-Carolina.   16218

Grand solar microscope. 38805

A grand sonata.   18086

Grand sport.   At the new tavern
in South Salem. 8868

Grand state lottery, for the improvement of internal navigation.   82

Grand State Lottery, of Pennsylvania.   1424

The grand theme of the Christian
preacher.   7697; 7698; 7699;

7700

The grand theme of the Gospel
ministry. 29066

Grande sonate pour le pianoforte.
3317

De grandest bobalition dat ever
vus be!! 29058

The grandmother's gift. 1425

Grandpapa's drawer opened.
33403

Granium gazette.   8870

Grants of land under Quapaw
Treaty. 31274

Graphical representation of the
coronation regalia of the Kings
of England. 20736

Gratitude always a duty.   1071

The grave.   A poem. 11903

The grave of Byron, with other
poems.   25160

The graves of the Indians, and
other poems. 29060

Gray's elegy in a country church
yard.   24733

Gray's letters & poems.   5490;
29061

Gray's narrative. 20740

"Great Anniversary Festival."
Philadelphia, July 5, 1776.
1441

The Great Chain of Truth. 2567

Great Christian doctrine of original sin defended.   20376;
33051

Great democratic and anti-tariff
meeting of the young men of
Portland. 34847

Great effects from little causes,
illustrated. 16337

Great effects result from little.
causes. 2827; 13817

The great moral duties of a free
and independent people. 26000

Great moral picture, the Court
of death. 1446

Great national object. 9224

Great official news. 35551

The great question answered--
What shall I do to be saved?
20616

Great Republican Meeting Rochester. 34388

The greatest sermon that ever

was preached. 11437; 23334

Grecian captive; or, The fall of Athens. 9721

Grecian daughter, a tragedy. 13427

The Grecian history. 8848; 8849; 8850; 8851; 12693; 16312; 24701; 24702; 24703; 29035; 33369

Grecian rondo. 16286

The Grecian waltz. 12715

The Grecian wreath of victory. 16338

Greece, in 1823 and 1824. 20819

A Greek and English dictionary. 33445; 38810

A Greek and English lexicon: adapted to the authors read in colleges. 40074

A Greek and English lexicon of the New Testament. 22113

The Greek ball. 19289

Greek course. 28653

Greek emancipation. 15918

Greek grammar. 8229; 15613; 23982

A Greek grammar of the New Testament. 23354

A Greek lexicon, adapted to the New Testament. 33916

The Greek lexicon of Schrevelius. 26022

The Greek march of liberty. 18180

The Greek reader. 12940; 29345; 29346; 39115; 39116

The Greek revolution. 16023; 16024

Greek tables. 10433

The green man. 39162

The Green-Mountain songster. 12718

The Green River almanac. 12719

The green room remembrancer. 33423

Green's New-England almanack, and farmer's friend. 20756; 20756a

Greene County almanack. 29072; 33418

The Greene County farmer's almanac. 5495

Gregory Strahan. 27010

Grigg's almanack. 16350

Grigg's city and country almanack. 38845

Grigg's Southern and Western songster. 38843

Griggs & Dickinson's American primer. 33439; 38844

The grocer's guide. 1463

Das grosse A B C - Buch. 1569

The grounds of a holy life. 10493

The grounds of the Christian's love to the church. 9529

Growth and manufacture of silk. 36324

Growth in grace. 1416

Grundverfassung der Evangelisch Lutherischen General Synode. 1129

The guards. A novel. 29095

Guatimala. 33021

Guess again! 24762; 38869

A guide for the home-domestick manufacturer. 5779

A guide for young disciples of the Holy Savior. 13779

Guide to acquaintance with God. 40404

A guide to Christ. 30715

The guide to domestic happiness. 16287

The guide to health. 21692

A guide to men and manners. 4971

A guide to national improvement. 12955

Guide to prayer. 4199

A guide to the English language. 1701; 5652

Guide to the Lord's Supper. 22404

A guide to the reading and study of the Holy Scriptures. 12575; 33231

A guide to the study of arithmetic and grammar. 11983

A guide to the true knowledge of Christian baptism. 31638

A guide to true peace. 1220

Guido, a tale. 33067

Guillermo Tell, o la Suiza libre. 25300

The guilt and danger of religious error. 5871

Guilt and punishment increased by abused privileges. 13082

Gunn's circular. To the voters of Knox and Anderson Counties. 38872

Gustavus Vasa. 15560

Gut gemeinter Rath an meine Deutscher Landsleute. 1345

Guy Mannering or the astrologer. 3135; 3136; 6741; 6742; 10198; 10199; 14059; 17916

Guy Mannering; or, The gipsy's prophecy! 14269; 14270

Guy's exercises in orthography. 16361

Gymnasium. The undersigned Committee, appointed to effect the establishment of a Gymnastic School in Boston. 23877

H

H. P. Cathell. 36325

Had I a heart. 1970

Hadad. A dramatic poem. 20891

The Hagerstown town and country almanack. 5513; 8915; 12741; 16369; 20778; 24773; 29104; 33452; 38878

Hail Columbia! 13759

Hail! LaFayette! 17860

Half an hour's amusement at York and James-Town. 15104

Half century discourse, delivered November 16, 1828. 40286

Half-century sermon; delivered at Warren March 8, 1822. 14190

A half century sermon, delivered at West-Hartford, on the 13th day of October, 1822. 9880; 13732

Halidon Hill. 10200; 10201

Hall of Union Lodge, No. 2, Madison, Indiana. 1292

Hallowell, Augusta & Bangor Mail stage. 23971

Hambly and Doyle. 27011

Hamilton. 8278; 8279; 12060; 12061; 12068; 19956; 19957; 19958; 19959; 19960; 19961; 19962; 19963; 19964; 19965; 19966; 19967; 19968; 15662; 15663; 15664; 15665; 15666; 15667; 15668; 15669; 24010

Hamlet. 3181; 10234

Hamlet travestie. 2806

Hampton L. Boon. 31275

The hand of Providence manifested. 8929

Handbuch für Deutsche. 33471

Handel's water music. 8932

The handsome horse Whip, will stand the ensuing season. 40100

Hannah, an authentic narrative of a Sabbath scholar. 38909

Hannah Jane: or, First reading lessons for children. 33474

Hannon's Georgia & South Carolina almanack. 1505

Hanoverian waltz. 16559

Happiness: a tale for the grave and the gay. 8935; 8936

The Happy boatman. 1506

The happy children. 29134

The happy choice; a sermon occasioned by the death of Mrs. Mallett. 16579

The happy choice: or, Potters' common. 22270

The happy cottagers. 1507

Happy days. 38911

The happy family. 32570

The happy harvest. 3304

Happy land. 3024

The happy man, and True gentleman. 4291

The happy man; or, The life of William Kelly. 1508

The happy nation. 21740

A happy New Year. Adapted to the favorite Scottish air. 12767

"A happy new Year" is tendered by the carrier of the Western Sun & General Advertiser. 27761

The Happy novice. 8937

Happy poverty. 5539

The Happy ship carpenter. 1509

Happy tawny Moor. 19460; 19461

The happy villager. 399

The happy waterman. 6114; 8938; 8939; 17225; 39637

The harbingers of the Reformation. 40426

Harbor of St. Mark's, Florida. 41131

Harbor of Stonington. 36326

Harbors - Marblehead & Holmes' Hole. 27012

Harbour Telegraph signals. 39964

Hardcastle's annual Masonic calendar. 5540; 8940; 12768

Hardcastle's annual Masonic register. 1510

Hard-scrabble calendar. 16405

Hark, I hear the bugles ring. 16583

Hark I hear the eve'ning drum. 17973

Hark, the bonny Christ Church bells. 19389

Hark! the vesper hymn is stealing. 6876; 6877; 14207

Hark! 'tis the breeze. 22144

Das harmonische Abend-Lied. 16435

Harmonisches gesangbuch. 1520; 1521; 29139

The harmony of Christians, the glory of God. 919; 5119; 8483

The harmony of divine and heavenly doctrines, demonstrated in sundry declarations on a variety of subjects. 9836

The harp in softly pleasing strains. 3327

The harp of Bendemeer. 19441

The harp of Columbia, or The American warbler. 20817

The harp of Delaware. 33895

The Harp of love. 8944; 11441

The harp of the beech woods. 10496

The harp of Zion. 29140

The harp that once through Tara's halls. 22376

The harper of the mull. 10299

The harper's song. 4280; 7657-7659; 11420; 14909

Harriet and her cousin; or, Prejudice overcome. 29142; 29143

Harriet and her scholars; a Sabbath school story. 33479

Harris and Farrow. 31276; 36327

Harry. 12779

Harry and Lucy. 5229; 20371

Harry Beaufoy; or, The pupil of nature. 33451

Harry Hobart. 33486

Hartford-bridge. 9830

Hartford city directory. 33488

The Hartford County Missionary Society present the following address. 8957

Hartford selection of hymns. 3358; 6908; 14231

Harvard University. Catalogue. 29163

The harvest festival. 24845

Harvest Home meeting of Chester and Montgomery Counties. 33494

The harvest home; or, The good farmer. 38930

Haste! haste! I pr'ythee haste away. 17299; 21587

"Haste idle time." 5533; 12756; 16391

Hasten, love! the sun hath set. 17432

Hasty-pudding; a poem. 323; 7959

The haunted inn. 39981

The haunted tower. 28527; 32743

Haupt Inhalt des Christlichen Lehre. 5559

Have you not seen the timid tear. 16524

Haverhill Social Library catalogue. 5560

Hawney's complete Measurer. 1546; 8975

Haydn's andante. 16487

Haydn's celebrated canzonet. 12792

He "lies like truth." 33773

He olelo no ke kanawai. 29173

Head of Medusa. 30319

Headlands in the life of Henry Clay. 29184

Health ordinances of the Corporation of the city of Baltimore. 15164

The heart of a woman. 15941

The heart of man, either a

temple of God, or a habitation
of Satan. 8988; 33512
Heart of Midlothian. 6743; 32978
The heart which condemneth not.
28526
The heart's ease. 1656
The Hearts of steel. 21279
Heaven lost. 7975
Heaven on earth. 22011
Heaven open to all men, condi-
tionally. 23454; 24824a
Heaven opened; or, A brief and
plain discovery of the riches
of God's covenant of Grace.
23453; 31938
The heavenly doctrine of the New
Jerusalem. 3373; 3374; 3375;
35448
The heavenly pilot. 8989
The heavenly sisters. 10244;
10245
A Hebrew and English lexicon of
the Old Testament. 16281
The Hebrew Bible. 8012
Hebrew canticles. 2725
A Hebrew Chrestomathy. 35433;
40570
A Hebrew grammar. 6912; 14233
The Hebrew mourner. 9545;
13388
The Hebrew student's pocket com-
panion. 12618
The hedge of thorns. 3204; 3205;
6787; 17964; 17965
Heidelbergh Catechism. 8991;
16500
Die heilige liebe Gottes und die
unheilige naturliebe nach ihren
unterschiedenen wirkungen.
33449
The heir at law. 818
The heir of the world. 38520
Heirs, &c. of William Drayton.
36328
Heirs of Caron de Beaumarchais.
27013
Heirs of Francis Valle. 27014
Heirs of Jean Baptiste Couture.
41132
Heirs of Joseph Jeans. 27015
Heirs of Louis de la Houssaye.
27016
Heirs of Philip Renaut. 36329

Heirs of Robert Fulton. 41133
Helen de Tournon. 10313
Helen Maurice. 33518
Helen of the glen. 21924; 30289;
40104
A hell for all the wicked, clearly
proved. 33185
Helon's pilgrimage to Jerusalem.
22395
Help from on high. 16282
Help to faith. 35100
A help to the Gospels. 38959
Helpless animals. 13666
Henderson's almanack. 1562;
5574; 8993; 12810
The Henriade of Voltaire. 14798
Henrich Stillings Alter, von ihm
selbst geschrieben. 5737
Henry and Eliza, a pathetic tale.
37094
Henry Bedinger. 27017; 36330
Henry Eckford. 41134
Henry Freeman. 27018
Henry G. Rice. 31277; 31278
Henry Huttleston. 36331
Henry Lee. 27019
Her hand were clasp'd. 4510
The herald of knowledge. 10459
Herbert Lacy. 33868
Here we meet too soon, to part.
3061; 13995; 13996; 17856;
17857; 17858; 22131
The hermit in London. 2050;
2051
The hermit in Philadelphia. 7561
The hermit in the country. 2052
The hermit of the forest. 1575
Hero and Leander. 16688
The hero of No fiction. 11749
Herodotus. 33534
Herr Cline's favorite dance La
Sabotiere. 38201
Der Herumträger des Unabhängi-
gen Republicaners an seine
Gönner beym Antritt des neuen
Jahres. 16513; 20868
Der Herumtraeger des Wahren
Amerikaners an seine geehrten
Rurden, beym Eintritt des
Neuen Jahrs. 20869
Hey dance to the fiddle & tabor.
12864
Das Herz des Menschen, ein

Tempel Gottes oder eine Wek-
stätte Satans. 9006; 12819;
24839; 29206; 38964
Heselrigge, or, The death of Lady
Wallace. 28719
Hibernicus; or, Memoirs of an
Irishman. 33538
A Hieroglyphical Bible. 406; 407;
408; 409; 11807
High church principles opposed to
the genius of our republican
institutions. 40269
The high churchman vindicated.
24870; 24871
High life; a novel. 29207
High life below stairs: a farce.
16254
Highest yet! Sam's last jump.
38973
A Highland laddie heard of war.
4721; 4722; 8075; 19744
Highland Mary. 12825
The Highlanders. 16533
The highlands. 27528
The Highway of all Nations. 1261
High-ways and by-ways. 16333;
20737; 29059
La hija del lechers. 35035
Hill and Moore's improved edi-
tion of the New-Hampshire
Register. 5585
Hill's Tennessee almanac. 20893;
24848
Der Himlische Wandersmann,
Oder Eine Beschreibung vom
Menschen der in Himmel
kommt. 32517
Hinda's appeal to her lover.
16800; 16801; 21114
Hinterlassene predigten, von Jo-
hann Georg Lochman. 33890
Hints for a general union of
Christians for prayer. 5589
Hints for American husbandmen.
30185
Hints for general union of Chris-
tians for prayer for the out-
pouring of the Holy Spirit.
12831
Hints for the improvement of
early education. 1624; 5596;
12840; 24864; 24865; 24866;
24867; 29231

Hints for the people, with some
thoughts on the presidential
election. 14024
Hints on banking. 29585
Hints on extemporaneous preach-
ing. 19186; 27553; 27554
Hints on female education. 34016
Hints on missions. 12394
Hints on public worship. 29219
Hints on the establishment and
regulation of Sunday schools.
5590
Hints on the importance of the
study of the Old Testament.
30790
Hints on the neglect of the Lord's
Supper. 19892
Hints to lawyers. 1595
Hints to mothers & infant school
teachers. 38983
Hints to my countrymen. 26040
Hints to parents. 20894
Hints to Pennsylvania Democrats.
24852
Hints to the farmers of Rhode Is-
land. 1596; 37997
Hints to young people on the du-
ties of civil life. 17241;
25433
His Excellency John Brooks,
Medford, Mass. Sir, at the
request of Mr. E.I. du Pont.
5166
Historia de la destruccion de los
templarios. 32012
Historia de Mejico. 32840
Historiarum liber primus et se-
lecta quaedam capita. 39309
Historical account of Christ
Church, Boston. 16036
Historical account of the First
Presbyterian Church and So-
ciety in Newburyport, Massa-
chusetts. 27667
Historical account of the North
American Indians. 4862
An historical account of the Prot-
estant Episcopal Church, in
South-Carolina. 941
A historical and classical atlas.
32450
Historical and critical observa-
tions on syphilis. 12970

Historical and descriptive lessons, embracing sketches of the history, character and customs of all nations. 33553

Historical and literary botany. 24670

A historical and mythological chart. 23902

The historical annals of Cornelius Tacitus. 40596

An historical atlas, containing the following charts. 27702; 31809; 37240

An historical catechism for children & youth. 27573

Historical collections. 8985

An historical discourse, delivered at Brookfield, Mass. 38603

An historical discourse, delivered at West Springfield. 22351

An historical disquisition concerning the knowledge which the ancients had of India. 10121; 40295

Historical documents and critical remarks on Unitarianism and Mahometanism. 1213

Historical eulogy of M. le Marquis de Laplace. 38614

Historical letters, including a brief but general view of the history of the world. 5039

An historical map of Palestine. 33671

Historical memoirs, of Napoleon. 2386; 2387

A historical narrative containing a brief sketch of the work of God in New-England. 14228

A historical narrative of the civil and military services of Major-General William H. Harrison. 15942

Historical notice of Saint Peter's Church of Perth Amboy. 20027

Historical notices, confession of faith, and covenant with the ecclesiastical principles and rules, and list of members, of the Congregational Church in Somers, Conn. 26102

Historical notices of Saint John's Church, Elizabeth-Town, New-Jersey. 22154

Historical notices of the New North Religious Society in the town of Boston. 8610

A historical outline of the American Colonization Society. 18068

Historical outline of the controversy respecting the text of the three heavenly witnesses. 12031

The historical pocket-book. 12832

Historical questions on the Kings of England. 1597

The historical reader. 4742; 11904; 15465; 19764; 23844; 28198; 28199; 32395; 37864

Historical religious events. 32205

Historical scenes in the United States. 28052

An historical sermon delivered at Brimfield. 41355

An historical sketch of Amherst. 1168

An historical sketch of the Ancient and honourable artillery company. 4278

Historical sketch of the convention of the congregational ministers in Massachusetts. 5052

A historical sketch of the formation of the confederacy. 19774; 23847

An historical sketch of the Greek revolution. 33598; 33599

An historical sketch of the various translations of the Bible. 1598

A historical sketch of Westfield. 24305

Historical sketches illustrative of the life of M. de Lafayette. 16538

Historical sketches of the rise and progress of the Methodist Society, in the City of New-York. 6897

Historical sketches: or The spirit of orthodoxy. 12541

Historical summary of the events which placed Joseph Napoleon, on the throne of Spain. 33607

Historical view of the literature of the south of Europe. 30615

An historical view of the public celebrations of the Washington Society, and those of the Young Republicans. 14837

Historico dramatic ambrosial eclogues. 1631

Historie de Charles XII. 37052

Die historie von Joseph und seinen Brudern. 37779

Historiettes morales. 25216

Historiettes nouvelles. 9355

The history and adventures of little Eliza. 20895

The history and adventures of little Henry. 20896

The history & adventures of Valentine & Orson. 20897

The history and analysis of the supposed automaton chess player. 23918

The history and mystery of Methodist episcopacy. 29559

The history and present state of the town of Newburyport. 24271

The history of a convert. 1599

History of a voyage to the China Sea. 14895; 27634

History of Agricultural Societies. 1599a

History of Alexander Selkirk, the real Robinson Crusoe. 1600

The history of all religions. 379; 4662; 15315

The history of America, by William Robertson. 6655; 10122; 10123

History of America...Mr. Everett, from the Committee of the Library. 31279

The history of an Indian woman. 552

The history of ancient Greece. 8837; 38759

History of Andover. 37344

The history of Andrew Dunn. 29220

History of animals. 16539; 20898; 20899; 24854; 33554

History of beasts. 16540; 20900; 20901; 24855

The history of beasts & birds. 9012; 33555

A history of Belfast. 31734

The history of Betsey Brown. 29221

History of birds. 16541; 20902; 24856

The history of Blue Beard and Fatima. 16542

History of Boston. 18024; 22313; 35241

History of Bunker Hill battle. 22410; 26164; 30750

The history of Capt. Thomas Parismas. 16543

The history of Charles XII. 11321; 23182; 37053; 41400

History of chivalry. 25375

The history of Chelmsford. 83

History of Christ. 19678

The history of Christian martyrdom. 1270

History of Constantius and Pulchera. 5591

The history of Daniel, the prophet. 10298

The history of Dedham. 31819

History of Edward Allen. 6359

The history of Elenor Williams. 1601

History of Emily and her brothers. 3206; 6788; 10261; 30595

History of England [Grimshaw] 1460; 12727; 24754

History of England [Hume] 5655; 33610; 33611

A history of England [Lingard] 29503

The history of England [Smollett] 10302; 35237; 35238

The history of fair Rosamond. 33556

The history of fidelity and profession. 650; 4902; 19927

The history of fish. 1602

History of France. 33442; 38851

The history of George Desmond. 9013

The history of George Gilbert. 1603

The history of George Hicks. 39623

History of good children. 1604

The history of Goody Two-Shoes.
16544; 16545; 20903; 24729;
33393; 38798

The history of Greece. 13366

History of Henry Fairchild, and
Charles Trueman. 6789; 10262;
17966

The history of Henry Milner.
14110; 17967; 30596; 35179;
40406

The history of honest Roger.
24857; 24858; 33557

The history of insects. 1605

The history of Ireland. 24178

The history of Jack Horner.
1606

The history of Jacob. 1607; 9014

The history of Jacob Newman.
33558

History of Jemina Wilkinson.
5650

The history of Jenny Hickling.
31975

The history of Joe Bennett. 20904;
33559

History of John Robins. 9015;
20905; 29222

History of John Wise. 1608;
16546

The history of Jonathan Brown.
32546; 32547

History of Joseph and his brethren. 5592; 37780; 37781

The history of Joseph Andrews,
and his friend, Mr. Abraham
Adams. 33172

The history of Joseph Green.
29223

The history of Kentucky. 17026

The history of King Philip's war
[Church] 20074

The history of King Philip's war
[Drake] 1049

The history of little Fanny. 5593;
20906

The history of little George and
his penny. 3207; 10263; 17968;
17969

History of little Henry and his
bearer. 3208; 3209; 10264;
40407

History of little Jackey Horner.
1609

The history of Little Jane. 20907

The history of little Lucy, and
her Dhaye. 17970

The history of Little Red Riding-
Hood. 5842

The history of Louisiana. 29632

History of Lucy Clare. 35180

The history of Lynn. 39288

The history of Margaretta C.
Hoge. 29360

The history of Mary Saunders.
14111

The history of Mary Wood. 1610

History of Massachusetts. 8165;
19845

The history of Mathew Wald.
16931

The history of Methodism. 37849

The history of missions. 601

The history of Mrs. Williamson.
2972

The history of modern Europe
[Coote] 8445

The history of modern Europe
[Russel] 10161; 10162

The history of modern Greece.
29224

The history of my own times.
28051; 32203

The history of New England.
23358

A history of New York. 16683;
24962; 39104

The history of North Carolina.
39436

The history of Nourjahad. 10253

The history of our Lord and Saviour Jesus Christ. 5823

The history of Pennsylvania.
38799

History of Peter and John Hay.
19240

The history of Philip's war. 749;
15761; 28488; 28489; 28490;
32707; 38165; 38166

A history of Pitcairns island. 2994

History of Queen Caroline. 5594

A history of Rasselas. 1803; 9160

The history of Rinaldo Rinaldini.
19163

The history of Robinson Crusoe.
983; 12352

History of Roman literature.
28741

History of Rome. 1989; 13121;
13122; 13123; 13124; 13125

History of Russia. 24859

History of St. Domingo. 5484

The history of Sally Preston.
20908; 29225

The history of Samuel Bonner.
1611

The history of Scotland. 10124;
40296

The history of Sindbad the sailor.
33560; 38984

History of Sir William Wallace.
502; 12391; 20331

The history of Sophia Carter.
1612

The history of Stanford and Mer-
ton. 38351

The history of Susan and Esther
Hall. 4903

The history of Susan Gray.
22271; 22272; 35181

The history of Susan Green.
29226

History of ten Baptist churches.
14260; 26180; 30771

History of the adventures, love
and constancy of Paul and Virginia. 17878; 17879

History of the American colony
in Liberia. 23547

A history of the American Revolution; comprehending all the
principal events both in the
field and in the cabinet. 7782

The history of the American revolution, in Scripture style.
14151

A history of the American revolution: intended as a reading-
book for schools. 19291; 27665;
31762

History of the American troops,
during the late war. 41501

History of the Battle of Lexington. 21888

History of the beasts and birds.
38985

History of the Bible. 1613; 1614;
9016; 12833; 12834; 16547;
20909; 20910; 20911; 24860;

29227; 33561; 38986; 38987

The history of the bucaniers of
America. 24473

The history of the celebrated
Mrs. Ann Carson. 8287

The history of the children in the
wood. 1105; 15739; 20045

The history of the Christian
Church. 16742; 16743

A history of the church from its
Establishment to the present
century. 30276

History of the church of Christ
[Allen] 11576; 15062

The history of the church of
Christ [Milner] 9498

History of the Church of England.
22165

History of the coal lands. 25568

History of the colonies. 17028

A history of the county of Berkshire, Massachusetts. 38567

The history of the crusades for
the recovery and possession of
the Holy Land. 25376

The history of the decline and
fall of the Roman empire.
8824; 24686; 38753

The history of the destruction of
the city and temple of Jersua-
lem. 19881

The history of the discovery and
settlement of America. 35058;
40297

History of the discovery of America. 10489; 35563

A history of the earth, and animated nature. 12694; 20692;
20693

History of the emperors who have
reigned in Europe. 5547; 16548

History of the erysipelatous inflammation that recently appeared in the Massachusetts
General Hospital. 24823

History of the expedition to Russia. 22237; 22238

The history of the Fairchild family. 35182

A history of the fight at Concord.
30459

The history of the Floridas. 19144

History of the French revolution.

29755

History of the General or Six
Principle Baptists in Europe
and America. 25048; 29431

History of the Greek revolution.
32790; 32791; 38244

A history of the haunted caverns
of Magdelama. 5730

The history of the Holy Bible.
1615

The history of the house that Jack
built. 1616; 16596; 20959;
24899

A history of the Indian wars with
the first settlers of the United
States. 35098

The history of the Inquisition of
Spain. 25125

History of the Island of St. Domingo. 15276

The history of the late province
of New York. 26094; 40466

History of the late war between
the United States and Great
Britain. 924

The history of the life, adventures, and heroic actions of
the celebrated Sir William Wallace. 1572

A history of the life and public
services of Major General Andrew Jackson. 33562; 33563;
33564

A history of the life and voyages
of Christopher Columbus.
33676

A history of the life of the Messiah. 37963

A history of the origin and progress of the doctrine of universal salvation. 23945

History of the Patriarch Abraham.
35202

The history of the pirates. 20912;
29228; 38988

History of the political system of
Europe. 38957

A history of the principal and
most distinguished martyrs in
the different ages of the world.
37252; 41598

History of the principal events in
the life of our Lord and Sav-

ior Jesus Christ. 5595

The history of the propagation of
Christianity among the heathens
since the reformation. 4852

The history of the Prophet Samuel. 1617

A history of the proceedings of
the Board of health, of the
city of New-York. 13538

A history of the Protestant "reformation," in England and
Ireland. 20104; 20105; 20106;
20107; 24135; 24136

The history of the rebellion and
civil wars in England. 28501

History of the reformation. Being
an abridgement of Burnet's
History. 80; 11577

A history of the Reformation, in
England and Ireland. 15795

The history of the reign of George
III.   8090; 32387; 32388

The history of the reign of the
Emperor Charles V.   10125;
40298

A history of the revolutionary
war between Great Britain and
the United States. 40437

The history of the rise, increase,
and progress of the Christian
people called the Quakers.
14083

History of the rise, progress,
and existing condition of the
western canals. 4187

History of the Sandwich Islands.
38506

History of the Spanish Inquisition. 25126

A history of the state of New
York, from the first discovery.
33035

History of the state of New York,
including its aboriginal and
colonial annals. 17242; 19349

History of the states of antiquity.
33517

History of the town of Hingham,
Plymouth county, Mass.
29501

A history of the Town of Shrewsbury. 27545

The history of the tread-mill.

spectfully requested to meet at the Church. 34769

Holding fast the faithful word. 39596

A hole in the wall. 33579

Holiday tales. 39013

Holiness preferable to sin. 40703

Holst's new village rondo. 16572; 16573

The Holy Bible on baptism. 5624

Holy holy Lord. 5536; 8930; 12172

Holy Scriptures, and the observance of the first day of the week. 1652

The holy war, made by Kind Shaddai upon Diabolus. 28319

Home. 1421

Home. In verse. 29249

Home missions. 24139

Home! sweet home! 11875; 11876; 11877; 11878; 15418; 15419; 15420; 15421; 15422; 15423; 15424; 15425; 15426; 15427; 19745; 19746; 23827

Homeri Iliadis. 9045

Homeri Ilias. 24884

The honest thieves. 9070; 16827

The honey moon; A comedy. 14292

Honig's owl-tower. 39021

Honor O'Hara. 30300

Hon. Cadwallader D. Colden's reply to the Committee of inquiry on the subject of freemasonry. 38217

Hrn. D. Philip Doddridge gewesenen öffentlichen Lehrers der Gottesgelahrtheit und Rectors bey der Academie zu Northampton. 12386; 32997

Hon. J. Bledsoe's introductory lecture on law. 28202

The Hon. Littleton W. Tazewell and John Randolph, Senators from Virginia, in the Congress of the United States. 28713

Honour to the brave. It is an act of justice to our worthy candidate for mayor, Captain Carberry. 9049

Honour to the brave. Merited praise to the disinterested. 16574

Hooker's new pocket plan of the city of New York. 16577; 24885

The hoop-pole law. 29641

Hope. 22303

Hope; a poem, delivered in the chapel of Harvard University. 5929

Hope for the dying infant. 29201

Hope Leslie. 30564

The hope of immortality. 41561

The hope of liberty. 39030

Hopkinsianism unmasked. 20814

Horace in New York. 24123

Horacio Español, ó poesias liricas. 33589

Horae Paulimae, Clergyman's companion. 6368

Horrid, brutish and bloody murder. Trial and sentence of Wm. Miller. 29259

Horrid murder and suicide being an authentic account of a most tragical event, which took place in the upper part of South Carolina. 9063

Hosfords' calendar. 20958; 24896; 24897; 29260

Hours of pleasure. 12876

Hours there were. 23186-23188

House of Representatives, 1820. 2151

The House of Representatives having, at the last session of Congress, passed a resolution. 27020

House of Representatives United States. 31280

House Representatives. No. 8. Commonwealth of Massachusetts. 34057

The house servant's directory. 30468; 35055

House surgeon and physician. 1501

How blissful those moments! 9546; 13389

How Christ's ministers are made. 21424

How comes it sad minstrel. 15806

1718; 1719; 1720; 5670; 5671:
5672; 9085; 9086; 12913; 16636;
16637; 20988; 24931; 24932;
29290; 39065

Hutchings' almanac. 5666; 9082;
9083; 12904; 12905; 16624-
16626; 20982; 20983; 24922;
24923; 29280; 29281; 29282;
29283; 33625; 33626; 33627;
33628; 39058

Hutching's improved. 12906;
12907; 12908; 24924; 29284;
39059; 39060

Hutching's revived. 1714; 9084;
12909; 12910; 12911; 16627;
16628; 16629; 16630; 16631;
16632; 20984; 20985; 20986;
24925; 24926; 24927; 24928;
29285; 29286; 33629; 33630;
33631

Huzza for Gen. Jackson! Down
with the Yankees! 29295

Huzza! for Gen. Jackson!! Undeniable and conclusive reasons
why General Jackson should be
elected President. 20990

Hyacinth Bernard. 36334

El Hyder. 11751; 32224

Hydraulicus. 33482

Hymen's recruiting sergeant.
7618; 14866

Hymn Book. [Rapp] 30403

Hymn book; containing a copious
selection of hymns, and spiritual songs. 20089

Hymn book for Sunday Schools.
40194

A hymn for December 22, 1820.
1724

Hymn, for the installation of the
officers of St. Paul's Royal
Arch Chapter. 9072

The hymn of eve. 4495

The hymn of Riego. 16609; 16610

Hymn, to be sung on laying the
corner stone of the Western
Reserve College, at Hudson,
Ohio. 23297

Hymn to the blessed virgin.
12914; 12915

Hymn to the evening star. 7660

Hymns adapted to the public worship
of the Christian church. 39067

Hymns and sacred songs for the
monthly concert and similar
occasions. 11660

Hymns and songs of praise, for
children. 1725; 1726; 3392

Hymns and spiritual songs, for
the use of Christians. 1727

Hymns and spiritual songs, in
three books. 11360; 11361;
14848; 14849; 14850; 19208;
19209; 19210; 23234; 27574;
27575; 27576; 31682; 31683;
37100; 37101; 37102; 37103

Hymns and spiritual songs, original and selected [Dupuy]
20347

Hymns and spiritual songs, original and selected [Foster]
12569

Hymns and spiritual songs, selected for the use of Christians. 1728

Hymns, composed on various
subjects. 8955

Hymns for children. 8003; 9091;
29298

Hymns for church and home.
1729

Hymns for conference meetings.
9354

Hymns for family worship. 5014;
5015

Hymns for good children. 16638

Hymns for infant minds. 3393;
3394; 3395; 3396; 3397; 3398;
3399; 5454; 16285; 20667;
20668; 24688; 29019; 33350;
33351; 33352

Hymns for little children. 1730;
20991; 24689; 33636

Hymns for social and private
worship. 29299

Hymns for Sunday schools. 1731;
16334; 16639; 29300; 33637;
39068; 39069

Hymns for the Lord's supper.
1525; 5548

Hymns for the use of the New
Church. 9658; 24665; 39070

Hymns for young persons and
children. 28104

Hymns in prose. 308; 309; 311;
312; 11744; 15260; 19600;

28050; 39071
Hymns in the Seneca language.
  40140
Hymns of the Protestant Episcopal Church. 30362; 34902;
  34903; 34904; 40165; 40166;
  40167a; 40168
Hymns of Zion.   38978
Hymns on the glorious, divine
  and important theme of the religion of Jesus Christ. 1700
Hymns on the works of nature for
  the use of children. 29192
Hymns on various subjects.
  16640
Hymns, original and selected, for
  the use of Christians [Foster]
  24541; 24562; 33218
Hymns, original and selected, for
  the use of Christians [Shaw]
  30580
Hymns, original and selected for
  the use of Christians [Smith]
  18001
Hymns, psalms and spiritual songs.
  38809
Hymns, selected from various authors, for the use of the Unitarian Church in Washington.
  7030
Hymns selected from various authors, for the use of young
  persons. 24768
Hymns set forth in General conventions. 40167
Hymns sung at a union meeting of
  the Sunday schools in Wheeling.
  29301; 33638
Hymns, written and adapted to the
  weekly church service. 29186
The hypocrite. 8053; 23821

                    I

I am a stranger here. 19989
I'm wearing awa' Jean. 4723;
  11879
I around the world have stray'd.
  17544
I canna live without thee. 5674
I do certify that a few days ago,
  Mr. John Downing came into

my counting room, and asked
  me if I thought he ought to be
  believed in a court of justice.
  33008
I fill this cup.   13291; 13292
I have a little heart. 1439
I have lov'd thee, dearly lov'd
  thee.   1657
"I know a bank whereon the wild
  thyme blows."   16584
I left thee where I found thee
  love! 12674
I love but thee! 28494
I never will deceive thee. 9816
I see them on their winding way.
  1593; 1594
I'll be a fairy. 9547
I will be a nun. 16641
I'll dream of thee on oceans
  rocking pillow. 12681
I'll love thee as the wild bee
  loves. 19164; 19165
I'll never do so any more. 1736;
  5626
"I'll ne'er forget thee, no!"
  14910
I'll pull a bunch of buds and
  flowers. 20122
I'll risk it! 33639
I'll think of thee! 15936
I'll watch for thee from my lone-
  ly bow'r. 3328; 17245; 17246;
  21530; 21531
I wish I was by that dim lake.
  19747
I won't be a nun.   1732; 1865;
  5675; 5676; 11511; 11512;
  12916; 12917; 12918; 16642;
  16643; 20992; 20993
I'd be a butterfly. 346; 347
I'd rather be excus'd.   5627;
  20941
Ichthyologia Ohiensis.   2934
Ida of Tokenburg. 5677
Ideas for infants.   21694
Ideas necesarias a todo pueblo
  americano independiente. 6658;
  6659; 13974
Idle Dick.   29610
Idle hours employed. 29302
The idle man. 5138
The Idle school boy. 1735
'If sleeping now fair maid of

An impartial and true history of
the life and services of Maj.
General Andrew Jackson.
16037; 33647; 33648; 33649

An impartial appeal to the reason, interest and patriotism,
of the people of Illinois.
16653

An impartial examination of the
case of Captain Isaac Phillips.
21884

An impartial history of proceedings of the church and people
of Goshen. 19271

An impartial investigation of the
nature and tendency of the
Unitarian doctrines. 5685

Impartial review. A general
brief view of the existing controversy between Unitarians
and the Orthodox. 1704

An impartial view of divine justice. 40366

An impartial view of the real
state of the black population of
the United States. 16654

An impartial view of the respec-
tive claims of Mr. Shulze and
Mr. Gregg. 14246

Impediments of speech. 20028

The import and practical use of
baptism. 38630

The importance and utility of the
faithful preaching of the Gospel. 24510

The importance of divine knowledge. 31813

Importance of doctrinal knowledge.
12923

Importance of early religious instruction. 30556

The importance of hearing the
word of God. 21713

The importance of mature preparatory study for the ministry. 39597

The importance of revivals as exhibited in the late convention
at New-Lebanon. 30244

Importance of right views of
Christ. 12444

The importance of spiritual
knowledge. 20109

The importance of the Gospel
ministry. 29761

The importance of the last promise of Jesus Christ to Christian missionaries. 24511

Importance of the ministerial office. 6370

The importance of the sciences
of anatomy and physiology as
a branch of general education.
25673

The importance of the scriptures
to a teacher of religion. 8120

Importance of true charity. 8223

Important act of the legislature
of South Carolina. 18054

An important discovery, or,
"Temper is everything."
10040

Important document! Massachusetts' claim. 18691

Important information! The national colours and coat of
arms of the United States fully
explained. 9095

Important notice. [Inquiries for
information about estate of
Isaac Cushing] 2212

Important questions. 1743

Important to the sick and lame!
18002

Imposition exposed. 40312

Impressment of seamen from
American vessels. 31281

The improved almanac. 5686;
5687; 5688

The improved arithmetic. 34641;
39961

An improved atlas. 30627

An improved chronological summary of the history of the
United States of America.
31704

The improved farmer's, mechanic's, and gentleman's almanack. 1744

The improved guide to English
spelling. 38617

Improved method of learning the
guitar or lyre. 29024

The improved New England
primer. 39737; 39738; 39739

The improved pocket reckoner.

20336

The improved system of botanic medical practice. 37696

An improved system of stenography. 7864; 37544

Improvement in Hall of House of Representatives. 31282

Improvement in the art of tanning. 40422

The improvement of the mind. 7604; 11362; 11363; 27577

Improvement of the navigation of the Kennebec River. 27021

Improvement of time. 13114

Improvements in the rotatory engine. 17165

Improvisatrice, and other poems. 21159

In answer to correspondents on the subject of hemp and flax. 8516

In Assembly, February 16, 1827. 29990

In Assembly, February 24th, 1820. 2516

In Assembly, Feb. 23, 1820. 2483

In Assembly, March 1, 1820. 2484

In Assembly, March 17, 1820. 2485

In Assembly, Mar. 28, 1828. 34499

In Assembly, March 29, 1826. 25549

In Assembly, March 27, 1826. 25548

In Assembly, November 13th, 1820. 2517

In Assembly, Oct. 23, 1827. 31867

In Assembly, Sept. 21, 1827. 31866

In Common Council, Nov. 4, 1822. 8130

In consequence of letters missive from the Chapel Church in North-Yarmouth. 8495

In diesem deutschen Alphabet, Viel guter Lehr geschrieben steht. 1745

In General Court, June 16, 1820. 2434

In happier hours. 478; 22367

In honor of the election of our distinguished fellow-citizen General Andrew Jackson. 33650

In House of Representatives of the United States. March 18, 1820. 3645

In my bower so bright. 16585

In my cottage near a wood. 5456; 13060

In relation to the Baltimore and Ohio Rail Road Company. 37085

In school and out of school. 29313

In Senate January 8, 1824. 17374

In Senate, January 10, 1826. 25550

In Senate. November 17, 1827. 31868

In Senate, Nov. 28, 1827. 31869

In the Court for the Trial of Impeachments and the Correction of Errors. Between Catherine Cunningham who is impleaded with William Erwin & C. L. Mattison. 21007

In the court for the trial of impeachments and the correction of errors between Philander Seward, survivor of William Seward, plaintiff in error, and James Jackson. 25551

In the court for the trial of impeachments and the correction of errors. Between Richard Abraham, Impleaded with Jonathan Thompson. Appellant; and Charles Berners Plestow. 34500

In the court for the trial of impeachments and the correction of errors. Between the Pacific Insurance Co., of New York, Plffs, and C. I. Catler and James Keith. 39792

In the court for the trial of impeachments and the correction of errors: between the town of North Hempstead...and the town of Hempstead... 21008

In the court for the trial of impeachments and the correction of errors, between Thomas Gibbons, Appellant, and Aaron Ogden. 6257

In the court for the trial of impeachments, and the correction of errors. James Jackson, ex dem. James Boyd, vs. John Lewis. 2487

In the court for the trial of impeachments and the correction of errors. Patrick Manahan, plaintiff in error, vs. James Gibbons. 9677

In the court for the trial of impeachments and the correction of errors. Samuel F. Lambert, plaintiff in error, vs. The People of the state of New York. 29991

In the district court of the U. S. of America for the Northern district of N.Y. James Jackson exdem. Martha Beadstreet vs Henry Huntington. 31323

In the House of Representatives. April 22, 1822. 10900

In the House of Representatives. April 26, 1822. 10901

In the House of Representatives. April 13, 1820. 3753

In the House of Representatives. February 1, 1821. 7300

In the House of Representatives. Feb. 16, 1827. 29667

In the House of Representatives. March 12, 1822. 11258

In the House of Representatives of the United States. April 18, 1820. 3755

In the House of Representatives of the United States, April 14, 1820. 3754

In the House of Representatives of the United States, April 20, 1820. 3756

In the House of Representatives of the United States, April 22, 1820. 3757

In the House of Representatives of the United States, March 22, 1820. 3752

In the House of Representatives of the United States, May 8, 1820. 3758

In the House of Representatives. The select committee to whom was referred the communications of his Excellency, the Governor. 25394

In the matter of proving the will of James R. Wilson. 39780

In the matter of William Kenner & Co. 34090

In the session of 1821, the Committee of pensions and revolutionary claims made the following report. 10902

In the Supreme Court of the United States, between John L. Sullivan & others, appellants, and the Fulton Steam-Boat Company. 7301

In the year of our Lord eighteen hundred and twenty. The joint committee on banks, submit the following report. 2152

An inaugural address delivered at Gardiner, Me. 12743

Inaugural address delivered at the first stated meeting of the board of directors of the Adams Athenaeum. 23191

Inaugural address, delivered before the board of trustees, of Madison College. 32230

An inaugural address, delivered before the directors of the Theological Seminary of the General Synod of the Evangelical Lutheran Church. 26021

An inaugural address delivered before the Medical Society of the County of New-York, on the 8th day of August, 1825. 21750

An inaugural address delivered before the Medical Society of the County of New York, on the 12th day of July, 1824. 16593

An inaugural address delivered before the Medical Society of the State of New York. 25218

An inaugural address, delivered before the New-York Historical Society. 1679

An inquiry into the human mind, on the principles of common sense. 17780

An inquiry into the importance of the militia to a free commonwealth. 14241

An inquiry into the moral character of Lord Byron. 17986

An inquiry into the nature and tendency of speculative Free-Masonry. 30703; 30704; 35393; 40531

An inquiry into the nature and treatment of diabetes, calculus. 25871; 34925

An inquiry into the nature of sin, as exhibited in Dr. Dwight's Theology. 38198

An inquiry into the nature of sin: in which the views advanced in "Two Discourses on the Nature of Sin," are pursued. 28888

An inquiry into the origin and effects of sulphurous fumigations. 10094

An inquiry into the privilege and duty of the Christian church. 19499

An inquiry into the propriety and means of consolidating and digesting the laws of Pennsylvania. 29054

An inquiry into the propriety of establishing a national observatory. 28611

Inquiry into the relation of cause and effect. 8195

An inquiry into the requisite ministerial authority and character of Congregational and Presbyterian clergymen. 21023

An inquiry into the rule of law which creates a right to an incorporeal hereditament. 27875

An inquiry into the Scriptural doctrine concerning the devil and Satan. 23584; 27936

An inquiry into the Scriptural import of the words sheol, hades, tartarus, and gehenna. 15158; 19504

The Inquisition and orthodoxy, contrasted with Christianity and religious liberty. 39096

The Inquisition examined. 21717

Inside out; or, An interior view of the New York state prison. 12194

Inside out; or, Roguery exposed. 30640

The insolvent laws of Maryland. 2121

Instances of early piety. 9114; 16670

Instituciones de derecho real de Castilla y de Indias. 23468; 31848

The institutes and practice of surgery. 16283; 29018

Institutes of Biblical criticism. 12664

The institutes of English grammar. 12001; 19874; 28296

Institutes of natural philosophy. 1104; 16061

Institution for Savings in the town of Salem. 22191

Instruction book for the guitar. 884

Instruction. In the Italian and Spanish languages. 34808

Instruction of youth in Christian piety. 12690

Instruction with amusement, in the tale of the blackbird's nest. 1757

Instructions and explanations for the use and direction of the agents. 25844

Instructions and observations concerning the use of the chlorides of soda and lime. 39241

Instructions for babes. 1758; 5700

Instructions for the relief of the sick poor. 1759

Instructions for the violin. 25954

Instructions from a father to his son on entering college. 12651

Instructions in the principles and duties of the Christian religion. 5701

Instructions to commissioners, treaty Indian springs. 41173

Instructions to land officers in

Arkansas. 41174

Instructions to officers in the United States revenue cutter service. 41175

Instructions to the assessors of the several towns and wards in the state of New-York. 17376

Instructions to the missionaries about to embark for the Sandwich Islands. 11592

Instructive alphabet. 9115

The instructor. 1827; 5746; 16767

Instrument of Association...prepared in Baltimore. 37290

Instrumental director. 24716; 39097

Integrity. 12855; 33574

Intellectual and moral culture. 37230

The intellectual and moral glories of the Christian temple. 17905

The intellectual and moral resources of horticulture. 35112

Intellectual and practical grammar. 40458

Intellectual arithmetic. 5020; 24152

Intemperance, a just cause for alarm and exertion. 30691

Intemperance: A sermon, delivered in the North Church in Newburyport. 15975

Intemperance destructive of national welfare. 34006

Intemperance. Extracts from an address upon the effects of ardent spirits. 29427a

Intention to have General Lafayette visit the State of Maine. 21305

Intercourse with foreign nations. 27096

Intercourse with the Indians. 27097

The interest and authority of the church and the privilege and duty of its members. 23914

Interest made equity. 25171

Interest to the state of Maryland. 27098

An interesting account of the

dreadful effects of the plague and yellow fever, at London. 18261

An interesting account of the plague, yellow fever, &c. as they have prevailed in different countries. 528

The interesting adventures of the industrious cobler. 1760

An interesting controversy between Rev. Lemuel Haynes, and Rev. Hosea Ballou. 33510

Interesting conversations with a cruel carman. 1761

Interesting events in the history of the United States. 32206; 37691; 37692

Interesting history of Mrs. Tooly. 39098

The interesting life, and daring engagements of the celebrated Paul Jones. 12929; 33674

An interesting narrative of the murder of John Love. 21024

Interesting particulars of the life of Major General La Fayette. 16671

Interesting report of the rise and progress of the Protestant Episcopal Church. 29332

An interesting sketch of the life of Dr. H-- T--. 4302

An interesting sketch of the life of Doctor Henry Todd. 4303; 11449

The interesting trial of William F. Hooe. 24955

Internal improvement [Carey] 19969; 19970; 19971; 19972; 19973-19977; 24011; 24012; 38062

Internal improvement [Lucerne County, Pa.] 29555

Internal improvement. At a numerous convention of delegates from the towns on the Kennebec River. 21025

Internal improvement. Letter from the Secretary of War. 36418; 36419

Internal improvement of South-Carolina. 9494

Internal improvement. Philadelphia, Dec. 21, 1825. 21850

Internal improvement. The acting
committee communicate to the
public the following. 21849

Internal improvements [N. C.]
39858

Internal improvements. Mr.
Bailey's resolutions proposing
to amend the Constitution.
22893

Internal improvements. Mr. Mercer's resolutions to provide a
fund for internal improvement.
27099

Internal improvements. Resolution submitted by Mr. Test.
22894

Internal improvements since
1824. 36420

Interpretation of the parable of
the unjust steward. 32741

An interpretation of the Rev. Doctor Ezra Stiles Ely's Dream.
21026

The interpreter's house. 622

An intolerant spirit, hostile to
the interests of society. 9079

The intolerants. 28565

Intrigue; or, Married yesterday.
2807

L'Introducteur François. 38289

An introduction to a course of
lectures on history. 11898

An introduction to algebra [Day]
970; 12339; 28670; 38350

An introduction to algebra [Bon-
nycastle] 8122; 19792; 28220;
37882

An introduction to algebra upon
the inductive method of instruction. 20113; 20114; 24153;
32762; 38213

An introduction to ancient and
modern geography. 921; 5120;
8486; 12304; 20227; 24260;
24261; 24262; 28634; 32867;
38317

An introduction to arithmetic.
19981

An introduction to chemistry.
8454

An introduction to Christianity.
22405

Introduction to English grammar.
8892

An introduction to farrierry. [!]
39046

Introduction to geography. 24799

An introduction to geology.
37546

An introduction to Latin syntax.
2088; 5925; 17010

An introduction to linear drawing.
20546; 33233

Introduction to mensuration &
practical geometry. 11918;
28221; 37883

An introduction to naval gunnery.
33672

An introduction to spelling and
reading. 4444; 15058; 23445

An introduction to spelling and
reading English. 39431

An introduction to systematic and
physiological botany. 30099

The introduction to the analytical
reader. 34942

Introduction to the art and science of music. 40665

An introduction to the art of penmanship. 5664

Introduction to the critical study
and knowledge of the Holy
Scriptures. 20954; 29256

An introduction to the elements
of algebra. 5268; 33087

Introduction to The English reader. 2374; 2375; 2376; 9588;
9589; 13457; 13458; 13459;
13460; 17278; 17279; 17280;
21573; 21574; 21575; 21576;
25468; 25469; 25470; 25471;
29865; 29867; 34244; 34346;
34347; 34348; 34349; 39678;
39679; 39680

An introduction to the geography
of the New Testament. 8282

Introduction to the Greek language. 39151

Introduction to the Latin language.
19495

An introduction to the mathematical principles of natural philosophy. 10133

Introduction to the mechanical
principles of carpentry. 29106

Introduction to the National spelling-book. 33068
Introduction to the Old Testament.
29349
An introduction to the practice of
midwifery. 5173; 20296;
38367
Introduction to the science of
government. 9116
An introduction to the study of
Grecian and Roman geography.
39314
Introductory address at opening
of Wesleyan Academy. 20527;
24541
An introductory address, delivered before the Utica Lyceum.
16721
Introductory address, delivered
by Frances Wright. 38335
An introductory address, delivered on Sunday, February 2,
1823, in the Unitarian Chapel
of Dundee. 13132
Introductory address on independence of intellect. 19924
An introductory address, on occasion of the opening of the
General Theological Seminary.
9021
Introductory arithmetic. 29545;
33918
An introductory catechism. 8281;
24029
Introductory discourse delivered
at New-Haven. 3500
Introductory discourse, delivered
to his congregation on his return from Europe. 40319
An introductory discourse, delivered to the lunatics in the
asylum, City of New York.
6855
Introductory discourse to a few
lectures on the application of
chemistry to agriculture.
21289
An introductory law lecture, delivered by Charles Humphreys.
24914
An introductory lecture, delivered at the College of Physicians and Surgeons of the City

of New York. 37735
Introductory lecture, delivered
at the commencement of the
session of the Medical College
of South Carolina. 24353;
32982
An introductory lecture delivered
at the opening of Washington
Medical College of Baltimore.
33695
An introductory lecture, delivered
before the Lexington Mechanic's Institute. 39987
An introductory lecture, delivered in the College of Physicians and Surgeons. 20957
An introductory lecture, delivered in the laboratory of Yale
College. 35201
Introductory lecture, on chemistry, delivered at the college
of South Carolina. 868
An introductory lecture on the
necessity and value of professional industry. 12398
An introductory lecture on the
study of the law, delivered in
the chapel of Transylvania
University. 8113
An introductory lecture, preparatory to a course of instruction on common and statute
law, delivered in the chapel
of Transylvania University.
11908
Introductory lecture to a course
of anatomy and physiology in
Rutgers Medical College.
24698; 29032
An introductory lecture to a
course of religious instructions for young persons. 9022
An introductory lecture to the institutes of medicine. 29338
An introductory lecture upon
criminal jurisprudence. 31726
Introductory lectures to John I.
M'Chesney's system of English grammar. 13169
Introductory observations and definitions in botany. 24767
Introductory report to the code of
evidence of the state of Louisi-

ana. 1988

Introductory report to the code of prison discipline. 29517; 29518

Inundated lands on the Mississippi. 41176

Invalid pensioners. 27100

Investigator: or A defence of the order, government & economy of the United Society called Shakers. 33962

The invincibles. 34204; 39647

Invisible realities, demonstrated in the holy life and triumphant death of John Janeway. 33696

The invisible girl. 5628

The invitation No. 79. American Tract Society. 11608

Ira Allen. 27101

Ira W. Scott's Albany directory. 26025

Irenicum; or, The peace maker. 1763

Irencium... reconciliation between the Bishop of North-Carolina and some of his "dissenting" brethren. 21028

The Irish freebooter. 12931

The Irish girl. 1764; 16672

The Irish tutor. 12687

The Irish widow. 16255

The Irishman in London. 5897

The iron chest. 28549

Iron store. James & McArthur. 21046

Irvine's Treatise on the yellow fever. 1768

Is he jealous? 7982; 15291

Is it a lie? 33678

Is't art, I pray, or nature? 19748

Is it well thee? 9552

Is there a heart. 1772

Is this religion? 30761

Isaac Hodsdon. 22895

Isaac Philips. 27102

Isaac Pool. 27103

Isaac Ricker. 27104

Isaac W. Norris. 36421

Isabel; A celebrated Spanish serenade. 479; 15429; 15430

Isabella; a novel. 12343

Isabella; or, Filial affection. 33679

Isabella, or The fatal marriage. 24661

Isaiah's message to the American nation. 16963

Isidore Moore. 27105; 27106

The island, or Christian and his comrades. 12040; 12041

Isle of beauty, fare thee well. 2943

Israel vindicated. 1681; 12877

It has been long the united wish of the most respectable merchants in this country, connected with the silk trade. 32503

It is better that ninety and nine guilty should escape. 23311

The Italian and English phrase-book. 34780

Italian convert. 5702

Italian pocket dictionary. 38803

The Italian villagers. 6134

Italy [Morgan] 6119

Italy, a poem. 13980

Italy during the consulate and empire of Napoleon Buonaparte. 37914

The itinerant sketch book. 33681

Itinerant sketches. 16687

The itinerary of a traveler in the wilderness. 22426; 22427

Ivanhoe. 3137; 3138; 3139; 3140; 6744; 14060; 14061; 14062;

Ivy castle. 19273

J

J. B. Cramer's Instructions for the piano forte. 901; 5102

J. B. Cramer's sequel to his celebrated book. 906

J. F. Carmichael. 36422

J. F. Ohl. 36423

J. Green proposes to publish The journals of the conventions of the province of Maryland. 21035

J. Haskin's defence of his conduct and opinions in relation to Dr. John H. Tomlinson. 12788

Jachin and Boaz; or, An authen-

tic key to the door of free
masonry. 22170
Jachin y Boaz; ó Una llave auten-
tica para la puerta de Fra-
masonería. 10164
Jack Halyard, and Ishmael Bar-
dus. 33682
Jackson a negro trader. 33961
Jackson almanac. 29340
Jackson and Liberty. An address
unanimously adopted by a gen-
eral meeting of the citizens of
Dauphin County. 32954
Jackson and the people's ticket.
33685
Jackson blasphemy. 21040
Jackson delegate ticket. 16698;
33686
Jackson ticket. 32960
Jackson triumphant in the great
city of Philadelphia. 16700;
33687
The Jackson wreath. 39114
Jackson's book-keeping. 4664;
5706
Jackson's duett. 16701
Jacob B. Clarke. 41177
Jacob Barker to David B. Ogden,
Esq. on the subject of the
United States loan of 1814.
4610
Jacob Barker to the electors of
the First senatorial district of
the state of New-York. 32213
Jacob Barker's letters, develop-
ing the conspiracy formed in
1826 for his ruin. 28055;
28056; 28057
Jacob Butler. 27107
Jacob Clements' assignees.
36424
Jacob Sights. 31328
Jacob Wilderman. 41178
Jacob's ladder. 7876
Jadin's favorite grand waltz. 5708
Jahn's History of the Hebrew
commonwealth. 33691
James A. Harper. 36425
James and his little sister.
21047
James Cooke. 27108
James D. Barry, and Bailey &
Torrey. 36426

James D. Cobb. 41180; 41181
James Devereux. 36427
James H. Mulford and all appel-
lants, vs. Abraham Bradley.
29829
James Hedge. 27109
James McCarty. 36428
James M'Ilvain. 36429
James May. 27110
James Miller, James Robertson,
Wm. H. Ellis, and Joshua
Prentiss. 31329
James Mitchel. 27111
James Mitchell. 36430
James Monroe. 27112; 41182;
41183
James Porlier & A. Gardipier.
41184
James Ray. 36431
James Riley et al. 31330;
36432
James River and Kenhawa Canal
route. 36433
James Ross. 27113
James Royal. 41185
James Russel. 36434
James Scull. 36435
James Somers, the pilgrim's
son. 29352
James Soyars. 41186
James Talbot. 6718; 17897
James Whitfield, by the Grace of
God and the appointment of the
Holy See,... See, Archbishop of
Baltimore. 41505
James Wolcott and wife. 27114
James Wood. 31331
Jane and her teacher. 21048;
21049
Jane Mary Lawrence. 36436
Jane Shore, a tragedy. 10149
Japanese air. 8826
La jardiniere. 16329
Jared E. Groce. 36437
Jason Warner, administrator of
Ferguson. 41187
The jealous wife, a comedy. 8391
Jean Baptiste Conture. 41188
Jean Baptiste Jerome. 41189;
41190
Jean Valery Delassize. 27115
Jefferson almanac. 24981; 33706
Jefferson County Republican

meeting. 29899

Jefferson, in reply to the Richmond anti-Jackson address. 33707

Jefferson Medical College: a representation of the conduct of the trustees and members of the faculty. 33708

Jefferson - No. III. 28399

Jefferson's letters to Samuel Kercheval. 39132

Jehial Bryan's patent daily account of time. 37974

Jelleff & Hull's patent pocket interest tables. 33709

Jemmy and Nancy. 1792; 5714

Jeptha's daughter. 4825

Jeremiah Buckley. 31333

Jeremiah Walker. 36438

Jesse Wilkinson. 36439

Jessie the flow'r o' Dumblane. 14145

Jessy. 16832

Jessy Allan, the lame girl. 16717

Jesus Christ, and Him crucified. 7774

Jesus Christ gloriously exalted above all evil, in the work of redemption. 16043

Jesus Christ magnified, and Mahomedan Christian exposed and warned. 21425

Jesus said unto him, follow me. 11487

The Jew. A comedy. 12297

The Jew and the doctor. 12371

The Jew; being a defence of Judaism, against all adversaries. 16696

Jim Crow. 33716

Job printing on the vertical press. 9151

Job Scott's last letter. 3128

Jockey and Jenny. 3409

Joe Miller's almanac. 33718

Joel Byington. 36440; 41191

Johann Friedrich Starcks tägliches Hand-Buch in guten und bosen Tagen. 22362; 35386; 40522

Johann Hübners zweymal zwey und fünfzig auserlesene Biblische

Historien. 24908

Johannis Markii Christianae theologuae medulla didacticoelenctica. 17019; 21326

John A. Webster. 27116

John, a witness of Christ. 12094

John Ab. Willink. 27117

John Adams. 27118

John Anderson, my Jo John. 8889

John B. Lamaitre. 31334

John Baker. Message from the President of the United States. 41192

John Brest and al, heirs of John P. Landerau. 36441

John Bruce, administrator of Philip Bush. 36442

John Bull in America. 21793; 21794

John Bull; or, The Englishman's fireside. 5025; 15815

John Burnham. 41193

John Burton, and al. 27119; 31335; 36443

John Buzzby: or A day's pleasure. 9194

John Culbertson. 36444

John Dorr. 31336

John Doyle's catalogue of books. 28728

John E. Dorsey. 27120

John Eustace. 27121

John F. Carmichael. 36445

John Gates, Jr. 36446

John Good. 27122; 36447; 36448

John Grigg's almanack. 33718a

John Gwynn--heirs of. 36449

John H. Mills. 27123

John Heard, assignee of A. Davis. 31337

John Heard, Jr. 36450

John Hendree's Proofs against the many falsehoods propagated by one Abel P. Upshur. 8994

John J. Rickers's catalogue. 25944

John Jackson. 31338

John Long. 36451

John McCartney. 27124

John M'Donnell. 36452

John Miles. 36453

John Moffett. 31339

John Moffit. 36454

John Nicks, tailor, respectfully
informs the inhabitants of Red-
hook and its vicinity, that he
has commenced the tailoring
business. 9715
John of Paris. 30284
John of the Score. 21059;
29364
John Overall. 31340
John Peters and Sabine Pond.
27125
John Pierre Landerau. 41194
John Randolph, abroad and at
home. 35079; 35080; 40329
John Reynold. 41197
John Rhea of Tennessee, to his
constituents. 6629
John Rodriguez. 31341; 31342;
41198
John Shirkey. 36455
John Slavan. 31343
John Slavin. 27126
John Steinman and others. 27127
John Stone. 31344
John Thompson, Christ. Adams,
and S. Spraggins. 36456
John Wells. 41199
John White, and Albert Williams.
39141
John Willard. 31345; 36457
John Williams, or The sailor boy.
29365
John Williams' reply to John
Blair. 41540
John Wilson against George
Graham. 31346
John Winton. 27128; 36458
John Woods. A Tennessean.
32027
John's Biblical archaeology.
12941
Johnny Bull my Joe. 21060
Johnny came a courting me. 9812;
39959
Johnson Goodwill. 41200
Johnson's almanac. 9163
Johnson's dictionary of the Eng-
lish language in miniature.
9159; 12960; 16736; 33725
Johnson's English dictionary.
33724; 39149
Johnson's march in The catarct
[sic] of the Ganges. 16727

Johnson's new cotillions and
march with the national airs.
16728
Johnson's Pennsylvania and New
Jersey almanack. 9164
Johnson's Pennsylvania, New Jersey, Delaware, Maryland, and
Virginia almanack. 12963
Johnson's Philadelphia primer.
5729
Johnson's Tennessee harmony.
5723
The joint committee on Roads and
Canals to whom was referred
the petition of Samuel Hinkley
and others to extend the Hampshire and Hampden canal respectfully report. 2153
The Joint Committee on Roads
and Canals, who were directed
"to consider the expediency of
providing for a Board of Commissioners for Internal Improvements," report the following resolutions. 29669
The Joint Committee on the petition of the President and Trustees of Williams College.
2154
Joint minutes of three separate
annual meetings, held by the
Baptized Churches of Christ,
Friends to Humanity. 37608
Joint resolution authorizing an examination of the claims to land
of John F. Carmichael. 36459
Joint resolution authorizing the
purchase of fifty copies of the
sixth volume of the laws of
the United States. 41201
Joint resolution authorizing the
purchase of Peale's portrait of
Gen. Washington. 18694
Joint resolution directing a system of cavalry tactics, and a
system of instruction for artillery, to be prepared for the
use of the cavalry and artillery
of the militia. 27129
Joint resolution directing experiments to be made to ascertain
the length of the pendulum, vi-
brating sixty times in a min-

ute. 27130; 31347

Joint resolution directing the Secretary of War to cause to be inspected and appraised the fortifications erected on Staten Island, at the expense of the State of New York. 31348

Joint resolution for procuring the laws of the several states. 41202

Joint resolution for the appointment of two extra clerks in the Patent Office, to record patents. 31349

Joint resolution for the purchase of a bust of Thomas Jefferson. 31350

Joint resolution in relation to the process of execution issuing from the courts of the United States. 27131

A joint resolution of the Senate and House of Representatives of the state of Alabama, disapproving certain resolutions of the Legislatures of the state of Delaware, Connecticut, Illinois, and Indiana. 37395

A joint resolution proposing an amendment to the Constitution of the United States, in respect to the election of a President and Vice President of the United States. 18695

Joint resolution providing for the care and preservation of the public buildings. 36460

Joint resolution providing for the distribution of certain public documents. 27132

Joint resolution providing for the more equitable operation of the acts granting pensions for Revolutionary services. 27133

Joint resolution, submitted by Mr. Walworth, proposing an amendment to the Constitution of the United States in relation to bankruptcies. 10904; 10905

Joint resolution to indemnify the Creek Indians for the land lying between the Chatahoochee River and the dividing line between

Georgia and Alabama. 31351

Joint resolution to provide for the care and preservation of the capitol, and capitol square, in the city of Washington. 27134; 27135

Joint resolution to repeal so much of the resolution of 27th April, 1816, providing for a biennial register of the officers and agents of government, as relates to the place of nativity of postmasters and mail contractors. 27136

Joint resolutions of the Mayor, Recorder, Aldermen, and Common Council, of the Borough of Norfolk. 10906

Joint resolutions providing for the distribution of certain public documents, and the removal of certain books from the Library. 31352; 36461

Joint rules of the Senate and Assembly. 29992; 34501

The jolly young waterman. 20310

Jonathan Eastman - widow of. 31353

Jonathan M. Blaisdell. 36462

Jonathan Postfree, or The honest Yankee. 28076

Jonathan S. Smith. 36463

Jos. Elliot, Peggy Stephens, & challenge. 41203

Joseph Burnett. 36464

Joseph Dixon. 36465

Joseph Ellis, the berry boy. 16746; 21074

Joseph G. Nancrede. 36466

Joseph Jeans - representatives of. 36467

Joseph Krittman. 41204

Joseph Le Carpentier. 27137

Joseph on the verge of eternity. 11956

Joseph; or, Sketches of scripture history. 21075; 29384

Joseph Shomo. 22900

Joseph Smith and John B. Dupuis. 36468

Joseph Smith--for J. B. Dupuis. 31354

Joseph Strahan and others. 27138

Joseph Towler--Treasurer; In account with the Trustees of Lexington.   25105

Joseph Young.   36469

Joshua Foltz.   36470

Joshua Fults.   31355

Joshua Maddox Wallace, of Burlington, N.J. 1806

Joshua Redivivus.   25993

Josiah Barker of Louisiana. 41205

The journal almanac for the state of Georgia.   9172; 16748

Journal, comprising an account of the loss of the brig Commerce.   3027; 6652; 6653; 10116; 13958; 22104; 25948; 35050; 40291

Journal de la chambre des representans [Louisiana]   2013; 5860; 9296; 13146; 16939; 21252; 25147; 29538; 33908; 33909

Journal du senat [Louisiana] 2014; 5861; 9297; 13147; 16940; 21253; 25148; 29539; 33910

A journal kept by Mr. John Howe. 29262

The journal of a convention assembled at the city of Raleigh, on the 10th of November, 1823.   13595

Journal of a Convention of delegates of the state of Pennsylvania, held for the promotion of the state agricultural and manufacturing interests.   28588

Journal of a convention of the Protestant Episcopal Church in the state of Maryland.   2888; 6553; 10028; 17713; 21990; 25855; 30365; 34909; 40173

Journal of a cruise made to the Pacific Ocean by Captain David Porter.   9978

A journal of a march performed by the corps of Cadets of the U.S. Military Academy. 1807; 9234

Journal of a residence in Chili. 12195

Journal of a residence in the Sandwich Islands.   35407; 35408

Journal of a second expedition into the interior of Africa, from the Bight of Benin to Soccatoo. 38187

Journal of a second voyage for the discovery of a northwest passage from the Atlantic to the Pacific.   17530

Journal of a third voyage for the discovery of a northwest passage, from the Atlantic to the Pacific.   25670

A journal of a tour around Hawaii.   20399

A journal of a tour in Italy. 16025

Journal of a tour of a detachment of cadets, from the A.L.S. & M. academy, Middletown. 29386

A journal of a tour through Connecticut, Massachusetts, New-York, the north part of Pennsylvania and Ohio.   8974

Journal of a voyage for the discovery of a north-west passage from the Atlantic to the Pacific.   6389

A journal of an excursion made by the corps of cadets, of the American Literary, Scientific and Military Academy. 9740; 15064

Journal of an excursion, performed by a detachment of cadets, belonging to the A.L.S. & M. academy.   25007

Journal of Daniel Coker. 807; 808

Journal of debates and proceedings in the convention of delegates, chosen to revise the constitution of Massachusetts. 5972

The journal of Rev. Francis Asbury.   4500

Journal of the Assembly of the state of New-York.   2488; 2489; 2490; 6244; 9678; 13548; 17377; 21658; 27747; 29993; 29994; 37322; 37323; 39793

Journal of the Board of public

works of the state of Georgia. 24677

Journal of the convention, began and held at Albany, the 13th of Oct. 1801. 6245

Journal of the convention of the Protestant Episcopal Church of the diocess[!] of Delaware. 34908

Journal of the convention of the State of New York. 6246

Journal of the convention, of the territory of the United States North West of the Ohio. 30094

Journal of the convention of Vermont. 11292; 37005

Journal of the Convention of Virginia. 31619

Journal of the convention of young men, of the state of New-York. 34389

Journal of the conversations of Lord Byron. 17092; 21385

Journal of the Council of censors. 7508; 37006

Journal of the Court of Impeachment for the trial of Robert Porter. 21811

Journal of the Court of Impeachment for the trial of Seth Chapman. 21812

Journal of the Court of Impeachment for the trial of Walter Franklin. 21813; 21814

Journal of the Court of Impeachment. The state of Tennessee vs. Nathaniel W. Williams. 40624

Journal of the General Assembly of the state of Vermont. 14776; 19131; 23152; 27502; 31599; 31600; 37007; 41370

Journal of the Honorable Senate, of the state of New Hampshire. 2435; 6206; 6207; 39745

Journal of the House of Delegates of the Commonwealth of Virginia. 4117; 27514; 31620; 31622; 31624; 37030; 37031

Journal of the House of Representatives of the Commonwealth of Kentucky. 1846; 1847; 29414; 33767; 39188

Journal of the...House of Representatives of the Commonwealth of Pennsylvania. 6411; 9845; 13702; 17556; 21816; 25693; 34677; 39995

Journal of the House of Representatives of the State of Alabama. 54; 4432; 4433; 7763; 11559; 15049; 19384; 23440; 27795; 31914; 37396

Journal of the House of Representatives of the state of Delaware. 988; 5170; 8528; 12356; 15954; 20285; 28680; 38360

Journal of the House of Representatives of the state of Georgia. 1374; 5442; 5443; 5444; 5445; 8814; 20658; 20659; 24678; 29011; 38748

Journal of the House of Representatives of the state of Illinois. 5682; 12920; 20997; 24940; 29306; 39075

Journal of the House of Representatives of the state of Indiana. 1747; 5692; 9101; 9102; 13621; 16659; 21010; 27741; 29316; 33652; 39084

Journal of the House of Representatives of the state of Louisiana. 2015; 2017; 5862; 9298; 13148; 16941; 21254; 25149; 29540; 33911; 33912

Journal of the House of Representatives of the state of Mississippi. 2290; 6072; 6073; 9507; 13355; 17174; 21476; 25395; 29776; 34158; 39610

Journal of the House of Representatives of the state of Missouri. 6081; 9513; 9514; 13360; 21480; 25400; 29779; 39615

Journal of the House of Representatives of the state of New Hampshire. 2436; 6208; 6209; 9630; 13502; 17321; 21617; 21618; 25507; 29934; 34436; 39746; 39747

Journal of the House of Representatives of the state of Ohio. 2587; |6334; 9761; 17478; 21728; 25625; 30105; 34600; 39902

Journal of the House of Representatives of the state of Tennessee. 3416; 6946; 10426; 14267; 18166; 22436; 26187; 30780;

Journal of the House of Representatives of the United States. 3760; 7302; 10907; 18765; 22901; 27139; 27140; 31356; 36471; 41206

Journal of the law-school, and of the moot-court attached to it. 10414

Journal of the legislative council of the territory of Michigan. 17142; 21450; 25357; 29747; 39582

A journal of the life and religious labours of Richard Jordan. 39164

A journal of the life, travels, and gospel labours of Job Scott. 3129

Journal of the life, travels and gospel labours of William Williams. 37195

Journal of the Missouri State Convention. 2297

Journal of the most Worshipful Grand Lodge of Vermont. 28956; 38680

Journal of the proceedings of a convention of the Protestant Church, in the Diocess [sic] of Mississippi. 25856

Journal of the proceedings of a convention of the Protestant Episcopal Church in the state of Delaware. 6552

Journal of the proceedings of a convention of the Protestant Episcopal Church of Virginia. 2896; 6560; 17722; 22000; 25870; 30377; 34920; 40185

Journal of the proceedings of the annual convention of the Protestant Episcopal Church, in the Diocese of Connecticut. 2885; 6551; 21989; 25853; 30364; 34907; 40171

Journal of the proceedings of the annual convention of the Protestant Episcopal Church, in the diocese of South-Carolina. 2894; 2895; 6559

Journal of the proceedings of the bishops, clergy, and laity of the Protestant Episcopal Church. 2879; 2880; 6548; 25850; 40169

Journal of the proceedings of the convention, holden at Windsor, Vt., February 16, 1825, for the purpose of taking preliminary measures to effect an improved navigation of the Connecticut River. 21080

Journal of the proceedings of the convention of the Protestant Episcopal Church in the state of Vermont. 10036; 13879; 17721; 21999; 25869; 30376; 34918; 40184

Journal of the proceedings of the eighth annual convention of the Protestant Episcopal Church in the state of North Carolina. 17716

Journal of the proceedings of the eighth annual convention of the Protestant Episcopal Church, in the state of Ohio. 21995

Journal of the proceedings of the eighth general convention of the receivers of the doctrines of the New Jerusalem. 24666

Journal of the proceedings of the eleventh annual convention of the Protestant Episcopal Church in the diocese of Ohio. 40179

Journal of the proceedings of the eleventh annual convention of the Protestant Episcopal Church in the state of North Carolina. 30369

Journal of the proceedings of the eleventh general convention of receivers of the doctrines of the New Jerusalem. 39776

Journal of the proceedings of the fifth annual convention of the Protestant Episcopal Church in the state of Ohio. 10032

Journal of the proceedings of the first branch of the city council of Baltimore. 37566

Journal of the proceedings of the first convention of the Protestant Episcopal Church in the diocese of Kentucky. 40172

Journal of the proceedings of the 40th annual convention of the Protestant Episcopal Church in the diocese of South Carolina. 34917

Journal of the proceedings of the fortieth annual convention of the Protestant Episcopal Church in the state of New Jersey. 13872

Journal of the proceedings of the fortieth convention of the Protestant Episcopal Church in the state of New-York. 21992; 25858

Journal of the proceedings of the fortieth convention of the Protestant Episcopal Church in the state of Pennsylvania. 17719

Journal of the proceedings of the forty-fifth annual convention of the Protestant Episcopal Church in the state of New Jersey. 34911

Journal of the proceedings of the forty-fifth convention of the Protestant Episcopal Church in the state of Pennsylvania. 40182

Journal of the proceedings of the 41st annual convention of the Protestant Episcopal Church in the diocese of South Carolina. 40183

Journal of the proceedings of the forty-first annual convention of the Protestant Episcopal Church in the state of New Jersey. 17714

Journal of the proceedings of the forty-first convention of the Protestant Episcopal Church in the state of New-York. 25859

Journal of the proceedings of the forty-first convention of the Protestant Episcopal Church in the state of Pennsylvania. 21997

Journal of the proceedings of the forty-fourth annual convention of the Protestant Episcopal Church in New Jersey. 30367

Journal of the proceedings of the forty-fourth convention of the Protestant Episcopal Church in the state of New-York. 40177

Journal of the proceedings of the forty-fourth convention of the Protestant Episcopal Church in the state of Pennsylvania. 34916

Journal of the proceedings of the forty-second convention of the Protestant Episcopal Church in the state of New York. 30368

Journal of the proceedings of the forty-second convention of the Protestant Episcopal Church, in the state of Pennsylvania. 25864

Journal of the proceedings of the forty-second annual convention of the Protestant Episcopal Church in the state of New Jersey. 21991

Journal of the proceedings of the forty-sixth annual convention of the Protestant Episcopal Church held in Christ's Church, New Brunswick. 40176

Journal of the proceedings of the forty-third annual convention of the Protestant Episcopal Church, in New Jersey. 25857

Journal of the proceedings of the forty-third convention of the Protestant Episcopal Church in the state of New-York. 34913

Journal of the proceedings of the forty-third convention of the Protestant Episcopal Church, in the state of Pennsylvania. 30372

Journal of the proceedings of the fourth annual convention, of the Protestant Episcopal Church, in the diocese of Mississippi. 40174

Journal of the proceedings of the fourth annual convention of the

Protestant Episcopal Church in the state of Ohio. 6556

Journal of the proceedings of the Grand Lodge of New-Hampshire. 8756; 12599; 16211; 20582; 38656

A journal of the proceedings of the Grand Royal Arch Chapter of the state of New Hampshire. 24610; 28942; 33268; 38657

Journal of the proceedings of the Grand Royal Arch Chapter of the state of Ohio. 38666

Journal of the proceedings of the House of Delegates of the state of Maryland. 29643; 34030; 39463

Journal of the proceedings of the Legislative council of the state of New-Jersey. 2449; 2450; 9648; 17343; 21631; 25522; 29951; 34454; 39763

Journal of the proceedings of the ninth annual convention of the Protestant Episcopal Church in the state of North Carolina. 21994

Journal of the proceedings of the ninth annual convention of the Protestant Episcopal Church of the state of Ohio. 25862

Journal of the proceedings of the ninth general convention of receivers of the doctrines of the New Jerusalem. 29958

Journal of the proceedings of the Protestant Episcopal Church of the diocess of Connecticut. 2886; 4386

Journal of the proceedings of the second annual convention of the Protestant Episcopal Church, in the diocese of Mississippi. 30366

Journal of the proceedings of the Senate of the state of Maryland. 29644; 39464

Journal of the proceedings of the seventh annual convention of the Protestant Episcopal Church in the state of North-Carolina. 13874

Journal of the proceedings of the

seventh annual convention of the Protestant Episcopal Church in the state of Ohio. 17718

Journal of the proceedings of the sixth annual convention of the Protestant Episcopal Church in the state of North Carolina. 10031

Journal of the proceedings of the sixth annual convention of the Protestant Episcopal Church in the state of Ohio. 13875

Journal of the proceedings of the special convention of the Protestant Episcopal Church in the state of Pennsylvania. 25865

Journal of the proceedings of the tenth annual convention of the Protestant Episcopal Church in the state of North Carolina. 25861

Journal of the proceedings of the tenth annual convention of the Protestant Episcopal Church in the state of Ohio. 30370

Journal of the proceedings of the third annual convention of the Protestant Episcopal Church, in the diocese of Mississippi. 34910

Journal of the proceedings of the third annual convention, of the Protestant Episcopal Church in the state of Ohio. 2892

Journal of the proceedings of the thirteenth annual convention of the Protestant Episcopal Church in the state of North Carolina. 40178

Journal of the proceedings of the 38th annual convention of the Protestant Episcopal Church in the diocese of South Carolina. 25868

Journal of the proceedings of the thirty-eighth annual convention of the Protestant Episcopal Church in the state of New Jersey. 6554

Journal of the proceedings of the 35th annual convention of the Protestant Episcopal Church in the diocese of South Carolina. 13878

Journal of the proceedings of the thirty-eighth convention of the Protestant Episcopal Church in the state of New-York. 17715

Journal of the proceedings of the thirty-fifth convention of the Protestant Episcopal Church in the state of New-York. 6555

Journal of the proceedings of the 34th annual convention of the Protestant Episcopal Church in the diocese of South Carolina. 10035

Journal of the proceedings of the thirty-fourth convention of the Protestant Episcopal Church in the state of New-York. 2890

Journal of the proceedings of the 39th annual convention of the Protestant Episcopal Church in the diocese of South Carolina. 30375

Journal of the proceedings of the thirty-ninth annual convention of the Protestant Episcopal Church in the state of New Jersey. 10029

Journal of the proceedings of the thirty-ninth convention of the Protestant Episcopal Church in the state of New York. 21993

Journal of the proceedings of the thirty-ninth convention of the Protestant Episcopal Church in the state of Pennsylvania. 13876

Journal of the proceedings of the 37th annual convention of the Protestant Episcopal Church in the diocese of South-Carolina. 21998

Journal of the proceedings of the thirty-seventh annual convention of the Protestant Episcopal Church in the state of New-Jersey. 2889

Journal of the proceedings of the thirty-seventh convention of the Protestant Episcopal Church in the state of New-York. 13873

Journal of the proceedings of the

36th annual convention of the Protestant Episcopal Church in the diocese of South Carolina. 17720

Journal of the proceedings of the thirty-sixth convention of the Protestant Episcopal Church in the state of New-York. 10030

Journal of the proceedings of the twelfth annual convention of the Protestant Episcopal Church in the diocese of Ohio. 40180

Journal of the proceedings of the twelfth annual convention of the Protestant Episcopal Church in the state of North Carolina. 34915

Journal of the proceedings of the twenty-ninth convention of the Protestant Episcopal Church in the state of New-Hampshire. 40175

Journal of the Senate of the Commonwealth of Kentucky. 1848; 1849; 13002; 29415; 33768; 39189

Journal of the Senate of the Commonwealth of Pennsylvania. 2688; 6410; 9844; 13703; 17555; 21815; 25692; 34676; 39994

Journal of the Senate of the Commonwealth of Virginia. 4118; 7533; 27515; 31621; 31626; 37032; 37033

Journal of the Senate of the state of Alabama. 55; 4434; 4435; 7764; 11560; 19385; 23441; 27796; 31915; 37397

Journal of the Senate of the state of Delaware. 989; 990; 5171; 8529; 12357; 20286; 24322; 28681; 38361

Journal of the Senate of the state of Georgia. 1375; 5446; 8815; 20660; 20661; 24679; 29012; 33345; 38749

Journal of the Senate of the state of Illinois. 5683; 12921; 20998; 24941; 29307; 39076

Journal of the Senate, of the state of Indiana. 1748; 5693; 9103; 9104; 16660; 21011; 27742; 29317; 33653; 39085

Journal of the Senate of the state of Louisiana. 2016; 5863; 9299; 13149; 16942; 21255; 25150; 29541; 33913; 33914

Journal of the Senate of the state of Mississippi. 2291; 6074; 6075; 9508; 13356; 17175; 21477; 25396; 29777; 34159; 39611

Journal of the Senate of the state of Missouri. 6082; 9515; 13361; 21481; 25401; 29780; 39616

Journal of the Senate of the state of New Hampshire. 9631; 13503; 17322; 21619; 21620; 25508; 29935; 34437; 39748

Journal of the Senate of the state of New York. 2491; 2492; 9763; 13622; 13623; 17479; 25626; 30106; 34601; 39903

Journal of the Senate of the state of Ohio. 2588; 6335; 9762; 9763; 13621; 13622; 13623; 17479; 25626; 30106; 34601; 39903

Journal of the Senate, of the state of Tennessee. 3417; 6947; 10427; 14268; 18167; 22437; 26188; 30781

Journal of the Senate of the United States of America. 3762; 7303; 10908; 18766; 22902; 27141; 31357; 36472; 41207

Journal of the thirty-eighth convention of the Protestant Episcopal Church in the state of Pennsylvania. 10033

Journal of the thirty-seventh convention of the Protestant Episcopal Church in the state of Pennsylvania. 6557

Journal of the thirty-sixth convention of the Protestant Episcopal Church in the state of Pennsylvania. 2893

A journal of the travels and sufferings of Daniel Saunders. 17895

Journal of the votes and proceedings of the General Assembly of the Colony of New-York. 2471

A journal of travels in England, Holland and Scotland. 3224

A journal of travels into the Arkansa [!] territory, during the year 1819. 6319

A journal of voyages and travels in the interiour of North America, between the 47th and 58th degrees of north latitude. 1518

Journals House of Representatives. 27142

Journals of a special session of the General Assembly of the territory of Arkansas. 32024

The journals of Madam Knight and Rev. Mr. Buckingham. 21135

Journals of the American Congress; from 1774 to 1788. 14545

Journals of the fifth session of the General Assembly of the territory of Arkansas. 27887

Journals of the fourth session of the General Assembly of the territory of Arkansas. 19459

Journals of the General Assembly of the state of Vermont. 4090; 7509; 11293

Journals of the Grand Lodge of Vermont. 8769; 16228; 24627

Journals of the ocean. 27581

Journals of the proceedings of the annual convention of the Protestant Episcopal Church in the diocese of Connecticut. 17712

Journals of the proceedings of the Bishops, clergy, and laity of the Protestant Episcopal Church in the United States of America. 13868

Journals of the Senate and House of Commons of the General Assembly of North-Carolina. 2562; 6306; 9728; 13596; 17440; 21701; 25602; 30072; 34570; 39859

Journals of the Senate during the first session of the fifth Legislature of the state of Louisiana. 2018

A journey round my room. 39420

A journey on horseback through the great West. 21247

A journey to Peekskill. 1808

Joy in Heaven over the penitent. 24407

The joys of harvest home. 6092

The jubilee of New England. 7690

The Jubilee rondo. 5457; 8827; 20669; 20670

Judah Alden. 36473

Judd vs. Trumbull. 1811

Judge Hopkinson's letter. 39026

Judge - Michigan. March 18, 1828. 36474

Judge Todd's answer and the court's decision, upon the article of impeachment preferred against him. 35533

The judgment, a vision. 5586

Judgment and mercy. 1053

Judicial specimens, and brief explanatory correspondence, submitted to the consideration of a free people. 32461

Judiciary System United States. 27143; 36475

Judith, Esther, and other poems. 594; 1812

Julia; an original song. 30581

Julia loves. A canzonett. 9913

Julia's wreath. 21395

Julian; a dramatic fragment. 14120

Julian, a tragedy in five acts. 13365

Julian Percival. 30597

Juliana. A favorite dance. 8828

Juliana Oakley. 22273; 22274; 22275; 22276; 30598

Juniatta, and Chesapeake and Ohio Canal. 27144

Junior exhibition. Williams College. 31768

Junior sophisters. 5557

Junius unmasked. 33741

Junta gubernativa de la Provincia de Texas. 14272

A Jurisprudencial [sic] Enquiry into the Grounds of the Old and New Grant Controversy. 33742

Just and true account of the Prison of the City and County of Philadelphia. 1816

Just like love. 969

Just published, a new, interesting and moral work entitled The sweets of solitude. 7680

Just published by H.C. Carey & I. Lea, Philadelphia; in one volume folio... Reports upon canals, rail-ways, roads. 23999

A just standard for pronouncing the English language. 5010; 8372; 15793; 20101

The justice and forbearance of God. 3238

The justice's guide; or, Directory for justices of the peace. 22452

The justice's manual: or, A summary of the powers and duties of justices of the peace. 23227; 41443

Justiciaris Pacis. 1817

Justification by faith. 619; 19895

Justification of the ways of God to Men. 1818

Justina; or, The will. 12977

The juvenile album. 25012

Juvenile anecdotes. 8204

The juvenile arithmetick, and scholar's guide. 30497; 35083

The juvenile class book. 35203

The juvenile companion. 28200

Juvenile correspondence. 7756

The juvenile English grammar. 39172

The juvenile expositor, or American school class-book. 2772; 6480; 30260

The juvenile expositor; or, Child's Dictionary. 340; 4625

The Juvenile forget me not. 33744

Juvenile geography. 39254

The juvenile harmony. 39231

The juvenile instructer. 2773; 25772

The juvenile mentor. 2774; 21897; 34795; 40078; 40079

A juvenile monitor. 12980

The juvenile national calendar. 1819; 16755

Juvenile pastimes. 1820; 1821;

21085

The juvenile philosopher. 13138; 25142

Juvenile piety. 1822

The juvenile Plutarch. 29394

A juvenile poem, entitled The Heliad. 33838

Juvenile poems. 9178; 33745

Juvenile psalmist. 39485

Juvenile psalmody. 29169

The juvenile reader. 12981; 13962; 25952

The juvenile sketch book. 33746

The juvenile souvenir. 29395

The juvenile speller. 21086

The juvenile spelling-book. 2775; 6481; 25013

The juvenile trial. 1823; 1824

Juvenilia. 25014

Juvenis, to the electors of the County of Madison. 21087

K

Katechismus, oder Kurze und einfaltig Unterweisung aus der Heiligen Schrift. 17124

Kau a nau so na na nono do wau gau ne u wen noo da. 29297

Kathleen O'Moore. 33748

Keep thy truth, sweet maid awhile. 16496

Kelley's first spelling book. 25018; 33751

Kelley's second spelling book. 29399

Kenilworth. 6745; 6746; 6747; 6748; 6749; 6750; 17917; 17918

Kent bugle quick step. 21062

The Kentucky almanac. 1853; 1854; 5757

The Kentucky farmer's almanac. 1855; 5759

The Kentucky harmonist. 2248; 25317

Kentucky harmony. 24309

Kentucky institution for the deaf and dumb. 22903

The Kentucky Miscellany. 5728

The Kentucky tragedy. 21109; 25030

Kenyon Seminary and College.

24073

Key adapted to the questions for Grimshaw's History of the United States. 9199; 16352; 21112; 38852

Key adapted to the questions for Grimshaw's improved edition of Goldsmith's Greece. 25031

Key adapted to the questions for Grimshaw's Life of Napoleon. 38853

A key containing the answers to the examples in the introduction to algebra. 28538; 38215

A key, containing answers to the examples in the Sequel to intellectual arithmetic. 24154; 28537; 38214

Key of Hitchcock's New method of teaching book-keeping. 24861; 38994

Key to a selection of Perrin's Fables. 28212

Key to a sequel to first lessons in arithmetic. 12201

Key to American tutor's assistant improved. 8230

Key to book-keeping. 11572

A key to Daboll's arithmetic. 32880

A key to English grammar. 5872

A key to introductory arithmetic. 33919

Key to Morse's picture of the House of Representatives. 13407

A key to knowledge. 16793; 16794

A key to Ryan's Algebra. 22166

Key to the American edition of Latin versification simplified. 39195

Key to the American Tutor's assistant. 2060

A key to the classical pronunciation of Greek, Latin and Scripture proper names. 4150; 7557; 14812; 23195

Key to the exercises adapted to Murray's English grammar. 2377; 9590; 13461; 13462; 13463; 16795; 25472; 29868; 34350

A key to the exercises for writing,

contained in The institutes of English grammar. 19875

Key to the first chart of the Masonic mirror. 21783

Key to the first eight books of the Adventures of Telemachus. 28213

A key to the last New York edition of Bonnycastle's Algebra. 25996

A key to the Latin and Greek languages. 39940

A key to the new Latin tutor. 39283

A key to the New Testament. 9877

A key to the revelation; or, Revelation revealed. 35165

A key to the second New York edition of Bonnycastle's algebra. 10163

A key to the shorter catechism. 9200; 41487

A key to the technical language and a few other difficulties of chemistry. 35217

A key to the third American edition of Bonnycastle's Mensuration. 15496

A key to the Western calculator. 27888

Key to Vivian Grey. 29421

A key to Willetts' arithmetic. 19285

The keys, a vision of Samaritams, in the year of the Christian era, 1820. 21113

Kill deer. 22258

Killing considered. 894

The kind little boy. 28366

Kind Robin loves me. 19290

The king and the country man. 34648

King and Thirber. 27145; 41208

King caucus. 23190

King-caucus, or "Secrets worth knowing." 16808

King Henry IV. 14091

King John. 10235

King Lear. 10236; 17947; 40393

The king of the peak. 11799

King's Bridge cottage. 27699

King's choice selection of Eng-

lish songs. 13020

King's choice selection of Scottish songs. 9207

King's Scotch song book. 9208; 9209

The Kingdom of Christ. A missionary sermon preached before the general assembly of the Presbyterian Church in Philadelphia. 5503

The Kingdom of Christ. A sermon delivered at the ordination of the Rev. Elderkin J. Boardman, to the pastoral care of the Church of Christ in Bakersfield, Vermont. 9992

The kingdom of grace merits universal patronage. 7624

The kingdom of Jesus Christ not of this world. 38977

Kingdom stories for juniors. 37165

Kingston academic exhibition. 16809

Kinloch of kinloch. 21396

Kinlock of Kinlock. 21122

Kirchen-ordnung der Reformirten Kirche in den Vereinigten Staaten von Nord America. 30417

Die kirchen-verfassung der Deutschen evanglisch-lutherischen gemeine in und um Philadelphia. 40044

Kirchliches Jahrbuch. Bericht von den Verrichtungen der Evangelisch-Lutherischen Tennessee Synode. 38494

Kirchliches Jahrbuch und Evangelische Bruchstücke. Bericht von der Verrichtungen der Evangelisch-Lutherischen Tennessee Synode. 33090

Kite's town and country almanac. 1872; 5773; 9914; 13029; 16816; 21126; 25034; 29425; 33784; 39215

Kittredge's third address delivered before the American Temperance Society. 39216

Das kleine A B C - Buch. 1570

Der kleine Catechismus. 2033; 9308; 21127; 25162; 33928;

33929; 33930; 33931; 39339
Des Kleine Davidsche Psalter-
spiel. 15363a; 37808
Das kleine Gebätbuch. 38877
Die kleine geistliche Harfe der
kinder Zions, oder auserlesene
geistreiche Gesänge. 2239
Die kleine harse. 39220
Der kleine Kempis, oder kurze
Sprüche und Gebelhlein.
35498
Kleine Lieder Sammlung. 25035;
28134; 29428; 39221
Das Kleine Lust-Gärtlein, oder
schöne auserlesener[!] Gebter
[!] und Lieder. 5775; 16817
Das Kleine Reformirten Gesang-
buch. 39222
Kleine Sammlung harmonischer
Lieder. 16444
Kleine Spruch-Bibel mit kurzen
Ermunterungen fur auf merkerk-
same Kinder. 9215
Kleines Liederbuch feur Sonntags-
schelen herausgegeben. 33095
Klinck's Albany directory. 9216;
13030
Kneeland's key to the new orthog-
raphy. 29429
The Knickerbocker almanac.
21132; 25043; 25044; 25045;
29430; 33795; 33796; 39228
The knight errant. 1059; 1674;
1675; 2333; 5638; 5639; 5640;
9064; 9065; 12874; 12874a;
20955
The knight of the needle, vs. the
knight of the bristle. 21136
Knight of the spotless banner.
15473
The knights of the orange grove.
33797
Know ye the land. 16267
Know your own mind. 13428
Knowledge. 29433
The knowledge and belief of
scriptural doctrines necessary
to true religion. 24125
Knowledge and holiness the
sources of morality. 4970
Knowledge essential to religion.
12835
"Knowledge is power." 30267

The knowledge of Jesus Christ.
25678
A knowledge of the Bible important to youth. 17726
Der könig Saul von Samuel best-
raft und vom Herrn verworfen.
33086
Koningsmarke, the long Finne.
13678
Koy e we "oos T'kau wen ea"
gweh Oo yad oas had o geh
teeh'gayh. 12776
Kremer & Clay. 21142
Kruitzner. 13081
Kurtzgefasste Anweisung über
die Anlegung von Weinbergen
die Behandlung des Mostes
und des Weines und andere
dahin gehörigen Gegenständen
mit besonderer Rücksicht auf
die Vereinigten Staaten.
33804
Kurze Lebens-Beschreibung des
Seligen Ezechiel Sangmeister.
1892
Kurze Nachricht von den Verrichtungen der ersten Confer-
enz, der Deutschen, Evangelisch Lutherischen Prediger,
gehalten in dem Staat Tennessee. 5271
Kurze und einfaltige Vorstellung
der aussern, aber doch eiligen
recht und ordnungen des Hah-
ses Gottes. 9318
Kurze Unterweisung in der christlichen Religion. 16502
Ein kurzer Auszug aus dem
Heidelberger Catechismus in
Fragen und Antworten. 40210
Kurzer Inbegriff der Christlichen
Lehre. 13038
Kurzgefasster Bericht des Mords,
Verhörs und Betragen des
James Quinn. 29439
The Kuzzelbash. 33245

L

The L.... family at Washington;
or, A winter in the metrop-
olis. 11356

L. Jackson's ornamental writing book. 29337
The La Bayadere Waltz. 165
La Clementina. 20097
La libertad de los mares, o el gobierno Ingles descubierto. 21212
La Plaisance Bay Harbor. 31358
Labor, subsistence, &c. and other reprinted articles. 25056
Labourers in the East. 29080
Lack of vision the ruin of the people. 23977
Lacon: or, Many things in few words. 5029; 5030; 8401; 12212; 12213; 15824; 15825; 24163; 32771; 32772
Laconics; or Instructive miscellanies. 29440
Laconies; or, The best words of the best authors. 40653
The Ladies' and Gentlemen's Diary and Almanack. 1894; 5785; 9225; 13039
The ladies' and gentlemens' diary; or, United States almanac. 1895; 5786; 5787
The ladies' companion. 16838
Ladies' diary. 25058
The ladies' lexicon, and parlour companion. 38853a
The lady and the devil. 5185; 15977
The lady at the farm house. 21147; 33809
The lady of the lake [Eyre] 16844; 24475
The lady of the lake [Scott] 14063; 14064; 14065; 17919; 26031; 30543; 40371
The lady of the manor. 3211; 22277; 26074; 26075; 31872; 35185; 40410
Lafayette [Song] 16847; 16848
LaFayette. A parody. 16849
The La Fayette almanac. 16850; 21148; 25059; 29444; 33810; 39243
Lafayette ball. 21149
LaFayette cotillions. 16729
La Fayette en Monte Vernon en 17 de octubre 1824. 21400

Lafayette in America in 1824 and 1825. 39281; 39282
La Fayette in Mount Vernon. A drama in two acts. 21401
Lafayette, or Disinterested benevolence. 21151
La Fayette, or The Castle of Olmutz. 19330
Lafayette; or, The fortress of Olmutz. 16879
The LaFayette primer. 17744
LaFayette, son of valor! heir of glory! 15145
Lafayette to the people. 21152
The LaFayette waltz. 16851; 16852
LaFayette's grand march. 16843
LaFayette's grand march and quick step. 17827
LaFayette's grand march for the piano forte. 15872; 15873
Lafayette's last visit to America. 16854
LaFayette's march. 15770
LaFayette's return, or The hero's welcome. 18181
LaFayette's waltz. 16853
LaFayette's welcome [Meineke] 17101
LaFayette's welcome. A new patriotic song. 16139
LaFayette's welcome to Philadelphia. 19353; 19354
LaFayette's welcome to the U. States in 1824. 15785
Lafitte; or, The Baratarian chief. 29445; 33811
Le lagrime. 16859
The laity's directory to the Church service. 9228
Lake Ponchartrain Canal. 41209
Lalla Rookh. 6102; 6103; 21503; 25413; 34184; 39631
The Lamb's book. 23219
Lamentation of freemasonry. 38138
A lamentation over the Rev. Solomon Froeligh. 28686
The lamp lighter's address. 29103
The lamp of life. 3195; 6777
The Lamplighter's New-Years Address. 1901

Lancaster agricultural almanac. 29450

Lancasterian geography. 123

The Lancasterian system of education. 5788

The Lancasterian system of tuition in needlework. 5789

Land agent's report. 29592

Land claims between the Rio Hondo and Sabine. 27146

Land claims in east Florida. 27147

Land claims in Florida. 22904; 27148

Land claims in Michigan. 27149; 36476

Land claims in Mississippi. 36477

Land claims in Opelousas. 31359

Land claims in St. Helena District. 27150; 27151

Land district--south of Tennessee. 36478

Land for Fort Washington. 36479

Land, Negroes, stock, &c. for sale. 28060

Land of love romance and glory. 18043

The Land of Powhatan. 4923

Land relinquished. 27152; 36480

Land to Cumberland Hospital. 41210

Land to Kentucky Asylum. 36481

Land to officers of the late war. 27153

Land warrants issued for revolutionary services. 27154

"The land which no mortal may know." 12174; 12175

The landing of Columbus. 21532

Lands between Ludlow and Roberts' Lines, Ohio. 41211

Lands for military post at Green Bay. 41212

Lands for schools and seat of government--Florida. 36482

Lands for support of colleges in Ohio. 36483

Lands granted to Indiana. 36484

Lands in Alabama. 36485; 41213

Lands reverted. 31360

Lands:--St. Helena and Jackson, C. H. Districts. 27155

Lands surveyed and not yet offered for sale. 27156

Lands to Alabama. 36486

Lands to Ohio--for canals. 36487

Lands within the state of Indiana. 41214

A landscape, sketched in New-Hampshire. 5101

Laneham's letter describing the magnificent pageants presented before Queen Elizabeth, at Kenilworth Castle. 9231

Der lange verborgene Freund. 1642; 1643; 33578

Langstroth & M'Dowell's almanac. 16856; 16857

Larger atlas, accompanying Rev. C. A. Goodrich's school geography. 24727

The larger catechism. 31724

A lash for petty tyrants. 29453

Lassie wi' the lint white locks. 11655; 29882

Lassie would Ye love me. 1647

Last appeal to the congregation of St. Mary's church. 5791

A last appeal to the stockholders of the Chesapeake and Delaware canal. 19978; 19979

The last bugle. 9914

The last day of the week. 21165; 29454; 33818

The last days of Lord Byron. 21788

Last legacy, or the useful family herbal. 31759

The last link is broken. 792

Last New Year's Day. 15069

Last night of Woodstock. 28252; 28253

A last notice. Citizens of Knox, a most scandalous handbill, and false as it is scandalous has been this day circulated. 12420

The last of the lairds. 28993

The last of the Mohicans. 24217; 28595

The last of the Plantagenets. 38965

The last solemn scene. 17253

The last token. 11880

The last trumpet. 15122
The last will and testament of Thomas Johnson of Greenfield. 29371
Last wills and testaments of thirteen patriarchs, and Gospel of Nicodemus, the believing Jew. 28135
The last word. A new song. 6384; 13667
The last words and dying confession of Wm. Gross. 12732
The late professors of the College of Physicans and Surgeons having seen fit to withdraw from that institution. 25989
Latent Calvinism detected. 13828
Later from hell. 21887
Latin grammar abridged. 15019; 37359
The Latin reader. 21041; 24968; 29347; 29348; 33689; 39117
The Latin translator. 28629; 38308
Latin versification simplified. 32571
Laugh when you can. 13937
The laughing philosopher. 21172
Laura & Lenza, a Rondo for the piano forte. 2308; 6093; 17193
Laura Somerville. 33821
The lavender girl. 1911; 5800; 9236; 13068; 13069; 16865; 16866; 17102
The law and the facts, submmitted [sic] to the consideration of the militia of the United States. 29457
Law catalogue, Dec. 1823. 14871
The law instructor. 16869
The law of contracts and promises upon various subjects. 24185
The law of executors and administrators. 18219
The law of infancy and coverture. 15405
The law of Java. 8395
The law of nations. 4083; 41363
The law of nisi prius, being reports of cases determined at nisi prius, in the Supreme court of the

state of New-York. 2495
The law of pleading and evidence in civil actions. 40357
The law of the Legislature of the state of New York. 9238
Law of the state of Maryland authorizing the incorporation of Christian congregations. 13231
Law opinion, in the case of the Paterson Manufacturing Society, against the Morris Canal and Banking Company. 39764
Law papers and documents relating to the management of the Old, or Fulton ferry. 9239
A law, to regulate the public markets. 13539
Lawrence & Lemay's North Carolina almanac. 5805; 29459; 33825; 39249
Lawrence the brave. 5579
Lawrie's History of Freemasonry. 39250
Laws and catalogue of the Library of Middlebury College. 13331
Laws and ordinances, made and established by the mayor, aldermen & commonalty of the city of New-York. 13540; 25537; 29963
Laws and ordinances of the Common Council of the City of Albany. 4437; 23443; 37399; 37400
Laws and ordinances ordained and established by the mayor, aldermen, and commonalty of the city of New-York. 6235
Laws and ordinances respecting the markets, in the city of Philadelphia. 34743
The laws and regulations of the Alert Eagle Fire Society. 11570
Laws and resolutions of the Medical Society of South-Carolina. 2202
Laws for the government of the Collegiate and Medical departments in the University of Pennsylvania. 2715
Laws for the government of the

Lead mines. Letter from the Secretary of War. 36489

Lead ore imported. 41215; 41216

The league of the Alps. 24829

A learned and honest clergy essential to the political and moral welfare of the community. 5828

Leave thy lone pillow. 18044

Leaves from a journal; or, Sketches of rambles in some parts of North Britain and Ireland. 4706

Leavitt's farmer's and scholar's almanack. 39257-39259

Leavitt's genuine, improved New-England farmer's almanack. 1921; 5808; 9242; 9243

Leavitt's improved New-England farmer's almanack. 21181; 21182; 25075; 25076; 29466; 33828

Leavitt's New-England farmer's almanack. 13076; 13077; 13078; 16873; 16874

Lebanon. 5809

Das Leben und Bekenntniss des Georg Swearingen. 40584

Das Leben und Wandel des in Gott ruhenten und seligen Br. Ezechiel Sangmeisters. 22199

Lebensgeschichte Napoleon Bonaparte's des ersten Kaisers der Franzosen. 8864

Der Lebenslauf von T. Jefferson und J. Adams. 29094

Lecciones da filosofia. 19126

Lecciones de retorica. 19117

Leçons françaises. 8004; 8005; 28106

Lecteur français amusant et instructif. 26192

Le lecteur français de la jeunesse. 24658

A lecture being the second of a series of lectures, introductory to a course of lectures. 20922

A lecture; being the third of a series in the University of Maryland. 24875

A lecture, delivered at Marlborough, Vt. 25730

A lecture delivered at the opening of the medical department of the Columbian College [Henderson] 20858; 24831

A lecture delivered at the opening of the medical department of the Columbian College [Sewall] 22252; 26054; 33830

Lecture delivered Sept. 2, 1823, in the Theological Seminary, Andover. 19325

A lecture, introductory to a course of law lectures in Columbia College. 15829; 16780

A lecture, introductory to a course of lectures, now delivering in the University of Maryland. 12852

Lecture introductory to the course of anatomy and physiology in Rutgers Medical College. 29031

A lecture, introductory to the course of Hebrew instruction in the General Theological Seminary. 21499

A lecture on a school system for New-Jersey. 39372

A lecture, on classical & national education. 25677

A lecture on existing evils and their remedy. 38336

A lecture on heads. 3321

A lecture on human happiness. 20741; 24732

A lecture on infant schools. 28412

A lecture on land surveying. 24764

A lecture on mysterious religious emotions. 40706

A lecture on popular superstitions. 41507

A lecture on rail roads. 39109; 39110; 39111; 39112; 39113

A lecture on sacred music. 13737

A lecture on some parts of the natural history of New-Jersey. 34172

A lecture on Symmes' theory of concentric spheres. 17079

A lecture, on the doctrine of universal salvation. 31937

Lecture on the medical systems.

38411
A lecture sermon delivered in
the Second Universalist
Meeting House in Boston.
4532
Lecture sermon, No. 1, deliv-
ered at the Lombard Street
Church, Philadelphia. 28884
Lecture sermon on the spring
season of the gospel. 14131
Lectures addressed to the young
men of Hartford and New-
Haven. 33506; 33507
Lectures, delivered at Bowdoin
College, and occasional ser-
mons. 7826
Lectures Françaises. 4499
The lectures of Sir Astley Cooper.
20187; 24216
Lectures on agriculture. 33770
Lectures on American literature.
39223
Lectures on anatomy, surgery,
and pathology. 31875
Lectures on ancient history.
7642
Lectures on Female Education.
1360; 20633; 20634
Lectures on future punishment.
40704
Lectures on geology. 23143
Lectures on infant baptism.
37232; 41587
Lectures on moral philosophy.
11466
Lectures on physiology, zoology,
and the natural history of
Man. 33824
Lectures on reading. 38937
Lectures on rhetoric and belles-
lettres. 501; 15463; 19762;
23834; 23835; 37858; 37860
Lectures on school-keeping.
38894-38896
Lectures on the adulteration of
food and culinary poisons.
12312
Lectures on the Book of Ecclesi-
astes. 11337
Lectures on the discovery of
America. 32889
Lectures on the elements of po-
litical economy. 24218; 38280;

38281
Lectures on the gospel of St.
Matthew. 40126
Lectures on the inspiration of the
scriptures. 41588
Lectures on the natural history
and management of the teeth.
2652; 6377
Lectures on the New Testament.
12333
Lectures on the parables. 2904
Lectures on the philosophy of
natural history. 27557
Lectures on the philosophy of the
human mind. 8196; 15575;
23946; 32495; 37966
Lectures on the Pilgrim's prog-
ress.   21183
Lectures on the progress and
perfection of the Church of
Christ. 4808; 11957
Lectures on the prophecy of
Isaiah. 25958
Lectures on the relations and duties of the middle aged. 33866
Lectures on the restrictive sys-
tem. 38375
Lectures on the sacred poetry of
the Hebrews.   39335·
Lectures on the science of as-
tronomy.   7722
Lectures on the shorter cate-
chism of the Presbyterian
Church. 1447; 38819
Lectures on theology. 23745
Lectures on various topicks of
morals, manners, conduct and
intellectual improvement.
28994
Lectures. The lectures of this
institution commence on the
1st Monday in November.
25990; 33340; 33341; 40336
Lectures to young men, on the
formation of character. 38938
The ledger hand. 12899
The Lee Rigg with variations.
1929; 1930; 13079
Leechmere's Point and Cambridge
Port and road to colleges.
3412
The legacy.   18099
A legacy for young ladies. 23690;

23691; 23692

The legal opinion of the Hon.
William Hunter. 39053

Legal outlines, being the substance of a course of lectures
now delivering in the University of Maryland. 1635; 39005

The legend of the rocks. 29877

The legendary. 37205

Leger[!] of Hitchcock's New
method of teaching book-keeping. 38995

Leghorn bonnet. 1931

Legislative directory for 1826.
27503

Legislative roll and lodgings.
20168

Legislature of Arkansas. 27159

Legislature of Georgia on tariff
and internal improvement.
36490

Legislature of New Jersey.
13517

Legislature of the state of Alabama. 36491

Legislature of the state of Mississippi. Mr. Harris, from
the Joint-Committee appointed
to meet General Andrew Jackson. 34161

Legislature of the state of Mississippi. Mr. Runnels, from
the Joint-Committee appointed
to meet General Andrew Jackson. 34162

Lehr und Zucht-Ordnung der
Vereinigten Brüder in Christo.
10506

Lehrbuch der deutschen Sprache
für Schulen. 25055

Lehre und Zucht-ordnung der
Vereinigten Brüder in Christo.
26265

Leichter Unterricht in der Vokal
Musik enthaltend die vornehm-
sten Kirchen-Melodien. 5197

Leisure hours. 25161

Leisure hours at sea. 21186

Lamprière's biographical dictionary. 25087; 29474

Lemprière's universal biography.
21191

A lenient system, for adjusting

demands, and collecting debts,
without imprisonment. 28673

Lenore. 4238

The Lenten monitor. 27931

The leper of Aost. 21319

Lesbia hath a beaming eye, or
Nora Creina. 6878

Leslie Linkfield. 24229

Lessee D. M'Arthur vs. John
Reynolds. 27921

Lessons for children. 314;
11745; 15261; 19601

Lessons for schools. 4453

Lessons from the Bible. 25097

Lessons in botany. 38342;
38343

Lessons in elocution. 3150;
3151; 3152; 3153; 3154; 6766;
14072; 22224

Lessons in English grammar.
9260

Lessons in Greek parsing. 38783

Lessons in practical anatomy.
12872; 29257

Lessons in simultaneous reading,
spelling, and defining. 25880

Let it alone till tomorrow.
33843; 37739

Let me live remov'd from noise.
21195

Let the dead bury the dead.
7648

Let us haste to Kelvin grove
[Nightingale] 2553

Let us haste to Kelvin Grove
[Smith] 18015; 18016; 18017;
22305; 22306

A letter addressed to a member
of the legislature of Virginia.
4624

A letter addressed to Elders
Calvin Hulbert of Warren,
Herkimer county, and William
Burch of Plainfield, Ostego
county. 11619

Letter, addressed to His Excellency John L. Wilson. 13091

A letter addressed to the Baptist Church in Orwell. 11614

Letter addressed to the chairman of the board of school
commissioners. 8906

A letter addressed to the citizens of Baltimore, 27932

A letter addressed to the Congregational clergy of Massachusetts. 39277

A letter addressed to the Danbury Association. 25003

A letter addressed to the King. 22465; 26209

A letter, addressed to the proprietors and managers of canals and navigable rivers. 20732

A letter addressed to Thomas L. M'Kenney. 1939

Letter and accompanying documents relative to the literary institutions of the state. 19919

Letter and circular from William Beaumont. 23727

Letter concerning the burning of the Philadelphia before Tripoli. 20280

Letter concerning the issue of new stock. 37857

A letter from a blacksmith to the ministers and elders of the Church of Scotland. 19313; 23362; 27686; 37218

Letter from a citizen of Philadelphia, to a member of the legislature at Harrisburg. 38063

Letter from a Congregationalist to a friend. 1940

A letter from a Friend in America, to Luke Howard, of Tottenham. 25100

A letter from a Friend in the country to a Friend in the city. 21197

Letter from a gentleman in Boston to a Unitarian clergyman of that city. 9255; 35463; 35464; 35465; 35466

A letter from a German doctor of the University of Strasburg. 33844

Letter from a member of the First Society of Free Enquirers in Boston. 39278

A letter from a soldier in America, to his wife in England. 2938

A letter from a son to his mother. 1941

A letter from a Trinitarian to a Unitarian. 1920

A letter from Anna Braithwaite to Elias Hicks. 19851

A letter from Bishop Chase, on the subject of his going to England. 12113

A letter, from David Holmes to the Church of Christ in Amherst. 12861

Letter from Dr. Daniel L. Green of Bethlehem, to Dr. Samuel L. Mitchell. 20752

Letter from Edward King and T. J. Wharton. 39199

Letter from Edward Livingston, Esq. to Roberts Vaux. 33888

A letter from Elias Hicks to William Pool. 12822

Letter from Gen. Jackson to Mr. Southard. 29336

Letter from James Mease. 36492

A letter from John Bowden. 19830

Letter from Jos. Strickland [pseud.] to Samuel F. B. Morse. 32914

Letter from Judge Brice. 37306

Letter from Lieut. Col. S. H. Long. 29524

A letter from Mr. Wiliam Cobbett. 32748

Letter from Mrs. Barney. 37704

Letter from Nathan Lufborough. 41218

Letter from Nathaniel Smith. 36493

Letter from Robert Hare. 16409

Letter from the commissioner of the treasury of the state, to the President of the Senate. 16996

Letter from the corresponding secretary of the Franklin Institute of the state of Pennsylvania. 16183

Letter from the Governor of Maryland. 12220

A letter from the Jackson committee of Nashville. 29344

A letter from the king to his people. 5111

Letter from the president of the

board of canal commissioners.
39997; 39998

Letter from the Reverend William
Adam. 23411

A letter from the son of man.
21198

Letter from the Treasurer of the
State. 13197; 21306; 25196;
25197; 29594; 29595; 39394

A letter from the wardens and
vestry of Christ Church, Cincinnati. 15762

Letter from Thomas Jefferson.
24978

Letter from Timothy Pickering.
17634

A letter from William Penn.
2679

Letter in explanation and vindication of Gen. Jackson's invasion and occupation of Florida.
15025

A letter in review of the proceedings and address of the meeting of Methodists. 31674

A letter lately written by - of
L-d, Me. to his friend.
13092

Letter of Elias Hicks. From the
Friend. 33540

Letter of Elias Hicks to Edwin A.
Atlee. 16530

Letter of Gershom Powers.
40139

Letter of Jos. Gist to his constituents. 20681

Letter of Moses Mendelsohn, to
Deacon Lavater. 6023

A letter of the celebrated Charles
Lewis de Haller. 8921

Letter of the committee of correspondence of Lancaster county.
13043

Letter of the Hon. Cadwallader
D. Colden, upon the secret
order of freemasonry. 38218;
38219

Letter of the Hon. John Quincy
Adams, in reply to a letter of
the Hon. Alexander Smyth.
11532; 31886

Letter of the Hon. Stephen Allen,
Mayor of the city of New-

York, to Joseph Bayley. 7783

Letter of the Hon. Thomas P.
Moore, representative in Congress, from Kentucky. 13382

A letter of vindication to His
Excellency Colonel Monroe,
president of the United States.
16766; 21090

Letter (A), of which the following
is an extract, was this morning picked up in one of the
streets of this city. 16889

A letter on Christian perfection.
2061

A letter on devotion at Church.
29482

A letter on speculative freemasonry [Merrick] 39562

Letter on speculative free masonry [Sumner] 40578

A letter, on the dispute of the
statements of Anna Braithwaite and Elias Hicks. 17975;
17976

A letter on the necessity of de-
fending the rights and interests of agriculture. 6941

Letter on the penitentiary system
of Pennsylvania. 31590

A letter on the principles of the
Christian faith. 3228; 10284

A letter on the principles of the
missionary enterprise. 23509;
30847

A letter on the sacred doctrine
of the divine Trinity. 8371

Letter on the use and abuse of
incorporations. 29483

A letter on the yellow fever of
the West Indies. 2618

Letter regarding the formation
of the American academy of
language and belles lettres.
675

Letter relating to the estate of
the late Jeremiah Allen.
15063

Letter, report and documents on
the penal code. 34680

Letter to a class of young ladies.
33071

Letter to a convert. 33845

Letter to a deist in Baltimore.

Letter to the Methodists of central Virginia. 33847

A letter to the parishioners of St. Luke's Church. 28632

Letter to the Presbytery of Oneida County. 30203

A letter to the Rev. Abner Kneeland. 9176

A letter to the Rev. Adoniram Judson, sen. 1813

A letter to the Rev. Charles B. M'Guire. 21202

A letter to the Rev. Dr. Beecher. 37553; 37554; 37555; 37556

A letter to the Rev. Edward Smyth. 5416

A letter to the Rev. Jackson Kemper. 12227; 12228

A letter to the Rev. Lyman Beecher. 21203

Letter to the Rev. Nathaniel Smith. 25101

Letter to the Rev. Parsons Cooke. 34643

A letter to the Rev. Samuel Miller. 6836

A letter to the Rev. William Boswell. 12030

A letter to the Rev. William Channing. 596

A letter to the Rev. William Vincent Harold. 9256

Letter to the Right Hon. Lord Kenyon. 16890

A letter to the Rt. Rev. Bishop Hobart. 12947; 12948

A letter to the Rt. Rev. James Kemp. 8972; 8973

Letter to the Right Reverend John Henry Hobart. 27804

A letter to the Roman Catholics of Philadelphia. 9257

Letter to the secretary of war. 30550

Letter to the Senate and House of Representatives of the United States. 5155; 5814

A letter to the Trinitarian Congregational Church in Waltham, Massachusetts. 29484

A letter to the trustees of Frederick Academy. 29432

A letter to the trustees of

South-Carolina College. 1943

A letter to the wardens and vestry of Christ Church, Cincinnati. 16891

A letter to Thomas Wistar. 28530

A letter to William H. Crawford. 5156

The letter writer. 29485

Letters addressed to a brother in the church. 40631

Letters addressed to John Sergeant, Manuel Eyre, Lawrence Lewis, Clement C. Biddle, and Joseph P. Norris. 32955

Letters addressed to Rev. Moses Thacher. 39280

Letters, addressed to several philanthropic statesmen, and clergymen. 24033

Letters addressed to the Agricultural Society of South-Carolina. 29368

Letters addressed to the commissioners appointed by the Legislature of New-York. 21204

Letters addressed to the daughter of a nobleman. 5524

Letters addressed to the members of the eighteenth Congress. 14077

Letters, addressed to the members of the General Conference of the Methodist Episcopal Church. 1944

Letters addressed to the people of the United States. 8830; 8831

Letters addressed to Thomas Bullock. 33180

Letters addressed to Trinitarians and Calvinists. 4163; 4164; 4165

Letters and documents in relation to the dissolution of the engagement of Loammi Baldwin, with the Union Canal Co. 14330

Letters and documents of distinguished citizens of Tennessee. 33848

Letters and journals of Lord Byron. 38018

The letters of the British spy.
4313

Letters of the Gospels. 15024

Letters of the late John Thorp.
6973

Letters of the late Lord Littleton.
5040

Letters of the Rev. Dr. Beecher
and Rev. Mr. Nettleton.
32254

Letters of the Secretary of War,
and opinions of the Attorney
General of the U. S. 10989

Letters of Thomas Gray. 1440

The letters of Wyoming. 19341

Letters on Christian baptism.
25138

Letters on Christian communion.
15974

Letters on clerical manners and
habits. 29762; 29763

Letters on education. 11467

Letters on female character.
32612

Letters on masonry. 39159

Letters on national subjects.
1902

Letters on practical subjects.
10325

Letters on religious persecution.
28400; 38064

Letters on religious subjects.
By a Bible Christian. 5816

Letters on religious subjects,
written since 1801, by sundry persons, whose name they
bear. 12708

Letters on slavery. 25900

Letters on the atonement. 29353

Letters on the constitutionality
and policy of duties, for the
protection and encouragement of
domestic manufactures. 39380

Letters on the constitutionality of
the power in Congress to im-
pose a tariff for the protection
of manufactures. 33965; 39381

Letters on the divinity of Christ.
12557

Letters on the eastern states.
2241; 3497; 7016

Letters on the elementary principles of education. 20791

Letters on the eternal generation
of the Son of God. 10369

Letters on the eternal Sonship of
Christ. 13339

Letters on the general structure,
government, laws and discipline of the Church. 24414

Letters on the Gospels. 23416

Letters on the immortality of the
soul. 37557

Letters on the importance, duty,
and advantages of early rising.
19891

Letters on the improvement of
the mind. 716; 8312; 24057;
28436

Letters on the logos. 36987

Letters on the ministry, ritual
and doctrines of the Protestant
Episcopal Church. 3286

Letters on the natural history and
internal resources of the state
of New York. 8370

Letters on the new theatre.
29107

Letters on the Richmond party.
13098

Letters on the sacrament of the
Lord's supper. 7978

Letters on the spiritual manifestation of the Son of God.
38595

Letters on the Union Canal of
Pennsylvania. 4523; 23582

Letters on Unitarianism. 6055;
13340

Letters proposing a plan for the
permanent encouragement of
the fine arts. 30845

Letters to a child. 6938

Letters to a friend, on ecclesiastical councils, discipline and
fellowship. 16894

Letters to a friend, on the evidences, doctrines and duties of
the Christian religion. 8891;
24747

Letters to a young gentleman com-
mencing his education. 14859

Letters to a young lady. 11797;
15317; 23750; 28102; 37760;
37761

Letters to Alexander Campbell.

20748

Letters to an anxious inquirer. 29202

Letters to Barton W. Stone. 8365

Letters to C. C. Biddle, Wm. McIlvaine, Mary Corvgille, and John Bacon. 10221

Letters to Congress, on national free schools. 40274

Letters to Dr. Priestley. 16895

Letters to James Blythe, D. D. 18110

Letters to James Monroe. 1868

Letters to John Quincy Adams. 12995

Letters to married ladies. 30632; 40449

Letters to Mr. Elias Lee. 20758

Letters to Rev. James Wilson. 13309

Letters to Richard Heber. 7744

Letters to the Hon. William Prescott. 15690

Letters to the Jews. 17696

Letters to the members, patrons and friends of the Branch American Tract Society in Boston. 19421

Letters to the people of Pennsylvania. 30650

Letters to the people of the United States. 35242

Letters to the Rev. A. M'Farlane. 30320

Letters to the Rev. John Potts. 29488

Letters to the Rev. William E. Channing. 35167

Letters to the Roman Catholics of Philadelphia, and the United States. 9258

Letters to Unitarians and reply to Dr. Ware. 11475

Letters to Unitarians occasioned by the sermon of the Reverend William E. Channing. 4326

Letters to young ministers of the gospel. 23596; 32095

Letters written by the late Right Honourable Philip Dormer Stanhope. 4972; 4973; 15735

Letters written in the interior of

Cuba. 37345

Lettre à l'Honorable Abraham Edwards. 31797

Lettre pastorale de Nosseigneurs L'Archeveque de Baltimore. 38089

Die letzte Ehre des christlichen Predigers in einer christlichen Gemeine. 20294

Lewis B. Willis. 31371

Lewis County Republican nominations. 16900

Lewis Neth. 41219

Lewis Rouse. 27177; 31372; 36509

Lewis Schrack. 36510; 41220

Lexicon manuale Graeco-Latinum et Latino-Graecum. 22205

Lexicon-medicum. 9054; 9055; 16578; 24886; 39024

Das lezte Bekenntniss von John Lechler. 9245

The liar. 16163

Liber primus. 5137; 15923; 28655

Liberal Christians, helpers to the truth. 38587

Liberal principles of Mr. Adams. 33860

The liberality of several gentlemen. 16461

La libertád de los mares. 322

Liberty saved, or The warnings of an old Kentuckian. 21213

Librairie de Behr et Kahl. 19652

Librairie Française, Espagnole, Italienne, &c. 15332

Library at auction. Catalogue of rare and valuable books; the library of the late Richard Peters. 35494

Library Company of Wilmington, Catalogue. 14941

Library fire-proof. 27178

Library of C. A. Rodney. 22118

Library of divinity. 1541

La libreria Masonica y general Ahiman Rezon. 8385

El libro primero de los niños, ó Nueva cartilla española. 13106

Licence to keep and sell gun

powder in the town of Providence. 10047

Licenses...to trade with the Indians.   27179; 31373; 36511;
41221

Lied eines lehrers, an seine con-
firmanten.   5824

Lieutenant Duncan. 27180

Lieutenant Isaac M'Keever. 27181

Lieutenant Weaver's vindicatory
address and appeal, to the public. 19216

The life, adventures & uncommon
escapes of Frederick, baron
Trenck. 26238

The life and acts of Saint Patrick.
9152; 12957

The life and adventures of Arthur
Clenning.   33202

The life and adventures of Bam-
fylde Moore Carew.   13107

Life and adventures of Col. Daniel
Boone.   12545; 16140

The life and adventures of Dr.
Caleb. 9307

The life and adventures of Humphrey Kynaston.   33805

Life and adventures of Israel R.
Potter.   1960

The life and adventures of James
R. Durand. 1058

The life and adventures of John
Dahmen.   5765

The life and adventures of Olau-
dah Equiano.   38484

The life and adventures of Peter
Wilkins. 34636; 34637; 39956

The life and adventures of Robert
Bailey. 7865

Life and adventures of Robert,
the hermit of Massachusetts.
40690

Life and adventures of Robinson
Crusoe. 24319; 32912

The life and character of Stephen
Decatur.   7549; 7550; 11324

Life and character of the Chevalier John Paul Jones. 22264;
22265

Life and confession of David D.
How.   15150

The life and confession of George
Swearingen.   40582; 40583

The life and confession of James
Hudson.   23375

The life and confession of John
Johnson.   16902

The life and confessions of Daniel
Davis Farmer. 8662

The life and confessions of George
B. Jarman.   33699

The life and confessions of Pere-
grine Hutton. 1723

Life and death of Eliza Thornton.
13108

The life and death of Isabella Turnbull and Ann Wade. 37210

The life and death of Lady Jane
Grey. 29498

Life and death of Stephen Decatur.
1961

Life and death of two young
ladies, contrasted. 16903; 25110

The life and exploits of...Don
Quixote de la Mancha. 20016;
28426; 32625; 32626

The life and genius of Goethe.
15174

Life and letters, together with poetical and miscellaneous pieces
of the late William Person.
2730

The life and religious experience
of the celebrated Lady Guion.
1476; 4381; 5511; 20775

The life and remains of Edward
Daniel Clarke.   30132

Life and remarkable adventures of
Israel R. Potter. 17676a; 17677

Life and sufferings of James Stil-
well.   10355; 18107

The life and surprising adventures
of Robinson Crusoe. 12353

The life and surprising exploits of
Rob Roy Macgregor. 6893

The life and travels of Father
Quipes. 2930

The life and times of Frederick
Reynolds. 25932

The life and voyages of Christopher
Columbus. 39105

The life and works of Robert
Burns. 15602

The life, condemnation, dying address and trial of the three
Thayers.   21214; 21215

The life of Mary, queen of Scots.
8303

Life of Michael Martin. 5946;
5947; 9368

Life of Michael Powers. 1839;
2840; 2841

Life of Miss Davis, the farmer's
daughter of Essex. 30166

The life of Mr. Henry Longden.
5849; 5850; 9288

The life of Mrs. Mary Fletcher.
2313

The life of Napoleon Buonaparte
[Scott] 30544; 30545; 30546;
35121; 35122

The life of Napoleon Buonaparte:
containing historical sketches,
and anecdotes. 1964

The life of Napoleon, with the
history of France, from the
death of Louis XVI, to the
year 1821. 38854

The life of Nelson. 22334

The life of Oliver Hazard Perry.
2554; 6299

The life of Orson C. Warner.
41429

The life of Our Blessed Lord and
Savior Jesus Christ. 1250;
5336; 8713; 12556; 24547;
33194; 38590

Life of Philip, the Indian chief.
30528

The life of Rev. David Brainerd.
1083

Life of Rev. Jeremiah Hallock.
37262

The life of Rev. Richard Baxter.
1965

The life of Saint Patrick. 13110;
21216; 33863

Life of Samuel Green. 8885

The life of Samuel Johnson, D.D.
The first president of King's
College. 15713

The life of Samuel Johnson,
LL.D. [Boswell] 15528

Life of Simeon Wilhelm. 1966

Life of Sir William Wallace.
15689; 20330

Life of T. H. Bowden Lambrith.
9268

The life of the Boston bard.
20111

Life of the Honourable William
Tilghman. 38765

The life of the late Dr. Benjamin
Franklin. 12577

The life of the late reverend and
learned Dr. Cotton Mather.
2186; 29698; 34084; 39531

Life of the Marquis de La Fayette. 23198; 27535; 27536;
27537; 27538; 31652

The life of the Rev. Freeborn
Garrettson. 37581

The life of the Rev. John W. de
la Flechere. 396

The life of the Rev. John Wesley, 17202; 25412

The life of the Rev. Thomas
Scott, D.D. 10190; 14055;
14056; 14057; 17912; 26027;
26028; 35116

The life of the Right Honourable
John Philpot Curran. 926

Life of Theobald Wolfe Tone.
26222

Life of Thomas Jefferson. 25163

The life of Thomas Scott. 17913

The life of Tom Thumb. 9269

The life of Washington, and history of the American revolution. 21217

The life of Wesley. 3284; 3285

Life of William Caxton. 35404

Life of William Grimes. 20763

The life of William Kelly. 9270

The life of William Penn, and
other poems. 11381

The life of William Penn [Hughs]
33606

The life of William Penn
[Weems] 11390; 41471

The life of William Vans. 27497

The life, travels, voyages, and
daring engagements of Paul
Jones. 13111

The life, trial, condemnation,
and dying address, of the
three Thayers!! 21218; 21219

The light and life of Christ within. 14899

Light - Bahama bank. 27182

Light brigade march. 20523

The light house. 4299; 11443

Light house on Dutch Island.
27183

Light-Houses. Letter from the
Secretary of the Treasury.
22965

The light of truth; an account of
some of the deeds of Andrew
Jackson. 33864

The light of truth, and pleasure
of light. 28378

The light of truth in the mind of
man. 16905

Light on masonry. 37766; 37767;
37768; 37769

Light vessel - Brandywine Shoal.
36512

Lights and shades of English life.
33865

Lights and shadows of Scottish
life. 11451; 11452; 11453;
19303; 19304; 27673; 31778;
31779

Lights of education. 21221; 25112

Like the gloom of night retiring.
480; 481; 4724; 8076

Die Lilie und die Rose. 16431

Lily Douglas. 29081; 29082

The lily of the vale. 20008

Lincoln's scripture lessons.
21223

Lines adjusted to an anthem, performed on the death of William
Eustis. 21225

Lines in memory of Porter Leavitt. 29462

Lines occasioned by the death of
Henry J. Feltus. 39296

Lines written by Simeon Dewey.
15971

Lines written on reading an account of the execution of Stephen M. Clark. 5831

Linnean Botanic Garden. 25834

Lionel and Clarissa, an opera.
8054

Lionel Lincoln. 15857; 28596;
38273

List of acts omitted in the revision of the statutes. 34502

A list of all the entries in the
Virginia military district. 5847

List of articles free of duty.
15272; 32219

List of balances on the books of
the Third Auditor. 41222

List of committees of the Senate
of the United States. 27184;
27185; 36513

A list of delegates by counties.
4119; 7534

List of delegates in Convention
Yeas and nays on the question.
2155

List of delegates in the convention. Nov. 1820. 2156

List of expulsions and suspen-
sions, as communicated to the
Grand Lodge of the state of
New York. 12604

List of freights charged by the
Pennsylvania Canal Boat Company. 34701

A list of invalid pensioners.
9375

List of jurors in the city of New
York. 29508

List of lands entered on the books
of the auditor of public accounts, for the state of Illinois. 33642

List of lands to be sold... for ar-
rears of taxes. 21663; 39796

List of literary publications, by
New Hampshire writers. 38533

List of members. Active Fire
Club, Salem. 10174

List of members of the House of
Representatives. 9411

A list of names and co-partnerships, that were taxed in the
year 1826. 27733

List of names of the members of
the Convention, and of the
Legislature of Virginia. 38811

A list of patents granted by the
United States. 1972; 13115;
36514

List of patents of lands, &c. to
be sold in January, 1822.
2497; 9682

A list of persons assessed in the
town tax of forty thousand dollars, voted by the freemen of
Providence. 30379; 40193

List of persons, co-partnerships,
and corporations, who were

taxed... in the city of Boston.
28231; 32419; 37890

List of postponements from June
to November session of the
House of Representatives of
New Hampshire. 17327

List of prices of the Philadelphia
Association of Journeymen
Book Binders. 21227

A list of prisoners' names, dis-
charged from the New-York
State-Prison.   2498

List of public officers and civil
appointments, in the state of
Maryland. 39466

A list of reports to be made to
the House of Representatives.
10990; 14625; 18831; 22966;
27186; 31374; 36515; 41223

List of Select Committees. 36516

A list of streets, roads, lanes,
alleys.   16913

A list of the attornies and counsel-
lors of the Supreme Court of
the state of New York. 5538

A list of the cargo taken on board
the Sloop Packet. 1973

List of the House of Representatives [Mass.] 21363

List of the lands entered on the
books of the auditor of public
accounts for the state of Illinois.   21003

A list of the meetings for worship and discipline, comprising
the yearly meetings of Ohio
and Indiana.   8785

A list of the members of the House
of Representatives [U.S.]
7362; 10992; 22967; 27187

A list of the members, subscribers and trustees, of the Free-
School Society of New York.
10050

A list of the musical composi-
tions performed by the Panharmonicon. 20970

List of the names of such officers and soldiers of the Revolutionary Army as have acquired a right to lands. 36517

A list of those qualified to vote
in the town affairs of Portland,

Maine. 10159

List of voters, in the city of
Boston. 11924

A list of young ladies, boarders,
who attend the Misses Martin's
school.   40129

The literary and scientific class-
book.   25094; 29477

The literary box.   25116

The literary fountains healed.
13341

The literary gem.   29509

The literary remains of the late
Henry Neele.   39708

Literature and science of the
United States. 9044

Little Agnes and blind Mary.
33871

Little Ann.   25118; 33872; 39300

The little bird teacher. 39301

Little Bo Peep.   9279

The little boy who minded trifles.
33873

Little Charles.   315

The little deceiver reclaimed.
1976

The little deserter.   16916;
21228

Little ditties for little children.
1977; 6849

Little dog.   21229

The little eagle.   33874

Little Edward.   33875

Little Ellen.   33806

Little Emma and her father. 187;
1540; 1978; 20956; 32070

The little farmer. 5838; 16917

Little George and his penny.
3212

The little girl who was taught by
experience. 29510

The little grammarian. 38596;
38597

The little graves.   1979

Little Helen.   21230

Little Henri, a German tale.
21154; 29446

Little Henry and his bearer.
5839; 10265; 30599

Little Henry.   A German tale.
21155

Little Henry's Sunday lesson.
33876

Little Jack and his rocking horse. 33877

Little Jane.   1980

Little Jane, the young cottager. 3015; 40279

Little Lizzie and the fairies.   900

Little Lucy: or The careless child reformed.   1981

Little Lucy: or, The pleasant day. 21231

The little manufacturer.   21232

The little missionary.   10041

Little Nancy, or, The punishment of greediness.   16918

Little Nannette.   21233

The little Osage captive.   8446

Little Patrick, the weaver's son. 29511

The little philosopher.   37350

Little plays.   28762; 28763

Little pocket looking glass.   39302

Little poems.   1982

Little poems for little readers. 5840; 33878

The little poulterer.   1983; 5841

The little present.   33879

Little Red Riding-Hood.   16920

Little Robert and the owl.   17971

The little rogue.   39303; 39304

Little Sally or the good girl. 29512

Little sermons on great subjects. 27669

Little sins.   1984; 1985; 21234

Little Sue.   1658

Little Susan and her lamb.   16921; 29513; 39305

Little Susan. Designed for children two or three years old. 33880

The little teacher.   25119

Little Tom, the huntsman's boy. 29514

Little Tom, the ploughman's boy. 39306

The little traveller.   21235; 33881

Little verses for good children. 31976

The little wanderers.   16922

Little Wentworth's morning lesson.   33882

The little woodman.   26076; 30600; 30601

Little Zoe and the spoiled children.   39307

Liturgy for the use of the church at King's Chapel in Boston. 32438

The liturgy of the New Jerusalem Church.   9657

Live oak timber.   27188; 31375

Lives of Adam Wallace and Waller Mill.   39308

The lives of Clemens Romanus, Ignatius, and Polycarp.   33887

The lives of distinguished foreigners.   25122

Lives of the ancient philosophers. 16132

The lives of the fathers, martyrs, and other principal saints.   8224

Lives of the novelists.   22217; 26032

Lives of the signers to the Declaration of Independence.   38780

Lives of the twelve apostles. 33425

The living and the dead.   29907

Living manners.   9281

Living plays.   16925

Llalla Rookh.   34183

Loan office and final settlement certificates, outstanding and unpaid.   27189

Location of Florida Indians.   27190

The lock and key.   16550; 16551

Locke's Essay for the understanding of St. Paul's epistles. 1990

Lodoiska; An opera.   12991

The log house. 24826

Logan, a family history.   9603

Logan, an Indian tale.   7608

Logan.   The last of the race of Shikellemus chief of the Cayuga nation.   12385

The logic and law of Col. Johnson's report to the Senate, on Sabbath mails.   39313

Logier's theoretical and practical study for the piano forte.   2000

The Lollards.   9286

London; a descriptive poem.   2001

The London and Paris union rule. 25130

The London march. 2002

The London Mathews. 17076; 17077; 17078

The London medical dictionary. 2654

The London practice of midwifery. 2004; 2005; 25131

The Long-Island almanack for 1828. 29525

The Long Island and farmer's almanack for 1830. 39317

Long Island Sound. 29526

The long lost friend. 1644

Long Tom's pilgrimage. 39988

The long wished secrets unfolded. 3186

Longworth's American almanac, New-York register, and city directory. 4382; 5851; 9289; 13135; 16934; 21246; 25137; 29527; 33902; 39319

Look out upon the stars my love [Gilles] 12679; 16290

Look out upon the stars my love [Meineke] 17103

The looking-glass, for the mind. 400; 15334; 19667; 37770

Die Loosungen und Lehrtexte der Brüdergemeine für das Jahr 1822. 6112

Lopez and Wemyss' edition. Acting American theater. 29528

Lord Byron and some of his contemporaries. 33617

Lord Nelson's hornpipe. 2008

Lord remember David. 8931

Lord Roland rose and went to mass. 23325

Lord Ullin's daughter. 10345

Lord's day. A hymn tune. 13363

The Lord's prayer. 25141

The Lord's supper, a sermon. 33774

The Lord's words are spirit and life. 4231

Loss of the ship "Beverly." 2009

Lost child. 29529; 32556; 39323

Lots in Buffalo. 9562

Lotteries exposed. 29531

Lotteries in the District of Columbia. 36518

Lottery draws on the 1st of June next. 15907

Lottery for promoting the sciences and useful arts. 2011; 7547

Lottery secrets. 1775

The lottery. The wonderful advantages of adventuring in the lottery. 2010

The lottery ticket: an American tale. 9294; 29532

The lottery ticket and lawyer's clerk. 32248

Loud and chill was the blast. 1384

Loud's almanack. 25143

Louden's bonnie woods & braes! 12539; 16937

Louisa's tenderness to the little birds in winter. 32278

The Louisiana almanac. 5865; 9300; 13153; 21258; 29543; 33915

Louisiana and Mississippi. 3384

Louisiana and Mississippi almanac. 13154

Louisiana Bank. 2007

Louisiana. Memorial of the Legislature of Louisiana praying for the final adjustment of land titles in the state of Louisiana. 36519

Louisiana. Memorial of the Mayor, Aldermen, and inhabitants, of New Orleans. 36520

The Louisiana merchants & planters almanack. 5866

Louisville and Portland Canal Company. 41224

Love à-la-mode. 13181; 16975

Love and friendship. 10346; 14208

Love and liberty. 788

Love & opportunity. 7056

Love and patriotism! 21260

Love & time. 1832; 9185; 9186

Love characteristic of the Deity. 12962

Love, good night! 16482

"Love has eyes." 482

Love in a village. 8055

Love is a little runaway. 14209

Love laughs at locksmiths. 15816

Love makes a man. 20077

Love my Mary dwells with thee. 18100

Love of admiration. 35573
The Love of God to a Lost World. 767; 24119; 32723
Love of popularity. 4327
The love of praise, and the love of virtue. 5867
Love sounds the trumpet of joy. 2020; 2951
Love thee dearest. 11304; 11305; 11306; 14785; 23168
Love to souls the mainspring of ministerial usefulness. 20841
Love to the church, the highest distinction. 15906
A love touch. 38919
Love wakes and weeps [Blangini] 19769
Love wakes and weeps. [Clifton] 12176
Love wakes and weeps [McMurdie] 5893; 5894; 5895
Love's eyes. 5154
Love's young dream. 3329
Lovely rose. 13156
Lovely's Purchase--Arkansas. 36521
Lovers, mother, I'll have none. 13158
Lovers' quarrels. 14767; 21117
Lovers' vows. 39238
The loves of the angels. 13377; 13378
Low's almanack. 2028; 5869;
Low's almanack and mechanic's and farmer's calender. 9303; 13159; 16951; 21266; 25156
Lucas' progressive drawing book. 29551
Lucinda; a dramatic piece in two acts. 33926
Lucinda; or, The mountain mourner. 17016
Lucretia and her father. 33927; 39337
Lucy and her Dhaye. 29552
Ludlow and Roberts' Lines. 27191
Luke the labourer. 615; 37978
Lullaby. Arranged as a rondo for the piano forte. 14224; 18112
The Lusiad. 8240; 19930
Luther Chapin. 27192; 31376;

36522; 36523; 41225
The lying valet. 12646; 12647; 16256
Lynchburg Adams meeting. 16954
The lyre of Tioga. 40639
Lyric poems. 26172
Lyrical and other poems. 30614
Lyrics. 10408

M

M. B. Roberts's almanac. 29557
M. Carey and Sons propose to publish by subscription. 4918
M. T. Ciceronis orationes quaedam selectae. 32709
M. T. Ciceronis quaedam selectae, notis illustratae. 32710
M. Tullii Ciceronis De republica librorum reliquae e palimpsesto ab angelo Maio. 12142
M. Tvllii Ciceronis Ad Q. fratrem dialogi tres De oratore, cum notis Jo Aug. Ernesti. 12139
Ma chere amie. 5874
Macbeth. 6773; 10237; 14092
M'Carter's country almanac. 33940; 39353
M'Carty & Davis' Franklin almanac. 2044; 5878
M'Carty & Davis' Pennsylvania almanac. 2045; 5879; 9312
M'Carty's American primer. 33941
McCartney, the builder of the viaduct over the Patapsco. 39354
The Macedonian cry. 5883
Mackenzie's Five thousand receipts. 39366
Madam de Neuville's favourite waltz. 17104
Mad. de Nouville's waltz. 2070; 5899; 9324; 9325; 16980; 16981
Madam, having had the honour of being appointed by a large and respectable meeting of the citizens of Philadelphia. 25740
Madam, Without being able to ascertain what degree of attention you may be desposed to

pay to the recommendation of
a town meeting. 28401

Madam. You are now addressed
as a member of a republic.
9551

Madame le Compte Piernes.
31377

Madeline, a tale. 9789

Maelzel's exhibition. 25183;
33968

Maey's tears. 6778

Maffit's trial. 39383

Magazine of wit. 5901

Magic harmonies. 6362

The magician, and "The holy alliance." 2344

Magnalia Christi americana.
2183; 2184

The magnitude of the ministerial
office illustrated from the value of the soul. 4521

The Magpie. 9961

The maid my heart adores. 4725

Maid of Athens. 1859; 16802;
16803

The maid of Devon. 5905

The maid of Llangollen. 770

The maid of the mill. 8056

Maids like the flowers. 20236

Maine branch of the American
Education Society. 11599

The Maine civil officer. 21862

The Maine farmer's almanack.
2085; 2086; 5923; 9351; 13205;
17008; 21317; 25209; 29605;
33987; 33988; 33989; 39413

The Maine justice. 13733; 40026

Maine. Memorial of merchants
and others of Portland. 36524

Maine not to be coupled with the
Missouri Question. 758

The Maine primer. 33990

The Maine register and United
States' calendar. 2087; 5924;
9353; 13206; 17009; 21318;
25210; 29607; 33991; 39414

Mair's introduction to Latin syntax. 33995

Le maitre de danse. 28590

Major Barry's hostility to the occupant and Green River settler.
33996

Major General William Lewis.
27193

Major R. Campbell bugle slow
march. 12958

Major Ross's march. 8809

Major's only son. 2089

Malaria; an essay on the production and propagation of this
poison. 39356

Malden Bridge to the people.
39421

The malignant or yellow fever in
Boston. 1753

Malvina: a National ballad opera.
2056

The man and the snake. 5927

The man of feeling. 5887; 33954

The man of God. 33569

The man of sin revealed. 37498;
37499

The man of the world. 16976

The man of two lives. 37876

Man responsible for his belief.
27549

Man's dependence, and God's
goodness. 23364

Man's first estate and high re-
volt. 38041

The manager in distress. 8392

A mandate for Lent. 41506

Mandates and decrees of the
Grand Council of Princes of
Jerusalem. 38652

Manfredi, a tragedy. 6799

Manhood. 2093

The maniac: a poem. 9356

The maniac song! 4762

The maniac's confession. 6800

The manifestations of the divine
goodness. 39154

Manifesto del Supremo poder ex-
ecutivo a la nacion. 13321

Manifesto que hace el Coronel
Español Don José Coppinger.
5081

Manifiesto que hace el Gobierno
de Colombia. 32769

A manifesto, to the people of the
United States. 16149

The manly heart. 2352; 6135

Manna gathered in the morning.
25672

Manners and customs of several
Indian tribes. 12897

Manners of the ancient Israelites.
20535

Manoeuvres of field batteries.
25219

Manual de practica parlamentaria.
24979

The manual for invalids. 38804

A manual for the Deist. 14802

A manual for the members of the
Briery Presbyterian Church,
Virginia. 32477

Manual for the use of children in
Episcopal Sunday Schools.
6549

Manual for the use of children in
Sunday Schools. 5930

Manual for the use of the stetho-
scope. 38225

A manual Hebrew and English lexicon. 33347

Manual Masonico conteniendo los
estatutos y reglamentos gener-
ales. 24586

Manual of botany. 8588; 16034;
38441

A manual of chemistry [Brande]
4830; 23922; 37930

A manual of chemistry [Webster]
27585; 37114; 41454

Manual of court forms. 25220;
34008

A manual of electricity. 21118

A manual of family prayer. 37870

A manual of French phrases.
9003; 16512

A manual of general anatomy.
32242

A manual of legislative practice.
30746

A manual of materia medica and
pharmacy. 38451

Manual of mineralogy and geology.
24425; 24426

Manual of mutual instruction.
25988

Manual of parliamentary practice;
comp. and arranged for the
use of the Senate and Assembly of the state of New York.
24114

A manual of parliamentary practice, composed originally for
the use of the Senate of the

United States. 1789; 9144;
12953; 33705

Manual of pathology. 29633

A manual of political economy.
34782

A manual of practical obstetrics.
33503

A manual of surgical anatomy.
33048

Manual of surgical operations.
20199

Manual of the Albany Lancaster
School.   942

A manual of the difficulties of
the French language. 38722

Manual of the Lancasterian system, of teaching. 2914

Manual of the physiology of man.
33635

The manual of the Superior Courts
of Chancery at Richmond and
Lynchburg. 41385

A manual of worship. 25221

A manual; or Hand book, intended for convenience in practical surveying. 6026

The manufacturer's book of wages.
21520

The manufacturer's, farmer's and
mechanic's guide. 8992

The manufacturers. 29619

The manuscript, comprising the
Fratricide, and miscellaneous
poems. 29702

The manuscript of Diedrich Knickerbocker.   17015

Manuscripts and printed books in
possession of Obadiah Rich.
31378

Map. [United States] 126

Map exhibiting the Farmington &
Hampshire & Hampden canals.
33717

Map of Asia. 37280

Map of Boston. 1492

Map of Louisiana, Mississippi
and Alabama. 24531

Map of Maine, New Hampshire
and Vermont. 24532

Map of Massachusetts, Connecticut and Rhode Island. 1230

Map of North and South Carolina
and Georgia. 25222

Maria of Genesee. 21327
Maria; or The good girl. 34013
Maria. The four sisters. 12271
Marianisches Blumen-Gärtlein.
2103
The Marietta pilot. 2108
Marigny D'Anterive. 27194;
27195; 31379; 36526; 41226
Marine hospital--Charleston, S. C.
36527
Marine hospital - sick and dis-
abled seamen. 31380
Marine telegraph. 12436
The mariners atmospherical reg-
ister. 21328
Marino Faliero, doge of Venice.
4893
Marinus W. Gilbert. 31381;
31382
Marion; or, The hero of Lake
George. 9722
Les maris garcons. 33325
Mark my Alford. 5580
Marmion for sale. 1952
Marmion, a poem. 30548
Marmion; or, The battle of Flod-
den Field. 23702
Marot & Walter's almanack.
17020; 21329; 25226; 29625
The Marquis de LaFayette's mili-
tary waltz. 17021
The Marquis de LaFayette's wel-
come to New York. 17022;
21330
The Marquis de LaFayette's wel-
come to North America. 17114
The Marquis of Huntley's fare-
well. 17023
Marriage. 20511
Marriage customs and ceremonies.
13374; 21501; 29788
The marriage feast, and happy
union. 3187
Marriage indissoluble, because of
divine appointment. 13729
The marriage of Fiagaro. 28191
A marriage in high life. 35115
Marrion Wilder. 29626
Marseilles march. 22138
Marshall's practical marine gun-
nery. 9364
Marshall's spelling book of the
English language. 25229;

25230; 25231; 29628; 39435
Marten and his two little schol-
ars. 19928
The martial Christian's manual.
12858
Martin and his two little schol-
ars. 28367
Martin's treatise on the powers
and duties of executors and
administrators. 2114
Martinique and Guadaloupe. 36528
The martyr of Antioch. 9497
Mary. A canzonet. 12680
Mary and Betsey. 29635; 34024
Mary and her cat. 13223; 34025
Mary and her little kid. 2117
Mary Ann Bond and Mary Love-
less. 36529
Mary Anne. The four sisters.
12272
Mary Hollis. An original tale.
10217
Mary James. 36530
Mary Jones. 34026
Mary, Mary list! awake! 7645;
7646; 14889
Mary Morison. A favourite
Scotch song. 19649; 19650;
19651
Mary of Scotland. 5949
Mary Queen of Scots. 3087
Mary Reynolds. 36531
Mary, the maid of the inn. 5950;
13224
Mary's book of hymns. 39482
Mary's dream, or Sandy's ghost.
10079
Mary's journey. 38807
The Maryland justice. 20233
Maryland. Memorial of farmers,
mechanics, and others. 36532
Maryland. Memorial of the Bal-
timore and Ohio Railroad Com-
pany. 36533
Maryland. Memorial of the Cham-
ber of Commerce of the city
of Baltimore. 36534
The Maryland resolutions. 9444
The Maryland spelling book.
40401
Maryland University lottery.
21352
The Mason's manual. 8737

A masonic address, delivered at Carmel. 28285

A masonic address, delivered at Colonel William Steele's, Woodford County, Ky. 12034

A masonic address, delivered at Herkimer. 31728

A masonic address, delivered on the 24 of June A.D. 1821. 6357

A masonic air. 16039

Masonic. An oration, delivered by Dr. Arthur Nelson. 2393

The Masonic casket. 12110

A Masonic discourse, delivered at the installation of Mexico Lodge. 9795

A masonic discourse: delivered before Franklin chapter, No. II, New-Haven. 2208

A Masonic discourse, delivered before Mt. Vernon Lodge, in Washington, N.H. 17994

A masonic discourse delivered before the Missouri lodge. 34859

A Masonic eulogy, delivered at Frankfort, Ky. 12895

Masonic lecture, spoken before the Brethren of Union Lodge, New-London. 37929

The Masonic manual, or Freemasonry illustrated. 18164

Masonic obligations: an address June 24th, A.L. 5826. 24165

The Masonic obligations from an entered apprentice to Knights Templar. 34049

Masonic obligations unlawful. 39530

Masonic Ode on the Dedication of the Grand Masonic Hall, Philadelphia. 688; 689; 3385

A masonic oration, delivered at Middleburg, Va. 646

A masonic oration. Delivered at the installation of Little-Falls Lodge. 16911

A Masonic oration, delivered before the Grand Lodge of Kentucky. 32467

A Masonic oration, delivered on the 24th June, 1825, in the city of Cincinnati. 19868

A Masonic oration, delivered on the 24th June, 1824 at Milford. 15326

Masonic oration delivered 24th June, 1826, at Hamilton, Ohio. 24224

A masonic oration. Pronounced before the brethren of Allen Lodge. 17158

A Masonic register and pocket magazine. 17042; 21357; 25227

A Masonic sermon delivered at the request of the several lodges in Lexington, Kentucky. 11335

A masonic sermon, delivered before the society of Free and Accepted Masons in Covington, Ky. 12424

A Masonic sermon, delivered in Masons' Hall, Lexington, Ky. 795

A Masonic sermon on general benevolence. 3229

A Masonic testimony. 38772

Masonick melodies. 20365

Masonry, by William Morgan. 34196

Masonry founded on the Bible. 24164

Masonry inseparable from religion. 31755

Masoth Hagojim. 5964

Massa George Washington and General LaFayette. 16483

The Massachusetts agricultural almanack. 2172

Massachusetts collection of martial musick. 3033; 25955

Massachusetts, Connecticut and Rhode Island, map. 3075

Massachusetts election. 2173

Massachusetts expects every man to do his duty. 17067

Massachusetts General Hospital Annual report of Board of Trustees. 34078; 39518

Massachusetts. Memorial of citizens of Boston. 36535

Massachusetts. Memorial of citizens of Duxbury. 36536

Massachusetts. Memorial of inhabitants of Boston. 41227

Massachusetts. Memorial of inhabitants of Nantucket. 36537

Massachusetts. Memorial of inhabitants of Scituate, Pembroke, Hancock, &c. 36538

Massachusetts. Memorial of merchants of Boston. 41228

Massachusetts. Memorial of the proprietors of the Hingham Umbrella Manufactory. 36539

Massachusetts militia claims. 27196; 27197; 36543

Massachusetts nomination. Eustis & Lincoln. 13931

Massachusetts. Petition of citizens of New Bedford. 36540

Massachusetts. Petition of sundry farmers and landholders of the town of Westborough. 36541

Massachusetts quickstep. 33475

The Massachusetts Register and United States Calendar. 2179; 5986; 5987; 9421; 13267; 17073; 21371; 25280; 29692; 34081; 39527

Massachusetts - wool growers of Berkshire. Memorial. 36542

A master-key to popery. 33326

Masters commandant--Navy United States. 36544

Masters of vessels as well as others therein concerned, are required... 28442

Matchett's Baltimore directory. 17074; 29697; 39529

A materia medica, of the United States. 31847

Materials for catechisation on passages of the scripture. 12801

Maternal instructions. 33945

Maternal solicitude for a daughter's best interests. 26174

The mathematical companion. 37191

The mathematical diary. 35087

A mathematical drawing chart. 8839

The mathematical expositor. 34627

Mathematical investigation of the motion of solids. 31999

Mathematical papers. 564

The mathematical principles of

navigation and surveying. 15943

Mathematical tables. 8908; 20769; 20770; 21372; 38870

Mathew's Invitations, and Yates' Reminescences. 25282

Mathew's trip to Paris. 9441

Mathews at home. 9438; 9439; 9440

Matilda, a tale of the day. 21890

Matilda Mortimer. 31801

La matinée. A favorite rondo. 5216; 5217; 12413; 16017; 16018

Matins and vespers. 28262

Matrimonial preceptor. 39532

Matter of fact, Versus Messrs. Huskisson & Peel. 32586

Matters of fact relative to late occurrences among professional Quakers. 29699

Matthias Roll. 36545

Maurice and Berghetta. 2653

Maxims and moral reflections. 29567

Maxims in law and equity. 16506

Maxims of equity. 12574

The may-bee. 14112

May day. 6094; 6095

A may eve dream. 12052

May it please the Court, as I am a very poor man... 330

May you like it. 10412

May's advice to children. 25289

Mayor and common council of Baltimore. 36546

Mayor and council of George Town, D. C. 31383

The mayor of Garratt. 8720; 16164; 16165

Mayor's communication and accompanying documents. 23590

The means by which the prosperity of the Church may be promoted. 15903

Means by which Unitarian Christians may refute misrepresentations of their faith. 35489

The means of curing and preventing intemperance. 560

The means of national prosperity. 363; 364

Measures, not men, illustrated

by some remarks upon the public conduct and character of John C. Calhoun. 13279; 25292

Mécanique céleste. 39247

The mechanic's and working man's almanac. 34095

Mechanics, be warned! 21380

The Mechanics' Almanac. 21379

The Mechanics' almanac, and astronomical ephemeris. 17085

The Mechanics' Assistant; or, Universal Measurer. 29711

Mecklenburg independence. 21381

The mediation of Christ. 26120

The mediatorial reign of the Son of God. 5487

Medical advice to European emigrants. 8564

Medical & physical memoirs. 23988; 28360

Medical College of New York. 25991

Medical college of South Carolina. 20032

The medical companion, or Family physician. 8649; 28820; 28821

Medical deception and imposition upon the public. 16133

Medical dissertation on the diagnosis and treatment of pertussis. 17545

Medical dissertations delivered at the annual meeting of the Massachusetts Medical Society. 9428

Medical dissertations on Hemoptysis. 4170

Medical education. 23735

A medical essay on drinking. 34594

Medical facts and inquiries. 20871

Medical flora. 34950

The medical formulary. 24416; 38461

Medical inquiries and observations, upon the diseases of the mind. 30494

Medical institution of Harvard University. 1536

Medical institution of Maine, at Bowdoin College. 4815

Medical notice. To parents, masters of ships, and such physi-

cians as do not prepare and compound their own prescriptions. 41401

The medical pocket-book, family physician. 10293

Medical police; and rules and regulations, of the Cincinnati Medical Association, 4994

Medical police of the New-Hampshire Medical Society. 6216

The medical practitioner's pocket companion. 9448

Medical school at Boston. 12786

Medical statistics: being a series of tables, showing the mortality in Philadelphia. 28786

Medical statistics; or a comparative view of the mortality in New-York, Philadelphia, Baltimore, and Boston. 30065

Medicine boxes, for any voyages. 1086

Medicine chest and instructive advice. 12869

Medicine chests carefully prepared for all climates. 24745

Medicine chests of all kinds. 20856

Medicine chests with new and approved directions. 30386

Medicine chests, with particular directions. 4210

Medicine chests, with suitable directions. 37329

Meditations among the tombs. 16514

Meditations & contemplations. 9005; 16515; 16516; 20870; 24838

Meditations for every day in the year. 7861; 11661

Meditations on various religious subjects. 34415

Meditations, representing a glimpse of glory. 19246

The medley. 2207; 9451

A medley of joy and grief. 8917

Meet me by moonlight. 4136; 4137

The meeting; a popular new song. 40399

A meeting of a number of citizens was held. 34754

A meeting of a number of gentlemen from several towns in the
County of Lincoln. 2209

A meeting of a number of Roman
Catholics was held at the
school-room of Joseph's.
25298

Meeting of the second...Univer-
salist Church. 2747

A meeting of the Suffolk Republican administration. 30427

The meeting of the waters. 3330

The meeting of the waters of
Hudson & Erie. 22377

Megen oh! oh Megen Ei! 1953

Melancholy! How are the mightly
fallen. 40622

Melmoth, the wanderer. 5990

Melodies, by Thomas Moore.
6104

Melodies, duets, trios, songs,
and ballads. 27700

Melodies, songs, sacred songs,
and national airs. 6105; 6106;
9535; 21504; 21505; 34185;
34186; 39632

The melodist. 3435; 17117; 21407

Member of Congress.   Fellow
citizens! On Monday next,
you will be called upon. 30428

Members and officers of the Assembly. 17382

Members of the class that graduated at Harvard University in
the year 1820. 1537

Members of the Pennsylvania So-
ciety for the Promotion of
Manufactures and the Mechanic
Arts. 31871

Memoir, by Lucy Aikin. 15044

Memoir, correspondence, and
miscellanies, from the papers
of Thomas Jefferson. 39133

Memoir of Ann Eliza Starr.
29722

Memoir of Ann Watson. 14843

Memoir of Anna Eliza Starr.
25305

A memoir of Barbara Ewing.
38512; 38513

Memoir of Barron Clarke. 29723

A memoir of Bowyer Smith. 7695;

14969

Memoir of Caroline-Ann Andrews.
6013

Memoir of Caroline Lee. 13297

Memoir of Catharine Brown.
19434; 23521; 27869; 32001

Memoir of David Acheson. 31977

Memoir of De Witt Clinton. 39031

Memoir of Dr. Bateman. 25306

Memoir of Edward A. Holyoke.
39522

Memoir of Elizabeth Davidson.
13298

Memoir of Elizabeth Matthews.
34085

A memoir of H--- G---, late of
Philadelphia. 17118

Memoir of Herbert Marshall.
35226

Memoir of Hon. William Tudor.
26253

The memoir of James Monroe.
34179

Memoir of Jane Evans.   21408

Memoir of John Arch. 39549

Memoir of John Gallison. 4945

Memoir of John Woolman. 11482;
23379

Memoir of Jonathan Leavitt. 8438;
9241

Memoir of Keopuolani. 22088;
22089

A memoir of Louisa Maw. 39533

Memoir of Lucy A. Pancoast.
2227; 2228; 16129

Memoir of Lucy Hurnard. 6014

Memoir of Mary Hallam Huntington. 1709

Memoir of Miriam Warner. 2229;
21409

Memoir of Miss Eliza Brainard.
6015

Memoir of Miss Hannah Sinclair.
10110

Memoir of Mrs. Ann H. Judson.
39232; 39233; 39234

A memoir of Mrs. Harriet Newell.   21410

Memoir of Mowhee, a young New
Zealander. 4321

Memoir of Rebecca M. Coit. 2230

Memoir of Rev. Levi Parsons.
17237

Memoir of Rev. Henry Martyn. 10182

Memoir of Rev. Thomas Baldwin. 24080

Memoir of Rev. Thomas Sumner Winn. 17119

Memoir of Samuel Hooker Cowles. 35030

Memoir of Sarah Knight. 39550

Memoir of Seth Burroughs. 39691

A memoir of some new modifications, of galvanic apparatus. 1515; 5541

Memoir of Susan B. Marble. 9462; 13299

A memoir of the French Protestants, who settled at Oxford. 24882

Memoir of the late Mrs. Susan Huntington of Boston. 27683; 27684

Memoir of the late William Harris. 39551

Memoir of the life and character of the Rev. Samuel Bacon. 152; 4501; 7842

Memoir of the life and character of the Right Hon. Edmund Burke. 21979

Memoir of the life and happy death of Wilberforce Smith. 9463

Memoir of the life and ministry of Mr. William Bramwell. 3223; 9464; 26080

Memoir of the life and writings of John Calvin. 29578

Memoir of the life, character, and writings of John Adams. 28617

Memoir of the life, character, and writings of Thomas Jefferson. 30641

A memoir of the life, death, and religious exercises of Harriet Dow. 21411

Memoir of the life of Josiah Quincy. 22017

Memoir of the life of Richard Henry Lee. 21184

Memoir of the Rev. Benjamin Goodier. 21412

Memoir of the Rev. Henry Martyn. 3109; 3110; 6717; 17894

Memoir of the Rev. Jesse Lee. 14285

Memoir of the Rev. Joshua Huntington. 2231

A memoir of the Rev. Legh Richmond. 38858; 38859; 38860; 38861; 38862; 38863

Memoir of the Rev. Pliny Fisk. 11917; 32410

Memoir of the Rev. Samuel John Mills. 40514

A memoir of the Rev. William Tennent. 553; 8152

Memoir of the Rev. William Ward. 29724

Memoir of Thomas Addis Emmet. 38879

A memoir of Thomas Hamitah Patoo. 21413

Memoir of Tristam Burges. 19839

Memoir on acupuncturation. 21516

A memoir on the antiquities of the western parts of the state of New York. 793

A memoir on the cultivation of the vine in America. 11545; 31902

Memoir on the discovery of a specific medicine, for the cure and prevention of the yellow fever. 20679

A memoir on the expediency and practicability of improving or creating home markets for the sale of agricultural productions. 22468; 30802

Memoir on the fracture of the lower extremity of the radius. 28073

Memoir on the geography, and natural and civil history of Florida. 5142

A memoir on the geological position of a fossil tree. 10187

Memoir on the organization of the army of the United States. 25307

Memoir on the recent surveys, observations, and internal improvements, in the United States. 40604; 40605

A memoir on the rise, progress, and present state of the Chesa-

peake and Delaware Canal.
5461

Memoir on the subject of aero-
lites. 24555

A memoir on the subject of the
wheat and flour of the state of
New-York. 814; 2524

Memoir on the topography,
weather, and diseases of the Bahama Islands. 26230

Memoir, prepared at the request
of a committee of the common
council of the City of New
York. 20118; 20119; 20120

Memoir read before the Historical
Society of the State of New-
York. 19663

Memoir upon the negotiations between Spain and the United
States of America. 6348; 6349

Mémoires historiques de Napoleon.
2388

Memoirs [Clap] 15769

Memoirs and letters of Mrs. Mary
Dexter. 12368

Memoirs and letters of Richard
and Elizabeth Shackleton.
14085

Memoirs and moral productions
and selections of Miss Eliza
Perkins. 13731

Memoirs and poetical remains of
the late Jane Taylor. 26179;
30769

Memoirs and recollections of
Count Segur. 22236

Memoirs and select papers of
Horace B. Morse. 38008

Memoirs and select remains of an
only son, who died November
27, 1821. 12411

Memoirs, & select remains, of
Charles Pond. 39955

Memoirs, from 1754 to 1758.
11323

Memoirs, including letters and select remains, of John Urquhart.
34622; 34623

Memoirs of a New England village
choir. 38760

Memoirs of Abigal Goodrich.
38773

Memoirs of Andrew Jackson. 4142;
33041

Memoirs of Andrew Sherburne.
35171

Memoirs of Captain James Wilson.
[Griffin] 8895; 29088

Memoirs of Captain James Wilson
[Tappan] 40606

Memoirs of Captain Rock. 17212;
17213

The memoirs of Charlotte Augusta,
princess of Wales and Saxe Cobourg. 6016

Memoirs of Commodore Stephen
Decatur. 979

Memoirs of David Brainerd.
25308; 29725

Memoirs, of Eliza Cunningham.
34553

Memoirs of Eliza Thornton.
17120; 17121

Memoirs of eminent female
writers. 29467; 29468

Memoirs of eminent persons.
29113

Memoirs of Fanny Newell. 17426

Memoirs of General Andrew Jackson. 16690; 16691

Memoirs of General LaFayette,
embracing details of his public
and private life. 21414; 21415

Memoirs of General Lafayette.
With an account of his visit to
America. 16822; 21129

Memoirs of Gilbert Motier La
Fayette. 16009; 16568

Memoirs of Göethe. 16302

Memoirs of Hannah Jerram.
39552

Memoirs of Harriette Wilson.
23344

Memoirs of John Horne Tooke.
33399

The memoirs of Joseph Fouché.
20542

The memoirs of Lafitte. 25309;
34108

The memoirs of Lorenzo da Ponte. 38328

Memoirs of Mary Hallam Huntington. 1708; 2232

Memoirs of military and political
life of Napoleon Bonaparte.
9783

Memoirs of Miss Eliza J. Drysdale. 34109

Memoirs of Miss Hannah Scofield. 3125

Memoirs of Miss Mary Campbell. 1524

Memoirs of Miss Polly Henderson. 1561

Memoirs of Mrs. Clarissa Wells. 27717

Memoirs of Mrs. Mary Cooper. 20192

Memoirs of Mrs. Siddons. 28207

Memoirs of Richard Lovell Edgeworth. 1079; 5233

Memoirs of Sergeant Dale. 6791

Memoirs of Simon Bolivar. 38425

Memoirs of the Agricultural Society of the county of New-Castle. 46

Memoirs of the American revolution. 5206

Memoirs of the Board of Agriculture of the state of New York. 6251; 13551; 25553

Memoirs of the campaign of the North western army of the United States. 16616

Memoirs of the Countess De Genlis. 20648

Memoirs of the Court of King James the First. 7757

Memoirs of the Court of Queen Elizabeth. 4424; 11553

Memoirs of the extraordinary military career of John Shipp. 40419

Memoirs of the Historical Society of Pennsylvania. 30192

Memoirs of the illustrious citizen and patriot, Andrew Jackson. 37060

Memoirs of the late Jane Taylor. 40614

Memoirs of the late Mrs. Susan Huntington. 41573

Memoirs of the late princess Charlotte Augusta. 6017

Memoirs of the late Rev. Abraham Marshall. 17027

Memoirs of the late Rev'd Samuel Pearce. 1340; 33310; 38711

Memoirs of the life and character of Mrs. Sarah Savage. 7071

Memoirs of the life and character of Rev. John Eliot. 9534

Memoirs of the life and character of the late Rev. Cornelius Winter. 12949

Memoirs of the life and character of the late Rev. George Whitefield. 1391; 12685

Memoirs of the life and eulogy on the character of the late Judge Waities. 32968

Memoirs of the life and ministry of the Rev. John Summerfield. 39014

Memoirs of the life and religious experience of Ray Potter. 40136

Memoirs of the life and religious experience of William Lewis. 5818

Memoirs of the life and travels of B. Hibbard. 20878

Memoirs of the life and writings of John Calvin. 13180; 29579

Memoirs of the life and writings of Lindley Murray. 29869

Memoirs of the life, character and writings of the late Rev. Philip Doddridge. 34625

Memoirs of the life of Anne Boleyn. 7999

Memoirs of the life of Caroline Eliz. Smelt. 4134

Memoirs of the life of David Ferris. 20512

Memoirs of the life of John Philip Kemble. 19776

Memoirs of the life of Joseph Alleine. 27803; 37418

Memoirs of the life of Martha Laurens Ramsay. 30399; 30400

Memoirs of the life of Miss Caroline E. Smelt. 4133

Memoirs of the life of the late Mrs. Catharine Cappe. 15638

Memoirs of the life of the Rev. William Tennent. 28257

Memoirs of the life of the Right Honourable Richard Brinsley Sheridan. 21506; 25414

Memoirs of the life of the Right Honourable William Pitt. 6982;

18220

Memoirs of the life, writings, and character, literary, professional, and religious of the late John Mason Good. 38836

Memoirs of the little man, and the little maid. 17122

Memoirs of the Marquis de La Fayette. 19908; 19909

Memoirs of the Mexican revolution. 3035; 40302

Memoirs of the military career of the Marquis de LaFayette. 17123

Memoirs of the Pennsylvania Agricultural Society. 17572

Memoirs of the Philadelphia Society for Promoting Agriculture. 25750

Memoirs of the private and public life of William Penn. 777; 28507

Memoirs of the private life of Marie Antoinette. 12048

Memoirs of the Protestant Episcopal Church in the United States of America. 4272

Memoirs of the public and private life of Napoleon Bonaparte. 40235

Memoirs of the Queen of England. 4919

Memoirs of the Rev. Ammi Rogers. 25962

Memoirs of the Rev. Claudius Buchanan. 29083

Memoirs of the Rev. David Brainerd. 8601

Memoirs of the Rev. Henry Martyn. 20759; 29084

Memoirs of the Rev. John H. Livingston. 38871

Memoirs of the Rev. Joseph Benson. 13172

Memoirs of the Rev. Joseph Eastburn. 33412

Memoirs of the Rev. Richard Whatcoat. 34790

Memoirs of the Rev. Samuel J. Mills. 3293

Memoirs of the Rev. William Tennant. 34110

Memoirs of the Rev. Zebulon Ely. 20402

Memoirs of the war in the southern department of the United States. 29469

Memoirs of the Wesley family. 15772

Memoirs of the youthful days of Mr. Mathews. 9465

Memoirs of William Ripley. 30460

Memoirs on the war of the French in Spain. 3036

Memoirs relating to the life and death of the Rev. David Badgley. 21416

Memoranda of Maryland. 34111

Memorandum of the different loans to the mayor, aldermen, and citizens of Philadelphia. 34744

Memorandums of the seasons. 39425

Memoria medica. 39553

Memoria politico-instructiva, enviada desde Filadelfia en agosto de 1821. 6660; 6661; 10129

Memorial [Auxiliary Society of Powhatan.] 37528

Memorial [To the New York Legislature] 2233

The memorial, a Christmas and New Year's offering. 25310; 29213

Memorial addresses to his excellency Governor Clinton. 27496

Memorial and argument in the case of the ship Blairean. 33573

Memorial and petition of Francis Henderson and Francis Henderson, Jun. 27198

Memorial & remonstrance of the Legislature of the state of Georgia. 18832

A memorial and remonstrance on the religious rights of man. 33966

Memorial and resolution of the Legislature of Louisiana. 22968

The memorial and resolutions adopted at the anti-tariff meeting held at Sumter district,

South Carolina. 30743; 36547

Memorial and resolutions of merchants and others, of the city of Philadelphia. 36548

The memorial and resolutions of the citizens of Philadelphia. 34753

Memorial de Sainte Helene. 13047; 13048; 13049; 13050

Memorial, &c. To the Honorable William Woodbridge, J. Kearsley, and Henry B. Brevoort. 6018

Memorial, &c. to the legislature of Virginia. 16233

A memorial for Sunday School Boys. 1565; 1566; 1567; 21417; 39554

A memorial for Sunday School girls. 21418

Memorial from the auctioneers of New York. 2234

Memorial from the General Assembly of North Carolina. 17441

Memorial from the professor of botany in the University of Pennsylvania. 334; 335

Memorial from the United Agricultural Societies of the state of Virginia. 3863

A memorial from two hundred and seven inhabitants of the District of Columbia. 18833

Memorial in behalf of sundry officers of the Revolutionary army. 27199

Memorial of a Christian life. 21269

Memorial of a committee appointed at a public meeting of the citizens of New York. 14626

The memorial of a Committee for the state of Maryland. 12119; 20040

Memorial of a committee of the citizens of Charleston, South Carolina. 18834

Memorial of a Committee of the Citizens of Philadelphia. 7363

Memorial of a committee of the inhabitants of the town of Fayetteville. 18835

Memorial of a committee, selected by the merchants of Portland. 18836

The memorial of a convention of delegates representing the merchants. 861; 3864; 3865

Memorial of a large number of delegates from most of the counties in the state of New York. 18837

Memorial of a revival. 9981

Memorial of Amos Binney. 41229

Memorial of certain hardware manufacturers, smiths and iron founders of Philadelphia. 36549

Memorial of certain merchant tailors of Boston. 36550

Memorial of certain surgeons of the United States. 36551

Memorial of citizens of the state of Ohio. 27200

Memorial of Edmund Winchester. 18838

Memorial of Garsed, Raines, and Co. of Frankford, Philadelphia County, Pennsylvania. 36552

Memorial of General Winfield Scott. 36553

Memorial of George Jones, and others. 18839

Memorial of James Gadsden and E. R. Gibson. 27201

Memorial of James M'Ilvain. 33949

Memorial of Jeremiah Elkins. 18840

Memorial of John Johnson Junior. 3866

Memorial of John M. Chapron. 3867

Memorial of John Mason. 27202

Memorial of John Owings. 22969

Memorial of John Ross, Geo. Lowrey, Major Ridge, and Elijah Hicks. 18841

Memorial of John S. Ellery and others. 1087

Memorial of John Wheelwright. 14627

Memorial of Josiah Meigs, and others. 3868

Memorial of Lewis Wernwag. 37135

The memorial of Lieut. Colonel
J. M. Gamble. 33318
Memorial of Major General And-
rew Jackson. 3869
The memorial of Martha Brad-
street. 37928
Memorial of merchants, trades,
and others, of Baltimore,
Maryland. 3870
The memorial of N. G. Cleary.
20094
Memorial of Paul Beck, jr. and
Thomas Sparks. 3871
A memorial of pious children.
6019
Memorial of Richard Bland Lee.
18842
Memorial of Richard W. Meade.
6003
Memorial of Rufus Davenport.
38337; 38338
Memorial of Samuel G. Perkins.
22970
Memorial of Samuel Slater.
18843
Memorial of sundry aliens, of
the city of New York. 18844
Memorial of sundry auctioneers
of the city of Baltimore.
18845
Memorial of sundry citizens of
Alleghany County in the state
of Pennsylvania. 36554
Memorial of sundry citizens of
Charleston, S. C. 3872
Memorial of sundry citizens of
Elizabeth city and county of
Pasquotank in North Carolina.
36555
Memorial of sundry citizens of
Hampshire County, state of
Virginia. 7364
Memorial of sundry citizens of
Missouri. 36556
Memorial of sundry citizens of
Montgomery County, Md.
41230
Memorial of sundry citizens of
Northumberland County, Penn-
sylvania. 36557
Memorial of sundry citizens of
Orangeburgh District, S. C.
36558

Memorial of sundry citizens of
Philadelphia. 36559
Memorial of sundry citizens of
Putnam County, in the state
of Georgia. 18846
Memorial of sundry citizens of
the city and county of Philadelphia. 18847
Memorial of sundry citizens of
the city of New York. 18848
Memorial of sundry citizens of
the county of Camden, in the
state of Georgia. 18849
Memorial of sundry citizens of
the District of Columbia, praying that a charter may be
granted by Congress, to enable them to institute a medical college. 27203
Memorial of sundry citizens of
the District of Columbia, praying that another medical college may not be incorporated
in the city of Washington.
27204
Memorial of sundry citizens of
the Districts of Chesterfield,
Marlborough, and Darlington,
South Carolina. 36560
Memorial of sundry citizens of
the state of New Jersey.
27205
Memorial of sundry citizens of
West Florida. 14628
Memorial of sundry farmers of
the state of Pennsylvania.
18850; 18851
Memorial of sundry holders of
land counter to the memorial
of the Chesapeake and Ohio
Canal Company. 39555
Memorial of sundry importers
and venders of hardware, of
the city of New York. 18852
Memorial of sundry inhabitants
of Albany. 18853
Memorial of sundry inhabitants
of Michigan. 36561
Memorial of sundry inhabitants
of Murfreesborough, N. Carolina. 36562
Memorial of sundry inhabitants of
Petersburg, in Virginia. 18854

Memorial of sundry inhabitants of that part of Florida attached to the state of Louisiana. 22971

Memorial of sundry inhabitants of the city of Baltimore. 3873

Memorial of sundry inhabitants of the state of Massachusetts. 7365

Memorial of sundry inhabitants of the upper counties of the state of South Carolina. 3874

Memorial of sundry inhabitants, to the legislature of Massachusetts. 18108

Memorial of sundry journeymen tailors, of Philadelphia. 36563

Memorial of sundry manufacturers, mechanics, and friends to national industry of the state of Connecticut. 18855

Memorial of sundry manufacturers of cordage, of the city of New York. 14629

Memorial of sundry masters of American vessels. 14630

Memorial of sundry merchant tailors, of New York. 36564

Memorial of sundry merchants and inhabitants of Salem, Massachusetts. 3875

Memorial of sundry merchants and other inhabitants of the city of Baltimore. 3876

Memorial of sundry merchants, and others, citizens of New York. 18856; 18857

Memorial of sundry merchants and traders of the city of New York. 3877

Memorial of sundry merchants, manufacturers, &c. of Baltimore. 18858

Memorial of sundry merchants of St. Louis. 22972

Memorial of sundry merchants, traders, and other citizens of Baltimore. 18859

Memorial of sundry merchants, traders, and other citizens, of the city of New York. 18860

Memorial of sundry persons, master tailors, of Philadelphia. 36565

Memorial of sundry persons, merchant tailors, of Philadelphia. 36566

Memorial of sundry residents of the city and county of Philadelphia. 36567

Memorial of sundry tallow chandlers, of Baltimore. 18861

Memorial of sundry umbrella-makers of Philadelphia. 36568

Memorial of the Agricultural Society of South Carolina. 36569

Memorial of the American Board of Commissioners for Foreign Missions. 18862

The memorial of the American Colonization Society. 23474

Memorial of the American Society of the city of New York, for the encouragement of domestic manufactures. 3878

Memorial of the auctioneers of the city of New York. 7366; 7367

Memorial of the Baltimore and Ohio Rail Road Company. 36570; 41231; 41232

Memorial of the Baltimore Chamber of Commerce. 36571

Memorial of the Bank of the United States. 7368

Memorial of the Bar Association of the state of Mississippi. 22973

Memorial of the Berkshire Agricultural Society of the Commonwealth of Massachusetts. 7369

Memorial of the board of managers of the Pennsylvania Society for the Encouragement of American Manufactures. 17578

Memorial of the Chamber of Commerce, and of other citizens of Charleston, South Carolina, adverse to the increase of duties on imports. 36572

The memorial of the chamber of commerce, and of the citizens of Charleston, against the tariff on woollen goods. 28439

Memorial of the Chamber of commerce of the city of New Haven. 3879

Memorial of the Chamber of Commerce of the City of New York. 3880; 14631; 18863; 18864

Memorial of the Chamber of Commerce of the city of Philadelphia. 3881; 3882; 3883; 18865; 18866; 18867

The memorial of the circuit judges of the state of Illinois. 29309; 30530

Memorial of the citizens of Beaufort, S. Carolina. 18868

Memorial of the citizens of Boston. 36573

Memorial of the citizens of Charleston, S. C. 720; 2235; 6020

Memorial of the citizens of Chester District, South Carolina. 36574

Memorial of the citizens of Georgetown, South Carolina. 36575

Memorial of the citizens of Kershaw District, South Carolina. 36576

Memorial of the citizens of Lancaster District, South Carolina. 36577

Memorial of the citizens of Laurens District, South Carolina. 36578

Memorial of the citizens of Madison, in Morgan County, in the state of Georgia. 18869

Memorial of the citizens of New Bedford, in the state of Massachusetts. 18870

Memorial of the Citizens of Norfolk. 18871

Memorial of the citizens of Petersburg, Virginia. 3884

Memorial of the citizens of Plymouth and Kingston, Mass. 36579

Memorial of the citizens of Richmond and Manchester, in Virginia. 18872

Memorial of the citizens of Savannah. 36580

Memorial of the citizens of the borough of Norfolk. 6021

Memorial of the citizens of Union District, South Carolina. 36581

Memorial of the citizens of Westborough, Massachusetts. 36582

Memorial of the city council of Charleston. 36583

Memorial of the Columbian Institute. 27206

Memorial of the committee on behalf of the Delaware and Raritan Canal Company. 24328

Memorial of the Comptroller General of South Carolina. 36584

Memorial of the convention of delegates assembled on the 22nd of August 1827. 29952

Memorial of the convention of the people of the state of Alabama. 7370

Memorial of the counties of St. Lawrence, Franklin and Clinton. 17383; 21664

A memorial of the dealings of God with the United States of America. 11916

Memorial of the delegates from the commercial and agricultural sections of the state of Maine. 3885

Memorial of the delegates of the United Agricultural Societies of Prince George Sussex, Surry, Petersburg, Brunswick, Dinwiddie and Isle of Wight. 3886

Memorial of the farmers, manufacturers, mechanics, and merchants, of the county of Rensselaer, in the state of New York. 18873

Memorial of the field officers commanding the Tennessee volunteer mounted gun-men, in the Seminole campaign, &c. 7371

Memorial of the General Assembly of Illinois. 22974

Memorial of the General Assembly of Indiana. 36585

Memorial of the General Assembly of Mississippi. 14632

merce in Salem and its vicinity. 2236; 3097

Memorial of the merchants, &c. of Portland. 18881

Memorial of the merchants of Baltimore. 3893

Memorial of the merchants of Bath, state of Maine. 3894

Memorial of the merchants of Boston. 36593

Memorial of the merchants of Savannah. 36594

Memorial of the merchants of the city of Philadelphia. 36595

Memorial of the merchants, ship owners, and manufacturers, of the city of Baltimore. 27211

Memorial of the merchants, ship owners, and mechanics, of Portsmouth, in the state of New Hampshire. 18882

A memorial of the Monthly Meeting of Baltimore. 28963

Memorial of the national institution for the promotion of industry. 7373

Memorial of the New York Chamber of Commerce adverse to an increase of duties on imported woollens. 36596

Memorial of the New York Chamber of Commerce praying that an uniform mode of settling protested bills of exchange by an act of Congress. 36597

Memorial of the New-York chamber of commerce, to the Hon. the Senate and House of Representatives. 17405

Memorial of the New York County Agricultural Society. 3895

Memorial of the Northampton Slate Quarry Company in Pennsylvania. 36598

Memorial of the owners of real estate in the vicinity of the Washington Military parade ground. 34112

Memorial of the Pennsylvania Society for the Encouragement of American Manufactures. 3896; 18883

Memorial of the people of the district of Spartanburgh, S. C. 7374

Memorial of the Philadelphia Chamber of Commerce. 36599

Memorial of the President and board of Managers of the American Colonization Society. 3897; 3898

Memorial of the President and Directors of the Chesapeake and Delaware Canal. 18884

Memorial of the president and directors of the Chesapeake and Ohio Canal Company. 41233

Memorial of the president and directors of the South Carolina Canal and Rail Road Company. 41234

Memorial of the professors in the medical department of the Columbian College. 27212

Memorial of the Rector and Visitors of the University of Virginia. 7375

A memorial of the Rev. John Chester. 39208

Memorial of the salt manufacturers in the town of Salina, Onondaga County, New York. 36600

Memorial of the Senate and House of Representatives of the state of Alabama. 7376

Memorial of the Sisters of Charity of St. Joseph. 36601

Memorial of the Society for Alleviating the Miseries of Public Prisons. 34770

Memorial of the South Carolina Canal and Railroad Company. 36602

Memorial of the state of Missouri. 27213

The memorial of the subscribers interested in printing, papermaking, bookselling. 9466

Memorial of the tallow chandlers of New York. 18885

Memorial of the trustees of Cumberland College. 27214

Memorial of the Trustees of the Mariner's Church for relief.

Memorial to the Senate and House of Representatives of the United States. 2711

Memorial, with accompanying documents, of Richard W. Meade. 22981

The memorial with resolutions adopted at the Anti-tariff meeting, held at Abbeville Court House, S. C. 27762; 36604

Memorials concerning deceased Friends. 5412; 8788

Memorials concerning several ministers, and others, deceased. 20612; 38696

Memorials of sundry citizens of Boston. 41235

Memorials, presented to the Legislature of the session of 1823, praying the repeal of the section of a law granting peculiar privileges to the Trustees of the Bethel Baptist Church. 13892

Memorias para servir de introduccion a la horticultura cubana. 30508

Memorie di Lorenzo Da Ponte. 12322; 24287; 38329

Memory. 29728

Memory, a favourite song. 4138; 23189

The memory of our fathers. 32255; 32256

The memory of the just. 35161

Men and manners, in verse. 29729

Men of different countries. 39556

Mengwe; a tale of the frontier. 19635

Menno's departure from Popery. 21422

Mental discipline. 28323

The mental friend. 13300

The mental guide, being a compend of the first principle of metaphysics. 34113

A mental museum, for the rising generation. 40661

Mental treasures. 26126

Mental vision on the ruins of the fall. 35028

Mentor, or Dialogues, between a parent and children. 33615

The mercantile arithmetic. 27542; 37073

Mercantile running hand. 1712

Mercein's city directory. 2242

Merchandise transported coastwise. 41236

The merchant and seaman's expeditious measurer. 19773

The merchant of Venice. 14093; 26058

The merchant; or, Practical accountant. 5464

The merchant's and shipmaster's assistant. 8116; 37874

The merchant's assistant, and clerk's new magazine. 16718

The merchant's memorandum and price book. 28895; 28896

Merchant's Murray. 17281

The merchant's table books. 22123

Merchants of Alexandria--District of Columbia. 36605

Merchants of Philadelphia--reduce duty on teas. 41237

The merchants tables. 8326

Merchants' and travellers directory. 2243

Merchants' and mariners' African guide. 11915

The merely amiable, moral man, no Christian. 37212

Merriam's American reader. 39561

Merrily goes the bark. 13273

The merry fellows' pocket companion. 592

The merry medley. 39567

The merry piping lad. 3410

The merry Swiss girl. 41357

The merry tales of the three wise men of Gotham. 25679

The merry wives of Windsor. 10238; 10239

Message, and accompanying documents, shewing the present situation of the Massachusetts claim upon the general government. 16997

Message du Gouverneur, Lewis Cass. 39583

Message. Fellows citizens of the Senate and House of Repre-

sentatives [Ohio] 9764
Message from David Lawrence
  Morril. 25510
Message from Governor Edwards.
  39079
Message from his excellency
  David Lawrence Morril. 17328
Message from His Excellency
  the Governor [N. H.] 2439;
  2440; 34440
Message from his excellency the
  governor transmitting memori-
  als respecting the Chesapeake
  and Ohio canal. 29646
Message from His Excellency the
  governor. To the Senate and
  Assembly [N.Y.] 2499
Message from his excel. Thom.
  B. Robertson. 5864
Message from Lawrence D. Mor-
  ril the Governor. 21622
Message from Martin Van Buren.
  39797
Message from the executive to the
  Legislature, enclosing commu-
  nications from the executives
  of the states of Maine, Connec-
  ticut, and Virginia. 37307
Message from the executive, to the
  Legislature of Maryland. 39467
Message from the Governor [Ohio]
  2590
Message from the Governor.
  [N. Y.] 34504
Message from the governor, ac-
  companied with the report of
  the canal commissioners.
  34681; 34682; 39999; 40000
Message from the Governor, J.
  A. Schulze. 25694
Message from the governor of
  Massachusetts. 17052
Message from the governor of
  New Hampshire. 30265
Message from the governor of
  Ohio. 6336
The message from the Governor
  to the Legislature of the state
  of New York. 21665; 25554;
  30000
Message from the Governor
  [John Clark] transmitting com-
  munications from the different

banks in this state. 8816
A message from the Lord. 19335
Message. Gentlemen of the Sen-
  ate. 1850
Message of De Witt Clinton to the
  Legislature. 21666
Message of Governor Hiester.
  6412
Message of His Excellency Gideon
  Tomlinson. 28574; 32806
Message of His Excellency Gov-
  ernor Clinton. 6252
Message of His Excellency Gov-
  ernor H. G. Burton. 30073
Message of His Excellency Gov-
  ernor Iredell. 34571
The message of His Excellency
  Gov. Van Buren. 39798
Message of his excellency James
  B. Ray. 24948; 33655
Message of His Excellency John
  Owen. 39860
Message of His Excellency Levi
  Lincoln. 25265; 29672;
  34060; 39499
Message of His Excellency Oliver
  Wolcott. 5058; 12236; 15844a;
  20169; 24197
Message of His Excellency the
  Governor, to the Legislature
  of Massachusetts. 13253
Message of His Excellency the
  governor, together with the
  report of the commissioners
  appointed on the part of the
  state of New Jersey. 34455
Message of Joseph Kent. 34032
Message of Levi Lincoln. 34061
Message of President Jackson to
  Congress. 41238
Message of the Acting Governor
  to the House of Representa-
  tives [Kentucky] 1851
Message of the executive to the
  General Assembly of Maryland.
  39468
Message of the governor of Kentucky, transmitting to the General Assembly the report of
  Henry Clay and John Rowan.
  13003
Message of the governor of Mary-
  land. 8410

Message of the Governor of New-
Hampshire. 13506
Message of the Governor of the
state of Connecticut. 12237
Message of the governor of the
state of Maine [William King]
2078; 5917
Message of the Governor of the
state of Maine [Parris] 9338;
16998; 21307; 25198; 25199
Message of the governor of the
state of Ohio. 30107
Message of the governor, to the
General Assembly of Connecti-
cut. 38255
Message of the governor to the
General Assembly of Maryland.
29640
Message to Legislature, Novem-
ber 17, 1824. 17329
Messrs. Gales & Seaton. 8272;
12062
Messers. Van Doren's Institute
for Young Ladies. 36994;
41360
The Messiah. 20802
The Messiah of the Scriptures.
14980; 23384
Messiah's advent. 28312
Messiah's question. 19293
The Messiah's victory. 8310
The Metamorphoses: or Effects
of Education. 1695
Metamorphosis, or, A transfor-
mation of pictures. 2247;
29733
Meteorological observations
(made) in the vicinity of Baltimore. 581; 4832; 8174;
11980
Meteorological register. 25153;
27226
Method of daily prayer. 9141;
9470
The method of grace. 1245
A method, to promote the spiritual improvement of the students
2084
Methode de traitement dans la
fieve jaune. 6590
A methodical treatise on the cultivation of the mulberry tree.
37016

The Methodist almanack. 25318
Methodist Episcopacy. 13311
The Methodist harmonist. 9474;
21434; 29739; 34116
The Mexican waltz. 21397
Mexico. 17139
México and Mr. Poinsett. 39577
M'Fingal. 26251
Mi opiniôn sobre la educación de
las mugeres. 21196
Miami University and Cincinnati
College. 9477
Michael Copp. 23006
Michael Lewis. 36621
Michigan Election. 27227
Microcosmus Philadelphicus.
21714
Middlebrook's almanack. 2254;
2255; 6039; 6040; 9479;
13324-13328; 17148-17152;
21451; 21452; 25359-25363;
29749; 29750; 34128-34133;
39586-39592
Middlebury College. 29752
The middling interest, Sir, pre-
sent you their respects. 2258
Midnight horrors. 13335; 29754
The midnight hour. 12924
The Midshipman. 2259; 10270;
17974; 22279
Das Milchmädchen. 35036
Military academy. 27228
The military & political life,
character & anecdotes of Na-
poleon Bonaparte. 13051
Military appropriations. 31426;
41243
Military! He took the field, not
as a victor crowned with glor-
ious deeds. 29757
Military journal during the Amer-
ican revolutionary war. 14275;
30784
Military laws. 4120
Military road--defence of north-
western frontier--Michigan.
36622
Military road--Fishkill Landing
to Cold Spring. 31427
Military road in Michigan. 27229
Military rondo. 7522
The military sketch-book. 29591
Military tactics. 24878

A military waltz. 6302; 9723
Militia and Patrol laws. [Ala.]
56; 11561
The militia and patrol laws.
[Miss.] 6076
The militia instructer. 6047
The militia law of the state of
Indiana. 9106
Militia law of the state of New
Hampshire. 2441; 6211
Militia law of the United States
and of the commonwealth of
Massachusetts. 41244
The militia law, passed by the
General Assembly of the state
of Illinois. 24943; 24944
Militia laws [Conn.] 5059
Militia laws of the state of New
Hampshire. 9633; 39750
Militia laws of the United States
and of the commonwealth of
Massachusetts. 17053
Militia of Maine. 5918
Militia of the United States. Let-
ter from the Secretary of War.
31428; 41245
Militia report of William H. Sum-
ner. 34062
The militia reporter. 463
Militia United States. 36623
The militiaman's pocket com-
panion. 5853; 9291
Milk for babes. 9493; 9484;
21455; 29758
The milkmaid. 3498
The mill of the muses. 33431
Mill site for sale, June 8, 1822.
8721
The millenniel kingdom of peace.
16768
The millennium. Extracts from
vol. III of the Moral Advo-
cate. 34139
The millennium; or, Twelve sto-
ries designed to explain to
young Bible readers the Scrip-
ture. 40411
Miller's agricultural almanac.
25371; 29764
The miller's daughter. 38036
The miller's maid. 1206; 8686
Miller's planters' & merchants'
almanac. 2267; 2268; 2269;

6056; 6057; 9491; 9492; 9493;
13344; 13345; 17163; 21458;
21459; 25372; 25373; 29765;
34142; 34143; 34144; 39598;
39599
Milton's familiar letters. 39600
Mina, a dramatic sketch. 20459
Mina. A favorite rondo. 20926
Miner's Agricultural Almanac.
2278; 13350
Miner's Agricultural and Miscellaneous Almanac. 2279
Miner's Pennsylvania & New-
Jersey almanac. 6060
Ming's Hutchins' Improved. 2284;
6062; 9500; 9501; 13351;
17168; 21467; 25386; 29769;
34148; 39603
Miniature Almanack. 2280; 2281;
2282; 2283; 9502; 9503; 6063;
6064; 13352; 13353; 17169;
17170; 21468; 21469; 21470;
25387; 25388; 29770; 34149;
34150; 39604; 39605; 39606
Miniature history of the Holy
Bible. 6065
Minister presenting his people to
Christ. 20528; 20529; 20530
The minister's affectionate exhor-
tation to his professing people.
362
The minister's rule of duty.
38991
Ministerial devotedness. 25284
Ministerial fidelity: a sermon
preached at the ordination of
the Rev. Daniel Fitz. 24281
Ministerial fidelity described in
a discourse delivered at Can-
ton. 9935
Ministerial gifts adapted to the
necessity of the church. 25726
Ministerial qualifications. 28737
Ministerial responsibility. 32466
Ministerial zeal. 711
Ministers must die. 6951
Ministers of Christ, labourers
with God. 4876
The ministers of Christ should
not miss their aim. 37715
Ministers' pocket companion, and
directory. 15529
Le ministre de Wakefield. 38767

The ministrel's returne'd from
the war. 1478
The ministry of good work.
37724
The ministry of the word com-
mitted to faithful and able
men. 17599
Minor catechism extracted from
the Evangelical primer. 5249;
38471
The minor literary exhibition of
the College of Georgetown.
5437
Minor Thomas. 36624
The minstrel. 354; 4643
The minstrel: A collection of
popular songs. 34151
Minstrel boy. 29772
The minstrel knight. 15684
The minstrel lyre. 28772
The minstrel, or, Pocket song-
ster. 29771
The minstrel's harp. 771
The minstrel's song. 14911
Mint of the United States. 27230;
36625; 41246; 41247; 41248
Minuet, in Don Giovanni. 6136
The minute gun at sea. 5769;
5770
Minutes, and circular [Western
Association of Universalists]
14760; 14761
Minutes and proceedings of the
Mutual Association of the vil-
lage of Rochester. 40307
Minutes of a Baptist Association
held at Coffee Creek meeting-
house. 27977
Minutes of a Convention held at
Salem Meeting House, in Gibson County, State of Indiana.
7906
Minutes of a convention held near
Marion, Shelby county, Indiana. 23615
Minutes of a convention of delegates from Baptist churches,
which met at Glenn's Creek
meeting house, in Woodford
county. 23623
Minutes of a discussion on the
question "Is the punishment of
the wicked absolutely eternal?

16824
Minutes of a General convention
[Universalist, Church. New
England] 4068
Minutes of a meeting held by the
messengers to compose the
Flat Rock Association. 11689
Minutes of an address, delivered
before the Anti-masonic con-
vention of Reading, Mass.
40352
Minutes of an adjourned session
of the American Convention
for Promoting the Abolition of
Slavery. 23476
Minutes of Concord Association
of Baptists. 15189
Minutes of evidence, taken before
the Committee on Manufac-
tures. 36626
Minutes of proceedings of Ebenezer Association of Baptists.
32193
Minutes of several conversations
between the Methodist preachers. 21472
Minutes of the Accomac Baptist
Association. 296
Minutes of the adjourned session
of the twelfth biennial American Convention for Promoting
the Abolition of Slavery. 31956
Minutes of the Alabama Association of Baptists. 19518; 37594
Minutes of the anniversary of the
Stonington Union Baptist Association. 19524
Minutes of the annual conferences
of the Methodist Episcopal
Church. 34117; 39571
Minutes of the annual meeting of
the Baptized Churches.
23613; 32112
Minutes of the annual meeting of
the Elkhorn Association of
Baptists. 37615
Minutes of the annual meeting of
the Friends of Humanity.
20605; 27975
Minutes of the Appomattox Bap-
tist Association. 15250; 19593;
23679; 28039; 37679
Minutes of the Ashford Baptist

Association. 19521; 23606

Minutes of the Associate Synod of North America. 10064; 19467

Minutes of the Baltimore Baptist Association. 251; 7914; 11701; 15204; 32143; 37633

Minutes of the Baptist Association [Ala.] 32104

Minutes of the Baptist Association, at a meeting held at Salt River Meeting-House. 27990

The minutes of the Baptist Association, in the Albemarle District. 297; 4601; 15249; 19592; 23678; 28038; 32191; 37678

Minutes of the Baptist Association, in the district of Goshen. 301; 4603; 11739; 28042; 32195; 37684

Minutes of the Baptist Concord Association. 285; 4596; 7944; 11730; 23674

Minutes of the Baptist Convention of Maine. 19546

Minutes of the Baptist Dover Association. 4602; 7952; 11737; 15252; 23681; 23682

Minutes of the Baptist General Association of Virginia. 19595; 23683; 28041; 32194; 37683

Minutes of the Baptist Goshen Association. 15255; 19596; 23684

Minutes of the Baptist Middle District Association. 304; 15256; 19597; 23685

Minutes of the Baptist Missionary Association of Kentucky. 15195

Minutes of the Baptist State Convention of South Carolina. 11729

Minutes of the Baptist Yearly Meeting. 15237

Minutes of the Barre Association. 7949; 11731; 32187; 37675

Minutes of the Barre Baptist Association. 28033

Minutes of the Beaver Baptist Association. 279; 4592; 15234; 32177

Minutes of the Becbe Baptist Association. 4546; 7896; 19519; 23604

Minutes, of the Berkshire Baptist Association. 23648; 32159

Minutes of the Bethel Baptist Association. 259

Minutes of the Bethlehem Baptist Association. 27966; 32105; 37595

Minutes of the Black River Ass'n. 263; 4575; 7922; 23649

Minutes of the Blue River Association. 232; 4556; 7905; 11688; 15188; 19535; 23614

Minutes of the Boon's Creek Association. 27986; 32124

Minutes of the Boston Baptist Association. 252; 253; 254; 4568; 7915; 11702; 19551; 23638; 27998

Minutes of the Bowdoinham Association. 245; 4563; 7909; 11696; 15199; 19545; 23632; 32136; 37624

Minutes of the Bracken Association. 234; 32125

Minutes of the Broad River Baptist Association. 282

Minutes of the Cahawba Baptist Association. 223; 4547; 7897; 11680

Minutes of the Cape-Fear Baptist Association. 19568

Minutes of the Cayuga Baptist Association. 264; 4576; 11709; 15213; 19561; 23650

Minutes of the Charleston Baptist Association. 283; 4595; 7943; 11727; 15239; 32183

Minutes of the Chattahoochie Baptist Association. 23611; 32110

Minutes of the Chemung Baptist Association. 7923; 11710

Minutes of the College of Electors of the state of Pennsylvania. 17558

Minutes of the Columbia Baptist Association. 298; 7901; 11736; 15251; 19526; 23680

The minutes of the Columbus Baptist Association. 272; 4587; 7934; 11719; 15226; 19570; 28019; 32169

Minutes of the Concord Baptist Association. 19583; 28032; 32184; 37671

Minutes of the constitution and first session of the Washington Baptist Association. 37603

Minutes of the Constitution [sic] of the Baptist Association, begun and held at Mount Zion Meetinghouse [sic] 15181

Minutes of the convention, and of the Grand Lodge of Alabama. 5371

Minutes of the convention at Hightstown, Middlesex County, N. J. October 25th A. D. 1828. 32157

Minutes of the convention, held at Portsmouth, N. H. Oct. 29, 1828. 32152

Minutes of the convention holden at Salem, October 16, 1827. 32148

Minutes of the course of chemical instruction in the medical department of the University of Pennsylvania. 8943; 12770; 16410; 20813

Minutes of the Cumberland Baptist Association [Me.] 247; 4564; 7910; 11697; 15200; 19547; 23634; 27995

Minutes of the Cumberland Baptist Association [Tenn.] 286

Minutes of the Cumberland Concord Baptist Association. 15241

Minutes of the Danville Association. 32188

Minutes of the Danville Baptist Association, 19586

Minutes of the Delaware Baptist Association. 227; 4551; 19525; 23610; 27974; 32109; 37601

Minutes of the doings of the Maine Baptist Convention. 23633

Minutes of the Dover Baptist Association. 299; 28040; 32192; 37681

Minutes of the Dublin Association. 260

Minutes of the Dublin Baptist Association. 7920; 28006

Minutes of the early proceedings of the Baptist Society. 34928

Minutes of the East Fork of the Little Miami Baptist Association. 273; 7935; 15227; 19571; 23657; 28021; 32170; 37659

Minutes of the Eastern Maine Association. 248; 4565; 7911; 11698; 15201; 19548; 23635; 27996

Minutes of the Ebenezer Association. 228; 4553; 7902; 19528

Minutes of the eighteenth anniversary of the Boston Baptist Association. 37634

Minutes of the eighteenth anniversary of the Cumberland Baptist Association. 37626

Minutes of the eighteenth annual meeting of Gasper's River Association, of United Baptists. 37617

Minutes of the eighteenth annual meeting of the Franklin Baptist Association. 37647

Minutes of the eighteenth session of the American Convention for Promoting the Abolition of Slavery. 11597

Minutes of the eightannual [sic] session of the Cahawba Baptist Association. 23605

Minutes of the eighth annual meeting of the Baptist Missionary Convention of the State of New York. 37592

Minutes of the eighth annual meeting of the Huron Baptist Association. 37661

Minutes of the eighth annual session of the Missouri Baptist Association. 19557

Minutes of the eleventh anniversary of the Eastern Maine Association. 37627

Minutes of the eleventh anniversary of the Salisbury Baptist Association. 37643

Minutes of the eleventh annual meeting of the Laughery Association of Baptists. 32116

Minutes of the eleventh session

38251

Minutes of the General Association of Virginia. 11738; 15254

Minutes of the General Conference of Maine. 32799; 38250

Minutes of the Genesee Baptist Association. 4578; 7925; 11711; 15214; 19562

Minutes of the Georgia Association. 37602

Minutes of the German Evangelical Lutheran Synod of Pennsylvania. 38495

Minutes of the Goshen Baptist Association [N. C.] 37657

Minutes of the Goshen Baptist Association [Va.] 7954

Minutes of the Grand River Baptist Association. 274; 4588; 7936; 11720; 15228; 23658

Minutes of the Hartford Baptist Association. 224; 4548; 7898; 11683

Minutes of the Hephzibah Baptist Association. 229; 4554; 19530

Minutes of the Highland Baptist Association. 37618

Minutes of the Highwasse Baptist Association. 15242

Minutes of the Holland Purchase Association. 266; 4579; 7926; 11712; 15215

Minutes of the Holston Baptist Association. 32185

Minutes of the Hudson River Baptist Association. 267; 4580; 15216; 19563; 23652

Minutes of the Huron Baptist Association. 7937; 15229; 19572; 23659; 28022

Minutes of the Illinois United Baptist Association. 11687; 19532; 19533; 23612; 27976

Minutes of the Indiana yearly meeting. 16234

Minutes of the Indianapolis Association. 27978; 32115

Minutes of the Juniata Baptist Association. 11723; 15235; 19578; 23665; 23665; 28028; 32179; 37666

Minutes of the Ketocton Baptist Association. 302; 7955; 28043

Minutes of the Lake George Baptist Association. 15218

Minutes of the Laughery Association. 11690; 15190; 19537

Minutes of the Leyden Baptist Association. 291; 4599; 7950; 11733; 15244; 28035

Minutes of the Licking Association of Particular Baptists. 239; 4561; 11694; 15197; 27991; 32130; 37620;

Minutes of the Licking Particular Baptist Association. 19544; 23627

Minutes of the Lincoln Association. 249; 4566; 7912; 11699; 15202; 19549; 23636; 32140; 37628

Minutes of the Little River Baptist Association. 37621

Minutes of the Little Rock Association of Regular Baptists. 15183; 19520

Minutes of the Little Wabash Baptist Association. 37605

Minutes of the Long Run Association. 240; 23628; 27992; 32131

Minutes of the Lost River Association. 23617; 27980

Minutes of the Mad River Baptist Association. 4589; 15230; 19573; 23660; 37662

Minutes of the Madison Baptist Association. 268; 4581; 7927; 11713; 23653; 28012

Minutes of the Mahoning Baptist Association. 4590; 7938; 11721; 15231; 19574; 23661; 28023; 32173

Minutes of the Maine Baptist Convention. 31849; 32137; 37625

Minutes of the Manchester Baptist Association. 292; 7947; 15245; 19589

Minutes of the Massachusetts Baptist Convention. 19552; 23639; 32146

Minutes of the meeting for Sufferings of New York. 38697

Minutes of the Meherrin Baptist Association. 303; 28044

Minutes of the Meigs' Creek Baptist Association. 23662; 28024;

37663

Minutes of the Meredith Baptist Association. 11705; 15210; 37640

Minutes of the Miami Baptist Association. 275; 4591; 7939; 11722; 15232; 19575; 23663; 28025; 32174; 37664

Minutes of the Middle District Association. 32197

Minutes of the Mohecan Association. 19576; 32175

Minutes of the Mount Pleasant Baptist Association. 19558; 23645; 28003; 37638

Minutes of the Muddy River Baptist Association. 19534; 32111

Minutes of the Muskingum Baptist Association. 276; 7940; 32176

Minutes of the New Jersey Baptist Association. 262; 4573; 7921; 11707; 15212; 19560; 23647; 28008; 32158; 37645

Minutes of the New-London Baptist Association. 225; 4549; 7899; 11684; 15184; 19523

Minutes of the New-York Baptist Association. 269; 4582; 7928; 11714; 15219; 19564; 23654; 28013; 32164; 37653

Minutes of the Niagara Baptist Association. 32165

Minutes of the nineteenth session of the American Convention for Promoting the Abolition of Slavery. 19406

Minutes of the ninth anniversary of the New-London Baptist Association. 23608

Minutes of the 9th anniversary of the Stonington Union Baptist Association. 23609

Minutes of the ninth annual meeting of the Columbia Baptist Association. 32144

Minutes of the ninth annual session of the Cahawba Baptist Association. 27967

Minutes of the ninth Gasper River Association of Baptists. 238

Minutes of the Nolachucky Baptist Association. 32186; 37673

Minutes of the North-Bend Association. 19538; 23618

Minutes of the North-Carolina Chowan Baptist Association. 15225; 19569

Minutes of the North District Association of Baptists. 241; 15198

Minutes of the Northumberland Baptist Association. 23666

Minutes of the Ocmulgee Association. 230; 4555; 7903; 15186; 19531

Minutes of the Old Colony Baptist Association. 15206; 19553; 23640; 27999; 32147

Minutes of the Oneida Baptist Association. 15220; 28014

The minutes of the Ontario Baptist Association. 4583; 7929; 11715; 15221

Minutes, of the organization and proceedings of the Forked Deer Baptist Association. 19584

Minutes of the organization of the Monroe Baptist Association. 32163

Minutes of the Otsego Baptist Association. 270; 4584

Minutes of the Oxford Maine Auxiliary Foreign Mission Society. 25643

Minutes of the particular synod in Albany. 30415

Minutes of the particular synod of New York. 2962

Minutes of the Pearl River Baptist Association. 4571; 32150

Minutes of the Penobscot Association. 27997

Minutes of the Philadelphia Baptist Association. 280; 4593; 7941; 11724; 15236; 19580; 23669; 28030; 32180; 37668

Minutes of the Portsmouth Association. 305; 15257

Minutes of the proceedings and trial in the case of John Milton Goodenow vs. Benjamin Tappan. 9505

Minutes of the proceedings, at the second annual meeting [Ebenezer Association of Baptists] 37682

Minutes of the proceedings of a convention, formed of delegates from the Baptist churches herein named. 28004

Minutes of the proceedings of the Baptist Convention of the state of New Hampshire. 23646

Minutes of the proceedings of the Columbus Baptist Association. 37658

Minutes of proceedings of the court of enquiry into the official conduct of Capt. Isaac Hull. 11057

Minutes of proceedings of the court of enquiry ordered by the Secretary of the Navy on the application of Cpt. James Biddle. 11058

Minutes of the proceedings of the Electoral College of Pennsylvania. 34683

Minutes of the proceedings of the Evangelical Lutheran Synod of West Pennsylvania. 28808; 38499

Minutes of the proceedings of the fifth General Synod of the Evangelical Lutheran Church. 38739

Minutes of the proceedings of the General Association of New-Hampshire. 28571

Minutes of the proceedings of the General Convention of Universalists. 7494

Minutes of the proceedings of the General Synod, of the Evangelical Lutheran Church. 12654; 20643; 29002

Minutes of the proceedings of the New Hampshire Baptist Convention. 28007

Minutes of the proceedings of the Western Association of Universalists. 4248; 7493; 11285

Minutes of the proceedings of the Yearly Meeting of Friends. 33288

Minutes of the Redstone Baptist Association. 23670

Minutes of the Regular Baptists, of the Little Rock Association. 27969

Minutes of the Rensselaerville Baptist Association. 19565

Minutes of the St. Lawrence Association. 271; 7930; 11716; 15222; 19566; 23655; 28016; 28017

Minutes of the Salem Association [Mo.] 37639

Minutes of the Salem Association of Baptists [Ky.] 242; 11695; 23629; 32134

Minutes of the Salem Baptist Association [Indiana] 32118; 37612

Minutes of the Salem Baptist Association [Mass.] 37636

Minutes of the Salem Baptist Association [Ohio] 277; 15233; 23664; 28026

Minutes of the Salisbury Association. 261; 4572; 11706; 15211; 19559; 32155

Minutes of the Saluda Baptist Association. 23673

Minutes of the Saratoga Baptist Association. 4585

Minutes of the Savannah Baptist Convention. 231; 7904

Minutes of the Savannah River Baptist Association. 11686; 11728; 15240

Minutes of the Scioto Baptist Association. 278

Minutes of the second anniversary of the Milford Baptist Association. 37641

Minutes of the second anniversary of the Monroe Baptist Association. 37652

Minutes of the second anniversary of the New-Haven Baptist Association. 27971

Minutes of the second annual meeting of the Baptist General Association of Pennsylvania. 37665

Minutes of the second annual session, of the Mulberry Baptist Association. 37596

Minutes of the second meeting of the Baptist Association,

Minutes of the tenth session of the Genesee Baptist Association. 32160

Minutes of the testimony taken by the Committee appointed by the House of Representatives to investigate the official conduct of Samuel D. Franks. 30173

Minutes of the third anniversary of the Penobscot Association. 32141

Minutes of the third annual meeting of the Lost-River Association. 32117

Minutes of the third Bethel Baptist Association. 27985

Minutes of the third meeting of the Baptist Association, which commenced on the first Saturday in October, 1829, at Glenn's Creek Meeting-House. 37619

Minutes of the thirteenth session of the Grand River Baptist Association. 37660

Minutes of the thirty-eighth anniversary of the Hartford Baptist Association. 27970

Minutes of the thirty-third anniversary of the Otsego Baptist Association. 37654

Minutes of the 12th anniversary of the Stonington Union Baptist Association. 37600

Minutes of the twelfth session of the Grand River Baptist Association. 32171

Minutes of the twentieth anniversary of the Black River Baptist Association. 37646

Minutes of the twenty-eighth Green River Baptist Association. 27989

Minutes of the twenty-fifth session of the Saratoga Baptist Association. 37656

Minutes of the twenty-first anniversary of the Madison Baptist Association. 37651

Minutes of the twenty-first biennial American Convention for Promoting the Abolition of Slavery. 37439

Minutes of the 24th Russell's Creek Association of Baptists. 32133

Minutes of the twenty seventh Green River Baptist Association. 23626

Minutes of the 26th meeting of the North-Bend Association. 32132

Minutes of the twenty-third Russel's Creek Association of Baptists. 27993

Minutes of the Union Association of Baptists [Ind.] 15192; 19540; 23620; 27982; 32120; 37606

Minutes of the Union Baptist Association [Miss.] 23643; 28002; 32151

Minutes of the Union Baptist Association [N.Y.] 7932; 11717; 19567

Minutes of the Union Baptist Association [Va.] 4605; 7957; 11742; 19599; 23688; 28047; 32201; 37687

Minutes of the Vermont Baptist Association. 294; 7948; 15247; 19590; 28036

Minutes of the Virginia Baptists General Meeting of Correspondence. 300; 7953

Minutes of the Virginia Portsmouth Baptist Association. 32198

Minutes of the Wabash Baptist Association. 27983

Minutes of the Wabash District Association. 4558; 7908; 11692; 15193; 19541; 23621; 32121; 37807

Minutes of the Waldo Association. 37631

Minutes of the Warren Association. 281; 4594

Minutes of the Warren Baptist Association. 7942; 23672

Minutes of the Warwick Baptist Association. 4586; 7933; 11718; 15224; 23656

Minutes of the Wendell Baptist Association. 19554; 23641

Minutes of the Westfield Baptist Association. 256; 4569; 7917; 15208

Minutes of the White River Association. 15194; 19542; 23622; 32122; 37613

Minutes of the White-Water Baptist Association. 27984

Minutes of the Woodstock Baptist Association. 295; 4600; 7951; 11735; 15248; 19591; 23677; 28037; 37677

Minutes of the Worcester Baptist Association. 257; 4570; 7918; 11704; 15209; 19555; 23642; 28000; 32149; 37637

The minutes of the yearly conference of the Methodist Society. 9475

Minutes of the Yellow River Baptist Association. 15187; 37604

Minutes of the York Baptist Association. 250; 4567; 7913; 11700; 15203; 19550; 23637; 32142; 37632

Minutes of three conferences of the African Methodist preachers. 7748

Minutes of two sessions of the Roanoke Baptist Association. 37685

Minutes on the Stonington Union Association. 226

Minutes taken at the several annual conferences of the Methodist Episcopal Church. 2250; 6031; 6032; 9471; 9472; 13313; 17133; 21435; 25322; 25323; 29735; 29736

Minutes. The Coffee Creek Association of Baptists. 32113; 37609

Miracles of God and the prophets. 39229

Miracles, wrought by the intercession of Prince Hohenlohe. 13354

Miraculous cure of Sister Beatrix Myers. 21473

Mirandola. 6542

A mirror for politicians. 34153

The mirror; or, Eighteen juvenile tales and dialogues. 34152

The mirror, reflecting the light of truth on the subject of manufactures. 35025

A mirror to Noah Webster's Spelling Book. 1092

Miscellaneous claims. 31429; 41249

Miscellaneous poems [Carter] 692

Miscellaneous poems, by a lady of Charleston. 25435; 29833

Miscellaneous poems on moral and religious subjects. 1905; 2286

Miscellaneous poems selected from the United States Literary Gazette. 25136

The miscellaneous prose works of Sir Walter Scott. 40372

Miscellaneous remarks on a pamphlet lately published. 16753

Miscellaneous selections and original pieces, in prose and verse. 4963

Miscellaneous sermons. 2287

Miscellaneous tracts. 6346

Miscellaneous works [Goldsmith] 29036

The miscellaneous works of the Rev. John Wesley. 37136

Miscellanies. 7017

Miscellanies, moral and instructive. 39630

Miscellanies selected from the public journals. 8211; 17171

The miscellany, being a selection from the writings of Benjamin Franklin. 1274

Miscellany containing a variety of anecdotes, religious experiences. 19856

The miscellany. Containing choice specimens in poetry and prose, an account of several modern shipwrecks. 25389

The miser. 12542

The miserable made happy. 6066

The misrepresentations of Anna Braithwait. 16531

Miss Billing's waltz. 12806

22153

Monumental inscriptions. 32382; 32383

The moon is on the hill. 16586; 16587

The Moorish lady's song. 21584

The moral and religious improvement of the poor. 15875

Moral and religious souvenir. 34189

The moral beauty and glory of the church. 13175

A moral catechism adapted to the capacity of children. 8332

The moral characters of Theophastus. 26196

The moral condition and prospects of the heathen. 19311

The moral dignity of the missionary enterprise. 19213; 19214; 19215; 23239; 27580; 31686

Moral duty and improvement. 513

Moral education. 20020

A moral inquiry into the character of man. 34190

Moral instructor, and guide to happiness. 14301

The moral instructor, and Guide to virtue. 18223; 22486; 26224

The moral plague of civil society. 6466

The moral providence of God. 37419

The moral purpose of ancient sacrifices of the Mosaic ritual. 4539

The moral responsibility of civil rulers. 38979; 38980

The moral responsibility of the American nation. 33694

A moral revolution. 41495

Moral sketches of prevailing opinions and manners with reflections on prayer. 6115

Moral stories, for boys and girls. 25415; 29795; 34191

Moral tales for young people. 5230; 24402; 38446

The moralist. 39607

The morality of the Bible. 28428

The morals of pleasure. 40380

Moravian waltz. 16019; 20351; 20352

The morbid anatomy of some of the most important parts of the human body. 185

Mordella. 17224

More calumny and persecution exposed. 999

More than 18,000 Vols. bound and unbound. 1148

More light on masonry. 29799

More than "One hundred and twenty reasons" for not "being a Universalist." 39639

More than one hundred Scriptural and incontrovertible arguments for believing in the supreme divinity of Our Lord. 2338

More wonders of the invisible world. 12046

Morgan confirmed. 29810

Morgan Magness. 27258

Morgan volunteer's march. 2339

Morgan's Freemasonry exposed and explained. 25424

Morgan's pamphlet. 29811

Morganiana, or The wonderful life and terrible death of Morgan. 34197

Morgiana in Ireland. 17229; 20671

Morgiana in Spain. 13399

Moritz Furst. 36632

Morning exercises, for every day in the year. 33703

Morning. From the hours of love. 9051

Morning its sweets is fingering. 3063

Morning thoughts, in prose and verse. 20234

Moron, a tale of the Alhambra. 41500

Morton; a tale of the revolution. 34205

Moses Hazen. 36633

Moses Shepherd. 27259; 36634

Moss roses. 2330

The most important tenets of the Roman Catholic Church fairly explained. 343

The Most Rev. Dr. James Butler's catechism. 4884

Mother Goose's melodies. 13413
Mother Hubbard.   2345
The Mother's catechism. 2346;
27672
A mother's journal, during the
last illness of her daughter.
6127
Motherless Mary. 34207
Motion of Mr. Gross, of New
York. 3927
Motion of Mr. Ingham for infor-
mation from the Secretary of
the Treasury. 14665
Motion of Mr. McDuffie to amend
the Constitution. 23010
Motives to early piety. 2864
Mount Carmel, February 1822.
8509
Mt. Holyoke, or, The travels of
Henry and Maria. 34211
Mount Pleasant Classical Institu-
tion. 34212
Mountain buds and blossoms.
20781
Mountain cottager. 13415
The Mountain Piper. 401
The mountain sprite. 19983
The mountain torrent, a grand
melo-drama. 1809
The mountaineer. 14180
The mountaineers; an opera.
24159
The mourner comforted. 4391
The mourners duty. 39321
The mournful tragedy of James
Bird. 17243
Mournful tragedy or, The death
of Jacob Webb, David Morrow,
John Harris, Henry Lewis,
David Hunt, and Edward Lind-
say. 34213
Mourning for the righteous. 3308
The mourning ring.   5689; 9097
Mozart's march. 21533
The much admired air Auld lang
syne.   13987
The much admired air Sul mar-
gine d'un rio. 13061
The much admired ballad of Rob-
in Adair. 2952
A much admired duett for two
performers on one piano forte.
13062; 16864

The much admired echo waltz.
19218; 19219
The much admired Hungarian
rondo. 3055; 6667; 17852
The much admired Hymn of Ri-
ego. 20972
The much admired Mantua waltz.
19992
The much admired New Orleans
Waltz. 1027
The much admired Turkish
march. 902
A much admired waltz. For the
piano forte. 6137; 13419;
17247
Much ado about nothing. 26059
Much instruction from little
reading. 29827
Mulberry--Silk worm. 27260
Das mundliche und documentar-
ische Zeugniss. 2689
Municipal ordinance, for the gov-
ernment of the municipality of
Austin. 38206
The Munster cottage boy. 3039
The mural diagrapher. 40580
Murder will out!! 32270
The murmurer corrected. 20508;
21538
Murray's English exercises.
17257; 17258; 25441; 34225
Murray's English grammar. 5334;
6149; 9580; 17264; 25437;
25443; 25447; 29850; 34230;
39663
Murray's English reader. 8859;
17275; 17277; 21569; 25448;
25450; 25454; 25455; 29864;
34239; 39664; 39669; 39672
Murray's introduction to the Eng-
lish reader. 29866; 34245
Murray's sure guide to the Eng-
lish language. 34353
Murray's system of English grammar. 29874; 39684; 39685
Murray's theory of the moods and
tenses of English verbs.
29070
A musant waltz. 3047
The muse of Hesperia. 13692
The muse; or, Flowers of poetry. 28543
Musette de Nina for the harp or

piano forte.   2378; 6170
Musette de Nina.   Pour la harpe
ou forte piano. 6171
Museum-Hall, over the New Mar-
ket, fronting Dock square.
4796
The museum of beasts. 17284
Museum of foreign animals.
34355
Music [Stevenson] 10347; 18101
Music, love & wine. 15312
Music of the church. 37058;
41403
Musica sacra.   8968; 17290;
20838; 29170; 33500; 38933
Musical bagatelles. 8283
A musical biography, or Sketches
of the lives and writings of
eminent musical characters.
17519; 21778
The musical cabinet, containing
a selection of all the new and
fashionable songs. 9593
The musical cabinet, or New-
Haven collection of sacred music. 15566
Musical catechism. 13465; 17203;
39628
Musical Fund Society of Philadelphia. 15th concert. 34356
Musical miscellany. 504
Musical monitor. 2948; 10068;
17765; 22042; 30408
The musical self instructor.
34776
Musing on the roaring ocean.
17105
The mutability of created things
a reason for active benevolence. 3345
The mutability of the world, and
the permanency of the Gospel.
37226
Mutius: an historical sketch of
the fourth century. 35047;
40289
Mutual insurance. Insurance
against loss by fire. 27677
Mutual love between a minister
and people. 27718
My ain kind dearie. 874; 8452
My aunt: a petit comedy. 146;
32030; 37503

My beautiful maid. 17289
My boat is on the shore. 21095
My childhood. A poem. 4072;
19116
My children's diary. 25475
My country no more. 11438
My dark eyed maid.   15431;
15432
My daughter; a poem. 16343
My dear Sir, I avail myself of
the earliest moment. 32482
My early days. 28870
My father, a poem. 16052
My fellow citizens- Behold I am
unfaithful and true and in
righteousness I will judge and
make war. 35550
My governess. A poem. 17290
My grandmother; a musical farce.
16552; 16553
My heart and lute. 2320; 13379;
17214; 17215; 17216; 21507
My heart is sair for somebody.
17291; 21582
My heart's in the highlands.
17106; 17292; 17293
My Henry is gone. 14210; 14211
My home. 22425
My life is like the summer rose.
18182
My love arise. 19484
My love will come to me. 2353
My Marie's ee's o' the deep,
deep blue! 10071
My Marion.   21042
My mind and its thoughts. 13411
My mother. A poem. 1380;
2381
My mother bids me bind my
hair! 1549
My native highland home. 483
My native land good night! 5356;
5357; 5358; 12572
My own native isle.   15433;
15434; 15435
My pretty Anne good night.
20098
My religious experience, at my
native home. 39690
My sister. A poem. 1090;
2382
My sister dear. 166
My soldier love. 4726; 4727;

4728; 11881

My son, a poem. 16344

My soul is dark. 19278; 34775

My sweet guitar. 327

My uncle; a farce. 28082

Mynehieur von Herrick Heimelman, the dancing-master. 16484

Mysteries of popery unveiled. 888; 889; 5093

The mysteries of trade. 19656

Mysteries of Udolpho, a romance. 6581; 34947

The mysterious picture. 20093

The mysterious stranger. 13466

Mystery developed; or, Russell Colvin (supposed to be murdered,) in full life. 1550; 1551

The mystery of Christ. 5836

The mystery of God's providence. 20995

The mystery of iniquity unveiled. 378

The mystery of revelation unfolded. 13034

The mystery; or, Forty years ago. 1362

The mystic beauties of Free Masonry developed!! 9597

The mystic mount and The voice. 12656

Mystische theologie. 3107

N

Nachrichters nützliches und aufrichtiges Pferd-Arzeneybuch. 8525

Nahant, or "The Floure of Souvenance." 29152

The Nahant waltz. 5581; 20874

Nahkahnoonun kanahnahkahmoowaudt ekewh ahneshueshenahpaigk anahmeahchik. 39161

Nahum Ward. 27261

The name of Christian the only appropriate name for believers in Christ. 33920; 33921

Names and place of residence of the members of the Hamilton Fire Club. 3094; 10178; 14037

Names of the members of the

First or North Church of Christ in Portsmouth. 34854

Namouna's song. 4999

Nancy Dolan. 36635; 41255; 41256

Nannetta amabile. An Italian song. 12285

Napoleon and the grand army in Russia. 20728

Napoleon in exile. 9780; 9781; 9782; 13635; 13636; 13637

Napoléon, poème, en dix chants. 13136

Napoleon's grave, a poem. 24652

A narration of facts, relative to the proceedings of the Methodist Episcopal Church, against certain local preachers. 33178

A narration of religious experience. 25121

A narrative and defence of the proceedings of the Methodist Episcopal Church in Baltimore City Station. 32411

Narrative journal of travels through the northwestern regions of the United States. 6729

Narrative of a journey from Constantinople to England. 37076

Narrative of a journey into Persia. 1884

Narrative of a journey through the upper provinces of India. 33514; 38951

Narrative of a journey to the shores of the polar sea. 16177

Narrative of a journey to the summit of Mont Blanc. 5644

Narrative of a pedestrian journey through Russia. 15796; 15797

Narrative of a private soldier in His Majesty's 92d regiment of foot. 9598

Narrative of a revival of religion in the Third Presbyterian Church of Baltimore. 19178; 23203; 27543

Narrative of a second expedition to the shores of the polar sea.

nary and distressing shipwreck of the whale-ship Essex, of Nantucket. 4964

Narrative of the murder of James Murray. 17297

Narrative of the mutiny on board the ship Globe. 33826

A narrative of the political and military events which took place at Naples, in 1820 and 1821. 9873

A narrative of the principal incidents in the life and adventures of Capt. Jacob Sherburne. 40402

Narrative of the revival of religion, in the County of Oneida. 25826; 30331; 30332

A narrative of the revival of religion, within the bounds of the presbytery of Albany. 6175; 6529

A narrative of the rise and fall of the Medical College of Ohio. 8569

Narrative of the shipwreck and sufferings of Miss Ann Saunders. 30525

Narratives of the shipwreck of the brig Betsey. 20126

A narrative of the state of religion, within the bounds of the General Assembly of the Presbyterian Church. 2852; 6528; 10002; 30327

Narrative of the state of religion, within the bounds of the Presbytery of Albany. 2854

A narrative of the sufferings and adventures of Capt. Charles H. Barnard. 37701

The narrative of the sufferings of J. Stephanini. 40534

A narrative of the sufferings of Massy Harbison. 20806; 33476; 38912

A narrative of the sufferings of Seth Hubbell & family. 20971; 24907; 29266; 39039

Narrative of the surprise and capture of Major-general Richard Prescott. 4619

Narrative of the surrender of Buonaparte. 25212

A narrative of the voyages round

the world performed by Capt. James Cook. 16811; 33778

Narrative of the wicked life, and death of Katherine Hayes. 2389

Narrative of travels and discoveries in Northern and Central Africa. 24334

Narrative of William Biggs. 23823

A narrative, shewing the promises made to the officers of the line of the Continental Army, for their services in the Revolutionary War. 25620

A narrative, showing the origin and progress of the difficulties in the Congregational Church in Rehoboth. 24192

Narratives of the lives of pious Indian children, who lived on Martha's Vineyard. 39535

Nashville Republican & State Gazette. 29884

Nathaniel B. Wood. 36636; 41257

Nathaniel Briggs. 36637

Nathaniel Childers. 27262

Nathaniel Hunt, et al. 31433

National and state rights considered by "One of the People." 5881

The national anniversary. In two sermons. 16915

National armories. Letter from the Secretary of War. 27263

National armory - Ohiopile Falls. 27264

National armory. Resolution of the General Assembly of the state of Tennessee. 27265

National blessings of Christianity. 38867

The national calendar. 2390; 29889; 34366; 39696

The National calendar, and annals of the United States. 6178; 9600; 17300

The national calendar and gentleman's almanac. 34365; 39695

The national calendar and people's almanac. 29888

National dangers, and means of escape. 6179

National debt. 36638
National defence. 41509; 41510
National divertimento for the piano forte. 5004
National hymns, original and selected. 39225
National independence. Order of performances at the North Meeting House. 14034; 17883
National industry. 13468
The National Journal. 38605
National jubilee. 23753
National militia standard. 8504
The national mirror of Masonry. 39699
National observatory. 27266
National orator. 38200
National paintings. 36639
National preceptor. 39921; 39922
National primer. 9601; 13470
National prosperity perpetuated. 33189
The national reader. 30268; 34802; 40085
National Republicans. At a numerous meeting of citizens. 39700
National road - Cumberland to Washington. 27267
National road. Memorial of the General Assembly of the state of Indiana. 36640
National road. Resolution of citizens of Adams County. 23420
National road--Washington to New Orleans. 36641
National Road -- Wheeling to Missouri. 31434
The national spelling-book, and pronouncing tutor. 33069; 38466
The national spelling-book, and scholar's guide. 39701
National tales. 20960; 20961
National turnpike from Washington to New-Orleans. 20559
National unity, in opposition to political controversy. 6182
The National Vaccine Institution. 2003; 10295
Native land, or The return from

slavery. 15978
The natural and aboriginal history of Tennessee. 12800
Natural history, abridged for the use of schools. 12695
A natural history of animals. 32379
A natural history of birds, fishes, reptiles, and insects. 32380
Natural history of quadrupeds. 17301; 38245; 39702
The natural history of superstition. 5845
The natural history of the Bible. 1526
A natural history of the most remarkable quadrupeds, birds, fishes, serpents, reptiles and insects. 40674; 40675
The natural history of the rise, progress and termination of the epidemic inflammation, commonly called yellow malignant fever. 8565
Natural history. Selected from the Youth's Friend. 29906
The natural, statistical and civil history of the state of New-York. 39379
Natural theology, or A demonstration of the being and attributes of God. 5255
Natural theology; or, Evidences of the existence and attributes of the Deity. 2637; 17512; 25654; 39951
The nature and design of the Lord's supper. 1468
The nature and duration of the punishment of the wicked. 16365
The nature and end of the Gospel dispensation. 13735
The nature and object of punishment. 35234
The nature and origin of civil liberty, with the means of its perpetuation. 13170
Nature and philosophy. 5214
Nature and reason harmonized in the practice of husbandry. 21248

eingerichtete Calender. 9608; 13479; 21597

Neue, Gemeinnützige Landwirth- schafts Calender. 2396; 6189; 13480

Der Neue Hochdeutsche Orwigs- burger Calender. 34419; 39712

Das neue Pennsylvanische ABC Buchstabier. 2397

Der Neue Pennsylvanische Stadt- und Land-Calender. 9609; 13481; 17308; 21598; 25488; 29914; 34420; 39713

Das Neue Testament. Neunte Auflage. 423

Das Neue Testament unsers Herrn und Heilandes Jesu Christi. 4683; 4684; 8025; 15364; 15365; 15366; 28136; 37810; 37811

Neuer Gemeinüzige Pennsylvan- ischer Calender. 39714

Neues Reformirtes Gesangbuch zum Gebrauch der Evangelisch Reformirten Gemeinen. 40230

Neuman and Baretti's dictionary of the Spanish and English lan- guages. 29915; 34422

Ne'er can the rose. 11882

A new abridgement of Murray's English grammar. 29870

A new addition of the demand of William Vans, on Stephen Cod- man. 19125

New American arithmetic. 9710

New American atlas [Finley] 24534

A new American atlas [Tanner] 14257; 22421; 26169

A new American biographical dic- tionary. 13981; 13982; 17847; 40313

A new American biography. 40324

The new American dictator. 30245

The new American gardener. 33168

The new American grammar of the elements of astronomy. 22167; 30504

The new American practical navi- gator. 4811; 23909

The new American primer. 6687

The new, American spelling-book. 21901

The new American spelling book and juvenile preceptor. 22162; 40334

New and cheap goods. Kurtz and Lodwick respectfully in- form their friends. 39239

New and cheap goods, whole sale and retail. C. Hotchkiss, Has this day received. 16595

A new and choice selection of psalms and hymns and spiritu- al songs. 31592

A new and complete dictionary of arts and sciences. 8890

A new and complete edition of Ossian's poems. 13185

A new and complete grammar of the French tongue. 37878

A new & complete preceptor for flageolets. 13484

A new and complete preceptor for the fife. 2398

A new and complete preceptor for the German flute. 2399; 17309; 25490

New & complete preceptor for the Spanish guitar. 29917

A new and complete preceptor for the violin. 2400; 9610

A new and complete system of Arithmetick. 9938

A new and complete system of naval and military tactics. 19282

A new and complete system of questions to Blair's Lectures on rhetoric. 493

New and complete system of short hand or stenography. 12820; 16517; 20873

A new and concise system of arithmetic. 10341

A new and correct plan of Port- land, Maine. 11968

A new and easy guide to the use of the globes. 28868

A new and elegant general atlas. 2401

A new and expeditious method for learning the French language. 8286

A new and improved English gram- mar. 4350

A new and improved school atlas.
39923

A new and improved system of
medical botanical practice.
39594

A new and improved system of
practical book-keeping. 24687

A new and improved theoretical
and practical grammar of the
Spanish language. 24332

A new and interesting view of
slavery. 2402

New and latest collection of
hymns, and spiritual songs.
2403; 2834

New & selected waltzes. 13485

A new and universal history of
the United States. 29918

New Arabian nights entertainments. 27883

The new arithmetical table book,
for the use of schools. 2404;
6190; 39718

New arithmetical tables. 9611;
21599

New-Bedford town accounts. 21600;
25491; 39719

A new bibliotheca legum Americana. 5472

The new birth; a lecture sermon.
199; 4534; 23585

New Brunswick, (N. J.) almanac.
2405; 6193; 9614; 9615; 11513;
13487; 17310; 21604; 25494;
25495; 29920; 29921; 29922;
34425; 39726; 39727

The New Brunswick collection of
sacred music. 9616; 31577;
31578; 41359

The new casket, containing rich
treasures for young minds.
34426

The new Christian almanac. 39728

The new Christian hymn-book.
29756

The new clerk's magazine and
farmer's safe guide. 4820

New collection of conference
hymns. 20388

A new collection of flute melodies. 8969

A new collection of hymns, for
conference meetings. 5128;
6194

New collection of spiritual hymns,
for the followers of the lamb.
4516

A new college atlas. 26170

New compilation of original & select hymns. 25780

New complete and universal natural history, of all the most
remarkable quadrupeds. 5890

New Concordance to the Holy
Scriptures. 4888; 4889;
32540

New constitution of the state of
the state of New York. 6253

The new constitution of the Western Association of Universalists in the state of New-York.
19113

A new constructed interest table.
2040

A new, copious and complete
system of arithmetic. 5903;
16985

New Cotillions for the piano forte.
9253

A new description of that fertile
and pleasant province of Carolina. 7828

A new dictionary of the Spanish
and English languages. 13482

The new Edinburgh Encyclopaedia.
38448

The new Edinburgh encyclopaedia.
To the public. 14900

A new edition of a Hebrew grammar. 12619

A new edition of Clementi's celebrated octave sonata for the
piano forte. 12167

A new edition of The blue bell of
Scotland. 16745

New elements of conversation.
21936; 40115

The New-England almanack. 2406;
6195

The New-England almanack, and
farmer's friend. 9618; 13488;
17312; 25496; 29923; 34427;
39729

The New England almanack, and
Masonic calendar. 29924;
34428; 34429

The New-England and New-York
  almanack. 6196
The New England anti-Masonic
  almanac. 34430; 39730; 39731;
  39732; 39733
The New-England calendar and
  almanac. 2407
The New England collection of
  hymns and spiritual songs.
  39178
New England distinguished.   A
  discourse. 35477
The New England drama. 20965
The New England farmer; or,
  Georgical dictionary. 8520
The New-England farmer's almanack. 13489; 17313; 21605;
  25497; 29925; 29926; 34431;
  34432; 39734; 39735; 39736
The New-England farmer's diary
  and almanac. 2408; 2409;
  6197; 9619
The New England farrier. 5722;
  9150; 16719
The New England farrier and
  family physician. 35033
The New England primer. 2413;
  2414; 2415; 2416; 2417; 2418;
  2419; 2420; 2421; 2422; 2423;
  6199; 6200; 6201; 9622; 9623;
  9623a; 9624; 9625; 9626; 9626a;
  13491; 13491a; 13492; 13493;
  13494; 13495; 13496; 17315;
  17316; 17317; 21608; 21609;
  21610; 21611; 21612; 21613;
  21614; 21615; 25500; 25501;
  25502; 29928; 29929; 29930;
  29931; 29932; 34433; 34434;
  34435; 39740; 39741; 39742;
  39743; 39744
A New-England tale. 10218;
  10219
New England's memorial. 25428;
  25429
The New English drama. 17503
New English reader. 2428
The new expositor. 29272
A new family receipt book.
  29933
The new fashioned bonnet of
  straw. 21615a
The new federal calculator.
  22293; 30628; 35225

The new forest. 40447
A new general atlas [Finley]
  16146; 20518; 24535; 28875;
  38573
New general atlas [Seaman]
  3160; 6204
A new general atlas, exhibiting
  the five great divisions of
  the globe. 34001; 39422
New general atlas of the West
  India Islands. 2429; 17318
New goods Burtch & Heberd,
  corner of Market and Water
  streets. 38010
The new grammar of the elements
  of astronomy. 25997
A new guide to conversation in
  Spanish and English. 16387
New guide to health; or, Botanic
  family physician. 10448;
  22464; 30795; 40646
A new guide to the English tongue.
  1029; 8549; 28705
The New-Hampshire agricultural
  repository. 9634
The New-Hampshire annual register. 29943; 34444; 39752
New Hampshire election. March
  9, 1824. 17334
The New-Hampshire justice of
  the peace. 17823
New Hampshire Medical Institution. 24297; 28663; 32894
New Hampshire. Memorial of citizens of New Hampshire in
  favor of further protection.
  36651
New Hampshire. Petition of
  farmers of New Hampshire.
  36652
The New-Hampshire register, and
  United States' calendar. 2445;
  9642; 13512; 13513; 13514;
  17338; 21628; 25519
New Hampshire. Reports of cases
  argued and determined in the
  superior court. 17824
The New Hampshire town officer.
  40275
The new harmony; or, A new collection of church music. 28105
New-Haven town and city register. 34451; 39760

A new hieroglyphical Bible. 424;
425; 426; 427; 15367; 37812

A new history of Blue Beard.
13515

The new hymn book. 40560;
40561

New ideas on population. 12482;
24453

A new, improved dictionary for
children. 9210

A new improvement in the art of
steam navigation. 17745

A new instruction for the piano
forte. 13293; 13294

A new interest table. 34004

A new introduction to book-keeping. 3499; 10497; 14323;
18252; 22527

The New-Jersey almanac. 6224;
6225; 9654; 9655; 13527;
13528; 17347; 17348; 21636;
21637; 21638; 21639; 25527;
25530; 29953; 29954; 29955;
34460; 34461; 39768; 39769;
39770; 39771; 39772; 39773;
39774

The New-Jersey and Pennsylvania almanac. 2461; 6226;
17349

New-Jersey and Pennsylvania.
Astronomical calculations.
2462

The New-Jersey farmer's almanac. 21641; 25529; 25531

New Jersey. Petition of the
manufacturers of Paterson.
36653

The New Jerusalem church defended. 17841

A new key to the exact sciences.
18200; 22473

A new Latin grammar. 38279

The new Latin reader. 41415

The new Latin tutor. 39284;
39285

A new little book containing the
shorter catechism. 6227

The new lover's instructor.
34463

New lunar tables. 14821

New manual of private devotions.
21643

A new map of the Hudson river.
38037

A new march. Arranged for the
piano forte. 17115

A new method of teaching book-
keeping. 24862; 38996

The new military guide. 8663

The new militia act. 13552

The new mirror for travellers.
34655

New moral tales. 20649; 20650

New Norwood gipsy. 13529;
34464

The new Ohio arithmetic. 35192;
40417

The new olive branch. 680;
4916

The New Orleans directory and
register. 9826; 13679

New Orleans waltz. 17107

A new picture book. 31978

The new pleasing spelling book.
5468; 24715

A new pocket atlas of the United
States. 35460

A new pocket dictionary of the
English and Spanish languages.
12295; 32860

A new pocket dictionary of the
French and English language.
6318; 13607; 25615; 30098;
39889; 39890

A new preceptor for the German
flute. 1437

A new preceptor for the piano
forte. 12087

A new pronouncing French primer. 40680

The new quizzical valentine
writer. 13902

New reports of cases argued and
determined in the Court of
Common Pleas. 1442

New riddle book. 34465

The new Robinson Crusoe.
12059; 15634; 15635; 28375;
32565; 38042

New St. Tammany almanac.
2464; 6228; 9659; 13530

New school act [N.Y.] 34506

The new school for boys. 38117;
38118

A new selection of hymns and
spiritual songs. From the

best authors. 29759

New selection of hymns and spiritual songs, designed for the use of the pious. 2465; 21644

A new selection of nearly eight hundred evangelical hymns. 8553; 20318

New selection of reformation melodies. 33219

A new selection of revival hymns. 29960

A new selection of sacred music. 1066; 20359

A new series of questions on the selected Scripture lessons for Sabbath schools. 33183; 33184

A new set of cotillions. 15324; 17352; 20350

A new society for the benefit of Indians, organized at the city of Washington. 7806; 7807

The new song, a poem. 19174

A new song book. 19879

A new song called Blue eyed Mary. 13531

New songs for the use of Christians. 10320

A new Spanish dance. 16730

A new Spanish grammar. 8476; 20218; 24249; 32861

The new speaker, or Exercises in rhetoric. 38618

New specimen of printing types from the foundry of William Hagar & Co. 24772

A new spelling book. 830; 5043; 8409; 15832; 20147; 28561; 38239

New State House--Boston. 7492

New steam boat. Proposals for raising by subscription 100,000 dollars. 2466

New store, Isaac N. Whittelsey, has just established himself in Carlisle. 41511

New store. The subscriber has just opened at his house, eight miles east of Washington. 37765

New stories. 30602

New story about Little Jack Horner. 2467

A new system of arithmetick.
40325

A new system of astronomy. 762

New system of cultivation. 4642

A new system of geography. 9555; 17234; 25425; 34201; 34202

A new system of mercantile arithmetic. 4157; 11333; 19177; 23200; 23201

A new system of mnemonic associations in chemistry. 6620

A new system of modern geography. 9560

A new system of shoeing horses. 5469

A new system of teaching writing. 24887

New tavern and boarding house. 4920

The new Tax law. 13553

The New Testament, by way of question and answer. 17681

New Testament stories and parables for children. 441

New (i. e., Park) Theatre. [Play bills] 6279; 9702

A new theory on the causes of the motions of the planetary bodies, belonging to the solar system. 40272

A new translation of the Epistle to the Hebrews. 28162

A new treatise on the use of globes. 13179; 25015

A new tutor for the Spanish guitar. 4935

A new tutor for the violin. 3021; 6229

A new universal atlas of the world. 9556; 21523; 25427

A new universal gazetteer. 6120; 13403

New universal letter writer. 17353

A new view of society. 21763; 21764

New views of penitentiary discipline. 38024

New views of the Constitution of the United States. 14261

The new Virginia justice. 1568

New vocal instructor. 789

A new way to pay old debts.
9433; 29696
The new week's preparation for a
worthy receiving of the Lord's
supper. 2881
A new world planted. 917
The New Year improved; or, Errors corrected. 6230
New-Year's address [Boston
News-Letter] 28246
New Year's address by the carrier of the Oracle. 12927
A New Year's address, delivered to the citizens of Center-
ville. 35240
New-Year's address, from the
carrier of the Free Press.
33248
New-year's address, of a street
sweeper. 30316
New Year's address of the carrier [Boston Commercial Ga-
zette] 8144
New Year's address of the carrier of the National Intelligencer. 39697
New-year's address of the carriers of the Columbian Centinel. 20136
New Year's address of the carriers of the New York Statesman. 13532
New Year's address of the lamplighter. 9660
New-Year's address to the patrons of The Annotator. 37476
New Year's address to the patrons of the Wheeling Gazette.
37158
A New-Year's Day, for 1820.
1756
New-Year's doggerels, for 1822.
4993
New Year's gift. Containing "A
picture of human life." 25532
A New-Year's gift. The result
of meditations at the Mansion-
House at the Boiling Spring
Farm. 5948
A New Year's lay, dedicated by
the carriers, to the patrons of
the Liberty Hall and Cincinnati Gazette. 12145; 17354

The new year's lay of the Columbian Centinel. 824
A New-Year's Lay, or retrospect. 1957; 8352; 13533
A New Year's memorial, for
minister and people. 23928
The New Year's Sabbath. 29961
A New Year's sermon preached
at Trinity Church. 20630
A new-Year's sermon, preached
on the first Sunday in January,
1825. 20879
New Year's sermons, delivered
in Deerfield, New-Hampshire.
11393; 14869
New-York almanack. 9690;
30032; 30033; 39810; 39811
The New-York and farmer's al-
manack. 39812
New-York and New-Jersey al-
manack. 2519; 6258; 9692;
9693; 13559; 13560; 17398;
17399; 17400; 21675; 25567;
30035; 39813
New-York and New-Jersey
Farmer's Almanac. 6259
The New York and Vermont al-
manac. 6260; 6261
New-York Athenaeum. 17402
New York canal lands on sale.
13775
New York Chamber of Commerce.
Memorial. 36654; 41263
The New York City Hall record-
er. 6264; 10132
New-York consolidated lottery.
34534
The New York cries, in rhyme.
25571
The New-York directory. 2525
The New-York expositor. 11421;
23323
New-York Farmer's almanac.
2527
New York Friendly Association of
Master Book-Binders' List of
prices. 9697
The New-York gardener. 15040;
27789; 31907
The New York guide in minia-
ture. 30044
The New-York medical almanac.
13568; 17416; 21687; 25577;

30048

New York. Memorial of agriculturists and manufacturers. 36655

New York. Memorial of inhabitants of Herkimer County. 36656

New York. Memorial of inhabitants of Otsego County. 36657

New York. Memorial of inhabitants of the city of Albany. 36658; 36659

New York. Memorial of the inhabitants of Dutchess County. 36660; 36661

New York. Memorial of the merchants of the city of New York. 41264

New York. Memorial of the Ontario Agricultural Society. 36662

New York. Memorial to merchants, traders, &c. 36663

New York. Petition of inhabitants of Red Hook. 36664

New York. Petition of sundry inhabitants of the county of Delaware. 36665

New York. Petition of the wool growers and manufacturers of Madison County. 36666

The New York preceptor. 4319; 9703; 13569

The New-York primer. 4320; 9704; 13570

New York reader. 6284; 25579; 30052; 34548

The New-York reporter. 2539

New York. Resolutions of the Legislature. 36667

New-York scenes. 30053

The New York selection of sacred music. 81; 7775; 11579; 23455; 31933

The New York serenading waltz. 2540; 2541; 2542; 2543; 23283

The New-York spelling-book. 2544; 9705; 13576; 25580

New York state convention. 34390

New York State literature lottery. 13577; 21689

The New-York state register.

39837

New-York State Tract Society. 13578

The New York Sunday school spelling book. 21690; 25581

The New-York telegraph and signal book. 10077

The New York, Vermont & Connecticut almanac. 2547

Newark Institute for Young Ladies. 25585

News-boy's address to the patrons of the Boston Yankee. 549

News carrier's address [Albany] 23444

News from Jerusalem. 20193

The Newtonian reflector: or New-England almanac. 9712; 13586; 17429; 21696; 25592; 30059; 34556; 39844; 39845; 39846

The Newtonian reflector: or Republican almanac. 9713

The next governor. To the people of Kentucky. 19190

Niagara. A poem. 9310

The Niagara almanac. 13587

Niagara Falls. 21938

Nicholas Hart. 27278

Nicolai's celebrated sonata. 30061

The night errand. 6297

Night thoughts on life, death, and immortality. 4358; 4359; 4360; 4361; 4362; 7723; 11499; 11500

The nightingale. A choice collection of patriotic, humorous, amorous and sentimental songs. 6298

The nightingale. A military air. 20210

The nightingale, or A new and choice selection of the most admired songs. 9717

The nightingale. With an introductory minuet. 13390

The night-watch. 2552a

Nina. 13592

Nina, an Icelandic tale. 30066

Nineteenth annual report [New Hampshire Missionary Society] 2443

Nineteenth annual report of the

trustees of the Free-School Society of New York. 17734

Nineteenth concert [Musical Fund Society. Philadelphia] 39687

The nineteenth report of the Bible Society of Philadelphia. 28179

Nineteenth report, of the trustees of the Hampshire Missionary Society. 1499

The Ninth and Tenth annual reports of the Board of Managers of the Bible Society of Baltimore. 451

The ninth and tenth annual reports of the Board of Public Works, to the General Assembly of Virginia. 27516

Ninth anniversary of the American Bible Society. 19401

Ninth annual meeting of the Baptist Education Society of the state of New York. 23603

Ninth annual report [Albany County Bible Society] 62

The ninth annual report, for the year 1825, of the managers of the Indigent Widows' and Single Women's Society. 24950

The ninth annual report of the American Society for Colonizing the Free People of Colour. 23475

Ninth annual report of the American Tract Society. 11609

The ninth annual report of the Association for the Relief of Respectable Aged Indigent Females. 7846

Ninth annual report of the Bible Society of Virginia. 8051

Ninth annual report of the Board of Directors of the Princeton Theological Seminary. 6537

The ninth annual report of the Board of Directors of the Washington County Bible Society. 7590

The ninth annual report of the board of managers of the New-York Protestant Episcopal Missionary Society. 25578

Ninth annual report of the Committee of Finance. 4771

Ninth annual report of the Controllers of the public schools. 30174

Ninth annual report of the directors of the American Education Society. 15083

Ninth annual report of the directors of the New-York Institution for the Instruction of the Deaf and Dumb. 34543

Ninth annual report of the directors of the Northwestern Branch of the American Education Society. 37442

Ninth annual report of the directors of the Penitent Females' Refuge. 34981

Ninth annual report of the Female Bible Society of Boston. 12527

The ninth annual report of the Female Missionary Society of the Western District, N. Y. 20507

The ninth annual report of the Long-Island Bible Society. 16932

The ninth annual report of the managers of the New York Bible and Common Prayer Society. 21680

Ninth annual report of the managers of the Religious Tract Society of the city of Washington. 34988

Ninth annual report of the Massachusetts Peace Society. 21370

Ninth annual report of the Missionary Society of the Methodist Episcopal Church. 34123

Ninth annual report of the New York Female Auxiliary Bible Society. 21684

The ninth annual report of the New York Religious Tract Society. 6285

Ninth annual report of the Philadelphia Orphan Society. 17614

Ninth annual report of the Presbyterian Education Society. 30335

Ninth concert of the Musical Fund

Society of Philadelphia. 21581
Ninth general report of the pres-
ident and directors of the
Chesapeake and Delaware Can-
al Company. 32660
Ninth report of the American
Bible Society. 19402
Ninth report of the directors of
the American Asylum at Hart-
ford. 19413
The ninth report of the Female
Bible Society of Philadelphia.
12528
Ninth report of the New Hamp-
shire Bible Society. 2442
The ninth report of the United
Foreign Missionary Society.
26266
Ninth report of the Vermont Col-
onization Society. 37011
The ninth report of the Young
Men's Bible Society of Balti-
more. 41623
No fiction: a narrative founded
on recent and interesting facts.
6594; 6595; 6596
No fiction; or, The test of friend-
ship. 6597; 6598
No flower can compare with the
rose of the valley. 15436
No hay unión con los tiranos.
17112
"No more by sorrow." 11977
No, no, no, to the woods I can-
not stray. 1660
No song no supper. 16554
Noah, a poem. 4451
Noches lúgubres...por el coronel
D. José Cadalso. 38021
The nomenclature, and expositor
of the English language. 23969;
28327; 32527; 38001; 38002
Nomination. At a respectable
meeting of the citizens of the
county of Monroe. 13372
Nomination of President & Vice
President of the United States.
12362
Non mi ricordo. A waltz. 5524
The non-personality, origin and
end of that old serpent, called
the Devil. 20533
Non-resident lands in the terri-

tories. 27279
Non vi fidate agli nomini. 1224;
1225
None so pretty. 12670; 12671
North America. 20519
North-American calendar; or, the
Columbian almanac. 2560;
6304; 9725; 13594; 17436;
21698; 25599; 30068; 34565;
39853
The North American spelling
book. 7662
North Bank. You are hereby
notified, that agreeable to a
vote of the stockholders.
34566
North Carolina. Act of the Leg-
islature. 41265
The North Carolina register and
United States calendar. 9731
North Carolina. Resolution of
the Legislature. 36668
The North eastern coast of North
America. 34586
North End Forever!!! 12525
North Paris Library. 34856;
40132
Der Northampton Bauern Calender.
2565; 6312; 9732; 13600;
17449; 21708; 25606; 30092
The Northampton Farmer's al-
manac. 9733; 13601; 17450;
21709; 25605; 30093
Northern and northwestern bound-
ary line. 36669
Northern boundary of Indiana.
36670
Northern regions. 30091; 39880
Northern section of the United
States, including Canada. 9458
A northern tour. 20678
The northern traveller. 20355;
24388; 33023
Northwest coast of America.
27280
Northwood; a tale of New England.
29110
The Norwich Female Seminary is
this day opened. 39885
The Norwood gypsy. 34588
The nosegay of honeysuckles. 651
Not a drum was heard. 19612;
19613

Not in the pictured halls.   15437

Notas históricas sobre la revolución de España.   25098

Note addressed to the Rev. Joseph Penney.   17454

A note from Corrector to William Jay.   12843

Note - Minister U.S. to Spain.   36671

The noted horse Hailstorm will stand this season in Gibson county.   9302

The noted horse Young Chester Ball will be let to mares the ensuing season.   24378

Notes and observations on Eliot's Indian grammar.   8577

Notes & reflections during a ramble in Germany.   30587

Notes, explanatory and practical, on the epistle to the Romans.   19610

Notes geographical and historical, relating to the town of Brooklyn.   16242

Notes of lectures on the theory and practice of medicine.   28757

Notes on a tour through the western part of the state of New York.   39886

Notes on Blackstone's commentaries.   26252

Notes on Colombia.   27920

Notes on Mexico.   17655

Notes on political economy.   23997

Notes on practice.   22523; 40682

Notes on (review of) "Europe by a citizen of the U.S."   1140

Notes on the cultivation and management of tobacco.   9504

Notes on the Epistle to the Romans.   18253

Notes on the origin and necessity of slavery.   23939

Notes on the parables of the New Testament.   7877

Notes, on the settlement and Indian wars, of the western parts of Virginia & Pennsylvania.   15990

Notes on the state of Virginia.   21052; 21053; 39135

Notes to his sketch of Bunker-Hill battle.   22411

Notes to the paper entitled Descriptions of ten species of South American birds.   19791

Notes to the trial of Commodore Barron.   13606

Nöthige Aufklärung in Betreff der Rödelsheim' schen und Streit' schen Legate.   25598

"Nothing is so Secret, but Time and Truth will reveal it."   30323

Nothing, by Nobody.   30450

Notice.   At a meeting of the Board of Trustees of the village of Utica.   14762

Notice extraordinary.   R.C. Weightman, a man of known liberal principles.   25613

Notice.   Fayetteville [N.C.]   20497

Notice.   Important to farmers, tavern-keepers cartmen, travellers, and economists in general.   2570

Notice.   In Chancery.   9683

Notice.   In conformity to an application made by Joseph Ricketson and ten other inhabitants of the town of New-Bedford.   39720

Notice is hereby given that the following causes are ruled for trial and argument in the Court of common pleas.   1842; 1843

Notice of a meeting of the Trustees of the Boston Central Wharf and Wet Dock Corporation.   23871

Notice of a meeting on the subject of Church music.   23885

Notice of a meeting, at Essex Coffee House.   3096

Notice, on the picture of the coronation of Napoleon.   22139

Notice.   Sir, At the semi-annual meeting of the Overseers of Harvard University.   16468

Notice.   The citizens of Wayne County are requested to meet at the council-house.   4207

Notice. The electors of the second ward, friendly to the nomination of a People's ticket. 17455

Notice. The subscribers, Agents of the Lehigh Coal Company of Pennsylvania, take this method of informing the public. 2038

Notice. To colonists in Austin's Colony. 37519

Notice to farmers, tradesmen and others. 21767

Notice to Land Debtors. 18937

Notice to St. Domingo Colonists. 24568; 24569

Notice to the friends of religion and learning. 24074

Notice. To the public. 748

Notices of East Florida. 10282

Notices of the early history of South-Carolina. 9485

Notices of the original and successive efforts to improve the disipline [sic] of the prison at Philadelphia. 27498

Noticias de govierno de Texas. 14273

Notification. Boston, April 4, 1828. 32448

Notification of annual meeting, dated, Boston, 22d December, 1825. 22400

Notification. The Freeholders and other inhabitants of the town of Boston. 4772; 4773; 4775; 8131

Notification. The freeholders and other inhabitants of the Town of Dorchester. 5202

Notification. The inhabitants of the city of Boston. 8132; 19799; 28232

Notification. The inhabitants of the town of Boston. 4774; 4776

Notions of the Americans. 32827

Notions on religion and politics. 25878

Nous, les soussignes, habitants de la Cote des Poux, de la Rivière Rouge. 6037

Le nouveau seigneur de village. 32850

Le Nouveau Testament de notre seigneur Jésus-Christ. 442; 15382

Nouveaux élémens de la conversation, en Anglais et en Français. 2822

Novela histórica mexicana relativa a la época de la conquista. 24985

Novels and tales. 20190

The novels of Charles Brockden Brown. 28292

The novels, tales and romances of the author of Waverley. 3145; 10203

The novice. 21892

Novum Testamentum, cum versione latina Ariae Montani. 4689; 15383

Novum Testamentum Graece ex recensione Jo. Jac. Griesbachii. 8036

Novum Testamentum graecum ad exemplar. 8035; 28163; 37830

Now at moonlight's fairy hour. 3431

Now by my troth. 9137

Now morn is blushing in the sky. 6879

Now or never. 39887

Noyes' system of practical penmanship. 39888

Le Nozze de Figaro. 24288; 24289

El nuevo Robinson Crusoe. 15636

Nuevo sistema de geografia. 28281

El Nuevo Testamento de Nuestro señor Jesu Cristo. 8037

The numbers of Carlton, addressed to the people of North Carolina. 32549

Nursery rhymes and tales. 25616

A nut shell of knowledge. 40611

Nützliche und erbauliche Anrede an die Jugend. 38005

Nützliches und sehr bewährt befundenes Weiber-Büchlein. 7830

O

O bless'd are the eye-lids that sleep sweetly closing. 11884

O Brigual banks are wild and fair. 40373

O by that blue eye's roguish brightness. 15439

O cold was the climate. 13368; 13369

O come my love! 5762; 5763

O, come smiling June. 3196; 14102

O dear what can the matter be. 13609; 17032

O dinna weep. 20821

O do you remember, Ding Dong, bell. 4139

O Dolce concerto. 630

O en ad o geh teeh soah Koy a noh soah. 12777

O for a thousand tongues to sing. 4071

O gin ye were dead gudeman. 1353

O happy fair! 4730; 11885

O! I feel sweet words impart. 16588

O! it was not for me that I heard the bells ringing. 23308

O lady love awake. 9881

O let me in this ae night. 9742; 9743; 9744; 10020

O Lord, have mercy upon me. 2717

O love with doubt should never dwell. 13610; 13611

O Mary turn away that bonnie e'e o' thine. 16702

O Nanny wilt though gang with me. 19998

O never doubt my love. 13612

O! no. We never mention her. 484

O pescator dell'onda. 17459

O praise the Lord in that blest place. 2220

O! rest thee babe, rest thee. 14890; 19264

O saw ye the lass wi' the bonny blue een. 2571

O! say not woman's heart is bought. 4266

O sing sweet bird. 2192

O soft with trembling motion. 15262

O surely Melody. 18133; 22413

O swiftly glides the bonnie boat. 29068

O swiftly glides the bonny boat. 7994; 16392; 17460; 21715; 21716

O, take the wreath. 4104

O! tell me how from love to fly. 15787

O then I'll cease to love. 19295

O, there's a mountain palm! 19749

O thou art all to me love. 4826

O 'tis love. 13613; 17767

O wat ye wha's in yon town. 16371

O well do I remember. 15440; 15441

O, what a row! 9745

O where will bonny Ann ly. 13988

O Willie brew'd a peck o' maut. 8368

O wilt thou go with me love. 16291

O woman shines brightly forever. 19279

Oaths and obligations of Free Masonry. 37487

The O'Briens and the O'Flahertys. 34194

The obedient son. 39892

Oberon; or, The charmed horn. 25176

Obi; or, Three-fingered Jack. 16029; 33032

An obituary memoir of Robert F. Mott. 28298

Obituary notice of Professor Peck. 13263

Obituary notice of Rev. John Bradford. 20742

Obituary notices of the Rev. John Chester. 37409

Obituary of Jackman J. Davis. 32648

Obituary of Mrs. Mary P. Clark. 6320

The object of the American So-

Wesley." 7598

Observations on the depravity of man. 37979

Observations on the efficacy of white mustard seed. 28591; 32822; 35572

Observations on the five candidates for the Commons. 25618

Observations on the floating dock. 30608

Observations on the genus Salamandra. 20816; 24793

Observations on the genus Unio. 39253

Observations on the geology and organic remains of the secondary, tersiary, and alluvial formations of the Atlantic coast. 36999

Observations on the growth of the mind. 25905

Observations on the importance of female education. 21528; 29822

Observations on the importance of Greek literature. 4352

Observations on the importance of improving the navigation of the River Schuylkill. 2573

Observations on the importance of the American revolution. 2868

Observations on the improvement of seminaries of learning. 21067

Observations on the lake fevers and other diseases of the Genesee country. 13161; 13162

Observations on the language of signs. 11554

Observations on the language of the Muhhekaneew Indians. 12433

Observations on the law passed the 27th of November, 1779. 6321

Observations on the medical character. 24895

Observations on the nature and cure of dropsies. 496; 2574; 19758

Observations on the nomenclature of Wilson's Ornithology. 23852

Observations on the nomination of a candidate for the presidency. 9749

Observations on the objects and progress of philological enquiries. 29493

Observations on the penitentiary system, & penal code of Pennsylvania. 34093

Observations, on the petitions to Congress of the inhabitants of the Counties of Mackinaw, Brown and Crawford. 6038

Observations on the Political Reforms of Colombia. 35093a

Observations on the present state of society. 17464

Observations on the principles of correct education. 7811; 12821

Observations on the relation between rolling and dragging friction. 39152

Observations on the religious instruction of youth. 32901

Observations on the religious peculiarities of the Society of Friends. 20774

Observations on the "Remarks on the constitutionality of the memorial of the city council for an extension of Faneuil Hall market." 17465

Observations on the report of the Committee of ways and means, made at Washington. 34708

Observations on the secale cornutum. 11514

Observations on the sermons of Elias Hicks. 27539

Observations on the silk worm. 32508

Observations on the slavery of the Africans and their descendants. 12823

Observations on the sources and effects of unequal wealth. 23983

Observations on the state of the currency. 39893

Observations on the surgical anatomy of the head and neck. 12026

Observations on the survey of the

sea coast of the United States.
30467

Observations on the Susquehanna
River and Maryland Canal.
9751; 11459

Observations on the tariff. 28313

Observations on the use and
abuse of mercurial medicines.
5526

Observations on the use of eme-
tics. 9068

Observations on the utility and
administration of purgative
medicines. 12748; 16385;
38901

Observations on the yellow fever.
9951; 9952

Observations on theatrical
amusements. 6322; 13614

Observations on those diseases
of females which are attended
by discharges. 15773; 24120

Observations on two epistles, re-
sponsive, of the Rev. Abner
Kneeland. 12974; 25010

Observations on yellow fever.
19195

Observations, reasons and facts,
disproving importation. 13985

Observations suggested by the
late occurrences in Charleston.
9750

Observations upon currency and
finance. 25619

Observations upon the automaton
chess player of von Kempelen.
29382

Observations upon the autumnal
fevers of Savannah. 24284;
32888

Observations upon the Floridas.
14781; 14782

Observations upon the memorial
and report of the citizens of
Boston. 34593

Observations upon the project for
establishing Geneva College.
16265

Observatory at Brunswick, Maine.
27281

Obstructions - The Ohio River.
36672; 36673

Obstructions to navigation, Wa-

bash. 36674

Occasional pieces of poetry.
19849

The odd volume. 28602

Odds and ends.   26163

Ode. Air---"Anacreon in
Heaven." 694

Ode. Air--"Rise Columbia."
3298

Ode for the canal celebration.
23377

Ode for the celebration of the
Battle of Bunker Hill. 21406

Ode, gesungen am Harmonie-
Fest, mit Musik. 16440

Ode suggested by Rembrandt
Peale's national portrait of
Washington. 16300

Ode sur le combat naval de Nav-
arin.   34820

Ode to LaFayette.   15269

An ode to science.   2780

Ode to Washington.   33592

An ode, written by request, on
the opening of the exhibition
at the Franklin Institute.
33947

Ode written for the celebration
on Bunker Hill.   23284

Ode, written for the Washington
Society. 20446

The odes of Horace in Cincinnati.
9834

Odes upon cash, corn, Catholics,
and other matters.   34187;
39633

Odofriede.   9173

The Odyssey. 9047; 9048;
33585

Of a' the airs. 13615

Of age to-morrow.   20312

Of the imitation of Christ. 9094

Of the state of the finances.
36675

An offering at the altar of truth.
28266

The offering for 1829. 39894

The office and duties of masters
in chancery. 16566

The office and duty of a justice
of the peace [Clayton] 15781

The office and duty of a justice
of the peace [Potter] 34857

Office and influence of evangelical pastors. 37916

Office-holders. 9753

The office of assistant bishop, inconsistent with the constitution. 40697

Office of institution of the Rev. Samuel Farmer Jarvis. 544

The office of surrogate. 19858

Office of the Democratic Press. 28188

The office of the Holy Week. 38087

The office work of a mediator explained. 32627

Officers and soldiers of the Virginia line. 2576

Officers, &c. of frigate Chesapeake. 27282

Officers, &c. pensioned under act of 1828. 41266

Officers of Revolutionary Army. 36676

Officers of the Agricultural Society of the County of Windsor. 4309

Officers of the General Grand Encampment of the United States of America. 33277

Officers of the New-York Horticultural Society. 17413

Officers on the pension list. 36677

Officia propria pro Diocesi Ludovicensi. 5207

Official army register. 3928; 7394; 11062; 14666; 36678

Official description of the Fancy Rag Ball. 39895

Official documents, containing a message of the state of Georgia to the Legislature. 20662

Official papers, printed for the Common Council of the city of Boston. 8133

Official Record from the War Department, of the Proceedings of the Court Martial which tried, and the Orders of General [Andrew] Jackson for shooting the six Militia Men. 2577; 36679; 36680; 36681

An official register of the deaths which occurred among the white population in the city of Savannah. 3077

Official Report. Jackson, 21st. June, 1828. 32981

An official report of the trials of sundry Negroes. 9192

Official reports on public credit. 5523

Oft in a stilly night. 30103

Oft in the stilly night. 2321; 6882; 6883; 22378; 22379

Oh banquet not. 4729

Oh! bid me die but leave me not. 22133

Oh Charlie is my darling. 9754

Oh come my love along the sea. 39884

Oh come to me when daylight sets. 6880; 14212; 18102

Oh! cruel. A comic song. 13617; 21720

Oh gaze on me. 2931

Oh lady fair. 2322; 6107; 13380

Oh lady ne'er think I'll prove false to thee. 22284; 22285

Oh! lady twine no wreath for me. 14912

Oh! let me only breathe the air. 5005

Oh! let the world deceive me love! 19996

Oh! listen 'tis the nightingale. 15438

Oh! maid of Marlivale. 6881

Oh! maiden fair. 17509; 17510

Oh! Mary when the wild wind blows. 1888; 16833; 16834

Oh! my baby. 1835

Oh ne'er can I the joys forget. 22299

Oh! no we never mention her. 32386

Oh! say not woman's heart is bought. 4267; 11406; 11407; 11408; 14891

Oh! say not woman's love is bought. 4268; 11409; 23309

Oh! soon return. 38968

Oh! still remember me. 8077

Oh strike again! 1867

Oh! sweet was the scene. 8078

Oh! talk not to me of the wealth

she possesses.   7504

Oh tell me how from love to fly.
  790

Oh tell me sweet Kate. 6329

Oh! then dearest Ellen. 14213

O think not.   15788

Oh this is the spot. 6138

Oh thou who dry'st the mourner's
  tear [Moran] 9548; 13391

Oh! thou who dry'st the mourner's
  tear [Wiesenthal] 14913

Oh 'tis love.   17468; 17469;
  17766; 17768; 17769; 17770

Oh! Tis the melody.   903

Oh turn away those mournful eyes.
  16731

Oh twine me a bower. 3037

Oh! why hast thou taught me to
  love thee. 39896

Oh woman.   9536; 9537

O'Halloran; or, The insurgent
  chief. 16970

Ohio. 16147

The Ohio almanac. 9773; 13628;
  21737

The Ohio and Mississippi pilot.
  1386

The Ohio canal. 14795; 39907

The Ohio gazetteer.   5766;
  25032; 39197

The Ohio justice and township officer's assistant. 7503

Ohio magazine almanack. 34604;
  39913

The Ohio manual.   25033

Ohio. Memorial of the inhabitants of Montgomery County.
  36682

The Ohio navigator. 17484

The Ohio pilot.   1387; 4817;
  24690

The Ohio primer. 25629; 39915

Ohio register.   2595; 6341; 9775

Ohio. Resolutions of the General Assembly. 36683

Ojibwa spelling book. 19731

Old and New Tariffs compared.
  4310

The Old and New Testaments connected in the History of the
  Jews. 13847; 13848

Old and young; or, The four
  Mowbrays. 34605

Old Christopher's almanac.
  39917

Old colony collection of anthems.
  12762

Old continental money. 36684

The old fashion farmer's motives
  for leaving the Church of England. 21738

Old hundred collection of sacred
  music. 17488

Old internal revenue and direct
  tax. 31439

The old maid.   25436

The old man's calendar. 8804

Old Mother Hubbard.   2597;
  17489

Old Mother Shipton's universal
  dream book.   6344

The old paths.   A sermon. 20915

The old soldier. 2629

Old Towler. 6793

The old woman and her pig.
  21739

The Olio, being a collection of
  poems. 12684

The olive tree.   21785

Omnifarious law exemplified.
  38415

The omnipresence of the Deity.
  34181

Omniscience, the attribute of the
  Father only.   1722; 24934;
  29294

Omnium botherum, or Strictures
  on "The Omnium gatherum."
  5618

On a bright sunny morn. 8502

On a new species of duck.
  15493

On altering election laws. 27283

On baptism.   21744

On civilization of the Indians.
  36685

On coming unworthily to the
  Lord's supper. 29834

On Confirmation.   13638; 34609

On cultivating a spirit of universal peace. 35064

On detraction, and curiosity
  about the affairs of others.
  5812; 21189

On drunkenness.   2973

On experimental religion. 27848

On faithfulness in little things.
40663

On false standards in religion.
38915

On fashionable amusements.
2600; 13397

On Friday, November 5, 1824,
was held at Marion, Perry
County, the first Anniversary
of the Baptist Convention of
Alabama. 15182

On General Lafayette. 22259

On hearing the word. 3159

On Hudson side. 15474; 15475

On human depravity. 26053;
30573

On Imprisonment for Debt. 2601

On intemperance. 9784

On man's accountableness.
33752

On Monday morning of this week.
37266; 37267; 37268

On paper money. 20849

On preaching the gospel. 37920

On preserving potatoes for sea
stores of foreign consumption.
7651

On religious phraseology. 24343;
28697

On retrenchment. 36686

On Saturday evening, Dec. 20,
at Pickering Hall, Mr. Stevens
will deliver a lecture on astronomy. 13639

On self-examination. 21745

On slander. 30558; 35137

On some corruptions of scripture.
31935

On surgical anatomy of the groin.
23140

On tests of true religion. 32974

On the aim of the order of the
Freemasons. 21746

On the amusements of the theatre. 25633

On the Baltimore rail-road carriage, invented by Ross Win-
ans. 40572

On the cultivation of forest trees.
11555

On the death of John Gale. 4383

On the death of Presidents Jefferson and Adams. 25328

On the death of Thomas Conden.
5048

On the distinction of two species
of Icterus. 28215

On the doctrine of two natures in
Jesus Christ. 33815

On the duties of consolation, and
the rites and customs appropriate to mourning. 20304;
24344; 38377

On the duty of parents to children. 7872

On the establishment of public
schools in the city of New-
York. 22008

On the evidence necessary to establish the doctrine of the
Trinity. 35481; 35482

On the first of March 1827, will
be published by H. C. Carey &
I. Lea, Philadelphia the first
number of The American Quarterly Review. 28387

On the Holy Scriptures. 2602

On the importance of constant attendance on Divine worship.
2974

On the importance of the study of
anatomy. 21747

On the Indian trade. 6347

On the influence of medicine.
32264

On the intercourse between the
soul and the body. 35449;
40587

On the internal improvement of
Virginia. 9785

On the knowledge of the Lord.
17908

On the loftiest and most important branch of all sciences.
28311

On the Lottery decision. 5478-
5482

On the mineralogy of Chester
county. 32604

On the mode of constituting presidential electors. 12382

On the nature and efficacy of the
cross of Christ. 2603

On the New Jerusalem, and its
heavenly doctrine. 40588

On the New Testament conformed

to Griesbach's text. 38834

On the original text of the New
Testament. 39925

On the pathology and treatment
of gonorrhoea. 2276

On the Peace of God, which pas-
seth all understanding. 2604;
34610

On the proposed alteration of the
tariff. 15863

On the religious phraseology, of
the New Testament. 1017;
24342

On the state of the finance.
27284

On the 10th of January, 1826, a
number of gentlemen met at
the Vestry of Parkstreet
Church, Boston. 23492

On the treatment of anchylosis.
28070

On the treatment of denuded
nerves of the teeth. 5780

On the true policy of states with
regard to bank charters.
12418

On the utility of country medical
institutions. 19642

On theatrical exhibitions. 19381

On this cold flinty rock. 579

On worship, ministry, and prayer.
2605; 9786; 9787

One hundred and twenty reasons
for being a Universalist.
32911

$100 reward. Stop the murderer!
20805

$150 reward. ran away from the
subscriber, on the night of the
27th October a negro man
named Ben. 28694

150 dollars reward. The store of
the subscribers was entered
last night. 8717

One hundred scriptural arguments
for the Unitarian faith. 19426;
23510; 27850

$1000 Reward. At the Battle of
Queenstown, Upper Canada, on
the 13th day of October, 1812.
15027

One thousand questions for the
examination of scholars in

Blairs rhetorick. 8106

One, two, three, four, five, by
advertisement. 17805

One year in Savannah. 2606

Onea: an Indian tale. 3226

The only copy of the life, & the
testimony that convicted
Michl. Monroe, alias James
Wellington. 17195

The only sure and true key to
the Holy Bible. 21027

The only sure guide to the English tongue. 2727; 2728; 6439;
6440

Onomasia: or, Philadelphia vocabulary. 10138

Onslow in reply to Patrick Henry.
23989

The Ontario almanac. 2608

Ontiva, the son of the forest; a
poem. 1916

Ontwa, the son of the forest. A
poem. 11413

Oolaita, or, The Indian heroine.
5165

Opera, ex recensione Io. Augusti
Ernesti. 30753

Opera. Interpretatione et notis,
illustravit Carolus Ruacus.
4085; 4086; 14771; 23148

Opera. Interpretatione et notis
illustravit Ludovious Desprez.
1667; 16580

Opera Omnia. 20078

The opera waltz. 3064

Operations of the mint. 27285;
36690

The operative mechanic, and the
British machinist. 25596

Opinion--Attorney General--
Treaty of Ghent. 36691

Opinion in case Stockton, R. F.,
vs. Ship Marianna Flora.
11063

Opinion in the case of John Healy
v. William Martin. 12331

Opinion in the case of Lansing,
appellant against Goelet re-
spondent. 29378

The opinion of Chief Justice Marshall, in the case of Garnett,
ex'r of Brooke v. Macon et al.
21334; 23011; 31440

Lodge.   29273

Oration before the Erin Benevolent Society of Pittsburgh.
15599

An oration before the Grand
Lodge of Freemasons in New
Hampshire.   11905

An oration before the Washington
Benevolent Society of Pennsylvania [Budd]   32509

An oration before the Washington
Benevolent Society of Pennsylvania [Dwight]   28747

An oration before Western Star
Lodge.   1688

An oration by Alexander Neil, the
Fourth of July, 1825, Long
Town, Fairfield district, S. C.
21591

Oration by Brother Dabney C.
Cosby.   15879

Oration by Mr. Custis, of Arlington.   934

Oration by Richard Henry Lee.
25079

An oration, by Thomas Rowland.
10150

An oration, commemorative of
American independence, delivered at Utica, July 5, 1824.
16722

An oration, commemorative of
American independence: delivered in the Presbyterian
Church in Litchfield.   6300

An oration commemorative of
American independence; delivered July 5, 1824, in the
Bowery church. 15904

Oration, commemorative of Col.
Philemon Hawkins, senior, deceased. 38940

An oration commemorative of the
birth of Washington; delivered
at the Baptist church, on the
23d of February, 1824. 16020

An oration, commemorative of
the birth of Washington; delivered in the Methodist Church,
Albany, February 22, 1826.
24380

Oration, commemorative of the
birth of Washington, delivered

on the twenty-third day of February, 1829. 37954

An oration, commemorative of
Washington, delivered Feb. 22,
1821.   5117

Oration, containing a declaration
of mental independence, delivered in the public hall, at
New-Harmony, Ind. 27749

An oration, delivered at Barre,
Massachusetts, before Mount-
Zion, Harris and Thompson
Lodges. 1794

An oration, delivered at Barre,
Massachusetts before Mount
Zion lodge of Free and accepted Masons. 29458

An oration, delivered at Bennington.   7686

An oration delivered at Brattleborough.   4925

An oration delivered at Burlington, Vt., on the anniversary
of American Independence,
July 4, 1828.   35218

An oration, delivered at Burlington, Vt., on the fourth of
July, 1828.   32063

An oration, delivered at Burlington, Vt., on the fourth of
July, 1826.   23740

An oration delivered at Cambridge. 24456; 24457

Oration delivered at Chapel Hill.
39025

An oration delivered at China.
25152

An oration delivered at Concord.
20441

An oration, delivered at Craftsbury. 37278

An oration, delivered at Dedham,
July 4th, 1823.   13210

An oration, delivered at Dedham,
June 24, A.D. 1820. 1875

An oration, delivered at Dorchester. 10294

Oration delivered at Dorset.
26064

An oration, delivered at East
Haverhill, Mass. 40066

An oration delivered at Germantown, Pennsylvania. 24995

An oration delivered at Gloucester. 30707

Oration, delivered at Groton.
4922

Oration, delivered at Halifax.
21918

An oration, delivered at Indian
Rock. 13310

An oration, delivered at Kinder-
hook. 19121

An oration delivered at Lancaster,
February 21, 1826. 24728

An oration delivered at Lancaster,
Mass. in celebration of American independence. 23329

An oration delivered at Lexington.
22373

An oration, delivered at Lyons.
24881

An oration, delivered at Meredith Bridge, N. J. 21278

An oration, delivered at Middlebury. 38709

Oration delivered at New-Castle,
Del. 14768

An oration delivered at Newark.
12301

Oration delivered at Newberry
court house. 30120

An oration delivered at Newburyport. 8472

An oration, delivered at Ogdens-
burgh, New-York. 31579

An oration, delivered at Old-
town, Ross County, Ohio.
28687

An oration, delivered at Oxford.
7968

An oration delivered at Paterson,
New-Jersey. 26077

An oration, delivered at Pittsfield. 24905

An oration delivered at Plymouth,
Dec. 22, 1824. 20442;
20443

An oration, delivered at Plymouth, December 22, 1802.
19

An oration delivered at Portland,
July 5, 1824. 16055

An oration, delivered at Portland,
July 4th, 1825. 21092

An oration, delivered at Potter's

Field. 31735

An oration: delivered at Princeton, New Jersey. 16231

An oration delivered at Providence. 21321

An oration delivered at Quincy.
15023

Oration delivered at Salem, Indiana. 24505

An oration, delivered at Salem,
Washington county, N. Y.
27654

An oration, delivered at Stockbridge. 610

Oration delivered at Swanzey.
37545

An oration delivered at the Baptist church in the City of Savannah. 8010

An oration delivered at the Baptist Church in the city of Troy.
37287

An oration delivered at the celebration of the forty-eighth anniversary of the independence
of the United States. 19120

Oration delivered at the Columbian
College in the District of Columbia, July 5, 1824. 15537

Oration, delivered at the Columbian College, in the District
of Columbia, July 4, 1825.
22392

Oration, delivered at the Columbian College, in the District
of Columbia, July 4, 1823.
13035

Oration, delivered at the court
house in St. Clairsville. 12655;
16266

An oration, delivered at the
court-house, Johnstown. 2636

An oration, delivered at the dedication of Thaxter's Academy.
22444

Oration delivered at the laying of
the foundation stone of a new
Masonic hall in Chambersburg.
12283

Oration delivered at the Methodist Reformed Church in Cincinnati, Ohio. 40546

An oration delivered at the public anniversary celebration of the Independent Order of 'Odd Fellows, ' in Odd Fellows' Hall Boston. 27723

An oration delivered at the request of Missouri Lodge. 24655

An oration, delivered at the request of Phoenix Lodge. 31932

An oration, delivered at the request of the Franklin Dialectic Society of Georgetown. 6870

An oration, delivered at the request of the Republicans of Boston. 8575

An oration delivered at the request of the selectmen of the town of Boston. 2036

An oration, delivered at the request of the town council, before the citizens and military of Columbia, S. C. 32541

An oration delivered at the State-House in Dover. 29269

An oration, delivered at the Union meeting house, in Westerly. 33496

An oration, delivered at Waltham. 6520

An oration delivered at Warren. 8358

An oration delivered at Wiscasset. 12450

Oration delivered before Capt. J. H. Byrd's company of volunteers. 24244

An oration, delivered before Harmony Lodge. 26155

Oration delivered before Missouri Lodge. 7971

Oration, delivered before St. Mark's Lodge. 34734

Oration delivered before the Adelphic Union Society of Williams College. 25479

An oration delivered before the Associated Alumni of Middlebury College. 29203

An oration, delivered before the Central Medical Society of Georgia. 39157

An oration delivered before the citizens of Charlestown. 33101

An oration delivered before the citizens of Hingham. 25113

An oration delivered before the citizens of Nantucket. 39645

An oration delivered before the citizens of Plymouth. 35166

An oration delivered before the Clarisophic Society incorporate. 30121

An oration, delivered before the Franklin Debating Club. 38347

An oration, delivered before the Maine Charitable Mechanic Association. 38417

An oration, delivered before the Mansfield Lodge. 28642

An oration delivered before the Masonic Society at Franklin. 875

An oration delivered before the Pennsylvania Peace Society. 12095

Oration delivered before the Phi Beta Kappa Society, September 10th, 1822. 9875

An oration delivered before the Phi Kappa Society of Franklin College. 32279

An oration delivered before the Phi Sigma Nu Society of the University of Vermont, at their anniversary celebration, August 13, 1823. 12731

Oration delivered before the Phi Sigma Nu Society, of the University of Vermont, Burlington, August 6, 1828. 32765

An oration delivered before the Philadelphia Medical Society [Hodge] 12848

An oration, delivered before the Philadelphia Medical Society [Jackson] 1776

An oration delivered before the Philadelphia Medical Society [La Roche] 29452

An oration delivered before the Philadelphia Medical Society [Meigs] 39548

An oration delivered before the Philadelphia Medical Society

[Mitchell] 21489

An oration delivered before the Philadelphia Medical Society. [Wood] 19318

An oration delivered before the Providence Association of Mechanicks and Manufacturers. 8499

An oration, delivered before the Republicans of Boston. 12944

An oration delivered before the Revolution and Cincinnati Societies of Charleston. 32908

An oration delivered before the Shamrock Friendly Association. 2596

An oration, delivered before the Society of the Alumni of William College. 20524

An oration delivered before the young men of Portland. 28871

Oration delivered before Wayne Lodge. 22475

An oration, delivered by appointment, at the anniversary meeting of the Medical Society of Delaware. 11990

An oration delivered by appointment before the Cincinnati Society of New-Jersey. 16509

An oration: delivered by appointment on the fourth day of July, A.D. 1828. 35370

An oration delivered by Chancellor De Saussure. 24335

Oration, delivered by Col. James Gadsden. 28988

An oration, delivered by Honorable Henry Baldwin. 27934

Oration delivered by Leonard Cassell M'Phail. 33964

Oration, delivered by Thos. Triplett. 7008

An oration delivered 4th July, 1828 [Jenkins] 33710

Oration delivered Friday, July 4, 1828 [Sumner] 35440

An oration delivered in Haverhill, Mass. 29182

An oration, delivered in Hopkinton, (Mass.) 14307

An oration delivered in Independence Square, in the city of Philadelphia. 26050

An oration delivered in Newburyport on the forty-fifth anniversary of American Independence. 5125

An oration, delivered in Newburyport, on the forty-seventh anniversary of American Independence. 14921

An oration delivered in Person Hall, Chapel Hill. 29835

An oration, delivered in Pittsburgh. 24526

An oration, delivered in St. Andrew's Church, on the Fourth of July, 1820. 1903

An oration delivered in St. Andrew's Church on the fourth of July, 1821. 5427

An oration, delivered in St. Michael's Church, Charleston, South-Carolina, on the fifth of July, 1824. 17156

An oration, delivered in St. Michael's Church, Charleston, South-Carolina, on the fourth of July 1822. 9248

An oration, delivered in St. Philip's Church, before the inhabitants of Charleston on the fourth of July, 1809. 38849

An oration, delivered in St. Philip's Church, Charleston, South-Carolina, on the fourth of July, 1821. 5244

An oration delivered in Salem. 24160

An oration delivered in the African Zion Church. 29122

Oration, delivered in the Capitol in the city of Washington. 20313

An oration, delivered in the Catholic Cathedral Church of St. Finbar. 19771

An oration, delivered in the chapel of the South Carolina College. 25779

An oration delivered in the chapel of Transylvania University. 10112

An oration, delivered in the church at Madison. 13471

Oration delivered in the church
of St. Andrew's parish. 17621

An oration, delivered in the College Chapel before the Clariosophic Society. 33406

An oration, delivered in the First Baptist Meeting-house in Providence. 16004

Oration, delivered in the First Presbyterian Church in Elizabeth-town, N. J. 12987

An oration, delivered in the German Reformed Church. 24085

An oration, delivered in the South parish, in Weymouth. 35032

Oration, delivered in the vicinity of Philadelphia. 23854

An oration, delivered in the village of Adams, Jefferson County, N. Y. 29815

An oration, delivered in the village of Fredonia. 15569

An oration, delivered July 5, 1824. 16085; 16086

An oration delivered July 4, 1820. 352

Oration delivered July 4, 1828. 37156

An oration delivered July 4, 1829, before the Anti-Slavery Society of Williams College. 39177

An oration delivered July 4, 1829, before the faculty and students of Williams College. 38027

An oration delivered July 4th, 1827. 27941

An oration, delivered July 4, 1826. 25040

Oration, delivered July 4, 1823. 13085

An oration, delivered on January 1, 1823. 12688

An oration, delivered on Monday, Fourth of July, 1825. 22346; 22347; 26116

An oration, delivered on Monday, the fifth of July, 1824. 15281

An oration delivered on the Anniversary Festival of St. John The Baptist. 607

An oration delivered on the anniversary of American Independence; at Blackstone Village, Mendon, Massachusetts. 11581

An oration delivered on the anniversary of American independence, at Edgefield courthouse, South Carolina. 20538

An oration delivered on the anniversary of Literary Fraternity of Waterville College. 40351

An oration, delivered on the fifth of July, 1824. 16370

Oration delivered on the fiftieth anniversary of American independence. 25675

Oration delivered on the 49th anniversary of American Independence. 19483

An oration delivered on the fourteenth anniversary of the Battle of New-Orleans. 37514

Oration, delivered on the 4th of July, 1830 [i. e. 1820] before the Republicans of Nowich, Franklin & Bozrah [Tracy] 3469

Oration delivered on the Fourth of July, 1820 [Cooper] 867

An oration delivered on the Fourth of July, 1820, before the Cincinnati and Revolution societies. 2920

An oration, delivered on the Fourth of July, 1829, at the celebration of American independence, in the city of Boston. 37518

An oration delivered on the Fourth of July, 1829, in Southbridge, Mass. 39960

An oration delivered on the Fourth of July, 1821, and published at the request of the Philomathean Society. 6915

An oration, delivered on the Fourth of July, 1821, before the Cincinnati and Revolution societies. 5525

An oration delivered on the 4th of July, 1821. Before the Tammany, Hiberian, Stone Cutters. 5771

Oration, delivered on the Fourth of July, 1827, at Newport,

R. I. 30464

An oration, delivered on the 4th of July, 1827, before the Cincinnati & Revolution societies. 28766

An oration delivered on the 4th of July, 1827, in the State house. 31725

An oration delivered on the fourth of July, 1826. 23594

An oration, delivered on the Fourth of July, 1823. 12309; 12310

Oration delivered on the 4th of July, 1822. 9563

An oration delivered on the occasion of the inauguration of Andrew Jackson as President. 39125

An oration; delivered on the 23d, February, 1829. 37877

An oration, delivered on Tuesday, the fourth of July, 1826. 25887

An oration delivered the fourth of July, 1820. 1484

An oration delivered Wednesday, July 4, 1827. 29658

Oration exhibiting the general principles of masonry. 21913

Oration, 5th February [1817] befor the alumni of Yale College. 3294

An oration, in celebration of American independence, pronounced at Natick. 15151

An oration, in commemoration of American independence delivered in the borough of Allegheny, Pa. 40455

An oration in commemoration of the forty-seventh anniversary of the Declaration of American Independence. 12720

An oration in honor of General Lafayette. 20978

An oration in vindication of Free-Masonry. 9165

Oration ... Newark, July 4, 1819. 6664

Oration of Charles Sprague. 22348

An oration on Bunker Hill Battle. 28793

An oration on Freemasonry. 22229

Oration on the absolute necessity of union. 38848

An oration on the aids of genius. 10468

An oration on the anniversary of the Declaration of American independence. 40640

An oration, on the causes of the mortality among strangers. 987

An oration on the death of Commodore Stephen Decatur. 3507

An oration on the evils of lotteries. 32469

An oration on the fiftieth anniversary of American independence. 24140

An oration on the forty-fifth anniversary of American independence. 5240

Oration on the forty-seventh anniversary of American independence. 12184

An oration, on the importance of cultivating the sciences. 33459

Oration on the importance of scientific knowledge. 25071

An oration on the improvement of the people. 25285

An oration on the influence of moral causes on the human character. 2556

An oration on the means of preserving our civil and religious liberties. 6987

Oration, on the occasion of laying the corner stone of the lunatic asylum, at Columbia, S. C. 8459

An oration on the permanency of republican institutions. 9039; 16570

An oration on the practicability and expediency of reducing the whole body of the law. 29091

An oration on the present state of Ireland. 30510; 33363

An oration on the progressive state of the present age. 30115

pendence before the citizens of Dedham. 8700

An oration pronounced in the Congregational meeting-house at Fairhaven. 4632

Oration pronounced in the Lutheran Church in the borough of Easton. 17844

An oration, pronounced July 4, 1821, at the request of the Republicans of the town of Boston. 5287

An oration, pronounced July 4, 1821, in the Baptist Meeting House in Southbridge, Mass. 4717

Oration pronounced on Friday, July 4th, 1823. 12535

An oration, pronounced on the anniversary of the KA Society of Hippocrates, in Lexington, Kentucky. 9488

Oration pronounced on the fifty-first anniversary of American independence, before the young men of the town of Providence. 29067

An oration, pronounced on the Fourth of July, 1821, at the request of the inhabitants of the town of Boston. 5854; 5855

An oration, pronounced on the Fourth of July, 1821, (by request) before the Republican citizens of Milford, Mass. 7653

An oration, pronounced on the Fourth of July, 1822, at the request of the inhabitants of the city of Boston. 8871

An oration pronounced [!] the Handel Society of Dartmouth College. 5350

An oration, recited in Newburyport. 21270

Oration, sermon, &c. delivered at the ceremony of laying the foundation stone of the Masonic Hall, in Hagerstown. 8740; 11432

An oration upon the dignity and utility of the art and science of agriculture. 21579

Orationes quaedam selectae. 750; 751; 24106

Orations by Robert Y. Conrad. 28581

The orations of Aeschines and Demosthenes. 37378

Orations on the death of Thomas Jefferson and John Adams. 23956

The orator's guide. 11391

An oratorio performed by the Handel and Haydn Society, at Boylston Hall. 12763

Oratorio, to be performed at the Rev. Dr. Nichols' Meeting-House. 9791

Oratorio to be performed by the Mozart Musical Society. 21535

Oratorio to be performed by the Psallonian Society. 2909; 6568; 13889

Ordenanzas, reglas, e instrucciones, para el servicio de la marina militar de los Estados Unidos. 11064

Order of arrangements, for the reception of Maj. Gen. Lafayette. 15500

The order of ceremonies and discourse delivered at the constitution of Rising-Star Lodge. 24631

Order of commencement, in Union College. 22542

Order of commencement of the Theological Seminary, Auburn. 32038

Order of consecration of Christ Church at Leicester. 17494

Order of consecration of St. Paul's Church, Boston. 545

Order of declamation, Tuesday evening, September 2, 1823. 11962

Order of exercise at the anniversary of the Theological Seminary, Andover. 27872

Order of exercises at commencement [Amherst College] 19430; 23515

Order of exercises at commencement [Dartmouth College] 12325; 15930; 24296

Order of exercises at commencement [Middlebury College] 25366

Order of exercises at commencement. Transylvania University. 10473

Order of exercises at commencement, Yale College. 4354; 11494; 19342; 37264; 41608

Order of exercises at Faneuil Hall. 23858

Order of exercises at Roxbury, April 10, 1822. 10153

Order of exercises at Seminary Sept. 22, 1824 [Andover Theological] 15107

Order of exercises at the anniversary of the Fatherless and Widows Society. 32434

Order of exercises at the anniversary of the Theological Seminary, Andover. 19436; 23523; 32002; 37470

Order of exercises at the annual exhibition of the Salem Grammar School. 6702; 10176

Order of exercises at the annual public declamation of the Scholars' Club. 32445

Order of exercises at the celebration [Brown University. Philermenian Society] 8201

Order of exercises at the consecration of Concord chapter. 24584

Order of exercises at the dedication of the Congregational Church in Purchase Street. 23893

Order of exercises at the dedication of the Evangelical Congregational Meeting-house at Bolton. 37880

Order of exercises at the dedication of the meeting house in Stow. 30724

Order of exercises at the dedication of the Methodist Chapel, in Salem. 17888

Order of exercises at the dedication of the new meeting-house of the Congregational Society in Salisbury. 30517

Order of exercises at the examination and exhibition of the Salem Grammar School. 22190

Order of exercises at the exhibition of the Alexandrian Society, in Amherst College. 27866

Order of exercises at the exhibition of the Junior Class [Yale] 14994; 31831

Order of exercises at the installation of Rev. Royal Washburn. 23518

Order of exercises at the installation of the Rev. Andrew Bigelow. 13280; 13643

Order of exercises at the installation of the Rev. Mellish Irving Motte. 32441

Order of exercises at the Junior exhibition [Amherst College] 23516; 37464

Order of exercises at the junior exhibition [Yale College] 4356; 19343

Order of exercises, at the ordination of Mr. Benjamin Blydenburg Wisner. 4798

Order of exercises at the ordination of Mr. Caleb Stetson. 29712

Order of exercises at the ordination of Mr. George Ripley. 23894

Order of exercises at the ordination of Mr. John P. B. Storer. 27540

Order of exercises at the ordination of Rev. E. S. Gannett. 15518

Order of exercises, at the Public Latin School. 19823

Order of exercises at the second anniversary of the collegiate institution, Amherst. 11617

Order of exercises, at the second annual examination and exhibition of the Salem English High School. 40347

Order of exercises at the second century lecture. 40349

Order of exercises for commencement [Bowdoin College] 566;

28260

Order of exercises for commencement [Harvard University] 1538; 29164

Order of exercises for exhibition [Bowdoin College] 8158; 8159; 11963

Order of exercises for exhibition at Franklin Academy, Andover. 5360

Order of exercises for exhibition at Phillips Academy, Andover. 2761; 9923

Order of exercises for exhibition at Phillips Exeter Academy. 2763

Order of exercises for the celebration of The Essex Historical Society. 20423

Order of exercises for the celebration of the forty-eighth anniversary of American independence. 17495

The order of exercises in the chapel of Transylvania University. 22501

Order of exercises, July 4, 1825. 21752

Order of exercises, of the exhibition at the College of Charleston. 38111

Order of performance, Anthems, Fast Day, April 4, 1822. 8151

Order of performance at the dedication of the Twelfth Congregational Church in Chamber Street. 15526

Order of performance at the East Meeting House. 6698

Order of performance, for the annual meeting of the Evangelical Missionary Society of Massachusetts. 1135

Order of performance of the New Hampshire Musical Society. 9641

Order of performance of the Pleyel Society, Nantucket. 9955

Order of performances at the Boylston Hall. 1204

Order of performances at the celebration of American independence, July 4, 1828. 34620

Order of performances at the exhibition of the Salem Private Grammar School. 14038

Order of performances for exhibition, April 24, 1821. 5556

Order of procession, at funeral of N. Hazard. 2610

Order of procession, at the dedication of the new Masonic Hall, in the city of Philadelphia. 2611

Order of procession for the funeral of Maj. Gen. Brown. 34621

Order of service, at the dedication of the New Stone Congregational Church in Quincy. 34945

Order of service at the ordination of Mr. Samuel Barrett. 19826; 21753

Order of service at the Young Men's commemoration of the death of Adams and Jefferson. 23872

Order of service in St. Paul's Church. 4799

Order of service on occasion of a sermon, before the Howard Benevolent Society. 12878

Order of service, on Wednesday evening, January 23, 1822. 7855

Order of services at Rev. Mr. Pierpont's Meeting-House. 5984

Order of services at the anniversary of the Howard Benevolent Society. 33596; 39034

Order of services at the dedication of the church at Lechmere Point. 28365

Order of services at the dedication of the Evangelical Congregational meeting-house. 28363

Order of services at the dedication of the new Masonick Hall in the old state-house, Boston. 6350

Order of services at the dedication of the Second Congregational Church in Lynn. 13166

Order of services, at the dedication of the South Congregational Church. 32442

Order of services at the eleventh anniversary of the Boston Asylum for Indigent Boys. 19808

Order of services at the Federal Street Church, Nov. 23, 1826. 24567

Order of services at the installation of a pastor in the Church in Barton Square. 22187

Order of services at the installation of Rev. David Perry. 38033

Order of services at the installation of Rev. Lyman Beecher. 23886

Order of services, at the installation of the Rev. Hosea Ballou. 6677

Order of services at the opening of the New Baptist Meeting House in Roxbury. 3072

Order of services at the ordination of Mr. Alexander Young. 19818

Order of services at the ordination of Mr. Charles C. Sewall. 28658

Order of services at the ordination of Mr. Charles Wentworth Upham. 17887

Order of services at the ordination of Mr. David H. Barlow. 39345

Order of services at the ordination of Mr. James Diman Green. 16955

Order of services at the ordination of Mr. Ralph Waldo Emerson. 37909

Order of services at the ordination of Mr. Warren Burton. 32553

Order of services at the Second Baptist Meeting-House in Boston. 19824

Order of services at the twenty-eighth anniversary of the Boston Female Asylum. 32436

Order of services at the twenty-seventh anniversary of the Boston Female Asylum. 28243

Order of services, Christmas Dec. 25 1824. 17889

Order of services for the dedication of the First Congregational Church. New York. 6270

Order of solemnities at the Old South Church, on Friday, April 26, 1822. 8141

Order of the Board of Health defining the duties of the superintendent. 10171

Order of the ceremony to be observed at the dedication of the Masonic Hall, Broadway. 28947

Order of the ceremony to be observed at the dedication of Union Hall Lodge-Room. 12602

Order of the day, for the First Brigade. 13254

Order of the exercise for an exhibition and examination of the pupils of the New-York Institution for the Instruction of the Deaf and Dumb. 6277

Order of the performance at the ordination of Mr. John Brazer. 3098

Order of the services at the installation of the Rev. Samuel Porter Williams. 6289

Order to parade. 3095

An order to regulate the stands of trucks, carts, sleds and other carriages. 8134

Orders. New England Guards' Armory. 25499

Orders of the day. 27286; 27287 27288; 27289; 27290; 31441; 31442; 31443; 31444

Ordinance. By Major General Andrew Jackson Governor of the provinces of the Floridas. 5340; 5341; 5342; 5343; 5344; 5346; 5347

An ordinance for preventing and extinguishing fires in the city of Savannah. 22202

An ordinance, for raising supplies

The origin of the harp. 690

Origin of the terms high and low Churchman. 30128

Origin of the theological school of Yale College. 8725

Original and miscellaneous essays. 38224

Original and select Hymns. 2802

Original and select poems. 30721

Original & selected beauties for the flute. 13644

Original and selected reformation hymns and spiritual songs. 39933

Original communications made to the Agricultural Society of South-Carolina. 18058

An original essay on the immateriality and immortality of the human soul. 38419

Original Hymns for Sabbath Schools. 3400; 3401

Original hymns for Sunday schools. 1381; 30763

Original hymns for the use of children. 1382

An original memoir, on the Floridas. 6351

Original moral tales intended for children and young persons. 30129

Original poems. 6342; 13630

Original poems, for infant minds. 5455; 10416; 10417; 30764

Original poems on different subjects. 5731

Original poems, on various subjects [M'Kissen] 39370

Original poems, on various subjects [Williams] 37189

Original poems, with imitations of Horace. 2612

Original poetic effusions. 8893

Origination, constitution and by laws of St. James' First African Protestant Episcopal Church. 37577

Orlando's farewell. 6812; 14147

Orlando's wedding. 6813; 18018

Orleans Navigation Company. 31445; 36692; 41272

The ornament of the American fireside. 37468

Orondalie: a tale of the crusades. 22399

The orphan boy. 10266; 10267

The orphan girl. 9792

The Orphan of the castle. 13646

The orphan sisters. 2630

The orphans; an American tale. 21757

The orphans of Normandy. 30603; 35186

Orsamus Holms. 27291

Orson Sparks and John Watson. 31446; 36693; 41273

Orthodoxy unmasked. A sermon, delivered in the Second Universalist Meeting in Boston. 27943

Orthodoxy unmasked; or, All is not gold that glitters. 37589

Orthographer and orthoepist. 39648

Orwigsburg almanac. 39939

Osagiitinin au Jesus, gibinibotanat inim mejüzhiuebizinijin. 2614

Osric and Lencastro. 25640

Othello. 10240; 14094; 25968

Otis' letters in defence of the Hartford convention. 17498

Ou peut on etre meiux qu'au sein de sa famille. 20673

Our chronicle of '26. 29720

Our country, and its laws. 34630

Our duty to our colured population. 24817

Our Saviour. A poem. 17499

Our village. 34174

Our way across the sea. 21758

Ourika; a tale, from the French. 38430

Outline of Bible history. 20717; 20718; 20719

Outline of eight lectures on astronomy. 12701; 16318; 20706; 20707

An outline of political economy. 33714

Outline of the course of geological lectures given in Yale College. 40424

An outline of the course of study

in the department of Christian theology. 7817

Outline of the course of study pursued by the students of the Theological Seminary, Andover. 19437

Outline of the history of England. 33389

An outline of the history of the church in the state of Kentucky. 15453

Outline of the lectures and demonstrations of William James Macneven. 2067

Outline of the plan of a bank. 590

Outline of the plan of education pursued at the Greenfield High School for Young Ladies. 38829

An outline of the system of education at New Lanark. 21765

Outline of the system of instruction recently adopted in the college at Amherst. 27863

Outlines of a course of lectures, on select subjects of natural philosophy. 39919

Outlines of a course of lectures on the institutes of medicine. 12045

Outlines of American political economy. 29505

Outlines of an arrangement of medical nosology. 12637

Outlines of ancient history and chronology. 13660

Outlines of chronology, ancient and modern. 33386

Outlines of ecclesiastical history. 38781

Outlines of lectures on materia medica and botany. 28071; 32228

Outlines of modern geography. 24724; 24725; 24726; 29046; 29047; 29048; 33382; 33383

Outlines of natural philosophy. 10088; 13924; 25923

Outlines of phrenology. 16246

Outlines of political economy. 21273; 21293; 33387

Outlines of scripture geography. 37241

Outlines of the experimental lectures in natural philosophy. 34607

Outlines of the history of ancient Rome. 33388

Outlines of the lectures on chemistry, delivered in the College of Physicans and Surgeons. 34533; 39944

Outlines of the life of Theodore Newell. 17427

Outlines of the principal events in the life of General Lafayette. 22470; 22471

Outlines of the science of life. 39852

O'er dales and mountains stray. 1834

The Overseers of the Poor of the city of Boston, to their constituents. 11925

Overture de Blaise et Babet. 1012

Overture de l'opera Jean de Paris. 4756; 4757

Overture for the pianoforte. 1908; 5706; 9223

Overture to Calife de Bagdad. 4755

Overture to Guy Mannering. 4731; 11886

Overture to Il barbieri di Seviglia. 22134

Overture to L'Italiana in Algieri. 13997; 13998

Overtrue to La donna del lago. 17859

Overture to Lodoiska. 1890

Overture to The Caliph of Bagdad. 11913

Overture to, The celebrated opera of Le Dieu et La Bayadere. 167

Overture to, The celebrated opera of Romeo and Juliet. 382

Overture to The deserter. 9524

Overture to the favorite opera of Semiramide. 3065

An overture to the General assembly of the Presbyterian Church. 34631

Overture to The impresario.
20079

Overtrue to the opera of Colu-
mela.   15641

The overture to the opera of
Otello.   13999

Overture to the opera of The two
blind men of Toledo.   13289

Ovid's art of love.   30134

Oxberry edition of the new English Drama.   4240

P

P. Canfield respectfully informs
his friends and the public that
he has contracted with the visitors and governors of Johns'
and Washington Colleges.
15637

P. Virgilii Maronis opera. 7505;
11307; 19128; 27500; 31594;
37002

Ps and Qs.   34938

Pacific overtures for Christian
Harmony. 37244

Paddy Carey.   2632; 6361; 17505;
21768; 25644

Paddy O'Carrol.   5083

Paddy O'Rafferty.   2633; 2634

Paddy's trip to America. 10403;
10404

The padlock.   19726; 23822

Paesiello's favorite air "Hope
told a flattering tale." 13652

The Pains of memory. 2245

Pains of the imagination. 15691;
15692

La paisana virtuosa.   20017

Paisiello's beautiful arietta
Quant'e piu bella. 17511

Palestine, and other poems.
33515

Paley's Moral philosophy. 25653;
34633

Palmer's manual.   13654

The pamphlet.   21773

Pamphlets and papers. 24013

Panama mission. Speech of Mr.
J.S. Johnston. 24997

Panama mission. Substance of
the remarks made by M.

Robbins.   25949

Panel of jurors.   25659

Panharmonicon march. 2638

Panorama, North 11th, near
Market St. 6371

Papers on agricultural subjects.
21702; 39861

Papers on various subjects connected with the survey of the
coast of the United States.
16480

Papers read before the general
assembly of the Presbyterian
church. 39126

Papers referred to in the annual
report of the Superintendent
of common schools. 17384

Papers relating to the state
agent, of the western shore.
13234

A papist misrepresented and rep-
resented. 33396

Par of weights.   37707

Parables and paroblic stories.
39957

Paradise lost.   2275; 21464;
25383; 25384; 34146

The Paradox solved. 2644

Parallel between intemperance
and the slave trade. 33616

Paraphrase on Genesis xlix. 10.
1042

The parent's assistant.   1077

The parent's assistant, and Sunday school book. 9808

Parent's assistant; or, Stories
for children. 28764

The parent's counsellor. 21774

The parent's monitor and
teacher's assistant. 37983

The parent's monitor; or Narratives, anecdotes, and observations on religious education.
37698

The parental character of God.
37944

Parental duties enjoined. 32229

Parental faithfulness. 25660

Parental fidelity. 37741

The parents' assistant; or,
young child's catechism.
9809

Paris & London. 34177

Parisian rondo. 7523

Parker's miniature almanack. 39965

A parlour-window book for dull times. 3265

The parole and documentary evidence, delivered before a committee of the House of Representatives. 2690

Part of a speech, delivered at Suffield, Con. 25085

Part III of the Missionary arithmetic. 11384

Partant pour la Syrie. 1676

A particular account of the battle of Bunker, or Breed's Hill. 19846-19848

A particular relation of the American Baptist mission to the Burman empire. 12973

Particulars of the piracies; committed by the commanders and crews of the Buenos Ayrean ship Louise. 2660

A parting address to a Sabbath-School child. 6390

Parting advice to a youth on leaving his Sunday school. 39970

The parting kiss. 6808; 14141

Pascagoula River. 36694

The passage of the sea. 24478

Passages cited from the Old Testament by the writers of the New Testament. 30153

Passenger ships and vessels. 41274

Passengers arriving in the United States. 27292; 31447

Passengers in 1827. 36695

Passions-Betrachtung. 16429

The pastor; a poem. 6393

A pastor's address on the season of Lent. 38449

The pastor's duty. 10009

The pastor's sketch book. 30407; 40222

A pastoral address to the members of St. Paul's Church. 17533

Pastoral address transmitted as testimonial of affection to his congregation. 29436

The pastoral care. 30791

A pastoral charge, and a specimen of classical latinity. 9028

A pastoral charge, delivered by the Right Rev'd. Henry. 6394

Pastoral charges delivered by the Right Rev. Bishop Henry. 6395

Pastoral letter addressed particularly to the churches, both settled & vacant, under the care of the Second Presbytery of the Carolinas & Georgia. 10007

A pastoral letter, addressed to the clergy and laity of the Protestant Episcopal Church. 39002

Pastoral letter addressed to the members of the Protestant Episcopal Church in the Diocese of Maryland. 9190; 16774

A pastoral letter, addressed to the members of the Protestant Episcopal Church in the eastern diocese. 5509

A pastoral letter, by the Associate Presbytery of the Carolinas. 23550

A pastoral letter, from the Presbytery of Chillicothe. 34870

A pastoral letter from the rector of Trinity Church, New Haven. 8473

Pastoral letter, Nov. 1, 1822. 10006

Pastoral letter of the Archbishop of Baltimore. 5934

Pastoral letter of the ministers of the Oneida Association. 28015; 28572

Pastoral letter of the Most Reverend the Archbishop of Baltimore. 38090-38092

Pastoral letter of the Piscataqua Association. 32801; 34810

A pastoral letter, of the Presbytery of Lexington. 30329

Pastoral letter of the Right Reverend Dr. England. 5258

Pastoral letter on the observance of Lent. 5257

A pastoral letter, relative to measures for the theological education of candidates for orders. 1630

A pastoral letter to the clergy and the laity of the Protestant Episcopal Church. 2882; 13869; 25851

A pastoral letter to the members of the Protestant Episcopal Church in South Carolina. 19840

A pastoral letter to the members of the Protestant Episcopal Church in the United States of America. 40170

Pastoral letters of Archbishop Carroll. 700

The pastoral office. 21540

Pastoral responsibility. 32375

Patent divitial invention. 25893

Patent lamp tea-kettle, boiler. 38566

Patent office. 31448

Patent Phenix Mill canvass. 27751

Patent sponge boots, for horses feet. 19842

Patents - 1827. 36696

Patents--1828. 41275

Patents for useful inventions in 1826. 31449

The path of the just as the shining light. 20306

Pathological anatomy. 28181

Pathological and surgical observations on diseases of the joints. 4839

Pathological reflections on the supertonic state of disease. 8797

The paths of learning strewed with flowers. 27650

Patience, a tale. 20924

Patriarchal times. 9776

Patrick O'Dermott the pride of Kildare. 6374; 13661

Patrick O'Neal. 4384

The patriot. 34653

The patriot's manual. 33587

The patriotic sailor. 39974

Patrol regulations for the county of Rowan. 22147

Patterson's magazine almanac. 2664

Patterson's Pittsburgh, Town & Country almanac. 2665

Paul, an example and proof of the peculiar excellence and usefulness of the missionary character. 15136

Paul and Virginia [Saint-Pierre] 3088; 10168; 14032; 22178; 30512; 30513

Paul and Virginia; a musical entertainment. 800

Paul Jones; a romance. 28639

Paul Jones; or The pilot of the German ocean. 37072

Paul Pry; a comedy. 25802; 30291

Paul Pry's almanac. 39976; 39977

Paulina. Swiss air. 12168

Pauperism. 28401a

Pause and think. Am I a Christian? 76; 77

The Pawtucket Collection of Conference Hymns. 386; 7998

Paymasters, &c. - marine corps. 27293

Payment on lands forfeited to the U. S. 27294

Payments to citizens of Georgia. 36697

Payments to jurors United States' Courts. 36698

Payments to Major General Brown. 36699

Peace and holy love. 8176

Peace be around thee. 15442

Peace campaigns of a cornet. 37731

The peace catechism. 31811

Peace Society of Windham County. 30159

The peaceful valley. 30160

A peacemaker. 12440

Peach trees for sale. 38291

The peacock "At Home." 20333

The pearl; or, Affection's gift. 39982

The peasant boy. 6378; 13668

The peasant girl. 13669; 17526

The peasant's joy. 8094

The Peasants waltz. 4214;

19221

The peculiar features of Christianity. 29077

A pedestrian tour of two thousand three hundred miles, in North America. 10333

The pedlar; a farce in three acts. 7640

Pedro Miranda. 27295

A peep at the Pilgrims. 15732; 24076

A peep at the various nations of the world. 2675

A peep into the banks. 34667

Pelham; or, The adventures of a gentleman. 33935; 39349

The Pelican Island. 29787

Pen Owen. 9053

Penelope Denny. 23012

Penmanship; or, The beauties of writing. 8866

Penmanship reduced to the simplest principles. 1080

The Pennsylvania agricultural almanac. 9864; 13717

The Pennsylvania almanac. 2705; 6429; 9866-9868; 13721; 13722; 17574; 17575; 21838-21840; 25704; 25705; 30186; 30187; 34698-34700; 40009

The Pennsylvania almanac and economist's assistant. 17573

The Pennsylvania almanac, and rural economist's assistant. 9865; 13720

The Pennsylvania & New-Jersey almanac. 2706; 9869; 17576; 21841; 30188; 30189

Pennsylvania and Ohio canal law. 30108

The Pennsylvania anti-masonic almanac. 40010; 40011

Pennsylvania canals. 32587

Pennsylvania--Chamber of Commerce. 36700

The Pennsylvania Farmer's almanac. 2706a; 6430

The Pennsylvania harmonist. 29292

The Pennsylvania Infirmary for Diseases of the Eye and Ear. 9870

Pennsylvania LaFayette march. 18150; 18151

Pennsylvania. Map. 38574

The Pennsylvania medical almanac and repository of useful science. 25710

Pennsylvania. Memorial and resolutions of citizens of Philadelphia. 36701

Pennsylvania. Memorial from citizens of Adams County. 36702

Pennsylvania. Memorial of citizens of Alleghany County. 36703

Pennsylvania. Memorial of citizens of the city and county of Philadelphia. 36704

Pennsylvania. Memorial of citizens of the state. 36705

Pennsylvania. Memorial of inhabitants of Blairsville. 36706

Pennsylvania. Memorial of inhabitants of Pennsylvania. 36707

Pennsylvania. Memorial of inhabitants of Philadelphia. 36708

Pennsylvania. Memorial of manufacturers of hardware. 36709

Pennsylvania, New Jersey, Delaware, Maryland, & Virginia almanac. 2709

Pennsylvania. Petition from inhabitants of Beaver County, Pa. 36710

Pennsylvania. Petition of inhabitants of Northampton County. 36711

The Pennsylvania primer. 17577; 39437

Pennsylvania. Resolutions and memorial, of inhabitants of the county of Washington. 36712

Pennsylvania. Resolutions of the Legislature. 36713

The Pennsylvania spelling book. 17584

Der Pennsylvanische Anti-Freimaurer Calender. 40019; 40020

Das Pennsylvanische Deutsche
Buchstabir und Lesebuch.
17031

The pensioner and his daughter
Jane. 13724; 17588

Pensions to widows, of deceased
seamen. 36714

People and customs of various
nations. 17589

The people's doctors. 38418

The people's rights reclaimed.
24837

The people's ticket. For Governor, De Witt Clinton. 1004;
17590

People's ticket. For President,
John Quincy Adams. 34403

The people's ticket. For presi-
dent-Wm. H. Crawford. 17591

Perche se mia tu sei? 20674

The Percy anecdotes. 6654;
10119; 10120; 13966; 13967

Percy Mallory. 16575

Percy's Masque. 1587

Peremtory [sic] sale at auction,
this day at 12 o'clock. 21691

The perfection of God, the foun-
tain of good. 2555

The Peri's song from Lalla
Rookh. 7627

Perils and safeguards of American liberty. 33798

Perils of the ocean, or, Dis-
asters of the seas. 2718

Periodical catalogue of fruit &
ornamental trees & shrubs.
32608

Periodical sketches, by an American patriot. 1019; 2719

Permanent lodge calendar. 25725

Perpetual almanack. 17593

Perry-patetic songs and other
jollification ditties. 15928

Perry's new pronouncing spelling-
book. 17596

Perry's revised and improved
pronouncing spelling book.
2729

The persecuted family. 40105-
40108

The persecution, which Daniel
Brocklebank suffered. 23927

Persia. 35196

Personal narrative of a journey
from India to England. 27800

Personal narrative of the first
voyage of Columbus to America. 28551

The personal narrative of the
sufferings of J. Stephanini.
40535

Personal sketches of his own
time. 28063; 32223

Personal sobriety, righteousness
to man, and piety to God.
2905

Persuasive to public Worship.
2731

Persuasives to early piety.
34806

The Pestallozzian primer.
29396

The Pestalozzian system of
arithmetic. 40338

The pestilence, a punishment for
public sins. 10365; 14232

Peter Ford. 36715; 41276

Peter Lohra vs. A. Morhouse.
29522

Peter P. M'Cormack. 36716

Peter Parley's method of telling
about geography to children.
38787-38789

Peter Parley's story of the
bird's nest. 38790

Peter Parley's story of the little
soldiers. 38791

Peter Parley's story of the
mocking bird. 38792

Peter Parley's winter evening
tales. 38793

Peter Prim's profitable present
to the little Misses and Masters of the United States.
6441

Peter Pry's puppet show. 6442

Peter Schlemiehl. 15711

Peter's letters to his kinsfolk.
1991-1993

Peters and Pond. 36717

Petit pot pourri. 6035

Le petit rien. 904

La petite sonate pour le piano
forte. 9036

La petite surprise! 4395; 4396

Petition and appeal of the Six

nations. 40033

A petition and memorial, addressed to the honourable legislature of the state of New York. 35029

Petition of a convention of the friends of national industry in New Jersey. 3930

Petition of Charles Dehault Delassus. 27296

The petition of Daniel Bussard. 29647

Petition of David Hale and Samuel Hale. 27297

Petition of George M'Dougall. 16965

Petition of James D. Cobb. 23013

Petition of James Le Ray de Chaumont. 11065

Petition of John Adlum. 36718

Petition of John Smith T. and Wilson P. Hunt. 27298

Petition of Joseph Forrest. 14667

Petition of Lewis A. Tarascon. 18939

Petition of Mary James. 27299

Petition of Moses Smith. 27300

Petition of Philander Chase. 36719

Petition of Reuben Shapley. 23014

Petition of Revolutionary officers. 23015

Petition of Samuel A. Lawrence and others. 16870

Petition of Sarah Chitwood. 27301

Petition of sundry inhabitants of the state of Missouri. 23016

Petition of sundry residents of Hertford, N. Carolina. 36720

Petition of the citizens of the counties of Lawrence and Franklin, in the state of Alabama. 7395

Petition of the president and directors of the Mohawk and Hudson Rail Road Company. 27798

Petition of the Sisters of the Visitation of Georgetown, D. C. 36721

Petition of Thomas Cooper. 23017

Petition of visitors and professors of William and Mary College. 19285a

Petition of William Dixon and James Dickson to Congress. 20316

Petition of William Hollinger. 27302

The petition of Wm. King. 18940

A petition, to the Congress of the United States, from the towns of Smithfield and Fenner. 40468

Petition to the General Assembly of Connecticut. 32814

A petition to the Senate and House of Representatives of Massachusetts. 37420

The petitions of Rufus Davenport. 38339

Peveril of the peak. 14066-14069

Phaedri Augusti Liberti Fabularum Aesopiarum libri quinque. 30208

Phaedri Fabulae expurgatae accedunt tractatus de versu Iambico. 30209

The phantom barge, and other poems. 10444

The phantom ship, from legendary ballads. 485

Pharmacologia. 9810; 13658; 17516; 21776; 21777; 34638

The Pharmacopoeia of the United States of America. 2733; 34737

Phelles, king of Tyre. 21954

Philadelphia almanack. 34748; 34749; 40042

Philadelphia. Arch Street Theater. [Playbills] 34750

The Philadelphia Cabinet and Chair Makers' Union Book of prices. 34751

Philadelphia chamber of commerce. 27303

The Philadelphia directory. 2742; 15967

The Philadelphia directory and register. 6451; 9891

The Philadelphia directory and

stranger's guide. 23350

Philadelphia, Dover and Norfolk Steam-Boat and Transportation Company. 34757

The Philadelphia grand waltz. 9895

The Philadelphia hop waltz. 1559

Philadelphia in 1824. 17612

The Philadelphia index. 13749

Philadelphia. Map. 38575

Philadelphia; or, Glances at lawyers. 25747

The Philadelphia practice of midwifery. 34102

The Philadelphia souvenir. 24781; 25752

The Philadelphia spelling book. 4612; 4613

Philadelphia Theatre. [Playbills] 6464; 9905; 13756; 17618; 25753; 30243; 34772

Philip Colville, or, A covenanter's story. 39182

Philip, or The aborigines, a drama. 9909

Philip Slaughter. 36722

The Phillipina waltz and gallopade. 1163

Philosophic grammar of the English language. 28382

Philosophical & practical grammar. 11377

Philosophical beauties. 33891; 33892; 39311

A philosophical enquiry into the origin of our ideas of the sublime and beautiful. 38003

Philosophical essays. 14125

Philosophical instructor. 16035

A philosophical treatise on the passions. 5016; 5017

Philosophy in sport. 34639

The philosophy of a future state. 38386; 38387

The philosophy of human knowledge. 33719

The philosophy of language illustrated. 26070

The philosophy of mind. 23947

The philosophy of natural history. 3239; 17997; 30626; 40445

The philosophy of religion. 38388

The philosophy of rhetoric. 12049

The philosophy of the active and moral powers of man. 35410

Philosophy of the human voice. 30495

Phinehas Underwood. 27304

Phinneys' calendar, or Western almanac. 2765; 6476; 9924; 9925; 13771; 17630; 21889; 25767-25769; 30255; 30256; 34785-34788; 40069; 40070

The phoenix chronicle. 22263

Physical sketches, or Outlines of correctives. 12329

A physician at hand. 40465

Physician's pocket synopsis. 7965

The physiognomist. 2767

Physiological and chemical researches on the use of prussic or hydro-cyanic acid. 2071

A physiological essay on digestion. 22302

A physiological inquiry into the structure, organization, and nourishment of the human teeth. 35557

A physiological memoir upon the brain. 33973

Physiological researches on life and death. 28182

A physiological system of nosology. 12699

The pianoforte primer. 631; 38009

The piano forte waltz. 15685

Picket's juvenile spelling book. 17638; 17639; 21898; 30262

Picknickery. 2777

Picolilly, or The critical chronicle of Ichabod Oculus. 12724

A picture of Greece in 1825. 25773

The picture of New York. 21899; 34796

Picture of Philadelphia, for 1824. 14950

A picture of war. 13139

The pictured alphabet. 17640; 21900; 25774

Pictures of Bible history. 2778; 34797

The pictures of events, foretold

in ancient prophecies. 12093

Picturesque piety; or Scripture truths illustrated. 6940

Picturesque views of American scenery. 3189

Pierpont's introduction to the national reader. 34801; 40084

Pierre and his family. 20760; 29085; 29086

Piety promoted in brief biographical memorials of some of the Religious Society of Friends. 1266; 38609

Piety promoted, in brief memorials and dying expressions of some of the people called Quakers. 14803

Pike's system of arithmetick abridged. 25776; 30269

The pilgrim fathers. 19871

The Pilgrim. Louse and flea. 2782

The pilgrim of India on his journey to Mount Zion. 35187

The pilgrim of love. 486; 8079; 11887-11890; 15443

Pilgrim sermon at Bridgewater, Mass. 1710

The pilgrim's companion. 29530

The Pilgrim's family's progress, from this world, to that which is to come. 2783; 2784

The Pilgrim's progress from this world to that which is to come. 4869; 8213; 15590-15594; 19896; 23966; 28320-28322; 32518-32520; 37987-37991

The pilgrim's progress in the nineteenth century. 27594

The pilgrim's songster. 33550

The Pilgrims. A sermon, preached in Wendell. 7663

The pilgrims, and Parley the porter. 2335; 2336

The Pilgrims of Hope. 2785

The pilgrims; or, First settlers of New England. 21906; 21907

The pilot; a tale of the sea. 12253; 15858; 28597; 38274

Pilots on the Ohio and Mississippi. 27305

Pinkey House. 13782

The pioneers. 12254; 12255; 20191; 28598; 32828; 38275

The pious and industrious sailor boy. 2788

Pious biography for young men. 32609

The pious dead blessed. 14800

Pious Edward. 40088

The pious gift. 30273

The pious guide to prayer and devotion. 21912; 30274

Pious Harriet. 13217

The pious Indian. 554-556

A pious inquirer with respect to the Lord's supper. 30275

A pious mother's love, illustrated. 38838

The pious parent's gift. 2140; 2141

Pious reflections for every day of the month. 1221; 12536

Pious resolutions. 2789

The pious shepherd. 33956

The pious stranger. 9944

The pious thresher. 13784

La pipe de tabac. 20635

La pipe tobac. 5424

The Pirate [Dibdin] 8544

The pirate [Scott] 10204-10210

The pirate lover. 15142; 15143

Piratical barbarity. 21779-21781; 25664

Pittsburgh almanac. 6485; 9945; 13785

Pittsburgh in the year eighteen hundred and twenty-six. 25002

Pittsburgh Magazine Almanac. 2790; 6486; 9946; 9947; 13786

Più dolci e placide. 6670; 14000

Pizarro; a tragedy. 29434; 29435

Pizarro, ó los Peruanos. 17113

Los placeres del tocador, publicados en Castellano. 39261

A plain account of Christian perfection. 7631; 27602; 37137; 41473

A plain account of the Lord's supper. 1623

A plain and easy catechism, suitable for children of a tender age. 34816

Plain and easy catechisms for
children [Watts] 4202; 4203;
11364; 14852; 19211

Plain and easy directions for
forming Sunday Schools.
25582; 34817

A plain and positive refutation of
the Rev. Samuel Pelton's unjust and unfounded charges.
12985

Plain and scriptural reasons why
I am a Chruchman. 1477

A plain and serious address to
the master of a family.
15992

Plain arguments by way of question and answer, from the
Gospel history. 10243

Plain catechetical instructions for
young communicants. 15274

A plain, comprehensive, practical English grammar. 31673

Plain directions on domestic
economy. 6820

The plain gold ring. 4215;
19222; 19223; 23256-23258

Plain hymns for Sunday schools.
34818

Plain matters of fact, undenied
and undeniable. 33355

The plain physician, giving directions for the preservation of
health. 30565

Plain questions, respecting attendance on public worship.
13789

Plain reasons of a plain man,
for preferring Gen. Jackson
to Mr. Adams, as president
of the U.S. 20818

Plain reasons why neither Dr.
Watts' Imitations of the
Psalms, nor any other human
composition ought to be used
in the praises of the great
God our saviour. 32721

Plain sense, on national industry. 2792

A plain statement. 18245

Plain statement of facts, submitted to the consideration of the
members of the Methodist connexion. 5327

Plain truth: containing remarks
on various subjects. 35394

Plain truth in a series of numbers. 6488; 6489

Plain truth on Christian baptism,
and communion. 3487

Plain truth. The following documents are submitted to the
consideration of a candid public. 34404; 34405

Plan, adopted by the Kentucky
annual conference, for raising
supplies. 25324

Plan and by-laws of the Institution for Savings in Haverhill.
38936

Plan and revised constitution of
the school [Monitorial School.
Boson] 15521

Plan del Peru, defectos del gobierno español antiguo, neces-
sarias reformas. 14780

Plan for promoting common
school education in Greece.
39824

Plan for raising by subscription
the sum of fifty thousand dollars. 16213

A plan for the gradual abolition
of slavery in the United
States. 21915

Plan for the melioration and
civilization of the British
North American Indians.
15585

Plan for the Theological seminary of the Synod of Kentucky.
40144

Plan in form of a bill submitted
by A. Blanding. 30665

Plan of a seminary for the education of instruction of youth.
20624

Plan of arrangements at the funeral of Dr. Bentley. 2793

Plan of proceeding in the formation of Sunday School Unions.
19419

A plan of public schools. 39862

The plan of reform in Transylvania University. 17491

Plan of Sunday schools for the
state of New Hampshire.

21629
Plan of the Boston Fuel Savings Institution. 4793; 4794
Plan of the city government [Providence] 34926
Plan of the City of Baltimore. 9304; 13235
Plan of the city of Philadelphia. 805
Plan of the city of Savannah. 2062
Plan of the City of Washington. 9949
Plan of the Fuel Savings Society of the City and Liberties of Philadelphia. 5415
Plan of the Methodist Episcopal Church in North Bennett Street, Boston. 32440
Plan of the Mississippi Baptist Education Society. 258
Plan of the New York City Mission. 21681
Plan of the theological seminary of the Protestant Episcopal Church. 2883; 2884
Plan of the town of Salem. 3112
Plan of York Town in Virginia. 2986
Plan showing the proposed route for opening Brown Street. 2794
Plane sliding sector, or Trigonometrical scale. 10437
The plans and by-laws of the Warren Institution for Savings. 41433
Plans and motives for the extension of Sabbath Schools. 39949
Plans and progress of internal improvement in South Carolina. 3277
Plans for improving the navigation of Hudson's River. 2500
The planter's almanack. 17648
The planters' & merchants' almanac. 6490
The platform of ecclesiastical government established by the Lord Jesus Christ. 24423
Platicas, ó Instrucciones familiares sobre las oraciones y

ceremonias del santo sacrificio de la misa. 31853
Playbill. Benefit of Mr. Holland. 32447
Playbills [Philadelphia. New Theatre.] 9898
Playbills [Walnut Street Theatre] 6465; 9906
Plays accurately printed from the text of the corrected copy left by George Steevens. 14095
A plea against religious controversy. 38710
A plea for a miserable world. 112
A plea for Africa. 19487
A plea for early piety. 5492
A plea for ministerial liberty. 16012
The plea for mercy of William Williams. 2798
A plea for religion and the sacred writings. 17987; 22283
A plea for religious charity schools. 21749
Plea for the American Colonization Society. 25380
A plea for the church in Georgia. 40450
A plea for the liturgy as it is. 40094
Plea for the orphan. 11436
A plea for the theological seminary at Princeton. 5829; 5830
A plea for the West [Chase] 24075; 28445
A plea for the West [Henry] 16511
Plea for union in erecting a house of God. 37263
The plea of the midsummer fairies. 29251
Pleasant stories. 18128
The pleasant walk in spring. 31659
A pleasing account of George Crosby. 2799
A pleasing companion for little boys and girls. 22487
A pleasing companion for little girls and boys. 26225

The pleasing instructer[!] 31979
The pleasing toy. 21916
Pleasing toy for children. 40095
A pleasing toy, for girl or boy.
  25790; 34822
The pleasure of your company is
  requested at the ball, at the
  Eagle Hotel. 16028
The pleasures of friendship.
  9316d; 9316e; 21280; 33948
The pleasures of hope. 660;
  8246; 32564
The pleasures of memory. 3046;
  17846
The pleasures of poverty. 14176
The pleasures of religion. 1020
The pleasures of sin. 33186
The pleasures of the imagination.
  4426; 4427; 7760; 7761
Pledge of the U. States to the
  governments of Mexico and
  S. America. 27306
The plenary inspiration of the
  Scriptures asserted. 34561
The plough boy. 1060
Plutarch's Lives. 9956-9958;
  21920; 25792; 34824
Pneumatologia. 30138
Pocahontas. 1590
A pocket almanac. 2803
The pocket companion. 2804;
  6493; 9959; 25986
A pocket dictionary of the Holy
  Bible. 37412
Pocket dictionary of the Spanish
  and English languages. 25489;
  39715
A pocket expositor. 34825
The pocket farrier. 37083
A pocket geographical and statis-
  tical gazetteer, of the state
  of Vermont. 12662
A pocket guide for the tourist
  and traveller, along the line
  of the canals. 18064
The pocket Lavater. 39248
The pocket lawyer. 34826
The pocket manuel of spiritual
  exercises. 28425
A pocket manual of the Lancas-
  terian system of education.
  30439
Pocket map of Maine. 20520

Pocket register for the city of
  Hartford. 21919
The pocket selection of hymns.
  9960
A poem...at the fifth anniversary
  of the Franklin Debating So-
  ciety. 29656
Poem delivered before the Con-
  necticut Alpha of the Phi Beta
  Kappa Society. 25720
A poem delivered before the
  Porter Rhetorical Society.
  38327
A poem, delivered in Bowdoinham
  (Maine). 25181
A poem, delivered on the cele-
  bration of Independence, in
  the free Meeting-House at
  Wilton. 34722
Poem in Latin and English.
  5502a
Poem on the last day. 7724
A poem on the restoration of
  learning in the East. 16297
A poem, spoken July 4, 1828.
  34635
A poem spoken on the summit of
  Wamaug mountain. 2995
Poema in comitiis collegii Co-
  lumbiani. 12725
Poems [Bancroft] 11674
Poems [Barbauld] 316
Poems [Bryant] 4861
Poems [Dana] 28656
Poems [Fairfield] 12492
Poems [Fisher] 1234
Poems [Goldsmith] 1402; 5466;
  16313
Poems [Knight] 5778
Poems [Lewis] 13101
Poems [Pinkney] 21911
Poems [Sigourney] 30612
Poems [Ward] 27547
Poems [Walter] 7562
Poems and essays. 28258
Poems and songs. 3383; 6932
Poems, by Bernard Barton.
  4618; 11756; 19620; 23713
Poems by Elizabeth Denning.
  5174
Poems by James G. Percival.
  6434; 13726; 40023
Poems by John Turvill Adams.

19369

Poems by Mrs. Felicia Hemans. 24830; 29193; 29194; 33520

Poems by S. Louisa P. Smith. 40462

Poems, by Selleck Osborn. 13647

Poems, by the Boston bard. 12196

Poems by Thomas Odiorne. 6327; 6328

Poems, by William B. Tappan. 10409

Poems by William Cowper. 5096- 5098; 12279; 15883; 24233

Poems by William Leggett. 9249

Poems for children. 3402; 13797

Poems: moral and religious for children & youth. 6495

Poems, moral and sentimental. 6172

The poems, odes, songs, and other metrical effusions. 7706

The poems of Ossiam. 29584

The poems of Robert Bloomfield. 4747

Poems on miscellaneous subjects. 23923

Poems, on religious and histori- cal subjects. 4230; 14861

Poems on religious subjects. 6775

Poems on several occasions [Brashears] 8175

Poems on several occasions [Guest] 12736; 16357

Poems, on various subjects [M'Kissen] 2063

Poems, on various subjects [Parsons] 25671

Poems, on various subjects [Ray] 6592; 25904

Poems, religious, moral and sa- tirical. 40637

Poems, selected from the works of Peter Pindar. 4314

Poems written on various sub- jects. 28304

Poesias. 20865

Poesias de un Mexicano. 34827

Poesias del Coronel Don Manuel de Zequeira y Arango, natur- al de la Habana. 41631

Poetic essays to aid the devo- tion of pious people. 8063

Poetic gift. 1091

Poetic tales for children. 2805

The poetical album. 37099

Poetical illustrations of the Athenaeum Gallery of paint- ings. 28623

Poetical lessons for children. 28714

Poetical miscellany, 17654

Poetical quotations. 37367

Poetical remains of the late Jane Taylor. 35470; 40616

Poetical sketches. 39938

The poetical works of Alexander Pope. 34842; 34843

The poetical works of James Hogg. 20925

The poetical works of James Montgomery. 6098; 21496

The poetical works of John Mil- ton. 6059; 9499; 17166

The poetical works of John Trumbull. 3493

The poetical works of Mrs. Fe- licia Hemans. 33521; 33522

Poetical works of Oliver Gold- smith. 20694

The poetical works of Robert Burns. 8220; 12028; 19902; 23975

The poetical works of Sir Walter Scott. 17920; 17921; 30549; 35123

Poetical works of Thomas Camp- bell. 661; 4906; 4907; 19933; 23993; 23994; 28373; 28374

The poetical works of Thomas Moore. 34188

The poetical works of William Collins. 20127

The poetical works of William Cowper. 20204

The poetical works of William Wordsworth. 19334

Poetischer himmelsweg, oder Kleine, geistliche lieder sammlung. 33536

Poetry for children. 1898; 9963

Poetry for schools. 35051

The poetry of numbers. 17597

Poetry without fiction. 21921

Polemic disquisitions on four general subjects. 33018

Polemical and other miscellanies. 29114

Police jury regulations of the parish of West Baton Rouge. 11397

The policy of Maryland, in relation to the Potomac and Susquehanna. 15908

Polish military waltz. 29131

The polite little children. 652

Politeness of manners and behaviour in fashionable society. 4659

A political and civil history of the United States. 34811

The political character of John Quincy Adams delineated. 32244

Political consistency. 17657

Political economy. 24015; 24016

The political memorial. 30286

Political miscellanies. 38758

Political reflections, delivered on Springfield-Hill, Massachusetts. 39148

Political running. 12403

The political state of Italy. 2037

Political tables. 34828

Political thoughts. 13798

The political works of Alexander Pope. 34844

The political works of Thomas Paine. 6365; 25650

The political writings of Thomas Paine. 17508

Politico-clerico-lay sermon. 29245

Politische Ausicht und Fortsetzung der Vertheidigung der Freyen Kirche. 8841

Pollok's Course of time. 34835

Polly Campbell. 36723

Polly Hopkins and Tommy Tompkins. 30290

Polonaise for the guitar. 885

A polyglot grammar of the Hebrew. 19609

The Polytechnic and Scientific College of Philadelphia. 25799

The polytechnic repository. 4639

Pomposo. 5181

Poor Barny. 2809

The poor but honest soldier. 13806

The poor gentleman. 819; 15817

The poor hindoo. 15070

Poor little Bess. 13670

The poor little maid. 3041

Poor little sweep, Exile of Erin. 21926

Poor man's catechism. 34007

The poor man's defence. 13825

The poor man's physician. 23972

The poor man's preservative against popery. 31732

Poor old Peggy. 2810

Poor Richard (revived) almanac. 25803; 25804; 30293; 40110

Poor Richard's almanack. 34836; 40111

Poor Robin's almanac. 2811; 6503; 9973; 13810; 17660; 21927

Poor Sarah. 557; 558; 4806; 4807; 8153; 11954

The poor soldier. 6343

Poor Will's almanac. 2812; 2813; 6504; 9974; 13807; 13808; 17661; 17662; 21928-21930; 25805; 25806; 30294; 30295; 34837; 34838; 40112

Poor Will's pocket almanack. 2814; 6505; 9975; 13809; 17663; 21931; 25807; 30296; 34839; 40113

Popery unveiled. 6325

The popular air Eveleen's Bower. 1999

The popular air. O! it was not for me that I heard the bells ringing. 14892

The popular ballad singer. 40116

Popular directions for the prevention and cure of headaches, colds, and indigestion. 13815

A popular exposition of the system of the universe. 33499

Popular fairy tales. 2823-2825; 4385

Popular lectures on the steam engine. 33817

Popular songs. 30299

The popular story of Blue Beard.
15476
Popular tales. 12431
The populous village. 24315
Port entry--Penobscot River.
31450
Port of Salem. Fire at Parama-
ribo. 6701
A portable advance book. 12111
The Portland directory. 12956;
13820; 30309
Portrait of Washington. 17541
Portraits from life. 2833
A portraiture of Shakerism.
9366
Ports of entry--Florida. 36724
The Portsmouth directory. 6515;
30315
Portsmouth Lyceum. Prospectus.
34855
A Portuguese and English gram-
mar. 176; 177
Positive facts, versus envious
assertions. 13822
Post at St. Mark's. 27307
The post-captain. 32904
The post-chaise companion. 6822;
35249
The post-horn waltz. 1891
Post office calendar. 22433
Post office clerks. 31451
Post-Office Laws. 3931; 23018;
36725
Post route--Litchfield to Norfolk,
Con. 27308
Postage accruing for year ending
31st March, 1828. 41277
Postage accruing in the U.S.
31452
Postage. Letter from the Post-
master General. 23019
Posthumous papers. 37109;
37110
The posthumous works of Capt.
William Morgan. 29055
The posthumous works of Junius.
39171
The posthumous works of the
Rev. John Fletcher. 16158
Postscript to Peter's letters.
1994
A postscript to the Rev. Mr.
Harold's address. 9987;

12773; 13823
A postscript to the second se-
ries of letters addressed to
Trinitarians and Calvinists.
14825; 23211
Pot calling the kettle black.
24539
The Potomac canal. 13824
The Potomac muse. 23385
Potter's compend. 17679;
23020; 25816
La poule. A popular French
quadrille. 6517; 13826
Pounder's Wesleyan almanac.
2838; 6518; 9988; 13827
The power, justice and mercy of
Jehovah exercised upon His
enemies and His people.
12406
The power of deception unveiled
and the man of sin revealed.
39160
Power of divine truth. 40510
The power of faith; exemplified
in the extraordinary case of
Ashnah Lawton. 5806
The power of faith exemplified
in the life and writings
the late Mrs. Isabella Graham.
19670; 33398
The power of faith, or, The entire safety of trusting in God.
16871
Power of God manifest in the
Gospel ministry. 16054
The power of Grace. 9991
The power of religion; exemplified in the life, sickness and
death of Job Scott. 2839;
3130
The power of religion on the
mind, in retirement, affliction,
and at the approach of death.
34351
The power of the church distinguished from the power of
Anti-Christ. 13017
The power of truth and love.
35027
The power of Unitarianism over
the affections. 37933
The powers and duties of the
town officer. 9748; 17462

The powers of fancy and other
poems. 9994
Powers of the general govern-
ment--rights of the states.
41278
Practica criminal de España.
24769
The practical accountant. 12717;
33415
The practical American gardener.
9995
The practical analyst. 25103
A practical and elementary
abridgement of the cases argued and determined in the
courts of King's Bench. 38814
Practical and internal evidence
against Catholicism. 27635
Practical and mental arithmetic.
22307; 30637; 30638; 40459-
40461
Practical and surgical anatomy.
8121
A practical application of the
principles of geometry.
20273
The practical arithmetic. 37532
Practical arithmetic, prepared
for the use of Mrs. Okill's
Female Boarding-School.
34863
Practical considerations founded
on the Scriptures. 12316
Practical conveyancing. 30114
Practical discourses on regenera-
tion. 8557
Practical education. 12432
Practical elucidation of the nature
of Hernia. 12887; 16611;
16612; 24910
A practical English grammar.
15572
A practical essay on typhus fever.
18013
The practical expositor, and sen-
tentious reader. 39022
The practical expositor; or,
Scripture illustrated by facts.
8207
Practical forms. 11551
Practical geography as taught in
the Monitorial School, Boston.
16172; 28903

Practical geography, for the use
of schools. 30116
A practical grammar of the Eng-
lish language [Buchanan] 23958
A practical grammar of the Eng-
lish language [Greene] 38827
A practical grammar of the Eng-
lish language [Nutting] 13608;
25617; 34592; 39891
A practical grammar of the Ger-
man language. 33209
A practical harmony of the four
Gospels. 32352
Practical hints to young females.
3388; 26175; 40609
Practical horse farrier. 693
Practical husbandry. 14219
Practical illustrations of typhus.
4494; 7836; 15123; 37496
Practical instructions and directions for silkworm nurseries.
39972
A practical method of learning
to speak correctly the Castil-
lian language. 37021
Practical morality. 13829;
20042; 35384
Practical observations on diseases of children. 21244
Practical observations on midwifery. 10062; 25896
Practical observations on popular
education. 23936
Practical observations on the lat-
eral operation of lithotomy.
17288
Practical observations on the nature and treatment of maras-
mus. 7858
Practical observations on the
Old & New Testaments. 2622
Practical observations on the
symptoms, discrimination,
and treatment, of some of the
most important diseases of
the lower intestines and anus.
5648
Practical observations on vaccin-
ation. 897
Practical piety. 13398
Practical reader. 4615; 7966;
11755; 19617
Practical reflections for every

day throughout the year.
25064

Practical researches on the nature, cure & prevention of gout. 5725

Practical rules for Greek accents and quantity. 38017

Practical sermons. 20751

A practical synopsis of cutaneous diseases. 15282; 38096

Practical system of arithmetic. 20753

A practical system of modern geography. 34608; 39924

A practical system of rhetoric. 30058; 39841

The practical teacher. 40213

A practical treatise of powers. 14235

A practical treatise of the law of vendors and purchasers of estates. 3362; 3363; 35435

A practical treatise on bills of exchange. 4980; 4981; 24083

A practical treatise on dying of woollen, cotton and skein silk. 13674

A practical treatise on parties to actions. 8924; 29124

A practical treatise on perspective. 4082

A practical treatise on poisons and asphyxies. 25638

A practical treatise on railroads and carriages. 22506

A practical treatise on the diseases of the foot of the horse. 19893

A practical treatise on the law of contracts. 28460; 32673

A practical treatise on the law of evidence. 26131; 35387

A practical treatise on the law of legacies. 30339

A practical treatise on the law of partnership. 20729

A practical treatise on the management of bees. 40627

A practical treatise on the ordinary operations of the Holy Spirit. 16095

A practical treatise on the settling of evidence for trials at

nisi prius. 8632

Practical treatise on the water delivered by the Manhattan Company. 20780

A practical treatise upon Christian perfection. 9237

A practical treatise upon the authority and duty of justices of the peace. 15940; 32902

A practical view of the prevailing religious system of professed Christians. 41516

The practice and doctrine of Christian ministers. 11750

The practice of privateering considered. 1352

Practice of the court of chancery of the state of New York. 15464

The practice of the court of Kings Bench. 11633; 27884; 35514

The practice of the high court of chancery. 25587

The prairie. 28599; 32829; 38276

Pratt's introduction to arithmetic. 17682

Pray Papa. 13392; 13393; 21515

Prayer and sermon. 21957

Prayer for the use of families. 39130

A prayer meeting and revival hymn book. 23352; 23353; 31787

Prayer the breath of a good man, as long as he breathes. 3419

Prayers and offices of devotion, for families. 5715-5717; 9147; 29359

Prayers and religious meditations. 5551; 38923

Prayers and sermons. 21295

Prayers for children. 34866

Prayers for children and youth. 13830

Prayers for the use of children and youth. 7603

Prayers for the use of families; or The domestic minister's assistant. 1787; 1788; 5711;

9143; 16706-16708; 29355;
33704
Prayers for the use of families.
With forms for particular oc-
cassions, and for individuals.
20243
The praying Negro. 2845
The preacher's manual. 2846;
4998
Preaching Christ in love. 19615
Preaching Christ, productive of
joy. 12682
Preamble and constitution.
[Friendly Association for Mu-
tual Interests] 24634
Preamble and resolution adopted
by the General Assembly of
Kentucky. 13004
The preamble and resolution of-
fered by Mr. Logan. 40001
Preamble and resolutions of a
meeting, in Richmond, Oc-
tober 24, 1827. 29904
Preamble and resolutions of the
legislature of Kentucky. 13005;
16784
Preamble and resolutions on the
subject of the Missouri ques-
tion. 4121
Preamble and resolutions submit-
ted to the House of Delegates.
7535
Precaution, a novel. 865
Precedents for the use of jus-
tices of the peace. 9996
The preceding map comprehends
all that is usually called the
"Louisiana purchase." 21962
The precepts of Jesus. 22021;
34953
The predestinarian. 14011
Prediction and fulfillment, two
political odes. 19433
Eine Predigt über die Kinder-
zucht. 8996
Pre-emption to actual settlers.
27309; 31453
Pre-emption to certain persons
in Florida. 36726
Preface to the American gram-
mar. 4849
Preliminary address, the Na-
tional Gazette and Literary
Register. 1336
The premium for the Sabbath
School boy. 13831
Premium history of the United
States. 38883
Premiums for 1820. 2607
Premiums for 1827. 30122
Prentiss's astronomical ephem-
eris. 21963
Preparation for the ministry.
20525
Preparative meeting libraries.
38694
A present for a good child.
2860
A present for an apprentice.
7960
A present for little girls. 17692;
21969
A present from New York.
25829; 34873
The present situation of the
Cherokee Indians is recom-
mended to the attention of
every citizen. 38040
The present state and prospects
of Unitarian Christianity in
Calcutta. 25830
Present state of Christianity.
35197
The present state of England.
16948
Present state of the law. 32486
Present system of education.
25831
A present to a dutiful child at
the Sabbath School. 24117
A present to children. 3296;
13841
A present to Sabbath schools.
40516
A present to the teachers and
rulers of society. 7678
Presentation of the Clinton
vases. 21970
Presente a las damas. 40147
Preservation and civilization of
the Indians. 27310
Preservation of the Cumberland
Road. 27311
A preservative from the sins
and follies of childhood and
youth. 2861

The presidency of the United
States. 23372; 23373

President Adam's [!] grand
march & quick step. 20251

President, Andrew Jackson.
Vice-President, John C. Calhoun. Virginia. Presidential
electors. 32961

President Andrew Jackson's
message to both houses of
the Congress. 41279

The president, directors and
company of the Bank of the
United States vs. Solomon
Etting. 34874

President Holley and infidelity.
15924

President Holley--not the Transylvania University. 16167

President John Quincy Adams'
grand march. 20513

President John Quincy Adams
grand march & quick step.
21398

President Monroe's inauguration march. 6111

President Monroe's march.
12902

The President of Hayti's
march. 22102

The President's march. 6467;
13760; 21880; 25756

President's message delivered
to both Houses of Congress.
Dec. 2, 1823. 13371

President's message. Mar-
tinsburg Gazette. Extra.
31454

President's message. Message
of the President of the
United States, transmitted
to both houses of Congress.
27312

President's message. National
intelligencer. Extra. 23021;
27313; 31455

The president's tour. 10060

The presidential contest.
34813; 34814

Presidential election. [Penn]
34670

Presidential election [Rich-
mond Enquirer] 13842

Presidential election. 1776.
Independence, liberty, and
glory! 37294

Presidential election. The
people's ticket, in support of
Andrew Jackson, for President. 15960

Presidential election. Washington, May 25th, 1824. 17693

The presidential election, written for the benefit of the
people of the United States,
but particularly for those of
the state of Kentucky.
13770; 17627-17629

Presidential nomination. Pittsburgh, Jan. 3, 1824.
15965

The presidential question.
30336

The presidential question. Addressed to the people of
the United States. 34875

The Presidential question. To
the friends of equal rights.
30337; 34876

Preston's complete time table.
34877

Preston's cure for intemperance.
37332

Preston's manual on book keeping. 30338; 40148

Preston's tables of interest.
34878; 40149

The presumption of skeptical
and careless contemners of
religion. 40120

Presumptive arguments in favor
of Unitarianism. 33622

A pretty painted toy for either
girl or boy. 803

Pretty pictures, with pretty
verses. 30340; 34881

The pretty rose tree. 21508

Pretty Sophy. 11891; 19750

A prey to tender anguish. 16693

Price book; or, Rules of carpenter work. 1682

Price list of quills, at John B.
Kreymborg's Manufactory.
2869

The pride of Minerva. 15270

The pride of Peter Prim. 17695;

40150

Pride shall have a fall. 15895

Pride's looking glass. 27597

Primary dictionary. 35052

The primary instructor and improved spelling book. 8986; 8987; 12802; 16494

Primary lessons in arithmetic. 28783

Primary lessons in geography. 37863

The primary spelling book. 26226

A primer of the English language. 27707; 37246; 41594

Primer; or, First book for children. 35188

The primer: or, Mother's spelling-book for children. 13013

Primitive Christianity revived. 39989

Primitive divinity. 11639; 15128; 27893; 37509

Primitive theology. 9031; 9032; 12859

Primitive Trinitarianism. 23570

The primrose. 10010

Prince Hohenlohe's prayer book. 29242; 29243

Prince Kutusoff. A much admired dance. 13659

Prince Leopold. The mermaid & The Tivolian favorite waltzes. 6536; 13852

The principal doctrines of the New Jerusalem church. 3376

The principal grounds and maxims, with an analysis of the laws of England. 17458

Principia leges et aequitatis. 15544

Principle and practice, or The orphan family. 34023

The principles and acts of Mr. Adams' administration. 34182

Principles and acts of the revolution in America. 9718

Principles and men. 13951

The principles of aristocratic legislation. 34889

Principles of Congregationalism. 41349

Principles of currency and banking. 39320

Principles of discipline and general regulations, confession of faith, and form of covenant, adopted by the Trinitarian Church of Christ in Northfield, Mass. 39882

The principles of midwifery. 625; 4877; 12027

The principles of moral and political philosophy. 6369; 9802; 21769; 30142; 30143; 34634; 39952

The principles of natural and politic law. 12024

The principles of peace exemplified in the conduct of the Society of Friends. 1500; 38905

Principles of political economy. 5926

The principles of progression and proportion, illustrated. 25836

Principles of religious equality. 25182

Principles of the Christian religion, in question and answers. 8641; 21239; 28803

The principles of the government of the United States. 12332

Principles of the reformation. 27488; 31567

Prindle's almanac. 17700; 21978; 25837; 30346; 34890; 40155

Printed petition of Wm. Belcher. 375

The printer's guide. 31586

Printing book and job printers. 38433

The prison house. 18037

The prisoner at large. 9778

Private acts of the State of Maine. 5919; 9339; 13198; 16999; 21308; 25201; 29596; 33976

Private acts of the third General Assembly of the state of Missouri. 21483

Private and special acts of the state of Maine. 39396

Private and Temporary Acts

[N. J.]   2451-2453; 6220;
9649; 13518; 13519

Private buildings on public lands
at Harper's Ferry. 41280

Private character of General
Jackson. 34893

Private claims of Florida. 36727

Private correspondence of William Cowper. 15884; 15885

Private devotions. 6539

Private hours. 32992

Private journal of a voyage to
the Pacific Ocean. 35409

The private journal of Captain
G. F. Lyon.   16958

The private journal of Madame
Campan.   19931

Private land claims - Florida.
41281

Private life; or, Varieties of
character and opinion. 39369

The private meditations and
prayers of the Right Reverend
Thomas Wilson.   31785

The private memoirs of Madame
Du Hausset.   28739

Private memoirs of the court of
Napoleon. 32235

Private or special laws of the
state of Maine. 33977; 33978

Private property taken for public
use. 36728

Private thoughts upon religion,
and a Christian life. 37772

Private thoughts upon the relics
of antiquity. 24820; 24821

The privateer, a tale. 6540

Privateer pension fund.   41282

The prize book of the Publick
Latin school in Boston. 543;
11944; 15523

Prize essay on the comparative
economy of free and slave
labour.   30404

Prize essays, on the institution
of the Sabbath. 29356; 29357

The prize for youthful obedience.
2873; 13856

The prize ode.   18073; 22349

The prize; or, The story of
George Benson and Wm. Sand-
ford.   17701; 21980

The prize, or The three half

crowns. 30350

The prize; or 2, 5, 3, 8. 29232

Prize poem, recited by Mr.
Caldwell at the opening of the
New American theater in New
Orleans. 17351

The prize poem writnen [!] for
the Boston Theatre. 19490

Pro and cons; or, Crawford and
Adams.   13857

The probate directory. 40157

The probate laws of Massachusetts. 37861

Probestück Wen das Gesetz
dereinst aus Zion ausgeht.
16414

Problems to illustrate the most
important principles of geography and astronomy. 33894

Proceedings and address of the
Anti-Jackson Convention of
Missouri. 34380

Proceedings and address of the
convention of delegates, that
met at Columbus, Ohio, Dec.
28, 1827. 29897

Proceedings and address of the
Convention of young men in
Rockingham councillor dis-
trict, Epping, 1828. 34382

Proceedings and address of the
New Hampshire Republican
state convention. 32933

Proceedings and address of the
New Jersey delegates in fav-
or of the present administration.   34383

Proceedings and address of the
New-Jersey state convention.
32935

Proceedings and address of the
Vermont Republican Convention.   32958

Proceedings and Constitution of
the Baptist Convention of Virginia.   19594

The proceedings and constitution
of the Pennsylvania Branch
of the General Union for Promoting the Observance of the
Christian Sabbath. 33334

Proceedings and constitution of
the South Carolina Anti-In-

Select Masters, held at Masons' Hall in the town of Frankfort. 37297

Proceedings of a convention of the people of Maine, friendly to the present administration. 34374

Proceedings of a court of enquiry held at the Navy Yard. 11066

Proceedings of a general court martial, held at Brunswick, in the state of New-Jersey. 13859

Proceedings of a Grand Annual Communication of the Grand Lodge of Virginia. 1320; 5400; 8770; 12616; 16229; 24629; 28957; 33282; 38683

Proceedings of a Masonic convention, held at Masonic hall, in Canandaigua. 5391

Proceedings of a meeting held at Princeton, New-Jersey. 17350

Proceedings of a meeting held in Boston to take into consideration the present state of the wool-growing and wool-manufacturing interests. 30352

Proceedings of a meeting held in Philadelphia on the 4th of November, 1824. 18030

The proceedings of a meeting of the citizens of Albany. 15051

The proceedings of a meeting of the democratic citizens of North Mulberry Ward. 32956

Proceedings of a meeting of the friends of African colonization. 34038

Proceedings of a meeting of the friends of civil & religious liberty. 24355

Proceedings of a meeting of the friends of the general administration. 29902

Proceedings of a meeting on the subject of Sabbath schools. 25839

The proceedings of a public meeting, held in the Middle Dutch Church. 37437

Proceedings of a special com-

munication of the Grand lodge of ancient Free-Masons of South Carolina. 12614

Proceedings of a town meeting [Philadelphia] 25840

Proceedings of Grand Chapter of Masonic Lodge in Connecticut. 28924

Proceedings of Grand Chapter of Masonic Lodge, in Massachusetts. 5386

Proceedings of Grand Commandery of Masonic Lodge, in Virginia. 28958; 33280; 33281

The proceedings of Lodge no. 43, Lancaster. 8746

Proceedings of sundry citizens of Baltimore. 27946

Proceedings of the Administration convention held at Indianapolis. 34370

Proceedings of the administration convention held in Frankfort, Kentucky. 29891

Proceedings of the Administration convention of Indiana, held at Indianapolis. 34371

Proceedings of the administration meeting in Baltimore County. 29894

Proceedings of the Albany Infant School Society for the further establishment of infant schools in the city of Albany. 37407

Proceedings of the Anti-Jackson convention held at the capitol in the city of Richmond. 34406

Proceedings of the Anti-masonick State Convention, holden at Montpelier. 37485

Proceedings of the Antiquarian and Historical Society of Illinois. 32010

Proceedings of the Auxiliary Foreign Mission Society of the Brookfield Association. 23565; 27910; 32048; 37524

Proceedings of the Auxiliary Foreign Missionary Society of the Worcester Central Association. 31814; 37526

Proceedings of the Auxiliary Mis-

New York. 39821

Proceedings of the first ten years of the American Tract Society. 15092

Proceedings of the fourteenth annual meeting of the Baptist Mission Society of Virginia. 28045

Proceedings of the fourth annual meeting of the Baptist Convention of the state of New Hampshire. 37644

Proceedings of the 4th annual meeting of the Baptist Convention of the state of Vermont. 37676

Proceedings of the Fredericksburg Auxiliary Colonization Society. 33246

Proceedings of the Friends of Convention at the meeting held in Raleigh. 9730

Proceedings of the friends of Gen. Jackson at Louisville & Frankfort, Ky. 30353

Proceedings of the Friends of Liberal Christianity in the city of New York. 38689

Proceedings of the friends of Mr. Richard, relative to the contested election. 21981

Proceedings of the G. R. A. Chapter, for the state of Maryland and District of Columbia. 1302; 16202; 16203; 20576

Proceedings of the G.R.A. chapter of the state of Maryland. 28934; 38647; 38648

Proceedings of the General Association of Connecticut. 838; 5051; 8417; 12231; 15844; 20161; 24188; 24189; 28568; 32796

Proceedings of the General Association of New-Hampshire. 841

Proceedings of the general convention of delegates from the members and local preachers of the Methodist Episcopal Church. 29738

The proceedings of the general county Anti-masonic meeting, held in Lancaster, Penn. 37481

Proceedings of the general court martial convened for the trial of Commodore James Barron. 11067

Proceedings of the General Grand Chapter of the United States. 38676

The proceedings of the General Grand Royal Arch Chapter, of the United States of America. 24626

Proceedings of the General Theological Seminary of the Protestant Episcopal Church. 39823

Proceedings of the German Evangelical Lutheran Synod of Pennsylvania. 33091

Proceedings of the graduates of Union College. 26262

Proceedings of the Grand Chapter of the state of Kentucky. 33259

Proceedings of the Grand Committee, held at Philadelphia. 12610

Proceedings of the Grand Encampment of the state of Virginia. 38682

Proceedings of the Grand Lodge of Alabama. 8734; 33253

Proceedings of the Grand Lodge of Ancient York Masons of North Carolina. 12607; 24617; 38663

Proceedings of the Grand Lodge of Connecticut. 5375; 8736; 16189; 16190; 24585

Proceedings of the Grand Lodge of free and accepted Masons, of the state of Mississippi. 12597; 16207

Proceedings of the grand lodge of Indiana. 38642

Proceedings of the Grand Lodge of Kentucky. 1295; 5378; 8743; 12588; 16194; 20574; 24596; 28929; 33260; 38643

Proceedings of the Grand Lodge of Missouri. 8754

Proceedings of the Grand Lodge of New Hampshire. 1305;

Proceedings of the Grand Royal Arch Chapter of the state of Vermont. 1319

Proceedings of the Grand Royal Arch Chapter of Virginia. 5401; 8771

Proceedings of the Great Indian Council, held at Tonawanta [sic] August 8, 1822. 9100

Proceedings of the M. W. Grand Lodge of Mississippi. 20580

Proceedings of the Maryland administration convention. 29895

Proceedings of the Maryland Grand Lodge of Free and Accepted Masons. 28933

Proceedings of the Massachusetts Episcopal Missionary Society. 29690

The proceedings of the Medical State Convention, begun and held in the town of Columbus. 34100

Proceedings of the meeting held at Lockport. 29246

Proceedings of the meeting of manufacturers and growers of wool, in the state of Vermont. 25841; 29620

Proceedings of the Missionary Society of the Middlesex Association. 37435

Proceedings of the most worshipful grand lodge of Connecticut. 1286

Proceedings of the Nassau-Hall Bible Society. 13855

Proceedings of the New-York Horticultural Society. 34541

Proceedings of the Northern Association of Universalists. 4069; 19114; 23139

Proceedings of the Pennsylvania Agricultural Society. 13718; 21837

Proceedings of the Pennsylvania Canal Convention. 21842

Proceedings of the Pittsburgh meeting, relative to the revision of the tariff. 17645

Proceedings of the Presbytery of Philadelphia. 2858

Proceedings of the president and directors of the Chesapeake and Ohio Canal Company. 32664

The proceedings of the president and fellows of Connecticut Medical Convention. 20174

The proceedings of the president and fellows of the Connecticut Medical Society. 24205; 32813; 38258

Proceedings of the R. W. Grand Lodge of the state of Georgia. 8739

Proceedings of the Reformed Church of Ohio. 40233

Proceedings of the Royal Arch Chapter of New-Hampshire. 8757

Proceedings of the School committee of the town of Boston. 530

Proceedings of the second annual meeting of the Auxiliary Foreign Mission Society of Essex County. 37525

Proceedings of the second annual meeting of the New Jersey Colonization Society. 25528

Proceedings of the seventeenth anniversary of the Auxiliary Foreign Mission Society of Boston. 32047

Proceedings of the sixth triennial meeting of the Baptist General Convention. 37674

Proceedings of the Synod of the Free Independent German Reformed Congregations of Pennsylvania. 38629

The proceedings of the Synod of the German Reformed Church in North America. 34976

Proceedings of the Temperance Society of Columbia, S. C. 38229

Proceedings of the tenth Evangelical Lutheran synod of Ohio and the adjacent states. 28806

Proceedings of the third annual convocation of the Grand Royal Arch Chapter of the state of Alabama. 24580; 24581

cified, the delight of God.
24055

Proclamation of the Governor convening the Senate. 30013

Proclamation of the Senate of Calamata, "one of those local assemblies which were organized in Greece..." 39568

A proclamation regarding contributions on any Lord's day in the month of September.
12239

A proclamation... "Resolved by this Assembly, that there may be contributions in the several religious societies and congregations in this state." 8428

A proclamation... that on any Lord's day, in the month of June next, contributions may be received for the above purpose. 12238

A proclamation...the State of Maine was admitted into the Union. 2079

Procrastination; or the evil of delay. 40412

The procrastinator's soliloquy and prayer. 17702

The prodigal daughter. 10019; 30354

The prodigal son. 30355

Profession is not principle. 16777; 25024; 29407; 29408; 33759; 39183

The profession of faith, and constitutional plan of government, of the Western association of Universalists. 4249

The profession of faith, bond of union and peace, and church organization and government, of the First Universalist Church of Christ. 9985

Professional reputation. 24700

Professor Hale and Dartmouth College. 2875

Professor Mitchell's report on the geology of North-Carolina. 34165

Professor Ripley's review of Dr. Griffin's letter on communion. 40287

Professorship of German literature and science. 11569

La profezia di Dante. 4894; 8234

Program for Le Macon and Le Bouffe et Le Tailleur, 30 September. 30224

The progress of Christianity retarded by its friends. 17821

The progress of divine truth. 8349

Progress of liberal Christianity. 37721

Progress of light & liberty. 28726

The progress of sin. 11498

The progress of the pilgrim Good-intent, in Jacobinical times. 32523

Progressive duets for two German flutes. 14984

The progressive primer. 40158

A progressive sonata. 6864; 14198

Prohibition of the slave trade. 31456

Prohibitory duties and domestic coasting trade. 41283

Projected salt works in Boston Bay. 35475

Prometheus. 9876

Prominent features of a northern tour. 10021

The promise of Paradise. 10467

The promised seed. 12261

The promissory note. 6956

The prompter: a series of essays on civil and social duties. 6543

The prompter; or, A commentary on common sayings and subjects. 31696

The pronouncing Bible. 37831

The pronouncing English reader. 17282

The pronouncing introduction. Introduction to the English reader. 29871; 39681

The pronunciation of the Latin language. 13860

The pronouncing spelling book. 5121; 8487; 12305; 20228; 20229; 24263; 28635-28637;

32868; 38318

The pronouncing Testament.
8038; 23809; 32353; 37832

Proof of Circular for consideration at an early meeting of
the council. 34710

Proofs that the common theories
and modes of reasoning respecting the depravity of mankind exhibit it as a physical
attribute. 18143

The proper mode of conducting
missions to the heathen. 41574;
41575

The prophecy of Dante. 4895

The prophecy; or, Love and
friendship. 5359

The prophetic history of the
Christian religion explained.
6727

A proposal for a plan of a
French school. 25217

A proposal for altering the eastern front of the city of Philadelphia. 358

Proposal for publishing by subscription, a work entitled experiments and observations on
the extraordinary effects of
phosphorus in the treatment of
different diseases. 16929

Proposal to alter the Eastern
front of the city. 359

Proposals by Amos Lay. 16872

Proposals by E. Morford. 6118

Proposals by James Thomas.
18184

Proposals, by Judah Delano.
8526

Proposals, by Kenton Harper.
29141

Proposals by Messrs. Warren &
Wood. 7587

Proposals by O. Wilder & Jas.
M. Campbell. 19280

Proposals by the proprietors of
the locks and canals on Merrimack River. 25842

Proposals by Thomas Morgan.
29800

Proposals, by W. Baxter.
11765

Proposals for a new school for

boys. 34894; 38119

Proposals for carrying mails.
3932; 7396

Proposals for erecting a large
and commodious Masonic hall
& city hotel. 33271

Proposals for making a geological and mineralogical survey
of Pennsylvania. 30356

Proposals for printing, by subscription, an Exposition of
the historical writings of the
New Testament. 34215

Proposals for publishing a newspaper in Taunton, Bristol
County. 12580

Proposals for publishing a religious & literary paper in the
town of Lexington, Ky. 19250

Proposals for publishing a weekly newspaper in the City of
Washington. 27566

Proposals, for publishing a work,
to be entitled The American
Economist. 29507

Proposals for publishing at Buffalo, N.Y. A new series of
Plain Truth! 30280

Proposals for publishing by subscription, a gazetteer of the
State of Vermont. 14283

Proposals for publishing by subscription, A Journal of Travels in New-England and New
York. 1065

Proposals for publishing by subscription, a map and gazeteer
of the Territory of Michigan.
16752

Proposals, for publishing by subscription a new work, en-
titled A System of pryotechny.
15912

Proposals for publishing by subscription, a new work, to be
prepared by Robert Walsh,
Jun. and entitled American biography. 14818

Proposals for publishing, by subscription a pamphlet on the
question of the next president.
13861

Proposals for publishing by subscription, in the city of Richmond, a semi-weekly and daily newspaper to be called The Virginia Times. 8463

Proposals for publishing by subscription, memoirs of the life and public services of Major-General William H. Harrison. 12338

Proposals for publishing by subscription, The history of America. 5660

Proposals for publishing in Mount Pleasant, Ohio, a quarterly magazine to be called "The Medical and botanical repository." 341

Proposals, for publishing in the city of Richmond, a new weekly paper, to be styled The Friend of the Union. 33286

Proposals for publishing in the village of Rome, a weekly newspaper, to be entitled The Oneida Plebeian. 14976

Proposals for publishing, in this city, a new semi-weekly paper, to be called The Boston Journal. 19816

Proposals for tobacco warehouses and accompanying documents. 29648

Proposals... for the sale of their mill power and land at Lowell. 25843

Proposals for the stock of the Ousatonic Canal Company. 9069; 9798

Proposals of Messrs. Warren and Wood for the erection of a new theatre in the city of Philadelphia. 31665

Proposals of the Maryland Institute for the Promotion of the Mechanic Arts. 29654

Proposals of the Massachusetts Hospital Life Insurance Company. 13264

Proposals, the following splendid work entitled The Presidency of the United States by A. B. Woodward is now in hand. 23374

Proposals, the subscriber proposes to publish a paper at Frankfort in Kentucky. 37590

Proposals to publish by subscription a selection of the miscellaneous works and essays of C. S. Rafinesque. 6584

Proposed amendment to the constitution of the United States. 21984

Proposed amendments to the Constitution of the U. S. 11068

Proposed new constitution of the state of North Carolina. 13598

Proposition for the better protection of the domestic industry of the country. 21983

Proposition to amend the Constitution. 27317

The propriety of introducing the fundamental doctrines of Christianity in the religious instruction of children. 39434

Proprium Dioecisis Baltimnensis, juxta rubrica breviarii ei octavorii Romani. 12080

Prose by a poet. 9530; 17199

The proselyte. 39240

The prospect before us. 8273

Prospective economy in the future public works of the state of New-York. 30740

Prospective theology. 22345

Prospecto. To the advocates of light & reason. 14274

The prospects and the claims of pure Christianity. 17514; 21771

The prospects of Christianity. 33426

Prospectus [N. Y. Horticultural Society] 17422

Prospectus and internal regulations of the American Literary, Scientifick and Military Academy. 21711

Prospectus and internal regulations of the Western Literary and Scientifick Academy, at Buffalo. 37981

Prospectus, by Catharine E. Beecher. 29155

Prospectus, by-laws and charter

of the Transylvania Botanic
Garden Company. 18233
Prospectus de l'Academie Clas-
sique et Militaire de Mantua.
31877
Prospectus. G. & C. Carvill,
New York, propose to publish
the American .annual register.
24032
Prospectus of a history of the
administration of John Quincy
Adams. 38606
Prospectus of a literary magazine to be published in Philadelphia. 30236
Prospectus of a literary and scientific journal, to be published, weekly, at the University of Virginia. 41390
Prospectus of a museum of arts
and sciences to be established
in Baltimore. 17542
Prospectus of a new and splendid publication The Hudson
River portfolio. 6009
Prospectus of a new journal to
be published at the City of
Washington. 15087
Prospectus of a new periodical
publication, to be called the
Theological Review and General Repository of Religious and
Moral Information. 5488
Prospectus of a new periodical
work, to be called the American Annual Register of History and Politics. 17703
Prospectus of a new plan to make
a large fortune by a new sys-
tem of power. 30448
Prospectus of a new work. Pres-
idents' speeches. 8404
Prospectus of a newspaper published at Bath. 17704
Prospectus of a school to be established at Round Hill,
Northampton, Massachusetts.
12197
Prospectus of a series of lectures
by Mr. Jonathan Barber. 4607
Prospectus of Alleghany [sic]
College. 37415
Prospectus of Morris Academy.
29812
Prospectus of the American Classical and Military Lyceum, at
Mount Airy. 23472
Prospectus of the Canton Company of Baltimore, 38046
Prospectus of the Female semi-
nary, at Wethersfield, Ct.
24423
Prospectus of the grand spec-
tacle and ballet of action, in
three acts, called "La belle
peruvienne" 6544; 11792
Prospectus of the intended pub-
lications of the life of the
Chevalier John Paul Jones.
22266
Prospectus of The National Jour-
nal. 13469
Prospectus of the National Pilot.
6181
Prospectus of the second Amer-
ican edition of the new Edin-
burgh Encyclopaedia. 7649
Prospectus of The Universal
Traveller. 19112
Prospectus of the Washington
Republican and Congressional
Examiner. 9320
A prospectus of Woodbine Insti-
tute, for Practical Education,
and Agriculture.   37225
Prospectus, or Concise view of
"A general abridgement and
digest of American law."
8497
Prospectus to form a new com-
pany for internal improvement.
40271
The protecting system. 38065
Protection to commerce. 27318
Protest against proceedings of
the first Church in Worcester.
4512
Protest of the Legislature of
Georgia, against the act of
Congress. 41217
Protest of the minority against
the act organizing the court
of appeals. 13006
Protest of the Minority of the
Senate of Maine, against the
Lottery Bill. 13199

The Protestant; a tale of the
reign of Queen Mary. 37931

A Protestant catechism. 16087

Protestant Episcopal Sunday
school book. 40677

Protestants not guilty of misrep-
resentation, as to Roman Catholic doctrines and pretensions.
40190

Protested bills of exchange.
36729

Protests, arguments, and address
against the whole of the proceedings of his prosecutors,
&c. in the Baltimore City Station. 30411

Protokoll der Sitzung der Evangelisch-Lutherischen Synode
von Maryland und Virginien.
16078

"Prove all things; hold fast that
which is good." 30279

The Providence directory. 17727;
25873; 34931

The providence of God displayed
in the rise and fall of nations.
37157

The Providence selection of
hymns. 2910

Provident Society. At a large and
respectable meeting of citizens. 17729

Providential care. 30522

Provincial letters. 34652

Provisional catalogue of Mr. Andrew Parmentier's fruit trees.
25669

Provisional ordinance of the Republic of Colombia for the regulation of privateering. 15822

Provisory rules and regulations
for the Government of Baltimore College. 4536

The provoked husband. 11287

The provost. 8798

Proyecto de un codigo penal.
37019

Prussian waltz. 6567

Prussian waltz for the harp or
piano forte. 4185

The psalmist, a collection of
Psalm and hymn tunes. 16936

The psalmists and hymnists, in

answer to a pamphlet of Mr.
Rankin. 33939

Psalmody; a sermon on Lord's
day, March 2, 1822. 14928

Psalms adapted to the public
worship of the Christian
church. 32354

Psalms and hymns, for social
and private worship. 9929

The psalms and hymns of Dr.
Watts. 31684

The psalms & hymns of the Reformed Dutch Church in North
America. 25910

The Psalms and hymns, with the
catechism, confession of faith,
and liturgy, of the Reformed
Dutch Church in North America. 2957-2960; 10074;
13913; 22047; 30416; 40228

Psalms carefully suited to the
Christian worship. 443; 4690;
8039; 8040; 11844-11846;
15384-15386; 23810; 28164;
28165; 32355

Psalms, hymns, and spiritual
songs, adapted to the Christian religion. 32560; 38039

The Psalms, hymns, & spiritual
songs [Watts] 14853; 19212;
31685

Psalms, hymns and spiritual
songs, selected for the use of
the United Churches of Christ.
12035; 28347

The Psalms of David, imitated
in the language of the New
Testament. 4691-4693; 8041-
8043; 11847-11849; 15387-
15389; 19714; 19715; 23811-
23813; 32356-32359; 28166-
28169; 37833

The Psalms of David, in metre.
4694; 4695; 8044; 8045; 19716;
23814; 37834

Der Psalter des Königs und
Propheten Davids. 4696-4700;
15390; 19717; 23815; 28170;
32360

The Psalter, or Psalms of David, with the Proverbs of Solomon, and Christ's sermon on
the mount. 15391

Public acts. Acts of the General Assembly of the state of New Jersey. 13520; 13521

Public acts of the state of Maine. 9340; 13200; 17000; 21309; 25202; 29598; 33979; 39397

A public address, to the Baptist society, and friends of religion in general. 2647

The public and general statutes passed by the congress of the United States. 31457; 36730

Public buildings [U.S. Government] 27319-27321; 31458

Public controversy: or, Universalism weighed in the balance and found wanting. 8065

Public defaulters brought to light. 8832

Public discourses, delivered (in substance) at Union Village. 12407

Public documents, concerning the Ohio canals. 33771

Public documents, relating to the New-York canals. 6265

Public hire of Negroes. 6110

Public lands in market from five to twenty years. 36732

Public lands. Letter from the Commissioner of the General Land Office. 36731

Public lands. Mr. Clay's resolutions. 41284

Public laws of the state of Maine. 9341; 13201; 17001; 21310; 25203; 33980; 39398

Public laws of the state of Rhode Island. 6635; 10102; 10103; 22080

Public meeting. A meeting of the young men of the city of Albany. 17730

Public meeting. At a numerous meeting of the friends of John Quincy Adams. 17731; 22006

Public meeting. At a very numerous and respectable meeting of the Canadian and American democratic citizens of the County of Wayne. 7606

A public oration, delivered by appointment, before the Phi Alpha Theta Society, July 4, 1826. 24362

Public oratorio performed by the Handel and Haydn Society. 12764; 12765

Public, parlour, and cottage hymns. 13890

Public printing. 41285

Public proceedings on the removal of the Hon. De Witt Clinton from the office of canal commissioner. 17732

Public property of the corporation of the city of New York, 1829. 39781

Public sale. I will offer at public sale, on my farm in Harrison township, Knox county. 19643

Public sale. On___the___day of October, 1822, at the residence of the subscriber, in Honey Creek Prairie, Vigo county, Ind. 8861

Public sale. Will be sold, at public vendue...John Swimley, ex'r. 17733

The public statute laws of the state of Connecticut. 845; 5060; 8430; 12240; 15845a; 15846a; 20170; 24198; 24199; 28575; 32807; 38256

The public universal friend. 6572

Public worship: A sermon. 30104

The publications of the American Tract Society. 15093; 23503

The publications of the New England Tract Society. 2426; 13498; 13499

Publii Ovidii Nasonis Metamorphoseon libri XV. Interpretatione et notis illustravit Daniel Chrispinus Helvetius. 13650; 25642; 30136

Publii Vergilii Maronis Opera. 31595; 41368

Published by the Society for the Promotion of Internal Improvement. 34707

Publishing of the laws. 27322

Publius Vergilius Maro Bucolica, Georgica, et Aenesis. 27499;

ments of Logick. 12803

Questions adapted to Hedge's Logick. 13663

Questions adapted to Morse & Parish's History of New England. 2921

Questions, adapted to Murray's Grammar. 25884

Questions adapted to Murray's observations on the principles of good reading. 10055

Questions adapted to study of general history. 2922

Questions adapted to the Arithmetic of S. F. Lacroix. 7644

Questions adapted to the constitution of the state of Massachusetts. 24999

Questions adapted to the constitution of the United States. 29376

Questions adapted to the study of Tytler's elements of history. 2923; 6577; 23368

Questions adapted to the use of the third edition of Worcester's Elements of History. 37242

Questions, adapted to Whelpley's Compend of history. 1099; 1100; 5250; 8621a; 16057; 20405; 24424; 33073; 38472

Questions adapted to Williams' History of the American revolution. 30718

Questions and answers upon the duties of the Christian religion. 13900; 22015

Questions and answers upon the truths of the Christian religion. 10056; 17742

Questions and counsel. 2975; 8879

Questions and supplement to Goodrich's History of the United States. 38473

Questions embracing the principal truths of religion, answered from Scripture. 39621

Questions for the examination of scholars in "Conversations on chemistry." 15466

Questions for the examination of scholars in "Conversations on natural philosophy." 8108; 15467

Questions for the examination of schools in Tytler's Elements of general history. 14084

Questions for the examination of students in Paley's Moral and political philosophy. 33309

Questions, geographical, historical, doctrinal, and practical, upon the Gospel according to St. Matthew. 8288

Questions in arithmetic. 17683

Questions in English grammar. 5508

Questions in sacred antiquities. 40207

Questions on Adam's Roman antiquities. 22016

Questions on astronomy. 24141

Questions on Christian experience & character. 29146; 33480

Questions on Hale's History of the United States. 25885

Questions on natural philosophy. 24757

Questions on natural philosophy for the use of the scholars of the Salem Street Academy. 10057; 17743

Questions on the Assembly's shorter catechism. 23519

Questions on the Bible for the use of schools. 2054; 2055; 9316; 9316a; 13173; 13174; 16967; 21275; 25172; 29568; 29569; 33942

Questions on the Bible, of the Old and New Testament. 2924

Questions on the collects. 30394

Questions on the confession of faith and form of government of the Presbyterian Church. 27591

Questions on the historical parts of the New Testament [Cummings] 922; 28638

Questions on the historical parts of the New Testament [Parmele] 17523; 21784

Questions on the historical parts

of the Old Testament. 2925
Questions on the sacred Scriptures. 326
Questions on the science of bookkeeping. 29071
Questions to Jamieson's Grammar of rhetoric. 2926; 6578
Questions upon the evidence of Christianity. 6678
Quick! we have but a second. 19751
Quiet and holy submission to the providential will of God. 7688
Quinti Horatii Flacci Opera. 5631; 12870; 20947; 20948; 24889; 29254; 33590; 33591
Quizzing glass, or Jackdaw exposed. 40208
Quotations from the British poets. 17748; 25890; 34946

R

A race for a dinner. 40309-40311
Rachel. 35538
Rachel Dyer: a North American story. 34411
The Raciad and other occasional poems. 2932
The radical. 6582; 6583
The rail road, a characteristic divertimento for the piano forte. 34104
Rail road company--Baltimore and Ohio. 36733
Rail road manual. 33897; 39316
Rail road march. 34105; 34106
Rail-road meeting. Chathcam County, N. C. 34951
Rail road resolutions. 39500
Rail-roads. [Carey] 28402
Rail roads in the United States of America [Hollins] 29247
The railway docks at Brooklyn. 26198
Railways. 21851-21853
Railways and canals. 19474
The rainbow after the thunder storm. 25894; 30398
The rainbow; or, Lights and shadows of fashionable life.

10001
Rainsford Villa. 22019
Raising the wind. 1841; 5751; 21104
The Ramble in the wood. 2936; 40211
The Rambler [Johnson] 5726; 9161; 16737; 29369; 37298
The rambler, or, A tour through Virginia, Tennessee, Alabama, Mississippi and Louisiana. 34954
Ramiro, conde de Lucena, Obra original en seis libros. 33609
Ramon: the rover of Cuba. 40212
Rand's system of penmanship. 6586
Randolph, a novel. 13473
Randolph's culinary gardener. 25899
La ranz des voches. 2091
Ne Raorihwadogenti ne Shonwayaner Yesus Keristus Jenihorihoten ne Royatadogenti Mark. 37835
Rapport, du comite des actionnaires, de la Banque de La Louisiane. 217
Rapport fait a l'Assemblée Générale de l'État de la Louisiane. 9282
Rapport. Le comité spécial, auquel on a renvoyé le rapport qu'on a fait sur cette partie du message du Gouverneur. 25355
Rapport publié au nom de la Société médicale de la Nouvelle-Orleans. 3254
Rasselas, a tale. 21065; 29370
Rasselas, prince of Abissinia. 16738; 24993
Rates of insurance in the port of Boston. 25901
Rates of toll on the Middlesex River canals. 6043
Ratio disciplinae, or The constitution of the Congregational churches. 41350
Ratio of representation under fifth census. 31461; 31462

The rational dame. 24524

The rational guide to reading and orthography. 16173; 33223

A rational illustration of the Book of common prayer. 4255; 23302

Rational sports in dialogues passing among the children of a family. 2940

A rational view of the Scripture doctrine of salvation by Jesus Christ. 17759

The ray that beams forever. 9187

Raymond and Agnes. 5817; 33856; 33857

Read and judge. 20387

Read & think. 10066

The reader. 7769

The reader's almanac for the middle, southern and western states. 22039

Reading lessons for primary schools. 20784

The ready calculator. 38825

The ready reckoner. 31751

Real estate purchased by United States, since fourth July, 1776. 27325

Real estate purchased for the U. States. Message from the President. 27324

The real principles of Catholics. 29258

The real Robinson Crusoe. 8524

A real treasure for the pious mind. 2946

Reason, folly and beauty. 6884; 18103

Reason versus prejudice. 34965

Reasons assigned by a number of ministers, elders, and deacons, for declaring themselves the True Reformed Dutch Church. 10487; 10488

Reasons for believing in Universalism. 19733; 23826

Reasons for believing that the future punishment of the wicked, will be endless. 8793

Reasons for temperance. 38757

Reasons for the necessity of si-

lent waiting, in order to the solemn worship of God. 4840

Reasons for the secession of a number of members from the Baptist Church in Hartford. 17761

Reasons for voting against the grant of $11,870.50 to Governor Tompkins. 33404

Reasons in favor of the General Theological Seminary. 5417

Reasons in favour of the erasure of the law which forbids a man to marry his deceased wife's sister. 29100

The reasons of the appeal court of equity for confirming the decree of the circuit court, in the case of Isaac Carr. 10067

Reasons of the author for his separation from the Methodist Society. 14247

Reasons of the committee on public land, for reporting against an appropriation. 25266

Reasons offered by Andrew M'-Dowell, for his opinions, to the Presbyterian Congregation of Carlisle. 2053

Reasons offered by Samuel Eddy, for his opinions, to the First Baptist Church in Providence. 5226; 24400; 24401

Reasons, principally of a public nature, against a new bridge from Charlestown to Boston. 22041

Reasons why Mr. Southard ought not to be elected by the Legislature to supply the vacancy in the Senate. 40219

Reasons why the present system of auctions ought to be abolished. 34546

Rebecca Blodget. 36734

Rebecca Guest. 36735

The rebels; or, Boston before the revolution. 20044

Recaptured Africans. 36736

The re-captured negro. 6792; 10268; 14113; 30604

Receipts and expenditures, Miami and Western Reserve

Road.   21729

Receipts and expenditures United States, 1825.   31463

Receipts and payments at the Treasury of Pennsylvania. 2691; 6413; 9846; 13704

Receipts at the treasury of the theological seminary, at Bangor.   11675

Receipts for the cure of most diseases incident to the human family.   29576

Receipts from the customs from 1815 to 1826.   31464

The recent attempt to defeat the constitutional provisions in favour of religious freedom, considered.   33924; 33925

The reciprocal duties of ministers and people.   5678

Reciprocal duties of parents and children.   22428; 30765

The reciprocal influence of knowledge, religion and civil freedom in supporting the union, and promoting the interest of the body politick.   39629

Reciprocal obligations of religion and civil government.   20184

The recluse.   7832

Recognition march on the Independence of Hayti.   21063

Recollections and reflections, personal and political, as connected with public affairs during the reign of George III. 9714

Recollections of a beloved sister. 2947

Recollections of an old soldier. 9884

Recollections of Egypt.   29773

The recollections of Jotham Anderson.   19187; 37081

Recollections of the Jersey prison-ship.   38420

Recollections of the last ten years.   24553

Recollections of the life of John O'Keefe.   30110

Recollections of the life of Lord Byron.   20248

Recollections of the peninsula.

17961

A recommendation of Bible Association.   24045

Reconciliation of all things. 29706

Record of the Proceedings before the Senate of Ohio.   2591

Records of patriotism and love of country.   19494; 23572

Records of the Congregational Church in Colebrook.   8386

Records of the life of the Rev. John Murray.   29839

Records of the Spanish Inquisition.   34966

Records of woman.   33523; 33524

La Récréation des demoiselles. 2800

Recreations of George Taletell. 9042

Recruiting march.   17763

The recruiting officer.   8683

The recruiting sergeant.   15399

Recueil choisi de traits historiques et de contes Moreaux. 4160; 14820; 23206; 41424

The red book.   32246

The red rover, a drama in three acts.   32640

The Red Rover, a tale.   28600; 32830

Redeeming the time.   20407

Redemption: A poem.   30749

Redfield: a Long-Island tale. 20617

Redgauntlet.   17922-17925

Reduce duties on wines.   36737

Reduction of all the genera contained in the catalogue of North American plants.   9567

Reduction of duty on tea.   36738

Redwood; a tale.   17936

The reference Bible.   23816; 28171

Reflections against the Baptists refuted.   40395-40397

Reflections for the New Year. 30259

Reflections occasioned by a public execution at Boston. 10072

Reflections, occasioned by the

late disturbances in Charleston. 9943

Reflections on death. 12383a; 12384; 15988; 28711

Reflections on intemperance. 27599

Reflections on prayer. 2337

Reflections on the character and public services of Andrew Jackson. 34971

Reflections on the dissention actually existing in St. Mary's congregation. 17771

Reflections on the important subject of full and free salvation. 17871

Reflections on the politics of ancient Greece. 16499

Reflections on the proposed plan for establishing a college in Philadelphia. 24017; 24018

Reflections on the relics of ancient grandeur. 38942

Reflections on the renewal of the charter of the Bank of Pennsylvania. 38066

Reflections on the Sabbath day. 40226

Reflections on the seven days of the week. 3381

Reflections on the statements and opinions published in the Free Enquirer. 38818

Reflections on the subject of emigration from Europe. 24019-24021

Reflections on the vanity of all things under the sun. 33509

Reflections on the works of God. 6916; 10371; 10372; 18121

Reflections suggested by the obsequies of John Adams and Thomas Jefferson. 25907

Reflections upon the law of libel. 13015

Reflections upon the perils and difficulties of the winter navigation of the Delaware. 9170

Reflexions medicales sur la maladie spasmodica-lipyrienne des pays chauds. 4934

Reflexions on the proposed plan for establishing a college in Philadelphia. 24022; 24023

Reformation melodies. 16171

Reformation principles exhibited by the Reformed Presbyterian Church in the United States of America. 17777

Reformed Edward. 40234

The Reformed Methodist pocket hymn book. 34979

The reformed pastor. 4636; 37727

Reformer's discipline. 34980

Reformirtes Gesangbuch, oder: ein Auszug von 270 Lieder aus dem Reformirten Gesangbuch. 40231

The refuge [Finley] 8705

The refuge. A romance. 21070

The refuge. By the author of "The guide to domestic happiness." 6603

A refutation of Arianism. 34654

Refutation of calumnies propagated by Abel P. Upshur. 8995

A refutation of certain calumnies published in a pamphlet. 2669

A refutation of certain calumnies, published in John Laws handbill. 28823

Refutation of certain misrepresentations issued against the author of the "Fauna americana." 24794

The refutation of error, and establishment of truth. 2965; 24544

Refutation of Mr. Colden's "Answer" to Mr. Sullivan's report to the Society. 35437

A refutation of sundry written charges, made by the Rev. Ravaud Kearney. 34982

A refutation of the calumnies circulated against the southern and western states. 9037

A refutation of the charges made against the public conduct of Gen. Andrew Jackson. 37295

Refutation of the reasons assigned by the arbitrators for their award in the case of the two Greek frigates. 26037

A refutation of the sophisms,

Arch Chapter of the state of New-Hampshire. 5390; 28943

Regulations of the Grand Royal Arch-Chapter of the state of Vermont. 20598

Regulations of the New Bedford Social Library. 25493

Regulations of the public schools in Concord, New-Hampshire. 32792

Regulations of the public schools in Danvers. 20258

Regulations of the school committee of the City of Boston. 28233; 37891

Regulations of the United States Military Academy. 14756

Regulations, recommended by the School Committee of the town of Ipswich. 12930

Regulations to ascertain the present occupiers or proprietors of sittings in the United Churches. 40058

Das Reich Gottes ist gekomen. 16436

The reign of Grace, from its rise to its consummation. 526

The reign of Jesus Christ. 31761

The reign of terrour. 32938

The reign of truth and righteousness about to commence. 17779

Das reine und lautere Evangelium. 20291; 24331

Rejected addresses; or, The new Theatrum poetarum. 35228

The rejected addresses, presented for the cup offered for the best address, on the opening of the new theatre. 14183

The rejected addresses; together with the prize address. 6605

The rejected lover. 12177

Rejected plays. 34985

Rejoinder to the reply of the Rev. Mr. Harold. 8274; 8275

Relating to settlers on the public lands. 27326; 27327

The relation of faith to missions. 19488

Relation of the fearful state of

Francis Spira. 27922

The relation the present state of religion bears to the expected millennium. 14029

Relations between the Cherokees and the government of the United States. 38123

Relative rank of officers of the Army and Navy. 41286

Relentless love. 16359

Relics of antiquity. 27674

Relief. The following persons voted for McCalla. 25916

Religion a social principle. 708; 709

Religion and its image. 28368

Religion at home. 41536

Religion exemplified in the life of poor Sarah. 2967; 10080

Religion in the cottage. 13918

Religion not traditional or theoretical. 40236

Religion of the Closet. 391-393

The religion of the sun. 25651

Religion productive of national prosperity. 12812

Religion profitable. 9805

Religion recommended to youth. 6955; 30785; 40633

Religion the one thing needful. 15993

Religious & moral poems. 35039

Religious cases of conscience, answered in an evangelical manner. 9939; 25777

Religious celebration of independence. 30692

Religious celebration of the fiftieth anniversary of American independence. 23890

Religious celebration of the fifty-third anniversary of American independence. 37907

A religious convincement and plea, for the baptism and communion of the spirit. 9820

Religious discourses. 35124; 35125

Religious duties. 25917

Religious education: a sermon. 25409

The religious education of the

youth in our society. 8789
Religious exercises. 6606
Religious fashion. 30604a
The religious informer. 34987
Religious institutions dear to the people. 22105
The religious instruction of the slaves in the West India colonies. 31675
Religious instructions enforced. 14008; 25983
Religious liberty. A sermon. 32751
Religious liberty and Unitarianism vindicated. 9280
Religious liberty of American citizens as found on the Constitution. 40237
Religious principle, the foundation of personal safety, and social happiness. 18257; 18258
The religious principles and forms of government, of the following denominations. 2578
Religious teachers tested. 30813
The religious tradesman. 14195
The religious world displayed. 4394
Reliques of ancient English poetry. 13727; 13728
The remains of Henry Kirke White. 4270; 11411; 14893
Remains of Joseph A. H. Sampson. 30519
Remains of my early friend. 34868
The remains of Nathaniel Appleton Haven. 29172; 33505
Remains of Samuel Bartlett Parris. 39969
Remains of the late Capt. O. H. Perry. 27328
Remains of the late Rev. Charles Wolfe. 31794; 37220
The remains of the late Rev. Truman Bishop. 38934
Remains of the Rev. Carlos Wilcox. 37179
Remains of the Rev. Richard Cecil. 15705; 24044
Remarkable & shocking deaths. 40238

The remarkable captivity and surprising deliverance of Elizabeth Hanson. 16403; 16404
A remarkable conversation. 5465
Remarkable events in the history of man. 27579
The remarkable history of Elizabeth Loveless. 17781
Remarkable shipwrecks and chronological tables. 16813
Remarkable visionary dreams of a mulatto boy. 10386
Remarks, accompanying the reading of the Declaration of American independence, Dedham, July 4, 1822. 9357
Remarks addressed to the citizens of Illinois. 17782
Remarks addressed to the consciencious [!] of all denominations. 10081
Remarks addressed to the Jefferson County Agricultural Society. 725; 726; 1935
Remarks and reflections upon the trial of Colonel Talbot Chambers. 28429
Remarks, by John Dwinel. 8580
Remarks, by John E. Howard. 16599
Remarks by Mr. Woodbury. 37228
Remarks, by Richard Sullivan. 18125
Remarks, by S. W. Pomeroy. 9972
Remarks, critical and historical, on an article in the forty-seventh number of the North American review. 21068
Remarks during a journey through North America. 12851
Remarks made in the Senate upon the manufacturing bill. 2771; 29168
Remarks, made on a short tour, between Hartford and Quebec. 3225; 17985
Remarks of Charles S. Morgan. 39641
Remarks of Gershom Powers. 34507

394 Remarks

Remarks of Mr. Allen, Counsel.
7778
Remarks of Mr. Buchanan.
32507
Remarks of Mr. Everett. 33102
Remarks of Mr. Foot. 38604
Remarks of Mr. Hayne. 38941
Remarks of Mr. James Barbour.
15264
Remarks of Mr. Sergeant.
35147
Remarks of Mr. Smith. 26093
Remarks of Mr. Webster. 37111;
37112
Remarks of Servius Sulpitius.
10374
Remarks of the Hon. James Hill-
house. 29216
Remarks of the Hon. Tristam
Burges. 37998
Remarks of the Rev. Mr. Nettle-
ton. 29910
Remarks of William T. Barry.
7963
Remarks on a late article in the
Wesleyan Journal. 22053
Remarks on a letter to the Right
Hon. Lord Kenyon. 17783
Remarks on a pamphlet entitled
"Auctions." 22054
Remarks on a pamphlet printed
by the professors and tutors
of Harvard University. 16950
Remarks on a pamphlet published
by a committee of the citizens
of Berkshire. 2982
Remarks on a popular error re-
specting the Lord's Supper.
24744; 29078
Remarks on a recent publication,
styled Memoirs of the life of
Mrs. Lucy Fairfield. 13112
Remarks on a report of a committee of the overseers of Harvard College. 17451
Remarks on a report of the late
general conference. 40415;
40416
Remarks on a review of Symmes'
theory. 30437
Remarks on a sermon, published
by the Rev. Isaac Robinson.
26157

Remarks on agriculture and a
method of improving soils.
9367
Remarks on Bishop Ravenscroft's
answer. 21487
Remarks on capital punishments.
5653; 5654
Remarks on changes lately pro-
posed or adopted, in Harvard
University. 22472
Remarks on Christian liberty.
30420
Remarks on delirium tremens.
30840
Remarks on Dr. Griffin's requi-
sition for 700,000 ministers.
15410
Remarks on Dr. Ware's answer.
11476
Remarks on duelling. 32773
Remarks, on Essay on the terms
of communion at the Lord's
table. 13971
Remarks on fractures. 31744
Remarks on "General Wm. Hull's
Memoirs." 22312
Remarks on Greek grammars.
21895; 25771
Remarks on John Francis Girod's
Exposition. 896
Remarks on liberty of conscience.
34989
Remarks on ministerial exchanges.
17784
Remarks on Miss Wrights' Moral
temple. 39352
Remarks on Mr. David Millard's
late publication. 16877
Remarks on our inland communi-
cations. 34990
Remarks on prayer meetings.
38865
Remarks on prisons and prison
discipline. 26171
Remarks on religious associa-
tion. 9227
Remarks on slavery in the United
States. 30574
Remarks on soiling. 2929
Remarks, on some of the provi-
sions of the laws of Massachu-
setts. 10058
Remarks on state rights. 17785

Remarks on 'temperate societies'
To the public. 40239

Remarks on the address delivered at Washington July 4, 1821. 6920

Remarks on the address of the Honourable John Quincy Adams. 10082

Remarks on the Amherst Collegiate Charity Institution. 13920

Remarks on the banks and currency of the New England states. 24777

Remarks on the bill for the relief of the revolutionary officers. 24458

Remarks on the Catholic layman's Desultory examination. 8946

Remarks on the censures of the government. 8863

Remarks on the character and narrative of the Rev. John Clark. 5712

Remarks on the character and writings of John Milton. 24053; 24054; 32636

Remarks on the character of Napoleon Bonaparte. 28433

Remarks on the charges made against the religion and morals of the people of Boston. 1527; 3161

Remarks on the condition, character, and languages, of the North American Indians. 24034

Remarks on the constitution of the Society for the Promotion of Theological Education in Harvard University. 20394

Remarks on the constituion of the Supreme and Circuit Courts of the state of New-York. 34991

Remarks on the constitutionality of the memorial of the City Council [Boston] 17747

Remarks on the cultivation of the locust tree. 11556

Remarks on the dangers and duties of sepulture. 11578

Remarks on the different senti-

ments entertained in Christendom relative to the weekly Sabbath. 28329

Remarks on the disorders of literary men. 20018

Remarks on the distinguishing doctrine of modern universalism. 20414

Remarks on the doctrine of the influence of the Holy Spirit. 2983; 10083

Remarks on the employment of females as practitioners in midwifery. 706; 4171

Remarks on the Farmington Canal. 34992

Remarks on the genius and writings of Soame Jenyns. 25062

Remarks on the importance of the teeth. 33190

Remarks on the influence of the mind upon the body. 29148

Remarks on the internal evidence for the truth of revealed religion. 5261; 12460; 24440; 38487

Remarks on the island of Cuba. 17786

Remarks on the late publications of the First Church in Worcester. 6607

Remarks on the law of imprisonment for debt. 12817; 20867

Remarks on the legal provisions for education in Pennsylvania. 39153

Remarks on the letter from a gentleman in Boston. 34993

Remarks on the letter of Domesticus. 30282

Remarks on the miraculous character of Our Lord. 13921

Remarks on the modern doctrine of the Universalists. 17787

Remarks on the opinion of the Right Rev. Servandus A. Mier. 6608

Remarks on the perseverance of the saints. 12667

Remarks on the plan of a college. 26016

Remarks on the policy and practice of the United States and

Remarks upon the writings of
Swedenborg. 10087
Remarks upon three of Mr. Bal-
lou's principal wide-spread
publications. 10248
The remember me. 40242
Remembrance of the righteous.
33195
The remembrancer. 33831
Reminiscences and Walpoliana.
4156
Reminiscences. Moral poems
and translations. 16127
Reminiscences of Charles Butler.
15607; 19905; 28335
Reminiscences of Michael Kelley.
25019
The reminiscences of Thomas
Dibdin. 32979
Reminiscences; or, An extract
from the catalogue of General
Jackson's 'juvenile indiscre-
tions.' 32028
Remonstrance and answer of the
Bethel Free School. 15335
A remonstrance & memorial to
the General Assembly of the
state of Tennessee. 20363
A remonstrance and memorial to
the legislature, by Joseph W.
Moulton. 13414
Remonstrance of sundry merchants, manufacturers, and
others, of the city of Boston.
18943
Remonstrance of the Chamber of
Commerce of New Haven.
18944
Remonstrance of the General Assembly of Alabama. 36740
Remonstrance of the Virginia Agricultural Society of Fredericksburg. 3937
A remonstrance of the Wilmington Monthly Meeting of Friends.
24643
A remonstrance to the Congress
of the United States. 16785;
18945
Remonstrances of Seth Sweetser.
37340
Removal of the Indians westward.
31465

Remove Indians westward. 41287
The rendezvous. 27919
The renegade. 7833
The renowned history of Richard
Whittington and his cat. 23318;
27641
Renowned history of Sir Richard
Whittington, and his cat.
19274
Repair Cumberland Road. 36741
Repentance explained and en-
forced. 6972; 35512
A reply & Remarks of Philo-
Jackson on the castigations of
Shelbyville & Co. 27964
Reply of a Unitarian clergyman
to the "Letter of a gentleman
in Boston." 34998-35001
A reply of Abraham H. Schenck.
35106
Reply of Colonel Orne. 39936
Reply of Dr. Hosack's inaugural
address. 23316
Reply of Krebs and Cromwell.
37299
Reply of Mr. Trimble. 26242
Reply of Mr. Vance. 27495
A reply of the Board of managers.
To a report of a committee of
the stockholers, of the Colum-
bia, Pa. Bridge Company.
821
Reply of the Committee of mer-
chants of Philadelphia to the
Memorial of the auctioneers.
17789
The reply of the committee of the
Associate Reformed Synod of
the West. 11641
A reply of the Genesee Consoci-
ation, to the letter of the Rev.
Joseph Emerson. 38741;
38742
A reply on the affair of Mr.
James Douglas. 15999
A reply to a Catholic layman.
8947
A reply to a discourse, deliv-
ered at Newark, New-Jersey.
24771
A reply to a discourse delivered
by Rev. Mr. Giles. 16912
A reply to a letter addressed to

the Right Rev. Bishop Hobart.
12844

A reply to a letter from a Trinitarian to a Unitarian. 6611

A reply to a letter in the Christian Examiner. 38270

Reply to a letter published by Henry Orne. 38826

Reply to a letter, published by James Creighton. 11480

A reply to a letter remonstrating against the consecration of the Rev. Henry U. Onderdonk. 30425

A reply to A letter to the Right Rev. Bishop Hobart. 12845

Reply to a letter, which appeared in the American Journal. 5651

A reply to a pamphlet [Haughton] 38935

A reply to a pamphlet entitled "Objections to Unitarian Christianity considered." 9971

Reply to a remonstrance and answer of the Bethel Free School. 17735

A reply to a second letter to the author. 12951

A reply, to a series of iniquitous letters to Alexander Campbell. 17790

Reply to Abolition of slavery. 3354

Reply to an anonymous letter, containing strictures upon the doctrine and conduct of the Baptist Church. 25924

A reply to an epistle. 38695

A reply to certain calumnious statements uttered and published by Francis S. Beattie. 24398

A reply to certain insinuations, published as an article, in the sixty-eighth [i. e., fifty-eighth] number of the Quarterly review. 16867

A reply to certain oral and written criticisms, delivered against an essay on lithotomy. 2670

Reply to Col. Pickering's attack upon a Pennsylvania farmer. 21959

A reply to Col. Troup's defence of the agency of the Pulteney estate. 8916

A reply to Dr. Miller's letter to a gentleman of Baltimore. 24377

A reply to Dr. Ware's Letters to Trinitarians and Calvinists. 7701

A reply to General Andrew Jackson's letter, of the 31st October, 1828. 32786

A reply to Judge Johnson's remarks. 23754

A reply to Mr. Balfour's essays. 39040

Reply to Mr. Carey's appeal. 22057

A reply to Mr. J. Sabine's Lectures on the "Inquiry." 15159; 19505

A reply to Mr. Robinson's review of remarks upon his sermon. 30741

A reply to Messrs. Daniel W. Coxe and Henry Turner's Remarks on my Exposition. 1394

A reply to objections against his performance on Primitive theology. 9033

Reply to Rev. Hubbel Loomis's Defence of letters on Christian baptism. 4283

A reply to Sir Walter Scott's History of Napoleon. 37881; 39325

Reply to strictures on Thomas G. Fessenden's Essay on the law of patents. 12538

Reply to Sundry letters of Dr. England to the Bishop Philadelphia. 9029

A reply to sundry pretexts and remarks of the friends of Mr. Southard. 40244

Reply to T. Roberts and William E. Ashton. 1645

A reply to the accusations of John T. O'Sullivan. 6612

Reply to the address of the male members of the Methodist

Church in Baltimore. 30866

A Reply to the Catholic Layman's Rejoinder. 8948; 8949

A reply to the criticisms by J. N. Barker. 34094

A reply to the goats of Columbia. 12189

A reply to the inquiries of a freeholder. 38728

A reply to the late Manifesto. 961

A reply to the little tract entitled Necessity of Christianity to India. 7569

A Reply to the Narrative and Strictures, &c. of Mr. Nathaniel Harris. 796

A reply to the Rev. Elisha Andrew's strictures. 11993

A reply to the Rev. Ethan Smith's two sermons. 1922

Reply to the Rev. Henry J. Feltus. 3175

Reply to the Review of Dr. Beecher's sermon. 19644

A reply to the review of Dr. Wyatt's sermon. 6613; 6614

A reply to the Right Rev. Bishop David's Vindication of the Catholic doctrine. 8920

Reply to the Shakers' statements. 17029

Reply to three letters of the Rev. Lyman Beecher. 39137

Reply to two letters of William Roscoe. 31591

Report. [Bible Society of Charleston] 37842

A report accompanied with sundry letters on the causes which contribute to the production of fine sea-island cotton. 30554

Report and accompanying documents on the petition of Lot Wheelwright. 23860

Report and address of a committee of the Association, addressed to the citizens of Massachusetts. 37986

Report and Bill for the relief of the sufferers by the Fire in Savannah. 2502

Report and correspondence of the

Commissioners for promoting the internal improvement of the state. 21820

Report and Documents respecting the University of Virginia. 4122; 6589; 14791; 14792

Report and observations, on the banks, and other incorporated institutions, in the state of New York. 32505

Report and proceedings in relation to a rail road from Baltimore to the Susquehanna. 32092

Report and resolution relative to internal improvement. 27947

Report and resolutions concerning the citation of the Commonwealth to answer a complaint before the Supreme Court of the United States. 7536

Report and resolutions of the directors of Salem Mill Dam Corporation. 26009

Report and resolutions of the legislature of Georgia. 31468

Report and resolutions on the subject of the Maryland Report. 9766

Report, as amended by the inhabitants of the town of Boston. 8135

A report before the bishops and South Carolina conference of the Methodist Episcopal Church. 8250

Report by James B. Finley, of the receipts and expenditures of the Wyandott mission. 21437

Report by the committee [Society for the Encouragement of Faithful Domestics, Philadelphia] 3258

Report by the Maryland commissioners on a proposed canal from Baltimore to Conewago. 13236

Report by the New Jersey Commissioners upon the subject of a canal, from the Delaware to the Raritan. 17344; 21632

Report - Committee of accounts on contingent expenditures.

31466

Report. Committee on the Hopkins Donation. 17056

Report concerning the pauper laws of New Hampshire. 6212

Report--Director of the mint. 31467

Report. Engineer's office. 40491

Report, &c. &c. containing a jurisprudential inquiry into the original ground of the old and new grant controversy in Tennessee. 40245

Report, &c. of the Fatherless widows' society. 1205

Report, 15th [Maine Missionary Society] 9352

Report for the year 1823. [Massachusetts General Hospital] 13261

Report from the auditor of state. 21730

Report from the commissioners appointed to revise the statute laws of the state of New York. 25555

Report from the committee of superintendence for the relief of the poor. 40039

Report from the Comptroller, of a general system of taxation. 13554

Report from the Secretary of State on the subject of the laws for the relief and settlement of the poor. 17385; 17386

Report from the Secretary of the Senate showing the expenditure of the contingent fund of the Senate. 31469

Report from the Secretary of the Treasury showing the amount of revenue from imposts and tonnage in Florida. 31470

Report from the Secretary of War, with abstract of licenses granted by superintendents and agents of Indian affairs. 31471

Report from the select committee to whom was referred the memorial of Benjamin S. Judah.

17387

A report from the Treasurer of the Western Shore. 37308; 37309

Report. In obedience to the duties assigned, the Director of the Ohio Pententiary [!]. 6337

Report, in relation to the instruction of the deaf and dumb, in the city of New York. 34508

Report in the Senate, ... relative to the accounts of Daniel D. Tompkins. 2503; 2504

Report made to the committee of the citizens of Elmira, (Tioga Co.) of the Tioga Coal and Iron Mines. 39042

Report made to the General Assembly of the state of Louisiana. 9283

Report made to the Institute of France on the 22d of March, 1824. 17592

Report made to the Mayor and Aldermen of the city of Boston. 22503

Report... May 1820; to the Female Domestic Missionary Society of Charleston. 1862

Report, 9 November, 1820 [Society for propagating the Gospel among the Indians and others in North America] 3257

Report, North Carolina Senate. 17442; 17444

Report No. 1, of the Civil and Military Engineer, of the State of South-Carolina. 3279

Report of a cause tried in the District Court of Philadelphia, April 24, 1822. 10089

Report of a committee [Ancient and Honorable Artillery Company] 117

Report of a committee, appointed by a resolve of the Legislature, June 30, 1826, to revise the laws of this state. 29938

Report of a committee, appointed by the High School Society of New York. 16532

Report of a committee appointed

by the Managers of the Protestant Episcopal Missionary Society of Pennsylvania. 2898

Report of a committee appointed by the Pennsylvania Society, for Discouraging the use of Ardent Spirits. 34704

Report of a committee appointed by the Society for the Prevention of Pauperism, in the City of New York. 14155; 18031

Report of a committee appointed for the purpose of ascertaining the most eligible route for a canal from the Seneca Lake to the Erie Canal. 10382

Report of a committee appointed to consider what changes it may be necessary to make in the "Plan of agreement..." 25925

Report of a committee at a meeting of the citizens of Providence. 34929

Report of a Committee of magistrates, on the act of Congress for extending the jurisdiction of justices of the peace, &c. 12381

Report of a committee of the Bank of Pennsylvania. 37586

Report of a committee of the board of supervisors of the county of Kings. 37946; 39202

Report of a committee of the citizens of Boston and vicinity, opposed to a further increase of duties on importations. 28239; 32428-32430

Report of a committee of the city council on the ordinance and resolutions relative to schools. 37892

Report of a committee of the Connecticut Medical Society, respecting an asylum for the insane. 5064

Report of a committee of the General Assembly of Kentucky. 16786

Report of a Committee of the Legislature, on the subject of a canal by the Ousatonic Valley. 8431

Report of a committee of the overseers of Harvard College. 20830; 20831

Report of a committee of the regents of the University, appointed to visit the College of Physicians and Surgeons in the city of New-York. 25556

Report of a committee of the Senate of Kentucky. 16787

Report of a committee of the Senate relative to the affairs of the Columbia Bridge Company. 6414

Report of a committee of the Senate upon the renewal of bank charters. 6415

Report of a committee of the trustees of the Free School Society. 22009

Report of a Committee on public instruction. 17036

Report of a committee on the memorial of the resident instructors. 20832

Report of a committee to the New York Senate. 39759

Report of a select committee upon the subject of prolonging the continuance of the mint of the United States at the city of Philadelphia. 14669

Report of a special committee appointed by the Chamber of commerce, to inquire into the cost, revenue and advantages of a rail road communication between the city of Charleston and the towns of Hamburg & Augusta. 35358

Report of a special committee of the American Institute. 37444

Report of a special committee of the Senate, of South Carolina. 30666

Report of a sub-committee of the school committee, recommending various improvements in the system of instruction. 32420

Report of a survey of a route for

a railroad from Taunton to
some point in the route previ-
ously surveyed between Boston
and Providence. 39501

A report of a survey of the
Genesee Valley. 25004

A report of a survey of the Tone-
wanda canal route. 27630

Report of a trial in the Supreme
judicial court, holden at Boston, Dec. 16th and 17th, 1828,
of Theodore Lyman. 35002

Report of both branches of the
City council, who were directed to consider the expediency of applying to the Legislature for an alteration of the
City charter. 15501

Report of Charles S. Daveis, esq.
agent appointed by the executive of the state of Maine.
33981

Report of Charles Trcziyulny,
appointed to explore the river
Susquehanna. 30826

Report of commissioners appointed to settle the line between New-Hampshire and
Maine. 34441

Report of committee including a
contract with the Boston Gas
Light Co. 19800

Report of committee on laying out
new streets. 23861

Report of committee on the free
passage over South Boston
bridge. 23862

Report of committee to whom
were referred the several subjects relating to the lands lying between the County Court
House and Court Street.
23863

Report of directors of the Salem
Turnpike and Chelsea Bridge
Corporation. 3099

Report of Ebenezer T. Andrews,
chairman, on the resignation
of Francis P. Greenwood.
4797

Report of General R. M. Saunders,
on the subject of Cherokee
lands. 34572

Report of Gershom Powers,
agent and keeper of the state
prison, at Auburn. 34509

The report of Hiram Maxwell's
case. 12713

Report of James Ferguson, Esq.
engineer relative to the surveys and examinations of the
French Creek section of the
Pennsylvania canal. 38565

Report of James Mebane, Esquire, concerning works on
Cape Fear River. 39540

Report of Jarvis Hurd, esq.,
civil engineer. 24787; 29279

Report of John Rowan. 14004

Report of Joint committee on the
expediency of adopting a more
systematic accountability for
publick moneys. 15506

Report of Mr. Stevenson, chairman of the Committee on Domestic Manufactures. 9848

Report of Messrs. Benj. Wright
and J.L. Sullivan. 19340

Report of proceedings in the District Court of the United
States for the southern district of New-York. 10090

Report of regulations of the
School committee of Boston.
11926

Report of Surgeons of New York
Eye Infirmary. 6662

Report of the Adjutant General
of North Carolina. 30074;
30075; 34573; 39863

Report of the adjutant general
of the Massachusetts militia.
17057

Report of the American Board
of Commissioners for Foreign
Missions. 96; 97; 4466; 7792;
11593; 15078; 19403; 23471;
27825; 31951; 37434

Report of the Attorney General
on the subject of the state
prison and criminal code.
39399

Report of the Auditor General,
giving a statement of the accounts of the commissioners
and engineers, of the Pennsyl-

vania Canal. 30175

Report of the auditor of the State
[Maryland] 9376

Report of the Auxiliary Bible Society of Lancaster Co. 11649

Report of the Auxiliary Missionary Society at Barnstable
County, West. 27916

Report of the Bible Society of
Massachusetts. 8049

Report of the Board for Domestic Missions, within the bounds
of the Presbytery of Albany.
17689; 25825

Report of The Board for Internal
Improvements. 30076; 30077

Report of the Board of Canal
Commissioners. 17480; 34602

Report of the Board of Commissioners for Common Schools.
37008

Report of the board of commissioners, for the survey of one
or more routes for a railway
from Boston to Albany. 34066

Report of the board of commissioners of internal improvement in relation to the examination of a route for a canal,
from Boston to the Blackstone
Canal. 34063

Report of the Board of Commissioners, of internal improvement in relation to the examination of sundry routes for a
railway from Boston to Providence. 17058; 34064; 34065

Report of the Board of commissioners of internal improvements, in relation to the survey of a route for a canal from
Boston to the Blackstone canal.
39502

Report of the board of counsel
[Massachusetts Society for the
Suppression of Intemperance]
2180; 2181

Report of the Board of directors
of internal improvements of
the state of Massachusetts.
39503

Report of the board of directors
of the Georgia Presbyterian

Education Society. 38751

Report, of the board of directors
of The Northern Missionary
Society. 9734

Report of the board of directors
of the Presbyterian Education
Society. 2859

Report of the board of engineers
to the Baltimore and Ohio
Rail Road Co. 37574

Report of the Board of Internal
Improvement to the General
Assembly of North Carolina.
21704

Report of the Board of Managers
of the Charleston Bible Society. 11854

Report of the board of managers
of the Lehigh Coal and Navigation Company. 33839; 39267

Report of the Board of managers
of the United society for the
spread of the gospel. 3516

Report of the Board of public
works to the General Assembly [Georgia] 24680

Report of the board of public
works to the general assembly
[Maryland] 29649

Report of the Board of Public
Works, to the Legislature of
South-Carolina. 3278; 6827

Report of the board of the corporation of the General Synod
of the Reformed Dutch Church.
2961

Report of the Board of Trustees
[Rhode Island Bible Society]
22083

Report of the Board of Visiters
[!], on the United States Military Academy. 27486

Report of the British Charitable
Society. 28282

Report of the Canal Commissioners [Illinois] 21000;
21001

Report of the canal commissioners [New York] 25557

Report of the Canal Commissioners [Ohio] 13624; 21731;
21732; 39904; 39905

Report of the canal commission-

ers [Pennsylvania] 21822;
25695; 30176; 34684-34686

Report of the canal commission-
nrs [!] [Pennsylvania] 21821

Report of the case of Alexander
and others against the president, managers and company
of the Schuylkill Navigation
Company.   21261

A report of the case of Jeune
Eugenie.   9399

Report of the case of Joshua
Stow vs. Sherman Converse.
10091

Report of the case of Thomas
Graham.   5425

Report of the central committee
of the Chesapeake and Ohio
Canal Convention. 24079

Report of the Chamberlain to the
corporation of the City of Albany.   7766

Report of the clerk of the council, transmitting the accounts
of Henry Thompson. 13237

Report of the commission by an
act of the legislature of the
21st of March, 1823 to view
and examine all the contemplated routes for connecting
the waters of Lake Erie and
French Creek.   17559

Report of the commissioner of
the school fund [Conn.]
24200; 28576; 32808

Report of the Commissioners, appointed by a resolve of the
22d February, 1825 [Mass.]
21364; 25267

Report of the commissioners, appointed by resolution of the
General Assembly of 1828 on
the claim of the state against
the U. States [N.C.] 39864

Report of the commissioners appointed by the act of April 21,
1825 [New York] 30001-
30011

Report of the Commissioners ap-
pointed by the Governor and
Council to examine banks
[Me.] 39400; 39401

Report of the Commissioners ap-

pointed by the governor and
council to examine into the
doings and transactions of the
banks in this state [Me.]
29599

Report of the commissioners appointed by the Legislature at
their last session to build a
new state prison [Conn.]
28577

Report of the Commissioners appointed by the Legislature of
the state of New-Jersey, for
the purpose of exploring the
route of a canal. 13522;
34456

Report of the commissioners appointed by the mayor of the
city of Baltimore, to explore
and survey the route for a
canal.   19508

Report of the Commissioners appointed to examine into the
practicability of a canal from
Baltimore to the Potomac.
13238

Report of the Commissioners appointed to explore the river
Susquehanna. 13705

Report of the commissioners appointed to perform certain duties relative to the salt springs,
in the county of Onondaga
[N.Y.]   21668

Report of the commissioners appointed to represent the state
in all general meetings of the
stockholders of the several
banks of N. Carolina.   39865

Report of the commissioners appointed to revise the statute
laws of this state [N.Y.] 30014;
30015; 34510-34512

Report of the commissioners appointed to visit the American
Asylum at Hartford.   21312

Report of the commissioners by
virtue of a resolution of the
house of representatives of the
22d February, 1826 [Mass.]
25268; 29673

Report of the Commissioners concerning the western limits of

the state [Maryland] 17035;
21343

Report of the commissioners,
directed by the act of 17th
April, 1826, to visit the state-
prison at Auburn. 30016

Report of the commissioners, for
promoting the internal improvement of the state [Penn.]
25696

Report of the commissioners for
the University of Virginia.
19157

Report of the commissioners of
Alabama and Tennessee, respecting the obstructions to
navigation at the Muscle
Shoals. 26191

Report of the commissioners, of
common schools [Ohio] 9767

Report of the commissioners of
New York, relative to the
boundary line. 34513

Report of the commissioners of
public schools to the city
council of Baltimore. 37568

Report of the Commissioners of
the Board of Internal Improvements, relative to a route for
a rail road from Plymouth to
Wareham. 39504

Report of the commissioners of
the canal fund [Ohio] 21733

The report of the commissioners
of the school fund of the state
of Connecticut.   20171

Report of the commissioners of
the state of Massachusetts,
on the routes of canals.
25269

Report of the commissioners on
the boundary line between New
Hampshire and Massachusetts.
25511

Report of the commissioners on
the controversy with the state
of New-York, respecting the
eastern boundary of the state
of New-Jersey. 25523

Report of the commissioners on
the penal code [Penn.]
34687; 34688

Report of the commissioners on

the Western Railway. 37149

Report of the commissioners under of the act of separation
[Maine] 17002

Report of the committee appointed at a meeting of Charleston
merchants, traders and others.
13926

The report of the committee appointed at a public meeting of
the friends of education, held
at the State house, in Trenton.
35003

Report of the Committee appointed at a town meeting of the
citizens of the city and county
of Philadelphia. 30213

Report of the committee appointed by an order of the legislature, in June, 1826, to aid
and assist such engineers as
might be appointed by the government of the United States.
39505

Report of the committee appointed by the Baltimore and Ohio
Rail Road Company, to ex-
amine the Mauch Chunck &
Quincy Rail Roads. 27954

Report of the committee appointed by the board of directors
of the Maryland penitentiary.
34033

Report of the committee appointed by the Board of Guardians
of the Poor of the city and
districts of Philadelphia.
30214

Report of the committee appointed by the directors of
the Winnipiseogee Canal.
27678

Report of the committee appointed by the House of Representatives of Ohio, to examine
Hines & Bain's machine.
17481

Report of the Committee appointed by the House of Representatives to inquire into the conduct of the governor of the
Commonwealth of Pennsylvania.   2692

Report of the committee appointed by the House of Repre-
sentatives to inquire into the
expediency of increasing the
banking capital. [R. I.]
25937

Report of the Committee appointed by the legislature of Connecticut to inspect the condition of New-Gate Prison.
20172; 24201

Report of the committee appoint-
ed by the Legislature of Maine,
June session, 1820, to investi-
gate the doings of the Hallowell
& Augusta, Wiscasset, and
Castine banks. 5921

Report of the committee appointed by the Legislature of
Maine, June 28, 1820, on the
subject of the state valuation.
5920

Report of the Committee appointed by the Legislature to contract for the state printing,
1829 [Maine] 39402

Report of the committee, appointed by the Philadelphia Medical
Society. 40054

Report of the committee, appointed by the South Carolina Agricultural Society. 14170

Report of the committee, appointed by the stockholders of the
Albany Female Seminary.
37402

Report of the committee appointed
by the Union Society of Cincinnati. 34120

Report of the committee appointed
November session, 1820, to
revise the probate laws of New
Hampshire. 9635

Report of the Committee appointed on the 29th Dec. 1826, on
a letter of John C. Calhoun,
Vice-President of the United
States asking an investigation
of his conduct. 31472

Report of the Committee, appointed the 22nd October 1821, "to
recommend a system for the
more efficient administrations

of the town and county government" [Boston] 4779

Report of the committee appointed to amend the constitution
of the New York Athenaeum.
21677

Report of the committee appointed to analyze the waters of
Chechunk spring.   2201

Report of the committee appointed to collect information, prepare and report a system of
common schools [Ohio] 21734

Report of the Committee appointed to enquire into the official
conduct of the Hon. William
W. Van Ness.   2505

Report of the committee appointed to enquire into the official
conduct of the judges of the
Court of Appeals. 16788

Report of the Committee appointed to enquire into the practicability and expediency of establishing manufactures in
Salem.   26005

Report of the Committee appointed to examine into the state of
the Bank of Pennsylvania.
40002

Report of the committee appointed to examine the accounts of
the Treasurer, and the general state of the finances of the
city of Annapolis. 37310

Report of the committee appointed to examine the state bank
[Alabama]   27797

Report of the committee appointed to inquire into facts relative to the Amherst Collegiate
Institution. 21365

Report of the committee appointed to inquire into the expediency of bringing in a bill to
enable the people to vote at the
next general election.   17560

Report of the committee appointed to inquire into the official
conduct of Robert Porter.
21823

Report of the committee appointed to inquire into the official

Report of the Committee of finance [Va.] 11310

The report of the Committee of Grievances and Courts of Justice. [Md.] 9380

Report of the committee of Harvard University to inquire into the state of the college. 16469

Report of the Committee of Merchants & Manufactures of Boston on the proposed tariff. 15516

Report of the Committee of merchants and others, of Boston; on the tariff.   831; 2164; 25927

Report of the committee of state directors of the Bank of Pennsylvania. 37587

The report of the Committee of the Agricultural Society of South-Carolina. 37387

Report of the committee of the association of the members of the Federal Street Society for Benevolent Purposes. 19814

Report of the Committee of the City Council on the relations of the Overseers of the Poor [Boston] 15503

Report of the committee of the city council on the several petitions of the Mercantile Wharf Corporation [Boston] 23866

Report of the Committee of the city council with the opinion of Messrs. Prescott, Jackson and Webster.   19801

Report of the committee of the First Parish. 25811

Report of the committee of the Franklin Institute. 24576

Report of the Committee of the House of Representatives of Pennsylvania to inquire into the extent and causes of the present general distress. 2693

Report of the committee of the Medical Society of the city and county of New York. 2203

Report of the committee of the Physico-Medical Society of New Orleans. 6477

A report of the committee of the Rhode-Island Coal Company. 22085

Report of the Committee of the Senate appointed to inquire into the extent and causes of the present general distress [Penn.] 2694

Report of the Committee of the Senate of Maryland on internal improvements. 5956; 9381

Report of the committee of the Senate to whom was referred the memorials of the Pennsylvania Institution and the Philadelphia Asylum of the Deaf and Dumb. 21826

Report of the committee of the Senate to whom was referred the resolutions relative to foreign corporations [Penn.] 21827

Report of the Committee of the Society for the Promotion of Theological Education in Cambridge University. 18035

Report of the committee of the West Parish Association on the state of religion. 19827

Report of the Committee of Valuation [Mass.] 9412

Report of the Committee of Ways and Means [Ala.] 31916

Report of the Committee of Ways and Means [Maryland] 9382; 13239; 21344

Report of the Committee of Ways and Means [Penn.] 2695; 9849; 13706; 25697; 30177; 34689

Report of the committee on a railroad from Boston to Providence. 39506

Report of the Committee on Agriculture [Penn.] 13707

Report of the Committee on banks [N. Y.] 21669; 39800

Report of the committee on banks [Penn.] 34690

Report of the Committee on Canals [New York] 2506; 25559; 30017; 30018; 34514

Report of the Committee on

canals [Ohio] 9769

Report of the Committee on
Claims. [Maryland] 37311;
37312

Report of the Committee on common schools [Conn.] 24202

Report of the Committee on Domestic Manufactures [Penn.]
2696

Report of the committee on education [Penn.] 34691

Report of the committee on elections [Boston] 37893

Report of the Committee on finance to the corporation of the
City of Albany. 4438

Report of the committee on further protection of the city
against ravages from fire
[Boston] 19802

Report of the Committee on inland navigation [Penn.] 21828-
21830

Report of the committee on inland navigation and internal
improvement [Penn.] 25698;
30178; 40003

Report of the committee on internal improvement [Md.]
34034; 34035; 39471

Report of the committee on internal improvement [Penn.]
34692

Report of the committee on laws
to the corporation of the city
of New-York. 21645

Report of the committee on literature [N.Y.] 30019

A report of the committee on petitions and memorials [Meth-
odist Episcopal Church]
34118

Report of the Committee on Public Schools [Providence] 34927

Report of the Committee on roads
and bridges [N.Y.] 34515

Report of the Committee on Roads
and Inland Navigation [Penn.]
2697; 6416; 13708

Report of the Committee on Roads
and Railways [Mass.] 34068

Report of the Committee on
roads, bridges and inland

navigation [Penn.] 40004

Report of the Committee on state
lands [Maine] 39403

Report of the committee on the
abduction of William Morgan.
39801

Report of the committee on the
accounts of the selectmen, and
of the overseers of the poor
[Portsmouth] 25813

Report of the Committee on the
claims of Connecticut against
the United States. 8432

Report of the Committee on the
College [South Carolina Uni-
versity] 14174

Report of the committee on the
correspondence between Governor Clinton & Governor
Williamson. 25524

Report of the Committee on the
expediency of applying to the
legislature for an alteration
of the city charter [Boston]
15504

Report of the Committee on the
incorporation of banking and
insurance companies, relative
to the Fulton Bank. 17388

Report of the committee on the
late governor's accounts
[N.Y.] 2507

Report of the Committee on the
laws regulating the election of
members of the Common Council [Boston] 11927

Report [of] the Committee on the
public buildings [U.S.] 31473

Report of the Committee on the
resolutions of Georgia relative to the election of president and vice president. [N.C.]
30078

Report of the committee on the
revenue system [Ohio] 21735

Report of the committee on the
sale of public lands [Boston]
37894

Report of the committee on the
state of the republic [Georgia]
20663

Report of the committee on the
subject of an extension of suf-

A report of the debates and proceedings of the convention of the state of New York. 6254

Report of the Directing committee of the Connecticut Bible Society. 851; 24204

Report of the directors [Hampshire Education Society] 1498; 5532; 20797; 24788; 29127; 33469

Report of the directors and warden of the Connecticut State Prison. 32809

Report of the directors of the Cayuga County Bible Society. 24043

Report of the directors of the Maryland Hospital. 39472

Report of the directors of the Maryland Penitentiary. 39473

Report of the directors of the Northern Missionary Society. 6311

Report of the directors of the Salem Mill Dam Corporation. 30515

Report of the directors of the Western Education Society of the state of New York. 19248

Report of the directors to the stockholders in the Roanoke Navigation Company. 17830

Report of the doings of the superintendant [sic] for erecting the state prison at Thomaston. 17003

Report of the engineer appointed by the commissioners for the improvement of the navigation of the river Susquehanna. 30179

Report of the engineer, to the Association for the Promotion of Internal Improvements in the state of Kentucky. 41541

Report of the engineers, employed to re-survey the location of the contemplated rail road in the vicinity of Philadelphia. 40005

Report of the engineers on the Lehigh Coal & Navigation Company. 25081

Report of the engineers, on the reconnoissance and surveys, made in reference to the Baltimore and Ohio rail road. 32088

Report of the evidence and reasons of the award between Johannis Orlandos & Andreas Luriottis. 25789

Report of the evidence, arguments of counsel, charge and sentence, at the trial of Stephen Merril Clark. 6615

A report of the evidence in the case, John Atkins, appellant, vs. Calvin Sanger. 10092

Report of the executive committee; and proceedings of the Auxiliary Foreign Mission Society of Worcester. 27915

Report of the executive committee of the Bible Society of Massachusetts. 454; 4703; 19723

Report of the executive committee; with an account of the proceedings of the Auxiliary Foreign Mission Society of Worcester North vicinity. 19481

Report of the Finance committee on the amount and value of the public property of the corporation of the city of New York. 2470

Report of the finances of the Commonwealth of Pennsylvania. 9850

A report of the finances of the several counties in the state of Delaware. 992

A report of the finances of the state of Delaware. 993

Report of the general committee to the Board of Agriculture [New York] 9684

Report of the guardians of the Washington asylum. 7592

Report of the Hampshire Bible Society. 12753

Report of the Health committee [Boston] 7883

Report of the House of Delegates,

by the Committee to whom was referred, the executive communication relating to the appointment of commissioners to inspect the Potomac River. 9383

Report of the inspectors of the penitentiary to the visiting committee of the general assembly of Georgia. 16276

Report of the investigation by council of the charges against General Geddes. 15722

Report of the joint Committee appointed to examine into the state of the penitentiary institution [Virginia] 31628

Report of the Joint Committee of both houses of the General Assembly [Ohio] 2592; 6338; 6339

Report of the joint committee of Conference on the controversy over management of the Maryland Hospital. 39474

Report of the joint committee of Council and Assembly appointed to view the Morris canal and inclined planes. 34457

Report of the joint committee of councils, relative to the malignant or pestilential diseases of the summer and autumn of 1820, in the city of Philadelphia. 6447

Report of the joint committee of the Council and Assembly [N. J.] 17345; 25525

Report of the joint committee of the house of bishops, and of the house of clerical and lay deputies. 25852

Report of the joint committee of the Legislature, respecting the University of Maryland. 25242

Report of the joint committee of the Senate and Assembly on canals and internal improvements. [N. Y.] 21670

Report of the Joint committee of the Senate and Assembly, in relation to the message of the governor [N. Y.] 6255

Report of the Joint committee of the Senate and Assembly, on the application for the relief of the Greeks [N.Y.] 30020

Report of the joint committee on a prospective plan and elevation of all the streets in the city [Boston] 15505

Report of the Joint committee on agriculture and internal improvement [Georgia] 29013

Report of the joint committee on common schools [Conn.] 32810

Report of the joint committee on petition for survey for railway on one or more routes from Boston to Hudson river. 29675

Report of the Joint Committee on roads and canals, to whom was referred the petition of Samuel Hinkley. 29676

Report of the joint Committee on the state prison [Mass.] 34069

Report on the Joint select committee appointed to investigate the accounts of the Treasury Department [North Carolina] 30079

Report of the Joint select committee appointed to make suitable arrangements to secure the debt due the state from the late treasurer [N.C.] 30080

Report of the joint select committee of the Senate and House of Representatives of the state of Maine in relation to the North eastern boundary of the state. 33982; 33983

Report of the joint select committee on so much of the Governor's message as relates to opening a communication from Albemarle Sound to the Ocean. 39866

Report of the joint select committee on the building of a penitentiary in North Carolina. 39867

Report of the joint select committee, on the propriety of establishing a medical board for the state of North Carolina. 21705

Report of the joint select committee on the subject of a penitentiary & lunatic asylum [N. C.] 34574

Report of the managers of the Apprentices' Library Company. 11631; 30221

Report of the managers of the Magdalen Society. 29589; 33971; 39384

Report of the managers of the North Carolina Bible Society. 6309

Report of the managers of the Protestant Episcopal Sunday and Adult School Society of Philadelphia. 13883

Report of the managers of the Richmond and Manchester Colonization Society. 22095

Report of the managers of the Schuylkill Navigation Company. 14054

Report of the managers of the Society for the Promotion of Temperance in Ware Village. 30655

Report of the managers, read at the fourteenth anniversary of the Cincinnati Miami Bible Society. 32713

Report of the Massachusetts General Hospital. 17068

Report of the Medical College. To the General Assembly of the state of Ohio. 25294

Report of the Miami University. 25332

Report of the Mississippi Bible Society. 34164; 39613

Report of the names of all persons holding offices under this commonwealth [Penn.] 9851

Report of the overseers of the poor [Salem] 3091; 6697

Report of the Overseers of the Poor [Boston] 11928

Report of the paymaster general to the Secretary of war. 9813

Report of the Pennsylvania Society for Discouraging the Use of Ardent Spirits. 40015

Report of the Philadelphia Auxiliary Society for Meliorating the Condition of the Jews. 17606

The report of the Philadelphia Sunday and Adult School Union. 17616

Report of the physician of the Connecticut Retreat for the Insane. 20825

Report of the practicability of navigating with steam boats, on the southern waters of the United States. 33312

Report of the president and directors [Yadkin Naviation Co.] 23387

Report of the president and directors of the Connecticut River Company. 24206

Report of the President and directors of the Literary Fund. 30088; 34575

Report of the president and managers of the Schuylkill Navigation Company. 10188; 26023; 30534; 35114; 40365

Report of the president and managers of the Union Canal Company of Pennsylvania. 3509; 7028; 10504; 14331

Report of the President and Trustees of the Miami University. 13322

Report of the principal engineer, on the rail-way from the coalpits to James river [Virginia] 37034

Report of the proceedings [Congregational and Presbyterian Female Association for Assisting in the Education of Pious Youth for the Gospel Ministry] 12230

A report of the proceedings in relation to the contested election for delegate to the Nineteenth Congress, from the

the memory of John Paulding. 29964

Report of the Select committee on that part of the governor's message relating to the abduction of William Morgan. 39802

Report of the select committee on the bill for the education of the poor children of North Carolina. 39869

Report of the select committee on the division of Haywood County. 34577

Report of the select committee, on the engrossed bill from the Assembly, relative to the construction of a rail-road from the Auburn state prison to the Erie canal. 34517

Report of the select committee, relative to the construction of a rail-road from Port Kent to the Sable river. 34518

Report of the select committee, relative to the construction of a rail-road from the Hudson river to Ithaca. 34519

Report of the select committee relative to the incorporation of the Susquehannah Navigation and Rail Road Company. 34520

Report of the select committee to whom was referred a resolution relative to the sale of the public land of the United States [North Carolina] 39870

Report of the select committee to whom was referred the bill from the House, respecting the Indians in Dukes county. 29678

Report of the select committee to whom was referred the message of the Governor [New York] 25561

Report of the several trials of R. M. Goodwin. 6663

Report of the Society for Promoting the Gospel among Seamen. 6817; 35245

Report of the Society for Propagating the Gospel among the Indians and Others. 26098

Report of the South Carolina Sunday School Union. 40495

Report of the speaker of the Senate [N.C.] 30081

Report of the Special committee on the duties of the city marshal [Boston] 11929

Report of the special committee on the subject of the free bridge [Boston] 23868

Report of the Standing committee of the Howard Benevolent Society. 24902; 29261; 33597; 39035

Report of the standing committee, to the board of visitors of the Maryland Hospital. 39475

Report of the State Agent, for the Western Shore. 9384; 25243; 39476

Report of the state convention held at the capitol in the city of Albany. 34391

Report of the State Librarian [Md.] 39477

Report of the state of the Land Office [Me.] 21313

Report of the state treasurer, shewing the receipts and expenditures at the treasury of Pennsylvania. 17563; 21831; 30180

Report of the state's agent of the Western Shore of Maryland. 29651

Report of the Street Committee [New York City] 25540

Report of the Sunday School Union for the state of Maryland. 34039

Report of the superintendent of public works [South Carolina] 18055; 30668; 35359

Report of the superintendent of public works on the Edisto canal. 22329

Report of the superintendent of the Christ Church Sunday-school. 23873

Report of the superintending school-committee of Concord. 32793

Report of the survey of a section

Report of the trustees of the New-York State Library. 25562

Report of the trustees of the Rhode Island Bible Society. 3002; 22084

Report of the trustees of the State Library [New York] 21671; 39803

Report of the trustees of the Theological Seminary of Auburn. 19473

Report of the trustees of the University of Maryland. 29655

Report of the Vermont Colonization Society. 19135; 23154

Report of the Visiting School-Committee of Concord. 28566

Report of the water committee to the city council of Baltimore. 37569

Report of the Watering Committee [Philadelphia] 2734-2737; 6448; 9888; 9889; 13744; 13745; 17604; 21868; 21869; 25734; 30215; 30216; 30694; 34745; 34746; 40040

The report of the Wyandott Mission. 13318

Report of the Young Men's Bible Society of Baltimore. 37284

Report of trial, Circuit Court of the U.S. involving the claim of J. J. Astor. 30678

Report on a disease afflicting neat cattle. 8496

Report on a plan for extending & more perfectly establishing the Mechanic and Scientific Institution of New York. 17415

Report on a system of municipal government for the town of Boston. 527

Report on an additional appropriation for the improvement of Cape Fear River. 34580

Report on banks made to the House of Representatives [Penn.] 21832; 25699

A report on church order and discipline, presented to the consocation of the Western district of Fairfield County. 15843

Report on compensation of chief engineer of fire dept. [Boston] 32422

Report on county academies [Georgia] 29014

Report on limited partnerships [Pennsylvania] 17564

Report on public schools [New York City] 21646

Report on punishments and prison discipline [Penn.] 34693

Report on roads, bridges and canals [Penn.] 9852

Report on so much of the governor's message as relates to the subject of railways [Mass.] 39507; 39508

Report on that part of the governor's speech relating to the tariff [Maine] 39404

Report on the affairs of the Bangor Bank. 7890

Report on the application of the Widow of C. Carpenter. 30200

Report on the Baltimore and Susquehanna Rail Road. 32093; 40591

Report on the charitable funds [Boston] 8136

Report on the Charleston and Hamburg railroad. 40492

Report on the concerns of the New-Hampshire Cent Institution. 9639

Report on the condition of the Bank of the United States. 7891

Report on the finances [Penn.] 2698; 6420; 6421; 9853; 13711; 17565; 21833; 25700; 34694

Report on the geological structure of the county of Saratoga. 10338

Report on the geology of North-Carolina. 17443

Report on the improvement of the navigation of Neuse River. 34581

A report on the medical virtues of Secale cornutum. 5774

Report on the memorial of sundry inhabitants of Buncombe and Burke for a new county.

39871

Report on the merits of the claim of the State of Massachusetts, on the national government. 9414

Report on the money necessary for the ensuing year [Boston] 28234

A report on the navigation laws, and a report and petition on the existing tariff of duties, from the delegation of the United Agricultural Societies of Virginia. 7031

Report on the organization of the board and on the prosecution of the surveys for proposed railroads in Massachusetts. 34070

Report, on the origin and increase of the Paterson manufactories. 35438

Report on the penitentiary system in the United States. 10093; 10305

Report on the penitentiary system, made to the Senate of Pennsylvania. 6419

Report on the petition of the trustees of Hamilton College. 2509

Report on the proceedings of the General Assembly of Ohio on a National Bank. 9772

Report on the progress and present condition of the Chester County Cabinet of Natural Science. 32666

Report on the proposed canal connecting the Altamaha and Ogeechee Rivers. 32857

Report on the reduction of the city debt [Boston] 28228

Report on the state of the Anatomical museum of the University of Pennsylvania. 16591

A report on the state of the Grand Lodge of Massachusetts. 15984

Report on the state of the Mariners' Church, at the port of Philadelphia. 30235

Report, on the subject of a com-

munication, between Canandaigua lake and the Erie canal. 4908

A report on the subject of connecting manual labour with study. 34763

Report on the subject of cotton and woollen manufactories, and on the growing of wool in North Carolina. 34582

Report on the subject of education, read in the Senate of Pennsylvania. 9854

Report on the subject of weights and measures [Pennsylvania] 9855

Report on the survey of a canal from the Potomac to Baltimore. 33595

Report on the Transylvania University and Lunatic Asylum. 16789

Report on the water power, at Kingsbridge. 30424

Report presented at the annual meeting of the American Antiquarian Society. 4464

Report read before the Auxiliary Union of Lowell and Vicinity for Promoting the Observance of the Christian Sabbath. 37529

Report, read to the stockholders of the Bank of Hamilton. 27960

Report relative to actual settlers [Penn.] 9856

Report relative to executive patronage [Penn.] 9857

Report relative to Ocracoke Inlet. 30082

Report relative to the Cherokee lands. 30083

Report relative to the rail road line, from the west end of Harrisburg bridge to the borough of York. 40006

A report submitted to the Phrenological Society of the City of Washington. 34791

Report. The enlarged Committee who were instructed by a vote of the town meeting held on

the 10th day of December,
"To report what is usually
called a system of municipal
government for this town.
4779

Report. The select committee
to whom was referred a report
made on the part of the Governor's speech, in relation to
claims due to the citizens of
Michigan. 25356

Report. The standing committee
on canals [Ohio] 21736;
30109

Report. The trustees of the Lon-
donderry Presbytery Missionary Society. 21965

Report to the City council of Savannah, on the epidemic disease of 1820. 7580

A report to the directors of the
Morris Canal and Banking
Company. 29813

Report to the guardians of the
poor of the regulations for the
government of the Children's
asylum [Philadelphia] 2738

Report to the honorable, the Senate and House of Representatives of the state of Ohio.
9478

Report to the Honorable the
Speaker and members of the
House of Representatives
[S. C.] 6829

Report to the president and directors of the Mohawk and
Hudson Railway Company.
38591

A report to the Secretary of War
of the United States, on Indian
affairs. 9557

Report upon the constitutional
rights and privileges of Harvard College. 5979

Report with sundry resolutions
relative to appropriations of
public land for the purposes
of education, to the Senate of
Maryland. 5957; 5958; 7510

Reports [Religious Tract Society,
New York] 2978

Reports and minutes of proceedings on so much of the Governor's message as relates to
the banks. [N.C.] 34583

Reports and proceedings of Col.
McKenney on the subject of
his recent tour among the
southern Indians. 36785

Reports and resolutions [House
of Representatives, S. C.]
6830

Reports made to the directors of
the Massachusetts Rail Road
Association. 39526

Reports of a Committee appointed by the Managers of the
Episcopal Missionary Society
of Pennsylvania. 1109

Reports of cases adjudged in the
Court of Chancery of New
York. 17391

Reports of cases adjudged in the
Court of King's Bench. 8875

Reports of cases adjudged in the
Superior Courts of Law and
Equity of North Carolina.
39872

Reports of cases adjudged in the
Supreme Court of Pennsylvania.
2699; 13712; 13713; 40007

Reports of cases adjudged in the
Supreme Court of the state of
Vermont. 7511

Reports of cases argued and
adjudged in the Supreme
Court of Errors and Appeals
of the state of Tennessee.
18169

Reports of cases argued and
adjudged in the Supreme
Court of North Carolina.
13599

Reports of cases argued and
adjudged in the Supreme
Court of the United States.
19082; 36786

Reports of cases argued and determined in the Circuit court
of the United States. 19083;
31476

Reports of cases argued and determined in the court of appeals of Maryland. 21346;
34036

Reports of cases argued and determined in the Court of Appeals of South Carolina.
26106

Reports of cases argued and determined in the court of appeals of Virginia. 14787

Reports of cases argued and determined in the court of chancery of the state of New York.
30021

Reports of cases argued and determined in the court of common pleas. 1443

Reports of cases argued & determined in the Court of King's
bench. 1444

Reports of cases argued and determined in the Court of the
Vice Chancellor of England.
38815

Reports of cases argued and determined in the English courts
of common law. 8876; 33408

Reports of cases argued and determined in the General Court
and Court of Appeals of the
state of Maryland. 5959

Reports of cases argued and determined in the High court of
chancery. 5491; 8877; 8878;
20744-20746; 33409

Reports of cases, argued and determined in the Superior
Courts of the Eastern district
of the state of Georgia. 16277

Reports of cases argued and determined in the Supreme court;
and in the Court for the trial
of impeachments and the correction of errors, of the state
of New-York. 17392

Reports of cases argued and determined in the Supreme Court
of Alabama. 37398

Reports of cases argued and determined in the Supreme Court
of Errors of the state of Connecticut. 846; 12241; 12242;
28578

Reports of cases, argued and determined in the Supreme
Court of Judicature [New Jer-
sey] 2456; 9651; 13523;
13524

Reports of cases argued and de-
termined in the Supreme
Court of Judicature [New
York] 39804

Reports of cases argued and determined in the Supreme
Court of Tennessee. 30782

Reports of cases argued and determined in the Supreme
Court of the state of Vermont.
31602; 37009; 41371

Reports of cases argued and determined in the Supreme
Court of Vermont. 19132

Reports of cases argued and determined in the supreme judicial court of Massachusetts.
17059

Reports of cases argued and determined in the supreme judicial court of the common-
wealth of Massachusetts.
34071

Reports of cases argued and determined in the Supreme Judicial Court of the State of
Maine. 9344; 17004; 25204;
25205; 33984; 39405

Reports of cases at common law
and in equity, argued and decided in the Court of Appeals
of the commonwealth of Kentucky. 21107; 25028; 29416;
33769; 39190

Reports of cases determined at
nisi prius, in the courts of
Kings bench. 12714

Reports of cases determined in
the Circuit court of the United
States. 27338; 31477

Reports of cases determined in
the Constitutional court of
South Carolina. 3280; 10311;
18056

Reports of cases determined in
the General court of Virginia.
41386

Reports of committees in relation to the Long Island Canal
Company. 30022

Reports of criminal law cases.

14879; 19259

Reports of equity cases, determined in the Court of appeals of the state of South Carolina. 22330

Reports of Generals Newnan and Harden to his Excellency Governor Troup. 16278

Reports of judicial decisions in the Constitutional court, of the state of South Carolina. 14167

Reports of select cases in chancery, and the Supreme court of the state of New York. 25563

The reports of Sir Henry Yelverton. 1445

The reports of that reverend and learned judge, the right honorable Sir Henry Hobart. 38816

Reports of the American Institute, in the city of New-York. 37445

Reports of the Auditor and Treasurer of State [Ohio] 2593

Reports of the Female Bible and Religious Tract Society of Kings County, L. I. 8694

Reports of the library and school committees [General Society of Mechanics. New York] 38736

Reports of the Medical Society of the City of New York. 29716

Reports of the missionaries employed by the Female Domestic Missionary Society of Charleston. 12529

The reports of the most learned Sir Edmund Saunders. 20747; 33410

Reports of the proceedings and debates of the convention of 1821, assembled for the purpose of amending the constitution of the state of New York. 6256

Reports of the trials of David T. Chase and John W. Fellows. 40250

Reports of the trustees of the board of overseers, December, 1828, Maine Wesleyan Seminary. 33994

Reports on canals, railways, roads, and other subjects, made to "The Pennsylvania Society for the Promotion of Internal Improvements." 26149

Reports on the Columbia Bridge Company. 822

Reports on the course of instruction in Yale College. 37265

Reports on the improvement of the Little Schuylkill. 39298

Reports on the stepping or discipline mill, at the New York penitentiary. 11582

Reports - registers &c. St. Stephen's. Letter from the Secretary of the Treasury. 36787

Reports relative to the Chenango Canal. 35054

Reports relative to the swamp lands in North-Carolina. 30084

Repository of sacred music. 27715

Representation of the members of the House of Representatives from that part of Massachusetts hitherto known as the district of Maine. 4041

Reps. John Ellis, deceased. 36790

Representatives of Benjamin Clarke. 41294

Representatives of G. S. Wise. 23112

Representatives of Gen. Wm. Hull. 31478

Representatives of James Davenport. 36788

Representatives of John P. Cox. 27339; 36789

Representatives of Joseph Falconer. 41295

Representatives of Joseph Jeans. 31479

The reproof. 22061

The Republic of Cicero. 38173

Republican Advocate Extra. 24668

Republican anti-caucus ticket. 17792

Republican Extra. Madison,

March 4, 1823. 13928

Republican meeting. Address to the Republican citizens of the state. 17393

Republican meeting. At a meeting of the Republican members of the legislature. 17793

Republican meeting. At a primary meeting of the Republicans of the town of Providence. 22062

Republican nomination for Governor and Lt. Governor, with an address to the electors of the state of New-York. 1005

Republican nominations. At a numerous and respectable meeting of the Democratic Republicans of the City of Albany. 15053

Republican nominations. Joseph Kirkland, for Congress. 6618

The Republican; or, A series of essays on the principles and policy of free states. 1783

The republican sentiment of New-Hampshire. 35008

Republican ticket. For mayor. Hon. Josiah Quincy. 22063

Republicans of Boston! Rally to the polls. 30429

Republikaner, Wahrheit mus bestehen. 22067

Republikanische documente. 2988

A republication of two addresses, lately published in Philadelphia. 6455

The requisite tables in acquiring a knowledge of arithmetic. 6619

Researches and observations on the use of phosphorus. 21238

Researches, philosophical and antiquarian, concerning the aboriginal history of America. 39357

Reservations under the Cherokee treaty. 36791

Resignation. An American novel. 20440

Resolution in opposition to proposed amendment to constitu-

tion establishing national banks [New Jersey] 2448

Resolution of the General Assembly of Indiana in favor of the encouragement of domestic manufactures and internal improvements. 36801

Resolution of the General Assembly of Indiana in relation to purchasers of public lands. 31482

Resolution of the General Assembly of Indiana, relative to the western mail route from Louisville. 36802

Resolution of the General Assembly of the state of Indiana, in reference to Major General Lafayette. 23115

Resolution of the General Assembly of the state of Indiana upon the subject of the lands set far apart for the use of schools. 31483

Resolution of the Legislative Council of Florida on the expediency of providing for the graduation of the price of public lands. 36803

Resolution of the Legislature of Alabama, proposing amendments to the Constitution. 36804

Resolution of the Legislature of Georgia, on the subject of militia claims. 31484; 31485

Resolution of the Legislature of Indiana requesting from the government, copies of the Journal of the Federal Convention. 36805

Resolution of the Legislature of Pennsylvania. Dec. 24, 1829. 41300

Resolution of the Legislature of Pennsylvania instructing their senators, and requesting their representatives in Congress to procure the establishment of such a tariff as will afford additional protection to domestic manufactures. 36806

Resolution of the state of Rhode

The resolutions of Virginia and
Kentucky; penned by Madison
and Jefferson. 25930; 27517;
35009

Resolutions of the state of Alabama in relation to the system
for the disposal of the public
lands. 31492

Resolutions passed at a meeting
of certain manufactures of
Philadelphia and others of the
city and county of Philadelphia
in favor of an increase of duties on imports. 36820

Resolutions presented by Mr.
Speaker, in committee of the
Whole on the state of the Union.
4051

Resolutions. Public lands for
popular education. 36821

Resolutions relative to slavery,
offered in Assembly, November 1, 1820. 3288

Resolutions submitted by Mr.
Davis, of S.C. 36822

Resolutions submitted by Mr.
Poinsett. 23121

Resolutions submitted to the senate by Thomas S. Grimke.
33440

Resolutions to amend the Constitution of the United States.
23122; 27353

Resolve regulating the choice of
electors of President and Vice-
President of the United States.
2165

Resolve that the commissioners
of internal improvements be
directed to survey the railway
from Boston, state line of
Rhode Island. 29679

Resolved by the Senate and House
of Representatives of the Commonwealth of Pennsylvania in
General Assembly met, that
the Committee on inland navigation be instructed to report
a bill constituting a board of
some commissioners for internal improvement. 21834

Resolved, That the resolutions
on the state of the College be

referred to a committee
[Penn.] 17586

Resolves establishing the seat of
Government [Maine] 29600

Resolves of the fourth Legislature of the state of Maine.
17005

Resolves of the fifth Legislature
of the state of Maine. 21314

Resolves of the General court of
the commonwealth of Massachusetts. 2166; 2167; 5980;
9416; 9417; 13255; 13256;
17060; 25271; 29680; 29681;
34072; 37318; 39509; 39510

Resolves of the legislature of the
state of Maine. 2080; 5922;
9345

Resolves of the ninth Legislature
of the state of Maine. 39406

Resolves of the seventh Legislature of the state of Maine. 29601

Resolves of the sixth legislature of
the state of Maine. 25206

Resolves of the state of Maine.
33985

Resolves of the third legislature of
the state of Maine. 13203

Resources of the adversary and
means of their destruction.
28090

Respected friend. By direction
of the Board of managers of
the Chester County Auxiliary
Colonization Society. 28453

A response, by a committee of
the First Baptist Church, in
Lexington, Ky. 29496

The response of Charles Miles
to the report of the president
of the Bank of Kentucky.
39595

The response of the judges of
the court of appeals, to the
preamble, resolutions and
address, proposed by a joint
committee of the Senate and
House of Representatives.
16790

Response to the celebrated ballad
of My heart & lute. 21509

Responses of Judges Saffold,
White and Crenshaw to cer-

tain charges preferred against them. 40342

The responsibilities of rulers. 32454; 32455

The rest of the nations. 25304

Rest! warrior rest! 21096-21099

Rest! weary traveller. 4827; 4828

Restoration of deserters. 27354

Result of a mutual ecclesiastical council, convened at Worcester, Nov. 14, 1820. 840

Result of an ecclesiastical council held at Dartmouth. 5053

Result of council, sermon, charge, address, (etc) at the installation of Ezekiel L. Bascom. 6621

The retired muse, or Forest songster. 21374

The Retort. 13932

Le retour de Kips Hill. 9370

Retratos politicos de la revolucion de España. 25077

The retreat, or sketches from nature. 6622

Retrenchment. 41301

The retrospect: or, Reflections on the goodness of providence, in the works of creation, redemption, &c. 19628

The retrospect; or, Review of providential mercies. 5940; 9361

Retrospection. A sermon. 12836

Retrospection: a tale. 10413

Retrospective theology. 20401

Return, O my love sung by Mrs. G. Barrett. 29022

Return of the state of Dismal Swamp Canal Company. 23123

Returning prodigal. 2989

Returns made by the trustees of the several incorporated literary institutions to the secretary of state [Maine] 39407; 39408

Reuben Apsley. 30631

A revelation of free masonry. 32820

Revelation the foundation of faith. 40215

Revelations in masonry. 30430

The revenge: a tale. 13641

The revenge; a tragedy. 11501; 11502

Revenue at Key West. 27355

Revenue laws and custom-house regulations. 4055; 5167; 15952

Revenue of the United States. 31493

Rev. Dr. Furman's exposition of the views of the Baptists, relative to the coloured population. 12633

The Rev. Legh Richmond's counsels to his children. 35037

Rev. Mr. Cooke's election sermon. 20185

Rev. Mr. M'Ilvaine in answer to the Rev. Henry U. Onderdonk. 29573; 33950

The Rev. Mr. Payson's interesting address to seamen. 17538

Rev. Mr. Sewall's poem, on the mode of baptism. 3176; 3177

Rev. Mr. Whittelsey's Seminary catalogue. 41512

Rev. W. V. Harold, D.D. Rev. Sir. - On the 24th ult. a large and respectable meeting of the pewholders and other Roman Catholics, worshipping in St. Mary's Church. 30240

A review and refutation of Haring's errors of Hopkinsianism. 17799

A review and refutation of short notices and reviews, contained in the Monthly Evangelical Witness. 18171

A review and refutation of the statements made in the late report of the canal commissioners. 37022

A review first published in the Christian Spectator for June 1829. 38784

A review of A debate on Christian baptism. 22020

A review of a discourse on the sovereignty of God. 40124

Review of a late pamphlet.
33463

Review of a Lecture Sermon, delivered in the Second Universalist Meeting-House in Boston. 4526; 4527

Review of a "Letter from a gentleman in Boston to a Unitarian clergyman of that city." 32396-32398

Review of a letter from Elias Hicks to Dr. N. Shoemaker. 40251

Review of a pamphlet, called "A testimony, and epistle of advice." 33346

Review of a pamphlet, entitled "An epistle and testimony, from the Yearly Meeting of Friends, held in New-York." 35564

A review of a pamphlet, entitled Observations on a sermon, delivered by John E. Latta. 13933

A review of a pamphlet entitled "The doctrine of the immediate happiness of all men." 14902

A review, of a pamphlet, entitled, Universalism, or, The rich man and Lazarus. 28819

Review of a pamphlet on the trust deed of the Hanover Church. 35010

Review of "A pedestrian tour of two thousand and three hundred miles in North America." 8647

Review of a report of the committee, to whom was referred the several petitions on the subject of mails on the Sabbath. 37745; 40252-40254

Review of a "Review of Dr. Freeman's sermons." 5744

A review of a sermon by Rev. Ebenezer Gay of Stoughton. 691

A review of a sermon delivered at New York, December 7, 1826. 25607

Review of a sermon, delivered by Stephen Bovell. 4809

A review of a sermon, delivered in the chapel of Yale College. 38931

Review of a sermon, entitled, "The Christian bishop approving himself unto God." 27685; 37217

Review of a sermon, recently published by Abner Kneeland. 24383

Review of a sermon, styled Baptism not regeneration. 5130

A review of an "Address," professing to be a vindication of the Baltimore annual conference. 28725

A review of "An appeal to the Christian public from the unprovoked attacks of the Reverend George Duffield, against the Methodist Episcopal Church. 35011

Review of An ecclesiastical memoir of the Essex-Street Society. 13934

Review of Brownlee on Quakerism. 22068

Review of Dr. Beecher's sermon at Worcester. 19166

Review of Dr. Chalmers's sermon respecting the theological sentiments of Sir Isaac Newton. 6623

A review of Dr. Church's two sermons, on the final condition of all men. 32080

A review of Doct. Emmon's theory, of God's agency on mankind. 6624

Review of Dr. Freeman's sermons. 4452

Review of Du Ponceau on the jurisdiction of the courts of the United States. 17800

A review of Elias Hicks' letter to Dr. Nathan Shoemaker. 17801

A review of Elias Hicks' letter to Thomas Willis, on the miraculous conception of our Lord and Savior, Jesus Christ. 17802

A review of Gen. Jackson's letters to Mr. Monroe. 22069

Review of Histoire de l'astronomie ancienne et moderne. 1203

Review of Johnson's English dictionary. 34793

Review of Lynn. 6625

A review of Mary M. Dyer's publication. 17943

Review of Mr. Beckwith's dissuasive. 37530

Review of Mr. McClintock's History and mystery! 30430a

Review of Mrs. Hemans' Forest sanctuary. 25608

Review of "Notions of the Americans, picked up by a travelling Bachelor. 32588

Review of pamphlets on the rights of the churches. 40255

Review of pamphlets on the Theological seminary of the Protestant Episcopal Church. 2990

A review of political opinions, published for the benefit of the people of Kentucky. 7892

Review of Prof. Frisbie's inaugural address. 13602

A review of Remarks by Rev. T. R. Sullivan. 30470

Review of Rev. Mr. Whitman's discourse on regeneration. 35012

A review of Rev. Mr. Whitman's discourse, preached before the Second Religious Society in Waltham. 30431

A review of Rev. Thomas Andros's essay on the doctrine of divine efficiency. 6959

A review of some parts of the Rev. S. W. Crawford's sermon on creeds and confessions. 29418

Review of the address by Hon. John Q. Adams, at Washington, on 4th of July, 1821. 6842

Review of the answer to the remonstrance sent to the bishops of the Protestant Episcopal Church. 30432

A review of the battle of the Horse Shoe. 35013

Review of the case of the free bridge between Boston and Charlestown. 30433

Review of the controversy between the Methodists and Presbyterians in central Virginia. 40256

A review of the correspondence between the Hon. John Adams, late president of the United States, and the late Wm. Cunningham. 17635; 17636; 21896

A review of the diseases of Dutchess County. 26071

Review of the "Doctrines of the Church vindicated from the misrepresentations of Dr. John Rice." 30447

A review of the efforts and progress of nations, during the last twenty-five years. 22281

A review of the evidence of the pretended general conspiracy of the Roman Catholics of Ireland. 12063

A review of the evidences of Christianity. 39226

A review of the general and particular causes which have produced the late disorders and divisions in the yearly meeting of Friends, held in Philadelphia. 38210

A review of the Layman's essay on the Sabbath. 39142

A review of the letters of the late Rev. John Bowden. 11448

Review of the "Life of Michael Martin, who was executed for highway robbery." 8398

Review of the Maryland report, on the appropriation of public lands for schools. 5960; 6837

Review of the mayor's report, on the subject of schools. 32064

Review of the memoir of Josiah Quincy Jr. 25888

A review of the minutes and proceedings of The Presbytery of Buffalo. 30328

Review of the opinion of the Supreme Court of the United States, in the case of Cohens vs. Virginia. 5531

Review of the pastoral charge delivered by the Rt. Rev. Henry, bp. of Pennsylvania. 4988

A review of The philosophy of the human mind. 19639

A review of the plan of education in South Carolina. 6626

A review of the present systems of medicine and chirurgery of Europe and America. 5200

A review of the principal doctrines of Elias Hicks. 22070; 25931

A review of The progress of religious opinions. 30616

Review of the report of a committee of the citizens of Boston and vicinity, opposed to a further increase to duties on importations. 35014; 35015

Review of the report of a committee of the Medical Society of the City of New York, on Dr. Chambers' remedy for intemperance. 30434

Review, of the report of the case of the Commonwealth versus David Lee Child. 40257

Review of the Reports of the American Colonization Society. 13935

A review of the Rev. Dr. Channing's discourse. 30435; 30436

Review of the Rev. Jared Sparks' letters on the Protestant Episcopal Church. 2991

A review of the Rev. Mr. Colman's sermon. 20196; 20197

Review of the sermon preached before the Bible Society of North Carolina. 23361

Review of the speech of Henry Brougham. 32489

A review of the testimony issued by the orthodox seceders from the monthly meetings of Westbury and Jericho. 39290

A review of the trade and commerce of New York from 1815 to the present time. 2992

A review of the trial of John Alley, Jr. and others. 13936

Review of the trial of O. Bachelor. 37535

A review of the whole truth. 10095

Review of three pamphlets lately published by the Rev. W. V. Harold. 8276; 8277

Review of tracts published by the American Unitarian Association. 27851

Review of Webster's American dictionary. 35016; 39203

The review, or The wag of Windsor. 28550

Review. The Reverend Rector of the Roman Church in Frederick-Town, vs. The Young Men's Bible Society. 37333

Reviews of Whilldin's essay on dropsy. 6627

A revisal of the laws of the state of North-Carolina. 30085

The revised act of the Legislature of the state of New York, respecting highways and bridges. 39805

The revised code of laws, of Illinois. 29310; 39080

The revised Code of the laws of Mississippi. 17177

A revised copy of The dying Christian. 8964

The revised form of government, and forms of process of the Presbyterian Church. 2853

Revised impression of the new system of practical arithmetic. 17803; 19661; 23751; 28103; 32268

The revised laws of Indiana. 16661

Revised report of the Board of Engineers on the defence of the sea board. 27356

Revised statute [N.Y.] 9686; 30023-30027; 34521; 39806

Revised Testament. 15392

The revised Twenty-five dollar
act. 9687
Revival hymns. 12919
Revivals of religion, considered
as means of grace. 29250
Revolutionary officers. 27357;
27358
The revolutionary officers. To
the Congress of the United
States. 32589; 32590
Revolutionary pensioners. 27359-
27361
The Revolutionary soldier's lullaby. 10357
The revolving alphabet. 617
The reward of ingratitude. 2993
Rewards and punishments. A
sermon. 28979
Reynaldo y Elena; o, La sacer-
dotisa peruana. 10463
A rhetorical grammar. 11330
The Rhode-Island Almanack.
3001; 6636; 10104; 13942;
17815; 22081; 22082; 25938;
30444; 35021; 40265
Rhode Island - citizens of Bristol. Memorial. 36823
Rhode Island. Memorial of a
committee in behalf of cotton manufacturers, of Providence. 36824
Rhode Island. Memorial of citizens of the town of Warren.
36825
Rhode Island. Memorial of the
auctioneers of Providence.
41302
Rhode Island. Memorial of the
farmers and manufacturers of
the county of Kent. 36826
Rhode Island. Petition of inhabitants of Newport. 36827
The Rhode-Island Register and
United States Calendar. 3003;
6637; 10106; 13944; 17817;
22086; 25939; 30446; 35023;
40266
Rhode Island. Representation of
sundry citizens of Providence.
36828
Rhode Island. Resolution of the
General Assembly. 36829
Rhode-Island tales. 39037

The rhyming alphabet. 40268
A rhyming dictionary. 14813;
37069
The rich man and Lazarus: a
discourse delivered in the
Universalist Church. 16366
The rich man and Lazarus! An
explanatory sermon, delivered
on the third Sabbath in July,
1822. 10363
The rich man in hell. 33187
Richard and James, or, The
duty of obedience. 3007
Richard Biddle, administrator
of John Wilkins. 36830; 41303
Richard Drummond. 36831
Richard Eppes. 36832
Richard G. Morriss. 36833
Richard H. Wilde. 36834;
36835
Richard Key--Insurance Company
of Baltimore, & Robert E.
Griffith, et al. 27362
Richard Livingston. 31494
Richard Peacock. 36836
Richard the Third. 10241;
37336
Richard W. Eppes. 41304
Richard W. Meade. 27363;
36837
Richard W. Steele. 27364;
31495; 36838
Richard Wall. 36839
Richardson's American reader.
13946
Richelieu: a domestic tragedy.
25680
Richelieu; a tale of France.
39118
Richmond alarm. 10108
The Richmond and Alexandria
Builder's Price Book. 3018
Richmond and Manchester Colon-
ization Society. 30454
Richmond; or, Scenes in the life
of a Bow Street officer.
30745
Richmond's march. 6646
Riddle, Becktill, and Headington.
36840
Riddle-book. 17825; 22096;
25945
Riego's celebrated quick step.

16608
Rienzi: a tragedy. 39622
Rifle drill. 23124; 29939
The right aim. 32898; 38340
The right object and use of religious investigation. 33951
The right of free discussion. 40282
The right of private judgement in religion. 6482
The right of Universalists to testify in a court of justice vindicated. 35042
The Right Rev. Dr. Doyle's letters to the Duke of Wellington. 33009
The right uses of afflictions. 24759
Righteousness the safe-guard and glory of a nation. 29112
Rights and disabilities of Brevet Rank. 22100; 22101
The rights of children defended. 6360
The rights of man to property. 40435
The rights of men and things. 13953
The rights of states to annul charters considered. 12419
The rights of the Congregational churches of Massachusetts. 28569; 28570
The rights of the Congregational parishes of Massachusetts. 29548; 29549
Rights of women vindicated in the following sermon. 38910
Riley's new instructions for the German flute. 6650
Riley's second sett of cotillions. 17828
Rime of the ancient mariner. 28545
Rinaldo Rinaldini der Räuber-Hauptmann. 4131
A ring of gold she gave to me. 39358
The ring; or, The thief discovered. 40284
Ringan Gilhaize; or The Covenanters. 12642
Rip Van Winkle. 1856; 39193

The rise and progress of religion in the soul. 5193; 8558; 8559; 12387; 20325; 28715; 32999
Rise gentle moon. 328
The rival queens. 5810
The rivals, a comedy. 10256; 10257; 26067
The rivals of Acadia, an old story of the New World. 28447
The rivals of Este, and other poems. 37951
The rivers of Pennsylvania. 21854
Road--Baltimore to Philadelphia. 31496; 36841
Road between Jackson and Columbus, Mississippi. 27365
Road - Cantonment Gibson to Natchitoches. 27366
Road - Cumberland to District of Columbia. 27367
Road - Detroit to Chicago. 27368
Road from Baltimore to Philadelphia. 27369
Road from Buffalo to Hanover. 27370
Road from Columbus to New Orleans. 36852
Road from Detroit to Lake Michigan. 27371
Road from Washington city to Buffalo. 31500
Road from Washington to New Orleans. 27372
Road from Wheeling to Missouri. 27373
Road from Zanesville, Ohio, to St. Louis, Missouri. 41307
Road--Homochitto Swamp. 36842
Road--La Plaisance Harbor, westward. 31497
Road - Lawrenceburg to Fort Wayne, Indiana. 36843
Road - Little Rock to Cantonment Gibson. 27374
Road, Miami of Lake Erie to Detroit. 27375
Road - Memphis to Tuscumbia. 36844
Road--Mobile to New Orleans. 41305

Romances of real life. 38801
Rome in the nineteenth century.
28753; 28754
Romeo and Giulietta; a serious
opera. 27731
Romeo and Juliet. 10242
The romp. 15400
Rondinetto, from Il Barbierre
de Seville. 1933
Rondo and introduction. For the
piano forte. 22098
A rondo for the piano forte.
5328
Roorbach's country almanack.
25965
Rosa, a melo-drama. 9090
Rosabell; or, The queen of May.
25966
Rosabella; or, The queen of
May. 30481
Rosalind. 13010
Rosamond. [Edgeworth] 1078;
5231; 5232; 24403
Rosamond, or The purple jar.
6665
Rose and Agnes: or, The dan-
gers of partiality. 31802
Rose & Emily; or, Sketches of
youth. 13961
The rose had been wash'd. 1879
The rose in June. 6090
The Rose of Arragon. 9174;
9175
The rose of love! 9059
Rose of Lucerne. 329
The rose of the valley. 11892;
15444
The rose that weeps with morn-
ing dew. 12873
Roses when they bloom the fair-
est. 23259
Rosina, a comic opera. 8183
Roslin Castle. 10137
Le rossignol. 21865
Rossini's celebrated cavatina "Di
piaca mi balza il cor."
17853
Rossini's grand march from the
opera Il barbiere di Sevigla.
22126; 22127
Rothelan. 20626
The roue. 32249
Rough notes taken during some

rapid journeys across the
pampas and among the Andes.
29183
Round Hill exhibition. 25970
Round my own pretty rose. 1927
The round table. 10146
Rousseau's dream, an air. 905
Route of the proposed canal
from Conewago to Baltimore.
14003
Row gently here. A popular
Venetian air. 8080; 8081
Rowlett's Tables of discount. 25974
Roy's wife. 1433; 1434
Roy's wife of Aldivalloch. 1435;
17868
Rudimental lessons in etymology
and syntax. 25950
The rudiments of architecture.
389
The rudiments of chemistry.
13664; 17521; 25668
The rudiments of English gram-
mar. 22338
Rudiments of geography. 7692;
7693; 11473; 14968; 23365;
27692; 37227; 41581; 41582
The rudiments of Latin and English grammar. 10-12; 23410
The rudiments of Latin grammar.
20726
Rudiments of the art of playing
on the piano forte. 1438;
20739
The rudiments of the Latin
tongue. 6680-6682; 10157;
30490
Rudiments of the Spanish language. 26011
Rufiana; or, The poetical sin-
nings of William Rufus.
25984
Rugantino; or, The bravo of
Venice. 9263
Las ruinas, escritas en frances
por el señor de Volney.
11319
Ruinous consequences of profan-
ing the Sabbath. 34005
The ruinous tendency of auction-
eering. 14012; 35077
The ruins of Paestum. 9933
Ruins of Troy. 23419

The ruins: or, A survey of the revolutions of empires. 11320; 14797

Rule a wife and have a wife. 355; 8716

The rule and exercises of holy living.   3403; 3404

Rules [New York Hospital Library.] 2531

Rules adopted by the president and directors of the Chesapeake and Ohio Canal Company. 32665

Rules adopted by the Supreme Court of Errors and Appeals in the state of Tennessee. 22438

Rules adopted by the Supreme Court of the state of Ohio. 13626

Rules adopted in joint-meeting, October, 1825 [New Jersey Legislature] 21633

Rules and By-Laws for the Universalist Society, in Roxbury. 3073

Rules and by-laws of the Salem Mechanic Library. 6704; 14036

Rules & catalogue of the Social Law Library. 18027

Rules and confessions of faith of the First Presbyterian Church constituted in Savannah. 30529

Rules and directions for cutting men's clothes. 9166

Rules and orderrs [!] of the Common Council [Boston] 8137

Rules and orders for conducting business, in the House of Representatives of the United States. 11274

Rules A(nd orders?) for regulating the practice in the courts of common pleas of the Ninth Circuit.   6422

Rules and orders of the Assembly of the state of New York. 39807

Rules and orders of the Common Council of the City of Boston. 11930; 15507; 23870; 28235

Rules & orders of the Court of Chancery and of the Court of the Trial of Impeachments and the Correction of Errors of the state of New York. 17394

Rules and orders of the Court of chancery of the state of New Jersey.   13525

Rules and orders of the Court of chancery of the state of New-York.   17395; 39808

Rules and orders of the Court of Common Pleas of Queens County.   17741

Rules and orders of the House of Representatives [U. S.] 11275; 36863

Rules and orders of the House of Representatives of the state of New Hampshire. 17330; 21623; 25512; 29940; 34442

Rules and orders of the Senate and House of Representatives [N. H.] 6213

Rules and orders of the Senate of the state of New York. 30028

Rules and orders of the Supreme court of judicature of the state of New-Jersey. 34458

Rules and orders of the United States supreme court. 41308

Rules and orders ordained and established for regulating and conducting business in this court [Maine] 21315

Rules and orders to be observed by the Fire Society, instituted in Falmouth. 30310

Rules and orders to be observed in the convention of delegates for the Commonwealth of Massachusetts.   2168

Rules & orders to be observed in the House of assembly of the state of New-Jersey. 9652

Rules and orders to be observed in the House of Representatives of the commonwealth [Massachusetts] 29682; 39511

Rules and orders to be observed in the House of Representa-

Rules and regulations of the Lexington Artillery. 25106

Rules and regulations of the Newton Theological Institution.
25591

Rules and regulations of the
Northern Dispensary. 6310;
25746; 30237; 34767; 40055

Rules and regulations of the Primary School Committee of the
city of Boston. 19803; 23869

Rules and regulations of the True
Republican Society in the City
and Liberties of Philadelphia.
14320

The rules and regulations of the
United Societies of the Wesleyan Methodists. 6033

Rules and regulations of the
Washington Light Infantry.
27567

Rules and regulations to be observed in the library of the
Legislature of Maryland.
29652

Rules and specifications, relating
to the construction of the Ohio
Canal. 39908

Rules and standing docket of the
Synod of Kentucky. 40145

Rules and statutes of the University of Pennsylvania. 2717

Rules for conducting business in
the Senate of Louisiana. 25151

Rules for government of St.
John's Church. 2745

Rules for holy living. 697

Rules for regulating the practice
of the Court of Common Pleas,
Quarter Sessions, and Orphan's
Court of Philadelphia County.
17566

Rules for regulating the practice
of the District court for the
city and county of Philadelphia.
21870

Rules for regulating the practice
of the District Court of the
United States, for the western
district of Pennsylvania. 19104

Rules for settling Militia claims.
27380

Rules for the admission of members into the Baptist Church
in Charleston. 32643

Rules for the construction of masonry on the Ohio Canal. 39909

Rules for the government of the
association of the Second Presbyterian Church, Charleston,
S. C. 20035

Rules for the government of the
board of guardians [Alms-
House of Philadelphia] 34747

Rules for the government of the
Charleston chamber of commerce. 32642

Rules for the government of the
Common Council. [Philadel-
phia] 2739

The rules for the management of
the Friends Asylum for the Insane. 34759

Rules for the Supreme Court and
the Court of Chancery for the
state of Vermont. 7513

Rules of Christ Church Academy,
at Cow Neck, Long-Island.
20054

Rules of college wood-yard.
[Yale University] 23391

Rules of court, S. J.C. [Mass.]
2169

Rules of discipline of the yearly-
meeting held on Rhode-Island
for New England. 24639

Rules of discipline of the yearly
meeting of Friends held in
Philadelphia. 20611; 33306

Rules of discipline of the yearly
meeting of Friends, held in
Virginia. 24642

Rules of order for the Board of
common council of the city of
Washington. 7591

Rules of practice at law and in
equity established by the judges
of the Superior courts of the
state of Georgia. 29015

Rules of practice for the courts
of equity of the United States.
11276-11279

Rules of practice in Baltimore
County Court. 37570

Rules of practice in the Courts
of equity, for the several cir-

cuits of the state of New-York. 13555

Rules of practice in the Superior Court of the city of New York. 34522

Rules of procedure adopted by the Consociation of the Eastern District of New Haven County. 15845

Rules of pronunciation, in reading Latin. 32003

Rules of prosody, for the use of schools. 30491

Rules of the American Education Society. 31957

Rules of the bar of the county of Suffolk. 30736

Rules of the bar of the county of Worcester. 37247

Rules of the Charleston Unitarian Book Society. 24067

Rules of the Courts of common pleas, and general quarter sessions of the peace, of the county of Gloucester. 13526

Rules of the Courts of Common Pleas and Mayor's Court [Albany] 4439

Rules of the District Court of the United States for the Northern District of New-York. 19105

Rules of the Female High-School in the City of New York. 24520

Rules of the General Assembly of the Presbyterian Church. 10003

Rules of the gymnasium of Harvard University. 24805

Rules of the House of Representatives [Vermont] 19133

Rules of the male confraternity of the Blessed Virgin Mary, established in Baltimore. 14013

Rules of the New-England Society, of Charleston, S. C. 2425

Rules of the Park Fire Society, formed Nov. 1825. 19820

Rules of the Philadelphia Dispensary. 9892

Rules of the Portland Dispensary and Vaccine Institution. 21950

Rules of the Senate and House of Representatives of New Hampshire. 17331

Rules of the Senate of New-Hampshire. 13507; 25513

Rules of the South Carolina Association. 14171

Rules of the South Carolina Society. 30673

Rules of the Southern Dispensary. 9902; 13754; 17615; 21878; 25751

Rules of the Superior Court of the Territory of Arkansas. 32025

Rules of the Supreme, Circuit and County Courts, of the state of Alabama. 57

Rules of the Supreme Court and Court of Chancery for the state of Vermont. 7512

Rules of the Supreme Court of Pennsylvania. 34695

Rules of Union chapter, no. 3, Royal-Arch Masons. 1317

Rules, orders, and by-laws, made by the freeholders and inhabitants of the town of Salem. 10172

Rules, regulations and by-laws for the government of the vestry and other officers of the Episcopal Church of St. Paul. 13752

Rules, regulations and instructions for the Naval service. 4057

Rules, regulations, and orders of the Boston board of health, relative to the police of the town. 4784

Rules, regulations, &c. [Albany Academy for Girls] 31918

Rules to be observed by the Assistant Guardians of the Poor. 4502

Rules to be observed by the House of Representatives in the choice of a president of the United States. 23125

Rumfustion innomorate, or The court of Quadlibet. 22156

Run Jerry run. 11637

The runaway: or A keen joke.

22157
Rural felicity. 14015
Rural hours, a poem. 16243
Rural rambles. 25987
Rural scenes, or A peep into the
country for children. 14016;
30770; 40617
Russian march. 14021; 22159-
22161
Russian march, and the Emperor
Alexanders waltz. 3081;
6686; 14022; 14023
Russian tales. 25211
The Russian waltz. 2643
The rustic reel. 2221; 17108
Rutgers Medical College. 30500
Ruth Lee. 32402; 40337
Rybrent de Cruce. 38950

S

The Sabbath. A discourse on the
duty of civil government, in
relation to the sanctification
of the Lord's day. 41557
The Sabbath as a rest to be oc-
cupied in personal, domestic
and social religion. 30097
Sabbath occupations. 20509;
22171; 40341
Sabbath recreations. 40610
The Sabbath scholar. 8536
Sabbath school addresses. 33992
The Sabbath school directory.
35088
The Sabbath school guide. 35193;
35194; 40418
Sabbath school hymns. 25998
Sabbath school psalmody. 32222
Sabbath school remembrancer.
3083
Sabbath school scenes. 40339
Sabbath school teacher's visits.
40340
The sabbatical institute, an Ora-
tion. 32017
Sabina ó Los Grandes sin dis-
fraz. 35089
Sacramental exercises. 5222
Sacramental meditations and ad-
vices, grounded upon Scrip-
ture texts. 7677

Sacramental meditations, upon
divers passages of scripture.
16155
The sacred and profane history
of the world. 17982
Sacred biography, or, the His-
tory of the Patriarchs. 33619
Sacred books of New Testament,
expounded. 31663
Sacred concert [Middlesex Har-
monic Society] 9481
Sacred concert, to be performed
at the Rev. Dr. Bancroft's
church in Worcester. 30507
A sacred concert, to be per-
formed at the Rev. Mr.
Ware's church. 17876
Sacred dramas. 25419
Sacred geography. 17999
Sacred manual. 6928
Sacred melodies. 32764
The sacred minstrel. 33478
Sacred music; an address deliv-
ered at Westhampton, May 23,
1827. 30842
Sacred music; containing a great
variety of psalm and hymn
tunes. 8616
The sacred origin and divine au-
thority of the Jewish and
Christian religions. 13118
Sacred poetry. 377; 35090
Sacred songs, duetts, anthems,
&c. 14103
Sacred songster. 21910
Sacred to the memories of two
youths who were poisoned by
eating Cicuta Aquatica or
water hemlock. 22174
Sacred to the memory of the
patriots John Adams and
Thomas Jefferson. 24435
The sacred writings of the
apostles and evangelists of
Jesus Christ. 23817; 32363
Sacred zoology. 32406
The sacrifice of the heart or A
choice collection of hymns.
37489
Sad tales and glad tales. 34107
Saddlery. The subscribers re-
spectfully inform their friends
and the public, that they have

entered into partnership, under
the firm of Graham & Dye.
33400

Safe & sound. A favorite rondo.
5629

The sagacity of dogs. 35090a

Sailing directions and remarks,
made on board the Sloop Orbit.
4161

Sailor boy; a novel. 22175

The Sailor boy. Or The first
and last voyage of little Andrew. 3086; 40343

The Sailor boy's first voyage.
26001

The sailor's candid appeal to his
shipmates. 6691

Sailor's physician. 2659; 17531

The sailor's son. 30509

Sailors and saints; or, Matrimonial manoeuvres [sic] 38762

Saint Chrysostom On the priest-
hood. 24104

A saint indeed, or The great
work of a Christian in keeping
the heart in the several conditions of life. 24546

St. Lawrence--County Corresponding Committee. 34393

The St. Louis directory and register. 6693

St. Patrick was a gentleman: a
celebrated Irish air. 24304

St. Patrick's day. Arranged as
a rondo. 5071; 12251; 14031

St. Paul a Universalist. 7878

St. Paul's Epistle to the Hebrews.
32364

St. Ronan's Well. 17927-17929

The saint's everlasting rest. 4634;
4635; 7976; 7977; 15285; 15286;
32237-32240

The saint's repose in death.
19854

La Sainte Bible. 444; 8046; 23818

Salathiel. A story of the past.
32855

Sale by the executors of the last
will and testament of the Hon.
William Winthrop. 21522

Sale of lands in the counties of
Oxford and Washington in
Maine. 13651

Sales of lands--lead mines Missouri. 36864

Salem Cadet's march. 3092

Salem witchcraft. 30516a

Salmagundi. 1769

Salt springs in Illinois. 31503

The saltworks case. 40470

The salvability and church membership of children and their
right of baptism explained
and vindicated. 32869

Salvation by Christ. 17909;
40367

Salvation by grace through faith:
a discourse delivered at a
quarterly meeting of the German United Brethren. 30647

Salvation by Grace, through
faith. A discourse on Ephesi-
ans, ii. 8. 12408

Salvation made sure. 23568;
27923; 32061

The salvation of all men strictly
examined. 16044

Salvation of Judas Iscariot.
9930

Eine Sammlung auserlesener Ge-
beter u. Lieder. 16507;
38962

Eine Sammlung nener Geistlicher
Lieder. 6709

Sammlung religioser deutscher
Gesange nebst einem kurzen
fasslichen Unterricht zum
singen. 17903

Sampson's Discourse, and correspondence with various learned
jurists, upon the history of the
law. 26014

Samtliche Neue Lieder. 14961

Samuel A. Ruddock. 27381

Samuel Angus. 27382

Samuel B. Crocket. 27383

Samuel Chestnut. 27384; 36865

Samuel D. Walker. 36866

Samuel Dubose administrator of
E. D. Dick. 36867; 36868

Samuel Sitgreaves. 41309

Samuel Sprigg. 31504; 36869

Samuel Ward. 36870

Samuel Youngs. 27385

The sanctification of the Sabbath.
23845

Sanctified afflictions. 9627
The sanctity, obligation, and
  benefit of the Sabbath, &c.
  considered and proven. 5122
Sand bars of the Ohio river.
  27386
Sandoval: or, The freemason.
  25124
Sandy and Jenny. 3106; 6716;
  22198
The sandy foundation shaken.
  2680; 21800; 30167
Sandy Walker. 36871
Santag's! Admired waltz. 1578
Sarah Chitwood. 36872
Sarah Jones. 36873
Saratoga; a tale of the revolution.
  15911
Sardanapalus; a tragedy. 8235;
  8236
Satan's wiles. A sermon. 27675
Satire on modern piety, and
  gilded prayers. 30524
Saul. Arranged for the organ.
  1502
Saul. Arranged for the piano
  forte. 16396
The savage beauty. 10328
The Savings Bank. At the ad-
  journed meeting of the Trus-
  tees of the Provident Institu-
  tion for Savings in the town of
  Boston. 2912
The saw-mill: or A Yankee trick.
  16485
Saw Ye Aught of my love? 1995
Saw ye my wee love. 17836
Saxe Cobourg. A rondo for the
  piano forte. 11773
The Saxe Cobourg waltz. 2309
Saxon rondo. 5451; 12665
Say my heart, why wildly beat-
  ing. 4216; 19224; 19225;
  23260
Say, what shall be our sport to-
  day? 8082; 8083
Sayings and doings. 16576;
  20942
Scales by contrary motion.
  20800
Scan Mag; or, The village gos-
  sip. 2808
"Scarce had the purple gleam of

day!" 6176
Scena de camera. 6725
Scena quarta del quinto atto di
  Adad. 20892
The scene was more beautiful
  far. 2325
Scenes at home. 14049
Scenes in Africa. 30766
Scenes in America. 22429
Scenes in Asia. 26176; 40612
Scenes in Europe. 10415; 14050;
  18157; 22430
Scenes in Georgia. 28733
Scenes of wealth. 26177
Schaeffer und Maund's Amerikan-
  ischer Stadt und Land-Calen-
  dar. 3116
Schatzkastchen enthaltend Bib-
  lische Betrachtung mit erbaul-
  ichen Liedern auf alle Tage
  im Yahre. 20725
Schedule of exercises for the ex-
  hibition at Hebron Academy.
  16497
Schism among the Quakers.
  12347
Der Schlüssel zur Offenbahrung
  von Jesus Christus selbst auf-
  geschlossen und entsiegelt.
  35108
The Scholar's arithmetic [Adams]
  16; 4398; 7738; 11527; 15022;
  19368; 23414; 27776a; 31885
The scholar's arithmetic [Wil-
  letts] 11429; 11430
The scholar's companion. 13400
Scholar's guide to chirography.
  35109; 40362
The scholar's guide, to the history of the Bible. 10366
The scholar's manual. 40363
The scholar's spelling assistant.
  19985; 32605
School atlas, to accompany the
  Rudiments of geography.
  41583
School atlas to accompany Woodbridge's Rudiments of geog-
  raphy. 7694; 11474; 23366
School atlas to Adam's geogra-
  phy. 17
School atlas to Cummings' an-
  cient & modern geography.

923; 12306

A school book for militia. 27745

The school boy's introduction to
the geography and statistics of
the state of New York. 22337

School committee of the city of
Boston. 37896

The school dictionary 40698

The school exercise. 5999;
13275

School exercises of the Lafayette
Female Academy. 25060

School for Boys in Franklin
Street. 37908

A school for grown children.
29819

The school for scandal. 3202;
17963; 30588

School fund for the several
states. 27387

School lands in Ohio. 23126

School lands in the Illinois Grant.
27388

School lands - Michigan. 27389;
36874

School lands - Ohio. 36875

School lands, St. Louis, Missouri. 36877

School lands--Union County, Indiana. 36876

School. Messrs. Dam & Hardy
take this method to inform
their friends and the public,
that their Spring quarter com-
mences on Monday. 28652

School of cavalry. 18222

The school of fashion. 40364

The school of good manners.
3119; 35110

The school of reform. 17239;
17240; 25430

The school; or, Lessons in morals. 30533

The school preceptor. 3120

The school-fellows; a moral tale.
10181

Schoolmaster's assistant [Daboll]
8492; 24276

The schoolmaster's assistant
[Dilworth] 12379; 20314

Schools, lyceums, and lyceum
seminary. To the public.
39011

Der Schul-Psalter. 6730;
35113

Schuylkill Canal navigator. 27815

The science of mechanics. 37424

Scientific agriculture. 29230

Scientific dialogues. 21081; 39169

The scolding wife. 3126

Scotch Betty. 2976

Scots wha hae wi' Wallace bled.
3127; 6380; 22209

Scott's exercises and manoeuvres
of infantry. 19777

Scott's militia tactics. 5144

The Scottish chiefs. 9980;
21942; 25809; 30305; 30306;
40122

The Scottish exiles. 32638

The Scottish orphans. 15458;
35416

Scriptual answer to the question,
How may I know that I am an
adopted child of God? 1063

Scriptural and philosophical arguments, to prove the divinity
of Christ. 20338

The scriptural doctrine of predestination. 29571

The scriptural doctrine of water
baptism. 17931

The Scriptural doctrines and
church government (also an
address and a sermon) of a
branch of the church of God,
called Christians. 25964

Scriptural evidence in favor of
female testimony in meetings
of Christian worship. 16923

A Scriptural exhibition of the
mighty conquest, and glorious
triumph of Jesus Christ, over
sin, death, and hell. 33634

A Scriptural exposition of the
declaration in the parable of
the sheep and goats. 10214

Scriptural hymns. 16875

Scriptural marks of salvation.
12323

Scriptural reasons for disbeliev-
ing the doctrine of the Trinity.
31661

A scriptural view of Baptism.
27929; 27930

A scriptural view of politics, ad-

dressed to serious-minded
Christians. 17932

A scripture account of the faith
and practice of Christians.
1363

A Scripture catechism. 16557

The Scripture doctrine concerning the Messiah. 26042

The scripture doctrine of Christian baptism. 21796

The Scripture doctrine of divine
sovereignty. 41420

The scripture doctrine of materialism. 12259

The scripture doctrine of the appropriation which is in the nature of saving faith. 11620

The Scripture doctrine of the
election of Jacob. 32526

Scripture extracts. Stating the
doctrines and duties of the
Christian religion. 6767

The scripture guide to baptism.
2677; 21799; 30164; 30165;
34668

A Scripture help, designed to assist in reading the Bible prof-
itably. 8057; 32373

Scripture histories; or Interesting narratives. 30271

The Scripture history [Watkins]
41444

Scripture History. [Watts] 4204

Scripture history, abridged.
35134

Scripture illustrations. 6768;
30553

Scripture instruction; or Christian doctrine and practice.
24872

Scripture invitations and promises
for little children. 2906

Scripture lessons. 11850; 14074

Scripture natural history of
birds. 27816

Scripture natural history of
quadrupeds. 31941

Scripture parables. 3155; 31980

A scripture peace tract. 8047;
10215

Scripture questions designed
principally for adult Bible
classes. 28334; 38012-

38014

Scripture questions; or, Catechetical exercises. 1968;
9274; 16908

Scripture scenes, being a selection of the most interesting
parts of the New Testament.
38557

Scripture truths demonstrated.
20307

The Scriptures an allegory.
9317

The Scriptures our only sure
guide. 4628; 4629

Sea bathing at Long Branch.
33955

The seaman's compass. 1246-
1248

The seaman's devotional assistant. 10216

The seaman's friend. 13218

Seamen. Letter from the Secretary of State. 27390

Seance de lecture. 150

The search after happiness. 3146

A search of truth in the science
of the human mind. 7980

Searsburgh poetry. 28756

The seasonable supply. 22231

The seasons. 3433; 10445;
10446; 18191; 18192; 22453;
26206; 26207; 35507; 35508;
40644

The seats and causes of diseases, investigated by anatomy. 17228

Second and third letters to S.
Miller on his charges against
Unitarians. 6838

Second anniversary of the Albany
County Agricultural Society.
61

Second annual convocation of the
Grand Royal Arch Chapter, of
North-Carolina. 16219

The second annual meeting of the
Lewis County Bible Society.
39291

Second annual meeting of the
Northern Sunday School Union.
34768

Second annual meeting of the
Western Auxiliary Foreign

Mission Society of Rockingham County. 31715

The second annual oration, delivered before the Belles Lettres and Union Philosophical Societies of Dickinson College. 29704

Second annual report. [Baltimore Unitarian Book Society] 7887

Second annual report. [Juvenile Finleyan Missionary Mite Society of Baltimore] 16754

Second annual report [Massachusetts Sabbath School Union] 29693

The second annual report [New York City Tract Society] 39819

Second annual report of the American Tract Society. 19423; 27846

Second annual report of the American Unitarian Association. 27852

Second annual report of the Board of Managers of the Charleston Port Society. 20033

Second annual report of the Board of Managers of the Prison Discipline Society, Boston. 30349; 34891

The second annual report of the Board of the New-Hampshire Baptist Domestic Mission Society. 6214

Second annual report of the Boston Sunday School Society. 37910

Second annual report of the Canal Commissioners. 2479

Second annual report of the Charleston Bethel Union. 15724

Second annual report of the Charleston Female Seamen's Friend Society. 32645

Second annual report of the Cincinnati Tract Society. 38179

Second annual report of the controllers of the public schools of the First school district of the state of Pennsylvania. 2700

Second annual report of the directors of the New Hampshire Branch of the American Education Society. 34447

Second annual report of the directors of the Pennsylvania Institution for the Deaf and Dumb. 13723

Second annual report of the Eastern Auxiliary Foreign Mission Society. 28751

Second annual report of the executive committee of the American Society for the Promotion of Temperance. 37448

Second annual report of the executive committee of the board of managers of the General Protestant Episcopal Sunday School Union. 34905

Second annual report of the Female Bible, Missionary, and Tract Society, of New-Utrecht. 28860

Second annual report of the Hartford County Sabbath School Union. 38921

Second annual report of the Maine Sabbath School Union. 33993

Second annual report of the managers of the Colonization Society of the state of Connecticut. 38227

Second annual report of the managers of the Lexington and Fayette County Auxiliary Colonization Society. 33858

Second annual report of the managers of the Society for the Encouragement of Faithful Domestic Servants in New York. 30653

The second annual report of the managers of the Society for the prevention of pauperism in the city of New York. 3259

Second annual report of the managers of the Society for the Reformation of Juvenile Delinquents in the City of New

York. 30656

Second annual report of the Marine Bible Society, Charleston, South-Carolina. 2105

Second annual report of the Marine Bible Society of Boston. 9360

Second annual report of the Massachusetts Charitable Eye & Ear Infirmary. 29687

Second annual report of the Missionary Committee of the South Carolina Conference. 14172

Second annual report of the Mississippi Baptist State Convention. 19556

Second annual report of the New Hampshire Auxiliary Colonization Society. 25516

Second annual report of the New-York Eye Infirmary. 13566

Second annual report of the New-York Peace Society. 2534

Second annual report of the Pennsylvania Branch of the American Tract Society. 37457

Second annual report of the Pennsylvania Institution for the Deaf and Dumb. 9872

Second annual report, of the Philadelphia Education Society. 2743

Second annual report of the Philadelphia Public Schools. 2740

Second annual report of the president and directors to the stockholders of the Baltimore & Ohio Rail Road Company. 32089; 32090

The second annual report of the president of Harvard University to the overseers. 33493

Second annual report of the Putnam Auxiliary Society, for colonizing the free persons of color. 5449

The second annual report of the Religious Tract Society of the City of Washington. 7593

Second annual report of the Seamens' Union Bethel Society of Baltimore. 22230

The second annual report of the Strafford County Bible Society. 40559

Second annual report of the Superintendent of public instruction, to the General Assembly of Maryland. 39481

Second annual report of the Theological Scholarship Society of St. Thomas' Church. 34549

Second annual report of the trustees of the High School Society of New York. 24841

Second annual report of the Vermont Sabbath-School Union. 31607

Second annual report of the Young Men's Missionary Society of New York. 23399

The second book of masonry. 28331

The second book of modern chronicles. 30562

A second check to Arianism. 27754

Second class book. 25154; 39329

The second cottage rondo. 20933; 20934

Second examination of the class of moral philosophy. 27523

The second exhibition of the South-Carolina Academy of Fine Arts. 14168

A second letter to the Rev. C. B. M'Guire. 22232

A second letter to the Right Hon. the Earl of Liverpool. 14053

Second letter to the Right Reverend John Henry Hobart. 27805

Second memorial of Joseph W. Brackett and Samuel Leggett. 11973

Second night of Paul Pry. 23897

The second part; or, A key to the higher degrees of freemasonry. 30563

The second report of the American Home Missionary Society. 31960

The second report of the American Society for Meliorating the Condition of the Jews.

15089
Second report of the American
Sunday School Union. 23497;
23498
The second report of the board of
trustees, of the Protestant
Episcopal Society, for the Ad-
vancement of Christianity in
Mississippi. 40189
Second report of the canal com-
missioners [Ohio] 13627
Second report of the canal com-
missioners [Penn.] 30181
Second report of the Chester
County Cabinet of Natural
Science. 38131
Second report of the committee
of ways and means, relative
to state lotteries. 13241
Second report of the directors
[American Education Society]
7798
Second report of the directors of
the Auxiliary Education Soci-
ety of the Young Men of Bos-
ton. 4513
Second report of the Domestic
Missionary Society of Massa-
chusetts proper. 1038
Second report of the Female
Bible Society of Lexington,
Kentucky. 20502
Second report of the instructer of
the Monitorial School, Boston.
32437
Second report of the managers of
the Episcopal Missionary As-
sociation of Zion Church.
9708
Second report of the Provident
Society for the Employment of
the Poor. 25875
Second report of the state agent
for the Western Shore. 13242
The second report of the Western
Sunday School Union. 31722
The second report of the Young
Men's Bible Society of Balti-
more. 11503
The second report of the Young
Men's Education Society of
New-York City. 31843
The second report on the Mon-

roe Sunday School Union.
25408
Second report on the United Do-
mestic Missionary Society.
18266
Second series of letters to Mr.
Elias Lee. 24748
The second set of quadrilles.
20854
A second statement of facts,
relative to the session (and
Presbytery) of the Reformed
Presbyterian Church, New-
York. 12395
Second statement on the part of
Great Britain, according to
the provisions of the conven-
tion concluded between Great
Britain and the United States.
38817
The second tour of Dr. Syntax
in search of consolation.
8406
Secondary lessons, or The improved reader. 31753; 37186;
41529-41531
The secret "customs," and reve-
nue of the sheriff's office.
3157; 3158
Secret journals of the acts and
proceedings of Congress.
4058; 7481
Secret memoirs of the royal fam-
ily of France. 25061
The secret mine. 12521
The secret of my heart. 4732
Secret proceedings and debates
of the convention assembled
at Philadelphia, in the year
1787. 7482
Le secretaire et le cuisinier.
35131
Secretion; the source of pleasur-
able sensations. 14234
Sections of canal, to be let at
Chillicothe. 39910
See from ocean rising. 2193-
2195
See, the dawn from heaven. Air.
8084; 8085
See the leaves around us falling.
12178
Seleccion de obras maestras

dramatics. 35095

The select academic speaker. 32835

Select airs. Arranged with variations for the piano forte. 16769

Select airs from the celebrated operas composed by Mozart. 13420

Select anecdotes of animals. 35142

Select aphorisms, or Moral and religious sayings. 4261

Select chants, doxologies, &c. 17041

A select collection of approved, genuine, secret, and modern receipts. 3163

A select collection of valuable and curious arts. 26043-26047

Select comedies from Shakespeare. 22254

The select committee, appointed on the subject of the poor laws, respectfully report [New York] 13556

The select committee to whom was recommitted the report of the committee upon foreign communications [Kentucky] 8744

Select dialogues of Lucian. 2030

Select dialogues, or Spanish and English conversations. 34815

Select edition of the British Prose Writers. 3164

Select harmony. 4335

Select hymns designed for social and private worship. 40383

Select hymns for the use of Sunday schools and families. 30567

Select hymns for youth. 40384

Select hymns: The third part of Christian psalmody. 14981

Select Oratorio [Handel and Haydn Society. Boston] 1503; 8933; 8934; 12766; 16399-16401; 20803; 20804

Select oratorio [Psallonian Society. Providence] 6569; 6570; 10049

Select plays of William Shakespeare. 3182

Select poems [Worgan] 11489

Select poems for small children. 35143

Select portions from the authorized version of the whole book of Psalms. 445

Select proverbs of all nations. 23185

Select psalms, Christmas hymns and other devotional and sentimental pieces. 4987

Select remains of the Rev. John Mason. 9393; 21353; 34042; 39483

Select Scottish airs. 509

Selectae e profanis scriptoribus. 1579

The selection and use of acceptable words. A sermon. 35162

Selection for the musica sacra. 33501

A selection from Tate and Brady's version of the Psalms. 19810

A selection from the ancient music of Ireland. 16962

A selection from the English prose works of John Milton. 25384a

A selection from the miscellaneous writings of the late Isaac Harby. 38913

A selection from the public and private correspondence of Vice-Admiral Lord Collingwood. 38226

Selection from the works of Jeremy Taylor. 22432

A selection from Walker's pronouncing dictionary. 14814

A selection, in prose and poetry, from the miscellaneous writings of the late William Crafts. 32846

Selection of Bible lessons. 3165; 3166

A selection of Christian hymns. 30555

Selection of Church musick. 22239

Selection of commissioned and

warrant officers - Navy.
36878

A selection of eulogies pronounced in the several states in honor of those illustrious patriots and statesmen John Adams and Thomas Jefferson. 26048

A selection of favorite conference hymns. 38004

A selection of favorite waltzes. 14078; 22240

A selection of hymns and psalms for social and private worship. 5131; 15915; 20244; 24274; 24275; 28647; 32874; 32875

Selection of hymns and spiritual songs. 14302; 18225

A selection of hymns, designed for the use of the Lutheran and German Reformed Sunday School. 40385

A selection of hymns, designed principally for the use of prisoners. 69

A selection of hymns for infant minds. 3167

Selection of hymns for the Sunday School Union of the Methodist Episcopal Church. 39572

A selection of hymns for the use of children. 30568

A selection of hymns for the use of Evangelical Lutheran Churches. 10222

A selection of hymns, for the use of social religious meetings. 3168; 9002; 17937

A selection of hymns for the use of Sunday schools. 10223; 22241; 26049

A selection of hymns for worship. 6770

A selection of hymns from the best authors. 25946; 30461

Selection of hymns: including a few originals designed to aid the Friends of Zion. 38631

A selection of Irish melodies. 4733

A selection of M. Perrin's Fables. 30206

A selection of more than three

hundred hymns, from the most approved authors. 4307

A selection of music from the operatic drama of The enterprise. 12179

A selection of one hundred of Perrin's fables. 34726; 40030

A selection of pleadings in civil actions. 40554

A selection of questions adapted to Pilkington's abridgement of Goldsmith's Natural history. 20764

A selection of sacred poetry. 33044

A selection of sepulchral curiosities. 13023

A selection of songs. Arranged for the Spanish guitar. 16820

A selection of speeches. To which is annexed a variety of poetry. 2635

A selection of the most celebrated sermons of M. Luther and J. Calvin. 39341

Selection of the New Testament rules. 10224

Selections from a poem, being a paraphrase of the book of Job. 446

Selections from his poems. [Frothingham] 1335

Selections from Mr. Mathews' celebrated memorandum book. 25283

Selections from Scripture, designed as lessons in reading for the use of adults. 30569

Selections from several literary works. 6324; 17467

Selections from the Chronicle of Boston and from the book of retrospections. 11378

Selections from the diary and other writings of Mrs. Almira Torrey. 14300

Selections from the oratorio of The creation. 8978

Selections from the Sibylline leaves. 28546

Selections from the tragedies of Aeschylus. 11547

Selections from the works of
Mrs. Barbauld. 32202

Selections from the writings of
Fenelon. 38563; 38564

Selections from tragedies of
Aeschylus, Sophocles, and
Euripides. 7746

Selections of a father for the use
of his children. 1408

Selections of hymns and spiritual
songs. 35541

Selections of hymns, from the
most eminent authors. 40276

Self conquest. 30570

Self-cultivation recommended.
3391

A self defence, with a refutation
of calumnies, misrepresentations and fallacies, which have
appeared in several public
prints. 32500

Self-denial. A tale. 33575

Self examination. 10225

A self-explaining grammar of the
English language. 5009

The self-interpreting Bible. 447

Self-knowledge essential to virtue
and happiness. 14079

The self-taught grammarian. 1451

The self-taught Latinist. 20755

The self-taught penman. 1580

The self-taught stenographer.
16518; 16519

The self vindication of Colonel
William Martin. 39438

Selling spirits to Indian tribes.
36879

Semblanzas de los miembros que
han compuesto la Camara de
diputados del congresso de la
union de la Republica Mexicana. 34124

Semi-annual report of the board
of directors, and of the South
Carolina Canal and Railroad
Company. 40493

Senda de les Luces Masonicas.
4932; 8302

Sendschreiben, des Ehrwürden
Herrn Benjamin Kurtz, der
jetzt Europa durchreist, als
Agent zum Boston des Theologischen Seminars. 29437

Seneca Indians--Ohio. 41310

Senior exhibition, in the chapel.
[Brown University] 15579

Senior exhibition. Williams College. 31769; 37203; 41549

Senior sophisters. 8961

The sentence of our Lord on
anger. 8327

A sentimental journey through
France and Italy. 18090;
30708; 30709; 35400

Sentiments of several eminent
persons on the tendency of
dramatic entertainments. 6168

Sentiments on resignation. 2246

The sentiments which should accompany the baptism of children. 15821

Sequel to American popular lessons. 30466

Sequel to Easy lessons. 39269;
39270

Sequel to Marrion Wilder. 32994

Sequel to the Analytical reader.
34943

Sequel to the English reader.
6169; 9591; 9592; 13464;
17283; 21577; 21578; 29872;
29873; 34352; 39682; 39683

Sequel to the Evangelical Rambler. 28085

The seraph; a collection of sacred music. 28542

The seraph: a new selection of
psalm tunes. 5021; 8382

The Seraph, part second. 8383

The serenade. 2092

Serenade for the guitar. 886;
887

The serenade of the troubadour.
15926

Serenade, waltz and rondo.
12672

A series of discourses on the
Christian revelation. 704

A series of easy lessons on the
Lord's Prayer. 40387

A series of essays on moral and
religious subjects. 26231

A series of extemporaneous discourses delivered in the several meetings of the Society
of Friends. 20880

A series of hymns. 26069
A series of lectures, delivered
in Park Street Church, Boston.
38841
A series of lectures on female
education. 34628
Series of lectures on the doctrine
of universal benevolence.
16825
A series of lectures, on the
most approved principles and
practice of modern surgery.
12965
A series of lectures on the most
important subjects in divinity.
28822
A series of letters [Andrews]
4482
A series of letters, addressed to
Rev. Hosea Ballou. 29267
A series of letters addressed to
the Protestant community, on
the secret causes of the increase of Catholics. 24656
A series of letters, addressed to
the Rev. William Hawley.
20415
A series of letters and other
documents relating to the late
epidemic of yellow fever. 3171
A series of letters, in defence
of divine revelation. 200
A series of letters on the mode
and subjects of baptism. 712
A series of letters, on the relation, rights, priveleges [!]
and duties of baptized children.
33944
A series of letters relating to the
late attempt at a reconciliation
between the members of the
congregations of St. Mary's
and St. Joseph's. 22242
A series of maps to Willard's
History of the United States.
27653; 37184; 41526
A series of numbers addressed
to the public. 8402
Series of political letters. 21917
A series of questions comprising
the history of the four gospels. 38569
A series of questions on the Gos-

pels of St. Matthew, Mark,
Luke and John and Acts of
the Apostles. 38568
A series of questions on the
Scriptures and religious subjects. 2034
A series of questions on the
selected Scripture lessons.
29391; 29392; 33738; 33739
A series of questions upon the
Bible. 14081
A series of sermons on practical and familiar subjects.
12809
A series of sermons on the divinity of Christ. 3031
A series of sermons, on the doctrine of everlasting punishment. 35144
A series of tracts on practical
religion. 17938; 22243
Series of Tracts. Published by
the Protestant Episcopal Female Tract Society of Baltimore. 13880
Serious actual dangers of foreigners and foreign commerce,
in the Mexican states. 25006
Serious address to children and
youth. 4205
A serious address to the clergymen and men of the Methodist
society. 17939
A serious address to the fre-
quenters of theatres. 3172
A serious address to Unitarians
and Trinitarians. 30572
Serious advice to youth. 2135;
2136
A serious and candid defence of
the polemical talents of William L. M'Calla. 17940
A serious and earnest expostulation. 22244
A serious and friendly address
to everyone who is halting between two opinions. 22245
Serious appeal! Read and reflect!! Fellow-citizens.
35148
A serious call in Christian love,
to all people [Hanchett]
16393; 20801

Serious call in Christian love to all people [Holme] 5620

A serious call; or, Masonry revealed. 40388

A serious call to a devout and holy life. 5802-5804

A serious examination. 40389

A serious expostulation with the followers of Elias Hicks. 38578

Serious reflections on the execution and death of Michael Powars. 3173

Sermon [Fairchild] 1157

Sermon addressed to the Bible class and Sabbath school in Granville. 15854

A sermon, addressed to the legislature of Connecticut, at New Haven, on the day of the anniversary election, May 3d, 1826. 23732

A sermon, addressed to the Legislature of Connecticut, at the annual election in New-Haven, May 5th, 1824. 16952

A sermon addressed to the Legislature of the state of Connecticut at the annual election in Hartford, May 2, 1827. 29492

Sermon, addressed to the Legislature of the State of Connecticut, at the annual election in Hartford, May 7, 1823. 14262; 14263

A sermon, addressed to the Legislature of the state of Connecticut, at the annual election, in New-Haven, May 1st, 1822. 8202; 8203

A sermon addressed to the temperate. 29708; 39536

Sermon and prayer by Anna Braithwaite. 19852

A sermon at Taunton. 7669

A sermon at the dedication of the meeting house in Foxborough. 14929

Sermon at the opening of the convention of the Protestant Episcopal Church of Virginia. 34092

Sermon at the opening of the Synod of Albany in Watertown,

Jefferson County. 27668

Sermon at the ordination of R. Anderson. 1209

A sermon at the ordination of Rev. Calvin Gardner. 21071

Sermon at the ordination of Rev. Moses Sawyer. 4336

A sermon before the Palestine Missionary Society. 28533

Sermon, by Elias Hicks. 38970

A sermon by Jacob J. Janeway. 39127

Sermon by the late Rev. James Smith. 30633

A sermon, by the Rev. John Wesley. 23289

A sermon by the Rev. Mr. John Chambers. 32630

Sermon, December 29, 1819. 1733

A sermon, delivered April 24, 1822. 8687

A sermon delivered at Acworth. 14245

A sermon delivered at Amesbury. 24397

A sermon, delivered at Bedford, N.H. 9814

A sermon delivered at Boston. 20496

A sermon, delivered at Bridge-Hampton, L.I. 6472

A sermon, delivered at Buxton. 5339

A sermon, delivered at Canaan, N.H. 33214

A sermon delivered at Castleton, Vermont. 6806

A sermon, delivered at Craftsbury. 1626

A sermon delivered at Deerfield, New Hampshire. 23708

A sermon delivered at Dorchester. 4166

A sermon, delivered at Dover, N.H. 19903

Sermon, delivered at Durham. 10292

Sermon, delivered at Enfield. 12291

A sermon, delivered at Epping, New Hampshire. 29074

A sermon, delivered at Exeter.

6676

A sermon delivered at Farmington. 30401

A sermon delivered at Fitchburg. 12426

A sermon, delivered at Fort Griswold. 7020

A sermon delivered at Fredericksburg. 22341

A sermon delivered at Friends' Meeting, Green Street, Philadelphia. 40518

A sermon, delivered at Friends' meeting-house, Rose-street, New-York. 38971

Sermon, delivered at Fryeburg, Maine. 34864

A sermon delivered at Glastenbury. 1544

Sermon delivered at Granville. 15855

A sermon, delivered at Hartford, Conn. 15161

A sermon delivered at Hopkinton. 11403

A sermon, delivered at Ipswich. 951

A sermon delivered at Kent. 38969

A sermon, delivered at Lansing. 32629

A sermon delivered at Lee, Dec. 22nd, 1820. 5673

A sermon, delivered at Lee, Massachusetts, May 15, 1822. 9089

A sermon, delivered at Leominster, Oct. 15, 1823, at the dedication of the new meeting-house. 12224

A sermon, delivered at Leominster, on leaving the old meeting-house. 12225

A sermon delivered at Lisle. 1465; 8901

A sermon, delivered at Lunenburg. 32882

A sermon delivered at Mason, N. H. 29212

A sermon, delivered at Monson, Massachusetts. 5245

A sermon, delivered at Montpelier. 33952

A sermon, delivered at North Bridgewater. 10359

A sermon, delivered at Northampton, before Jerusalem Lodge. 10367

A sermon delivered at Northampton before the Hampshire Missionary Society. 4910

Sermon delivered at Northwood. 9998

A sermon, delivered at Plymouth, N. H., July 4, 1825. 27546

A sermon, delivered at Plymouth, on Thanksgiving day, December 5, 1822. 11414

A sermon delivered at Randolph 15152

Sermon delivered at Rose Street Meeting, New York. 27621

A sermon, delivered at Rutland West parish. 12797

A sermon delivered at Salem Church. 4810

A sermon, delivered at Salisbury, Mass. 19608

A sermon, delivered at S. Reading. 1101; 1102

A sermon delivered at Sandwich, New-Hampshire. 31731

A sermon delivered at Southborough, Mass. 30151

Sermon, delivered at Springfield, Mass. [Dickinson] 38390

A sermon delivered at Springfield, Mass. [Osgood] 30131

A sermon, delivered at Stoughton, Mass. 1242; 1243

A sermon delivered at Taunton. 38902

Sermon delivered at the consecration of the temple of the Second New Jerusalem Church, of Philadelphia. 40303

A sermon, delivered at the consecration to the episcopacy of the Rt. Rev. Wm. Meade. 41503

A sermon delivered at the dedication of the Baptist Meeting House in New Haven. 16536

A sermon delivered at the dedication of the church, erected by the Second Congregational

Society in North Bridgewater.
24918
A sermon delivered at the dedication of the college chapel in
Amherst.   29277
A sermon, delivered at the dedication of the First Congregational Meeting House, Malone,
N. Y.   33601
A sermon delivered at the dedication of the First Evangelical
Congregational Meeting House
in Eastport, Maine.   38718
A sermon, delivered at the dedication of the First Universalist meeting house, in Milford,
Mass.   4531; 15162
A sermon, delivered at the dedication of the First Universalist Meeting House in Roxbury.
4530
A sermon delivered at the dedication of the "Free Church,"
Clinton.   10300
Sermon, delivered at the dedication of the new Congregational
meeting-house, in Berlin.
14132
A sermon delivered at the dedication of the New Congregational Meeting House, in New
Preston, Conn.   19779
A sermon, delivered at the dedication of the New Meeting
House in Waterville Village.
24056
A sermon delivered at the dedication of the new meeting
house of the First Baptist
Church & Society, Union
Street, Boston.   38868
A sermon, delivered at the dedication of the new Universalist
meeting house in Duxbury
[Mass.]   23586
A sermon delivered at the dedication of the New Universalist Meeting House in Norway
Village.   41579
A sermon delivered at the dedication of the North Congregational Church in Hartford.
20842

A sermon delivered at the dedication of the Second Congregational Church, in Worcester.
37579
A sermon delivered at the dedication of the Second or South
Congregational Church in
Hartford.   29504
A sermon, delivered at the dedication of the Universalist
meeting-house in Cambridgeport.   7879
A sermon delivered at the dedication of the Universalist
Meeting-house in Halifax,
Mass.   40072
A sermon, delivered at the
fourth anniversary of the Auxiliary Education Society, of
the Young Men of Boston.
12434
A sermon, delivered at the funeral of Capt. William A.
Fanning.   25727
A sermon, delivered at the funeral, of Deacon Josiah Torrey.   8377
A sermon delivered at the funeral of Miss Sarah Potter
Williams.   17595
A sermon, delivered at the funeral of Mr. Jacob White
Dawes.   22449
Sermon, delivered at the funeral
of Mrs. Achsah Snow.   15563
A sermon delivered at the funeral of Mrs. Anna B. Bush.
29550
A sermon, delivered at the funeral of Rev. John Marsh.
4948
A sermon delivered at the funeral of Samuel P. Crafts.
20025
A sermon, delivered at the funeral of the Hon. John Treadwell.   13819
A sermon delivered at the funeral of the Rev. Araetius B.
Hull.   25480
A sermon delivered at the funeral of the Rev. David Osgood.
9041

A sermon delivered at the funeral of the Rev. Edwards Whipple. 9605

A sermon, delivered at the funeral of the Reverend Eliab Stone. 10337

A sermon delivered at the funeral of the Rev. Federal Burt. 33285

A sermon, delivered at the funeral of the Rev. John Rodgers Coe. 13976

A sermon delivered at the funeral of the Rev. Joseph Pope. 25481

A sermon delivered at the installation of Rev. Frederick Freeman. 20383; 20384

A sermon, delivered at the installation of Rev. Jacob Frieze. 40073

A sermon delivered at the installation of Rev. Jacob Scales. 28768

A sermon delivered at the installation of the Rev. Andrew Bigelow. 11673

A sermon delivered at the installation of the Rev. Daniel Dana. 8498

A sermon delivered at the installation of the Rev. Ebenezer Peck Sperry. 1323

A sermon, delivered at the installation of the Rev. Hosea Ballou. 5162

A sermon delivered at the installation of the Rev. Lorenzo D. Johnson. 28448

A sermon, delivered at the installation of the Rev. Sebastian Streeter. 18115

A sermon delivered at the installment of the Rev. John W. Doak. 1030

A sermon delivered at the interment of Elder James Pinkerton. 39962

A sermon delivered at the interment of Mrs. Betsy Bartlett. 21134

A sermon delivered at the interment of Mrs. Lucretia Colton. 5246

A sermon delivered at the interment of the Hon. Jacob Abbot. 1075

A sermon, delivered at the ordination of Rev. David Page Smith. 28752

A sermon delivered at the ordination of Rev. Freeman P. Howland. 29248

A sermon delivered at the ordination of Rev. Moses G. Grosvenor. 28769

A sermon, delivered at the ordination of Richard Varick Dey. 14005

A sermon, delivered at the ordination of the Rev. Abijah Cross. 17518

A sermon delivered at the ordination of the Reverend Abner Morse. 1233

A sermon, delivered at the ordination of the Reverend Absolom Peters. 511

A sermon, delivered at the ordination of the Rev. Asa Cummings. 4454

A sermon delivered at the ordination of the Rev. Asa Hixon. 39072

A sermon, delivered at the ordination of the Reverend Caleb Hobart. 18113

A sermon delivered at the ordination of the Rev. Edmund Quincy Sewall. 3026

A sermon, delivered at the ordination of the Rev. Ezra Stiles Gannett. 15714-15717

A sermon, delivered at the ordination of the Rev. Hosea Hildreth. 20931

A sermon, delivered at the ordination of the Rev. Jacob C. Goss. 19397

A sermon delivered at the ordination of the Rev. Jared Sparks. 710; 4946; 4947; 12096; 15718

A sermon delivered at the ordination of the Rev. John M. Merrick. 32226

A sermon delivered at the ordination of the Rev. John Samuel Thompson. 27944

A sermon delivered at the ordination of the Rev. John W. Ellingwood. 14972

A sermon, delivered at the ordination of the Rev. Jonathan Cole. 37934

A sermon, delivered at the ordination of the Rev. Jonathan Ward, Jr. 23208

A sermon delivered at the ordination of the Rev. Moses G. Thomas. 37711

A sermon, delivered at the ordination of the Rev. Robert Page, jr. 9292

A sermon delivered at the ordination of the Rev. Royal A. Avery. 16477; 16478

A sermon, delivered at the ordination of the Rev. Samuel Cook. 8311

A sermon delivered at the ordination of the Rev. Thomas M. Smith. 11477

A sermon delivered at the ordination of the Reverend Wales Tileston. 22352

A sermon delivered at the ordination of the Rev. William Henry Furness. 23214

A sermon delivered at the ordination of the Rev. William Parsons Lunt. 33427

A sermon delivered at the South Church in Andover. 24408

A sermon, delivered at the taking up of a collection, for the benefit of the Greeks, in the congregation of St. John's Church. 16258

A sermon, delivered at the Universalist chapel, in Pawtucket, R.I. 38704

A sermon, delivered at the Universalist Church, in the city of Hudson. 9931

A sermon delivered at Thomastown. 514

A sermon, delivered at Torrington. 24801

A sermon delivered at Townshend. 7018

A sermon delivered at Upton. 11470

A sermon delivered at Vassalboro' [Adams] 4404

A sermon delivered at Vassalboro' [Tappan] 6934

A sermon, delivered at Waterville. 18244

A sermon delivered at West-Boylston. 4829

A sermon delivered at Wilkesbarre. 28261

A sermon delivered at Winthrop. 22467

A sermon, delivered at Woburn. 2766

A sermon, delivered at Woodstock. 23712

A sermon, delivered Aug. 25, 1825. 23381

A sermon delivered August 25, 1822. 14140

A sermon, delivered before Columbus Lodge, No. 6. 24730

A sermon, delivered before his Excellency John Brooks. 7575

A sermon delivered before his Excellency Levi Lincoln [Fisk] 38581-38583

A sermon delivered before His Excellency Levi Lincoln [Stuart] 30734

A sermon delivered before His Excellency Levi Lincoln [Walker] 37062

A sermon, delivered before Morton Lodge. 12780

A sermon, delivered before the American Board of Commissioners for Foreign Missions. 6121; 9553

A sermon delivered before the ancient and honourable artillery company in Boston, June 5, 1820. 642; 804

A sermon delivered before the Ancient and Honourable Artillery Company. June 6th, 1825. 20615

A sermon delivered before the Auxiliary Education Society of

Norfolk County at their annual meeting in the East Parish in Medway. 24147

A sermon delivered before the Auxiliary Education Society of Norfolk County, at their annual meeting in the Union Society of Braintree and Weymouth. 39958

A sermon, delivered before the Congregational Church and Society in Lempster, N. H. 32637

A sermon, delivered before the convention of the Congregational ministers in Massachusetts. 6373

A sermon, delivered before the convention of the diocese of New-York. 18254

A sermon, delivered before the ecclesiastical society in Williamsfield and Wayne, Ashtabula county, Ohio. 27695

A sermon, delivered before the Female Benevolent Society, in East Randolph. 22262

A sermon delivered before the Female Benevolent Society in Exeter. 948

A sermon, delivered before the First Baptist Church in Lowell. 38632

A sermon, delivered before the First Restoration Society, in Shrewsbury, Massachusetts. 7687

A sermon, delivered before the First Universalist Church and Society in Charlestown. 38508

Sermon delivered before the First Universalist Societies in Washington and Langdon. 4616

A sermon delivered before the First Universalist Society, in Cambridge, on the evening of the second Sabbath in February, 1823. 14903

A sermon delivered before the First Universalist Society, in Cambridge, on the evening of the third Sabbath in March, 1824. 19272

A sermon, delivered before the First Universalist Society in Gloucester. 39201

A sermon delivered before the First Universalist Society in Haverhill. 38555

A sermon delivered before the First Universalist Society, in Woburn, Mass. 40438

Sermon delivered before the General Convention of Universalists. 20277

A sermon, delivered before the Hampshire Missionary Society [Lord] 9290

A sermon delivered before the Hampshire Missionary Society [Miller] 17159

A sermon, delivered before the Legislature of the state of Connecticut. 933

A sermon delivered before the Massachusetts Society for Promoting Christian Knowledge [Homer] 33584

A sermon, delivered before the Massachusetts Society for Promoting Christian Knowledge. [Huntington] 16619

A sermon delivered before the Massachusetts Society for Promoting Christian Knowledge [Jenks] 21056

A sermon, delivered before the Massachusetts Society for the Suppression of Intemperance. 5718; 5719

A sermon, delivered before the Mount Vernon Lodge. 1095

A sermon, delivered before the Palestine Missionary Society. 34721

A sermon delivered before the Sabbath School Union Society of Providence. 13163

A sermon delivered before the Second Baptist Church and Society in Providence, Rhode-Island. 338

A sermon, delivered before the Southampton Ministerial Association. 40564

A sermon delivered before the

Third Congregational Society
in Greenfield, Mass.   23573

A sermon delivered before the
Universalist Society in West
Cambridge.   11416

A sermon, delivered before the
Vermont Colonization Society
[Hough]   24898

A sermon, delivered before the
Vermont Colonization Society
[Yale]   31826

A sermon, delivered before the
Village Lodge, Number 142.
954

A sermon, delivered before the
Warren Association, in Newport.   4663

A sermon, delivered before the
Westminster Association, at
Phillipston.   927

A sermon, delivered Dec. 18,
1821.   7576; 7577; 11339

A sermon delivered Dec. 18,
1823.   15481

A sermon delivered December 14,
1825.   23412

A sermon delivered December 13,
1820.   1734

A sermon, delivered Dec. 31,
1820.   5252

A sermon delivered Dec. 12,
1821.   10247

A sermon delivered Dec. 12,
1822.   13945

A sermon delivered February 15,
1826.   23458

A sermon, delivered February 4,
1824   [Jenkins]   16711

A sermon, delivered February 4,
1824   [Putnam]   17739

A sermon, delivered February 20,
1822.   8612

A sermon delivered Feb. 28,
1821.   5320

A sermon, delivered February
25, 1820.   194

A sermon, delivered February
27, 1820.   383

A sermon, delivered Feb. 23,
1825.   20782

A sermon, delivered February
23, 1827.   28780

A sermon, delivered in Adams,

N.Y.   26051

Sermon delivered in Augusta.
31887; 31888

A sermon delivered in Bangor.
16339

A sermon delivered in Boston
before the convention of Congregational ministers.   14973

A sermon delivered in Boston,
May 26, 1829.   38167

A sermon, delivered in Boston,
on the anniversary of the
American Education Society.
2828; 6511

A sermon delivered in Boston,
September 17, 1823.   12340

A sermon delivered in Brunswick.
21486

A sermon delivered in Chillicothe.   41563

A sermon delivered in Christ
Church.   19997

A sermon, delivered in Clinton.
6313

A sermon, delivered in Concert
Hall, Bath.   24134

A sermon delivered in Farmington.   7784

A sermon delivered in Franklin.
14878

A sermon, delivered in Gorham.
32865

A sermon, delivered in Hanson.
19396

A sermon, delivered in Haverhill.   5194

A sermon, delivered in Holliston.
24542

A sermon delivered in Ipswich.
20256

A sermon, delivered in Kennebunk Port.   24994

A sermon delivered in Killingly,
Conn.   4506

A sermon delivered in King's
Chapel, Boston.   27550

A sermon, delivered in Littleton,
Mass.   14308

A sermon, delivered in Madison.
23831

A sermon delivered in Malden.
8880

A sermon delivered in Mount-

Vernon. 17507

A sermon, delivered in Northampton. 32029

A sermon, delivered in Plymouth.
10461

Sermon delivered in Pomfret.
17672

A sermon delivered in Portland.
13137

A sermon, delivered in Princeton. 12162

A sermon, delivered in Randolph,
Mass. 18183

A sermon delivered in St. Luke's
Church, Rochester. 32864

Sermon, delivered in St. Paul's
Church, in Schoharie. 1971

A sermon delivered in Scituate,
Mass. 31745

A sermon, delivered in Shoreham,
December 2, 1824. 21526

A sermon, delivered in Shoreham,
January 31, 1827. 29818

A sermon, delivered in Shrewsbury. 19512

Sermon, delivered in the Capitol
of the United States. 26135

A sermon delivered in the chapel
of the College of New Jersey.
16909

A sermon; delivered in the chapel of the General Theological
Seminary. 37208

A sermon, delivered in the chapel of Waterville College.
20021

A sermon, delivered in the Col-
lege-Hall at Cannonsburgh,
Pa. 3377

A sermon delivered in the Court
house, Bangor. 38403-38404a

A sermon, delivered in the first
Congregational Church of Pittsfield, Mass. 5118

A sermon, delivered in the First
Parish Meetinghouse, in Haverhill. 33042

Sermon delivered in the First
Universalist Church, Lombard
Street, Philadelphia. 40463

Sermon delivered in the Friends'
Meeting, Baltimore [Hopkins]
20945

Sermon, delivered in the Friends'
meeting, Baltimore [Wether-
ald] 23299

A sermon delivered in the Independent Presbyterian Church,
Savannah. 20963

A sermon delivered in the meeting-house of the first parish
of Beverly. 33198; 33199

A sermon delivered in the meeting-house of the Second Baptist Church in Boston. 7702

A sermon delivered in the Middle Church, New Haven, Con.
9489

A sermon, delivered in the Murray Street Church, New York.
14883

A sermon, delivered in the Presbyterian Church, Lancaster.
38391

A sermon delivered in the Presbyterian Church, Washington,
Pa. 14988

A sermon delivered in the Reformed Dutch Church at English Neighbourhood, N. J.
35468

Sermon, delivered in the rotunda
of the University of Virginia.
39538

A sermon, delivered in the Second Presbyterian Church,
Charleston, S. C. 2966

A sermon, delivered in the Second
Presbyterian Church, in the city
of Pittsburgh [Jennings] 9149

A sermon delivered in the Second
Presbyterian Church, Pittsburgh
[Swift] 22412

A sermon, delivered in the Second Universalist meeting house,
in Boston, on the evening of
the first Sabbath in January,
1818. 201

A sermon, delivered in the Second Universalist meeting house,
in Boston, on the morning of
the third Sabbath in November,
1819. 202; 4533

A sermon delivered in the Second
Universalist Meeting in Boston,
on Fast Day morning, April

3, 1828. 32081; 32082

Sermon delivered in the South meeting house, Norwich, Vermont. 23306

A sermon, delivered in the Tabernacle Church, Salem, Mass. 12262

A sermon delivered in the Universalist Chapel in Portland. 32385

A sermon, delivered in the Universalist Meeting House in Roxbury. 7880

A sermon, delivered in the Universalist Meeting House, Norway Village. 29837

A sermon, delivered in the village Meeting House, Bowdoinham. 28528

A sermon, delivered in the West Parish Meeting House, Boxford. 38443

A sermon, delivered in the West Parish of Andover. 33684

A sermon, delivered in Union Village, Paris (N. Y.) 10301

A sermon delivered in Waldoborough. 37365

A sermon delivered in Weathersfield, Vt. 8437

A sermon delivered in Wells. 6935

A sermon delivered in Winthrop. 10407

Sermon delivered January 1, 1822. 8688

A sermon, delivered January 17, 1821. 7578

A sermon delivered July 9th, 1826. 23593

A sermon delivered July 7, 1825. 20103

A sermon, delivered July 13, 1823. 13086

A sermon delivered July 29, 1829. 40353

A sermon, delivered June seventh, 1823. 13342

A sermon delivered June 26, 1821. 9468

Sermon, delivered Lord's Day, January 6, 1828. 35431

A sermon, delivered March 7, 1821. 5321

Sermon, delivered March 6,

1820. 4145

A sermon, delivered May 10, 1820. 1455

A sermon, delivered Nov. 5, 1823. 19258

A sermon, delivered November 19, 1827. 28625

A sermon, delivered November 2, 1825. 20254

A sermon, delivered November 7, 1821. 8484

A sermon, delivered November 3, 1821. 11412

Sermon, delivered Oct. 17th, 1824. 17822

A sermon, delivered October 16, 1822. 9235

A sermon delivered October 12, 1820. 4167

A sermon delivered on occasion of constituting a church at Ware factory village. 24420

A sermon, delivered on Sabbath evening, Sept. 30th, 1827. 29379

A sermon delivered on Sabbath, July 5th, 1829. 37384

A sermon delivered on taking leave of the Second Universalist Society in Philadelphia. 21524

A sermon delivered on Thanksgiving Day at Mattapoisett, Rochester. 12016

A sermon delivered on the anniversary of the Female Benevolent Society, Raleigh. 17755

A sermon, delivered on the day of general election, at Montpelier, October 14, 1824. 15712

A sermon, delivered on the day of general election, at Montpelier, October 9, 1823. 14047

A sermon, delivered on the day of general election at Montpelier, October 13, 1825. 19619

A sermon delivered on the day of general election, at Montpelier, October 12, A.D. 1820. 1934

A sermon, delivered on the twenty-fifth anniversary of the Boston Female Asylum. 20757

A sermon delivered on the 27th December, 1826. 30140

A sermon, delivered September 14, 1825. 22298

A sermon delivered Sep. 14, 1826. 24525

A sermon delivered September 16, 1821. 7652

A sermon delivered September 25, 1827. 35229

A sermon delivered to the church and congregation on Jamaica Plain, Roxbury. 5489

A sermon delivered to the First Society in Mendon. 38405

A sermon delivered to the First Society in Winchester. 13219

A sermon delivered 24th June, A. L. 5820. 1542

Sermon, delivered Wednesday, October 29th, 1823. 12003

A sermon, describing the sin and danger of self-love. 8490

A sermon, &c. Acts XI. 26. 21454

A sermon exhibiting some of the principal doctrines of the Protestant Episcopal Church. 4346

A sermon for children. 33016; 38428

Sermon, funeral of Miss Charlotte Lindsey. 6960

A sermon, illustrating the human and official inferiority and supreme divinity of Christ. 25956; 30471

A sermon, in commemoration of the landing, of the New-England Pilgrims. 730

A sermon in Madison. 9191

A sermon in memory of the Rev. Samuel Bacon. 2355

A sermon in vindication of the religious spirit of the age. 2046

A sermon in which is attempted a full and explicit answer to the common and highly important question, "What wilt Thou have me to do?" 16347

A sermon occasioned by the completion of the New college edifice for the use of the Theological Seminary at Andover. 6913

A sermon occasioned by the death of Edmunds Mason. 16831

A sermon, occasioned by the death of Elizabeth Kilbourn. 32851

Sermon, occasioned by the death of his excellency Dewitt Clinton. 34145

A sermon occasioned by the death of John Gorham, M. D. 39953

A sermon, occasioned by the death of Miss Hanna Leverett. 27626

A sermon occasioned by the death of Mr. Edmund P. Sanford. 24936

A sermon occasioned by the death of Mr. Samuel Hoadley. 12683

A sermon occasioned by the death of Mrs. Abigail Lothrop. 30264

A sermon occasioned by the death of Mrs. Beulah Clark. 28760

Sermon, occasioned by the death of Mrs. Carile Mary Whitmore. 9819

A sermon, occasioned by the death of Mrs. Deborah Dunham. 1085

A sermon, occasioned by the death of Mrs. Eleanor Wilcoxon. 25973

A sermon occasioned by the death of Mrs. Miriam Phillips. 14956

A sermon, occasioned by the death of Royal W. Smith. 4286

A sermon occasioned by the death of the Hon. William Phillips. 31789

A sermon, occasioned by the death of the Rev. John H. Livingston. 20242

A sermon occasioned by the
death of the Rev. Matthias
Bruen.   40440
A sermon occasioned by the
death of the Rev. Samuel Worcester.   7703
A sermon occasioned by the decease of the Rev. Levi Hart-
shorn.   949
A sermon occasioned by the late
death of Mrs. Charlotte
Sprague.   5247
A sermon, occasioned by the sud-
den death of Mrs. A. Fisher.
28883
A sermon of Chandler Robbins.
3028
A sermon on baptism. [Anderson]
15103
A sermon on Baptism, delivered
at Upton.   14962
A sermon on Christ's sheep.
13155
A sermon on Christian baptism.
35395; 40532
A sermon, on Christian perfec-
tion.   3472
Sermon on conversion.   35032a
A sermon on creeds and confes-
sions.   28618
A sermon on divine decrees.
32481
A sermon on election. 16810
A sermon on final perseverance.
20362
A sermon on future punishment.
15541
A sermon on human depravity.
22251
A sermon on infant baptism.
1389; 1390
A sermon on intemperance.
27778
A sermon on John IV. 35. 1236
Sermon on meetness for heaven.
24935
A sermon on national righteous-
ness and sin.   28192
A sermon on Nebuchadnezzar's
dream.   3241
Sermon on nonconformity to the
world.   6591
A sermon on practical infidelity.

6904
A sermon on preaching the cross.
29093
A sermon on predestination.   De-
livered in the Methodist Epis-
copal Church at Bridgeton,
W. N. J.   30321
A sermon on predestination,
preached in Milledgeville, Au-
gust 1826.   26141; 30712;
40539
A sermon on regeneration. 2941
A sermon on religious and moral
brotherhood.   34728
A sermon on revivals of religion.
31774
A sermon on small sins.   31662
A sermon on speculative Free-
Masonry.   40294
A sermon, on the adaptation of
Christianity. 21157
A sermon on the annual election.
3174
A sermon on the apostolic mis-
sion. 23554
A sermon on the art of preaching.
20762
A sermon on the atonement.
15922
A sermon, on the authenticity of
the holy scriptures. 21971
Sermon on the benefits, extent,
and nature of the atonement.
38592
A sermon on the Book of life of
the Lamb.   23345
A sermon on the character and
mission of the son of man.
10130
A sermon on the Christian min-
istry delivered in St. Peter's
Church, Washington. 22031
A sermon on the Christian ministry, preached in Christ
Church, Cincinnati.   12115
A sermon on the church. 17756;
22032
A sermon on the communion.
23218
A sermon, on the confession of
faith & covenant of the church
in Paris. 14863
A sermon on the death of his

Excellency, William Eustis.
20743

A sermon, on the death of Mr.
John Russell. 16168

Sermon on the death of Mrs.
Sarah Lanman. 39619

A sermon on the death of the patriots and statesmen, Thomas
Jefferson and John Adams.
24347

Sermon, on the death of the Rev.
Abel Flint. 22106

Sermon on the death of Thomas
Gilbison. 37949

A sermon on the Devil. 19307;
19308; 27676

A sermon on the divinity of
Christ [Church] 28487

A sermon on the divinity of
Christ [Pond] 40109

A sermon on the divinity of our
Lord and Saviour Jesus Christ
[Cumming] 12302

A sermon, on the doctrine of
election [Fessenden] 1226

A sermon on the doctrine of
election [Morse] 13405

A sermon on the doctrine of the
Trinity [Cornelius] 24220;
24221

Sermon, on the doctrine of the
Trinity [Parker] 13662

A sermon, on the duty and advantages of affording instruction to the deaf and dumb.
16248; 16249

A sermon on the duty of constant
communion. 4242

A sermon on the duty of the
church. 19759

A sermon on the effects of the
Hebrew slavery as connected
with slavery in this country.
21790

Sermon on the foreknowledge of
God. 5253

A sermon on the freeness of divine grace. 9180

A sermon on the glory and security of the church of God.
23346

A sermon on the importance of
good moral principles in

rulers. 20406

A sermon on the inability of man
to believe in Jesus Christ, ex-
cept the Father draw him.
12441; 33062

A sermon, on the intercession of
saints. 1640

A sermon on the introduction to
the gospel of St. John. 20677;
33358

A sermon on the Lord's Supper.
21124

A sermon on the manifestation of
God. 13947

Sermon on the manner in which
the Gospel was established.
5749

A sermon on the manner of forming and conducting Bible
classes. 24409

A sermon of the modes and the
subjects of baptism. 12733

A sermon on the nature and influence of faith. 27697

A sermon, on the nature and tendency of the opposition to the
true doctrine of Jesus Christ.
7881

A sermon on the nature, author
and necessity of regeneration.
24411

A sermon on the new birth.
32613

A sermon, on the occasion of the
death of the Rev. Oliver Norris. 25291

A sermon on the occasion of the
lamented death of the Rev.
Joseph Galluchat. 19937

A sermon, on the only true
foundation. 23313

A sermon on the parable of the
rich man and Lazarus. 41513

Sermon on the perdition of Judas.
28789

A sermon on the possibility of
final apostacy. 11645

A sermon on the propriety of the
Christian name. 2260

A sermon on the qualifications of
a spiritual shepherd. 28788

A sermon, on the religious opinions
of the present day. 8872

Sermon on the repentance of the
  unchaste woman. 14045
Sermon on the sacred doctrine
  of the Divine Trinity in Unity.
  22246
A sermon on the sacred import
  of the word Christian. 8510
A sermon on the salutary nature
  of punishment. 19319
A sermon on the sin of duelling.
  37260
A sermon on the sinner's inability to obey the law of God.
  32405
A sermon on the study and interpretation of the Scriptures.
  22033
A sermon on the subject of bap-
  tism. 37867
A sermon on the Supreme God.
  6815
A sermon on the worship of God.
  11486
Sermon on Thursday, Nov. 7,
  1822. 12019
A sermon on universal charity.
  30617
A sermon, preached April 4,
  1820. 1263
Sermon, preached April 16, 1823.
  12875
A sermon preached at a two-
  days meeting. 12547
A sermon, preached at Alstead
  (N. H.) 23545
A sermon preached at Amherst,
  N. H. 11340
A sermon, preached at Attlebor-
  ough, Mass. 10440
A sermon preached at Belfast,
  Maine. 27527
A sermon, preached at Benning-
  ton, Vt. 9885
A sermon preached at Billerica.
  11583; 15065
A sermon, preached at Bosco-
  wen East Society. 14964
A sermon, preached at Brandon,
  on the sixth anniversary of
  the Northwestern Branch of
  the American Education Soci-
  ety. 27529
A sermon preached at Brandon,

Vt. , Oct. 1827. 29063
A sermon, preached at Cam-
  bridge. 25641
A sermon preached at Canter-
  bury. 13286
A sermon, preached at Caven-
  dish, Vermont. 40441
A sermon, preached at Charl-
  ton, Massachusetts. 24279
A sermon, preached at Concord,
  before His Excellency Samuel
  Bell [Bradford] 4819
A sermon, preached at Concord,
  before His Excellency Samuel
  Bell [French] 8773
A sermon, preached at Concord,
  before His Excellency Samuel
  Bell [Howe] 1684
A sermon preached at Concord,
  Massachusetts, May 15th,
  1823. 12318
A sermon, preached at Concord,
  N. H. , on the day of public
  thanksgiving, Nov. 23, 1826.
  23907
A sermon, preached at Danvers,
  April 12, 1826. 23921
A sermon, preached at Danvers,
  January 23, 1826. 24283
A sermon preached at Danvers
  on the day of annual thanks-
  giving, November 30, 1826.
  28268
A sermon preached at Dorches-
  ter, Mass. on Sabbath eve-
  ning, January 18, 1829.
  41514
A sermon, preached at Dorchester, on the Lord's day after
  the interment of Mr. Nathaniel Topliff. 1528
A sermon, preached at Dorchester, third parish, June 24,
  1827. 30449
A sermon, preached at Edwards-
  ville, Illinois. 34665
Sermon, preached at Enfield.
  24405
A sermon, preached at Epson,
  New Hampshire. 5124
A sermon, preached at Free-
  hold. 19876
A sermon preached at Friends'

meeting-house, Burlington,
New Jersey. 11469
A sermon, preached at Goffstown,
New Hampshire. 16450
A sermon, preached at Grace-
Church-Street, London. 38378
A sermon preached at Hanson.
37714
Sermon, preached at Killingworth,
Connecticut. 14255
A sermon preached at Leominster. 6100
A sermon preached at Manchester. 22107
Sermon, preached at Manlius
Square. 33539
A sermon preached at Mansfield.
15771
A sermon, preached at Merrimac.
4875
A sermon, preached at Middle
Granville. 13410
Sermon preached at Middle-Haddam. 21789
A sermon, preached at Montpelier,
before the Legislature [Goodwillie] 29052
A sermon, preached at Montpelier,
before the Legislature
[Walker] 41408
A sermon, preached at Needham.
9202
A sermon, preached at New-Ark.
13343
A sermon, preached at New London. 26184
A sermon, preached at New-
York. 32257
A sermon, preached at North
Guilford. 8623
A sermon preached at North
Wrentham. 26194
A sermon preached at North-Yarmouth. 20026
A sermon preached at Norwich,
Vermont. 4330
A sermon preached at Pittsfield.
23571
A sermon preached at Pittsford.
4631
A sermon, preached at Plymouth,
N. H. 19182
A sermon preached at Poultney.

20967
A sermon, preached at Provincetown. 3341
A sermon preached at Rehoboth.
6962
A sermon, preached at St. Philip's Church. 20618
A sermon preached at Salem.
25169
A sermon preached at Sanford.
28201
A sermon, preached at Seekonk,
Mass. 21902
Sermon preached at Shrewsbury.
5698
A sermon preached at Springfield. 14185
A sermon, preached at Stoughton.
1364
A sermon preached at Templeton.
11392
A sermon preached at the anniversary meeting of free and accepted Masons at St. Albans,
Vt. 24989
A sermon, preached at the anniversary of St. John the Baptist. 24843
A sermon, preached at the annual
meeting of the Prayer Book
and Homily Society of Maryland. 23567
A sermon preached at the dedication of the church in Hanover
Street, Boston. 26156
A sermon, preached at the dedication of the Congregational
Church at the Upper Falls,
Newton. 35046
A sermon, preached at the dedication of the First Congregational Church in New York.
5278; 5279
A sermon preached at the dedication of the meeting house belonging to the East Evangelical
Church & Society in Ware,
Mass. 28592
A sermon, preached at the dedication of the new Congregational meeting-house, in Buxton.
5857
A sermon, preached at the dedi-

cation of the new meeting
house in the First parish in
Deerfield. 23330

A sermon preached at the dedication of the Presbyterian
meeting-house in Hunter,
N. Y. 40118

A sermon preached at the dedication of the Second Congregational Church in Milton.
39331

A sermon, preached at the dedication of the Second Congregational Church in Northampton.
23215

A sermon preached at the dedication of the Union Meeting-
house in Chester, Vermont.
40574

A sermon preached at the dedication of the "Union St. Brick
Church," Bangor. 39056

A sermon preached at the formation of the First Congregational Church in Lowell. 28491

A sermon, preached at the funeral of Doctor Daniel Sawin.
10434

Sermon preached at the funeral
of George Holcombe. 34720

A sermon, preached at the funeral of George Washington Peck.
30792

A sermon preached at the funeral of his Excellency William
Eustis. 22255

A sermon, preached at the funeral of Mr. Nathan Bliss.
6963

A sermon preached at the funeral of Mrs. Lucy Moulton.
30793

A sermon, preached at the funeral of Mrs. Naomi F. Harlow.
22443

A sermon, preached at the funeral of Mrs. Susanna Martin.
6964

A sermon preached at the funeral
of the Hon. Tapping Reeve.
28091

A sermon: preached at the funeral of the Rev. John Elliott.

20531

A sermon preached at the funeral of the Rev. Samuel Eaton.
11585

A sermon, preached at the house
of Dr. Calvin Martin. 6965

A sermon, preached at the installation of the Rev. James
Flint. 5027

A sermon, preached at the installation of the Rev. Luke
A. Spofford. 23973

A sermon, preached at the installation of the Rev. Thomas
G. Farnsworth. 23588

A sermon, preached at the interment of Deacon John Brown.
10441

A sermon preached at the meet-
ing house of the people called
Quakers in Grace Church
Street, London. 22387

A sermon preached at the opening and on the thirty-first day
of May, 1821 of the Cathedral. 4637

A sermon preached at the opening of the General Assembly
of the Presbyterian Church.
25972

A sermon preached at the opening of the new Presbyterian
Church in Rochester. 17548

A sermon preached at the ordination of Mr. George Wads-
worth Wells. 29547

A sermon preached at the ordination of Mr. Samuel Barrett.
21265

A sermon preached at the ordination of Rev. Elam Smalley.
40642

A sermon preached at the ordination of the Rev. Benjamin
Kent. 24570

A sermon preached at the ordination of the Rev. David Star-
ret. 6975

A sermon, preached at the ordination of the Rev. Moses
Thacher. 14282

A sermon, preached at the ordination of the Reverend Silas

Shores. 10442

A sermon preached at the ordination of the Rev. William Batchelder. 13685

A sermon preached at the Pacifick Congregational Church. 3430

A sermon preached at Torringford, Conn. 31828

A sermon, preached at Warren, Connecticut. 40597

A sermon, preached at West Rutland, Vt. 38423

A sermon preached at West Springfield. 40511

A sermon, preached at Woodstock, Vt. 30856

A sermon preached August 9, 1826. 26210

A sermon, preached before His Excellency John Brooks. 1795

A sermon preached before the annual convention of the Congregational ministers of Massachusetts. 33435

A sermon preached before the Auxiliary Education Society, of Norfolk County. 19899

A sermon, preached before the Auxiliary Education Society of the Young Men of Boston. 9142

A sermon preached before the Bible Society of Darlington District, S. C. 21045

A sermon, preached before the Bible Society of N. Carolina. 22034

A sermon preached before the board of directors of the Domestic and Foreign Missionary Society of the Protestant Episcopal Church. 37059

A sermon preached before the Cumberland conference of churches. 25290

A sermon preached before the First Congregational Society in Burlington, Vt. 24952

A sermon preached before the First Universalist Society in Providence, R. I. 5882

A sermon, preached before the Masonic Societies of Richmond and Manchester. 5550

Sermon preached before the North Society of Greenwich. 37193

Sermon preached before the Presbytery of Lexington. 19630

A sermon preached before the Society for the Education of Pious Young Men for the Ministry. 12815

A sermon, preached before the Vermont Colonization Society. 23305

A sermon, preached before the Vermont Domestick Missionary Society. 27627

A sermon, preached before the Washington County Bible Society. 13970

A sermon preached by Edward Mitchell. 2302

Sermon, preached Dec. 13, 1826. 28790

A sermon preached December 30, 1819. 950

A sermon, preached December 31, 1821. 9532

A sermon, preached February 15, 1826. 25665

A sermon preached Feb. 20th, 1825. 20852

A sermon preached for the Young Ladies Missionary Society of Philadelphia. 25676

A sermon preached in Acworth, N. H. 8440

A sermon, preached in behalf of the American Colonization Society. 21285

A sermon preached in Biddeford. 17431

A sermon, preached in Boston before the Massachusetts Society for Promoting Christian Knowledge [Kimball] 5767

A sermon, preached in Boston before the Massachusetts Society for Promoting Christian Knowledge [Stearns] 3313

A sermon preached in Brooklyn, Connecticut. 19167

A sermon preached in Christ Church, Alexandria. 21377

A sermon preached in Christ Church, Quincy. 32873

A sermon, preached in Cohasset. 12348

A sermon, preached in Dedham. 5679

A sermon preached in Ellington. 32480

A sermon, preached in Foxborough. 10431

A sermon, preached in Franklin. 1237

A sermon, preached in Gardner. 23342

A sermon preached in Grace Church, Waterford, and Trinity Church, Lansingburgh. 33005

Sermon, preached in Haddam. 2109

A sermon preached in Harrisburg. 24348

A sermon preached in Hopkinton. 24937

A sermon preached in Lemster, N. H. 8710

A sermon preached in Medway West parish. 39073

A sermon, preached in Poultney. 24736

A sermon, preached in Presbyterian Church in the City of Richmond. 3005

A sermon preached in Rutland. 33013

A sermon, preached in St. James' Church, Philadelphia. 39926

A sermon preached in St. John's Church, Elizabeth-Town. 6679

A sermon preached in St. Patrick's Cathedral. 31653

A sermon preached in St. Paul's Church, Alexandria. 2942

A sermon, preached in Saint Paul's Church at Troy. 28336

A sermon preached in St. Paul's Church, Boston. 22398

A sermon preached in St. Paul's Church, Troy. 8008

A sermon preached in St. Thomas's Church, New York, at the funeral of the Rev. Cornelius R. Duffie. 30118

A sermon preached in St. Thomas's Church, New York, on August 26, 1827. 31637

A sermon, preached in the chapel of Nassau Hall. 23449

A sermon preached in the church in Brattle Square. 21772

A sermon preached in the church of St. Augustine, in Philadelphia. 39043; 39044

A sermon, preached in the Congregational Church, in Chelsea. 17183

A sermon preached in the First Baptist Meetinghouse in Haverhill. 39176

A sermon, preached in the hall of the House of Representatives in Congress. 10317; 10318

A sermon, preached in the meeting House in Park Street, Boston. 12551

A sermon, preached in the newly rebuilt St. George's Church, Hempstead. 12781

A sermon, preached in the Old South Church, Boston. 6944

A sermon preached in the Presbyterian Church at Troy. 28876; 28877; 33175

A sermon preached in the Presbyterian Church of Drumacose, Newton-Limavady, Ireland. 38455

A sermon, preached in the Reformed Dutch Church, in Nassau-Street. 10375; 10376

A sermon, preached in the Second Presbyterian Church, Charleston, May 24, 1829. 37510

A sermon, preached in the Second Presbyterian Church, Charleston, October 6, 1827. 29020

A sermon preached in the South Parish in Weymouth. 9741

A sermon, preached in the state prison, in the city of New-York. 20327

Sermon, preached in Wintonbury meeting-house, Windsor. 7964

A sermon preached January 14,
1829.   40512

A sermon preached January 3,
1821.   6844

A sermon preached July 5, 1829
[Mead]   39537

A sermon preached July 5, 1829
[Strong]   40567

A sermon, preached July 6, 1824.
15801

A sermon preached June 9, 1824.
19327

A sermon, preached June 24th,
1822.   9009

A sermon preached March 8,
1826.   26211

A sermon, preached May, 1820.
1592

A sermon preached May, 1821.
5332

A sermon, preached May 15,
1821.   6845

A sermon preached May 10, 1826.
26212

A sermon preached November 19,
1826.   40203

A sermon, preached November
29, 1821.   6961

A sermon, preached November
23, 1826.   25879

A sermon, preached October 2,
1827.   28216

A sermon preached October 12,
1827.   28092

A sermon preached Oct. 24,
1787.   33547

A sermon preached on Thanksgiving day, to the Chapel Society, in North Yarmouth.
24240

A sermon, preached on the day
of general election, at Montpelier.   4630

A sermon preached on the occasion of the death of Nathaniel
Conkling.   9486

A sermon preached on the seventeenth of March, in the Irish
Franciscan Church of S. Isidore.   5543

A sermon, preached on the twentieth anniversary of his ordination [Tuckerman]   7015

A sermon, preached Sept. 18,
1825.   20100

A sermon preached September
14, 1826.   24751

A sermon, preached Sept. 14,
1823.   12396

A sermon preached September 2,
1828.   33436

A sermon preached September 2,
1827.   29087

A sermon, preached Sept. 12,
1821, at the ordination of the
Rev. George Fisher.   9092

A sermon, preached September
12, 1821, at the ordination of
the Rev. Richard Manning
Hodges.   5868

A sermon preached Sept. 24,
1823.   13187

A sermon, preached September
29, 1824.   16059

A sermon preached to the First
Congregational Church and Society in Exeter.   7674

A sermon preached to the Society in Brattle Square June 8th
1823.   13653

A sermon pronounced before
Vernon Lodge.   2768

A sermon pronounced in Milford,
Mass.   11417

A sermon showing the nature
and evil of church schism.
4243

A sermon.   The perdition of
Judas.   24429

A sermon, the substance of which
was delivered at the Third Parish in Gloucester.   29476

A sermon, the substance of which
was delivered before the Vermont Legislature.   21525

A sermon upon duelling.   7981

Sermon upon 1st Timoth, 3. 16.
17951

A sermon wherein is shown that
sin is finite, or limited, in
its nature and consequences.
29817

Sermons   [Blair]   8102; 23836
Sermons   [Cunningham]   12307
Sermons   [Moore]   17201
Sermons   [Smalley]   6805

Sermons adapted to revivals.
37206

Sermons and plans of sermons on
many of the most important
texts of holy scripture. 15325

Sermons, by Elias Hicks, Ann
Jones, and others. 33541

Sermons by Joseph Butler.
28342

Sermons by the late Rev. Cornelius R. Duffie. 38429

Sermons by the late Rev. David
Osgood. 17497

Sermons, by the late Rev. Edward Payson. 34659

Sermons by the late Rev. Henry
Martyn. 9371

Sermons by the late Rev. John
Emery Abbot. 37346; 37347

Sermons by the late Rev. Joseph
Lathrop. 5794

Sermons by the late Rev. Joseph
S. Buckminster. 37977

Sermons by the late Rev. Samuel
C. Thacher. 18172

Sermons by the Rev. John Venn.
11290

Sermons by Thomas Wetherald,
and Elias Hicks. 27622

Sermons, by Thomas Wetherald,
delivered at Friends' meetings
in Baltimore and Washington.
27623

Sermons by Thomas Wetherald:
delivered in the Friends' meeting, Washington City. 23300;
23301

Sermons; by Timothy Dwight.
33024

Sermons chiefly of a practical nature. 5352

Sermons, chiefly on sacramental
occasions. 3184

Sermons collected from the manuscripts of the late Rev. John
D. Blair. 19763

Sermons, delivered at Middleborough. 9800

Sermons delivered by Elias Hicks
and Edward Hicks. 12824;
20881

Sermons delivered on various occasions. 32258

Sermons for children. 13604;
17457; 34591

Sermons, illustrating the method
of interpreting the Sacred
Scriptures. 37964

Sermons illustrative of several
important principles of the
New Jerusalem Church.
25959

Sermons illustrative of the influence of life according to the
commandments. 19333

Sermons in a series of volumes.
14930

Sermons, left for publications by
John Taylor. 1804

Sermons of Samuel Johnson. 5727

Sermons of Samuel Stanhope
Smith. 6811

Sermons of the late Dr. James
Inglis. 1755

Sermons of the late Rev. J. S.
Buckminster. 4866

Sermons of the Rev. James
Saurin. 30527

Sermons on baptism. 39184

Sermons on important subjects
[Backus] 15147

Sermons on important subjects
[Davies] 32900

Sermons on important subjects
[Harris] 5544

Sermons on important subjects of
doctrine and duty. 21162

Sermons on important subjects,
selected from the manuscripts
of the late Rev'd James M'-
Chord. 9314

Sermons on particular occasions.
5367

Sermons; on philosophical, evangelical, and practical subjects.
29717; 34101; 39547

Sermons on practical subjects.
4151

Sermons on Psalm, CIII. 15, 16.
2274

Sermons on several occasions.
31708; 31709; 41474

Sermons on some of the distinguishing doctrines of divine
revelations. 21121

Sermons on the distinguishing

doctrines and duties of experimental religion. 16876

Sermons on the principal events and truths of Redemption. 16558

Sermons on the public means of grace. 5169

Sermons on the unity of God. 7866

Sermons on those doctrines of the gospel, and on those constituent principles of the church, which Christian professors have made the subject of controversy. 7889

Sermons on two subjects. 14938

Sermons on various subjects [Bowers] 568

Sermons on various subjects [Colman] 820

Sermons on various subjects [Kollock] 9219

Sermons on various subjects [Paley] 30144

Sermons on various subjects, chiefly practical. 31763

Sermons on various subjects of Christian doctrine and duty. 12453; 20410; 24430

Sermons on various subjects, practical and doctrinal. 14982

Sermons on war. 40543

Sermons, or homilies, appointed to be read in churches in the time of Queen Elizabeth. 12137; 35149

Sermons, practical and doctrinal. 25662

Sermons preached in England. 38952

Sermons preached in India. 38953

Sermons preached in St. John's Church. 15708; 15709

Sermons, preached in the Parish Church of High Wycombe. 8168

Sermons preached March 23, A.D. 1828. 35426

Sermons selected from the manuscripts of the late Moses Hoge. 5617

Sermons to children. 7666; 7667

Sermons translated from the original French of the late Rev. James Saurin. 10183

Sermons upon religious education and filial duty. 41404

Sermons upon the ministry, worship, and doctrines of the Protestant Episcopal Church. 32639

Sermons, upon various subjects and occasions. 25801

Servile spirits and spiritual masters. 600

Set of Mon's Labasses quadrilles. 2094

A set of new cottilions for the year 1825. 20855

A set of quadrilles. 22247

Seth Knowles. 36881

Sett of Monsr. Labasses quadrilles. 3311

Settlement of accounts of Farrow & Harris. 27391

Settlers - Michigan and Indiana. 36883

Settlers on Choctaw lands. 31505

Settlers on land--Choctaw district--Mississippi. 36884

Settlers on the Oregon River. 36882

The seven against Thebes. 23431

The seven champions of Christendom. 22248

Seven conversations between Athanasius and Docilis. 4505; 19470

The seven last plagues. 34984

Seven lectures on female education. 16252; 16253

Seven letters to Elias Hicks. 23199

Seven nights. 6566

Seven sermons. 3076

The seven wonders of the world. 10229; 26052

Seven years of the King's theatre. 33043

Seventeen discourses on several texts of scripture. 17840

Seventeen letters by B. C. 38480

Seventeenth annual report of the Vermont Bible Society. 41372

Seventeenth concert of the Musical Fund Society of Philadelphia. 34357

The seventeenth report [Bible Society of Philadelphia] 19724

Seventeenth report of the city auditor [Boston] 37897

The seventeenth report of the New-Hampshire Bible Society. 34446

Seventh annual meeting of the Baptist Education Society of the state of New York. 15177

Seventh annual report of the American Society for Colonizing the Free People of Colour. 15081; 15082

The seventh annual report of the Association for the relief of respectable aged indigent females. 156

The seventh annual report of the Auxiliary Missionary Society of New Haven, West. 27917

The seventh annual report, of the Board of Directors [Massachusetts Domestic Missionary Society] 21369

Seventh annual report of the board of directors of the Presbyterian Education Society. 21968

The seventh annual report of the Board of Managers of the Charleston Protestant Episcopal Sunday School Society. 24065

The seventh annual report of the Board of Managers of the General Convention of the Baptist denomination. 4598

The seventh annual report of The board of managers of the Missionary Society of The Reformed Dutch Church in North America. 40229

The seventh annual report of the Board of Managers of the New-York Protestant Episcopal Missionary Society. 13571

The seventh annual report of the board of managers of the New-York Protestant Episcopal Sunday School Society. 17419

Seventh annual report of the Committee of Finance [Boston] 4785; 15508

Seventh annual report of the Controllers of the Public Schools of the first district of the state of Pennsylvania. 21835

Seventh annual report of the Directors of the Boston Society for the Religious and Moral Instruction of the Poor. 11950; 15525

Seventh annual report of the directors of the New-York Institution for the Instruction of the Deaf and Dumb. 25576

The seventh annual report of the Female Society of Boston. 12532

The seventh annual report of the Managers of the Auxiliary New York Bible and Common Prayer Book Society. 13562

Seventh annual report of the Massachusetts Peace Society. 13266

Seventh annual report of the missionary society of the Methodist Church. 2251

Seventh annual report of the Missionary Society of the Methodist Episcopal Church. 25325

The seventh annual report of the New-York Religious Tract Society. 6286

Seventh annual report of the Philadelphia Orphan Society. 9899

The seventh annual report of the Religious Tract Society of Baltimore. 13919

Seventh annual report of the Rhode Island and Providence Plantations Peace Society. 17816

Seventh annual report of the trustees of the Female Missionary Society of the Western District, N. Y. 12530

Seventh annual report of the Washington Orphan Asylum Society. 14836

The shipwreck, a comic opera. 7838

Shipwreck! a memorial account of the Brig Ardent. 12903

The shipwreck and dreadful sufferings of Robert Barrow. 24351

The shipwreck, and other poems. 28838

The Shipwreck; or, Humanity rewarded. 3218

The Shipwreck; showing what sometimes happens on our sea coasts. 3219; 31982

Shocking calamity! Particulars of the tragical death of Mrs. Ann Taylor. 6794

Shooting match. At the new tavern in South Salem. 10273

A short account of a long travel; with Beauties of Wesley. 12397; 28727

A short account of Robert Cutts Whidden. 41493

A short account of Sierra Leone and Sherbro. 5079

A short account of the experience of Mrs. Hester Ann Rogers. 3042; 3043

A short account of the formation and proceedings of the Education Society of Nassau Hall. 8599

A short account of the Hartford convention. 13165

A short account of the life, last illness and death of Elizabeth C. Secor. 6795

A short account of the life of Jesse Cadbury. 10274

A short account of the life, sickness and death of Elizabeth Merritt. 2244

A short account of the small-pox which prevailed at Bridgeport. 26147

A short address, delivered before the sufferers by the late fire in Wiscasset and Alna. 17504

A short address to the Roman Catholic congregation of St. Mary's Church. 10275

Short and easy method with Deists wherein the certainty of the Christian religion is demonstrated. 25096

A short and plain catechism for children. 5799

A short and plain introduction to the better understanding of the Lord's Supper. 11454

Short appeal from the decrees of King Caucus and the Albany regency. 17977

A short Biblical catechism. 7664

Short biographical notices. 26078

A short biography of the illustrious citizen, Marquis de Lafayette. 17978

A short but comprehensive grammar. 13036

A short catechism, containing the most of what is necessary to be known in order to admission to the Lord's table. 8188

A short catechism for the use of the Catholic Church in the U.S.A. 20005; 24039

A short catechism, for young children. 598; 4850; 8187; 12007

A short defence of diocesan episcopacy. 3220

A short epistle, addressed to the people, who are called Baptists. 458; 15398

A short essay to do good. 35140

A short extract from the Heidelberg Catechism. 6585; 16501

A short historical account of the early society of Methodists. 17979

A short history of a long travel from Babylon to Bethel. 5109

A short history of a moral & political scoundrel. 32607

Short history of LaFayette. 26066

A short history of the African Union Meeting and School House. 6564

A short history of the life of Joshua Comstock. 8416

A short history of the life of William Vans. 23144

A short instruction in the Christian religion. 16503; 24827

A short introduction to Latin grammar. 960; 12330; 20268

A short memoir of Andrew Underhill. 26079

A short method with Peter Edwards: in which the Baptist tenets are vindicated. 5713

Short method with the deists. 13090

Short missionary discourses. 17658

A short narrative of the revival of religion in Ithaca. 30505

A short, plain, comprehensive, practical Latin grammar. 13989; 30482; 40318

A short poem, containing a descant on the universal plan. 2673; 30163

Short poems: including a sketch of the Scriptures. 28882

Short practical essays on the Sabbath. 24127

A short reply to a pamphlet published at Philadelphia. 32377

Short review of a project for uniting the Courts of Law and Equity in this State [S. C.] 10312

A short scriptural catechism. 14118

A short sketch of the author's life, and adventures. 19999

A short statement of the excellency of Doctor Horwitz's anti-bilious pills. 13167

Short stories. 30610

Short stories, moral & religious. 35199

A short system of polite learning. 1785; 12946; 24976

A short system of practical arithmetic. 9212; 13022; 21123; 29423; 39206

A short treatise: containing, observations on the duty of believers. 13072

Short treatise on horticulture. 13851; 34887

A short treatise on operative surgery. 11650

A short treatise on prayer. 1967

A short treatise on the superior excellency of the Scripture Psalms. 7655

A short view of the history of the Christian church. 2949

A short view of the whole Scripture history. 11365

Shorter catechism. 4252; 6796; 6797

The shortness of time. 21961

Should those fond hopes. A favorite Portuguese air. 3331; 6885

Siamese youths. 41432

Sibyline leaves and wayward criticisms. 22286

Der sichere Himmels-Weg. 1271; 12576; 33232

Sicilian air, on which is founded the popular ballad of Home! sweet home. 15445; 15446

Sicilian mariners hymn. 14119

The sick man's friend. 189; 17983

The sick monkey. 35200

Die siebenlezten Posaunen oder Wehen. 1815

The siege of Algiers. 14143

The siege of Belgrade. 12190

The siege of Constantinople. 8658

The siege of Tripoli. 8285

Sigh not for love. 13018

Sigh not for the summer flowers. 348

Signiorina's concert. 30611

Signs of the moral age. 32376

Signs of the times. A sermon delivered in Brookfield. 18022

The signs of the times. A sermon delivered in Rochester. 34644; 39963

Signs of the times: A sermon preached in the chapel of the Theological Seminary, Andover. 13818

The signs of the times: being the substance of a discourse delivered in Chillicothe, Ohio. 5885

Signs of the Times--Extra. Message of His Excellency DeWitt Clinton. 34505

Silent glances. 15937

The silent stream. 16589

Silent submission under affliction. 518

Silk-worms. Letter from James Mease. 36885

Silver mines in Mexico. 40425

The silver sixpence. 26081

Simple innocente et joliette. 11914

Simple hymns for children. 37187

Simple memorials of an Irish family. 40429

Simple stories, in words of one syllable. 14123; 22282

Simple truth, illustrated in eight short discourses. 6967

Simplicity in the Christian faith alike scriptural and powerful. 29825; 34210

The simplified German grammar. 11867

Simpson & Co., a comedy. 13804; 30292

The sin against the Holy Ghost illustrated. 9277

Sin destitute of the apology of inability. 3227

Since the promulgation of the General Order, of the 9th July, 1821, the President of the United States directs the commanding General to announce the following promotions. 7043

Since then I'm doomed. 1625; 13063; 21170; 21171

The sincere Christian instructed in the faith of Christ. 8976

Singing exemplified in a series of solfeggi [sic] and exercises. 32826a

Single rail railway. 30618

Sinking fund. Annual report of the Commissioners. 41311

Sinners in the hands of an angry God. 24115

Sir, ... [form letter sent by chairman of the Democratic Committee of Correspondence for the City and County of Philadelphia.] 12365

Sir: Agreeably to the request of the General Assembly, I transmit you a copy of their resolutions. 2586

Sir: Accompanying this letter, you will receive a copy of the proceedings. 32011

Sir. Although I have very recently issued a long circular letter. 32591

Sir and Brother, I beg leave to transmit you a copy of the Annual publication of the R. W. Grand Lodge. 16223

Sir Andrew Wylie, of that ilk. 8799

Sir. As I am about to retire from public life. 35406

Sir, As very erroneous impressions prevail on that portion of the proceedings of the convention at Harrisburg. 28403

Sir, At a meeting of Persons "opposed to the election of General Jackson." 34364

Sir, at a town meeting on Friday last. 19980

Sir, At an interview which took place on the 18th instant. 25863

Sir, At the request of the Legislature of this State, I have the honor to transmit to you, their decided opinion. 2510

Sir, Being appointed a committee to procure an exhibition. 15834

Sir David Hunter Blair's favorite reel. 17988

Sir Francis and Henry. 3230

Sir. Having been appointed by a public meeting held in this city. 17084

Sir, Having had the honour of being appointed by a large and respectable meeting of the citizens of Philadelphia. 25741

Sir, Having, on mature consideration, resolved to withdraw from the discussion of the tariff question. 15670

Sir, I am induced by the critical situation of the application for the protection of the woolen and other manufactures, to adress a circular. 32592; 32593

Sir: I have the honor to enclose an address to the Legislature. 4116

Sir. I have the honor to hand you a copy of a memorial, which I propose to submit to the Legislature. 4821

Sir, I have the honor to lay before you the following resolution. 41392; 41393

Sir, I regret to say, that the favorable anticipations, which. 41391

Sir: I take the liberty of directing this to you. 1144

Sir. I trust your honorable station, and the magnitude of my subject, will excuse the liberty I take. 24264

Sir. In behalf of the Genesee Missionary Society. 5433

Sir, In compliance with the direction of the standing committee of the General Theological Seminary. 34537

Sir, It has been determined by a number of the citizens of Fayette County. 16013; 16124

Sir, It is highly gratifying to find that sound opinions are rapidly spreading. 24014

Sir, It is well known that Mr. Jefferson has been compelled to seek relief. 23875

Sir, Men are liable to be imposed upon by unfounded pretensions. 40096

Sir, Notwithstanding the very ungenerous, ungentlemanly and ungrateful manner in which I have been treated. 32594

Sir, On the 4th of May, I received a letter from Lewis Tappan. 28404

Sir, Pursuant to a request of three Trustees of the Theological Seminary of the Protes-

tant Episcopal Church, it has become my duty. 4858

Sir. Sincerely desirous to promote the reputation of the American Philosophical Society. 15671; 15672

Sir, the annexed resolution, and the appended papers, are respectfully submitted. 30229

Sir. The annual meeting of the contributors to the Boston Dispensary will be holden. 37905

Sir: The board of officers assembled at this city to report "A completes system of cavalry tactics." 27395

Sir. The Central corresponding committee, appointed by the friends of the administration in convention on the 23d July last. 34395

Sir, The enclosed memorial is submitted to your consideration. 27962

Sir. The Legislature of this state, desirous of establishing a system of criminal jurisprudence. 5843

Sir. The Light Infantry Company of New-England Guards are hereby ordered to appear. 2411

Sir, The officers of the militia being required by the 13th section of the militia law to wear an "uniform dress..." 9347

Sir. The outrage committed on Wednesday last on my person, is doubtless known to you. 35515

Sir, The rejection of the electoral law. 16375

Sir, The result of the approaching election. 13930

Sir, The salutary bill for the protection of the woolen manufacture failed. 28405

Sir: The trustees of the Boston Library. 19817

Sir, the undersigned, a committee on the part of the citizens of the metropolitan county of the Territory of Michigan. 11369

Sir, The undersigned are a committee appointed by the Agricultural Society of Albermarle. 7754

Sir, the undersigned being a committee appointed by their fellow citizens of both political parties friendly to the state and national administrations. 30619

Sir - The undersigned, members of the Democratic Republican Committee. 17126

Sir, we beg to announce to you, the establishment of an association, under the title of "The Pennsylvania Society for the Promotion of Internal Improvements." 17580

Sir, we have the honor to address you as a committee appointed by the citizens of Columbia and Richland. 30620

Sir. We have the pleasure to inform you, that at length, after much difficulty, we have succeeded in chartering a vessel. 30230

Sir, we take the liberty to enclose the plan of a society for the promotion of national improvements. 17989

Sir: We take the liberty to enclose the plan of the Society for the Promotion of National Improvements. 17581

Sir. When I undertook the editorship of the Political Economist, it was in the fond expectation that there would be no difficulty. 15673

Sir--Wishing to collect all the information, possible, on the subject of the culture of the vine, within the United States. 20344

Sir--You have already been informed through the medium of the press, that Congress adjourned on the 15th of May. 1511

Sir, You will herewith receive a copy of the New Olive Branch. 681

Sir. You will herewith receive the first of four codes, which form a system of penal law. 16927

Sir, You will perceive by the subjoined resolution of the faculty of this institution. 37042

Sir: Your favor of the twelfth ult. has been received. 17500

Sistema politico moral. 6574

A sister's gift. 35207; 40431

The Sisters. A selection of popular & esteemed airs. 3231

The sisters. Being the first of a series of interesting stories. 6868

The sisters of St. Clara. 20460

The sisters of the cavern. 12816

Sisyphi opus: or, Touches at the times. 4154

Site for an armory - Louisville, Kentucky. 27396

Site United States Arsenal, Mount Dearborn, South Carolina. 27397

Sive collectanea Graeca majora. 15920

Six divertimentos in a familiar style. 3318; 6802; 6865-6867

Six duettos for juvenile performers. 8829

Six favorite waltzes for two performers on the piano forte. 19122

Six favourite airs. 13986

Six hundred questions deduced from Goldsmith's History of England. 10286

Six letters proving the residency and episcopacy of St. Peter in the city of Rome. 38481

Six letters to the editor of the Charleston Observer. 32567

Six months in the West Indies. 24157

Six months residence and travels in Central America. 24775

Six progressive sonatas for the
piano forte. 15686
Six sermons, containing some
remarks, on Mr. Andrew Ful-
ler's reasons for believing that
the future punishment of the
wicked would be endless.
14201
Six sermons on the nature, occa-
sions, signs, evils, and rem-
edy of intemperance. 28093;
32259; 32260; 37746-37749
Six short sermons adapted to the
aged. 40520
Six waltzes. 8834
Sixteen short sermons. 3232
Sixteenth annual exhibition of the
Pennsylvania Academy of the
Fine Arts. 30184
The sixteenth annual report of the
Association for the Relief of
Respectable, Aged, Indigent
Females. 37513
Sixteenth annual report of the
Auxiliary Foreign Mission So-
ciety, of Franklin County.
32050
Sixteenth annual report of the
Bible Society of Virginia.
37843
Sixteenth annual report of the re-
ceipts and expenditures of the
city of Boston. 32423
Sixteenth annual report of the
trustees of the Free-School
Society of New York. 6571
Sixteenth annual report of the
Vermont Bible Society. 37010
Sixteenth annual report on the
concerns of the Female Cent
Institution. 38560
The sixteenth report of the Bible
Society of Philadelphia. 15396
The sixteenth report of the New-
Hampshire Bible Society.
29945
Sixth and seventh letters to Rev.
Samuel Miller. 6839
Sixth annual convocation of the
Grand Royal Arch Chapter of
North Carolina. 33269
Sixth annual meeting of the Bap-
tist Education Society of the

State of New-York. 11679
Sixth annual meeting of the Rich-
mond and Manchester Coloni-
zation Society. 40280
Sixth annual report [Rhode Is-
land. Peace Society] 13943
The sixth annual report of the
American Society for Coloniz-
ing the Free People of Colour.
11596
The sixth annual report of the
Board of Managers of the
Charleston Protestant Episco-
pal Sunday School Society.
20034
Sixth annual report of the board
of managers of the Kentucky
Bible Society. 9197
The sixth annual report of the
Board of managers of the New
York Protestant Episcopal
Missionary Society. 2536
The sixth annual report of the
Board of Managers of the New
York Protestant Episcopal
Sunday School Society. 13572
Sixth annual report of the board
of managers of The Protes-
tant Episcopal Female Tract
Society of Baltimore. 13881
The sixth annual report of the
board of trustees of the New
Hampshire Baptist Mission
Society. 21625
Sixth annual report of the Boston
Society for the Religious and
Moral Instruction of the Poor.
8150
Sixth annual report of the Charles-
ton Bethel Union. 32644
Sixth annual report of the Charles-
ton Port Society. 38114
Sixth annual report of the Controllers of the Public Schools
of the first school district of
the state of Pennsylvania.
17569
Sixth annual report of the directors of the Domestic Missionary Society of Connecticut.
8563
Sixth annual report of the directors of the New York Institu-

tion for the Instruction of the
Deaf and Dumb. 21686

Sixth Annual Report of the Executive Committee [New England
Tract Society] 2427

Sixth annual report of the Female
Auxiliary Bible Society of Cincinnati. 8692

The sixth annual report of the
managers of the Auxiliary New-
York Bible and Common Prayer
Book Society. 7856

Sixth annual report of the managers of the New-York Asylum
for Lying-in Women. 39814

The sixth annual report of the
managers of the Society for the
Prevention of Pauperism.
14156

Sixth annual report of the managers of the Union Female
Missionary Society. 40708

Sixth annual report of the Massachusetts Peace Society. 9430

Sixth annual report of the Middlesex Bible Society. 6042

The sixth annual report of the
Missionary Society of the Reformed Dutch Church. 34974

Sixth annual report of the New
York Female Auxiliary Bible
Society. 9696

Sixth annual report of the New
York Sunday School Union Society. 9706

Sixth annual report of the Philadelphia Orphan Society. 6452

Sixth annual report of the trustees
of the Connecticut Reserve
Bible Society. 452

Sixth annual report of the trustees
of the Female Missionary Society of the Western District.
8695

Sixth annual report of the Young
Men's Missionary Society of
New York. 7725

Sixth annual report of the Young
Men's New York Bible Society.
39816

Sixth general report of the president and directors of the
Chesapeake and Delaware Canal Company. 20038

Sixth report of the American
Bible Society. 7791

Sixth report of the board of directors of the Presbyterian
Education Society. 17690

Sixth report of the directors of
the American Asylum at Hartford. 7790

Sixth report of the directors of
the American Education Society. 4470

Sixth report of the directors of
the Penitent Female's Refuge.
22051

Sixth report of the New York
Bank for Savings. 21678

The sixth report of the Philadelphia Sunday and Adult School
Union. 13755

The sixth report of the United
Foreign Missionary Society.
14337

The sixth section, act of 23d
March, 1826 [Penn.] 25701

Sixtieth anniversary. Minutes of
the Warren Baptist Association. 28031

Sixtieth annual commencement of
Brown University. 37969

Sixty-first anniversary. Minutes
of the Warren Baptist Association. 32182

Sixty progressive lessons arr.
either for one or two clarinets.
8806

Sixty-second anniversary. Minutes
of the Warren Baptist Association. 37670

The 62d annual publication. Minutes of the Ketocton Baptist
Association. 32196

The skaters. 35208

The sketch book. 1770; 1771;
9130; 16685; 24963; 33677;
39106

Sketch of a journey through the
western states of North America and the city of Cincinnati.
29615

Sketch of an argument delivered
before the District court of the
U. States. 21268

Sketch of an Indian Irruption into the Town of Shawanqunk, in 1780. 3233

Sketch of Connecticut. 17984

Sketch of etymology, syntax, punctuation, [sic] and prosody. 3234

A sketch of medical chemistry. 33156

Sketch of Mr. Teackles remarks. 35474

A sketch of my friend's family. 2111-2113; 5942; 5943; 9365; 25233; 29630; 29631; 34021

A sketch of old England. 9822

A sketch of several distinguished members of the Woodbee family. 14126

A sketch of the botany of South-Carolina and Georgia. 5243; 16053

A sketch of the character of John Adams. 24161

Sketch of the character of Mr. Canning. 35081

A sketch of the character of the late Hon. Samuel Howe [Strong] 35427

A sketch of the character of the late Hon. Samuel Howe [Williams] 37192

A sketch of the claims of sundry American citizens on the government. 24042

A sketch of the condition of the science of law in the United States. 5658

A sketch of the ecclesiastical history of Ipswich. 13014

A sketch of the first settlement of the several towns on Long Island. 19320; 27689; 37224

Sketch of the geographical rout of a great railway. 40221

A sketch of the geography of the town of Huntington. 19321

Sketch of the geology, mineralogy and topography of Connecticut. 12837

Sketch of the history, articles of faith, rules of discipline [Congregational Church in Newport, N. H.] 39842

A sketch of the history of Alabama Presbytery. 25824

A sketch of the history of Framingham. 27938

Sketch of the history of the church. 38304

A sketch of the history of the grammar school, in the easterly part of Roxbury. 25666

A sketch of the insolvent laws of Pennsylvania. 9112

Sketch of the internal condition of the United States. 25794

Sketch of the Irish code. 12064

Sketch of the laws [Virginia] 11311; 23170; 31629

A sketch of the laws relating to slavery in the several states of the United States. 30732

A sketch of the life and character of Matthew Irvine. 28985

A sketch of the life and character of the Hon. Samuel Howe. 33458

Sketch of the life and character of the late Rev. Joseph Mottey. 10287

A sketch of the life and dying words of William Hillhouse Barron. 40432

Sketch of the life and military services of Gen. LaFayette. 17990

A sketch of the life and public services of John Quincy Adams. 30621; 35209

Sketch of the life and public services of Nathaniel Peabody. 17991

A sketch of the life and services of John Quincy Adams. 30622; 35210; 35211

A sketch of the life and singular sickness of Heman Doane. 24357

A sketch of the life, condemnation and death of the three Thayers. 22287

Sketch of the life of Alexander Wilson. 34619

A sketch of the life of Brig. Gen. Francis Marion. 5709

A sketch of the life of elder

Benj. Putnam. 6575

A sketch of the life of General Thomas Metcalfe. 35212

Sketch of the life of James Bennington. 17992

Sketch of the life of John Quincy Adams. 17993; 30623

A sketch of the life of the late Rev. John Cowper. 891

A sketch of the life of Thomas Jefferson. 24694

A sketch of the most important events of the life of Andrew Jackson. 35213

A sketch of the olden times. 37872

A sketch of the Pilgrims of Plymouth. 3235

A sketch of the politics, relations and statistics of the Western World. 28454

A sketch of the practice of physic. 34937

Sketch of the resources of the city of New-York. 28710

A sketch of the state of Nineveh. 14127

A sketch of the theory of protecting & prohibitory duties. 35214

A sketch of the tour of General Lafayette. 16170

Sketch of the trial of the Hon. Nathaniel W. Williams. 40433

A sketch on the difference between the doctrines of the people commonly called Newlights and the Methodists. 6966

Sketches [Clarke] 24121

Sketches [Willis] 31771

Sketches, essays and translations. 33360

Sketches from the Bible, written for the American Sunday School Union. 40434

Sketches, historical and topographical, of the Floridas. 5351

Sketches of a tour to the Lakes. 29575

Sketches of Algiers. 26060

Sketches of American character. 38884

Sketches of an address read before the Hartford County Agricultural Society. 2548

Sketches of character; or Facts and arguments, relative to the presidential election. 35215

Sketches of history, life, and manners, in the United States. 25978

Sketches of Irish character. 38885; 38886

Sketches of Moravian missions. 30624; 35216

Sketches of naval life. 39158

Sketches of Persia. 33998

Sketches of scenery and manners in the United States. 38436

Sketches of sermons preached to congregations in various parts of Great Britain. 26083

Sketches of the domestic manners and institutions of the Romans. 10288; 14128

Sketches of the early history of Maryland. 5504

Sketches of the earth and its inhabitants. 14978

Sketches of the ecclesiastical history of the state of Maine. 5497

Sketches of the elements of natural philosophy. 26063

Sketches of the history, manners, and customs of the North American Indians. 15586

Sketches of the History of literature. 30759

Sketches of the life and character of William H. Crawford. 15606

Sketches of the life and correspondence of Nathanael Greene. 9162

Sketches of the life and public services of Gen. Andrew Jackson. 16244

Sketches of the primitive settlements on the river Delaware. 28059; 32214

Sketches of the public services of Adams, Clay, and Crawford. 14129

Sketches of the trial of Stephen

joint committee on rivers and canals, relating to the proposed improvements of Connecticut River.   35353

Some remarks on a pamphlet entitled "Rev. Mr. McIllvaine in answer to the Rev. H. U. Onderdonk."   40482

Some remarks on education. 33313

Some remarks on the assassination of Julius Caesar.   30644

Some remarks on the "Toleration act" of 1819.   14149

Some remarks upon a publication by the Philadelphia Medical Society concerning Swaim's panacea.   35443

Some rules for the investigation of religious truth.   27716

Some Scripture facts and prophecies illustrated in a treatise. 28563

Some serious considerations on the present state of parties. 30392

Some strictures on church government.   14163

Some thoughts on the doctrine of justification.   24314

Some thoughts upon population. 14164

Some unkindly wou'd persuade me. 6824

Some very gentle touches to some very gentle men.   3269

Somerseter calender.   3270; 6824a

Somerville's plume of the classics.   3271

Something must be done: a New Year's sermon.   6847

Something new; or, A budget of Calvinism.   31873

La somnambule, comedie-vaudeville.   35132

The son of a genius.   24876

A son of the forest.   37490

A sonata [Beethoven] 11789

A sonata [Dussek]   12414

A sonata [Nicolai]   2552

A sonata [Pleyel]   13795

Sonata [Steibelt]   10340; 14199

Song. By Frederick S. Hill. 29214

Song, for the celebration of the 4th of July.   8952

The song of ascent.   Sermon. 20862

A song of 4 stanzas, on the Marquis de Lafayette's visit. 18049

Song of the angels at the birth of Christ.   35462

Songs by the way.   15985

Songs. Divine and moral. 4206

Songs, duetts, & chorusses. 13367

Songs for gentlemen, patriotic, comic, and descriptive. 3272

Songs for ladies.   3273

Songs in the night.   5549

Songs of Judah, and other melodies.   3386

Songs of Zion: being a collection of hymns, for the use of the pious of all denominations. 18075; 26125; 30695; 40515

Songs of Zion; being imitations of Psalms.   13373

Songs of Zion, containing a choice collection of Psalm and hymn tunes.   16899

Songs of Zion: or, The Christian's new hymn book.   10308

Songs, patriotic, humorous, and sentimental. 22327

The Songster's magazine.   3274

The songster's museum.   10309; 14165; 18050; 26103; 26104; 40484

The songster's new pocket companion.   6825

Sophia Morton.   30660

Sophia: or, The bandit of the forest.   35355

Sorrowful Sam.   40485

The sorrows of Werter.   12692; 16303-16307; 38764

The sorrows of Yamba. 3275

Sound doctrine intolerable. 23739

Sound the loud timbrel. 4515; 7857

Sound the trumpet. 16537

The source of public prosperity.

37422
South America. 6933
South Carolina - Abbeville District. Memorial. 31506
The South Carolina almanac. 40489
South Carolina Canal and Rail Road Company. 40494
South Carolina - Edgefield District. Memorial 31507
South Carolina. Memorial of citizens of Chesterfield, Marlborough, and Darlington. 36887
South Carolina. Memorial of the canal and rail road company. 36889
South Carolina. Memorial of the Charleston Chamber of Commerce. 36890
South Carolina. Memorial of the citizens of Columbia. 31508
South Carolina. Memorial of the citizens of Laurens District. 36891
South Carolina. Memorial of the citizens of Orangeburg, S. C. 31509
South Carolina. Memorial of the inhabitants of Barnwell District. 31510
South Carolina. Memorial of the inhabitants of Fairfield District. 31511
South Carolina. Memorial of the inhabitants of Newberry District. 36888
South Carolina. Memorial of the Legislature of the state. 36892
South Carolina. Remonstrance of the citizens of Beaufort District. 36893
The South Sea islander. 3282
The southern and western songster. 30674
Southern bend of Lake Mighican. 36894
Southern boundary - Lake Michigan. 36895
The southern excitement, against the American system. 40496
Southern excitement, or A view

of the opinions and designs of the friends of General Andrew Jackson. 22332
The southern preacher. 16971
Le souvenir. Air. 14278
Souvenir, or Moral and religious selections. 40500
Le souvenir, or, Picturesque pocket diary. 18062; 22335; 26110; 26111; 30677
The sovereignty of God. 4325
The spaewife. 16250
The Spanish constitutional march. 18065
The Spanish dance. 18066; 20676; 22339
The Spanish daughter. 15611; 15612
Spanish grammar. 25099
A Spanish minuet. 22340
Spanish rondo. 16839
Spanish telegraph. A new and easy method to read Spanish. 21194
Spanish waltz. 2252; 6834
The speaker; or, Miscellaneous pieces, selected from the best English writers. 12455
Speakers for the Parkerian Premiums. 29753
Special acts passed at the eighth session of the General Assembly of the state of Indiana. 16662
Special meeting of the Foreign Mission Society of Boston. 12567
Special message. 39906
Specification for a lock. 39911
Specification of a patent for an apparatus denominated the dormant balance. 38079
Specification of a patent for locomotive engines or carriages propelled by steam, on rail. 39032
Specification of an improvement or combination in the art of constructing rail roads. 40573
Specification on certain improvements in the locomotive engine. 25133

Specifications for a stone and wood lock. 39912

Specifications of a patent for an improved rail-way carriage. 39033

Specifications of patents for improvements in rail-roads and cars. 41600

Specimen florae Americae septentrionalis cryptogamicae. 6732

Specimen impressions of Congreve patent bank checks and Rewards of merit. 567

A specimen of divine truths. 5570; 5571; 20851; 33519

Specimen of modern printing types and stereotype cuts from the Boston Type and Stereotype Foundry. 23899

Specimen of ornamental type and printing ornaments cast at A. Chandler's foundry. 8308

Specimen of ornamental types & embellishment, cast at the foundry of A. Chandler. 705

A specimen of printing type cast in the Franklin Letter Foundry. 39207

A specimen of printing type, from the foundry of O. & H. Wells. 31706

Specimen of printing type from the letter foundry of James Ronaldson. 10135

A specimen of printing types [Boston Foundry] 537

Specimen of printing types, by R. Starr & Co. 26133

A specimen of printing types, cast at the letter-foundry of D. & G. Bruce. 606

A specimen of printing types, cast in the Franklin letter foundry. 33777

Specimen of printing types from the Boston Type and Stereotype Foundry. 32449

A specimen of printing types from the foundry of E. White. 7647; 27632

A specimen of the consistency of Universalists. 26112

Specimens of American poetry. 39194

Specimens of bank note engraving. 20348

Specimens of Irish eloquence. 2755

Specimens of metal ornaments and job types cast, and for sale at the stereotype foundry of J. Howe. 12879

Specimens of the Russian poets. 8163

The Spectator. 10319; 18070; 26113; 26114; 40502

The spectre bridegroom. 6090

The spectre mother. 14179

The spectre of the forest. 13176

Speech delivered at the bar of the Senate of South-Carolina. 1554

Speech delivered at the fourth anniversary of the American Bible Society. 559

A speech delivered before the American Bible Society. 1458

Speech delivered before the overseers of Harvard College. 20833; 21710

A speech, delivered before the Senate of the state of Louisiana. 30484

Speech delivered by John S. Tyson. 30858

Speech delivered by Mr. Lewis Louaillier. 29535

Speech delivered in the United States House of Representatives, on the Seminole War in 1819. 34969

Speech in support of an American system for the protection of American industry. 15778; 15779

Speech in the Senate, on the bill for the repeal of the laws prohibiting private banking. 22342

Speech of Abel P. Upshur. 41351

Speech of Alexander Smyth. 35239

Speech of Ben. Hardin. 16407

Speech of Colonel Leslie Combs. 38237

Speech of Col. Richard M. John-

ges. 28325

Speech of the Hon. Wm. Smith of South Carolina, delivered in the Senate of the United States, December 8, 1820. 14148

Speech of the Hon. William Smith, of South-Carolina, in the Senate of the United States, on the bill making appropriation for internal improvements. 35236

Speech of the Rev. Isaac Clinton. 32739

Speech of Thomas Kennedy, esq. at the Jackson meeting. 29409

Speech of Thomas Kennedy, Esq. in the Legislature of Maryland. 12999

Speech of Thomas P. Moore. 29793

Speech of Thomas R. Joynes. 39169a

Speech of Thomas Smith Grimké. 38850

Speech of W. T. Barry. 28064

Speech of William C. Jarvis. 12952

Speech of William Maxwell. 25286

Speech of William T. Barry. 23709

Speech on the admission of Missouri. December 12, 1820. 2065

Speech on the Canal Bill. 5619

Speech on the Indian Bill. 342

Speech on the Missouri question. 3131

A speech on the operation of the tariff on the interests of the South. 33465

Speech on the Panama mission. 24988

Speech on the preamble and resolutions protesting against the decision of the Supreme Court of the United States. 15932

Speech on the proposition to amend the constitution of the United States. [Everett] 24462

Speech on the proposition to amend the Constitution of the

United States [Henry] 24834

Speech on the proposition to amend the constitution of the United States [Stevenson] 35402

Speech on the tariff bill. 17656

Speech upon taxing bank stock. 9057

The speeches, addresses and messages, of the several presidents of the United States. 23128

The speeches of Charles Phillips. 2756; 2757; 6471; 13765

The speeches of Governor Clinton. 12188; 13557

Speeches of Henry Baldwin. 192

The speeches of Henry Clay. 28517

Speeches of J. J. Ormond and A. F. Hopkins. 39934

The speeches of Mr. Jacob Barker and his counsel. 23701; 28058

Speeches of Mr. Randolph. 17752

Speeches of Mr. Wilde. 37180

Speeches of Mr. Wood. 27690

Speeches of Mr. Wright. 31824

The speeches of the different governors, to the Legislature of the state of New-York. 21672

Speeches on Increasing the number of delegates; and address to the Convention of the Two Republican Parties in the Western District. 5483

Speeches on the Jew bill. 37923

Speed the plough. 9561

The speller and definer. 38946-38948

The speller's guide. 10276; 17980

Spelling book, being a just standard for pronouncing the English language. 20102; 24132

A spelling book containing exercises in orthography, pronunciation, and reading. 19785; 28211; 32408

A spelling-book containing the rudiments of the English language. 13083; 33834; 39263

A spelling-book for the United

States. 41595

A spelling book of the English language. 2110; 5944; 9363; 13221; 17024; 17025; 21332; 25232; 29629

A spelling book, written in the Chahta language. 23386

A spelling book written in the Chato language. 31822

The spelling reader. 38785

The spinning wheel. A favorite ballad. 16525

The spirit of Methodism. A poem. 39986

The spirit of Odin. 24836

The spirit of orthodoxy. 33045

The spirit of prayer [Law] 13070

The spirit of prayer [More] 25421

The spirit of '76. 40503

The spirit of the gospel essential to a happy result of our religious inquiries. 28430

The spirit of the Old Dominion. 29784

The spirit of the Pilgrims. 30720

Spiritous liquor to the Army. 41313

Spirits in prison. 3079

Spiritual and experimental regeneration. 40504

Spiritual blessings. 23537

The spiritual combat. 14075

A spiritual exposition of the declaration, in the parable of the sheep and goats. 10322

Spiritual gleanings. 16330

The spiritual guide. 6089

Spiritual lessons from a military school. 30130

The spiritual mirror or looking glass. 22343

The spiritual mustard pot. 17227

A spiritual poem on animated graves. 39941

A spiritual retreat, for eight successive days. 561

Spiritual songs. 15550

Spiritual temple. A sermon. 2726

The spiritual testimony. 6484

A spiritual treasury. 2142

The spiritual voyage, performed in the ship Convert. 23903; 32451; 32452

Spirituous liquors pernicious & useless. 39235

Splendid original paintings, at auction. 339

Splendid, rare and valuable foreign books at auction. 14280

Splendid triumph of principle. 18071

The splendid wedding. 13500

The spoil'd child. 16555; 32371

Spoliations of the French, prior to 1800. 30686

Spoliations on the commerce of the United States. 31512; 31513

Spooner's Brooklyn directory. 10324; 14182; 18072; 22344; 26115; 40506

Sporting anecdotes, original and selected. 8606; 12435

The sports of New York. 18023

Sprigs of laurel. 30111

Spring flowers. 10327

The spring time of the year is coming. 3429

The springtime of love. 15447

The Spy. 5075; 8441; 8442; 15859; 28601; 32831; 38277

The spy unmasked. 32220; 37708

Squire Hartley, a farce. 30756

The squirrel's family. 40517

The stage, canal and steamboat register. 3299

Stage register. 22366; 27924

The Stand. 3301

A standard spelling book. 26036; 30559; 35138; 35139

The standards of the Reformed Dutch Church, exculpated from the charge of teaching indefinite atonement. 13908

Standing orders, for conducting the business of the "Columbian Institute." 24172

Standing rules and orders, for the government of and conducting business in the Senate of the state of Indiana. 21013

Standing rules for conducting business in the first and second branches of the city council of the city of Baltimore. 27949

Standing rules for the government of the legislative council of Michigan. 17147

Staniford's practical arithmetic. 3307

Stantz waltz. 13213; 17221

The star of Bethlehem [Banister] 215

The Star of Bethlehem. A sacred song. 1426; 1427; 5477; 8869

The star of the west, being memoirs of the life of Risdon Darracott. 37759

The star of the west, or Kenyon College. 32653

A star of Virginia. 28987

The Star Spangled Banner. 1581; 3245; 6809; 14142; 18008; 22300; 22361; 38967

State convention. At a meeting of Republican delegates of the several counties in the State of New-York. 15054

The state convention on internal improvements. 21351

State convention. Proceedings and address of the Republican young men. 34394

State of agriculture in Italy. 2663

State of Alabama. A remonstrance of the General Assembly of Alabama. 36896

The state of business in the Supreme Court of the state of New-York. 18078

State of Maine. State prison. 21311

State of New-Jersey, Secretary's office. 2460

State of New-York agricultural almanack. 3309; 6858; 10334; 10335; 14192; 14193; 18079; 22364

State of New-York. Secretary's office. I certify, that licenses have been issued to the following persons. 25564

State of New York. In the Court for the trial of impeachments and the correction of errors, between Peter McCartee, one of the executors of the last will and testament of Philip Jacobs. 30029

State of New York. In the Court for the trial of impeachments and the correction of errors. Between the Orphan Asylum Society, in the City of New York, respondents, and Peter M'Cartee. 30030

State of Ohio agricultural almanac. 30698

State of the accounts of the Pennsylvania Hospital. 34702; 40013

State of the Asylum for the relief of persons deprived of the use of their reason. 1333; 9894; 13748; 25742

The state of the case and argument for the appellants, in the case of the Bank of the United States versus the auditor and treasurer of the state of Ohio. 12751

The state of the departed, set forth in a funeral address. 20916

State of the finances. 23129; 27401; 31514

State of the New-York Hospital. 6274; 14159

State of the Treasury of Massachusetts. 13257

State of Vermont, Chittenden County, ss. Heman Allen against Usal Pierson and Silas Hathaway. 7779

State prisons and the penitentiary system vindicated. 6859

State register of civil, judicial, military and other offices of Connecticut. 40525; 40526

Stated communication of the Grand Lodge of Delaware. 33255; 38638

Statement addressed by the association of the Fifth Presbyterian Church to the members of the congregation. 40047

Statement and evidence of the
doctrine of the Trinity. 41571

Statement and exposition of the
title of John Jacob Astor to
the lands purchased by him.
30699; 30700

Statement, and remarks of The
Caledonia County Bible Society.
647

The statement and substance of
a memorial, &c., of John
Nicholas. 2550

Statement by James C. Biddle
and William M. Meredith.
8058

Statement by the trustees of the
Theological Seminary in Ohio.
21110

Statement from the late States[!]
Agent of the Western Shore.
37317

Statement from Thomas L. Mc-
Kenney. 36897

Statement, furnished by the Com-
missioner of the General Land
Office, at the request of the
Hon. Mr. Benton. 23130

Statement in relation to the lead
mines and salt springs in
Missouri. 27402

Statement in relation to the United
States' Mexican Company.
26134

Statement. In the year 1763,
Thomas Greene, Esq. 18080

Statement of a committee of the
Eye and Ear Infirmary, Boston. 34076

Statement of a theory of life,
founded on observations & ex-
periment. 40119

Statement of allowances to the
officers of the Army. 7483;
7484

Statement of articles paying ad
valorem duties. 11280

A statement of bank reports from
the Auditor General, to the
Senate [Pennsylvania] 17570

Statement of deaths with the diseases and ages, in the city
and Liberties of Philadelphia.

40041

Statement of expenditures on internal improvements [N. C.]
30086

Statement of expenses, of the
Town of Billerica. 4708; 8061

A statement of fact relative to
the Six Principle Baptist
Church, Cranston, R.I. 2837

A statement of facts [McClellan]
9315

A statement of facts, exhibiting
the causes that have led to
the dissolution of the connexion which existed between
Philadelphia Quarterly meeting and the Monthly Meeting
of Friends, held at Green
Street, Philadelphia. 28972

A statement of facts, in relation
to the call and installation of
the Rev. Mark Tucker. 17448

Statement of facts, in relation to
the claims of the inhabitants
of the County of Tompkins.
37871

A statement of facts, presented
by Captain Scallan, of the
United States' army. 3115

Statement of facts relating to the
building of the Presbyterian
Meeting-House in Zanesville,
Ohio. 21460

Statement of facts, relating to
the claim of Major Moses
White upon the U. S. 30702

Statement of facts relative to the
claims of J. Aubin, and others. 3310

Statement of facts, relative to
the last will of the late Mrs.
Badger. 18081

A statement of facts relative to
the late fever which appeared
in Bancker-street and its vicinity. 6237

A statement of facts, relative to the
session of the Reformed Presbyterian Church, New-York. 8567

A statement of facts, showing
the debt due to Vans. 41361

A statement of facts, with remarks, &c. In answer to a

A statement of the grievances, on
account of which, that section
of the church now called the
"Associate Reformed Synod of
the West," separated from and
declared themselves independent of, the "Associate Re-·
formed Synod of North America." 11642

Statement of the income of Harvard College.   16470

Statement of the objections to the
passage of the bill entitled
"An act to regulate the sale of
lottery tickets." 31835

Statement of the organ cause in
St. Andrew's Church. 6861

Statement of the origin, nature
and operations of the Pennsylvania Domestic Missionary Society. 30191

Statement of the Overseers of the
Poor [Charlestown, Mass.]
12109

Statement of the plan and object
of the Mariner's Church, Portland. 40128

A statement of the proceedings of
the Presbytery of Glasgow.
4990

A statement of the receipts and
expenditures of the United
States. 14753

A statement of the revenue of
North Carolina. 30087;
34585; 39873

Statement of the trade between
the port of New-York and Ber-
muda. 4060

Statement of the treasurer [Har-
vard University] 16471

A statement of the trial of Isaac
B. Desha. 22451

Statement of the trial of John P.
Sheldon. 40528

Statement of the Turnpike Company of the Commonwealth.
9859

A statement of warrants drawn on
the treasurer [Georgia] 8818

Statement of what has recently
been done to supply the destitute of New Jersey with sacred Scriptures. 34462

Statement on the part of the
United States, of the case referred, in pursuance of the
convention of 29th September.
41314

Statement, prepared in conformity to the order of the General Synod. 22365

Statement read at the anniversary
of the opening of the Mariner's
Church. 21873

Statement, shewing the actual sit-
uation of the funds of the
Towns' branch of the Mutual
Assurance Society. 9596

Statement shewing the amount of
funds remitted to the officers
of the quarter-master's department. 14754

A statement showing, in detail,
the particulars of the item of
$240, 75 *59, which appears in
the report of the 30th January,
1828, on the claim of the state
of Massachusetts. 34074

Statement showing the quantity of
land surveyed in the several
land districts. 27404

Statement showing the quantity,
quality, and average value of
the unsold and unsaleable public
lands. 36899

Statement submitted by Mr. Cam-
breleng. 14755

Statement transmitted to the parent of each student concerned,
Aug. 1, 1828 [Yale Univer-
sity] 37270

A statement with regard to the
Moorish Prince Arduhl Rahhah-
man. 33317

Statements accompanying the report of the Committee on Manufactures. 7486

Statements by Colonel William H.
Winder. 41568

Statements, calculations and
hints, relative to rail-roads.
30478

Statements of the affairs of the
State Bank of North Carolina
and the Bank of Cape Fear.

40524
Statements of the treasurer of the Western Shore. 25244
The Statesman. 18082
Statesman's manual. 12334
Stationery--Custom House, Philadelphia. 36900
The stations or devotions on the passion of our Lord Jesus Christ crucified. 34651
Statistical account of the town of Middlebury. 5517
Statistical notices of some of the lunatic asylums of the United States. 37737
A statistical report of the county of Albany. 13843; 17694
Statistical tables of the state of New-York. 35390
A statistical view of the United States. 9459; 21403
Statistics of South Carolina. 25379
Statute of Washington. 27405
Statutes. [American Academy of Arts and Sciences] 15072
Statutes and laws of the university in Cambridge, Mass. 20834; 24806
Statutes of Columbia College. 5032; 5033; 28554
Statutes of Dickinson College. 8545; 24352
The statutes of Rutgers College. 22163; 22164; 35084
The statutes of the Albany Female Academy. 19386
Statutes of the British Parliament, in relation to the colonial trade. 27406
Statutes of the Medical School of Maine. 4816; 11966
Statutes regulating the practice of physic and surgery in the state of New York. 9449; 13283; 17089; 34098; 39544
The steam-boat. 12643
The steam-boat Superior, Captain Milner, will commence running up and down daily, for the season, on Friday the 18th. 14194
Steamboat tonnage United States.

36901
Steam boats Henrietta & North Carolina. Rates of freight. 21286
Steele's Albany almanack. 10339; 14196; 18085; 22370; 26136; 30705; 35397; 35398; 40533
Steibelt's celebrated storm-rondo. 3315
Steibelt's favorite waltz. 18087
Steibelt's much admired waltz. 18088
Stellarota. Invented by Rev. Amos Pettengill. 34733
Stenographic synopsis. 1418; 1419
Stephen Hook's statement and oath. 36902
Stereotype laws--United States. 41315
Steward's Healing art. 30710
Stewards of the mysteries of God. 13383
Stockbridge Indians. 31515
Stoddard's calendar. 26143
Stoddard's diary. 3340; 6899; 10356; 14221; 30716; 35413; 40540
The stop waltz. 14222; 14223; 18111; 22384; 22385
Storia della lingua e letterature Italiana in New York. 28659
Stories about Captain John Smith. 1414; 38794
Stories about Dr. Franklin. 40547
Stories about General LaFayette. 40548
Stories explanatory of the church catechism. 14114-14116; 35189
Stories for Adelaide. 39274
Stories for children [Hughs] 1696
Stories for children [Plumptre] 17651
Stories for children, with plates. From the French. 40549
Stories for Emma. 39275
Stories from scripture. For small children. 3344
Stories from the Scriptures. 30719; 40550

Stories of the miser. 40551

Stories on the history of Connecticut. 38782

Stories selected from the history of England. 20217

Stories selected from The lights and shadows of Scottish life for youth. 14944

The storm [Dix] 32995

The storm [Jackson] 1777

The storm [Steibelt] 3319; 3320

The storm; one of old Daniel's stories. 14225

The storming of Quebec. 40620

The story of a life. 22267

The story of Ahmed the cobler. 35421

The story of Aladdin. 35422

The story of Aleck, or Pitcairn's Island. 38586

The story of Ali Baba and the forty thieves. 72; 11632; 15060

The story of Dinah Doudney. 16348

Story of Jack Halyard. 15643; 19940-19942; 28383; 38048

The story of Kate Higgins. 22388

The story of little Benjamin. 3348; 40555

Story of Little John. 40556

Story of little Thomas and Betsey. 6905

The story of Mary and her cat. 22389

Story of Quashi. 3349

The story of the kind little boy. 22390

Story of the third old man. 8119

Story of William and Ellen. 22391; 30722; 35423

Stoughton collection of church music. 40557

A strange thing. 22393

Stranger, a play. 9221

The stranger in Charleston! 5204; 8568; 24361

Stranger of the valley. 22394

The stranger's grave. 18114

The stranger's guide [Philadelphia] 3352; 35461

Stranger's guide thro' Baltimore. 2029

The strangers' guide to the City of Charleston. 10360

A stranger's offering to infant minds. 3353; 30727

Stratton Hill. 38072

Stray cow. On Monday the 17th of April. 4312

The stray lamb. 35424

Strayed from the Fort Harrison prairie, on the 26th July last, two horses. 5886

The strayed lamb. 3355; 10361

Strength, wisdom, and virtue. 37836

La strenna. A divertimento. 20211; 20212

Strictures addressed to James Madison on the celebrated report of William H. Crawford. 15864; 18116

Strictures by Robert Hare, M.D. 1516

Strictures on a book entitled, "An apology for the book of Psalms." 10158; 22155

Strictures on a pamphlet written by William Vincent Harold. 9030

Strictures on a publication entitled, Clark's gas blowpipe. 1517

Strictures on a sermon, entitled, "Religion a social principle." 203

Strictures on a sermon, entitled An account of a revival of religion in Jerusalem. 11638

Strictures on a Voyage to South America. 3357

Strictures on Article II of the North American Review. 37695

Strictures on Dr. John M. Mason's plea for sacramental communion on Catholic principles. 6906

Strictures on health. 34970

Strictures on "Mr. Pattison's reply to certain oral and written criticisms." 1377; 1378

Strictures on Mr. Samuel Hutchinson's apology for believing in universal reconciliation. 40679

Strictures on Professor M'Vickar's pamphlet. 40202

Strictures on Rev. Mr. Brooks's essay. 7818

Strictures on Rev. Mr. Sullivan's last pamphlet. 40299

Strictures on Reverend O. Thompson's review of Andros's essay. 4483

Strictures on seven sermons. 24528

Strictures on strictures of William Hogan upon the Rev. William Harold's pamphlet. 8296

Strictures on the doctrine of universal salvation. 5113

Strictures on the letters written by the Right Rev. Dr. England, and the Rev. Mr. M'Encroe. 14229

Strictures on the present state of the medical profession among the foreign practitioners in Havana. 16567

Strictures on the religious system of Baron Swedenborg. 19287

Strictures on the review of Dr. Spring's Dissertation on the means of regeneration. 40702

Strictures on the sentiments of the Kehukee Association. 39709

Strictures on three letters respecting the debate at Mount Pleasant. 8242

Strictures upon Arator's attack. 13719

Strictures upon the Constitutional powers of the Congress and courts of the United States, over the execution laws of the several states. 20796

Strictures upon the 2d ed. of a pamphlet recently published by the followers of Elias Hicks. 22396

Strike the cymbal. 13894

The striking similitude between the reign of terror of the elder Adams, and the reign of corruption, of the younger Adams. 32943

Stroke at the root. 20890

Strong's almanack. 30731

Stubborn facts. 10370

The student's companion. 20183

The student's walk. 24749; 33432

The study of medicine. 12700; 16316; 20698; 24713; 29041; 38770

Sturm's reflections on the works of God. 30735

The subaltern. 20683

The subaltern's log-book. 40571

Sub-committees of the several schools [Boston] 11931; 15509; 19804

The subjection of kings and nations to Messiah. 4304

The subjects and mode of Christian baptism. 1861

The sublime and beautiful of scripture. 37331

Submission to "The powers that be," scripturally illustrated. 35056

Subscribe stock Tenth Turnpike Road Company, N.H. 36905

The subscribers hereby give notice that the concerns of the Essex Bank will be closed. 8636

The subscribers, the Acting Committee of "The Pennsylvania Society for the Promotion of Internal Improvements in the Commonwealth," respectfully submit the following essay. 17582; 17583; 21855; 21856

Subscription for the Southern and Western Theological Seminary. 3283

Subscription paper for the Knoxville Register. 1882

Subscriptions for the "Society for bettering the condition of the Poor." 40057

Subscriptions in the city and state of New-York to the General Theological Seminary of the Protestant Episcopal Church. 25860

Substance of a discourse, delivered April 23, 1823. 11868

The substance of a discourse, delivered at the public recognition of the First Universalist Church in Roxbury. 10495

The substance of a discourse delivered before a moral society on the subject of intemperance. 18122

Substance of a discourse delivered before the Hibernian Society of the City of Savannah. 16064

The substance of a discourse, delivered in the First Universalist meeting-house, in Portsmouth. 30852

Substance of a discourse delivered June 4, 1823. 11869

The substance of a discourse, delivered to seamen, in Marblehead. 12787

Substance of a discourse illustrating, the sin against the Holy Ghost. 24840

The substance of a discourse in two parts. 8707; 8708

The substance of a discourse, on the subject of Baptism. 12082

The substance of a discourse on the validity of presbyterial or elder ordination. 16002

The substance of a discourse preached in the hall of the House of Representatives. 24436

Substance of a discussion between the Rev. W. L. McCalla and the Rev. Abner Kneeland. 16961

Substance of a discussion in the Senate, on the report of a committee in favor of incorporating Amherst College. 17061

Substance of a protest and arguments against the competency of the court and jury to try the members of the Union Society. 29150

The substance of a sermon, delivered at the Methodist chapel in Cazenovia. 32963

The substance of a sermon, delivered in the Methodist Chapel, Middlebury, Vt. 4367

The substance of a sermon in favor of aiding the Greeks in their present contest with the Ottoman power. 16015

Substance of a sermon on Christian perfection. 39196

The substance of a sermon on particular providence. 24731

The substance of a sermon on the doctrine of atonement. 25041

The substance of a sermon on the supreme Deity of Christ. 29187; 38955

The substance of a sermon, preached at the Methodist Chapel. 25184

Substance of a sermon preached in Augusta, Georgia. 30661; 35356

Substance of a sermon preached in Cincinnati, Ohio. 37254

Substance of a sermon, preached in the Methodist chapel, Shockoe Hill, Richmond, Virginia. 39968

Substance of a sermon, preached June 10, 1827. 28743

Substance of a speech of Mr. Randolph. 34958; 34959

The substance of Col. Benton's argument. 32274

The substance of Leslie's method with the deists. 1937

Substance of Mr. Bradish's remarks in Committee of the whole House. 37925

Substance of Mr. Haine's remarks. 12742

Substance of Mr. Storrs' remarks. 35418; 35419

Substance of Mr. Van Buren's observations. 36993

Substance of the Hon. John C. Spencer's remarks. 30684

Substance of the remarks of Mr. Edwards. 8605

Substance of the semi-centennial sermon, before The New-York Annual Conference.

28995

The substance of two discourses, delivered in New York. 20882

The substance of two discourses on the mode of Baptism. 27890

The substance of two sermons, preached in Columbia, South Carolina. 24379

Substance of two speeches, delivered in the House of commons. 24920

Substances of a sermon delivered in Leicester, Vt. 11656

Substitute intended to be offered to the next meeting of the citizens of Richmond, on the subject of a convention. 16881

Substitute proposed by Mr. Morris of Hanover, to the instructions offered by Mr. Stevenson, on the subject of the United States' bank. 2340

Successful ligature of the common iliac artery. 29824

Succinct account of the case, Sarah Walker, vs. John Martin. 31649

A succinct view of the primitive apostolic church. 8468

Sufferers of the late war - Michigan. 36906

Suffering condition of the emigrant Indians. 36907

Sufferings and death of Christ. 29276

The sufferings, support, and reward of faithful ministers, illustrated. 1552

The sufficiency of divine Grace exemplified in the dying experience of Mary Ann. 18123

The sufficiency of the spirit's teaching without human learning. 20962

Suggestions for the improvement of the commerce of the state of South-Carolina. 30737

Suggestions in vindication of Sunday-Schools. 37413

Suggestions on education. 14020

Suggestions on presidential elections. 22401

Suggestions on the canal policy of Pennsylvania. 18124

Suggestions respecting improvements in education. 37743

Les suivantes. 13381

Sukey. 7563; 7564

Sul margine d'un rio. 5797; 13064

Sull' Italia. Discorso apologetico in risposta alla littera dell' avvocato Carlo Phillips al Re d'inghilterra. 5141

Sullivan County farmer's almanac. 6919

Sullivan's island. 899

The sultana; or, A trip to Turkey. 7862; 7863

A summary account of the evidence and the nature of revealed religion. 1932

Summary confession of faith, and form of covenant: adopted by the Presbytery of Geneva. 2855

A summary declaration of the faith and practice of the Baptist Church of Christ in Salem. 10177

Summary declaration of the faith and practice of the Baptist Church of Christ in Woburn. 31792

A summary declaration of the faith and practice of the Federal Street Baptist Church of Christ in Boston. 32435

A summary declaration of the faith and practice of the Second Baptist Church of Christ in Boston. 4800; 28248

Summary notice concerning Bible societies in general. 30742

Summary of Biblical antiquities. 13483; 34423; 34424; 39717

A summary of Christian doctrine. 23760

Summary of Church discipline. 15253

A summary of physiology. 9328; 16984

A summary of the course of law lectures in Columbia College. 16781

Summary of the first ten lectures of the professor of law in Columbia College. 16782

A summary of the law and practice of real actions. 18083

Summary of the law of bills of exchange. 23720

A summary of the law of lien. 9527; 17197

A summary of the law of set-off. 21494

A summary of the law relative to pleading and evidence in criminal cases. 15118

Summary of the persecutions of the Rev. Wm. Hogan from Bishop Conwell & others. 8628

Summary of the practical principles of political economy. 24272

A summary of the principal evidences for the truth and divine origin of the Christian revelations. 2830; 9982; 9983; 26159

Summary of the proceedings in Congress, in 1828-29. 40575

Summary of the trial of Robert M. Goodwin. 3364

Summary proofs of the Catholic doctrine. 37543

Summary view of the American Bible Society. 40576

A summary view of the houses for public worship in the city and county of New York. 37125

A summary view of the Millennial church. 14086

A summer month. 14240

The sun going down at noon. 38992

The sun that fails to light the dawn. 13295

The sun that lights the roses. 4293; 7670

Sunalei Akvlvgi No'gwisi Alikalvvsga Zvlvgi Gesvi. 19315

Sunday mail. 41316

Sunday mails. Mr. Johnson's report. 39147

The Sunday scholar. 28690

The Sunday school children. 3367; 10377

Sunday school conversations. 40579

Sunday school facts. 6921

Sunday school gleanings. 18129

The Sunday school hymn book. 6922; 10378; 14242; 27839; 35441

The Sunday school music book. 25639

The Sunday school; or Village sketches. 3368

The Sunday school prayer book. 6923; 26160

Sunday school regulations. 30311

The Sunday school spelling book. 10379; 17617; 21879

The Sunday school teacher's guide. 16703; 21044; 33692

The Sunday sliding party. 10380

The Sunday spelling book. 6924

Sunday tract. 32399

Sundry documents addressed to St. Mary's congregation. 6925

Sundry memorials, resolutions, and petitions from states, territories, and individuals, on the subject of graduating the prices of the public lands. 36908

Superintendency of Indian Affairs. 27407

Superintendent Armory--Harper's Ferry. 36909

The superior glory of gospel worship. 12097

The supplement to a lecture on the stars. 33159

A supplement to a "New-year's gift." 4867

Supplement to A treatise on pleading. 4982

Supplement to Andrew Jackson's negro speculations. 33082a

Supplement to Picket's juvenile, or universal primer. 30263; 40080

A supplement to the act, entitled, An act for the promotion of internal improvement. 34037

A supplement to the act to incorporate the Union Canal Company of Pennsylvania. 7029

A supplement to the address of Henry Clay to the public. 32734

Supplement to The American ornithology. 21751

Supplement to the catalogue of books [Yale University] 41610

A supplement to the catalogue of books, &c. belonging to the Library Company of Baltimore. 13105

Supplement to the catalogue of books, &c. belonging to the Maryland Circulating Library. 9392

A supplement to the Catalogue of the Library of Congress. 4061; 23131; 31516

Supplement to the India sailing directory. 24893

Supplement, to the Kentucky Harmony. 20272

A supplement to the New-Orleans directory. 17536

Supplement to the Pittsburgh Mercury. 17646

Supplement to "The Political character of Mr. Holmes." 20932

Supplement to the Stoughton collection of church music. 40558

Supplement to the tract, entitled conversation in a boat. 14243

Supplement to the U.S. register. 38457

A supplement to Vesey, junior's reports of cases in chancery. 33411

Supplemental account of some of the bloody deeds of General Jackson. 35458

Supplementary appropriation (military) for 1828. 36910

Supplementary Catalogue of the Essex Circulating Library. 1123

The supplementary directory, for 1820 [Philadelphia] 4387

Supplementary enactments [University of Virginia] 37043

Supplementary memorial of Joseph W. Brackett and Samuel Leggett. 14244

A supplementary report of the committee appointed to ascertain the fate of Captain William Morgan. 30744

Supplementary rules and regulations, for the government of the Penitentiary of Maryland. 13245

Support in death. 3305

Suppression of the slave trade. 27408

The supreme and exclusive authority of the Lord Jesus Christ, in religious matters. 26173

Supreme court. Bank of United States vs. January. 16791

Supreme Court of the U.S. James Foster and Pleasants Elam vs. David Neilson. 28899

Supreme Court of the United States. January 2, 1829. Mr. P. P. Barbour, from the Committee on the Judiciary. 41318

Supreme Court of the United States of America. James Carver, plaintiff in error, vs. James Jackson. 41317

The supreme deity of Christ proved. 8990

The supreme divinity of Jesus Christ. 30150

Sure methods of improving health, and prolonging life. 33401

Surgeons of the Navy. 31517; 36911

The surgical and physiological works of John Abernethy. 19358

Surgical essays [Cooper] 5073; 5074

Surgical essays [Larrey] 13046

The surprising adventures of Baron Munchausen. 29831

The surprising adventures of four Russian sailors. 3369; 10381

The sword of justice wielded by mercy. 10389

The sword; or Christmas presents. 40059

Swords's pocket almanack. 3379; 6929; 10390; 10391; 14251; 18134; 22415; 26165; 30751; 35454; 40593

Sylla; a tragedy. 25008; 29387

Syllabaire françois. 10054; 30390; 40205; 40206

Syllabus of a course of lectures on chemistry. 22417

Syllabus of a course of lectures on law. 1636; 5608

Syllabus of a course of lectures on materia medica and pharmacy. 37965

Syllabus of a course of lectures, on the elements of geological mineralogy. 5078

Syllabus of a course of lectures on the history and criticism of Spanish literature. 14288

Syllabus of a course of medical examinations. 13979

Syllabus of a part of the lectures given in the department of sacred rhetoric, Theological Seminary, Andover. 37471

Syllabus of the lectures on medical jurisprudence. 28740

The sylph, and other poems. 35506

The sylph cotillion. 11909

Sylvester Daggerwood. 5026; 15818

Sylvia Sweet.   English melody. 15789

The sylviad, or Minstrelsy of Nature in the wilds of N. America. 12804; 20850

The symbolical primer. 38949

Symmes's theory of concentric spheres. 25166

Sympathy, its foundation and legitimate exercise considered. 33760

Symptoms of a falling church. 10392

Symzonia; a voyage of discovery. 3156

A syndesmological chart. 11508

Synodal-Verhandlungen der Hochdeutschen Reformirten Kirche. 22049; 30418; 34977

A synopsis of chemistry. 5129

A synopsis of didactic theology. 8615

A synopsis of J.R. Smith's perspective lectures. 26091

Synopsis of Latin grammar. 8566

Synopsis of mercantile laws. 2311

A synopsis of pharmacology. 11580

A synopsis of rules and directions for exciting electricity. 20445

A synopsis of the diseases of the eye.   22502

A synopsis, of the several resolves, relating to a City Government, submitted to the people of Boston. 8138

Synopsis of the universal practice of medicine. 1959

A synopsis of theology. 6931

System of accountability for clothing and camp equipage issued to the army. 31525

A system of anatomy. 14957; 23360; 31790

A system of astronomy.   31636

A system of Bible-class instruction.   39654

A system of Bible questions. 35455

A system of constitutional by-laws, for the present government of New-York Nautical Institution. 2533

A system of dental surgery. 38588

A system of divine truth. 33603

A system of education proposed for the improvement of common schools. 38442

The system of education pursued at the free schools in Boston. 14253

The system of education, the code of discipline, and the professorships, adopted by the trustees of the Western University of Pennsylvania. 7773

A system of English grammar.

39640
A system of exercise and in-
struction of field-artillery.
41324
System of fortifications. 27419
A system of geographical ques-
tions. 30117
System of geography. 34002
A system of geometry and trig-
onometry. 20536
System of instruction, for the
use of Protestant Episcopal
Sunday schools. 29001
A system of materia medica and
pharmacy. 6141; 17252; 34216
A system of medical ethics.
13284
A system of penal law for the
United States. 33889
A system of penal law prepared
for the state of Louisiana.
16943-16945
A system of pharmacology.
31934
A system of practical nosology.
5641
System of pyrotechny. 20239
A system of rhetoric. 18105
A system of speculative masonry.
10464
A system of stenography. 4519;
4520; 20349
System of surgical anatomy.
7813
A system of universal geography.
19324; 31798; 41584
A systematic arrangement of
Lord Coke's First institute of
the laws of England. 24148
A systematic introduction to English grammar. 2651; 6376;
17522
Ein systematischer Auszug aus
des Gottseligen und hocher-
leuchteten Deutschen Theo-
sophi. 8118
Systeme de la loi pénale pour
l'état de la Louisiane com-
prenant les codes. 21256;
21257

T

T. V. Cuyler's Albany directory.
18135; 22418; 30752
A table book and primary arithmetic. 37549; 37550
A table of fees, adopted by the
bar of Windham county. 7684
A table of fees, and rates of
charging, for sundry articles
and services in medicine and
surgery. 2200
Table of post offices in the
United States. 11281; 23132
A table of the corresponding
prices of cotton. 16897
A table of the votes for Governor and electors of President,
in Ohio. 18136
Table Talk at a Club in Boston.
3380
Tables by which the price of any
quantity of staves, wood or
bark, may be ascertained.
1223
Tables containing the assays,
weights & values of the principal gold and silver coins of
all countries. 10394
Tables of arithmetic. 22537;
30861; 35581
Tables of comparative etymology.
33854
Tables of contemporary chronology. 40594
Tables of discount, or interest
on every cent from one to
one hundred. 27793
Tables of discount or interest,
on every dollar from one to
one thousand. 22148
Tables of interest, calculated
according to equitable and
legal principles. 28434
Tables of interest and discount,
calculated on the only true
principle. 714
Tables on chemical equivalents.
19669
Tables to facilitate the necessary
calculations in nautical astronomy. 6857; 10332
Tables with easy examples under

25810
Tales to my daughter. 18138
The talisman. 30758; 35459;
    40601
The talisman: a tale for boys.
    40600
Talyho, or The fox chase.
    16758
The tambarine dance. 12989a
Tamerlane and other poems.
    30285
Tancred, or The rightful heir to
    Rochdale Castle. 16906
Tancred; or, The siege of Anti-
    och. 30717
Il Tancredi. 22135; 30483
The tank. A favorite air. 4887
Tanning and currying in their
    various branches. 27937
Di tanti palpiti. 3066; 10144;
    10145
Tariff correspondence. 40607
Tariff or duties, on importa-
    tions into the United States.
    4062; 5168; 15953; 32913
Tariff, or rates of duties, on all
    goods, wares, and merchan-
    dise, imported into the United
    States. 13409
Tariff; or rates of duties payable,
    according to the existing laws.
    35467
Tariff, or rates of duties payable
    after the 30th of June, 1828.
    32562
Tariff, or rates of duties, pay-
    able after the 30th of June,
    1824. 16957
Tariff, or rates of duties payable
    from and after June 30, 1828.
    33934
Tariff, or rates of duties, pay-
    able on goods, wares, and
    merchandize, imported in the
    United States. 20340
Tariff; or, rates of duty con-
    formably to the existing laws
    on July 1, 1824. 18146
Tariff; or, rates of duty on all
    goods, wares & merchandise,
    imported. 18147; 33344
The task. 892; 20205; 24234;
    32845

The task, and Tirocinium. 5099
Tasso's Jerusalem. 22423
Tax for the year [Massachusetts]
    2170; 5983; 9420; 13258; 17062;
    39513
Tax on domestic spirits of 1813.
    36925
A Te Deum. In four vocal parts.
    6010
The tea party. 22434
The teacher and pupil's assistant.
    943
Teacher's assistant and scholar's
    guide to shorthand writing.
    23418
The teacher's assistant, or A
    system of practical arithme-
    tic. 2781; 6483; 9940-9942;
    17644; 21905; 25778; 30270;
    40086
The teacher's manual. 21237;
    25129; 37300
The teachings of Christ. 30643
Tears of contrition. 5900
Teatro scelto italiano. 37538
Tekeli; or, The siege of Mont-
    gatz. 12866; 20943
Tell her I'll love her. 10271
Tell me where is fancy bred!
    6886
The tell tale eye. 15144
Temper, or, Domestic scenes,
    a tale. 9790
Temper; or The story of Susan
    and Betsy. 20875
Temperance and revivals. 39710
Temperance Notice. 6303
The templar. 10422
Templar's chart. 915; 5112;
    15896
The temple harmony. 7589;
    14832
The temple of sensibility. 10329
A temple to friendship. 6887;
    14214
Temple's arithmetick. 22435;
    30774
Templi Carmina. 595; 4845;
    10423; 11997; 15567; 19872;
    23938; 28291; 32488; 37953
"Tempora mutantur." 11754
Ten chapters of the Book of Job.
    22149

The ten commandments. 30775

Ten new lessons for the piano forte. 26019

Ten sermons, preached on various important subjects. 4274

Ten years' exile. 6851

The tendency of evil speaking against rulers. 35163

The tenets of Freemasonry. 9796

The Tennessean. 30489

The Tennessee Almanac. 3418

The Tennessee farmer. 6950; 10428; 18170

Tennessee militiamen. 36926

Tennessee to issue grants. 31526

Tenth anniversary of the American Bible Society. 23469

Tenth anniversary of the Fairfield County Bible Society. 16098

Tenth annual exhibition of the Pennsylvania Academy of the Fine Arts. 6428

Tenth annual meeting of the Baptist Education Society. 28009

The tenth annual report [Protestant Episcopal Tract Society] 2903

The tenth annual report for the year 1826 of the managers of the Indigent Widows' and Single Women's Society. 29320

The tenth annual report of the American Society for Colonizing the Free People of Colour. 27828

Tenth annual report of the American Tract Society. 15094

Tenth annual report of the Bible Society of Virginia. 11858

Tenth annual report of the Board of Directors of the Princeton Theological Seminary. 10016

Tenth annual report of the Board of Managers of the Kentucky Bible Society. 25029

The tenth annual report of the board of managers of the New York Protestant Episcopal Missionary Society. 30050

Tenth annual report of the Bos-

ton Society for the Religious and Moral Instruction of the Poor. 23895

Tenth annual report of the Committee of Finance [Boston] 8140

Tenth annual report of the controllers of the public schools of the first school district of the state of Pennsylvania. 34697

Tenth annual report of the directors of the American Education Society. 23480

Tenth annual report of the directors of the Hampshire Bible Society. 29126

Tenth annual report of the directors of the New-York Institution for the Instruction of the Deaf and Dumb. 39829

The tenth annual report of the Education Society of Connecticut. 20373

The tenth annual report of the Female Missionary Society of the Western District, N. Y. 24521

The tenth annual report of the Long Island Bible Society. 21245

Tenth annual report of the Massachusetts Peace Society. 25279

Tenth annual report of the New-York Female Auxiliary Bible Society. 25572

Tenth annual report of the New York Sunday School Union Society. 25583

Tenth annual report of the Philadelphia Orphan Society. 21756

Tenth annual report of the trustees of the Society of the Protestant Episcopal Church for the Advancement of Christianity in Pennsylvania. 10034

Tenth annual report on the state of the Asylum for the Relief of Persons Deprived of the Use of their Reason. 30233

Tenth general report of the pres-

ident and directors of the
Chesapeake and Delaware Canal Co. 38125

Tenth report of the American
Bible Society. 23470

Tenth report of the Bible Society
in the County of Middlesex,
Massachusetts. 19721

The tenth report of the Board of
Managers of the Albany Bible
Society. 4440

Tenth report of the Board of
Managers of the New Jersey
Bible Society. 2463

Tenth report of the Cincinnati
Miami Bible Society. 15763

Tenth report of the directors of
the American Asylum at Hartford. 23491

Tenth report of the directors of
the Western Education Society.
37146

Tenth report of the New-Hampshire Bible Society. 6215

Tenth report of the trustees of
the Ohio Bible Society. 9774

Term reports in the court of
King's bench. 29062

Terms of admission, courses of
studies, expenses [Trinity
College, Hartford] 26245

Terms of communion. 15217

The Terpsichorina. 22440; 35478

Territorial government--Huron.
36927

Territorial taxes. 27420

Territory of Huron. 36928;
41325

Territory west of the Rocky
Mountains. 36929

Testamentary cases decided in
the colony of New York.
39782

Testimonials, in favour of the
Carstairion system of writing.
35479

Testimonials of Captain Jesse D.
Elliott. 5242

Testimonies concerning the character and ministry of Mother
Ann Lee. 30577

A testimony against that anti-
Christian practice of making

slaves of men. 20124

A testimony and epistle of advice issued by Indiana Yearly
Meeting. 28974-28976

The testimony of Christ's second
appearing. 15003

The testimony of God on some
important doctrines of Christian revelation. 12249

The testimony of Jesus Christ,
and a study of Divinity. 21128

The testimony of three who bear
witness in earth, on the fact
and mode of purification.
31782

Text book...modern geography.
4741

Textbook of a course of lectures
on the theory and practice of
physic. 21038

A text book of chemical philosophy. 38820

Thaddeus Laughlin. 31527

Thaddeus of Warsaw. 2829;
6512; 17673; 21943; 21944;
30307; 40123

Thadeus Laughlin. 41326

The thane of Fife. 10424

Thanksgiving anthem. 40632

Thanksgiving ball. 35483

A thanksgiving discourse from
107th Psalm and 8th verse.
16835

A thanksgiving discourse, on the
means of increasing public
happiness. 37170

Thanksgiving sermon. 13816

That part of South America
which the New York South
American Steam Boat Association contemplates making the
field of their operations, is
at present little known. 30054

The thatcher's wife. 29623

Thatsachen und Beweisse, bezie-
hend auf Joseph Hister und
William Findlay. 3421

Theater. The doors will be
opened at 6, and the curtain
rise at 7 o'clock, precisely.
25737

Theatre. (By particular request,)
the Vincennes Thespian Society

will perform on Saturday.
23165

Theatre. Master and Miss Blan-
chard's benefit. 15511

Theatre. The managers have the
pleasure of announcing that
Mr. Cooper, is engaged for
eight nights. 11951

Theatre. The managers have the
pleasure of announcing the engagement of Mr. & Mrs. Bart-
ley. 534

Theatre. The Vincennes Thespian society will perform. 23166

Theatre. This evening Monday
Nov. 7, [1825] 19809

Theatre. This evening Thursday
October 14, 1824. 15512

Theatre. Will be performed by
the Vincennes Thespian society,
on Saturday. 23164

The theatrical budget. 37341

Theatrical comicalities. 35490

The theatrical contributions of
"Jacques." 24969

The Theban Club. 18174

Thema original. 9080

Then, fare thee well. 490; 3069

Then fly with me. 5764

Theodora; a dramatic piece.
35491

Theodore; or, The crusaders.
16564

Theodore, or The Peruvians.
21904

Theodric; a domestic tale. 19934;
19935

A theological dictionary. 611;
612; 4863; 12017; 15587;
19890; 23959; 37976

Theological institutes. 23229;
27570

The theological questions of President Edwards. 8603

Theological school at Cambridge.
29166

Theological works. 6366

Theology, and not religion, the
source of division and strife in
the Christian church. 39330

Theology; explained and defended,
in a series of sermons. 12416;
20356; 33025; 38437

Theology, in a series of sermons. 21276

Theophilus Cooksey. 36930

A theoretical and practical arithmetic. 19672

A theoretical and practical grammar of the French tongue.
1949; 13099; 13100; 16896;
25102; 29490; 33851; 39287

Theory and practice of seaman-
ship. 15477

The theory and practice of surveying. 5453; 33349

The theory of moral sentiments.
10290

A theory of thunder showers.
12867

Theory tested by experience.
3423

"There is nothing true but Heav-
en!" 30526

There's a bower of roses. 3424

There's a tear that flows when
we part. 24291

There's nae luck. 3425; 6957

There's nothing true but Heaven.
3197; 6779; 10250; 17957;
40400

There's nought on earth so fair
as you. 38732

Therese, the orphan of Geneva.
6399; 6400; 28735

Thesaurus poeticus. 26197

Theses hasce Juvenes. 1539

They're a' noddin. 6385; 6942;
9817; 10419; 15927; 18176;
18177; 21787

They're noddin. 17109

They don't propose. 512

They know not my heart. 19753;
23337

They tell me thou art cold of
heart. 22446

Thine am I my faithful fair.
4269

Thinks I to myself. 17295; 29878

Third and fourth annual reports
of the female society of Boston
and its vicinity. 1217

Third anniversary [Albany County
Agricultural Society] 4441

Third annual convocation of the
Grand Royal Arch Chapter, of

North Carolina. 20587

Third annual meeting and report of the Auxiliary Foreign Mission Society of New-Haven. 32052

Third annual meeting of the Baptist Education Society, of the State of New York. 221

Third annual report [Auxiliary Foreign Mission Society, Hartford] 23562

Third annual report [Episcopal Missionary Society of Philadelphia] 1110

Third annual report [Female Sunday School Society. Philadelphia] 2746

Third annual report. [Juvenile Finleyan Missionary Mite Society of Baltimore] 21084

Third annual report [Lexington, Va. Missionary Society] 1955

The third annual report for the year 1819, of the managers of the Indigent Widows and Single Women's Society. 1750

Third annual report of the African Improvement Society, of New-Haven. 37382

Third annual report of the American Branch Tract Society of Utica. 37436

The third annual report of the American society for colonizing the free people of colour of the United States. 100

Third annual report of the American Tract Society. 31983

Third annual report of the Auxiliary Foreign Mission Society. 27907

The third annual report of the board of directors of the Franklin Bible Society. 5365

Third annual report of the Board of Managers of the Charleston Port Society. 24064

The third annual report of the Board of managers of the Charleston Protestant Episcopal Sunday School Society. 8320

Third annual report of the Board

of managers of the New York Protestant Episcopal Sunday School Society. 2537

Third annual report of the board of managers of the Prison Discipline Society, Boston. 34892

Third annual report of the board of managers of the R. I. Sunday School Union. 35024

The third annual report of the Board of Trustees of the New Hampshire Baptist Domestick Mission Society. 9636

Third annual report of the Charleston Bethel Union. 20031

Third annual report of the Committee of Management of the Tract Association of Friends in New York. 3468

Third annual report of the controllers of the public schools of the first school district of the State of Pennsylvania. 6427

Third annual report of the Eastern Auxiliary Foreign Mission Society. 33034

Third annual report of the executive committee of the board of managers of the General Protestant Episcopal Sunday School Union. 38735

Third annual report of the Female Bible, Missionary, and Tract Society of New-Utrecht. 33161

Third annual report of the Female Union Society for the Promotion of Sabbath Schools. 211

Third annual report of the Maine Sabbath School Union. 39416

The third annual report of the managers of the Female Domestic Missionary Society of Philadelphia. 1215

Third annual report of the managers of the Missionary Society. 17137

Third annual report of the managers of the Society for the Encouragement of Faithful

22544

The third report of the United
Foreign Missionary Society.
3515

The third report of the Western
Domestic Missionary Society.
41481

The third report of the Western
Sunday School Union.   37151

The third report of the Young
Men's Bible Society of Baltimore.   15001

Third trial of Jacob Barker.
30787; 30788

Thirsty souls invited by Christ to
come to him for spiritual
blessings.   23202

Thirteen letters addressed to the
Right Rev. Doctor Bowen.
33078

The thirteenth anniversary of the
Hudson River Baptist Association.   32162

Thirteenth annual exhibition of the
Pennsylvania Academy of the
Fine Arts.   17571

Thirteenth annual meeting of the
American Bible Society.
37433

Thirteenth annual report of the
American Bible Society.
37432

Thirteenth annual report of the
American Tract Society.   27844

The thirteenth annual report of
the Association for the Relief
of Respectable Aged Indigent
Females, established in New-
York.   23552

Thirteenth annual report of the
Board of directors of the
Theological seminary.   21975

The thirteenth annual report, of
the board of managers, of the
New York Protestant Episcopal Missionary Society.   39832

The thirteenth annual report of
the board of missions of the
General Assembly of the Presbyterian Church.   40142

The thirteenth annual report of
the board of trustees of the
New York Protestant Episco-

pal Tract Society.   13573

Thirteenth annual report of the
directors of the American Education Society.   37441

The thirteenth annual report of
the Hampshire Bible Society.
38903

The thirteenth annual report of
the Long Island Bible Society.
33899

The thirteenth annual report of
the managers of the Auxiliary
New York Bible and Common
Prayer Book Society.   34529

The thirteenth annual report of
the New York Sunday School
Union.   39838

Thirteenth annual report of the
Philadelphia Orphan Society.
34624

Thirteenth annual report of the
president and directors of the
Board of Public Works, to the
General Assembly of Virginia.
41387

Thirteenth annual report of the
receipts and expenditures of
the city of Boston.   19805

Thirteenth annual report of the
Washington Orphan Asylum
Society.   37091

The thirteenth report of the Bible
Society of Philadelphia.   4704

Thirteenth report of the New
Hampshire Bible Society.   17333

The thirtieth annual report, of
the Massachusetts Missionary
Society.   39523

Thirty four psalm tunes.   813

The thirty-nine articles of religion.   12573

Thirty-six animals, drawn from
nature.   20009

The thirty-sixth anniversary of
the Hartford Baptist Association.   19522

This blooming rose.   6469; 9915;
13763

This college will commence the
course of lectures, for the
ensuing Winter session [Gen-
eva College]   30501; 33342

This day is published, No. I of

the Philosophical Library. 30789

This exposé was prepared for the press the first week in July and Mr. Test was per mail advised of its intended publication. 19262

This indenture, made this twenty-second day of May, in the year of our Lord one thousand eight hundred and twenty-seven, between the rector, church wardens, and vestrymen of Trinity Church, in the city of New-York. 30057

This institution will commence their course of lectures for the ensuing Winter session [Rutgers Medical College] 25992

This is the House that Jack built. 16597

This plate of the town of Fayetteville, North Carolina. 21292

Tho' clouds by tempests may be driven. 23261

Tho love is warm awhile. 11978; 15542a

Tho' the day of my destiny's over. 6936

Tho' thou hast broke thy plighted vow! 12043

Tho' 'tis all but a dream. 11894; 15448-15450; 19754; 19755

Tho' you leave me. 8514; 12336

Thomas Blackwell. 36932

Thomas Brown and his pretended history of Shakers. 14870

Thomas Buford. 41327

Thomas C. Withers. 27421; 31528

Thomas Cooper. 27422

Thomas Crown. 41328

Thomas Cutts. 27760

Thomas D. Arnold to the freemen. 27892; 37505

Thomas F. Cornell. 36933

Thomas Flournoy. 31529

Thomas Gulledge. 31530

Thomas H. Bradford. 27423

Thomas Hunt. 36934

Thomas Jefferson's opinion of DeWitt Clinton. 18186

Thomas McClanahan. 31531

Thomas Marsh and Joseph Yaw. 31532

Thomas R. Williams. 36935

Thomas Shiverick. 41329

Thomas Wheatley. 36936

Thompson's new arithmetic. 35503; 35504

The Thomsonian practic revealed. 40647

The thorough--base primer. 32534

The thorough bred and imported horse, Winter's Arabian will stand in Lexington. 19309

Those evening bells. 3332; 6888-6890

Those, who are appointed [Hampden Sydney College] 12752

Thou faithful guardian. 15687

Thou lov'st no more. 19756

Though love is warm awhile. 3436

Thoughts, in five propositions on the following: vii. Verse, II Chapter of Psalms. 9369

Thoughts in prison. 28712

Thoughts of Peace in time of war. 9794

Thoughts on Christian baptism. 18196

Thoughts on Christian Communion. 1918

Thoughts on domestic education. 40649

Thoughts on Masonry. 39227

Thoughts on Missions. 3405; 3406

Thoughts on political economy. 2944

Thoughts on reason and revelation. 403

Thoughts on religion, and other subjects. 39971

Thoughts on religion, by M. Diderot. 32984

Thoughts on revivals. 35227

Thoughts on some parts of the discipline of the Methodist Episcopal Church. 37693

Thoughts on the Anglican and American-Anglo churches. 8182

Thoughts on the Baptist contro-

Thro' the forests thro' the
meadows. 23262
Throg's Point, Long Island.
27424
A thumb paper and Captain Me
Big. 39377
The thunderstorm. 30800
Thurber and King. 36937
"Thy cheek has borrowed from
the rose." 8977
Thy fatal shafts. 19994
Thy kingdom come; a sermon.
1064
Thy last farewell. 16821
Thy smiles are all decaying love.
15688; 19995
Tickets in all the following lot-
teries can be obtained at Cle-
utt's Lottery Office. 22469
Tiller's Lafayette badge. 18199
The timber measurer's, merch-
ant's, and shipmaster's as-
sistant. 8194
Timber merchant's guide. 12738
The time and lunar register.
26215; 28086
Time has not thin'd my flowing
hair! 21037
The time-piece; or, almanac.
40654
Time's almanac. 22474; 26216;
30804; 35516
The timely remembrancer. 6977
The times. 3442
Tink a tink. 21100
Tirolienne. Parole de Dubois.
12634
Tis all a farce. 31939; 37425
'Tis love. 3442a
'Tis love in the heart. 1670;
1671; 20953
'Tis not his form, so fair to
view. 4734; 11893
'Tis not the beam of a languish-
ing eye. 15483
'Tis the last rose of summer.
3333
'Tis thee I love. 7572
Titi Livii Patavini historiarum
libri priores quinque. 5844;
13126; 29519
Titles, and legal opinions there-
on, of lands, in East Florida.

8914; 24770
Titles of the Acts passed by the
Legislature of the Common-
wealth of Pennsylvania at the
session of 1821-22. 9862
Titles of acts passed by the Leg-
islature of the state of New-
York, at its forty-eighth ses-
sion, 1825. 21673
Titus march. 3443; 16840; 16841
The Titus waltz. 3444; 16842
Tivolian waltz. 3445
To. Agreeably to the advice of
many Democratic Republicans
in various parts of the state.
28689
To all benevolent and charitable
Christians. 40655
To all those who may be desir-
ous of emigrating to the West-
ern Country. 31721
To all who love Zion. 7793
To all whom it may concern. Take
notice, that application will be
made to the Legislature of the
state of Illinois. 21002
To all whom it may concern.
This is to certify, that ____
is duly authorized to collect
the names of subscribers for
"The Infant School Society of
Southwark." 33662
To all whom these present shall
come to...in pursuance of the
several acts of the General
Assembly. 5447
To amend the Constitution. 27425-
27431
To amend the rules. 27432
To Chandler Price. 24396
To Charles Shaler. 31927
To commend truth to the con-
science. 20843; 20844
To day! 3446; 3447
To distribute proceeds of sales
of public lands. 41330
To Drs. Miller, Carnahan and
Alexander. 17461
To emigrants of industrious hab-
its. 28376
To friends of Indiana yearly
meeting. 20607
To Friends of the yearly meet-

ing of Indiana. 22116

To gentlemen residing in the vicinity of the Erie Canal. 8589

To His Excellency Martin Van Buren. 37700

To hold a treaty with the Seneca Indians. 27433

To Honorable men. 35577

To Irishmen and adopted citizens. 14291

To John Hunt. 12558

To ladies eyes. A favorite Irish melody. 10348; 14215; 14216

To love thee, night and day, love! 491; 4735; 4736; 8086

To members of the Protestant Episcopal Church in the parish of St. James's Mecklenburg County. 17757

To mill owners. 16458

To Mr. Charles Adams. 35518

To Messrs. N. Goddard, Shaw, Winslow. 32596; 32597

To my fellow citizens. A gross, scandalous and unprovoked libel appeared in the "City of Washington Gazette." 580

To My Fellow-Citizens of Kentucky and the West. 3448

To my fellow-citizens, of Knox, Daviess and Martin counties. 38514

To my friends. 34664

To my friends and fellow citizens. 16090

To Philip S. Physick, M.D. 38067

To procure state laws. 41331

To remove the defects in the Returns of the Militia. 2150

To S.C. Phillips, Benja. Hankes and Perley Putnam. 35554

To sigh yet feel no pain. 1548; 8980; 8981; 12793-12795; 16488

To Stephen C. Stevens, esq. 38288

To sweep the Augean stable. 18201; 32949

To the Aqueduct Corporation. 533

To the aged. 3449

To the assessors of the town of Westbrook. 9348

To the Baptist churches throughout the United States. 21871

To the Bishops and Members of the next General Conference of the Methodist Episcopal Church. 17134

To the Board of Directors of Middlesex Canal. 6044

To the calm, considerate and reflecting. 35519

To the catholic voters of the city of Baltimore. 35520

To the citizens of Albany. 37401

To the citizens of Baltimore. 16451; 40200

To the citizens of Boston. 7795

To the citizens of Charlestown. 4959

To the citizens of Crawford and the counties adjacent. 75

To the citizens of Jefferson, Oldham, Nelson & Bullitt Counties. 31747

To the citizens of Knox county, Fellow citizens--at the invitation of John D. Early. 11771

To the citizens of Knox county. Fellow citizens--I flattered myself that I should not be compelled to appear in the present manner. 12252

To the citicizens [sic] of Knox county. In all governments of the republican kind. 12421

To the citizens of Knox county. Seeing my name announced as a candidate to represent you in the next legislature. 20408

To the citizens of Knox county... Vigo. 26217

To the citizens of Knox, Daviess & Martin counties. 29455

To the Citizens of Mercer County. 2042

To the Citizens of Montgomery County. 16451

To the citizens of Ohio County. 32906

To the citizens of Pennsylvania. 21861

To the citizens of Perry, Henderson, Humphreys and Stewart Counties. 38492

To the honourable Superior Court of the state of Connecticut. 34137

To the honourable, the General Assembly of North Carolina. 21539; 29836

To the Honourable the Legislature of the Commonwealth of Massachusetts. 22380

To the honourable the Legislature of the state of New York... The petition of Felix Pascalise. 35525

To the honourable the legislature of the state of New York. The petition of the stockholders and dealers of the Mechanics' Bank. 39541

To the Honourable the mayor and Council of the city of Baltimore. 6979

To the Honourable the Senate and House of Representatives of the Commonwealth of Pennsylvania. 9900

To the Honourable the Senate and House of Representatives of the United States [District of Columbia] 15982

To the Honourable the Senate and House of Representatives of the United States.. The memorial of the Board of Manufactures. 2712

To the honourable the Senate and House of Representatives of the United States. The memorial of the subscribers [New York City] 39815

To the honourable the Senate and House of Representatives of the United States... The memorial of the subscribers [Philadelphia] 30225; 30226; 30807

To the honourable the Senate and House of Representatives of the United States: The petition of Samuel Ward. 41425

To the honourable the speakers and members of the Senate and House of Delegates of Virginia. 32650

To the independent electors of all parties of the fifth senatorial district. 22477

To the independent electors of Massachusetts. 17047

To the independent electors of the Somerset and Penobscot congressional district. 35526

To the independent voters of Crawford & Clark counties. 8478

To the independent voters of Knox county. 12422

To the independent voters of the 1st Reg't. of Indiana militia. 13052

To the independent voters of Vigo county. Under the influence of many of the people of this county, I introduce the following. 9305

To the independent voters of Vigo county. Under the influence of many of you, I have given my name. 8360

To the inhabitants of Boston. 22478

To the inhabitants of Concord. 18209

To the inhabitants of Pennsylvania. 25709

To the inhabitants of South Carolina. 6006

To the inhabitants of the City of New York. 14157

To the inhabitants of the County of York. 7721

To the inhabitants of the Western district of the state of New York. 7033

To the intelligent & philanthropic in the United States. 23478

To the intelligent and upright citizens of Knox county. 20447

To the laboring poor of Kentucky. 3455

To the ladies of the Presbyterian Congregation. 1096

To the landholders of the state of Maryland. 22479

To the lay members of the Protestant Episcopal Church.

24437

To the Legislature of the state of ____ one of the United States of America. 32899

To the legislature of the state of New York. 14087

To the Legislature of Virginia. 8884

To the mechanics and working-men of the fifth ward. 40656

To the members and friends of the Protestant Episcopal Church of the Diocese of North Carolina. 17717

To the members of Mount-Pleas-ant Church. 6117

To the members of the Baltimore annual conference. 17135

To the members of the Boston seat in the Legislature. 19807

To the members of the General Court. 13334

To the members of the Honour-able General Court of the Com-monwealth of Massachusetts. 13116

To the members of the legisla-ture of the state of New-York. 16655

To the members of the legisla-ture of the state of New York. 18210

To the members of the Method-ist Episcopal Church, in the city of Baltimore. 30808

To the members of the Methodist Episcopal Church in the City of New York. 18173

To the members of the parish of Grace Church. 41405

To the members of the Pennsyl-vania Society for the Promo-tion of Manufactures and Me-chanic Arts. 32600

To the members of the Protes-tant Episcopal Church, in the state of Massachusetts. 2174

To the members of the Roman Catholic Church. 35527

To the members of the senior class. 5126

To the members of the Society of Friends...residing in...

Cecil County, Maryland. 35040

To the members of the United Episcopal Churches of Christ Church, St. Peter's Church. 34774

To the members of the United States Military and Philosophi-cal Society. 18132

To the memory of George Dill-wyn. 3456

To the memory of Mrs. Ann Carter Francis. 35528

To the officers and soldiers com-posing the first regt. of Indi-ana militia. 5707

To the officers of the army [Webb] 31688

To the officers of the army, the following is submitted. 26088

To the officers of the late war. 24182

To the patrons of Geneva Col-lege. 24669

To the patrons of the Salem Ga-zette. 3093

To the patrons, the carrier of the Columbian. 24169

To the people. 10454

To the people. How the bank and treasury "pigeons flutter!" 23320

To the people of Berkeley county. 28613

To the people of Cayuga County. 34398

To the people of Charlotte, Prince Edward and Halifax. 18211

To the people of Harrison. 37962

To the people of Harrison county. 28303

To the people of Illinois. 18212

To the people of Illinois [Cook] 15851

To the people of Kentucky [Ar-gus] 32925

To the people of Kentucky [Nich-olas] 17430

To the people of Kentucky [Re-garding the Nicholas Circuit Court] 22480

assembled, the memorial of the subscribers. 9511

To the Senate and House of Representatives of the United States in Congress assembled. The trustees of the American Literary, Scientific and Military Academy. 25611

To the Senate and House of Representatives of the United States. The undersigned, citizens of the village of Cleaveland. 24128

To the settlers in Austin's settlement. 11648

To the speakers and members of both houses of the General Assembly of Virginia. 33484

To the stockholders of the Bank of the United States [Smith] 22304

To the stockholders of the Bank of the United States [Swann] 22407

To the stockholders of the Bank of the U. S. [Weightman] 23281

To the stockholders of the Chesapeake & Delaware Canal. 18217

To the stockholders, or charter members and patrons, of the New York Academy of the Fine Arts. 30635

To the thinking few. 28409

To the tribunal of the American people. 21940

To the voters and citizens of the eleventh congressional district, in the state of Kentucky. 38137

To the voters of Baltimore County. 15576

To the voters of Knox county fellow citizens, I had fondly hoped that no circumstance would have rendered it necessary. 7983

To the voters of Knox county. Fellow citizens, I only hand you this bill that you may know I have become a candidate. 16739

To the voters of Prince George's and Ann Arundel counties, and the city of Annapolis. 41467

To the voters of the City of Washington. 10456

To the voters of the congressional district, composed of the counties of Bourbon, Nicholas, Mason and Bracken. 37742

To the voters of the eighth Congressional district. 39145

To the voters of the first congressional district. Fellowcitizens, I am informed that a certificate has been shewn to many of you. 8110

To the voters of the first congressional district. Fellow citizens, the period will shortly arrive, when your duty to your country will again call. 8543b

To the voters of the first congressional district. Fellow citizens--You will be called to the polls in a few days. 10457

To the voters of the first congressional district of Indiana. 15468

To the voters of the second electoral district of Maryland. 16764

To the Voters of the 10th Congressional District of Kentucky. 3074

To the voters of the Third Congressional District of the state of Louisiana. 32468

To the voters of the third ward. 26220

To the West Point cadets. 6980

To the yeomanry of York District. 30812

To thinking men. 35531

To Thomas Scott. 31651

To travellers. The subscriber has opened a tavern. 21274

To Wm. A. Fletcher. 12894

To William Jenkins. 35532

The tobacconist. 12657

Tobias E. and Wm. Stansbury. 31533

The Tocsin! or, Another alarm.
18218
Together let us range the fields.
11970
Tokeah; or, The white rose.
40379
The token, a Christmas and New
Year's present. 30815; 35535;
40658
Token for children. 9138; 29354;
33697
A token for mourners. 1249
Token of respect to a departed
brother. 32512
Tom & Jerry; or, Life in Lon-
don. 14295; 17190; 21491
Tom and Sue. 14296
Tom, the piper's son. 22483
Tom Thumb. 17470
The tomb of Henry. 12181
Tommy Duff. 30816
Tommy Wellwood. 18221;
35537
Tompkins and Republican Prin-
ciples. 1000
Tonnage duties. 36939
Tonnage of the United States.
31534
Tonnewonte. 16456; 20822
Tony; ou, Cinq annees en deux
heures. 32463
Too late for dinner. 9167; 9168
Tooke's Pantheon of the heathen
Gods. 3460; 14298; 21925
The tooth-ache. 28270
A topographical and historical
sketch of Epsom, New Hamp-
shire. 12311
A topographical and historical
sketch of the town of Andover.
9533
Topographical and historical
sketches of the Town of Lancaster. 27655
Topographical and historical
sketches of the town of Leicester. 27560
Topographical and historical
sketches of the town of North-
borough. 23457
Topographie physique et médicale de la ville de Philadel-
phie. 13129

The Tor hill. 26090
Torch light. 24265; 24266
Total abstinence from ardent
spirits. 37541
Touches on agriculture. 17738;
22013
The touchstone of sincerity.
33192
The tour of Doctor Syntax. 10462;
38236
The tour of General La Fayette.
20977
The tour of James Monroe. 4143
A tour in Germany. 22158
The tourist's map of the state of
New York. 35542
Towar & Hogan's farmer's and
citizen's almanack. 40662
Tower of Helvin. 29417
Town accounts for the town of
Lynnfield. 16956
Town and country; a comedy.
29820; 29821
Town and country almanac. 3463;
3464; 6984-6986; 10465; 10466;
14303; 18226; 22490; 26229;
30819-30821
Town meeting, Monday, 9th Oc-
tober 1820. 3465
Town Meeting. Philadelphia,
January 24, 1825. 22491
Town of Boston. At a legal
meeting. 4786
Town of North Hempstead vs.
Town of Hempstead. 21674
The Town of Providence, Indi-
ana. 6563
The town officer. 1285
Town officer: or, Laws of Mas-
sachusetts. 20722; 38796
Town officer's guide. 19486
Trabajos de Persiles y Sigis-
munda, historia setentrional.
28427
A tract for Sunday Schools. On
lying. 40664
A tract on the proposed altera-
tion in the tariff. 15865;
15866
Tracts before the General Asso-
ciation of Georgia. 19529
Tracts; designed to inculcate
moral conduct on Christian

Travels in the central portions of the Mississippi Valley. 22204

Travels in the north of Germany. 38435

Travels into several remote nations of the world. 3378; 40592

The travels of Anacharsis the younger, in Greece. 37716

The travels of True Godliness. 39174

Travels through North America. 32277

Travels through part of the United States and Canada. 12404

Travels through Upper and Lower Canada. 6994

A treasure for the honest inquirer after truth. 29832

Treasurer's accounts. 31536

Treasurer's report [N. C.] 39874

Treasurer's report [Maine] 9349

Treasurer's report [Maryland] 9389

Treasurer's report [Mississippi] 34163

Treasurer's statement [Massachusetts] 21367

Treasury clerks. 36942

Treaties with Lubeck, Bremen, and Hamburg. 41332

Treaties with several tribes of Indians. 27436

A treatise and catalogue of fruit and ornamental trees. 10013

A treatise concerning divine love and divine wisdom. 35450

A treatise concerning Heaven and its wonders. 22408

A treatise concerning religious affections. 5234; 16045; 16046; 33053

A treatise concerning the last judgement and the destruction of Babylon. 35451

A treatise concerning the sanctification of the Lord's day. 4296

A treatise of algebra. 6801

A treatise of church discipline. 4574

A treatise of domestic medicine. 15867

A treatise of equity. 204; 1260

A treatise of infant baptism. 15730

A treatise of pathology and therapeutics. 32823

Treatise of plane trigonometry. 15944

A treatise of the diseases of the chest. 13041

A treatise of the law of arbitration. 8238; 19925

A treatise of the law relative to contracts. 12223

A treatise of the law relative to merchant ships. 37348

A treatise of the materia medica and therapeutics. 8590; 20367

A treatise of the rights, duties, and liabilities of husband and wife, at law. 32719

A treatise on adulterations of food, and culinary poisons. 8

A treatise on agriculture. 143; 4493

A treatise on artillery. 1897

A treatise on atonement, containing an account of the creation and formation of man. 12568

A treatise on atonement; in which the finite nature of sin is argued. 32083

A treatise on baptism; being a reply to a book entitled A debate on Christian baptism. 19172

A treatise on baptism, containing a faithful citation of all the texts of the new Testament which relate to this ordinance. 27679

A treatise on bowel complaints. 14799

A treatise on Christian doctrine. 21465

A treatise on church discipline. 17910; 17911

A treatise on church government. 7956

A treatise on contracts. 6290

A treatise on crimes & misdemeanors. 17872

Treatise on criminal pleading. 18077

A treatise on derangements of the liver. 21064; 24991; 24992

A treatise on descriptive geometry. 5114

A treatise on diet. 25661; 34640

A treatise on diseases of females. 28696

A treatise on dislocations and on fractures. 15856; 20188; 20189

A treatise on domestic medicine. 10436

A treatise on female equitation. 22504

A treatise on fever. 4865

Treatise on fruit and ornamental trees. 2871

A treatise on Gunter's scale. 15910

A treatise on gymnasticks. 33690

A treatise on indigestion. 9907; 9908; 13761; 17619; 17620; 21881

A treatise on inland navigation. 2270

A treatise on keeping the heart. 33193

A treatise on maritime contracts. 6516

A treatise on natural philosophy. 25402

A treatise on nervous diseases. 15852

A treatise on pathological anatomy. 39029a

A treatise on physiology applied to pathology. 23937; 32487

A treatise on political economy [Say] 6722; 17900; 30531

A treatise on political economy [Stirrat] 18106

A treatise on practical surveying. 8825

A treatise on prayer. 32374; 37845

A treatise on pride. 37728

The treatise on religious affections. 5235; 5236

A treatise on religious experience. 8208

A treatise on repelling the paroxysm of intermittent fevers. 23941

A treatise on self knowledge. 2137; 2138; 5963; 9394; 13247; 17040; 21354; 25246-25248; 34043; 39484

A treatise on slavery. 16011

A treatise on soils and manures. 6995

A treatise on some practical points relating to the diseases of the eye. 6720

A treatise on special and general anatomy. 24892

A treatise on sulphureous waters. 23543

A treatise on surgical anatomy. 817

A treatise on surveying. 1470; 1471; 20771; 24766; 33446

A treatise on Swaim's panacea. 10384; 10385; 18131; 22406

Treatise on the authenticity & canonical authority of the Scriptures. 38454

A treatise on the blood. 12896

A treatise on the civil jurisdiction of a justice of the peace, in the state of New-York. 5095

A treatise on the common law, in relation to water-courses. 15111

A treatise on the conduct of the understanding. 21242; 33893

A treatise on the construction of the statutes. 22110

A treatise on the courts for the trial of small causes. 17549

A treatise on the cultivation of ornamental flowers. 33414

A treatise on the culture and growth of different sorts of flower roots. 4928

Treatise on the culture of the vine. 12099

A treatise on the disease of the eye. 12620

Treatise on the diseases incident to the horse. 5211

A treatise on the diseases most
prevalent in the U.S. 6996;
22505; 30827

A treatise on the diseases of females. 24339; 32972

A treatise on the diseases of seamen. 37154

A treatise on the divine nature.
17204

A treatise on the education of
daughters. 1222; 5326

A treatise on the forms of actions, and on pleading with
second and third volumes, containing precedents of pleadings.
32674

A treatise on the French verbs.
28109

A treatise on the law of actions
on penal statutes in general.
8633

A treatise on the law of des-
cents. 2950; 22043

A treatise on the law of evidence.
2753; 9922; 13766; 40065

A treatise on the law of idiocy
and lunacy. 9008

A treatise on the law of injunc-
tions. 8997

A treatise on the law of insurance. 13768

A treatise on the law of legacies. 40317

A treatise on the law of mercantile guarantees. 20500

A treatise on the law of mortgages. 34861

A treatise on the law of nisi prius. 12750; 20795

A treatise on the law of obligations, or contracts. 25815

A treatise on the law of Pennsylvania. 20724

A treatise on the law of principal and agent. 9803; 9804

Treatise on the law of property
arising from the relation between husband and wife.
17851

A treatise on the law of slander.
26132

A treatise on the law relative to
merchant ships. 7729

A treatise on the law relative to
sales of personal property.
13133

A treatise on the laws of wills
and codicils. 13963

A treatise on the limitation of
actions at law, and suits in
equity. 37474

Treatise on the Lord's supper.
37846

A treatise on the materia medica. 8060

A treatise on the millennium.
17680

A treatise on the nature and constitution of the Christian
Church. 40536

A treatise on the nature and effects of heat. 30828

A treatise on the nature, cause,
and treatment of contagious
typhus. 38974

A treatise on the parties to actions, the forms of actions,
and on pleading. 20051

A treatise on the patriarchal, or
co-operative system of society. 33776; 39204

A treatise on the philosophy of
the human mind. 28306

A treatise on the physical and
medical treatment of children.
20303; 24340; 38376

A treatise on the pleadings and
practice in real actions.
33683

A treatise on the practice of the
supreme court of New York
in civil actions. 5212

A treatise on the principles and
practice of the action of ejectment. 4399

A treatise on the principles and
practice(s) of the High court
of chancery. 9326; 29586

A treatise on the principles of
pleading in civil actions.
18089

A treatise on the retention of
urine. 28734

Treatise on the revocation and
republication of wills and
testaments. 3053

A treatise on the right of property in tide waters. 23524
A treatise on the Schrofulous disease. 39041
A treatise on the statute of frauds. 13964
A treatise on the statute of limitations. 37559; 37560
A treatise on the structure, diseases, and management of the human teeth. 16284
A treatise on the subject of baptism. 12250
Treatise on the theory and practice of physic. 24746
A treatise on the union, affinity, and consanguinity between Christ and His Church. 25918
A treatise on the use of Prussiate of iron. 11504
A treatise on wall-coloring. 4073
A treatise upon the eternal generation of the Son of God. 6997
A treatise upon theological subjects. 37473
Treatises on various theological subjects. 10192; 17914
Treaty between the United States and Sweden. 31537
Treaty between the United States of America and the Chippewa, Menomonie and Winnebago tribes of Indians. 41195
Treaty between the United States of America and the Crow tribe of Indians. 27437
Treaty between the United States of America, and the Eel river or Thorntown party of Miami Indians. 36943
Treaty between the United States of America and the Hunkpapas band of the Sioux tribe of Indians. 27438
Treaty between the United States of America and the Kansas nation of Indians. 27439
Treaty between the United States of America and the Maha tribe of Indians. 27440
Treaty between the United States

of America and the Mandan tribe of Indians. 27441
Treaty between the United States of America and the Ottoe and Missouri tribe of Indians. 27442
Treaty between the United States of America and the Pawnee tribe of Indians. 27443
Treaty between the United States of America and the Poncar tribe of Indians. 27444
Treaty between the United States of America, and the Potawatamie tribe of Indians. 41196
Treaty between the United States of America and the Ricara tribe of Indians. 27445
Treaty between the United States of America and the Shawonee nation of Indians. 27446
Treaty between the United States of America and the Sioune and Ogallala tribes of Indians. 27447
Treaty between the United States of America and the Teton, Yancton, and Yanctonies bands of the Sioux Indians. 27448
The Treaty of Ghent. 18234
Treaty of limits between the United States of America, and the united Mexican states. 36944
Treaty of San Lorenzo el Real. 41333
Treaty with Creek Indians. 27449
Treaty with Eel River Indians. 36945
Treaty with Spain. 31538
Treaty with Sweden. 36946
Treaty with the Creek Indians. 36947
Treaty with the Florida Indians. 27450
Tremaine; or The man of refinement. 23209
Tremont Theatre. [Playbills] 37911
The trial and confession of John Johnson. 18235
Trial and confession of Reynolds.

22507

Trial and defence of First Lieutenant James Hall. 1493

Trial and dying confession of
Henry Evans. 35558

The trial and life and confessions of John F. Van Patten.
22508

Trial and sentence of John Johnson. 16733

The trial balance, or the book
keepers directory. 20684

Trial: Commonwealth vs. J. T.
Buckingham. 10474; 14315

The trial, confession, &c. of
John Funston. 22510

The trial, conviction and sentence of Jesse Strang. 30830

Trial etc. at a court of general
sessions of the peace, held in
and for the city and county of
New York. 6998

Trial, etc. for slander, Superior
court, Windham county,
(Conn.) 13897

Trial, &c. The people vs. Israel Thayer, Jr. and Isaac
Thayer. 22509

Trial for a rape. 26239

Trial for murder. 20334

The trial in full of Edward Ar-
rowsmith. 3473

Trial of a suit, brought in the
district court for the city and
county of Philadelphia. 18236

The trial of a young lady. 40669

Trial of Amos Furnald. 22511

Trial of Benjamin Shaw, John
Alley Junior, Jonathan Buf-
fum, and Preserved Sprague.
10475

The trial of Cain. 11998; 11999;
15570; 28293; 32490

Trial of Captain John Shaw.
11282; 11283

The trial of Charles Stevens.
14316

Trial of Daniel Davis Farmer.
7000

Trial of 1819. 3474

Trial of Elsie D. Whipple.
30831

Trial of Gamaliel H. Ward.

10476

The trial of Georg Swearingen.
40670

The trial of Gulian C. Verplank.
7001

Trial of Isaac, Israel, Jr., and
Nelson Thayer. 22512

Trial of Israel Thayer Jr.
Isaac Thayer, and Nelson
Thayer. 22513-22516

Trial of Jacob Barker, Thomas
Vermilya, and Matthew L.
Davis. 30832

Trial of James Lackey, Isaac
Evertson, Chauncey H. Coe.
30833

Trial of James Robertson. 15478

Trial of Jesse Strang. 30834

Trial of John Blaisdell. 10477

Trial of John Lechler. 10478

Trial of John Moore, John Mul-
len, John Lowry and Henry
Bush. 19260

The trial of Joseph Mason. 3475

The trial of Joshua Barney.
18237

The trial of Joshua Randell.
26240; 30835

Trial of Levi Kelley. 30836

Trial of Lieutenant Joel Abbot.
10479; 10480

Trial of Medad M'Kay. 7002

Trial of Michael Martin. 7003

The trial of Michael Powars.
3476-3478

Trial of missionaries. 14137

Trial of Moses Parker, James
Buckland, Joseph Wade.
22517

Trial of Richard Johnson. 14317

The trial of Robert Douglass.
22518

Trial of Robert M. Goodwin.
3479-3482

Trial of S. and J. Boorn. 3483

The trial of Samuel Perry.
26241

The trial of Samuel Yardley
Thornton, Jacob Hellings and
others. 7004

Trial of Seth Elliot. 18238

Trial of Stephen and Jesse Boorn.
3484

Trial of Stephen Videto. 22519

Trial of the British soldiers. 18239

Trial of the case of the commonwealth versus David Lee Child. 40671

Trial of the commonwealth versus Origen Bacheler. 40672

The trial of the Rev. William Hogan. 10481

Trial of Tobias Watkins. 40673

Trial of twenty-four journeymen tailors. 29056

The trial of universal charity. 16621

Trial of William and Peter C. Smith. 19261

The trial of William Holmes, Thomas Warrington and Edward Rosewain. 3485

Trial. Rev. Menzies Rayner, vs. Col. Agur Judson. 22520

Trial, sentence, and execution of Israel Thayer, Jr., Isaac Thayer and Nelson Thayer. 22521

Trials; a tale. 16772

The trials and encouragements of Christ's faithful ministers. 16775

Trials between E. M. Blunt vs. I. Greenwood. 10482

Trials, experiences and changes addressed to the patrons of the New-England Galaxy. 13490

Trials of John Duncan White. 30837

The trials of life. 38837

Trials of Margaret Lyndsay. 14945-14947; 31780

The triangle. 7005

The tribute of a mourning husband. A sermon. 6846

Tribute of affection to John Roulstone, Jr. 8248

A tribute of respect to the memory of Mrs. Sarah Bowdoin Dearborn. 24797

Tribute of the muses through the carriers of the Columbian Centinel. 28558; 32781

A tribute to New-England. 6848

Tribute to the memory of DeWitt Clinton. 35380

A tribute to the memory of Jacob Dyckman. 12401

A tribute to the memory of James A. Powell. 39047

Triennial catalogue... Vermont Academy of Medicine. 38081

The trim built wherry. 20311

The Trinitarian controversy. 2025; 33922; 33923; 39332

Trinitarians rational. 15545

A trip to camp meeting. 10420

Trip to Nahant. 5582

Trip's history of beasts. 3486

The triumph of philanthropy. 3432

Triumph of religion. 22522

Triumph of truth. 28782

The triumphal march of General LaFayette. 18152

Triumphs of intellect. 15719

Triumphs of liberty. 19491

The triumphs of truth. 22458

El triunfo de la libertad sobre el despotismo. 6666

The troubadour, and other poems. 5876; 9311

The troubadour; catalogue of pictures and historical sketches. 21160

The troubles of Israel. 40635

The Troy directory, for 1829. 40683

The truant boy. 7011

A true abstract. From the returns of the president and directors of the several banks. 2171

A true abstract from the statements of the presidents and directors of the different banks. 29686

The true and affecting history of Henrietta de Bellgrave. 4660; 11793

A true and candid statement of facts, relative to the late affairs and proceedings of the government of Brown University. 26248

A true and concise narrative of the voyage and sufferings of James Washburn, Jr. 11347

A true and correct account of the confession of Perregrine Hutton. 3488

True believers, hated by the world. 35235

The true Christian faith in our Lord Jesus Christ, plainly asserted. 10485; 10486

The true copy of a manuscript, found hanging on a post at Gorham Corner. 6896

True copy of the excommunication of the Church of Rome. 4930

The true English grammar. 28904; 38619

The true glory of the church. 25021

True history of the rise & progress of the difficulties between Rev. Wm. Clark & people of Wolcott. 3489

The true history of Zoa. 7012; 14319; 34656; 34657

True love! 23326

The true masonic chart. 916; 15897; 24247

The true Messiah exalted. 21456

The true Messiah, in Scripture light. 13337

True moderation; a sermon. 19857

The true object of Christian worship demonstrated. 34562

True piety. 5152; 15934; 15935; 20267; 24302

True prophecies. 3490

A true relation of the holy war. 37992

The true Scripture-doctrine concerning some important points of Christian faith. 12372

The true sentiments of the writer of the last appeal to the congregation of St. Mary's Church. 7013

True way of turning to God. 1915; 25069

The true Yankee sailor. 14259

The trumpet march. 10490

The trustees' account of the agricultural exhibition, at Danvers. 8635

Trustees' account of the cattle show, and other exhibitions at Topsfield. 1121; 5262

The trustees of the Methodist Episcopal Church in Bridgeport, Connecticut, respectfully submit the situation. 15549

Truth advocated. 11302; 11509

Truth and falsehood, exemplified in a true history. 20876

Truth espoused, relative to the difficulties that existed in the town of Manchaster. 13673

Truth illustrated. 30685

Truth is no slander. 28519

The truth of the gospel demonstrated from the character of God manifested in the Atonement. 32610

Truth Teller, No. 1. 28885

The truth teller, the people's ticket. 37321

Truth triumphant. 38914

Truth versus a Wesleyan Methodist. 3494

Truth vindicated, in a letter to a friend. 8519

Truth without controversy. 18014

The truths of the Bible harmonious, and inseparably united. 29470

The tulip, or Selina's favourite. 30571

Il Turco in Italia. 25969

Turkey. 38080

Turkish barbarity. 34089

Turn out! A musical farce. 9195; 33761

The turnpike gate. 16828; 25049

The Tuscaloosa almanac. 14325; 26254

Twas his own voice. 6891

'Twas I, or, The truth a lie. 30158

'Twas within a mile of Edinburgh. 2916

Tweed side. 3501

The twelfth anniversary of the Hudson River Baptist Association. 28011

Twelfth annual exhibition of the

Pennsylvania Academy of the Fine Arts, Philadelphia. 13716

Twelfth annual meeting of the American Tract Society. 23500

Twelfth annual meeting of the Baptist Education Society. 37591

The twelfth annual report, for the year 1828, of the managers of the Indigent Widows' and Single Women's Society. 39088

Twelfth annual report of the American Bible Society. 31948

The twelfth annual report of the American Society for Colonizing the Free People of Colour. 37438

Twelfth annual report of the American Tract Society. 23501

Twelfth annual report of the Board of Directors of the Princeton Theological Seminary. 17697

The twelfth annual report of the board of managers of the Auxiliary New-York Bible and Common Prayer Book Society. 27918

The twelfth annual report of the board of managers of the New-York Protestant Episcopal Missionary Society. 34914

The twelfth annual report of the board of managers of the New-York Protestant Episcopal Sunday School Society. 39834

Twelfth annual report of the Board of Public Works, to the General Assembly of Virginia. 37035

The twelfth annual report of the Cincinnati Miami Bible Society. 24108

Twelfth annual report of the directors of the American Education Society. 31958

The twelfth annual report of the directors of the Hampshire Bible Society. 33468

Twelfth annual report of the directors to the Boston Society for the Religious and Moral Instruction of the Poor. 32446

Twelfth annual report of the Female Episcopal Benevolent Society. 33163

The twelfth annual report of the Long-Island Bible Society. 33898

Twelfth annual report of the Massachusetts Peace Society. 34080

The twelfth annual report of the New-York Female Auxiliary Bible Society. 34536

Twelfth annual report of the New York Religious Tract Society. 17420

The twelfth annual report of the New-York Sunday School Union. 34550

Twelfth annual report of the president and directors of the Board of Public Works. 37036

Twelfth annual report of the receipts & expenditures of the City of Boston. 15510

The twelfth annual report of the Society for Educating Pious Young Men for the Ministry of the Protestant Episcopal Church. 40473

Twelfth concert. [Musical Fund Society of Philadelphia] 25474

Twelfth night; or What you will. 14096

The twelfth report of the Bible Society of Philadelphia. 455

The twelfth report of the Bible Society of Salem. 11857

Twelfth report of the directors of the American Asylum, at Hartford. 31945; 31946

The twelfth report of the Female Bible Society of Philadelphia. 24519

Twelfth report of the New Hampshire Bible Society. 13509

Twelfth report of the trustees of the Ohio Bible Society. 17482

Twelfth report of the Vermont Bible Society. 19134

Twelve English songs. 12737

Twelve favourite songs. 17111

Twelve letters on the energies of the human mind. 34632

Twenty-sixth annual narrative of missions. 21475

Twenty-sixth annual report of the New Hampshire Missionary Society. 29949

The twenty-sixth report of the trustees of the Hampshire Missionary Society. 33470

Twenty-third annual narrative of missions. 8435

Twenty-third annual report of the trustees of the New Hampshire Missionary Society. 17337

Twenty-third annual report of the trustees of the Public School Society of New York. 34940

Twenty-two plain reasons for not being a Roman Catholic. 35574

Twilight dews. 3334

The Twin Brothers. 1697

The twin sisters; or beauty without sense. 18255

The twin sisters, or the advantages of religion. 14044

The twin sisters; or, Two girls of nineteen. 7021; 13296; 29719; 35575

The twinkling star. 30853

The twins. 10042

The twins: or, An account of the happy lives and triumphant deaths of Sophia Crocker. 32852

Two addresses to "The Associated Members of the Bar of Philadelphia." 17758

Two admired waltzes. 5535

The two Americas, Great Britain, and the Holy alliance. 16007

The two apprentices. 10498; 14326

The two arrows. 22530

The two birth-days. 26255

Two Bohemian waltzes. 9139

The two brothers. 8245

Two celebrated polonaises. 21719

The two circulars. 18256

The two cocks. 3504

Two dialogues with children. 40700

Two discourses, containing the history of the church and society in Cohasset. 8718; 8719

Two discourses containing the history of the Old North and New brick churches, united as the Second church in Boston. 7579

Two discourses delivered at Rye, N. H. 21941; 21945

Two discourses delivered at the new Universalist Chapel in Westminster Street. 25770

Two discourses delivered at the Universalist Meeting House, in Medway. 17632

Two discourses, delivered before the First Society of United Christian Friends, at Saratoga Springs. 26084

Two discourses, delivered in the Universalist Church in Pawtucket. 38705

Two discourses designed to illustrate in some particulars, the original use of the Epistles of the New Testament. 28698

Two discourses, exhibiting an historical sketch of the First Baptist Church in Boston. 4308

Two discourses on a new system of society. 21766; 21766a

Two discourses on the Atonement. 6914; 18120; 35434

Two discourses on the Christian revelation. 12090

Two discourses, on the completion of the second century from the landing of the forefathers of New England at Plymouth. 1650; 5622

Two discourses on the membership, obligations, and privileges of the seed of the church. 4298

Two discourses on the most important duties of townsmen. 16534

Two discourses on the nature of sin. 24543

Two discourses to townsmen. 16535

Marblehead. 3496

The two shoemakers. 39638

Two short catechisms. 599

The two sisters. 3213

The two sisters, or The cavern. 7023

The two sisters; or, The exiles of Roseville castle. 22532

Two speeches, delivered in the New-York state convention. 16376; 17396

2 tes verzieichness der buecher welche in der deutschen-buch-andlung. 1571

Two tracts. 12260; 15868

The two visions. 14175

Two waltzes. 13065

The two witnesses. Rev. XI. 14896

Two wives. 9818

Typhus syncopalis. 21466

Tyranny unmasked. 10418

Tyrant! soon I'll burst thy chains. 22136; 22137

Tyrolese air. 5428

Tyrolese evening hymn. 32499

The Tyrolese song of liberty. 2326

Tyrolese waltz. 14327; 18259

Tyrolesian air. 6173

Tyrolian waltz. 3059

Tyronis thesaurus. 8627

U

U. S. Ship Constitution on a four year's cruise. 41342

Ugolino; a tragedy. 19795

The Ulster County Farmer's almanac. 3506; 10500; 14329; 22535; 22536; 26260

Ulster County Republican nominations. 10501

Unanimous address of the Council of Censors to the freemen of Vermont. 31603

The uncertainty of obtaining justice by the law. 8533

Unclaimed dividends. 27451

Uncle Sam's almanack. 30859; 30860; 35580; 40705

The unconditional freeness of

The Gospel. 33081

The undersigned delegates, from a meeting of the citizens of Philadelphia. 16475

Undine: a tale, from the German. 16855

Undine; or The spirit of the waters. 14152

The unfortunate concubine. 7026; 10502

The unfortunate lovers. 9827; 34658

Uniform dress for the students of Yale College. 19345

The uniform of the general staff, field and platoon officers, shall remain as prescribed. 2289

Union Canal Company. 28187

A union catechism. 5251

The union grammar. 33701

Union harmony. 38221

The union hymn book. 15268

Union--No union. 6981

The union of Prudence. 23406

Union of sentiment among Christians not essential to peace. 39333

Union, or a Treatise of the... affinity between Christ and his church. 1830; 2981

Union questions. 1814; 38580

The Union Republican Ticket for 1820. 3513

Union spelling & reading book. 23499; 27842

Union ticket. At a convention of the "United Committees of Conference." 12361

Union ticket. Representatives. Nathaniel P. Russell. 22543

The Unique. 40444

The Unitarian Baptist exposed. 2043

The Unitarian Baptist of the Robinson school exposed. 25168

Unitarian Christianity free from objectionable extremes. 33359; 38761

Unitarian worship vindicated by the precepts and example of Jesus Christ. 22308

The Unitarian's answer. 20305;

upon Mr. Balfour's ground.
22172

The universal songster. 41347

The universal spelling-book.
33166

Das Universal-Traumbuch oder
der vollstandige Traum-Aus-
leger aller Arten von Traumen.
4067; 7490

The universal writer. 18091;
18092

Universalism exposed. 14759

Universalism not of God. 22301

Universalism; or, The rich man
and Lazarus. 16946; 27746;
29544

Universalism refuted. 12975

Universalism vindicated. 22455;
27757; 35501

The universalist Bible. 37536

The Universalist, consisting of
essays. 22456

Universalist hymn-book.   4528;
4529; 15163; 32084; 37563

The universality of the atonement.
6588; 25898

Universitatis Transylvaniensis
Curatoribus AEstimandis et
Honorandis. 3470

University in Cambridge, Order
of performances for exhibition.   12785; 16473; 24807-
24809; 29165

University of North-Carolina.
17446

University of the State of New-York.
College of Physicians and Surgeons. Catalogue. 39820

University of Vermont. Commencement. 19138; 23157;
31609; 37014

University of Vermont. Exhibition of the Junior Class.
11298; 19137

University of Vermont. Junior
Exhibition. 27507; 37015

The University of Virginia.   Its
origin and endowments. 19158

University of Virginia. This institution was opened on the 7th
day of March. 23173

The unlawfulness of the subscription required of the ministers
of the Gospel. 38688

An unparalled[!] law case.
19115

The unpardonable sin. 8387

Unpartheyisches gesang-buch.
4070; 39557

Unproductive post roads. 31540;
36951; 36952

Unproductive post routes. 27455

Unseasonable and irreligious
mirth. 17210

Unsettled accounts. 23133; 31541-
31543; 36953

Unsettled balances. 27456; 31544;
31545; 36954; 36955

Der Underschied Zwischen wahren
und falschen Bekehrungen. 31984

"Until fifteen dull years." 7574;
14823

The upright character and peaceful end of the righteous.
9806

The Uranian harmony. 14264

Uriah Brown. 36956; 36957

The use of strong drink, contrary to the Scriptures. 38306

Use of the dead to the living.
30642

A useful guide for grocers.
37732

Useful selections, from ecclesiastical records and printed
sermons. 23417

Useful tables of scripture. 30822

Useful tables of Scripture names.
27646; 37176; 37177; 41519

The usurper. 39364

Usury, or interest, proved to be
repugnant to the divine and ecclesiastical laws. 17466

The Utica [City] directory. 36991

The Utica library. 41354

The utility and importance of
creeds and confessions. 17160

The utility of apprentices' libraries. 9223

Utility of natural history. 12838

V

Vacant lands in Tennessee.
36958; 36959

10140

Vida de Fernando Septimo.
25078

Vida de Jorge Washington.
22023; 25895

La vida de Lazarillo de Tórmes.
5807

La vie et aventures de Robinson
Crusoe. 985

Vienna grand waltz. 4105

The Vienna waltz. 16705

View of all religions. 17834;
22108; 25951

View of General Jackson's domestic relations. 33466

View of Holliston. 28887

A view of religious covenanting.
74

A view of South America and
Mexico. 21697; 25597; 30064;
34558

View of the agency of Jesse Hopkins. 12868

View of the American Board of
Commissioners for Foreign
Missions. 15079

View of the city of New-Orange.
21529

A view of the civil administration and political character of
Napoleon Bonaparte. 7521

A view of the claim of Alexander
Nisbet. 30067; 31612

View of the claims of American
citizens. 38094

A view of the constitution. 22035;
40216

A view of the course of studies
and system of education pursued in the Polytechny. 38140

A view of the covenant of grace.
28222

View of the doctrine of the Trinity. 24222

A view of the evidences of Christianity. 21770; 25655

A view of the expected Christian
millennium. 30342; 34882-
34884; 40151

A view of the finances of the
state of Maryland. 16778

A view of the grand canal.
23162

View of the heavens. 25728

View of the Hebrews. 14138;
22295

A view of the history, literature
and religion of the Hindoos.
19185

View of the human heart. 22280;
35204

A view of the insolvent laws of
Pennsylvania. 29331

A view of the internal evidence
of the Christian religion.
16714

A view of the jurisdiction and
proceedings of the Court of
Probate in Massachusetts.
11410

View of the Livingston County
High-School on Temple-Hill.
33336

A view of the metaphysical and
physiological arguments in
favour of materialism. 15869

View of the missions. 98;
11594

A view of the Pilot. 17864

A view of the policy of permit-
ting slaves in the states West
of the Mississippi. 1919

A view of the present state of
the African slave trade.
16238

View of the present state of the
slave trade. 1326

A view of the question in controversy. 23569

A view of the ruinous consequences of a dependence on
foreign markets. 684

A view of the sentiments of Elias
Hicks. 37723

View of the state of Europe.
5520; 16382

View of the Trinity. 18004

A view of the United States.
32890

A view of the utmost researches
of human reason. 19141;
19142

View of the very great natural
advantages of Ireland. 12069

A view of West Florida. 31760

Views in New Haven. 19602

Views of Niagara. 7628

Views of religion. 20131; 22188

Views of society and manners in America. 5148; 5149

Views of the missions under the direction of the American Board of Commissioners. 19404

Views of the President of the United States. 9523

Views of the Reformer. 30706

Views of the Society for the Prevention of Pauperism in the City of Baltimore. 10394; 11300

Views on political economy. 9461

Views on the subject of internal improvement. 20929; 20930

Views on the two seeds. 25663

Views respecting the Chesapeak and Delaware canal. 19143

The vigneron. 29293

The village almanack. 41378

Village conversations. 32907

Village dialogues, between farmer Littleworth, Thomas Newman, Rev. Mr. Lovegood, and others. 20888

Village dialogues. By the author of "William's return." 190; 1698; 9074; 12886

Village harmony. 4106; 7524; 31613

The village holyday. 4107

Village hymns. 17304; 21593; 25483-25485; 29911; 34417

The Village in the mountains. 4108; 31614; 37020

The village lawyer. 9322

Village lots. 24239

The village milkmaid. 4109

The village nurse. 14783

The village of Mariendorpt. 6508-6510

Village plans and domestic sketches. 41379

Village poems. 3297

The village rambler. 1358

The village reformed. 23163; 31615

Village register. 41380

The village school. 31616

Village sermons on the chief articles of faith. 19666

Village sermons: or one hundred and one plain and short discourses. 4872; 19898

Village sketches. 20024

Village tales. 30322

The villager's daughter. 19145

Villany unmasked. 5474

The Vindication and Reply of Henry Banks to Certain Writers. 219

Vindication of An address to the Catholic voters of Baltimore. 33712

The vindication of John Banks. 23602

A vindication of Mark Langdon Hill. 20887

A vindication of Methodist episcopacy. 214; 4542

A vindication of Mr. Adams's oration. 6101

Vindication of Mr. E. C. Genet's Memorial. 29005

A vindication of publick justice and of private character. 13188

A vindication of the argument, a priori, in proof of the being and attributes of God. 19640

A vindication of the character and public services of Andrew Jackson. 33832

A vindication of the character of Alford Richardson. 11303

A vindication of the character of the Apostle Paul. 6841; 14181

Vindication of the character of the late Col. Solomon P. Sharp. 30579

A vindication of the claim of Elkanah Watson. 7010

A vindication of the conduct and character of Henry D. Sedgwick. 26038; 26039

A vindication of the doctrine contained in a sermon, entitled the Universality of the atonement. 22025

A vindication of the doctrine of the final perseverance of the saints. 30318

A vindication of the end of religious controversy. 21463

Vindication of the land agent. 32044

A vindication of the laws, limiting the rate of interest on loans. 1393

Vindication of the liberty of conscience. 10387

A vindication of the pastoral letter of the Right Rev. Bishop Hobart. 41381

Vindication of the recent and prevailing policy of the state of Georgia. 28518

Vindication of the rights of the Churches of Christ. 37023

A vindication of the Thomsonian system. 22461; 40391

A vindication of the truth. 37024

Vindiclae Hibernicae. 12070

The vine. 31617

The vine-dressers' theoretical and practical manual. 40634

Viola. 550; 37913

The violet of the vale. 15603

The violin instructor. 37026

Viotti's, grand concerto in G. 4111

Viotti's pollacca. 19148

The Virginia address. 34408

Virginia almanack. 4123; 7538; 7539; 11313-11315; 14788; 14789; 19152; 19153; 23175; 23176; 27519; 37037

Virginia and North Carolina almanack. 23177; 27520; 31633; 37038; 41388

The Virginia and North-Carolina Pocket almanack. 4124; 7540; 11316; 14790; 19154; 41389

Virginia electoral ticket. 32962

The Virginia housewife. 17753; 22026; 34960; 34961

Virginia: in the High court of chancery. 27518

Virginia - Mecklenburg County. Memorial. 36963

Virginia military land warrants. 27458

Virginia; or, The fatal patent. 23174

The Virginia-Pennsylvania farmers' almanac. 7541

The Virginia reel. 19155; 19156

The Virginian Orator. 11865

Virginius. 1880; 21137; 25050

Viri illustres urbis Romae. 21210; 25109

De Viris Illustribus Urbis Romae. 1956; 5820; 33859

Virtue in a cottage. 11317

The virtuous woman. 563

The vision of Columbus. 324; 15271

The vision of Cortes, Cain, and other poems. 40427

The vision of Hell, Purgatory, and Paradise. 20257

The vision of Isaac Child. 24082

The vision of liberty. 19188

The vision; or Hell, purgatory and paradise. 8501

Visions for the instruction of younger minds. 881

The visions of John Bunyan. 37993

The visit concluded. 37044

Visit for a week. 30161

Visit of General Lafayette. 21150

A visit to a Sabbath School. 4126; 4389; 41394

A visit to Colombia. 24368

A visit to my birth-place. 32513

A visit to the Isle of Wight. 33433

A visit to the sea-side. 37045; 37046

A visit to the West. 41395

Visite a bedlam. 35133

Visite du General La Fayette a la Louisiane. 23178

The visitor. 41396

Visits of mercy. 38465

Visits to a cottage. 31634

Visits to the Blessed Sacrament. 21222

De vita excellentium imperatorum. 25482

Vive l'amour. 5018

Vivian Grey. 23721; 28077

Vocabulary, containing an explanation of certain chemical

terms. 27524

Vocabulary of all the places contained in the map of the countries. 41565

Vocabulary of the Massachusetts Indian language. 38287

The vocal cabinet. 14793; 19159

The vocal companion. 41397

The vocal lyre. 23179

The vocal standard. 19160

A voice from Greece. 34540

A voice from Kentucky. 37047

A voice from the interior. 37048

A voice from the people. 21055

The Voice of free grace. 772

The voice of her I love. 2655; 6386-6388; 13672

The voice of Israel. 12206

Voice of Maine! At a full and respectable meeting of the members of the Legislature of the State of Maine. 17007

Voice of Maine! Office of the Independent Statesman and Maine Republican. 14794

Voice of Rhode-Island! 19161

Voice of the people. A review of the principles and conduct of Messrs. Vance, Sloane, Wright & Co. 27525

Voice of the people!!!...De Witt Clinton, as a candidate for the office of Governor. 65

The voice of the people! General Republican address. 1006

The voice of truth. A secret printed circular, misnamed the Voice of the People, accidentally fell into my hands. 7542

The voice of truth. To the citizens of Pennsylvania. 37049

The voice of truth. To the electors of the State of New York. 66

The Voice of Virginia! 34409

Der Volksfreund und Baltimore Calender. 4128

Volksfreund und Hagerstauner Calender. 4129; 7544; 11318; 14796; 19162; 23180; 27526; 31635; 37050; 41398

Volney's ruins. 37051

A volume of sermons. 24116

Volunteer mounted gunmen. 36964

Von der himmlischen arzeney, oder dass Jesus Christus der wahre arzt. 3123

Von dreyerley leben der menschen. 3124

Vorbericht. 11322

Die Vorsehung. 16433

A vote for the slave trade. 4130

Votes and proceedings of the ... Assembly of the state of New Jersey. 2457-2459; 6222; 6223; 9653; 17346; 21634; 21635; 25526; 34459; 39767

Votes and proceedings of the General Assembly of the State of Maryland. 9390; 13243; 17038

Votes and proceedings of the House of Delegates of the state of Maryland. 2128; 5961; 21347

Votes and proceedings of the Senate [Maryland] 2129; 2130; 9391; 13244; 17039; 21348

Votes for Ward no. 1. For aldermen. 22064

Votes for Ward no. 1. For mayor. 22065

Votes of the electors of President and Vice President. 23134

Votes of the overseers and corporation of Harvard University. 24810

Vox Populi Vox Dei. 37054

A voyage around the world. 8243

A voyage from the United States to South America. 11798

The voyage of Captain Popanilla. 32245

The voyage; or, Reflections on the mutability of human life. 17093

Voyage to South America. 24566

Voyage to the Eastern seas. 29111

A voyage to the moon. 30846

The voyages and adventures of Captain Robert Boyle. 23184;

step. 5572
The Washington Grays' grand
march. 12807
The Washington guide. 8613;
24412
Washington medals. 31547
The Washington miracle refuted.
19199
Washington Turnpike Road Com-
pany. 27464
The Washington waltz. 20252
Washington's farewell address.
31667; 41437
Washington's favourite the brave
LaFayette. 18009
Washington's grand march.
14839
Washington's march. 7595; 12427;
23225
Washington's papers. 30680
The Washingtoniana. 7594
The watchmaker and his family.
13207
The watchman. A favorite song.
2327
The Watchman's address. 11350;
23226
The water drop. 21802
The Waterman. 7596
Waters of Elle. 1860; 13011;
19203; 19204; 21115
Waterville College. 8380
Watts' Divine and moral songs.
41450
Watts' Divine songs. 14847;
23231; 27571
Watts' First catechism. 23233
Watts' Plain and easy catechism
for children. 4201
Waverly [Scott] 3149; 6763-
6765; 10212; 10213; 17930;
22223; 40376
Waverly. A divertimento. 5452
The way of living. 11366
The way to be good and happy.
23235; 37107
The way to be happy. 23236
The way to divine knowledge.
29101
The way to get married. 6122
The way to happiness. 11367;
17226
The way to keep him. 9569

The way to wealth [Franklin]
1275; 1277; 20549; 24571
Way to wealth and prosperity.
11368
The way-worn traveller. 15124
Ways and means. 15819
We're noddin at out house at
hame. 8971
"We have broken the chain."
23240
We invite your candid and seri-
ous attention. 13929
We met! 350
We part forever part tonight!
5546
We the subscribers, being desir-
ous to circulate the sermon.
11949
We'll rove at break of day.
17529
Wealth of society. 4208; 4209
The wealth of the cottage is love.
13911
The wealthy fool. 10272
Weariness in well-doing. 14226
The weathercock. 23461
Webster's Calendar: or the Al-
bany Almanack. 4226; 7616;
7617; 11379; 11380; 14860;
19238; 23278; 27589; 27590;
31697; 31698; 37123; 37124;
41465; 41466
The wedding day. A favorite
song. 9052
The wedding waltz. 3351
Week days and Sunday. 37127
A week in a cottage. 4227
The week; or, The practical du-
ties of the fourth command-
ment. 27592; 37126
Weep not for those. 9549;
13395
Weeping: A funeral sermon.
40360
Weeping for ourselves the duty
of all men. 32459
Der Weg zum Glück. 1278
Weighty considerations. 37131
Welcome Fayette! 18153-18155
Welcome, freedom's noblest son.
16377
Welcome, Lafayette. 4305;
19302

Welcome the nation's guest.
17958

The well bred horse Ball, a beautiful dark sorrel. 10193

The well spent hour. 31703

Wellesley Grey. 30776

Wells and Lilly, Boston [Works in press] 23285

Wells' calendar. 41472

The wept of Wish-ton-wish. 38278

Werner, a tragedy. 12042

Wesleyan almanack for 1826. 23290

Wesleyan camp-meeting hymn-book. 9467; 39560

The Wesleyan harmony. 1974; 5833

The Wesleyan Juvenile Benevolent Society, of Boston. 14873

Wesleyan selection. 4244

The West-Chester County Farmer's Almanac. 4246

The West Indian. 8479; 15902

West Point foundery and boring mill. 5748

West Point march. 21439; 23338

West's paintings. 27465

Westchester and Putnam farmers' almanac. 37140

Western agricultural almanac. 7634; 7635; 11398

The Western Almanack. 4247; 7633; 14874; 14875; 19247; 23292; 23293; 27610-27613; 31710-31714; 37143-37145; 41477-41479

The western almanack, and Michigan register. 23291; 27609; 37142

The Western almanack, for the state of Ohio, Kentucky, and Indiana. 41480

Western boundary of Arkansas. 41335

The western calculator. 3338; 14220; 26142; 35412

Western emigration. 26250

The western farmer's almanack. 4250; 7636; 11399; 14876; 19249; 23295; 27615-27617; 31717-31720; 37147; 37148; 41482

The western farmer's magazine almanac. 41483

"The Western Harmonic Companion." 25657

The western harmony. 15644

Western land agency and commission office. 357; 4251

The western miscellany. 30713

The western navigator. 8481

The western pilot. 20223; 38315

The western preceptor. 4626; 4627

Western Railway. 38553

The Western Reserve almanac. 19251; 23296

The Western souvenir. 37150

The western spelling book. 6898

Der Westliche Menschenfreund u. Schellsburger Calender. 7638; 11400; 14877; 19253; 23298; 27620; 31723; 37152

The Westminster Shorter Catechism. 37153

What a ploughman said about the "Hints to farmers." 37999

What detains him. 16770

What fairy like music. 2787

What hath God wrought? A narrative of the revival of religion. 6530

"What hath God wrought!" A sermon. 8970; 12791

What is done away; and what remaineth. 22296

What is gentility? 35231

What is the character of the late tariff law? 35546

What is truth? A sermon. 7979

What is truth? or, A search after, and defence of, the doctrine taught in the sacred scriptures. 24241

"What shall we do to be saved?" 4254; 19255

What think ye of Christ? 13777; 17642

What tho 'tis true I've talk'd of love. 1661

The wheel of fortune. 8480; 12298

When a Christian may be said

to have done his duty to the heathen. 31727

When Charles was deceived. 12182

When darkness brooded o'er the deep. 8384

When Freedom on the battle storm. 12658

When he tells of a lover. 3102

When I gaz'd on a beautiful face. 13019

When I left thy shores o Naxos. 14885

When I was a girl of eighteen years old. 4259

When love was a child. 8087; 11895

When merit's rewarded, ambition will rise. 41492

When night was spreading o'er me. 14217

When oft at twilight hour. 16569

When pensive I thought of my love. 1836

When rays of summer. 29397

When shall we three meet again. 1673

When the day with rosy light. 3337

When the following letter was written, it was without the slightest idea of its ever being published. 32602

When the hollow drum. 19462

When the rosebud of summer. 14218

When the warrior returns. 20936

When the weary sun declineth. 14160

When the wild wind blows. 1889

Whene'er I see those smiling eyes. 12677

When zephyr comes freshning. 20195

Where can peace of mind be found. 4833

Where Hudson's murm'ring billows. 13764

Where is lover? 21133

Where is the smile? 2222

Where roses were blowing. 18005

Where roses wild were blowing. 4260; 6807

Where shall I dine? 13977

Whereas a resolution proposing certain amendments to the constitutions of the State of Delaware, aforesaid, was adopted. 994

Whereas, Dr. Wm. Mosher has thought proper wantonly to assail my character. 727

Wherefore sweet maid sigh you so. 11896

Which society shall you join, liberal or orthodox? 37160

Whilst I listen to thy voice! 6892

Whims and oddities. 33586

Whimsical incidents. 4264

Whimwhams. 37160a

The white bosom'd maid with the blue rolling eye. 23322

The white cockade. 13066; 13067

The white kitten. 14898

White lies, a moral tale. 13642

The white palfrey. 41504

The white pony. 19268; 23314

The white rose. 12549

Who ever saw the like! 30636

"Who goeth a warfare at his own charges?" 34804; 34805

Who's the dupe? 12278; 15882

Who ought we to send to Congress. 655

Who shall be our next sheriff? 14904

Who'll be King but Charlie. 25416

"Who'll buy my love knots?" 8088; 11897

Whole art of bookbinding. 19276

The whole book of Psalms. 449; 4701; 11851; 11852; 15393; 15394; 23819; 23820; 32365; 37838-37840

The whole duties of men and women. 11418

The whole duty of woman. 5753

The whole of the documentary evidence, relative to the controversy between the regents of the University, and the trustees of Union College. 14334

The whole of the proceedings...
Andrew Ure, M.D. vs Catharine
Ure. 7654
The whole quantity of down-
freight. 39809
The whole truth, relative to the
controversy betwixt the Ameri-
can Baptists. 1646
Wholesale prices current at Cin-
cinnati, Ohio. 12146
The whore of Babylon unmasked.
28214
Why are you wand'ring here I
pray. 21588; 21589
Why does azure deck the sky.
1702
Wicked men ensnared by them-
selves. 22353; 26122; 26123
Wide awake. Warden. Prince
Snow. 17796
The widow's son. 23378
Die Wiedervereinigung der Lu-
theraner und Reformierten.
25838
Wild flowers; or, The May day
walk. 31750
Wild oats. 9779; 13633
Wild roses. 12442
The wilderness; or Braddock's
times. 13178
The Wilderness; Together with
The Union of the States. 4284
Wilhelm Meister's apprentice-
ship. 33365
Wilhemina. 27647
Wilkins Tannehill. 27466
The will. A comedy, in five
acts. 10097
The will of God. 9278
Will you go to the ewe-bughts
Marion. 13336
Will Watch. 12337
William A. Tennille. 36965
William and Eliza; or, The visit.
4288; 41533
William and Hugh Shannon. 36966
William and Jacob. 4289
William and John Peirce. 31548
William and Mary. 15071
William Benning. 27467
William Bishop. 31549
William Brown. 27468
William C. Grissam & Co's.

Mississippi and Louisiana al-
manac. 41534
William Cloyd. 27469; 31550
William Cooper and his family.
31754
William H. Bassett. 27470
William Hallaway and Westgate
Watson. 31551
William Hubble and Daniel Gano.
36967
William Hull - representatives of.
31552
Wm. J. Quincy and Charles E.
Quincy. 36968
William Jacocks. 41336; 41337
William King. 27471
William L. D. Ewing. 27472
William Legg and James Feland.
27473
William M. Dever. 23135
William M'Clure. 36969
Wm. Mendenhall. 27474
William Montgomery: or, The
young artist. 41535
William Morrison. 27475;
31553
William Morrisson. 36970
William Otis. 36971
William R. Maddox. 27476;
36972
William Schley, executor of J. G.
Posner. 31554
William Tell; a play. 21138;
21139; 33800
William Tell; or Swisserland
delivered. 1258; 24554;
28892
William the brave. 12678; 20337
William Thompson. 27477;
31555; 31556
William Tipton. 36973; 41338
William Vance's Oath of allegi-
ance. 37188a
William Young. 27478
William's return. 1699
Williams College celebration of
American independence. 41550
Williams' calendar, or the Utica
almanack. 31764; 31765;
37196-37198; 41543; 41544
Willie Blount. 27479
Willig's edition with additions &
improvements of J.B. Cram-

er's Instructions for the piano
forte. 38297
Willig's instructions for the vio-
lin. 4294
Willig's pocket companion. 11429
The willow basket. 9746
Wilm's variations to Dear Augus-
tine. 23343
Wilson's farmers' almanac. 11456
Wilson's Tennessee farmer's al-
manac. 11457; 14951; 19305;
23351; 31786
Wilt thou be my dearie. 11458
Wilt thou say farewell love. 2328
Wilt thou tempt the waves with
me. 41564
Wind thy horn, my hunter boy.
492; 15451; 19757
The winds of the winter are over.
11460
Windsor Park. A favorite rondo.
12461
"Wine is a mocker, strong drink
is raging." 34206
Wines imported, and duties there-
on. 36974
Winnebago Indians. 36975
Winter. 27680
Winter evening tales. 1641
Winter evenings: A series of
American tales. 38891
Winter evenings conversations.
37214
A winter in Washington. 18011
Winter; ornamented with cuts.
23357
A winter's evening. 16694
Winter's evenings conversations
between a father and his chil-
dren. 24124
The Winterville waltz. 16526
Wisdom, a poem. 23328; 37182
Wisdom displayed, and Lorenzo's
villany detected. 38416
Wisdom in miniature. 11464;
11465; 19310
The wisdom of God in the selec-
tion of his ministers. 33566
The wisdom of winning souls.
20022
Wisdom's voice to the rising gen-
eration. 28522; 41572
The Wise Builder. 763

The wise sayings of the Honorable
Isaac Hill. 33546
The wish; a pleasing and instruc-
tive fable. 23359
The wishing cap. 3214; 3215
The witch of New England. 16960
With the advice of the Council I
appoint Thursday a day of
thanksgiving and praise. 29604
With verdure clad. 8982
Witnesses imprisoned to secure
their attendance in court.
27481
The witty exploits of George Bu-
chanan. 31791
Wives as they were. 21009
"Woe unto the wicked!" 14289
The wolf and lamb. 2187
Woman and her accusers. 6140
A woman never vext. 30485
Woman's eulogy. 12183
The wonder: a comedy. 8301
A wonderful and horrible thing is
committed in the land. 9010
The wonderful cure of Naaman.
19317
The wonderful dealings of God to
Andrew Jaquith. 33698
The wonderful history of the Mor-
ristown ghost. 27724
The wonderful life and adventures
of Robinson Crusoe. 12354
Wonderful mechanism. 7686a
The wonders of nature and provi-
dence; displayed. 21972;
25832
The wonders of the horse. 35471
The wonders of the invisible
world displayed. 4000; 32550
The wonders of the world. 9921
Wood for sale. 31571
The wood pecker. 21101
The wood robin. 11471
Wood's almanac. 4328; 4329;
7704; 7705; 11478; 11479;
14974; 14975; 19328; 19329;
23370; 23371; 27698; 31806
37233; 41589
The woodlark. 21220
The woodman's hut. 7839;
23369
Woodstock; or the cavalier.
26033-26035

The works of Virgil. 14772; 23149; 23150

The works of William Paley. 17513

Works, preparing for publication by G. & C. Carvill. 38077

The world described, in easy verse. 9309

The world, on a globular projection. 27494

The world to be reclaimed by the Gospel. Missionary paper. 31923

The world to come. 37104

Worse and worse!! 37250

The worship of the church on earth. 12846

Of worshipping in the beauty of holiness. 27636

Worsley & Smith's Kentucky almanac. 4340

Worsley's Almanac. 7713

The wounded hussar. 5583

Wragg's improved flute preceptor. 14983; 14983a

The wreath: A collection of poems. 7715; 19337; 27711; 31820

The wreath of the west. 32724

The Wreath, or, Verses on various subjects. 1986; 33883

The wreath you wove. 9954

The wreck of honor. 17899; 26018

Wrifford's Mercantile penmanship. 19338; 19339

The writer. 8166

Writing simplified. 41356

Writings of Miss Fanny Woodbury. 41585

Wyeth's repository of sacred music. 4347; 4348; 14987

X Y Z

X, Y, Z. 32768

Xenophontis De Ciri Institutione. 37261

Yale College: Junior exhibitions. 27721

Yale College. The theological department of this institution. 31832

Yamoyden. 1069; 3104

Yankee Doodle! 1560; 11497; 14995; 19347

The Yankee in London. 27722; 37274

The Yankee or farmer's almanack. 41613

The Yankee. The farmer's almanack and annual register. 31834; 37373

The Yankee songster's pocket companion. 19348

Ye banks and braes of Bonny Doon. 1969

Ye shepherds tell me. 13274

A year in Europe. 12730; 16354

A year in Spain. 39365

The year of jubilee. 21973

The yearly Meeting's Epistle, 1820. 1327; 1328

Yearly messenger or New town and country almanac. 31836

The yellow shoe-strings. 34666

Yes and no: A tale of the day. 34789

Yesterday at 4 o'clock, the Governor transmitted by Mr. Pettus, his private secretary. 9516

Yesterday in Ireland. 38307

Yorktown: an historical romance. 24273

You are requested to attend the funeral of Mr. Robert Douthat. 37276

Young against Chipman. 31838

The young Americans. 39276

The young botanist. 41621

The young builder's general instructor. 39244

The young cadet. 33576; 39006

The Young Child's A, B, C. 4363

The young child's natural history of birds. 41622

The young child's prayer book. 17515; 31839

Young Christian's companion. 24306; 28666

The young Christian's guide. 613; 4864

Young churchman's guide. 12292

The young clergyman. 37281

The young communicant's catechism.   4297; 19301; 23339; 41555

The young convert: A collection of Divine Hymns.   4364

The young convert's apology. 11805

The young convert's pocket companion.   7728

The young cottager.   3016; 3017; 6643; 6644; 22094; 25942

The young gardener's assistant. 37938

The young gentleman and lady's monitor.   17206-17208

The young Jewess.   31840

Young ladies' astronomy.   19618

Young ladies' high school, Boston.   31841

The young lady's piece book. 35493; 40636

A young man came.   14824

The Young Man's Monitory. 1231

The Young May moon.   10349

Young men of Cortland county. 32945

The young merchant's manual. 71

The young mill-wright and miller's guide.   5277; 24450; 38503

Young Montezuma, an excellent claybank horse.   22526

The young moralist.   27713

The young naturalist.   29617

The young philosopher.   31845

The young pilgrim.   33577

The young preacher's manual. 40121

The young puzzler.   41625

The young rifleman's comrade. 29614

Young Roscius's strathspey. 14052

The young scholar's manual. 3360; 6910; 10368; 30730; 40565

The young sea officer's sheet anchor.   1947

The young widow.   22119

Young's Ephemeris, or almanack. 23400-23402; 27729; 27730

Youth a flower. A discourse. 7545

The youth and manhood of Cyril Thornton.   29120; 29121

The youth in his blooming array. 8089

The youth's almanack.   37286; 41626

Youth's arithmetic.   4370; 20721

The youth's arithmetical guide. 4188

The youth's assistant.   22459; 26204; 35505; 40643

The Youth's companion.   4371

The youth's ethereal director. 8218

The youth's guide.   3335; 10354

The youth's instructer and guardian.   15004

The youth's library.   31970

The youth's miscellaneous sketch book.   41627

The youth's monitor.   2314

The youth's natural history of animals.   41628

The youth's prayer book.   30148

Youthful piety.   4368

Youthful religion exemplified. 5195

Youthful sports.   4369

The youths' easy guide to a knowledge of arithmetic. 26082

Ypsilanti village lots at auction. 29556

Ysabel Osorno de Valverde. 36978

Zeal employed upon the mere circumstantials of religion. 30458

Zembuca.   17653

Zillah.   40448

Zion triumphant over all opposition.   25897

Zion's harp.   17305

Zion's pilgrim.   29174

Zion's songster.   21356; 34048; 39486

Zion's temple. A sermon. 15459

Zodiac of Dendera.   25648

Zoological and medical miscellany.   24795

Zoological text-book. 24395
Zophiel, a poem. 19869
Die Zukunft des Herrn. 16442
Zum neuen Jahr. 27732; 37288
Zum 17ten Juny, 1822. 11505
Zur Christnacht, den 24sten De-
    cember, 1822. 11506
Zuschrift der Verwalter der Bi-
    belgesellschaft von Philadel-
    phia. 28180
Der Zweyte Theil des Systema-
    tischen Auszugs aus des gott-
    seligen und hocherleuchteten
    deutschen Theosophen Jacob
    Böhmens Sämmtlichen Schriften.
    15489